FAMILY CHANGE AND FAMILY POLICIES IN THE WEST

A series of country studies and comparative analyses examining major changes in the family and the broad spectrum of family policies in Western industrial society in the second half of the twentieth century.

Series Editors: Peter Flora, Sheila B. Kamerman, and Alfred J. Kahn

Volume I:
Family Change and Family Policies in
Great Britain, Canada, New Zealand,
and the United States

FAMILY CHANGE AND FAMILY POLICIES IN THE WEST

A series of publications by the
Mannheim Centre for European Social Research

Volume II:
Family Change and Family Policies in Consociational Democracies:
Belgium, Switzerland, and The Netherlands

Volume III:
Family Change and Family Policies in France and Southern Europe:
A Pioneer Versus Latecomers?

Volume IV:
Family Change and Family Policies in Capitalist and Socialist
Central Europe: Austria, the Germanies, Hungary, and Poland

Volume V:
Family Change and Family Policies in the Scandinavian Welfare States

Volume VI:
Family, Industrial Society, and the Welfare State in the West:
Early Variations and Long-Term Developments in Comparative Perspective

Volume VII:
Family Policies in the West Since World War II: A Cross-National Analysis

Family Change and Family Policies in Great Britain, Canada, New Zealand, and the United States

Edited by
Sheila B. Kamerman and Alfred J. Kahn

CLARENDON PRESS • OXFORD
1997

Oxford University Press, Great Clarendon Street, Oxford OX2 6DP

Oxford New York
Athens Auckland Bangkok Bogota Bombay
Buenos Aires Calcutta Cape Town Dar es Salaam
Delhi Florence Hong Kong Istanbul Karachi
Kuala Lumpur Madras Madrid Melbourne
Mexico City Nairobi Paris Singapore
Taipei Tokyo Toronto Warsaw
and associated companies in
Berlin Ibadan

Oxford is a trade mark of Oxford University Press

Published in the United States
by Oxford University Press Inc., New York

British Library Cataloguing in Publication Data
Data available

Library of Congress Cataloging in Publication Data
Data available

ISBN 0–19–829025–X
Series ISBN 0–19–961857–7

1 3 5 7 9 10 8 6 4 2

Typeset by Mannheim Centre for European Social Research, Mannheim, Germany
Printed in Great Britain on acid-free paper by Biddles Ltd, Guildford and King's Lynn

Acknowledgements

The volume editors wish to thank the German Science Foundation for its generous support of this project. We also wish to thank manuscript editor Gretchen Wiesehan and the staff of the Mannheim Centre for European Social Research (MZES), especially Astrid Pfenning, for their diligence in formatting the tables and figures and preparing the camera-ready copy.

The authors of the Canadian report wish to acknowledge the generous support of National Welfare Grants (Human Resources Development Canada) in Ottawa, and especially wish to thank Fran McIninch for her encouragement and enthusiasm for this project. Several colleagues were kind enough to provide valuable comments on earlier drafts of this paper, including Roderic Beaujot (University of Western Ontario), Peter Burton (Dalhousie University), Martha Friendly (University of Toronto), Antonia Maioni (McGill University), Lars Osberg (Dalhousie University), and our fellow contributors Sheila Kamerman and Alfred Kahn (Columbia University). But most of all we want to thank our research assistants—Barbara Mitchell from McGill and Suzanne Chisholm, Stefanie Fischel, and Richard Lim from Dalhousie—who worked long hours to produce the research and statistics for this report.

The authors of the New Zealand report acknowledge the support of Statistics New Zealand, especially the Chief Demographer Mansoor Khawaja; the Department of Inland Revenue; the Social Policy Agency of the Department of Social Welfare, especially Mary Mowbray; the Ministry of Women's Affairs; the Ministry of Education; and the Roy McKenzie Foundation for its support of the Family Policy Programme at the Social Policy Research Centre, Massey University. Chapter 1 owes much to research undertaken by Natalie Jackson, (Demography Ph.D. candidate, Australian National University) when she was a Research Fellow at the Population Studies Centre, University of Waikato (PSC). Kim Johnstone, Research Fellow, PSC, co-authored with Ian Pool an early draft of Chapter 2 and a longer paper, on which the chapter draws. The work of Tracy Eagle, Gillian McCrae, and Janet Milne is gratefully acknowledged in the typing of the manuscript.

List of Contributors

MAUREEN BAKER is Professor at the McGill University School of Social Work in Montreal, Quebec.

ALFRED J. KAHN is Professor Emeritus and Special Lecturer at the Columbia University School of Social Work and Co-Director of the Cross-National Studies Research Program.

SHEILA B. KAMERMAN is Compton Foundation Centennial Professor for the Prevention of Children's and Youth Problems at the Columbia University School of Social Work and Co-Director of the Cross-National Studies Research Program.

PEGGY KOOPMAN-BOYDEN is Professor of Sociology and Dean of the School of Social Sciences at the University of Waikato, New Zealand.

SHELLEY PHIPPS is Associate Professor of Economics at Dalhousie University in Halifax, Novia Scotia.

IAN POOL is Professor of Demography at the University of Waikato, New Zealand, and Director of the Population Studies Centre.

STEIN RINGEN is Professor of Sociology and Social Policy at Oxford University. His most recent book is *Families, Citizens, and Reform* (Oxford University Press, 1996).

IAN SHIRLEY is Professor of Social Policy at Massey University, New Zealand, and Director of the Social Policy Research Centre.

SUSAN ST. JOHN is Senior Lecturer in Economics in the Department of Economics at the University of Auckland, New Zealand.

Table of Contents

List of Figures and Tables

NEW ZEALAND

UNITED STATES

Abbreviations and Symbols

LIST OF ABBREVIATIONS

AWE	average weekly earnings
GDP	gross domestic product
GNP	gross national product
LFPR	labour force participation rate
LIS	Luxemburg Income Study
OECD	Organization for Economic Co-operation and Development
TFR	Total Fertility Rate

LIST OF SYMBOLS

—	Data not available
…	Category not applicable
0	Magnitude nil or less than half of the unit employed
x	Included in another category

Introduction

Sheila B. Kamerman
Alfred J. Kahn

Introduction

This volume is the first in a series reporting on a multi-country exploration of the family policy of the modern welfare state. This introduction therefore defines terms, explains the choice of subject matter, and comments on the four countries featured here: Great Britain, Canada, New Zealand, and the United States.

Much about the welfare state has been analysed and reported on, but there has been no systematic effort to look in historical context at the evolution of its family policy or to explicate paths taken in some countries but not in others. More recently, there have been multi-country overviews of particular programmes—child care or family allowances, for example—or more comprehensive comparisons of a few countries, but the larger task remains. If the welfare state represents a modification or correction of market outcomes in the interest of certain other values, and if one set of such values relates to a concept of child and family well-being as a prerequisite for individual development and well-being, in which domains do the modifications appear? How and where do they develop, and what is their current direction as welfare states face economic globalization and political changes?

The term 'family policy' includes laws, regulations, benefits, and programmes (sometimes) deliberately and explicitly designed to achieve specific objectives with or for individuals in their family roles or for the family unit as a whole. We follow here the common practice of using the term 'family policy' to refer to families with children: policy with regard to 'the elderly', 'senior citizens', or 'the aged' is a separate domain. As we shall see, family policy may be implicit or explicit, intended or inadvertent, a consequence of actions with other goals or an indirect way of achieving child- and family-related goals without necessarily articulating their value base. Family policy usually refers to government actions, but may occasionally refer to the workplace, the church, political parties, or other associations. Since most family policy is enacted by government or private-sector employers, the others usually develop family policies as instruments of advocacy.

THE TWO DIMENSIONS—AND OTHER VARIABLES

Although we shall return to these matters and elaborate the domains and instruments of family policy later, it is useful initially to note that the major rationale for family policy is as a response to *family change* in a way expected to promote family well-being. The latter could mean helping with problems caused by social pressures or internal dysfunction; or moving family behaviour and structure in directions believed desirable in the light of the economic, political, and/or social goals of the larger society, or of a moral vision. Thus, family change is one of the two anchors for the country studies.

But the fact of change does not tell one what to do. *Family policies* therefore provide the other anchor: what is or is not done, how, for whom, with what financing, with what programmatic choices, and so on. Here, the focus is on the *content* of the actions. Further consideration also suggests that family policies may be among the forces creating family change. Thus an exploration must consider both family changes and family policies as potentially dependent or independent variables. Nor need we assume that the causal dynamics are necessarily limited to what occurs within a country. Countries that interact culturally or compete economically learn from one another—or at least some of their policy-makers or advocates do. And in recent years, within the European Community and European Union (as earlier in the institutions of 'communist' Europe), specific supra- or multi-national directives or recommendations have encouraged a degree of convergence.

If we are interested in the interactions of family changes and family policies, why not carry out a single quantitative investigation employing multi-variate techniques? There are precedents for this approach, for example, in expenditure studies by Wilensky (1975), Pampel, and others (1988 and 1992), in Mitchell's income transfer studies (1991), and other efforts. We choose a different approach: too little has been specified about family change in the industrial world, and a detailed overview will lead to more precise development of the variables for future quantitative work. Even less has been said about the various types of family policies and what they actually represent in their societal contexts. It is too early to conceptualize their combined alleged 'responsiveness' to family changes and to respecify them as variables in the ultimate multi-variate quantitative studies.

Our strategy is to begin on the ground. Within each country we look historically at the story of family changes, then at the evolution—or lack thereof—of family policies in various domains. Then we ask about possible interactions between the two in the context of political developments in the country, the institutional attention to these matters, interest and advocacy or pressure-group actions, and other relevant factors. The next step is to look at each country *vis-à-vis* others, since in effect it takes cross-national comparisons to highlight the idiosyncratic and the shared. Using a concept similar to that developed by Francis Castles and his colleagues (1993), the country volumes are clustered variously by religion, shared political history, geography, language, and culture.[1] The groupings are neither mutually exclusive nor completely rigorous, but could generate further insights. The current volume groups Britain and some of her former colonies in the 'Anglo-Saxon' tradition, with the addition of Canada's important French tradition. Australia, which belongs in the grouping, could not be included in the research within our time frame for reasons not relevant to the issues. Beyond the shared history of colonialism, some experts would stress the economic liberalism of our four countries, rather than the cultural and historical traditions, as being most salient.

The issue is broader socio-economic, -political, and -cultural contexts. As already suggested, the interactions between family changes and family policies may be mediated by important 'macro' variables. In fact, each of our two main dimensions may reflect such variables rather than the influence of the other. Some theories of the welfare state feature the political economy and differentiate countries among the social democratic, liberal (in the European sense), and the corporate types (Esping-Anderson, 1990). Other theories stress the role of labour and social democratic parties, social cleavages, national solidarities, or other dimensions. Still others do focus on country-specific historical dimensions (Castles, 1993; Levine, 1988; Pierson, 1991; Ringen, 1987; Mishra, 1990; Rose and Shiratori, 1986). Therefore, just as our country-specific historical reports are intended to deepen and enrich the content under the two major dimensions, family changes and family policies, our country-clustering permits fundamental and multi-faceted exploration of some of the 'macro' variables which may belong in future hypotheses. Indeed, it may well be that the current major theories and classifications of welfare states based substantially on pensions and other income transfer policies, and, perhaps, on expenditures, may require modifications when family policy is factored into the equation (Baker, 1995).

FAMILY CHANGES

A subsequent volume in this series will systematically report on family changes in Europe, focusing particularly on the twentieth century. It will consider the family as an institution and a social grouping, as well as examine the family at work. It will offer a foundation for reviewing family changes in the past half-century and particularly since the 1960s, for purposes of current research.

Prior scholarship in the field has documented the patterns of demographic transition during modernization and industrialization, established the nuclear family as the norm in the countries studied, and noted the shedding of family functions and the rise of governmental and other societal institutions to carry responsibility for such elaborated and more specialized functions as education, social control, religion, health care, and work (Mitterauer and Sieder, 1982). The family changes of the period studied here (post-World War II) all had earlier beginnings but posed new challenges to society from the middle of the century. We refer particularly to the later age of marriage, the declines in fertility and in family size, the major increases in out-of-wedlock births[2] and teenage non-marital births, and the increase in non-marital cohabitation.

The sum result of such changes is a major shift in family structures in many countries, including the growth of lone-parent (especially female-headed) families with children led by divorced, separated, or never-married women, while the lone-parent family headed by a widow is now relatively rare. The rise in labour force participation of women—in recent decades especially of married women with young children—has been even more dramatic. The gradual decline in male labour force participation rates, especially among older men, and the stagnation or decline of male wages have other implications. Despite significant national variations, there have been important shifts in gender roles in the home, at work, and in the society generally.

As suggested earlier, it is possible for public and workplace policies to accommodate and ease these transitions and, perhaps, also to encourage and accelerate them. Are there more or less 'responsive' societies and workplaces? These are matters to be investigated.

FAMILY POLICIES

The term 'family policy' was used first in European social policy discussions (Myrdal, 1941; Kuusi, 1964; Wynn, 1970) to describe what government does to and for children and their families, in particular those public policies (laws and administrative policies) designed to affect the situation of families with children— or individuals in their family roles—and those that have clear, though possibly unintended, consequences for such families. Characteristic of family policy internationally is: (1) concern for all children and their families, not just poor families or families with problems, although these and other family types may receive special attention; and (2) an acknowledgement that doing better by children requires help for parents and the family unit as well.

The increased attention to family policy in the latter part of the twentieth century derives from developments that either threaten this role of the family or are believed to do so. Demographic and social trends suggesting changes in the family as an institution and changes in the roles of family members have been the primary catalysts in generating support for family policies.

As already noted, family policy may therefore be explicit or implicit. Explicit family policy includes those policies and programmes deliberately designed to achieve specific objectives regarding individuals in their family roles or the family unit as a whole. (This does not necessarily mean general agreement as to the objective, but only that the actions are directed toward the family; various actors may have different goals in mind.) Explicit family policies may include population policies (pro- or anti-natalist), income security policies designed to assure families with children a certain standard of living, employment-related benefits for working parents, maternal and child health policies, child-care policies, and so forth. Implicit family policy includes actions taken in other policy domains, for non-family related reasons, which have important consequences for children and their families as well. For instance, an income tax measure designed to raise more revenue may create a work disincentive for a low-earner wife in a husband/wife family.

Family policy is a sub-category of social policy, and as such can be viewed as a policy field or domain, a policy instrument, or as a criterion by which all social policies can be assessed as to their consequences for family and child well-being. The family policy field includes those laws that are clearly directed at families, such as family law; child or family allowances; social assistance benefits contingent on the presence of children; maternity and parenting benefits; tax benefits for dependants; and child-care services. Family policy can also be an instrument to achieve other objectives in other social policy domains. For example, family policy may be used to achieve labour market objectives, encouraging more women to enter the work-force, or discouraging them from entry. Family policies may be designed to encourage parents to bear more children and thus achieve population goals. Thus, in family policy, the family may be both object and vehicle of social policy. Family policy as 'perspective' assumes that sensitivity to effects and consequences for families informs the public debate about all social policies. Family policy as perspective is concerned with monitoring a broad range of actions in terms of their potential or actual impact on children and their families. Viewing family policies from this vantage point is particularly important in those countries that do not have explicit family policies but rather a series of categorical policy initiatives directed toward different aspects of child and family functioning and designed to achieve different and sometimes contradictory objectives.

Family policy, therefore, in the sense discussed in this book, suggests:

- a view of the family as a central institution in the society;
- a definition of 'family' that allows for drawing distinctions while encompassing a variety of types, structures, roles, and relationships usually involving at least one adult and one child;
- a definition of 'policy' that assumes a diversity and multiplicity of policies rather than a single, monolithic, comprehensive legislative act;
- a definition of 'family policy' that therefore encompasses *families* and *policies*, and includes both the policy field or domain (specific laws, regulations, and activities such as those mentioned above explicitly designed to affect families) and family and child well-being—or family impact—as a criterion for assessing the outcomes of relevant governmental and non-governmental policies.

Family policy instruments include cash benefits, services, laws, and administrative directives. The major instruments are:

- income transfers including child and family allowances, social insurance, social or public assistance, and tax policies, among others;
- parenting policies including paid and job-protected leaves from employment following childbirth or adoption, and during children's illnesses or school transitions;
- child-care policies, both services and various forms of cash and tax subsidies;
- the laws of inheritance, adoption, guardianship, foster care, marriage, separation, divorce, custody, and child support;
- family planning and abortion laws and policy, and related educational and service programmes;
- personal social service programmes;
- housing allowances and policies;
- maternal or family and child health services;

- legislation, policy, and programmes affecting the status of women;
- employer and governmental policies affecting work schedules and the interrelationship of work and family life generally.

The roots of family policy are found in Europe. The first policies explicitly labelled 'family policy' or 'family policies' date from the late nineteenth and early twentieth centuries in France and Sweden and reflected concern with demographic and economic developments regarding families, in particular the problems of low birth rates and low wages. Family or child allowances (cash benefits provided to families based on the presence and number of children) were the primary policy instrument used to respond to these problems. They were first provided by employers as a supplement to the low wages of employees with large families (or by governments to their civil service employees with several children). It was understood that basic wage structures did not take account of the number of family members who depended on a given salary. Designed as an alternative to more general wage increases, by the 1930s family allowances also began to be viewed increasingly as a pro-natalist strategy for providing parents with an incentive to have more children.

Major growth in family allowances followed World War II. Whether in response to the devastation experienced by children and their families, a conviction about the need for social solidarity, or as the child-related part of welfare state developments following the war, family allowances were established throughout most of Europe. Indeed, in many countries, the 1950s were the 'golden age' of family allowances.

The second major stage in the development of family policy began in the 1960s, in the context of the highest rates of economic growth in history. Some countries 'discovered' poverty generally while others discovered the particular problems of low-income families with children. All the western industrialized countries expanded their systems of social protection in all areas during this decade: income transfers, health care, education, housing, employment, and personal social services; social policies for the aged burgeoned as well. In particular, income supplements designed to fill the gap between wages and family needs were expanded.

We have talked throughout of 'family policy' although, as we shall see in this volume, the reality is family *policies*. Family policy implies an integrated, holistic, coherent construction, something difficult to achieve in heterogeneous societies. Some countries, however, do have more explicit policies and more comprehensive provisions than others, differences which are central to this exploration.

The years from 1960 to the early 1990s are the primary focus of this book and the four country studies. How have families changed and how do these developments compare across these countries? To what extent have family policies in each country been responsible for—and shaped—these changes? Alternatively, to what extent have these policies responded to the changes experienced by families? For example, have policies supported new efforts concerning the education, socialization, and emotional support of young children as children become more likely to live in a mother-only family, a reconstituted family, and/or in a family in which the lone parent or both parents are employed? Has attention been paid to issues of equity between men and women as more women join men in the labour market? What other family policy developments have been generated by the growth in female labour force participation as a consequence of changes in the economy and the need for women's labour, on the one hand, and the economic and personal needs of women on the other?

Ultimately, no effective modern society can ignore labour force or family structural changes, demographic trends, or expanding child poverty. What shape have these responses taken in these four countries, with what known consequences?

FOUR COUNTRIES

Context

In the context of the industrialized world, as defined by the 28 pluralistic, industrialized democracies of the Organization for Economic Co-operation and Development (OECD) or of what are now the 15 countries of the European Union, we see a startling similarity in family changes and family policies in the four countries here in focus. Nonetheless, as one looks closely at these four, their individual histories and characteristics are visible in family patterns and family policies that make significant differences to their citizens.[3]

Canada, New Zealand, and the United States are all countries whose social policies come at least in part out of a shared language, culture, value system, and tradition, shaped by their histories as British colonies. In addition, the French tradition has a powerful and continuing influence in the Canadian province of Quebec. As indicated earlier, the concept of 'family policy' has its roots in continental Europe, emerging first in policy discussions in France and the Scandinavian countries, especially Sweden. In no way could family policy be considered a concept integral to the policy histories and debates of the four countries discussed here, except for French Canada. Indeed, the common theme in every discussion of the historical roots of family policy in these countries is that none has ever had an explicit, national, comprehensive child or family policy, or any such cluster of policies. Over time, however, all their governments have adopted a range of measures, directly or indirectly targeted at children and their families, that have had a significant impact on their standard of living and could be considered implicit child/family policies.

To the extent that implicit family policies exist in these countries, they can be identified and assessed only in the context of the countries' social policies more broadly defined, and only with reference to certain historical and philosophical themes. These themes reflect a remarkable degree of similarity across the four countries. The following list is derived from the four reports and, with minor caveats and modifications, describes the group:

- an emphasis on *laissez-faire* economic and social policy ('liberalism' in the European sense) as the dominant ideology, limiting the role of the state in providing social protection;[4]
- a dominant Protestant ethic despite a religiously-diverse population and a strong Catholic presence in three of the countries, with a resulting stress on individualism, self-reliance, the work ethic, voluntarism, and a strong private sector;
- a shared history of poor law as the point of departure for social policy and concern with poverty as a reference point in family policy;
- a comparatively heavy reliance on means-tested rather than universal benefits, with a particular stress on social assistance as a major policy instrument directed toward the very poor;
- a trend away from universalism in those countries (Britain, Canada, New Zealand) that had launched their post-World War II social policies with a significant commitment to universalism;
- a strong commitment to the primacy of the family in child care and child-rearing and the importance of family privacy;
- a bias toward a traditional family model (in contrast to the Scandinavians' more active acceptance of family diversity) or at least ambivalence regarding women's changing roles;
- the lack of concern over birth rates or population policy (except recently in Quebec);
- a long and early tradition of compulsory public education (except in Britain);
- the use of tax benefits as an instrument of social and family policies;
- a highly categorical and fragmented system of social protection;
- a related emphasis on personal social services targeted on the poor, handicapped, and severely deprived;
- a history of social reform focused on children and women beginning in the late nineteenth and early twentieth centuries;[5]
- subsequent periods of social reform in the 1930s, after World War II (in Britain, Canada, and New Zealand), and in all four countries in the 1960s, with particular attention in the last period to the poor;
- a history of low social spending at or below the OECD average for 1960–1990 (Kamerman and Kahn, 1991 and 1995, forthcoming), a recent conservative backlash in response to low rates of economic growth, high debts and deficits, high rates of unemployment (except in the US), high costs of social programmes, and some anxiety about the future of the family.

Especially important, the former colonies share a pattern of population diversity based on a history of relatively open immigration as well as the presence of indigenous peoples (Inuit and Native people in Canada, Maori in New Zealand, Native American in the US) making for a highly pluralistic society. Although not truly comparable, Britain has the most diverse population of any country in Europe.

Acknowledging all these similarities, each country also has a particularly distinctive aspect to its history that has also left an imprint on its social/family policies: the US is by far the largest of the countries, with a population of about 260 million as compared with 58 million in Britain, 29 million in Canada, and 3.5 million in New Zealand. The US is also the most heterogeneous, especially in recent years, with Asians, Latin Americans, African-Americans, and Europeans contributing to its population mix. Most important is the history of slavery in the US and the strong strain of racial prejudice that remains in the society.

Britain is increasingly seeing itself as part of Europe. Developments in the European Union over the last two decades have begun to bring about a modest 'Europeanization' of British social policies despite its refusal to sign the Social Chapter of the Maastricht Treaty. Canada has had a dual system of culture/language/values dominating its family policies with an increasingly strong French Quebec presence in all policy debates. Both Canada and the US have federal governmental structures, with an ongoing debate about the allocation of policy domains and responsibilities between national and provincial/state governments.

Because of the nature of the New Zealand economy, characterized until recently by full employment, its social protection system was built on the concept of a family wage (a male wage adequate to support a man, his wife, and three children). Unlike the other three countries, New Zealand did not rely on an income transfer or social insurance benefit system. In New Zealand, ethnicity has played by far the most important role in family change and family policy, even more so than gender.

This then is the context for our exploration of family change and family policies in Canada, Great Britain, New Zealand, and the United States—countries that emerged largely from a common heritage, though each has distinctive elements affecting both patterns of family change and family policies.

The Challenges of Demographic Change

The general pattern of family change is very similar across the four countries, with the trends that began more than a century ago in Britain, Canada, and the US continuing intermittently during the first half of the twentieth century and accelerating rapidly and consistently since the 1960s. Age at marriage, which has fluctuated over the years, has increased in all four countries, although it is not as high as in the other Western European countries. Marriage rates have declined across the four countries, as have remarriage rates, but both are higher in the US than in the other three countries. Divorce rates rose in all and levelled off somewhat in the 1980s. Britain's rates are the highest in Europe though not as high as in the US, the highest among the four. Cohabitation rates have increased in all the countries, compensating in part for the decline in marriage; however, cohabiting-couple unions are more likely to break up than legal marriages. In Britain and the US more than half of those marrying in the 1990s had cohabited before marriage. British cohabitation rates are the highest among the four countries and are similar to the French, though not nearly as high as the Scandinavian rates. Although cohabitation has increased dramatically over the last two decades, it clearly has not replaced marriage in these countries as it may yet do in Denmark and Sweden.

All four countries experienced a baby boom after World War II, with fertility rates peaking between the late 1950s (US) and the end of the 1960s (New Zealand). All have experienced a decline in fertility rates since then with some levelling off (in Britain since the 1970s) or rising slightly (in the US) in the late 1980s/early 1990s. First births are occurring at later ages in all four countries but still earlier than in other Western European countries. Fertility rates are also quite similar, at about the OECD average, with Canada having the lowest rate (lower still in Quebec), while New Zealand currently has the highest rates in the group, comparable to Sweden's. The British fertility rate is similar to rates in France and Norway, while the US rate falls in the middle of the four. In all four countries, the typical family includes two children, with a major decline in larger families and some apparent increase in childlessness.

Marriages and family formation among minority groups follow the overall trends in their respective countries yet differ visibly from the dominant group in the society. For example, in the US black women, who previously tended to marry at earlier ages than white women, now marry at even later ages than whites, at lower rates, and remarry at still lower rates, thus ending up far more likely to be single mothers than are white women. Hispanic women follow patterns somewhere between the two. Out-of-wedlock fertility also varies by race and ethnicity, with blacks and Hispanics having significantly higher out-of-wedlock rates than whites, and higher rates among adolescents in particular. In New Zealand too fertility rates vary significantly by ethnicity. Maori fertility rates declined dramatically over the last two decades as did rates for the population of European descent, but adolescent fertility is far higher among the Maori population.

Contrary to conventional wisdom, adolescent fertility rates declined in all these countries, declining in numbers and proportion in Canada since 1960 and in New Zealand since the 1970s, and declining in numbers since 1970 in the US and in proportion from 1960 to the late 1980s. British rates are the highest in Western Europe though significantly lower than those in the US, about the same as in New Zealand, and higher than in Canada. The major changes are that in earlier decades most teenagers were married when they gave birth or soon after, and if they remained single they gave their babies up for adoption. Since the 1970s, most teen births are out-of-wedlock, and more teenagers are keeping their babies. In Britain, teen births increased by more than 70% between 1980 and 1990, with 80% of these out-of-wedlock—double the rate in 1980. In New Zealand almost all births to teens aged 15–19 were out-of-wedlock in the 1990s. Births to teenagers comprised about 33% of all out-of-wedlock births in Canada, 30% in the US, 21% in New Zealand, and 19% in Britain.

Since the 1960s, out-of-wedlock births generally have increased dramatically in these countries as they have throughout most of the advanced industrialized west, and most by far are to non-adolescents. The numbers of such births have tripled in the US since 1960, while the proportion of all births out of wedlock increased by an astonishing six times between 1960 and 1992. Current rates are remarkably similar across the four countries: 31% in Britain, 29% in Canada, 36% in New

Zealand, and 30% in the US, as compared with 33% in France, 15% in Germany, 46% in Denmark, and 50% in Sweden.

In the four countries, families have become smaller and family households less likely to include children. Among families with children, the biggest change is the increase in single-parent, mother-only families. Since about 1970, the increase in this family type has been dramatic in all four countries. Not all unmarried mothers are living alone, however. Although the data are not precise, it appears that a growing portion of unmarried mothers are cohabiting with a partner in Britain, Canada, and the US, and a still larger portion (more than one-quarter) are living with extended family in New Zealand.

Lone-parent families, the focus of much policy attention in these countries, are headed overwhelmingly by women and have rapidly increased as a percentage of all families. In the 1970s, this family type was dominated by divorced women, but since the 1980s unmarried mothers are the most rapidly growing group. Lone-mother families constitute about 18% of all families with children in Britain. Of these, in 1991, one-third were headed by never-married single women (more than double the percentage in 1971), another third by divorced women, and 22% by separated women. In New Zealand, 25% of families with children are lone-parent families. Of these, 19% are headed by one parent living alone with children, while the other 6% live as sub-families in a larger household. In Canada, lone-parent families constituted 20% of families with children in 1991, almost double the proportion in 1961 (11%). The largest group is headed by divorced women, while 25% are separated, 20% never-married, and the remainder widowed. During the past two decades lone-parent families in the US also increased as a proportion of all families with children to 30%, with almost half of these headed by divorced or separated women and one-third by never-married women.

Lone-mother families are particularly vulnerable economically and socially, largely because they have only one earner in the family and that earner is a woman, likely to be receiving a low wage. These families are also vulnerable to stress because they are likely to be 'time poor' and experience social isolation as well. Some are protected because they live with a partner (Britain, Canada, and the US) and may not technically even be counted as a lone mother, and some live with an extended family (New Zealand). But for the most part these families are likely to be deprived and disadvantaged. The poverty rate for mothers living alone with their children is more than 50% in all four countries.

Racial and ethnic differences are almost as significant as gender differences in these countries (and in New Zealand, possibly more so). The portion of black lone-parent families with children in the US is far greater than the comparable portion of white families; in New Zealand a similar pattern can be found among the Maori as opposed to the population of European descent. (There are no official data on lone-parent families by race or ethnicity in Canada.) Although extended families are a significant family type only in New Zealand, largely among the Maori, they also exist among some minority groups in other countries as well, mainly among the households that contain lone-mother families.

Challenges from New Divisions of Labour

One major aspect of family change in the latter half of the twentieth century is the shifting division of labour in families: an increased proportion of women, especially wives and mothers, are in the labour force and displaying a growing attachment to it regardless of childbearing and child-raising. The trend may have begun earlier in some countries but World War II was something of a watershed, with women born after the war increasingly likely to be in the paid labour force during their adult years. Regardless of the reasons—higher education and therefore greater opportunity costs of not working; fewer children and therefore more time for paid employment; greater risk of divorce and therefore labour force attachment as a kind of personal insurance; an expanded service sector and therefore greater job availability at better wages; stagnating or declining male wages and rising male unemployment and therefore the growing need for an additional income source—women have found it economically and personally worthwhile to take on market work in addition to household and family work.

Male labour force participation has declined in all these countries, with earlier withdrawal from work and as a consequence of a weaker economy; when men do have jobs these often pay less and provide fewer benefits. Women's wages make an essential contribution to family income. Indeed, in the US working wives have sustained real family income over the last two decades and protected their families from declines in income they would have experienced had they depended solely on husbands' earnings. The pattern has been similar in Canada and New Zealand, where working wives compensated in part for the demise of the family wage, and seems to be emerging in Britain.

Although the division of labour inside and outside the home has become somewhat more equitable, by and large women are working two jobs, one in the paid labour force and a second in the home. For the most part, women's total working hours exceed those of men: men work longer hours in the labour market while women put in more hours at home. Over the last two decades, however, all women have begun to reduce their time investment in housework while struggling to maintain their time commitment to their children. Over the same period, men, especially those with wives in the labour force, have begun to spend more time in child-related tasks. Working wives may find themselves confronted by a time crunch but family income has been protected, at least in part, and husbands' contributions to home and family work have increased modestly.

Although the overall pattern of changes in gender roles is similar in all four countries, there are several significant differences. Canada and the US appear to have experienced the largest changes in women's roles, followed by Britain, with New Zealand apparently remaining the most traditional. Thus, whereas in 1965 only 35% of Canadian husband/wife families were dual-earner families, in 1991 56% were. In the US, by 1980 53% of husband/wife families were dual-earner families and by 1990, over 60% were. Moreover, the highest labour force attachment now in both countries is among women aged 25–34, the peak childbearing years, and the next highest is among those aged 35–44. In Britain, by 1990 two-thirds of husband/wife families were dual-earner families, but most of these wives worked part-time, whereas in the US and Canada most worked full-time.

Britain, Canada, and the US have relatively similar patterns of labour force participation rates (LFPR) among women with children: about two-thirds of the mothers in these countries are in the work-force. Moreover, in contrast to many continental European countries, it is not generally the number of children but rather the age of the youngest child that determines women's likelihood of working. In Britain, Canada, and the US, women with very young children are less likely to be working than are women with older children, though more likely in the US than in the other two countries.

In all four countries LFPR are higher among married than single mothers, but the gap between the two is greater in the other countries than in the US, especially among women with very young children. For example, 63% of lone mothers in Canada are in the labour force, nearly comparable to the more than two-thirds of wives in the labour force. Among women with very young children, however, 64% of wives are in the labour force as compared to only 41% of lone mothers. LFPR of lone mothers in Britain are still lower, and lowest by far in New Zealand at 28%.

Finally, in both the US and New Zealand LFPR vary by race and ethnicity. Married black women in the US are far more likely to be in the labour force than whites, while black lone mothers are less likely. In New Zealand both Maori women in couple families and those who are lone parents (living alone or not) are less likely to be in the labour force than are women of European descent. The issue of policy responsiveness to these family changes is obviously significant.

The Income Challenge

Here, too, the four countries reflect a common pattern, especially with regard to overall trends in the economic situation of families. As we shall see, the differences emerge more strongly in the policy responses. Although not completely consistent across the countries, the picture is one of economic growth and rising earnings and income in the 1960s and early 1970s, followed by economic slowdown and the impact of restructuring, stagnant or declining real wages and real family income (even when adjusted for family size), rising unemployment or underemployment (part-time and contingent work), increasing income and wage inequality, and rising child poverty. Finally, although family expenditure patterns vary little by family type in all four countries, the portion of the family budget allocated to food declined, while housing costs became a growing burden. Only the decline in family size, the rising contribution of wives to the family economy, and the availability of government income transfers (in some countries) kept the economic situation of families with children from worsening still further; while the growth in the proportion of families headed by a women alone exacerbated their economic problems. Young families, large families, and families headed by women or by minority members were especially vulnerable in all four countries.

With earnings and transfers as the core components of family income, the balance between the two changed dramatically in Britain, Canada, and New Zealand beginning in the mid-1970s, as families depended increasingly on transfers. In Britain the share of family income made up by transfers almost doubled between 1961 and 1991. The shift was especially dramatic for lone mothers, with transfer payments increasing from 36% of family income to 72% during these years, and the proportion of these families totally dependent on transfer income rose dramatically as well. Even in the US, with its more limited income transfer system, transfer payments emerged as an important source of income for poor single mothers and their children. At the same time, middle-class families and husband/wife families in general increasingly depended on wives' earnings.

Despite the high proportion of women in the work-force and the declining numbers of children per family, the economic situation of children worsened too during these years, above all in lone-mother families and families with no wage-earner. Using an international definition of poverty as less than half the median family income in the country under consideration, and drawing on a comparative household income database, Rainwater and Smeeding (1995) found that of the 18 countries for which they had data, three of the six countries with the highest child poverty rates were Britain, Canada, and the US (and two more of these countries, Australia and Ireland, come out of the same common tradition). New Zealand is not part of this database but appears to have similar poverty rates. US child poverty rates of 22% in the early 1990s are by far the highest of the 18, far higher even than the 10–14% rates in the other three countries here in focus.

Minority-group families are more likely to have lower incomes than the dominant population group in all four countries, but differences in immigration laws have meant that immigrant families in Canada are better off economically than the average family while they are worse off in other countries. Regional variations are also significant in Britain, Canada, and the US, reflecting differences in the nature of regional economies and the availability of jobs.

We turn now to the central question: in what sense are policies responsive to family changes or do changes appear to be created by policies?

THE MODEST AND RELUCTANT RESPONSE OF FAMILY POLICIES

It should come as no surprise that in the context of EU or OECD norms these four countries do not lead in family policies; on the contrary, most or all are distinct laggards in many areas. When choosing among family, market, and state as the responsible institutions for helping families adapt to or cope with demographic, workplace, and economic change, these four countries leave most up to the family even where others have assigned larger roles to the state. Even marketplace responses are modest. Thus, as will be specified below and documented in the country reports, despite major shifts in the labour market roles of mothers, these are among the less-generous countries in offering maternity, parental, and related leaves; indeed, the US lags behind the entire industrialized world in these areas. Childcare provision has developed, more in some places than others, but remains generally inadequate for preschoolers by international standards. Here, New Zealand has moved fastest, followed by the US, then Canada and Britain.

It is more difficult to generalize about income transfer specifics, a domain in which some of a country's unique features make a difference. Yet we note (New Zealand not reporting) that these countries, comparatively, lead in post-transfer child poverty. Government policy, whatever its specifics, achieves less here than in northern and western Europe, despite a shared awareness of poverty. The income transfer/family benefit packages are categorical, fragmented, and not easily comprehended. Social assistance, the last-resort safety net, is particularly important. The US is unique in its lack of a universal child or family allowance or a universal, refundable (non-wasteable) child tax credit; Canada's and New Zealand's limited and income-tested policies set them apart as well.

Health care in the industrial world is not standardized, but only the US is a laggard in this area. Indeed, until recently the British health service was regarded as the 'jewel in the crown' of its social policy. Housing policy is not consistent cross-nationally: Britain and New Zealand are among the countries with more generous housing policies, while Canada and the US may be said to lag.

Quite consistent with the ethic is a tendency toward personal social services: child and family welfare services; family counselling; social support services for those 'in need'. Thus, the poor law tradition ensures an ongoing emphasis on personal and behavioural aspects of social problems where others may turn to inadequacies in social policies, social institutions, or the economy. On the positive side, these countries, especially Britain and the US, pioneered in the social work methods these services require. But, as already seen, the overall balance of the policy response to change may be affected.

Family Law

In Britain, Canada, and New Zealand, family law—the family policy most concerned with family formation, structure, and dissolution—is the responsibility of the national government. By contrast, in the US it is the responsibility of state governments. In Canada, while the legal system in nine provinces and two territories is based on English common law, the Napoleonic (French) legal code remains influential in Quebec. Despite the decentralization of responsibility for family law in the US, trends in family law, too, seem quite similar across the countries. Significant reforms were carried out between the late 1960s and 1980s in all four, making divorce easier, equalizing the status of children born in and out of marriage, legalizing abortion, and stressing the importance of non-custodial parents' child support obligations. Nonetheless, as seen in the country reports, legal changes and reforms lagged far behind family change in these countries, although once in place they may have made it easier for those wanting to explore different lifestyles.

Introduction

Workplace Adaptations and Child Care

Despite the dramatic changes in women's roles and the high and growing LFPR among women with young children, public policy responses in these four countries have been very limited. The major policies usually associated with these developments are paid and job-protected parental leaves following childbirth or adoption, child-care services, and flexible work schedules. Only Canada has statutory provision of any significance, and even there it is modest. Britain ranks second among the four but remains a laggard in Europe, and the four countries resemble one another more than any of the European countries.

Canadian provinces now provide about 17 weeks of unpaid, job-protected maternity or parental leave. In addition, the federal government has provided maternity benefits since 1971, adoption benefits since 1984, and parental benefits since 1990 under the Unemployment Insurance Program. Employed mothers may be eligible for 25 weeks of benefits at childbirth, while fathers and adoptive parents may be eligible for 10 weeks. However, the cash benefit to replace wages at childbirth has declined in value in recent years and is significantly lower than comparable European benefits. Furthermore, only 40% of women giving birth qualify for maternity benefits. Several provinces also provide for brief, unpaid additional family-related leaves.

Britain first enacted a maternity leave policy in 1956 and has amended it several times since. Because of fairly restrictive qualifications it has been criticized for its limited coverage and for the problems some women have faced when returning to work. A cash benefit was made available in 1956 and amended in 1987. Britain rejected European Union efforts at enacting a parental leave (1994) but was forced to accept the EU directive providing a 14-week leave for all working women at the time of childbirth, to be paid at the level of sick pay. This could be seen as a modest example of the European effect on British social/family policy.

After a long and arduous political fight, the US enacted a 12-week unpaid, job-protected leave for working parents in the case of childbirth, adoption, personal illness, or the illness of a dependent child, parent, or spouse requiring care. Five states covering about 22% of the work-force provide for a paid maternity disability leave. New Zealand has an unpaid 14-week maternity leave and a 52-week parental leave, but neither is fully job-protected although seniority is protected.

In all four countries, statutory provision is supplemented by collective bargaining agreements and voluntary employer provision, but none provides full coverage for working parents at the time of childbirth which is comparable to the typical European policy. Nor do these countries have statutory provision for flexible working hours or for paid time off from work to care for an ill child, attend a child's school, facilitate a young child's entry into school, or phase in return to work after childbirth by working part-time (as in Sweden and Finland). There is no recognition of the value of 'family work' in the pension system, as in Germany and Austria.

These four countries avoid or minimize government intervention in employer/employee relations. The result is inadequate and uneven coverage and limited policies for most employed parents, with somewhat better provision for those employed in the public sector or in one of the leading companies. In addition, some policies to increase equity for women in the work-force have also had positive consequences for women in their family roles. Of particular importance are the several equal opportunity and equal pay laws enacted in Britain, Canada, New Zealand, and the US in the 1970s and the gradual though slow improvement in women's wages (now about 72–75% of male full-time wages).

Economic Well-Being

Despite many similarities, the policy responses reflect how country specifics have shaped the common core. First, the similarities: during the 1960s, Britain, Canada, and the US 'rediscovered' poverty and expanded their family benefits and their social protection systems in general. In the 1980s and 1990s, in response to resource constraints, rising public social expenditures, and changed public attitudes toward the poor in some countries, all have imposed cuts and restrictions on these systems. Overall, the income transfer/family benefit systems in these countries can be described as fragmented, categorical, extremely complicated, and as the British report indicates, almost always in a state of change and revision. In Britain, Canada, and to a lesser extent New Zealand, policy has shifted from providing a package of benefits that included a significant universal component to one that is largely means-tested and targeted on the very poor. Britain is the only one of the four that still has an important universal child benefit, although its real value has declined significantly over the years. The US and New Zealand have always had a targeted and selective social protection system for families with children, but the trend has been toward even narrower targeting.

All four countries have stressed the use of tax benefits as a social and family policy device, reducing tax exemptions for dependants (except for the US) and using instead some form of refundable tax credit targeted on low-income working families. All have also emphasized the enforcement of child support or maintenance obligations as a strategy for protecting the economic situation of some lone-mother families while reducing public expenditures. And all have the usual social insurance benefit systems with dependants' benefits for children and special benefits for children with disabilities.

The major differences have to do with the specifics of the policy package and policy regimes. In these as well as most other countries, social assistance is the final safety net. But it plays a much larger role in these four (and the other countries of the same tradition) than in most of northern and western Europe. Lone mothers are especially likely to claim assistance in all four countries.[6] But only in the US, which lacks both unemployment assistance and a national assistance entitlement for adults with no children and who are not aged or handicapped, and New Zealand, do they constitute the largest group of social assistance beneficiaries.

Between 40% and 50% of lone-mother families in Canada and the US and well over half in Britain and New Zealand receive social assistance. The four countries vary significantly, however, in the additional or alternative benefits available to these families. In contrast to the other three, until the mid-1970s New Zealand stressed full employment and a family wage adequate to cover the needs of the male employee, his wife, and three children as the cornerstone of its social protection system, instead of income transfers and a social insurance system. With growing economic problems including a high and rising unemployment rate, its family wage declined in real value as did the value of its universal family allowance, and its residual means-tested benefits became increasingly important in the 1980s. The increase in lone-mother families also put additional pressures on its social protection system. In effect, family benefits in New Zealand evolved from a selective approach early in the century to a universal one in the immediate post-World War II period to one that is now highly targeted on the poor.

Canada's most distinctive strategy has been its use of unemployment insurance both to reduce regional economic inequities and protect those with seasonal employment, and to provide sickness, maternity, and parenting benefits. Nonetheless, the number receiving social assistance doubled between 1981 and 1993 as unemployment increased and eligibility for unemployment insurance became more restricted, paralleling the rise in assistance claims in the other countries.

Although Britain still maintains the largest component of universal child benefits among the four, it provides far less through universal benefits than do the other northern European countries. Its core 'Income Support' programme is a means-tested assistance programme available to all low-income individuals and families but used extensively by lone-mother families. Canada has a similar programme, but it reflects provincial variations in generosity. The US social assistance programme Aid to Families with Dependent Children (AFDC) (abolished in 1996 and replaced by Temporary Assistance to Needy Families, or TANF) was the most narrowly targeted, focused overwhelmingly on lone-mother families with children; it also allowed great variations in eligibility criteria and benefit levels across the 50 states. The only assistance programme available to all the poor in the US is an in-kind benefit providing a guaranteed minimum income for food. All these programmes are or have been under attack in the four countries, and in 1996 the value of the US Food Stamp benefit was cut.

The general trends in pre-transfer family incomes are remarkably similar, but poverty rates for children and families vary significantly, largely because of differences in the availability and generosity of government income transfers either as substitutes for earnings or as supplements to low earnings. In this domain the policy responses differ most among the countries. New Zealand stressed work and wage regulation, only to discover that when its economy collapsed in the course of economic restructuring, so did its social protection system. Britain provides a complicated package of universal and selective categorical benefits, accepting the right of lone mothers to be supported at home until their children are grown. Their standard of living remains quite minimal, however, and British policy-makers are currently focusing further on lone parents and work. Canada follows a similar pattern but has recently dropped the universal component, and in most provinces, welfare mothers are expected to enter the work-force when their children reach school age. The US has pursued the most narrowly targeted assistance policy of all and has recently restricted it still further because of widespread concern about out-of-wed-lock births and the view in some quarters (despite research results to the contrary) that social assistance encourages unmarried childbearing. In fact, all four countries are now becoming concerned about possible perverse incentives created by their social assistance policies, especially work or marriage disincentives or incentives for women to have children out of wedlock that they cannot support. Thus, once again these countries are in the process of changing—or debating changes in—their family-benefit transfer systems.

Social Infrastructure and Social Services for Those with Special Needs

Health care, housing, food, child care, and treatment-orientated and support serv-ices for children and their families are all visible components of the social protec-tion systems in these countries, but to varying degrees. Like all the advanced in-dustrialized countries, the countries in this volume, except for the US, all devel-oped a system of national health care coverage: New Zealand at the end of the 1930s, Britain after World War II, and Canada in the mid-1960s. This coverage took the form of either national health insurance or a national health service and assured all children and their families access to health care. Recently, the British National Health Service has been subject to criticism and reorganization, the Ca-nadian system has experienced funding cuts, and the New Zealand system has been reorganized in a way that restricts access and coverage. Nonetheless, the US is unique in its limited statutory provision.

Housing, a growing burden on family budgets, also receives less attention in public policy in the US than in the other countries. Home-ownership is important in all four countries, with about two-thirds or more of all households living in owner-occupied housing. (This figure has been declining in the US while increas-ing in Britain.) Seventy-two percent of all families in Canada and 71% in New Zealand (but fewer Maori) own their own homes. Public housing, the inclusion of housing costs in assistance benefits, and various cash and tax subsidies exist in all four countries, but have been most extensive in Britain and New Zealand and least in the US. In the US, most housing assistance has been targeted on middle- and upper-class families, while housing policy in the other countries has been targeted on the poor or on first-time home buyers (New Zealand).

School meals exist in all the countries but are more available in Britain than in the others; yet even in Britain provision is not universal in the same sense as in the Scandinavian countries. The US is unique in that one of its core assistance pro-grammes is a food voucher (Food Stamps), providing the poor with a minimum guaranteed income for food, as mentioned earlier.

Given the relatively high proportion of employed women, child-care services remain inadequate in all four countries, although New Zealand and the US have slightly greater coverage than the other two countries. Neither of the two major

22   *Introduction*

child-care patterns seen in continental Europe are found in these four: neither the Scandinavian pattern, in which child care is designed to respond to the needs of working parents as well as the developmental needs of children, nor the alternative European pattern of universal preschool education for all children from age two or three regardless of mothers' employment status. Instead, these countries have followed a third pattern, in which until very recently child care was largely a dual system of early-childhood education for middle-class children and day care for children from deprived or disadvantaged families who need special attention or compensatory education. Most care of the very young remains informal, either as child-minding or unregulated family day care; most care is provided privately, and most preschool programmes for 2–4 year olds are only part-day. Although primary school begins at age 5 or 6, school schedules still leave full-time working parents with less than complete coverage, and after-school provision is also far more limited than in a country such as France. At best, child-care services may be available to children with special needs, but are not yet universal as in some European countries, and often cost more than many working parents can afford.

In Britain, where compulsory schooling begins at age 5 and most 4-year-olds are already in preschool, care for younger children is limited to those with special needs, and provision is made through child welfare and child protective services. Having an employed mother is not defined as a special need. Other young children may be in part-day, part-week playgroups. Some effort is being made to integrate child care and early-childhood education in the education system.

In the US, public funding supports care for children in low-income families either to facilitate their mothers' exit from social assistance (AFDC or the new TANF) via employment, or to help them avoid going on assistance by making work feasible. A tax credit helps offset some of the child-care costs for middle-class working parents, and a tax deduction fulfills a similar function for middle- and upper-income families in Canada; but overall the cost burden on parents remains disproportionately high compared to the continental European pattern, especially for low-income or working poor families. The US has begun to integrate the care and education functions, though this is occurring primarily in private programmes; it has only begun to move in this direction for 3- and 4-year-olds in the public education system. The Canadian pattern is similar to that of the US; in both countries primary responsibility for child care is assigned to the state or provincial level, but the federal (national) government helps with funding.

In short, child-care services expanded significantly in all four countries during the 1980s and early 1990s, and the two functions have been merged into the education system in New Zealand and begun to merge in Britain and the US. Nonetheless, they are far behind the continental European countries, and there is a long way to go before any of these countries achieve a fully integrated, accessible, and affordable child-care system that provides care to meet the needs of children with working parents, let alone one that is also of high quality.

Finally, all four countries stress the provision of supportive and treatment-orientated social services for troubled children and their families, and appear to invest far more heavily in these services—comparatively—than many other countries. In the 1960s and 1970s these services saw significant growth in public funding. Particular attention has been paid to abused, neglected, handicapped, and deprived children, to family crises, battered women, the mentally ill, and most recently to the homeless. Children from lone-parent, low-income, and minority families are overrepresented in this service system in all four countries. Growing concern with children's rights in relation to parents' rights was reflected in legislation enacted in Britain and Canada in the late 1980s and early 1990s. A stress on 'deinstitutionalization' and a shift to community-based services and initiatives, family-focused interventions, and increased sensitivity to diverse racial and ethnic cultural patterns in delivering these services characterize all four countries, as does a general trend away from public provision to delivery through voluntary, private non-profit social agencies, often publicly financed.

FAMILY POLITICS AND FAMILY POLICIES

While the review called for examining each country's institutionalization of family policy, there was little reason to expect all-embracing family ministries even in countries with explicit, deliberate, and relatively comprehensive family policies, and much less so in these countries without explicit or holistic approaches. In a review almost two decades ago, we found that governments assign the family's policy and programmatic interests to many different units, and that the few that try to organize specifically and comprehensively for family matters discover that it is difficult and debatable. Government ministries tend for good reason to be organized functionally (trade, defence, justice, housing, education, etc.), not by population groups; and cross-cutting assignments are difficult. One expert said: 'A family ministry, then, can be thought of as a government department of everything—or nothing' (Kamerman and Kahn, 1978: 489).

Thus it is hardly surprising that these countries have no focused governmental centre for family policies nor a ministry or cabinet-level post or high-level government office with that responsibility. Indeed, only in Britain is there even a semblance of this since 1994, with the assignment to the Minister for Health of special responsibility for family matters. Quebec established a Secretariat for the Family and an Advisory Council for the Family in 1988.

Although all the major political parties stress the primacy of the family, and clear differences exist in their positions, no party in these countries uses family policy as the focus of its political platform. Conservative parties or parties of the right stress traditional values, families, and gender roles and are supported by employers, fundamentalist Christian groups, and conservative politicians. Liberal (in the US sense), Labour, or left parties recognize diversity of families and family lifestyles, are more tolerant toward gender-role changes, and support equitable treatment of men and women, but are hardly radical advocates of change. They are supported in some countries by feminists, organized labour, advocates for the poor, and social reformers. Despite almost ritualistic pro-family rhetoric, the parties generally do not advance and run on family policy agendas. Family-related items may occasionally be included in a party platform (e.g., the Republicans' anti-abortion stance in the US). More recently, as noted in the income-transfer discussion, points of view about lone-mother families and child support have been taken up by the parties.

Nor have any of the other major interest groups played a leadership role in advocating for family policy. The trade unions have not been any more at the forefront in the three countries where they have been relatively strong than in the US, where unions were not strong to begin with and have grown still weaker. Indeed, in earlier years the British trade union movement had a visibly anti-feminist stance. Feminist groups have emphasized political, legal, and social rights of women as individuals far more than child and family policy issues.

Child advocacy organizations and related pressure groups like the Child Poverty Action Group and the National Council for One-Parent Families in Britain, the Child Poverty Action Group in Canada, and the Children's Defense Fund in the US have been effective advocates for specific issues affecting poor or minority children and their families, but have not sought support for a comprehensive or coherent universal family policy. Royal commissions, blue-ribbon panels, task forces, religious organizations, and think-tanks have also played a more or less successful role with regard to specific issues. Some have projected more comprehensive visions but have not seen results in the form of broad family policy legislation. Conservative 'pro-family' organizations in the US have been moving closer to advocating a comprehensive (and traditional) policy, dealing with divorce, abortion, school curricula, and so forth—in dramatic contrast to efforts of liberal and feminist groups to pre-empt the family policy vehicle in the 1970s.

Nonetheless, social policies benefiting children and their families expanded in the 1960s and early 1970s and contracted, for the most part, in the 1980s and 1990s. Why? In the 1960s and early 1970s the left and centre-left dominated politically, economies were strong, resources were available, public support for social protection was high, and government social expenditures increased dramatically. In the 1980s and early 1990s the economy was weak, unemployment or underemployment was high, resources were constrained, the future seemed uncertain, and the centre-right and right dominated the social policy debate, holding the poverty and children's lobbies at bay. Funds for social programmes were cut and these programmes became more narrowly targeted, the challenges presented by changes in the family were largely disregarded, and family policies contracted. One result has been increased income inequality among families with children and increased child poverty—or more specifically, less reduction of such market-generated inequality through government action.

Placing these countries in the context of the OECD countries generally, we see these trends confirmed even more strongly. Overall social spending between 1960 and 1990 in Britain, Canada, and the US increased steadily but remained below the OECD average. Only in Britain was social spending at about the average; New Zealand showed a significant decline in the 1980s. Of the four, only in Britain was family benefit spending as a portion of social spending significantly above the OECD average at any point during these years. Nor can demography account for these differences, because Canada, New Zealand, and the US have younger populations than the OECD average, and Britain is just at the average.

The dominant theme in these four reports is that between 1960 and the late 1970s, the role of the state expanded steadily in relation to the family. This expansion did not involve intervening in or taking over for the family, but instead responded to the challenges presented by changes in the family as an institution. Our New Zealand colleagues point out that for most of the twentieth century women and children were dependent on men—first their fathers and then their husbands—and on male wages. Indeed, New Zealand institutionalized this as the heart of its social protection system: full employment and a family wage—for men. This assumption seems to have been implicit in the other countries as well. When the economy changed and male wages could no longer fulfil that function, and women clearly could not provide adequate support for themselves and their children as divorce rates and extra-marital births rose, some women and children became increasingly dependent on the state. Others were able to increase their economic independence by attaining higher levels of education and earning higher wages. These processes each raised distinct problems of their own: economic costs to the state and a potential threat to men. While there are no significant advocates for a diminished family, given the broad recognition of the role of primary group experience in child-rearing, socialization, and development, these trends suggest a larger—if still secondary—role for state policy and perhaps for private-sector employers.

In effect, given family change in these countries, governments had two clear policy options: to make gender equity a high priority and therefore make family policy explicit and in accordance with that end, as in Scandinavia; or to support family work in the home and provide increased financial recognition for parenting, as in Austria and Germany. The countries in this volume have done neither deliberately nor on a sufficient scale, attempting either to deny or reverse family change via a 'do-nothing' policy, or to get by with a reluctant and minimalist one.

The conclusion to the British report lays out a profile of British family policy that includes many elements shared by all four countries and thus provides a useful summary. The British authors note first that governments enact policies with regard to the family when there is consensus about specified problems in the family, when pressures for government intervention are not overridden by constraints on the scope for government action, and when they believe it is within their power to intervene effectively with regard to the identified problems. They characterize current British family policy as:

- reluctant and based on the premise that the state should do less, not necessarily that the family should do more;
- emphasizing family, rather than government, responsibility for family problems;
- concerned about poverty, not family well-being, as the driving force for social policy;

- increasingly stressing selectivity and means-testing, rather than universalism;
- showing an absence of concern or even interest in the birth rate;
- demonstrating a desire and intention to hold down public spending;
- reflecting traditional attitudes toward women, or at best ambivalence about gender-role changes, and a conviction that gender inequities at home are a private matter while inequities in the market may warrant modest attention;
- accepting both horizontal and vertical inequities in family income but concerned more about the latter than the former;
- minimizing the regulation of employers with regard to their responsibilities toward employed parents;
- and, overall, implying a rolling-back and modest retrenchment of the welfare state generally as well as the welfare state of the family in particular.

Taking account of the other three countries, too, we would add that they display:

- fragmented and categorical policy responses targeted on delineated family problems rather than holistic policy responses targeted on the enhancement of family functioning;
- a system of family law that is more tolerant of family diversity than are other social policies;
- concern with single mothers as a growing moral problem, not only as a burden on the public purse;
- racial and ethnic differences that may be as significant as gender differences in their effects on the family change/family policies equation.

TO CONCLUDE

Patterns of family change in these four countries since World War II, and especially since the 1960s, have been very similar, with variations within countries linked to racial and ethnic subgroups and some modest differences in timing or degree of change. Demography generally, and fertility in particular, have never been significant factors in the policy debates in these countries, except during the 1920s and 1930s in Britain and the late 1980s in Quebec, and then without any real policy impact nationally. By contrast, race, ethnicity, and immigration have entered into the public discussion of both family change and family policies.

In describing the changes occurring to families, one could talk either about how the traditional family is disappearing or how it has changed, leading to the emergence of new family forms. Instead of a legally-married couple with a male breadwinner and a female at-home parent, the new family is a cohabiting couple (legally married or not) with a male full-time worker and a female part- or full-time worker (working part-time when children are very young). Instead of constituting a 'permanent' two-parent, husband/wife family, the new family is likely to experience a series of variations in status over the lifetime of the individual members, on a continuum between legal marriage, cohabitation, and living alone, as a lone parent with children, or as a couple with no children.

The major differences across the countries, however, are in their policy responses to these family changes; here, except with regard to family law, differences are significant. Overall, the generosity of family policy seems linked to periods of economic growth or crises, but not necessarily to changing demographic or social realities.[7] Geography, politics, and culture also appear to have a role. Britain's proximity to Europe and its membership in the European Union seem to be making the British more aware of how their social policy lags behind much of Europe and may have played a role in maintaining universal child allowances, in recent adoption of new maternity policies, and in the current (belated) debate about child care. Regardless of the general trend toward greater targeting, Britain has managed to retain a greater degree of universalism, especially in its child benefit, than the other countries in the group, providing a significant if declining benefit to all children that is weighted especially toward the first child and lone-parent families.

While Quebec has certainly influenced Canadian social policy, Quebec's family policies have not led the federal government to modify its child and family benefits. The US and New Zealand (recently) appear to have been intransigent in the targeting of their social policies and in their greater reliance on a market response. But all four countries have emphasized work-related benefits, even in their meagre family policies, and all reveal the vulnerability of such benefits, whether statutory or voluntary, in times of major economic dislocation or recession.

Federalism, a characteristic of Canada and the US, and decentralization generally may also have led to slower growth in family policies in those two countries; certainly the greater centralization and stronger emphasis on the role of federal governments in the 1960s led to more progressive social policies. Racial and ethnic diversity has been far more important in Canada, New Zealand, and the US than in Britain. Indeed, although Britain has a more diverse society than any other European country, obtaining British family change and family policy data that are disaggregated by race and ethnicity remains largely impossible.

Despite shared concern about poverty, none of the four has been as successful as several other European countries in keeping children out of poverty. Yet protecting children against poverty seems to have been a stronger motive and a more successful strategy in Britain and Canada than in New Zealand and the US. Although all four governments have assumed responsibility for the financial support of the elderly, Britain has moved furthest toward direct sharing in the economic responsibility of families for rearing children, especially poor lone-mother families, but it is not clear that this will be continued in the future.

Finally, on a central issue: family change has posed problems for policy-makers and families but has not assured a policy response. Some family policies are responsive to family change, some apparently to other factors; these reports offer little evidence to suggest that family policies instigate family change. The evidence may not all be in, which is not to say that some family policies do not facilitate family change, even where they do not cause it. A research agenda remains.

Notes

1 The concept of 'families of nations' as developed by Castles refers to groups of countries that share certain national attributes and, as a result, also share in the development of particular policy patterns. He argues that recent research in the comparative history tradition and in comparative policy studies 'demonstrate[s] conclusively that historical events and their assimilation into an individual nation's accumulative policy experience can decisively shape policy outcomes for many decades thereafter; also that a failure to contextualize policy decisions in the particularity of their historical context renders them substantially incomprehensible to contemporary observers.'

2 The preferred New Zealand term is 'ex-nuptial childbirth'.

3 Australia is missing from this volume but has been sufficiently reported elsewhere for us to make occasional references to it and to note that it does share major characteristics with our cluster.

4 Here, New Zealand is an exception since the liberalism ideology is more recent. Indeed, it became strongly evident only during the restructuring of the economy from 1984 on.

5 Britain enacted unpaid leave for childbirth in 1895, free school meals in 1906, and home health visiting; Canada enacted restrictions on female and child labour in 1884 and compulsory education in 1891; New Zealand enacted the first women's suffrage law in the world in 1893 and the first minimum wage law in 1894; the US established a special juvenile court, a special Children's Bureau in the federal government, mothers' or widows' pensions and a national programme of maternal and child health in this period.

6 Other recently published empirical research provides statistical documentation of the uniqueness of this pattern for these four countries and others in the same tradition (Australia and Ireland). See for example, Eardley et al., 1995, and Ditch et al., 1995.

7 This point is made as well in a recent report from the European Observatory on National Family Policies (Ditch et al., 1995: 132), in which the authors note that it is impossible to establish causal links between demographic indicators and policy initiatives.

Family Change and Family Policies: Great Britain

Stein Ringen, editor

This monograph is a team effort. Most of the participants have contributed material to various parts of the monograph and participated in the editorial process. The members of the team: Ann Buchanan, David Coleman, John Dewar, John Eekelaar, Anne Gauthier, Jay Gershuny, Mavis Maclean, Susan McRae, Michael Noble, Joan Payne, Katherine Rake, Stein Ringen, George Smith, and Teresa Smith. The team is at the University of Oxford, with the exception of Susan McRae who during the project was at the Policy Studies Institute, London, whence also Joan Payne moved during the project. Jay Gershuny moved from the University of Oxford to the University of Essex during the project.[1]

Introduction: Historical Roots
of Family Policy

Some main themes in the changing picture which emerge and re-emerge in the following study are:

- concern with poverty as a reference point in family policy;
- heavy reliance on social assistance as a policy instrument, and the persistence of poor law residuals;
- the (comparative) persistence of traditional attitudes to women and the family, regarding, for example, child-care provision and income support;
- a highly categorical approach to social policy and the diverse character and low level of public provision of non-educational child-care service;
- the National Health Service as the jewel in the crown of the British welfare state;
- privacy of the family as a value both in public opinion and policy formulation, and the absence of 'population policy' or pro-natalist intentions in family policies.

Britain does not have, and has never had, an explicitly formulated policy with regard to families and children. Over time, however, British governments have adopted a range of measures directly or indirectly targeted at families which have had a significant impact on their standard of living. Mothers and children constitute a major group of welfare beneficiaries.

In the period between 1867 (the Reform Act) and 1914 (World War I), 'British politics moved from a very limited notion of citizens' rights to a much more comprehensive one' (Harris, 1993). In terms of social policy, Britain entered this period in the spirit of the 1834 Poor Law, which 'embodied the principle that economically-active individuals should be financially responsible not merely for their children, but for their parents, grandparents, and grandchildren', and left the period in the spirit of the benefit reforms of the 1911 National Insurance Act and the tax reforms of Lloyd George's 'people's budget' of the same year. After World War II, Britain entered a new phase of social policy development in the spirit of the Beveridge Report with a range of reforms based on the principle of universality. This phase is characterized by a high degree of consensus that lasted until the 1979 Conservative government under Mrs Thatcher, which challenged the post-war consensus and argued in favour of a change of direction towards (again) more individual and family responsibility and curtailment of state welfare.

Britain*

Although a system of cash family allowances was operating in much of the country from about 1790 until the 1834 Poor Law reform, the earliest radical state social intervention with regard to the family was in education. Compulsory education was introduced nationally in 1876 and enforced by a network of school attendance officers. Otherwise, until the turn of the century, state involvement as a welfare provider or welfare regulator was minimal by later comparison. Most relief activities were carried out by philanthropic organizations, although Poor Law activity in Britain was more extensive than comparable welfare provisions elsewhere up to the 1880s.

This situation was considerably challenged in the 1890s and the early decades of this century. During this period, the health and well-being of children and mothers gained increasing attention, encouraged in part by the emergence of information showing the severity and magnitude of poverty. A four-week unpaid leave for working mothers, introduced in 1895, and an established system of training and certification of midwives, introduced in 1902, were intended to reduce infant mortality. Free meals and medical inspections for school children, introduced in 1906 and 1907, were intended to improve children's standard of living. Cash benefits at childbirth came in 1911, and a separation allowance for widows and orphans of soldiers in 1914.

In 1914, the government decided to grant Local Authorities matching funds to establish child and maternal welfare services, and in 1918 this initiative was reinforced by the Maternity and Child Welfare Act. The range of services provided under these new provisions was wide, although none was obligatory: 'provision of hospital services for children under five, maternity hospitals, "home helps" (i.e., domestic workers to take over the housework of the mother after childbirth, free of charge for needy women), food for expectant and nursing mothers and for children under five, crèches and day nurseries, homes for the children of widowed and deserted mothers and for illegitimate children, and experimental work for the health of expectant and nursing mothers and of infants and children under five years of age' (Thane, 1991).

The decline in fertility also received considerable attention. From an average of nearly five children per woman in 1870, the total fertility rate for England and Wales had briefly declined below two children per woman by 1930. At a time when population growth was viewed favourably, such a declining fertility trend was to raise concern in several circles. However, no explicitly pro-natalist policy was adopted, then or later. The 1944 Royal Commission on Population dismissed the existence of a demographic crisis.

World War II with its devastating consequences marked a turning point in state support for families. Whereas state support had previously been limited to specific groups, it was now gradually extended in various ways to cover all families, especially universal family allowances and comprehensive health services. These policies were not introduced without controversy. Family allowances were initially proposed as benefits to be paid to fathers, but after strong pressure (in particular from Eleanore Rathbone), the bill was amended and allowances were paid to mothers. With these reforms, state support for families had been given a firmer grounding. All families, no longer only those in greater need, were now legitimate welfare beneficiaries.

During the late 1960s and the 1970s, a series of measures helped improve the position of women. The Family Planning Act 1967 enabled Local Authorities to provide free contraceptive supplies and advice. The Abortion Act 1967 represented a major departure from the previous legislation in allowing abortion on medical and social grounds, as well as if the continuation of the pregnancy would involve greater risk to the physical and mental health of the woman than if the pregnancy were terminated. A new free-fault divorce law was passed in 1971 and removed the previous obligation to demonstrate a 'matrimonial offence'. With regard to female employment, legislation on equal pay and equal work was adopted in 1970, and on equal opportunity in 1975. The right to reinstatement after maternity was then introduced in 1976 allowing women to be absent from work for a period of up to 40 weeks with job security.

Although there were clear signs of change in public and fiscal policy under the Labour government before 1979, the next phase in family policy followed the 1979 election of a Conservative government under Mrs Thatcher. New objectives were made explicit: (1) containing and reducing state expenditure on welfare benefits and universal measures; (2) reducing citizens' dependency on state benefits and services; and (3) promoting occupational and private welfare benefits. The universal child benefit was also questioned on the grounds that means-tested benefits could more effectively target families in greater need. The value of the child benefit was frozen in 1987, but pressures from both within and outside the Conservative Party forced the government in 1991 to upgrade slightly, though not restore, its value; the future of the universal child benefit remains under fierce attack from some Members of Parliament. Finally, the government gave further visibility to children in 1989 through the Children Act which aimed to provide a coherent legislative framework for children's rights.

By European standards, the support provided by British governments to families has been and remains limited and hesitant—and deliberately so. After 1945, for about thirty years the trend was towards a less limited and hesitant family policy, but since 1979, the trend has been in the opposite direction, with government systematically opposed to further legislation which could increase the welfare dependency of families or impose additional burdens on employers. These considerations were also behind the decisions of Britain not to endorse the EC Social Charter in 1988 and to opt out of the Social Chapter of the Maastricht Treaty at the Maastricht conference in 1991.

1

The Formation of Families

The population of the United Kingdom numbered 57.4 million in 1990. Northern Ireland comprised 1.6 million, Scotland 5.1 million, and England and Wales 50.7 million.

The demographic transition in Britain from the eighteenth century used to be regarded, at least by the British, as a paradigm of the process. A decline in the death rate preceded a decline in the birth rate by a considerable interval, permitting a period of population growth in the nineteenth century which was unprecedented in British history. By around 1870 a fall in the birth rate became apparent and continued, except for the severe disruption of World War I, as a more or less linear decline for sixty years until the 1930s, when it reached a low at about the same level as that today.

From an average Victorian family size of five to six children ever-born (about one would die in infancy, another before maturity), fertility had already declined considerably by 1900. By the end of their childbearing careers, women married in 1900–09 had produced on average 3.4 children. World War I reduced births by about 600,000 over four years, compared to what might have been expected in peacetime. That loss was not entirely restored by the short baby boom which followed (although that baby boom was bigger than the better-known baby boom which followed the end of World War II). As in a number of other Western European countries, 1933 saw a nadir of fertility unmatched for a further forty-five years (total fertility rate = 1.72). Despite that one-year low, the completed family size of women at peak childbearing age at this time was about two children. In the 1930s, fears of the 'twilight of parenthood', future underpopulation, and of 'race suicide' became lively topics in academic and some political circles in Britain and elsewhere. The fertility decline was given added bite by the earlier decline of middle-class fertility compared to that of the working class, and of European fertility compared to that of other nations. While many European countries responded to the fear of population decline with policies designed to prevent abortion and the dissemination of contraceptive knowledge, in Britain the only response was to appoint a Royal Commission on Population. Its report was a pioneering work in demography, and it conducted the first British official enquiry on family planning in 1946. But no practical pro-natalist policies were adopted.

MARRIAGE, DIVORCE, AND CHILDBEARING

Marriage

From the sixteenth until well into the twentieth century, marriage in Britain conformed to the long-established Western European pattern of delayed marriage with relatively high proportions of men and women remaining single all their lives. Mean age at first marriage in 1931 was 27 for men and 25 for women, figures not much different from what they had been a hundred years before.

Starting in the late 1930s, more men and many more women began marrying at earlier ages and in greater numbers, a trend common throughout Western societies. First marriage rates for teenage bachelors increased sixfold from 1945 to peak in the early 1970s. Marriage rates of men in their early twenties doubled; those of young women almost trebled. These rates greatly increased the proportions of men and women ever married in their twenties to levels not seen for centuries. In the peak year of 1971, 60% of women aged 20–24 had been married (compared to about a quarter before the war); by their late twenties, 87% had been married. Of men aged 20–24, 37% had been married, twice the pre-war level. These cohorts have broken all records for nuptiality as they age. Before the 1940s, about 15% of women would remain single all their lives, and about 8% of men. Among the 1940s birth cohorts, only about 5% will remain spinsters and 7% bachelors (Kiernan, 1989). For the first time the proportions of women ever marrying by age 50 or more are exceeding those of men.

The record low mean ages at marriage of the early 1970s are likely to stand for a long time. Since 1972, again in common with the rest of Western Europe, the statistics show a return to a pattern of later and less popular marriage. These statistics, however, do now not reflect the tendency to form unions. In the new pattern, later marriage is usually preceded by cohabitation and often by extra-marital childbearing, and many cohabit without any intention to marry. Of first-married couples in 1979–82, 24% lived together before their marriage; of remarrying couples the figure was 65%. Ten years later, 50% of first-marrying couples and 75% of remarrying couples had lived together before marriage. What proportion lives together but never marries is uncertain. According to the General Household Survey, in 1983 12% of unmarried women aged 18–49, and 7% of all women aged 20–24, were cohabiting. By 1992, 9% of women aged 18–49 were cohabiting, as were 21% of never-married women and 28% of divorced women. Cohabitation, however, does not yet appear to have replaced marriage as a stated expectation of most young people; over 90% of young women interviewed in the late 1980s expected to marry. Cohabitation in Britain is not as general as in Scandinavia, but is much higher than in Southern Europe and at about the same level as in France.

Divorce and Remarriage

Divorce became more frequent in the twentieth century than ever before. Before 1858, civil divorce in England was impossible without a private Act of Parliament.

Successive legislation has gradually broadened its availability in terms of grounds and access, and each measure has stimulated at least a temporary rise in frequency. In general, however, the increase in divorce has not depended on legislative steps but preceded them and has occurred within most divorce law regimes, especially in the unsettled conditions during and after both world wars. After reaching peaks following each world war, divorce in fact declined in the 1930s and 1950s, periods which can be regarded both in terms of family stability and the level of illegitimate births as 'golden ages'. Because of the much-reduced chances of dissolution by death and the scarcely-awakened threat from divorce, marriages enjoyed a stability in these periods without precedent in history—and one which is unlikely ever to be revisited. Since then, divorce rates have increased rapidly.

Life table calculations applied to period rates of divorce give the proportion of marriages surviving at current risks of divorce. Such calculations show that 8% of marriages would have ended by the husband's age of 50 at the divorce rates of 1951, 13% at the 1966 rate, and 35% at the 1975 rate. In relation to the duration of marriage, the divorce rates of 1979 would end 33% of all marriages, and 56% of teenage marriages, by their 25th anniversary. The same calculation on the 1987 rates yields 35% dissolved by 25 years' duration. The acceleration of the divorce rate somewhat slackened in the 1980s; age at marriage increased in the 1970s and therefore made the average recent marriage less divorce-prone, other things being equal.

Most marriages which are going to break up, break up fast. The 1984 Act permitting divorce after one year of marriage (not three as before), precipitated a renewed tide of petitions. British data show that premarital cohabitation is associated with a higher risk of subsequent marital breakdown. The most important determinant of divorce, however, more than social class, length of previous acquaintance, and civil versus religious ceremony, is the age at marriage—the younger, the worse risk.

No natural limit to the increase in divorce is yet in sight, except that determined by ability to afford the costs (which the 1991 Child Support Act has increased). UK divorce rates are the highest in Europe, but still lower than in the USA, where about 50% of marriages are likely to end in divorce after 25 years at current rates.

Remarriage is an increasingly frequent and important social phenomenon. In 1985, more than one wedding in three involved at least one formerly married person and 12% of marriages two divorced persons. As recently as the late 1960s, 83% of marriages were still first marriages, compared to 88% in 1901–05. Because the high level of divorce is relatively recent, the proportion of remarried people in the population has not yet caught up with current rates of divorce and remarriage; at the 1981 census, only about one in ten married couples were remarried (one or both partners).

Although the frequency of remarriage has greatly increased, remarriage rates themselves have changed little over the years; since the 1980s they have been in decline. Cohabitation precedes three-quarters of remarriages, and many couples see no reason to remarry. Many separated spouses move in with someone else but cannot, of course, remarry immediately. The late twentieth century is revisiting a pattern typical of previous centuries when almost one wedding in three was a re-marriage for one or both partners. Then, remarriage arose through premature mor-tality; now, through divorce.

Births

The demographic transition was not absolutely over in the 1930s—there were still many large families and their number continues to decline slowly up to the present—but a new fertility regime emerged, as elsewhere in Western Europe. This new regime was characterized by an unprecedented volatility in fertility, especially in its timing, made possible by parents' ability to adjust the pace of their childbearing with precision hitherto impossible. This generated much bigger swings in fertility over a short time than previously when the short-term trends depended on delaying or forgoing marriage.

The late 1940s reinforced the pattern of the 1930s, with fertility apparently drift-ing down again towards replacement rate (the total fertility rate (TFR) in 1951 was 2.14, and the net reproduction rate 1.00). Official projections made even in the early 1950s assumed continuing low fertility and consequent slow population growth. The most interesting feature of post-war fertility in the developed world, the great boom in births from the early 1950s until the late 1960s, was entirely unexpected in the UK as elsewhere. It peaked in the UK in 1964 (TFR in England and Wales = 2.94). This baby boom added about two million births to the number that would have occurred had fertility remained at its 1955 level up to the 1970s. Until its equally unpredicted end, the baby boom and the modest population growth it generated provoked a new concern about overpopulation.

The final phase of fertility trends has lasted from the early 1970s to the present. Fertility fell from 1964 to below the replacement level in 1972 and has since lev-elled out at about 1.8. This twenty-year period is the longest period of stability in the British birth rate so far in the twentieth century. Similar patterns are shared by other countries in Western Europe, although at a lower level of average birth rate. The UK has experienced neither the rise in fertility since the mid-1980s which is evident in Sweden, nor the chronic low fertility of Germany, nor the rapid decline of the Mediterranean countries. Married women have moved, irreversibly it is be-lieved, into the work-force in large numbers, which is one of the main factors in keeping fertility low, because of rising relative wages for women and increasing opportunity costs of taking time off work for childbearing. While there are, then, good reasons for not expecting another period of high fertility, it is not so clear why fertility does not fall lower. Britain's comparatively higher fertility is regarded as being somewhat anomalous in the wider European context, although it is close to that of its neighbours France and Norway.

The most marked difference between the fertility of the 1980s and that of half a century before is not so much its average level, which is about the same, but its distribution in terms of family size. The fall in the number of families with over three children has continued from the previous century, and family size has become more concentrated around two children. While two-child families resulted from 22% of the marriages of 1911–15 and 44% of the marriages of 1961–65, they are still not quite the majority of families. Almost a quarter are larger; almost a third comprise one or no children.

During the 1950s and 1960s, the trend was for women to have their babies earlier in life than had previously been usual, the result, in part, of a lower average age at marriage and the increased popularity of marriage. The birth rates of women in their early twenties and among teenagers more than doubled from 1938 to 1964. Since the 1930s, women had increasingly been completing their families within the first ten years of marriage, which also raised the birth rates of women in their twenties and made childbearing among women over 30 relatively rare. Since the 1970s, this pattern of relatively early and condensed childbearing has been displaced by yet another phase of later sub-replacement fertility. The age pattern of fertility is returning to something like the temporal pattern of the pre-war world, although in other ways it is radically different.

Following the decline in marriage rates since the 1970s, teenage births became less common, and women more often had children into their thirties as in the early twentieth century. The delay in the timing of births continues into the 1990s. Mean age at all births, having fallen to a low of 26 years in 1973–5, had risen to 27.5 in 1990. Mean age at first birth, having fallen to about 24 years around 1970, had risen to about 25.4 in 1990. (By Western European standards, this is still relatively precocious childbearing.) During the 1980s, conception rates for teenage girls increased slightly, from 62 per 1,000 teenagers per year in 1979 to 69 in 1990. Only a slightly increased proportion (36% compared with 30%) were terminated by legal abortion (available since 1967); most of the remainder produce live births outside marriage. Britain has by far the highest rate of teenage childbearing in Western Europe—33.3 births per 1,000 teenagers in 1990—almost four times the Western European average. As teenage pregnancies are problematic in a variety of ways, this is regarded as a considerable failure of sex education and family planning (although there may also be perverse consequences of the welfare system).

Consolidation of the small nuclear family continues, but further reduction in the number of large families has ceased, probably for the first time since about 1870. Annual data on birth order are only available for births within marriage. Comparing births within marriage in 1980 with those in 1990, births of all orders up to four have fallen: first births by 17%, second births by 11%, third births by 8%, and fourth births by 6%, while fifth and higher order births have increased by 4%.

Because of the post-war rise in divorce and remarriage, births to remarried women have increased: 41,311 in 1990 (8.2% of all births within marriage), a number which has changed little since 1980 (38,487, 6.6%) but is much higher than in earlier years (25,119 in 1975, 16,794 in 1966). A disproportionate number of higher-parity births to older women are now born to immigrant mothers and women belonging to ethnic minority groups of immigrant origin. Those in Britain from Third World countries mostly come from the countries of the 'New Commonwealth'

(NC), especially the West Indies, India, Pakistan, Bangladesh, Hong Kong, and African countries. Mothers born in these countries have accounted for about 8% of all births for some years; the proportion is probably now about 10%, including births to ethnic minority mothers born in the UK. Initially, the NC immigrants had much higher fertility than the native British. In some cases (Indians, East Africans, Asians, West Indians), the TFR of immigrant mothers has declined to about the UK average. Others, notably Muslim minorities (mostly Pakistanis and Bangladeshis) have higher fertility (TFR 4.7 in 1990). The NC group as a whole had a TFR of 2.6 in 1990 compared with a national average of 1.8 and a British native average of 1.7.

Perhaps the most dramatic change in fertility in Britain is in the proportion of children born outside marriage. Until the 1950s, illegitimacy accounted for less than 5% of births. Its frequency had declined throughout most of the nineteenth century in Britain as in the rest of Western Europe. After the inevitable wartime increases, it resumed particularly low levels in the 1930s and the 1950s. Since the 1960s, illegitimacy has been increasing fast, as it has generally in Europe. England and Wales is now top of the European league outside Scandinavia, with 29% of all children in 1991 born outside marriage.

Over two-thirds of the recent increase in illegitimacy has been to cohabiting couples. 'Traditional', mostly unwanted, illegitimate births still occur in large numbers, especially to teenage girls. There were 44,600 teenage births in 1990 compared with 25,900 in 1980; 80% of the former and 43% of the latter were illegitimate.

A substantial number of births are reported to be unwanted: at least 10% of births even within marriage.

The analysis of current birth rates, including the distribution of births by birth order and the results of questions on family intentions in such surveys as the General Household Survey, leads to official projections of modest rises in fertility, toward a TFR of 1.9. Although this is below replacement, population decline is not forecast until well into the next century (even though the projections assume, unrealistically, that immigration will cease). These demographic developments have not stimulated much interest in the issue of population decline. In the most recent official analysis (by the Central Policy Review Staff in 1973), zero population growth was not regarded as a problem.

HOUSEHOLD AND FAMILY STRUCTURES

Size and Composition

Some of the most interesting developments have been taking place in family and household composition. Average household size has declined from 4.6 in 1901, to 3.0 in 1961, and to 2.5 in 1991. This decrease is due to the modern decline in fertility and the rarity of very large families, but also to the departure of resident domestic servants and lodgers. Of all households in 1861, 14% had at least one residential domestic servant, as compared to just 1% in 1951. The fall in household size has certainly not been due to any great change in the residential pattern of different generations of the same family. Contrary to popular myth, there never was any time in recorded history when 'extended families' were very common in Britain, either vertically (three or more generations) or horizontally (relatives outside the nuclear family). Average household size was about 4.6 for several centuries before the present (Laslett, 1972). About half of Victorian households (47% in 1861) consisted of one or both parents with their children but no other relatives, exactly the same as in 1961 and 1966. In 1861, 15% of households contained relatives of the household head, the same as in 1951, although this fell to 10% in 1966.

The number of single-person households has multiplied at both ends of the age range: young people leaving home and elderly people living on their own. The type of single-person households has changed: earlier in this century there were relatively more widows but almost no divorced persons; many lived alone, though many lived with siblings. Many more adults, especially women, remained unmarried, and these now predominate in the elderly single population. Since the 1970s in particular, the number of older single-person households has increased.

Lone-parent families comprised 18% of all families with dependent children in 1991, almost three times the proportion of 1971 (7%). Up to the 1970s, the increase in lone-parent families was due more to the effects of divorce and separation than to illegitimacy. In the 1980s, lone-parent households headed by never-married single mothers increased much more than those headed by divorced or separated women. Of all one-parent families with dependent children in 1991, a third were headed by never-married single women (more than double the proportion of 1971), another third by divorced women (a category almost non-existent at the beginning of the century), and 22% by separated women.

In 1991, over a quarter of households (26%) comprised just one person, compared with 17% in 1971 and 5% in 1911. For the first time, such households were more numerous than married couples with dependent children (24%). At the other end of the scale, only 2% of households included six or more people in 1991, down from 6% in 1971. Naturally the picture looks different when analysed in terms of persons rather than households. Almost half the population (41% in 1991) lives in households of a married couple with dependent children, and only about one person in ten lives alone.

Family Planning

The first family planning clinic in Europe was set up by Marie Stopes in London in 1921. Modern methods of contraception, the contraceptive pill and the IUD, became available in the UK in the early 1960s, although only under medical supervision, which has sometimes been felt to restrict access. Contraception became freely available on social grounds through the National Health Service (Family Planning)

Act 1967. Public involvement in providing family planning is exclusively orientated toward health and welfare of mothers, children, and families, with no goals either to increase or to reduce fertility.

Modern contraception is not necessary for fertility decline. The initial decline in British birth rates in the 1870s, as elsewhere in Europe, was accomplished by such simple methods as *coitus interruptus*, the condom, and the cap, which had become nearly universally practised by the 1930s. These methods were backed up to an unknown extent by illegal abortions, possibly up to 100,000 per year just before their legalization on broader grounds (not 'on demand') by the Abortion Act of 1967. In 1992, 160,000 legal abortions were performed upon residents of England and Wales, of whom 106,000 were unmarried.

Unlike some continental countries, the UK placed no legal obstacles to the sale and dissemination of contraceptive materials or information, other than those deemed to require medical supervision, after the acquittal on obscenity charges of birth control propagandists Charles Bradlaugh and Annie Besant at a sensational trial for publishing obscene material in 1877. The possibility of the moral use of family planning within marriage was endorsed by the Lambeth Conference of the Church of England in 1930, decades after most clergy were already limiting their own families. However, there were and remain some restrictions on advertisement (for example, on the London Underground system) arising out of concerns for public decency, and controversies, as yet unresolved, about the rights of young girls to obtain medical contraceptive advice and material in confidence.

By the 1990s, the annual General Household Survey, which in some years asks questions about contraception, revealed that 80% of currently married or cohabiting women aged 16–69 were currently using at least one method of birth control: 21% used the pill, 18% the condom, 6% the IUD, 4% withdrawal, and 2% the safe period. In 33% of cases, one or other partner had been sterilized for contraceptive reasons. Sterilization is the most rapidly growing method; pill use has declined somewhat, especially among more educated women, and the use of the condom correspondingly risen, following medical concerns. But the pill remains by far the most common method used by young women, especially unmarried women.

FAMILY LAW

The Divorce Reform Act 1969 (effective 1 January 1971) had a profound effect on family relations. The fundamental shift from fault-based divorce to divorce on proof of irretrievable breakdown of marriage breaks with a concept going back to the Protestant Reformation. The divorce reform paved the way for the Law Commission's radical proposals in 1990 that divorce should (virtually) automatically be granted at the behest of one party one year after either party lodged a sworn statement of belief that the marriage had broken down. The net effect of these legal changes was to increase the number of divorce decrees for every 1,000 of the married population from 2.1 in 1961 to 12.7 in 1987.

As part of the 1971 divorce reform, courts were granted very wide powers to transfer either spouse's property to the other (formerly only the wife's property could be transferred) and to make other financial orders. In this respect wives rather than husbands were the main beneficiaries of the relaxation of the divorce law.

Some detected an even more profound revolution originating in the divorce reform. Following the Matrimonial and Family Proceedings Act 1984, which introduced new 'clean break' provisions, long-term income transfers between former spouses became rare except when there were children. As far as legal mechanisms for economic adjustment were concerned, the significant distinction no longer lay between married and unmarried people, but between people who had children and those who did not. Those without children usually settled matters by agreement, often dividing their capital between them. For those with children, primary (though not sole) consideration in most disputed cases was 'what should be provided for the children?', an issue overlooked by the 1984 Act, and there was strong evidence that child support awards were inconsistent and compliance poor.

The Child Support Act 1991 established a formula for calculating an absent parent's liability to children. Effective April 1993, assessment was moved from the courts into the Child Support Agency, an administrative agency with wide investigatory and enforcement powers. The new legislation gave precedence to child support obligations over obligations owed to former spouses. However, policy-makers were primarily motivated by a wish to raise higher contributions from absent parents (usually fathers) to offset social security payments to one-parent families. This aspect of the agency's work dominated its public image in its first years, causing many public protests. In 1995, changes were introduced which reduced the financial burdens that the original assignment had placed on absent fathers and their new families.

Child support payments cease when children grow up, but a former spouse may still wish to look to the other for support during later life. English law has failed to deal directly with the loss of pension prospects faced by elderly divorced women. There are no provisions for pension-splitting between former spouses. Usually the courts try to compensate for the loss by awarding the whole of, or a share in, the capital value of the former matrimonial home, where possible. (Possible pension-splitting schemes are currently under consideration by the government.)

Since the 'rediscovery' of domestic violence in the 1960s, the law has developed remedies to safeguard a spouse's occupation of a home free from violence inflicted by the other. Since 1967, courts have the power to exclude a spouse from the home or otherwise regulate its occupation, and since 1976 also a power of arrest under certain conditions. The protection offered remained limited, however, and in 1995 recommended comprehensive reforming legislation was enacted in the Family Homes and Domestic Violence Act, the effects of which remain to be seen.

If a couple live together without marrying, neither will acquire any obligation to support the other, although the fact that their finances may be amalgamated will be taken into account in assessing for social security entitlements. If they separate, the

courts have no power (as they would if the couples were married) to order maintenance payments or to require the transfer of property. During the 1970s it was
nevertheless established that a partner who makes a financial contribution to the
household might acquire a vested interest in property or capital acquired by the
other, reflecting the extent of the contribution. Purely domestic work, including
raising children, is not sufficient to establish such an interest. If the unmarried
couple separate, leaving one of them with their children, the courts can transfer
property (for example, a house) from one to the other if this will benefit a child.
After 1993, the absent parent can be required to pay child support maintenance,
including an element of support of the caregiving parent. There is no provision
allowing homosexual cohabitation to attract any of the legal effects of marriage.

In deciding disputes between parents over their children's upbringing, courts are
to give 'paramount consideration' to the welfare of the child. In 1969 the House of
Lords interpreted this principle to mean that the child's welfare was the sole consideration.

In the Children Act 1989, the legal rights and duties of separated parents regarding their children were completely restructured. Parents who are married to one
another automatically acquire 'parental responsibility', defined as 'all the rights,
duties, powers, responsibilities and authority' the law gives parents over their children. They lose this responsibility only when the child reaches full age or is adopted.
If the parents divorce, they both still retain parental responsibility. The Children
Act retained the principle that in determining disputes over the upbringing of children, courts are to give paramount consideration to the welfare of the children. It
attempts to structure the exercise of the discretion by setting out a 'checklist' of
factors to be taken into account, but the list makes no attempt at 'weighting' the
various factors. The Act also seeks to achieve a more fundamental attitudinal change.
Courts are to decline to make any orders unless they are convinced that making the
order would be better for the child than not making it. The purpose is to send a
strong signal to parents—and their lawyers—that they should resolve problems
without going to court.

Since 1950 (the Matrimonial Causes Act), opportunities for the legitimation of
illegitimate children have been gradually expanded, and by 1982 the position of
children born within and outside wedlock was completely assimilated, except as
regards succession to British nationality.

FAMILY VALUES

The very considerable changes which have occurred in fertility, marriage and divorce, and in family and household composition, in particular since the 1970s, are
outward signs of dramatic shifts in the economics of the family and the values and
attitudes of individuals. Increased opportunities for women to follow careers and
the steady return of married women to the work-force have contributed to these
developments.

The economics of child-rearing have been altered by substantial increases in the costs of children, particularly by rises in their indirect cost resulting from the greater propensity for married women to go out to work. While raising the average family may keep a woman away from work for about seven years, in terms of lost opportunities for promotion and career advancement a more realistic estimate of earnings lost is about thirteen years (Joshi, 1989).

The British Social Attitudes surveys show general agreement that women should go out to work before they have children and after the children have left home, but only one in 20 thinks that a woman should work if she has a preschool child, and only one in five if there are school-aged children. Nearly nine in ten reject the view that the husband should be the breadwinner and the wife's job is to look after the home; more than three-quarters dispute that what most women want is a home and children; more than two-thirds feel that a job is the best way for a woman to be independent, and disagree that family life suffers when the mother has a full-time job; nearly as many disagree that a preschool child suffers if his or her mother works (Kiernan, 1992; Witherspoon and Prior, 1991).

Age is the most important predictor of attitudes towards working women. Three-quarters of the 60-year-olds, but only half of the 20- to 40-year-olds, think that women with preschool children should stay at home (Scott, Braun, and Alwin, 1993). Most women who stay at home give family responsibilities as the reason ('looking after children at home'). Three-quarters of the women with children under 12 think it is important for them to spend time at home with their children, and say they enjoy doing so. The lack or cost of child care, unsuitable hours or type of work, and the difficulties of combining work and child care are also important factors.

How important is work in relation to the family? The National Child Development Study (Wiggins and Bynner, 1993) shows a certain ambivalence about 'having a job' as the key to a full and satisfied life: nearly half of those interviewed thought a job was essential for 'a full member of society' while only one-third thought it was essential in order to 'get satisfaction out of life'. Most respondents, however, thought that it was possible for a woman to be out of the labour market and still be an interesting person (91% disagreeing with the statement that 'women who do not have a job are dull'), and a fair number were prepared to opt for being a housewife (41% agreed that it was 'just as fulfilling as working for pay').

There is general—if not complete—acceptance of equal opportunities. Most people think that men and women should have the same employment and training opportunities (97%) and should do the same kind of work (88%). But only six out of ten think that it is equally important for women to go out to work. A substantial number of men with wives working full-time continue to feel uncomfortable about it (Kiernan, 1992).

Marriage remains a popular institution in Britain. Most people in Britain would advise young people to marry—in due course, at any rate. A slender majority favours cohabitation before marriage, though living together without eventual marriage is still seen as undesirable. Only one in three of the British public thought that a single mother can bring up her children as well as a married couple can. One in two says that marriage without children is 'not fully complete' (and one in four that people without children 'lead empty lives'). In the National Child Development Study (Wiggins and Bynner, 1993), seven out of ten of the 33-year-olds interviewed thought that it was 'all right for people to have children without being married' and for 'couples who have children . . . to separate', and nearly nine out of ten agreed that women 'should have the right to choose an abortion if they wish'. Only one in ten thought that married people were 'generally happier than unmarried people'. On the other hand, almost half thought that divorce was 'too easy to get these days' and six out of ten said that marriage was 'for life'.

No-child families and one-child families remain consistently unpopular in attitude surveys as ideal or intended family sizes. For most people, two children is the desired family size. Survey research consistently points to an average expected family size somewhat above that currently being achieved, both in the United Kingdom and in other countries in the West (Simons, 1986a).

The British Social Attitudes survey regularly asks people for their views on how family tasks such as shopping, cooking, washing, and ironing should be shared. Over the last decade, both egalitarian views and practices have steadily if slowly increased (Heath and McMahon, 1992). In 1991, 47% reported that shopping was shared equally, compared with 39% in 1984; for washing and ironing the figures were 12% and 9%; for cooking 20% and 16%. The gap between attitudes and practice has grown over the years; numbers of those saying that household chores should be shared have grown more than of those actually sharing (Kiernan, 1992).

Women's participation in the labour market does not seem to make all that much difference to the domestic division of labour (Witherspoon, 1988; Kiernan, 1992). Whether a woman works outside the home or not, work inside the home continues to be largely her responsibility—even if traditional household tasks are more likely to be shared when she works full-time. But egalitarian arrangements may be slowly creeping in: while women carried the main responsibility for domestic tasks in 72% of the families where both partners worked full-time in 1987, this had dropped five percentage points to 67% in 1991.

CONCLUSION

The story of the British family during recent decades is a story of change: from larger to smaller families, from many to fewer children, from marriage to cohabitation, and to increasing family instability with more frequent divorce and more single-parent (single-mother) families. Although 'extended families' were never common in Britain, today's nuclear family is very different from the nuclear family at the start of the century or in the early period after the Second World War. Whether these changes add up to a 'decline of the family' is a contentious question, but for many families, no doubt, the trend is towards increasing strain; and for many children, towards less stability of family support.

Family change has not been linear. Birth rates, in particular, have moved dramatically up and down in the course of relatively few years, and usually in ways which were not expected or foreseen.

While family circumstances have changed, attitudes have remained more stable. Popular attitudes to the family in Britain remain 'conventional'. Changes in family and fertility have not resulted in pressures on government for the introduction of 'population policies'. Family law has been modified to accommodate changing patterns of family behaviour, most notably, perhaps, with respect to divorce.

While overall birth rates have declined, teenage birth rates have remained stable. Britain has by far the highest rates of teenage childbearing in Western Europe.

2

Families and the Division of Labour: Employment and Family Work

The period from the 1960s into the 1990s was characterized by growth in married women's employment, particularly on a part-time basis; decline in male employment, particularly in manufacturing; increasing unemployment; and by a modest movement towards less segregation in the family division of labour.

Britain has a profile of employment policies for parents and of related child-care policies which must be characterized as conservative and hesitant in European comparison.

PAID AND HOUSEHOLD WORK

While attitudes to the distribution of responsibility within the family have clearly shifted from 'sexism' toward 'egalitarianism', behaviour has changed less. British time-use studies comparing the mid-1970s and the mid-1980s show that activities remained strikingly segregated by gender, with women doing the great majority of unpaid work and men the larger part of paid work. Nevertheless, within the general pattern of persistent segregation, there is also a sub-pattern of change: women moving to less time in housework and (some) more time in paid work, men moving to more time in housework and (much) less time in paid work, and both women and men moving to (much) more time in child care.

From the mid-1970s to the mid-1980s, time spent in housework increased for men in about the same measure as it decreased for women. Time in child care increased from 6 to 13 minutes for men and from 24 to 39 minutes for women (minutes per day, averaged out for all days). Adding all categories of unpaid work (housework, shopping, child care, and odd jobs), women's unpaid work increased by an average of 10 minutes, and men's by about an hour. Despite the substantial change in balances, segregation is still evident. Overall, women did nearly three times as much unpaid work as men in the mid-1970s, and in spite of the very considerable growth in men's unpaid work, still more than twice as much in the mid-1980s.

In paid work, when measured in time use, there has been more change for men (reduced time) than for women (increased time). This contrasts with the picture that emerges on labour market behaviour (see next section): labour force participation has changed more for women than for men. Hence, the increase in the number of women in paid work does not carry through to a similar change in women's average time in paid work. Nor does it carry through to a similar change in the contribution of female earnings to family income. For example, in families whose head of household is in the age range 20–50, the contribution to family income from wives' earning increased from only 15% to 17% of gross income in the period 1976 to 1986 (Ringen and Halpin, 1995).

The distribution of parents' work and responsibility inside and outside of the family depends in large measure on the presence of children. Comparing couples, the following trends emerge from the mid-1970s to the mid-1980s:

• Women's participation in paid work remains sensitive to the presence or absence of children. Measured in time use, it is highest for young women without children. Women with young children continue to spend a relatively insignificant (although increasing) part of their time in paid work.
• Men's participation in paid work continues to be relatively independent of children; it remains at about the same level for men with and without children and independently of the age of children, and has been reduced in about the same measure across the board.
• In couples with children, both men and women spend more time in work, paid and unpaid work combined, in the mid-1980s than they did a decade earlier. For men, unpaid work has increased more than paid work has decreased; for women both main categories of work have increased—but for those with small children notably unpaid work and for those with older children notably paid work.
• Most of the increase in time spent on child care, for both men and women, has taken place in families with young children.

Who works more, women or men? Total work time (paid and unpaid work combined) has increased for both men and women by some minutes per day. This increase reflects principally a growth in paid work time for women and in unpaid work time for men. While women clearly work less than men in paid work, it has been suggested that they work more than men when unpaid work is added. This does not appear to be the case in Britain during the period for which we have reasonably accurate data; rather it seems that total work time is remarkably similar for women and men. This comparison, however, is only in the amount of time spent. While the 'dual burden' may not represent a substantial quantitative difference in the total of work time, the type of work women and men do still differs qualitatively. Women, including those who are in full-time employment, work fewer hours per day for money than do men. In addition, women not only spend more time than men in household unpaid work, they also tend to take more responsibility for organizing it. Both of these factors, less time in paid work and more responsibility outside of paid work, may make it more difficult for women than for men to invest fully in a work career and to build up experience and human capital towards that end. It is perhaps this difference in the mix of work activities, rather than in the overall work load, which constitutes the most significant issue of gender inequity in the contemporary division of labour within and outside of families.

LABOUR MARKET BEHAVIOUR

Since the 1960s the labour force participation of women has risen continuously. In 1991, the proportion of women who were economically active (persons 15 years and older, employed and unemployed combined) was 71%, with no difference between married and not-married women. Since 1961, the proportion increased steadily from 30% for married women and 38% for all women. Men, in contrast, have experienced a drop in economic activity rates, from 86% in 1961 to 75% in 1991. The decline in male employment during the period has been brought about mainly through a shift in overall employment from full-time manufacturing jobs to part-time service jobs. It seems likely that by the end of the 1990s, about equal numbers of men and women will be in the labour force (although not working equal numbers of hours). Indeed, in certain regions of the UK in mid-1993, the number of women in the labour force exceeded the number of men.

In large measure, the rise in women's employment may be accounted for by increasing proportions of women married to men in white-collar or higher-level occupations returning to work after having children. Between 1957 and 1980, the proportion of middle-class wives who were in employment by the time their youngest child was 11 years old grew from 45% to 86%. The corresponding rise in the participation of women married to manually-employed men was much less marked, largely because two-thirds were already in employment by 1957. By 1981 there were no differences by social class in the labour force participation of women by the time their youngest child reached 11 years of age (Joshi, 1985).

Both full-time and part-time employment among women have increased, with part-time employment mainly in service industries. The rate of part-time employment among married women increased threefold, from 12% in 1961 to 33% in 1990, compared to a doubling from 17% to 34% in the rate of full-time employment. Eight out of ten part-time workers are married women. The proportion of couples with both partners in full-time employment remains low—at about 10% to 15% of all households—and did not increase during the 1970s and 1980s.

Most of the change in women's employment during the post-war period has come through increases in the employment of mothers. In 1961, only about 1 in 4 women with dependent children was in the labour force. This proportion rose steadily to 2 in 3 either in paid work or looking for work by 1991. Mothers have increased their labour force participation in two ways: by returning to work more often between births, and by returning to work more quickly after childbearing. The bulk of the growth in mothers' employment has been on a part-time basis. Not surprisingly, the proportion of mothers working full-time declines with rising numbers of dependent children. Growth in the rate of economic activity has occurred for mothers with children of all ages, for example, from 27% of mothers with four-year-old or younger children in 1973 to 50% in 1991. Economic activity rates of mothers increase as their children get older, a pattern which has been consistent across the post-war period.

As a result of the increasing labour force participation of women, the proportion of dual-earner families has increased from half of all couples with dependent children in 1981 to almost two-thirds in 1990. The employment of women married to unemployed or economically-inactive men did not increase over this period.

The growth in employment among married women has also been accompanied by a growth in unemployment. Thirty years ago, there was only insignificant unemployment among married women/mothers; at the beginning of the 1990s, 5% of wives and mothers aged 15 and over and 6% of mothers with dependent children were unemployed. The rate of unemployment for mothers is about constant independent of the number of children and the age of the youngest child. Reliable statistics of unemployment among women are difficult to obtain because many married or cohabiting women are not eligible for unemployment benefits.

For men, unemployment is strongly associated with family circumstances. Single men have higher rates of unemployment than married men: for example, in 1985, 15% of single men of working age were unemployed compared with 7% of married men. Both marital breakdown and lone parenthood reduce the probability of employment. In 1985, 14% of widowed, divorced, or separated men of working age were unemployed, compared with 7% of married men. The number of non-working lone parents is rising: in 1981, 70% of lone fathers were employed; by 1989 the proportion in work had fallen to 58%. Similarly, the proportion of lone mothers in work fell from 45% to 41% (Harrop and Moss, 1993).

Unemployment tends to be concentrated within families, thus increasing the risk of family poverty. In the early 1980s, 35% of unemployed 16- to 19-year-olds lived in a family in which at least one other person was unemployed (Payne, 1987). The same study produced evidence that parental unemployment increases the risk of unemployment among sons and daughters.

EMPLOYMENT AND PARENTING POLICIES

Maternity rights were introduced by a Labour government as part of the Employment Protection Act 1975 in order to reduce the disadvantages that women experience as a result of leaving paid jobs to have a baby. Maternity rights were amended by successive Conservative governments through the 1980 and 1982 Employment Acts and the Social Security Act 1986. Each amendment restricted women's maternity rights or rendered them more complex. Implementation of the EC Pregnant Workers Directive in October 1994 improved maternity rights in Britain, but they remain among the poorest in the European Community.

Pregnant women employees have four rights under the employment protection legislation:

- the right to Statutory Maternity Pay;
- the right not to be unreasonably refused time off for antenatal care and to be paid when allowed that time off;
- the right to complain of unfair dismissal if dismissed because of pregnancy or for reasons connected with pregnancy;
- the right to return to work with the previous employer, subject to certain limitations, up to 29 weeks after confinement.

UK legislation does not grant women a right to maternity *leave* (although this term is common currency). Nor are employers required to give a woman any benefits attached to her contract of employment while she is absent from work for reasons of pregnancy or confinement.

These rights generally are available to all women employees, married or unmarried, but from their introduction they have been subject to conditions and limitations which restrict eligibility. Until the early 1990s, for example, women who were members of the police or armed services were not eligible for maternity rights. Furthermore, until 1994 all rights except those relating to time off for antenatal care required a minimum period of continuous employment.

When the right to reinstatement after an absence for reasons of pregnancy came into effect in June 1976, qualifying women had the right to return to the jobs that they had held before pregnancy. During the 1980s, this right was weakened: firms with six or more employees could offer a woman suitable alternative employment rather than her original job, if the employer thought it was not reasonably practicable for her to return to her old job. Firms with fewer than six employees were exempted from the obligation to reinstate a woman who qualified for reinstatement if they could show that it was not reasonably practicable to offer the woman either her original job or a suitable alternative.

Suitable alternative work could also be offered if the woman's former job was no longer available because of redundancy. In all three situations, 'suitable alternative work' denoted work which was both suitable and appropriate for the employee, with terms, conditions, and location not substantially less favourable than those of her employment before maternity absence.

Legislative changes during the 1980s also allowed employers to require women to provide written confirmation of their intention to return to work, within 14 days of being requested for such confirmation. Failure to comply with a request would result in forfeiture of the right to return. In addition, women were required to notify their employers in writing of their intended date of return at least 21 days before returning. Legislative changes also meant that the qualifying period for protection against unfair dismissal on grounds of pregnancy was extended during the 1980s from six months to two years (or five years in the case of part-time employees).

In 1979, survey research found that 54% of women employees qualified for the right to return by virtue of their hours of work and years of continuous employment. Of these qualifying women, 41% gave formal notice to return and 15% returned to their same employer after the birth (Daniel, 1980). Since the 1979 survey, it has become more common for women to return to work relatively soon after having a child and to take up their entitlement to reinstatement. In 1988, 60% of women employees qualified, 72% gave formal notice of return, and 36% returned to their same employer (McRae, 1991).

To qualify for reinstatement and protection from unfair dismissal, until 1994 women were required to have worked for the same employer for at least two years if employed for 16 or more hours per week, or for five years if employed for more than eight hours but fewer than 16 hours per week. They needed to remain in employment until 11 weeks before the expected week of confinement in order to qualify for reinstatement. Women employed for fewer than eight weekly hours were not eligible for maternity rights.

With implementation of the EC Pregnant Workers Directive in 1994, pregnant employees qualify for a minimum of 14 weeks' maternity leave, irrespective of length of service. All employees are protected against dismissal from employment for reasons connected with pregnancy, and the burden of proof lies with the employer to justify a dismissal. All contractual employment rights are to be maintained during maternity leave and during any absences from work for reasons of health and safety while pregnant. Pregnant employees retain the right to paid time off for antenatal care.

Women returning to work after maternity absence do not have the right to return to part-time working hours, and employment continuity may be jeopardized if working hours after pregnancy fall below 16 hours weekly. However, although there is no statutory right to return to work part-time, there have been a number of successful cases involving the right to reduce working hours brought under the Sex Discrimination Act.

The Employment Protection (Consolidation) Act 1978 provided a right, under certain qualifying conditions, for pregnant women in employment (employees and self-employed) to receive maternity pay upon leaving work to have a baby. In April 1987, the maternity pay provisions in the Act were replaced by the Statutory Maternity Pay provisions introduced in the Social Security Act 1986. From the initial introduction of maternity pay in April 1977, the amount of maternity pay has been linked to women's employment continuity.

With implementation of the EC Pregnant Workers Directive in October 1994, pregnant British employees acquired the right to payment during 14 weeks' maternity leave at a level not less than statutory sick pay. The length of service qualification was reduced to 12 months for higher rate payments. The UK government was instrumental in linking the level of maternity pay to the level of sick pay, despite objections from the Equal Opportunities Commission, other interested bodies in the UK, and other Community Member States.

Adoptive mothers in the UK currently are not legally entitled to maternity rights or benefits. There is no statutory provision for parental leave or leave for family reasons in the UK. Nor is there any statutory provision for paternity leave.

The Second Community Action Programme on the promotion of equal opportunities for women, 1986–90, included a draft directive on parental leave and leave for family reasons. Parental leave is defined as a period of leave to look after a child, available to employees after the expiry of maternity leave. Leave for family reasons would include time off work to care for an ill child or spouse. The draft directive stipulates that payment for parental leave should be made from public funds, but does not include any specific requirements on member states as regards payments of allowances.

The UK government blocked the draft directive in December 1985. Legislation in this area is regarded by the government as inappropriate. Government takes the view that any provisions for parental leave should arise through the voluntary agreement of employees and employers. The matter was considered also by a House of Lords Select Committee which agreed that parental leave was not a matter appropriate for legislation.

The need to develop employment policies for families came to prominence during the 1980s as the employment of women with young children increased radically. During the 1970s, policy-making had focused on the creation of equal opportunities for women; the 1980s brought the recognition that most women workers were also mothers and that so long as traditional views about the parental responsibilities of men and women prevailed, arrangements were needed in the workplace to help women to accommodate their double role. It was also hoped that flexible and family-friendly working arrangements would encourage men to take up a greater share of domestic obligations.

However, an increasing need for employment policies for families coincided with the advancement of Conservative government policies committed to non-intervention in the relations between employer and employee. Proposals for policies designed to improve working arrangements for employees with children were regularly resisted by government on the grounds that enforced policies would entail an unacceptable burden on employers and make them reluctant to hire women with children or of childbearing age. In the place of explicit employment policies for families, the government has encouraged employers to be more flexible and to provide satisfactory arrangements for workers with children, where these can be justified on economic grounds.

The outcome of government non-intervention is an uneven distribution of working arrangements to help employed parents. Workers in the public sector—where trade unions are strong—have substantially better access to such arrangements than workers in the private sector, apart from a handful of highly-visible large corporations. Women in higher-level white-collar and professional occupations are substantially more likely than women in manual or lower-level non-manual work to have access to flexible working arrangements and child-care facilities.

The hours of work of women (and children) were restricted by a series of measures in the nineteenth century that were gradually extended and consolidated during the twentieth century. Protective legislation for women workers evolved alongside the developing concepts of 'housewife' and 'family wage'. The introduction of sex discrimination and equal pay legislation in the 1970s brought widespread discussion about the possible repeal of protective legislation governing women's hours of work. The Confederation of British Industries was in favour of lifting restriction and the Trades Union Congress against; the House of Commons in favour and the Lords against. While deciding to retain the regulations provisionally, the 1974 Labour government asked the newly-formed Equal Opportunities Commission to review them. The Commission reported that the regulations provided some limited protection for some women, but argued that by creating differences between men and women, the legislation also perpetuated unequal pay. Accordingly, the EOC decided in favour of repeal. The European Commission also favoured repeal of laws which specifically prohibited women from doing particular jobs or jobs with particular hours or work regimes. But in addition, the EC endorsed legislative protection for both men and women from harmful working practices. Hence the development of the Social Chapter.

The Conservative governments elected since 1979 have supported the repeal of legislation which interferes with the freedom of employers and employees to determine for themselves appropriate working practices. However, these governments have opposed attempts to extend general protective employment legislation and refused to sign the EC Social Chapter. Accordingly, restrictive legislation on the hours and workdays of women was repealed in the late 1980s, and the UK is currently at the extreme of lack of such regulation among Community Member States.

There is no statutory entitlement in the UK to flexible working hours or reduction in working hours to accommodate family responsibilities. Current government policy is that flexi-time, annual hours, term-time working, part-time working, and so on are matters to be decided between employers and employees, not matters for legislation. Some lead is provided to employers by way of example, and government departments have been encouraged to provide flexible working arrangements for staff provided these arrangements can be justified on economic grounds. The Employment Department, for example, promotes flexible working arrangements in two ways: (1) through booklets intended to provide information and raise awareness among employers and employees of the benefits of flexible working; and (2) by setting a good example to others. The Department has a range of 'family-friendly' measures in place such as part-time employment, job-sharing, term-time working, annual hours, working from home, and so on.

However, few employers have done much more than introduce part-time working arrangements. Other 'family-friendly' practices tend to be concentrated in certain industries, such as the public sector, and among larger private sector employers (Brannen et al., 1995). Moreover, where they are accessible, flexible arrangements tend to exist at management's discretion only—that is, they are often available only to a limited extent and to a limited range of staff. For example, survey research carried out in the late 1980s indicated that 46% of employers, but only 12% of new mothers, reported that flexi-time was available in their workplace. Similar disparities between employers' and employees' accounts were also found in relation to job-sharing, career break schemes, working at home, and help with child care (McRae, 1991).

CONCLUSION

A critical chapter in the story of family change is the increasing participation of married women in paid work (and some reduced participation by men). This has created pressures on the family, including pressure for more equitable sharing of household duties between women and men, and pressure on the labour market for arrangements to accommodate working mothers. For children, the result is that fewer are likely to have a home parent, although very small children are still likely to have a mother at home.

The pressure on families has resulted in a change of attitudes in the direction of egalitarianism and also in some change in actual sharing of tasks and responsibilities in family work, although less in the latter than in the former. Here, it seems, changing attitudes are ahead of changing behaviour.

The pressure on the labour market has not resulted in a similar change in attitudes to gender and paid work, as was seen in Chapter 1. The issue of policies to accommodate working mothers became a political battleground within Britain and between Britain and (some of) its partners in the European Union. British governments in the last 15 years have adopted a 'hands-off' approach, arguing that social issues are for the labour market partners, rather than government, to sort out. This approach has resulted in comparatively underdeveloped employment policies for parents, disparate responses by employers, and an uneven distribution of arrangements to support working parents.

3

The Income of Families:
Earnings and Transfers

Over the last fifty years, the distribution of income in Britain has changed dramatically, moving towards more equality up to the mid-1970s, and then shifting again towards greater inequality. During the 1980s, the income gap widened, and by the early 1990s, the distribution of income in Britain was more unequal than at any time since World War II. The shift towards inequality was a result of labour market developments, demographic trends—notably the increasing polarization between two-earner and no-earner households—and new policies. In the latter category, in particular the move from wages to prices as the basis for upgrading state benefits was significant, as was also the reduced real value of the child benefit.

PATTERNS OF INCOME

The first-ever analysis of trends in the distribution of family income over a reasonably long period of time (from 1961 to 1991) based on consistent time-series of statistical data was published by the Institute for Fiscal Studies in 1994 (Goodman and Webb, 1994). The present overview draws heavily on this report. (For consistency with the rest of this monograph, we use the term 'family' rather than 'household' although the analyses we draw on are of household income.)

The Composition of Income

Families have income from a range of sources: earnings, self-employment, investments, private pensions, social security, and other sources (e.g., private transfers). Considering all types of families together, earnings are by far the most important source of income. The second most important source, although contributing much less than earnings, is social security benefits. The big story on the composition of income over the last three decades is the declining contribution of earnings to family income, down from about 77% of total family income in 1961 to 61% around 1991. This is the result of many underlying pressures, including demographic changes such as the ageing of the population. However, the declining contribution of earnings is also characteristic of younger households, including families with children.

The contributions of income from self-employment, investments, and private pensions have increased somewhat over the period, but the source of income showing the strongest growth is social security, from contributing 9% to total family income in 1961 to 16% in 1991. The increasing importance of social security income is characteristic of most types of families, including families with children.

The composition of income for couples with children has changed moderately: earnings down from 80% to 73% of total family income, self-employment income up from 10% to 12%, and social security income up from 6% to 10%. For single-parent families (mainly headed by women), however, the composition of income has changed dramatically: the contribution of earnings to family income fell from 64% to 28%, while the contribution of social security income rose from 25% to 53%. Single-parent families also have significant income from 'other' sources, mainly maintenance from previous partners, which on average contributes about 10% to total income, with probably some slight increase over the period.

Income Inequality

Income inequality is commonly described by the Gini coefficient. A coefficient of 0 would indicate income equally distributed in the population; a coefficient of 1 represents total inequality.

In 1961, the Gini coefficient (disposable income after housing costs) was 0.27. It fell to a low of 0.25 in 1977, then increased again and had by 1991 reached 0.37. The share of total income held by the bottom 10% of families went down from 4.2% in 1961 to 3% in 1991, while the share of the top tenth of families increased from 22% to 25% over the same period. Most of the increase in this income gap occurred during the 1980s. The ratio of the real income of the top tenth of the population to that of the bottom tenth was roughly 3:1 up to the late 1970s, and then increased to about 4.3:1 by the beginning of the 1990s.

Measured in 'poverty' terms, the proportion of the population (persons) whose family income after housing costs is below half of the national mean was down from 11% in 1961 to 7.4% by 1977, then rose to 24% by 1990/91. This kind of relative poverty standard, when applied to comparison over time, may be considered to exaggerate the trend in poverty by not taking into consideration the increasing absolute standard of living. However, even when the poverty line for both points of observation was set at 50% of the average 1979 real income, Hills (1993) reports the number of persons in poverty to have increased from 1979 to 1990/91, if only moderately.

The increasing inequality after 1977 has occurred despite a tendency for social security benefits to equalize the distribution of income. Final income inequality has become more unequal both because other factors than state transfers have pulled in this direction, notably increasing inequality in the distribution of 'market' income, and because the equalizing impact of transfers has been modified. The latter is due to a variety of factors reducing the value of social security benefits. These are outlined in the third section of this chapter.

The value of state benefits is illustrated in a study of the cost of living in 1993 (Bradshaw, 1993). The study estimated a 'low-cost budget' which includes items which more than two-thirds of the population regard as necessities or which more than three-quarters of the population actually have. The weekly costs of this budget for a couple with two children were £36 more than the family would receive if they were unemployed and dependent on Income Support.

Children and Income

A study covering the first ten years of the period of increasing income inequality (1976 to 1986), and limited to families with household heads in the age range 20 to 50, shows a relative deterioration of the economic situation of children and families with children. Families with children have a lower standard of living than the population average (measured in income adjusted for family size and composition), and this difference has increased since 1976. If we assume that children and parents in each family have the same standard, it still turns out that children as a group have a lower standard of living than parents (and a much lower standard than all adults), because families with children, and more so the more children, do not have enough additional income to 'cover' their additional needs. The gap in standard of living between children and parents/adults has increased as overall inequality has increased.

Poverty is more prevalent among children than adults. Measured by adjusted income, the proportion of children in relative poverty was 7.7% in 1976 and 11.2% in 1986, as compared to 3.1% and 7.1% respectively among adults (families in the 20–50 age range). Relative poverty is defined as persons below half of the median adjusted disposable income of all persons.

Family income is sensitive to children in the sense that there is generally an 'opportunity cost' of children (actual family income tends to be lower than 'expected income' without children, other things being equal). The opportunity cost of children appears to be higher in Britain than in some other European countries, probably in part because of the relative lack of child-care facilities and other forms of family support (Joshi and Davies, 1993). With increasing female labour force participation and increasing female contribution to family income, the opportunity cost of children has increased (Ringen and Halpin, 1995).

Family Types

The composition of income groups has changed a great deal over the last thirty years. In the poorest tenth of families, by income after housing costs, there are more families with children and fewer pensioner families. In 1961, 35% of the families in this bottom income group were couples with children and 3% singles with children; by 1991 these family types represented 46% and 11% respectively. The proportion made up by single or married pensioners went down from 42% in

1961 to 10% in 1991. This shift in the composition of the 'poverty' population occurred mainly after the mid-1970s and is in some measure explained by the rise in unemployment (from 1.3 million in 1979 to 2.8 million in 1991) which pushed many non-pensioner families into poverty.

The changing composition of low-income groups is shown even more dramatically if we look at persons rather than families. The number of persons belonging to low-income families was on a falling trend until the mid- or late 1970s and then increased sharply. In 1961, there were 5.3 million persons in families below half of the median income, in 1977 there were 3.3 million, and in 1991 the number was up to 11.5 million.

These trends are in line with the latest Department of Social Security figures on Income Support which show that in 1993 approximately one in four of all dependent children lived in households on Income Support, a rise from just over one in five children in 1991 (Department of Social Security, 1994). These children are concentrated within the younger age groups: 36% (1.12 million) are under five years, and about the same proportion (1.14 million) are of primary-school age. The latest 'Households Below Average Income' report for 1991/92 shows that 30% of dependent children were living in households without a full-time worker, up from 18% in 1979, and notes with calculated understatement that this change 'gives the family a higher than average risk of being on a low income' (1994: 53). The number of children in England entitled to free school meals has risen nearly 40%, from 821,400 in 1991 to 1,141,300 in 1993.

The composition of the top tenth of the distribution shows much more stability. Pensioner families are more or less steady at about 10% and there are virtually no single-parent families. While families with children have hence maintained their relative position in the top of the distribution, they have added to the numbers at the bottom of the distribution, which implies an increasing polarization of income inequality among families with children. Again, this has happened mainly during the 1980s.

Expenditure

The composition of family expenditure has changed a good deal in recent decades. On average in all families, from 1960 to 1980 food was down from 30% to 18% of the budget, housing up from 9% to 18%, and motoring and travel up from 10% to 16%.

Families with children have higher expenditures than the average for all families, but the lowest level of expenditure is in lone-parent families. Generally, expenditure is higher in large than in small families, but family expenditure depends more on income than on family size.

The composition of expenditure in families with children differs only marginally from that of all families: 20% for food, 17% for housing, and 16% for motoring and travel. In lone-parent families, a somewhat larger share of the budget than average goes to food and housing.

TAXATION

During the period under review, three trends in taxation policy relevant to the family can be identified: first, tax penalties associated with marriage have been eliminated, leading to the separate taxation of husband and wife and to the elimination of anomalies that enabled unmarried couples to claim twice allowances that married couples could claim only once (such as the Additional Personal Allowance and Mortgage Interest Relief, both discussed below).

Second, reliance on the tax system to assist with the costs of children has been reduced in favour of means-tested benefits (such as Income Support and Family Credit) and non-means-tested benefits (such as Child Benefit). Child Benefit, for example, was in part a replacement for the Child Tax Allowance, an income tax allowance set against the earned income of fathers that was abolished in the 1970s. As a result, the direct tax burden on couples with children has increased significantly. For a couple with two children under 11, the burden has increased from 9% of average gross earnings in 1964–5 to 22% in 1994–5 (Utting, 1995). For single taxpayers and childless married couples, the incidence of direct taxation has decreased over the same period.

Third, most marked since 1979, is a shift from direct to indirect taxation coupled with a reduction in the rate of direct taxes. Taxes on goods and services are now the second most significant source of tax revenue behind income tax, which is one reason why the changes in tax and benefit structures since 1979 have benefited richer households to a far greater extent than poorer.

Allowances

The most significant tax exemption is the 'married couple's allowance' (MCA), introduced in 1990 to replace the 'married man's allowance' (MMA). The MCA is an income tax exemption available only to married couples on top of the single person's income tax exemption. Current government policy is to restrict the value of the MCA, both in terms of the size of the allowance and the rate of tax from which it provides exemption. In 1995, for example, the MCA was not uprated in line with inflation, and the rate of tax from which it provided exemption was reduced to 15%, cutting its value by a quarter.

An additional personal, or single parent, allowance (APA) is available to unmarried parents responsible for a child or children. It is equivalent in value to the MCA, which, until recently, was seen as a major source of fiscal discrimination against married couples, because it could be claimed by both members of a cohabiting couple with two or more children. Recent legislation has prevented this, in line with government policy of removing all forms of fiscal discrimination against marriage.

A limited tax exemption for employers who provide child care was introduced in 1990; it does not cover the costs of nannies or child-minders employed by the parents, nor does it apply to allowances or vouchers provided by employers towards the cost of child care. It has no relevance to the self-employed. Whether the scope of this allowance should be widened is a controversial question. Some argue that it would be appropriate to abolish the MCA and replace it with more extensive tax reliefs for child-care costs; while others, bearing in mind that the tax system is a necessarily crude and potentially inequitable mechanism for distributing state welfare, would prefer to see any money saved from the removal of the MCA applied to greater social security benefits for parents and carers (see, e.g., Commission on Social Justice, 1994).

Another important form of income tax exemption relevant to families is the exemption for interest repayments on loans of up to £30,000 taken out for the purpose of purchasing a primary residence. This is a direct subsidy to owner-occupiers and is not therefore concerned with families as such. However, like the APA, it was until recently regarded as a further source of fiscal discrimination against married couples, because the full allowance of £30,000 could be claimed by each borrower unless the borrowers were a married couple, in which case only one allowance was given. Thus an unmarried couple could obtain relief on a loan of up to £60,000, but a married couple only on a loan of up to £30,000. Since 1988, however, only one allowance may be claimed per residence, thereby removing the tax advantages of the unmarried state in this respect. In any case, the value of this exemption has been progressively restricted in recent years and it is likely that it will eventually be abandoned.

The Tax Treatment of Marriage

Before 1990, the tax treatment of married couples was based on the principle that the taxable income of a married couple was aggregated and treated as the income of the husband. The principle of aggregation is as old as income tax itself (1799) and survived the scrutiny of two Royal Commissions (1920 and 1954) until the 1990 changes. Aggregation for tax purposes meant that a married couple were potentially exposed to a higher rate of tax than they would have paid if they were two unrelated individuals, although this was offset to some extent by the fact that the husband (and only the husband) was entitled to claim a 'married man's allowance' (MMA), an income tax allowance equivalent in value to approximately 1.5 the value of the single person's allowance.

The wife was not entitled to a personal exemption in her own right, but the husband was entitled to claim an earned income exemption on her behalf. Any unearned income of the wife was taxed in full at the husband's marginal rate. Further, the wife was not entitled to any privacy in her tax affairs: matters were resolved between the husband and the Inland Revenue. This situation was mitigated to some extent in 1970 by the introduction of separate assessments for husband and wife (which left intact the means of calculating the amount of tax payable); and by the 1971 introduction of the wife's earnings election, which meant that spouses could be taxed as separate individuals. However, since this modification did away with the MMA, it was only worthwhile for the comparatively well-off, for whom the savings entailed in avoiding aggregation more than offset the loss of the MMA.

This structure of personal taxation attracted much criticism, most significantly from the Conservative government in two Green Papers issued in 1980 and 1986. The Green Papers singled out three features of the regime for criticism: (1) the lack of privacy and independence for married women in tax matters; (2) the system's discrimination against marriage itself; and (3) the difficulty of ensuring that increases in tax thresholds would benefit primarily the poorer taxpayers.

In 1990, the government introduced separate taxation of husband and wife within a system of non-transferable personal exemptions, coupled with an additional transferable exemption for married couples now termed the 'married couple's allowance' (MCA).

When initially introduced, the MCA was to be set against the husband's earnings, just like the old MMA. Since 1993, however, it is possible for married couples either to allocate the whole exemption to the wife or to split it equally between them. Even so, it is difficult not to see the MCA as simply the MMA in only a slightly different guise. The new system still penalizes single-earner couples in exactly the way that was so cogently criticized in the Green Papers, since the wife's non-transferable personal allowance is only of value where she is earning. It is current government policy to restrict the value of the MCA and possibly to phase it out altogether in the long run. The size of the exemption has not been uprated annually in line with the rate of inflation since 1990, thereby reducing its significance further.

FAMILY BENEFITS

Social security benefits for families divide into two main categories: non-means-tested benefits and means-tested benefits. Non-means-tested benefits subdivide further into non-contributory benefits and National Insurance benefits where payment is contingent on contributions paid to the National Insurance fund. For families whose income (after receipt of any non-means-tested benefit to which they are eligible) falls below specified minima, means-tested 'topping-up benefits' are available. For families where the parent or one of the parents is working 16 or more hours a week, the relevant benefit is Family Credit. For families where neither parent is so employed, the family may be eligible for Income Support (social assistance). The main elements of the British social security system are displayed in Figure 1.

Non-Contributory Benefits

From the inception of the post-war welfare state in 1948 until 1977, families received a universal non-means-tested social security benefit, the Family Allowance, paid at a flat rate for each child except the first. This benefit was complemented by tax exemptions for each child for those with earned income. Family allowances

FIGURE 1. The British social security system, 1996

	Contributory	Unemployment Benefit [1] Incapacity Benefit [1,2] Maternity Allowance [1] Widows Benefits [1] Retirement Pensions [1]
Non-means-tested benefits	Non-contributory	Child Benefit [1] One Parent Benefit Guardian's Allowance Severe Disablement Allowance [1] Attendance Allowance Disability Living Allowance Invalid Care Allowance Industrial Injuries Scheme War Pensions
	Employment-related [3]	Free prescriptions for certain groups, e.g. pensioners, children
		Statutory Sick Pay [1] Statutory Maternity Pay [1]

Means-tested benefits		Income Support
		Family Credit
		Disability Working Allowance
		Housing Benefit
		Council Tax Benefit
		Social Fund
		    Budgeting Loans
		    Crisis Loans
		    Community Care Grants
		    Maternity Payments
		    Severe Weather Payments
		Health Benefits
		    passported for IS or FC claimants
		    otherwise a separate means test e.g.
		    prescriptions, dental treatment,
		    vouchers for glasses, patient's hos-
		    pital fares
		Education Benefits
		    free school meals for IS claim-
		    ants; discretionary uniform grants

[1] Overlapping benefits; claimants may receive only one of these even if eligible for several.

[2] Replaced 'Invalidity' and 'Sickness Benefits' in 1995.

[3] Paid by employer.

were paid to the mother (or the lone father), while tax exemptions accrued to the principal earner, usually the father.

In 1977, the Family Allowance and tax exemptions were abandoned in favour of a universal Child Benefit. Initially, it was paid at a lower rate for the first child and a higher rate for each additional child. From 1978 to 1991, the benefit was paid at a flat rate for all children. Since 1991, it has been paid at a higher rate for the first child. Child Benefit is paid until the child reaches 16 and continues up to the age of 19 if the child is in non-advanced education (i.e., secondary school or equivalent).

Before 1976 there was no universal benefit specifically for lone parents. With the introduction of Child Benefit in 1977, an additional non-means-tested benefit was made available for lone parents, named 'Child Benefit Increase' and renamed 'One Parent Benefit' in 1981. One Parent Benefit is payable only with respect to the eldest child living with the family. It ceases to be paid when there are no children for whom Child Benefit is in payment. In 1994/5, the number of families receiving the benefit was 818,000 (with 1.3 million children), up from 508,000 families (779,000 children) in 1981.

Introduced in 1977, the Guardian's Allowance is paid to those looking after children whose parents are both dead. The total number of families receiving this allowance in 1991 was 1,850. The Child Special Allowance is paid to divorced women whose former husbands are dead, providing the women have not remarried and are not cohabiting. The benefit is being progressively withdrawn as no new claims have been allowed since 1987. It was never a significant benefit; the number of cases peaked at 919 in 1982 and had fallen to 187 in 1991.

Contributory Benefits

The Widowed Mothers' Allowance is a National Insurance benefit paid to widows who have not remarried or who are not cohabiting, providing they are either pregnant by the late husband or have at least one child living with them for whom they receive Child Benefit. It was introduced in April 1977 and has not been substantially altered since. The number of families receiving the benefit has remained fairly constant at around 1,500 since its introduction.

Until 1982, a flat rate one-off Maternity Grant was payable to all mothers on the birth of a child where the appropriate National Insurance contributions were met. In 1982 the National Insurance conditions were dropped; in 1987 the grant was replaced by a means-tested maternity payment from the Social Fund.

The Maternity Allowance is a weekly National Insurance benefit, normally paid for 18 weeks, starting 11 weeks before the baby is due. It is paid with increases for dependants. Since 1987, most women who worked for an employer immediately preceding pregnancy became entitled to statutory maternity pay instead, payment for which is made by the employer. In 1991 the number of Maternity Allowance awards was 67,000, down from 244,000 in 1977 and 332,000 in 1987.

National Insurance benefits are earnings-replacement benefits and can be classified as either short- or long-term. Unemployment Benefit, Sickness Benefit, and

Maternity Allowance are regarded as short-term benefits, whereas Invalidity Benefits, Widows Benefits, and Retirement Pensions are long-term benefits.

Before 1980 all earnings-replacement benefits had additions for dual dependants. Since that time, however, additions for children for short-term benefits have been withdrawn.

Social Assistance

The current British social assistance scheme—Income Support—has its origins in the National Assistance scheme introduced in 1948 to replace 'poor law' provisions. National Assistance existed until 1966 when it was transformed to Supplementary Benefit, which was then transformed to Income Support in 1988. It is currently payable where neither claimant nor any partner works for 16 or more hours a week.

National Assistance was paid at a rate which reflected family composition. It also allowed for those with special weekly needs to seek additional help through a series of discretionary weekly exceptional circumstance additions (ECAs). ECAs became an important component of the weekly benefit for many claimants, particularly pensioners and those with young children. The proportion of claimants receiving ECAs had risen from 28% in 1948 to 60% in 1965. In order to receive an ECA, home visits were required so that the claimant could 'prove the need'. In order to address both the increasing dependence on ECAs by some groups and the stigma attached to claiming National Assistance, the benefit was renamed Supplementary Benefit in 1966 and made payable at a higher rate for certain groups.

The 1966 reforms achieved only limited success in tackling the weaknesses of the National Assistance system because they did not fundamentally address the problem of fitting a 'last resort' residuary system to the 'first resort' role it had come to play. Following a recommendation contained in the 1975 Annual Report of the Supplementary Benefits Commission, in 1976 the government set up a review of the entire system. The review was reported in 1978 in a document entitled *Social Assistance*, and several of the recommendations were implemented in the Social Security Act 1980. In particular, the much-criticized discretionary nature of the pre-1980 scheme was in large measure replaced by a system of entitlements, but it is questionable both whether claimants benefited by this shift from a system of discretion to one based on legal rights specified in extremely lengthy, complex, and formal regulations, and whether the objective of a simpler scheme was achieved.

In 1985, the government issued a Green Paper in three volumes entitled *Reform of Social Security*. In addition to a series of changes in other social security benefits, the Green Paper proposed a radical overhaul in Supplementary Benefit. One of the problems identified was that Supplementary Benefit did 'not target resources to those who need help most as effectively as it could . . . There is good evidence to support some re-allocation of help towards families with children'. This apparent 'client-centred' agenda was also driven by Treasury pressures to cut overall social security expenditure.

A new scheme of Income Support, to replace Supplementary Benefit, was enacted in the Social Security Act 1986 and came into force in 1988. The reforms implemented in 1988 represented the most fundamental overhaul of income maintenance policy since the implementation of Beveridge forty years earlier. Social assistance in the form of Supplementary Benefit had become the most important part of the income maintenance system for all, save pensioners. Changes to it inevitably had major consequences for the poor.

The introduction of Income Support meant that the complex set of entitlements geared to meet individual family circumstances under Supplementary Benefit was replaced by less complex arrangements based on family type. Families with high needs lost as a result of this process, and other groups, such as individuals aged between 16 and 25, were singled out for benefit reduction. Receipt of Income Support also gives entitlement to free school meals and may trigger eligibility to other locally-administered education benefits such as school clothing grants or educational maintenance allowances.

Under the Child Support Act (as of 1991), lone parents on Income Support (or Family Credit) are required to disclose the name and whereabouts of the other parent so that maintenance payments can be recouped (and thus reduce the amount of Income Support due to the claimant). Failure to disclose will result in reductions to the Income Support payable.

For families and other claimants of social assistance, a system of grants for exceptional items has been available since 1935. With the introduction of National Assistance in 1948, these were referred to as 'exceptional needs payments' (ENPs). The rationale for payment was that the weekly benefit rates were insufficient to cover the larger items of expenditure which arose on an occasional basis. Such payments have always raised controversy, notably on where to draw the line as to what is or is not covered by the weekly scale rates. Moreover, the discretionary and therefore arbitrary nature of the system was frequently called into question.

The Social Security Act 1980 attempted to specify more clearly the scope for exceptional payments. The discretionary nature of ENPs was eliminated, and the grants were renamed 'single payments', to be established through entitlement regulations. During the 1980s, however, expenditure on single payments escalated. The government reacted by first reducing eligibility for certain items, e.g., furniture (1986), then by removing certain items from the scope of the system, e.g., payments for the needs of the newborn baby (1987), and finally by abolishing the system altogether (1988). Instead, a new system of discretionary payments was introduced, to be drawn from a cash-limited budget—the Social Fund.

Although there is some limited scope for obtaining grants from the Social Fund, most payments for items previously covered by the single payment/ENP system are now in the form of interest-free loans. Families did particularly badly from these changes, losing on average the equivalent of £3–5 a week (Noble et al., 1989).

Free prescriptions, dental treatment, vouchers for glasses, and maternity payments from the Social Fund are triggered by receipt of either Income Support or Family Credit.

Family Credit

The late 1960s saw a 'rediscovery' of family poverty for those both in and out of work. Two major candidates considered for tackling the problem of low-income working families were a Negative Income Tax (NIT) and a substantial increase in family allowances with a clawback mechanism through taxation for the better-off. On gaining power in June 1970, the Conservative government saw the latter as the most effective short-term solution, although the legislation it brought in did not build on universal benefits but introduced a new means-tested benefit, the Family Income Supplement (FIS). Although both NIT and the prospect of increased family allowances with clawback had their critics, commentators at the time emphasized that these schemes would have had the advantage of 100% take-up, whereas many were sceptical about the take-up for the new FIS. This pessimism proved justified. Costings when the benefit was introduced were based on a take-up of around 85%. However, a year after introduction, actual take-up had reached only about 50%, and by the time the benefit was discontinued in 1988, take-up rates had not significantly altered.

In addition to reviewing Supplementary Benefit, the 1985 Green Paper also considered the future of FIS. A new system of 'Family Credit' came into effect through the Social Security Act of 1986. Family Credit differs from FIS in several respects: eligibility still depends on the claimant having dependent children and being in paid work. However, the minimum hours which Family Credit claimants need to work are 24; under FIS it had been 30 for couple parents and 24 for single parents. The computation itself also changed. Net earnings rather than gross earnings are used as the basis for calculation. A maximum benefit is determined by the number and ages of the children. Earnings and other relevant income are compared to a fixed 'applicable amount' (uprated annually).

An award of Family Credit is itself taken into account in assessing entitlement to both Housing Benefit (HB) and Council Tax Benefit (CTB) (and indeed Income Support if a person becomes eligible for this benefit during the period of a Family Credit award). No other means-tested benefit itself becomes a resource in the calculation of other means-tested benefits. Because excess income reduces HB by 65% and CTB by 20%, an award of Family Credit to recipients of both those benefits is effectively taxed at 85%, until eligibility for HB and/or CTB is exhausted. Awards of Family Credit to owner-occupiers are only subject to marginal 'tax rates' of 20%, as under the present system they are eligible only for CTB. In theory, therefore, it might be expected that owner-occupiers would be more likely to claim Family Credit than would those in rented accommodation where the marginal tax rate could be 85%. However, owner-occupiers moving from Income Support lose reimbursement of mortgage interest.

In April 1992, the hours-of-work eligibility criterion was reduced from 24 to 16 hours. This meant that a significant number of lone-parent families in which the parent was working between 16 and 24 hours and drawing Income Support would in principle have shifted from this benefit to Family Credit. While the numbers will be small against the overall numbers on Income Support, this change marks a further step in making benefits a supplement to income earned at work, rather than a substitute for it. The intention is to provide such benefits in a way that encourages labour market participation.

Housing Costs

Housing costs for those on Income Support are supported in two ways. If the claimant is buying a house with a mortgage, s/he will receive 50% of the mortgage interest for the first 16 weeks of a claim and thereafter 100% of the mortgage interest (subject to certain restrictions). S/he will also receive 100% rebate of Council Tax eligibility. For those in rented accommodation the Local Authority will meet 100% of the rent and Council Tax due (subject to certain restrictions and deductions).

Rent and Council Tax liability for anyone on a low income (including recipients of Family Credit) may, depending on circumstances, be rebated up to 100% by the Local Authority. The scheme is not discretionary, but amounts of rebates depend on many factors including household composition (the presence of children enhances entitlement) and level of income. Those not on Income Support get no help with mortgage interest, which acts as a perverse incentive for owner-occupier families on Income Support against sentencing the labour market. If they take on low-paid jobs, they become entitled to Family Credit but lose all help with mortgage costs.

Pension Entitlement for Those Caring for Children

The basic state retirement pension and the State Earnings Related Scheme (SERPS) both depend on recipients having a full contribution record. People outside the labour market because they are caring for children, for example, might obtain only a reduced pension. However, for people outside the labour market with children under the age of 16 (or, in some circumstances, looking after a person who is disabled), some protection is afforded through the 'home responsibilities' scheme. This scheme helps satisfy some of the contribution requirements for long-term benefits such as retirement pensions.

CONCLUSION

The system of cash benefits to families in Britain is extremely complicated and in a state of almost permanent change and revision. The universal Family Allowances, later Child Benefit, which were a cornerstone in the welfare state reforms at the end of World War II, have gradually declined in real value (and, surprisingly, also in popular support). Since the early 1980s in particular, gradually more emphasis has instead been put on social-assistance type means-tested benefits, based on the theory that these could be targeted better to those most in need.

The overall effectiveness of the system of cash benefits is difficult to assess, but in a sense it was put to the test when the distribution of income shifted towards increasing inequality since the late 1970s. Although the various benefits are clearly of great importance to many families, families with children found themselves on the losing end of the redistributions that took place with rising inequality. Obviously, not all families with children lost out in this period, but these families, and hence children, on average found themselves unprotected against increasing relative poverty when total inequality increased. Child poverty increased drastically.

Taxation has moved towards being 'neutral' with respect to family and marriage, a trend that has been controversial in Britain, where the view remains relatively strong that taxation should encourage 'conventional' family arrangements.

4

Families and Social Services

In addition to policies concerning work and income, many families rely on a range of public or private services including child care, health, and housing.

Children in Britain start school at age five, hence the education sector takes care of a year-group or two more of children than in some other European countries. Outside the education sector there is a range of albeit patchy services for preschool children and for children with special needs. UK child-care provision is piece-meal, heavily reliant upon the private and voluntary sectors, and only inadequately meets the needs of employed parents.

Health care in Britain has been predominantly public through the National Health Service, which has done a good job of meeting the needs of families. The NHS is presently undergoing far-reaching reorganizations, the effects of which on service delivery are not yet clear. Housing policy has been dominated by public housing (Council Housing), mainly for low-income families, and mortgage tax relief to encourage home-ownership. Both of these policies have in recent years been strongly scaled back.

CHILD CARE

Post-war government policy towards the provision of child care falls roughly into three broad, overlapping phases. The first phase entailed the dismantling of public day nurseries established during World War II. The second phase saw government policy heavily influenced by psychoanalytical theories suggesting that maternal separation was harmful to young children, which led to the development of part-time nurseries and to child-minding rather than group care. From 1975 to 1985, the number of children receiving nursery education all but doubled, largely through part-time attendance. Educational provision has been the only publicly-provided form of institutional child care to increase in the post-war period. Nonetheless, there were fewer than 800 Local Authority day nurseries in 1985, catering for less than 1% of children under five.

The third phase in the provision of child care has seen responsibility for provision passed to the hands of parents, with some limited assistance from employers. Current government policy takes the view that employed parents are responsible for making, and paying for, their own child-care arrangements. Various government-led or -supported initiatives exist to encourage employers to collaborate with parents and the voluntary sector in the provision of child care for employees: in 1989, for example, Local Education Authorities and school governing boards were encouraged to offer the use of school premises for after-school and holiday play schemes; and in 1992–3, Training and Enterprise Councils were invited to take part in a pilot scheme to provide out-of-school care for children aged 5–14. Funding for such projects is generally restricted to start-up grants, and projects are expected to be self-financing or operated with financial assistance from employers.

In 1990, the tax liability on employees whose employers provided a 'benefit-in-kind' through a workplace nursery was removed. This tax had been imposed in 1983, and for seven years workplace nurseries had attracted a higher rate of taxation than company cars. Lifting the tax was intended to encourage greater provision of workplace nurseries by employers, particularly through partnerships with Local Authorities and voluntary organizations. At the end of 1990, however, there were only about 130 workplace nurseries, providing care for about 3,000 children of preschool age. The economic recession in the UK since 1990 has slowed, if not extinguished entirely, the development of additional workplace nurseries.

An exception to government child-care policy concerns children designated as 'in need'. To some extent, the Children Act represents an improvement in provision, but it also signifies the continuing trend towards the deregulation and rationing of child care.

The following themes have been prominent in Britain over the last thirty years in the provision of child-care services for preschool-aged children—that is, out-of-home provision, whether 'educational' or 'care' in type, provided by statutory authorities or the voluntary or private sectors:

- a slow expansion in nursery schools and classes, with a rapid expansion at the end of the 1980s of 'rising fives' (children entering school before the statutory age of five) in primary-school reception classes;
- Britain's unchanging position, however, towards the 'bottom of the league' of provision compared with its European partners;
- the continued importance of voluntary (and, more recently, not-for-profit and private) provision, particularly for working parents;
- increasing demand, particularly from women in the work-force and from lone parents;
- pressure to integrate services fragmented between different statutory, voluntary, and private organizations; and
- the shifting debate about educational, social, and economic arguments underpinning child care.

By the 1990s, the educational arguments for nursery provision for three- and four-year-olds have been generally accepted (Sylva, 1994). Constraints on this type of provision are financial rather than in terms of effectiveness. However, the social, economic, and political debates about the impact of out-of-home provision on children below the age of one and about the compatibility of care and work for mothers with small children remain fiercely contested.

Current discussion of Britain's fragmented services and the impact and desirability of child care can best be understood in the context of historical developments. Throughout this century, we can see four main arguments played out, concerning, first, women's role in the labour market; second, the social and psychological effect on young children of out-of-home care away from their mothers; third, the educational impact of early years' programmes; and fourth, the role of the state in such provision.

At the turn of the century, the education system catered for a surprisingly high number of preschool children. In 1901, 43% (more than 600,000) of three-year-old children were in elementary schools established under the 1870 Education Act, a percentage only now being reached again with the large numbers of 'rising fives' in reception classes. By 1919, the percentage of preschool children in school had dropped to 17% following the removal in 1902 of grants for children under three and the inspectorate's recommendation in 1905 that elementary school was an inappropriate setting for under-fives. Nursery schools were permitted by the 1918 Education Act, but by 1938 only 118 of these had been established with just over 9,500 places.

Both world wars provided the impetus for child care to release women into the work-force. During the first, 108 day nurseries were established. In World War II, the number of nurseries increased during the three years 1940–43 from 14 to 1,345. By the end of the war there were nursery places for 62,000 children in England and Wales—more than double the figure for 1988. As the Minister for Labour, Ernest Bevin, explained in 1941, 'Married women not previously employed [must] supply most of the necessary additional power for industry. From that point of view the provision for the care of children is a matter of first importance to the war effort.' It is thus not surprising to find a policy of nursery closures following the end of the war as men returned to the work-force. Within a year the number of nurseries had dropped to 914; within twenty years only a third remained open. In 1945, the Ministry of Health was asserting that 'the right policy to pursue would be positively to discourage mothers of children under two from going out to work' and 'to make provision for children between two and five by way of Nursery Schools and Nursery Classes' (Penn and Riley, 1992).

Even during the war, there were conflicting medical, social, and psychological arguments for and against day nurseries. *The Lancet*, for example, quoted the view of the Medical Women's Federation in 1943 that war nurseries were places with 'a high incidence of infection and a low incidence of happiness'. A lead article in the *British Medical Journal* in 1944, entitled 'War in the nursery', argued that mothers of young children should not go out to work: 'In the years from two to five the battle between love and primitive impulse is at its height . . . Winnicott, Buhler, Isaacs, Bowlby, and others all note the turbulent characteristics of the age . . . Destructive impulses let loose in war may serve to fan the flame of aggression natural to the nursery age' (Penn and Riley, 1992). Thus even before the end of the war, psychoanalytic theories about the damage to young children of separation from their mothers were increasingly influential.

In education, priority lay with the statutory age group during the 1950s and 1960s. This period was summed up in the 1972 White Paper, *Education: A Framework for Expansion*, as follows:

although local education authorities were required by the 1944 Education Act to 'have regard' to the need for the provision of nursery education, its claims on resources have had to be subordinated to the needs of children of compulsory school age . . . While the school-leaving age has been raised twice, Local Authorities were asked to restrict the number of under fives in school (other than 'rising fives') to the number in 1957. This has been mitigated only by a concession to enable local education authorities to establish new nursery classes where these would allow married women to return to teaching, and by the approval of some 20,000 new places in nursery schools and classes under the Urban Programme.

Expansion in the 1960s occurred elsewhere: in the self-help playgroup movement, characterized by adult learning and parental involvement.

TABLE 1. Children using day-care services, Great Britain 1990 (in %)

Day-care service	Age of child last birthday[1]					All preschool children (in %)
	0	1	2	3	4	
No services	48	30	20	5	3	22
Father	19	18	24	24	24	21
Grandparent	22	24	25	22	18	23
Brother or sister	2	2	2	1	1	2
Other relatives	4	4	5	5	5	4
Friend or neighbour	6	6	7	8	7	7
Registered child-minder	4	6	7	7	6	6
Nanny, mother's help, or au pair	2	3	3	3	3	3
Playgroup	—	1	18	50	42	21
Nursery class or school	—	—	4	30	54	15
Day nursery	2	6	8	13	9	8
Parent and toddler group	12	36	31	13	7	21
Base[2]	*626*	*739*	*713*	*685*	*480*	*3,243*

[1] Columns total more than 100% because children may use more than one service.
[2] Numbers taken from a 1990 Department of Health survey with a total sample of 5,525 children from 3,705 households.
Source: Meltzer, 1994.

Research in the 1960s on young children's learning and the possibility of reducing disadvantage by intervention in the early years—part of the War on Poverty in the United States and compensatory education movements in Britain (G. Smith, 1975)—provided evidence for those pressing for a change in priorities. The Plowden Report published in 1967, *Children and Their Primary Schools*, drew heavily on these studies and added to the pressure. The first example of government recognition of the 'importance of the years before five in a child's education' came in the 1972 White Paper and the following circular 2/73: 'The value of nursery education in promoting the social development of young children has long been acknowledged. In addition we now know that . . . children may also make great educational progress before the age of five.' The White Paper argued for the first significant increase in educational nursery provision in the thirty years following the end of the war, drawing directly on the Plowden Report's recommendation in 1967 that part-time nursery education should be provided for all three- and four-year-olds whose parents wished them to have a place. Demand was estimated at 90% for four-year-olds and 50% for three-year-olds.

Although the White Paper was rapidly dubbed 'the framework for contraction' as government expenditure was squeezed throughout the 1970s and 1980s, there was still some expansion of nursery provision. Expenditure on under-fives by Local Authorities increased from under 10% of the total spent on primary education in 1979/80 to nearly 20% in 1992/93. A breakdown of the use of child-care services by preschool children is given in Table 1.

Assumptions about the damage to young children of separation from their mothers have continued to undermine pressure for any expansion of day care. In 1968, a Ministry of Health circular spelling out the criteria for Local Authority day nurseries restricted places to children designated as 'at risk' and 'special needs', with the exception of single parents who had no option but to go out to work. Notions of good/bad parenting are still powerful in the family centres which have largely replaced publicly-funded day nurseries, catering for families 'at risk' and children 'in need' following the Children Act 1989 (van der Eyken, 1984; T. Smith, 1992). This is despite research which shows that children over the age of one year benefit from well-run day care (Sylva, 1994; Melhuish and Moss, 1991). It remains to be seen whether the Children Act 1989, with its emphasis on a joint approach to educational and care services for children under eight, and its emphasis on a proactive rather than crisis approach to provision for children and families under stress, will result in any expansion of provision.

Despite known heavy demand for publicly-funded day care (Witherspoon and Prior, 1991), child care for children of working women is still largely a private matter (Meltzer, 1994), relying on family and friends or privately-funded care by nannies (for the middle classes) or child-minders (for the working classes). Conservative government positions on provision for the under-fives have always contained mixed moral and economic undertones. Prime Minister John Major was quoted in 1990 as follows: 'We have always made it clear that it is not for the government to encourage or discourage women with children to go out to work' (*Independent* 21 Mar. 1990). In 1979 Patrick Jenkin, then Secretary of State for Social Security, stated: 'Quite frankly, I don't think mothers have the same right to work as fathers. If the good Lord had intended us to have equal rights to go out to work, he wouldn't have created man and woman. These are biological facts; young children do depend upon their mothers' (*Guardian* 6 Nov. 1979). A 'child-care disregard' for working parents came into effect in October 1994 for claimants receiving Family Credit, Housing or Council Tax Benefit, or Disability Working Allowance. It is too soon to say whether these limited measures will encourage more employers to set up provision or unemployed claimants to return to work.

In the mid-1990s, all-party support is growing in Britain for some expansion of preschool provision. At the Conservative Party Conference in October 1994, the Prime Minister promised nursery places 'for all four-year-olds whose parents wish it.' In the summer of 1995, the government introduced a voucher scheme, although only a few Local Authorities have initially agreed to participate. Vouchers worth about £1,100 annually to parents of four-year-olds will buy education places (in nurseries, reception classes in primary schools, or playgroups) but not day care intended for working parents. The government's stated intentions are to increase 'choice and diversity' in preschool education, and to stimulate the private and voluntary sectors to provide new places to satisfy parental demand. The scheme will be funded partly by new money and partly by recouping some of Local Authorities' current expenditure.

Services in Britain for children under five are piecemeal and fragmented between the statutory and voluntary or not-for-profit and private sectors, and vary according to region, Local Authority and neighbourhood, function, age of child, and socio-economic status of the parents (Meltzer, 1994; Moss, 1994; Owen and Moss, 1989; Penn and Riley, 1992). Broadly speaking, services cover educational provision for children, day care for children of parents in employment or education or training, play and care for children and families with 'welfare' needs, and self-help or community-run groups providing play, education, and care for children for short periods of time, as well as support services for parents. It is not always possible to draw clear distinctions between the functions or uses of different types of provision. Working parents, for example, may use a combination of services to provide care for their children. Most groups would aim to provide good learning experiences for young children, even if they were not run by trained teachers.

Costs vary. Commercial or private nurseries catering for working parents charge high fees and tend to cater for high-earning groups, while state educational provision intended for the developing child is free, and voluntary or self-help groups aimed at parent and child together make small charges. Thus the economics of child-care provision neatly illustrate the underlying ideologies.

Educational provision for children under five may be provided in separate nursery schools or nursery classes in primary schools, or by early entry into reception classes in primary schools. Care may be provided by day nurseries, family centres, community nurseries, workplace nurseries, private nurseries, or child-minders. A mixture of play and family support services is provided by playgroups, parent and toddler groups, family centres, and a wide variety of other types of preschool group—crèches, drop-in centres, one o'clock clubs, playbuses, family centres, family projects, parents'/children's resources centres, and after-school clubs. Table 2 gives an overview of day care and preschool education services in Britain.

Both public and private child-care services have expanded over the last thirty years. In education, the proportion of children aged three and four in school in the

Great Britain

TABLE 2. Day care and preschool education: provisions and costs, Great Britain, 1991

Type of provision	% of children[1]	Hours	Age	Cost	Provided by
Day care (% of 0–4 year-olds)					
Child-minders	7%	All day	0–4	£1.50/hr £50/wk	Private arrangement
Local Authority day nurseries/ family centres	1%	All day or sessional	0–4 (few under 2)	Means-tested	Local Authority social services
Private day nurseries, partnership and workplace nurseries	2.5%	All day	0–4	£45–150/wk dep. on child's age and subsidy availability	Employers, private organizations, individuals
Education and play (% of 3–4-year-olds)					
Local Education Authority nursery schools and classes	26%	Termtime: most 2½ hrs/day	3–4	Free	Local Authority education
Infant classes	21%	Termtime: 9am–3.30pm	Mainly 4	Free	Local Authority education
Playgroups	60% (1.8 children/ place)	Most 2½ hrs 2–3 days/wk, some all day	2½–4	£1.70 per 2½ hr session	Parents and voluntary groups
Private nursery and other schools	3.5%	Most 9am–3.30pm	2½–4	Various fees	Private individuals, organizations
Services on which there are no national statistics					
Combined nursery centres	Approx. 50 centres	All day	0–4	Education free, day care means-tested	Local Authority education and social services[2]
Family centres (may include some Local Authority day nurseries)	Approx. 500 members of Family Centre Network[3]	Usually all day	Vary	Vary	Local Authority social services, health authorities, voluntary sector
Out of school/ holiday clubs	700 clubs[3]	Before and after school, holidays	Vary	Vary	Schools, leisure depts., voluntary sector

[1] % do not add up to 100 because some children attend two types of provision.
[2] Some health and voluntary sector input.
[3] As of December 1993.

Source: Ball, 1994.

UK rose sharply from 15% in 1965/66 to 53% in 1991/92. (This is in both the state and private sectors; the proportion in state schools only would be slightly lower.) The proportion of two- to four-year-olds in state nursery education in England (separate nursery schools, or nursery classes in primary schools) increased slightly, from 22% in 1984 to 26% in 1993. Most of the expansion, however, has been in primary schools as four-year-olds or 'rising fives' in reception classes: over the same period, this group has increased from 19% to 25% of the age group. By contrast, full-time nursery education places in the United Kingdom have actually declined between 1965/66 and 1991/92 from 26,000 to 16,000 (Department for Education, 1994; *Social Trends* 1994 and 1995).

The term 'day care' covers many different types of provision, including voluntary and private day nurseries for working parents, Local Authority day nurseries and family centres (increasingly restricted to children with health or behaviour problems and families with social needs where children are considered to be 'at risk'), child-minders and crèches, and part-time voluntary groups such as playgroups (which provide play and learning opportunities for children and self-help support for parents, usually mothers). Over the last thirty years the number of day-care places in the UK has increased significantly. This increase has taken place mostly in the private and voluntary sector: between 1980/81 and 1991/92, the number of day nurseries provided by Local Authorities actually fell (from 32,000 to 30,000), while in the voluntary and private sectors the number of nurseries is estimated to have more than quadrupled (from 23,000 to 105,000). Playgroups also increased over the decade, but less significantly (433,000 to 496,000), although they still serve the largest number of children aged four and under. The increase in registered child-minders (from 110,000 to 297,000) again reflects working parents' demand for full-time day care.

Working parents seeking full- or part-time day care look to day nurseries run by Local Authorities or the voluntary and private sectors, and to child-minders. According to the Department of Health's survey of day-care provision in 1990 (Meltzer, 1994), day nursery places catered for 8% and child-minders for 6% of the 0–4 age group. Workplace nurseries are used by only about 1% of families for their under-fives (Bridgewood and Savage, 1993). A small number of playgroups have moved to providing full-day care, which is an important move away from the part-time nature of playgroups and their ethos of parental involvement.

What does this variety look like in practice? For one example, we can turn to the General Household Surveys for 1986 and 1991 showing the different patterns of education and care provision between private and public sectors, as well as variations in use by age of the child, family type, working status of the mother, father's socio-economic status, and mother's education. In 1986, 55% of the under-fives were being cared for outside the home. Nearly half the two-year-olds did not use any form of out-of-home care; a fifth of the three-year-olds and one in ten of the four-year-olds stayed at home. Once the break from home was made, playgroups catered for the younger and nursery school or primary school for the older age groups. Children using different types of group also showed very different patterns of attendance. Nurseries tended to be full-time or half-time, and playgroups and mother and toddler groups tended to be very part-time. Child-minders provided for a very small minority of the under-fives.

The picture from the 1991 survey has similarities and differences. Rather more families with children under five (64%) used some form of out-of-home care. Nursery or primary schools were used by a quarter (this probably represents a real increase in four-year-olds and 'rising fives' in reception classes), private or voluntary services by just under a fifth, and child-minders or nannies by one in ten. As in the 1986 survey, working mothers were more likely than non-working mothers to use out-of-home care for their under-fives, and full-time working women tended to use child-minders/nannies. Mothers' education was also important: the higher their qualification, the more likely they were to look for a day-care place.

Access to and use of provision varies considerably between regions, Local Authorities, and by type of neighbourhood, ethnic group, and social class (Bone, 1977; Osborn et al., 1984; Cohen, 1988; Cohen and Fraser, 1991). In 1993, the proportion of three- and four-year-olds in English Local Authority nursery schools and in nursery classes in primary schools, combined with four-year-olds and 'rising fives' in primary school reception classes, ranged from a low of 31% in the southeast region to a high of 77% in the north, with London at 55% slightly above the national average. Hence, access to provision in England still depends largely on where you live.

Despite increases in out-of-home provision for preschool children, working parents still have to rely largely on informal rather than formal care. According to the Department of Health's 1990 survey of day care (Meltzer, 1994), family and friends still look after nine out of ten preschool children whose mothers work. Working women with under-fives have to devise 'packages of care' including family and friends as well as statutory, voluntary, and private care.

Child-care services are recognized as particularly important for lone parents. From 1981 to 1991, the number of lone mothers with preschool children increased by nearly a quarter of a million, but the proportion in employment fell from 21% to 19% (just over half in part-time employment), in sharp contrast to the increase in married women's employment.

Married or cohabiting mothers with under-fives are more likely to be working than are lone mothers, and increasingly so, if we compare the 1981 and 1991 censuses. At the beginning of the 1980s, the employment profile of the two groups looked similar, with 'couple' mothers slightly more likely to be working but in part-time jobs, while lone mothers were more likely to be in full-time jobs. By the beginning of the 1990s, however, employment patterns of the two groups had diverged sharply. 'Couple' mothers were twice as likely to be employed, whether part- or full-time, than were lone mothers, presumably reflecting both the growth of part-time, low-paid work for women and the lack of child care.

Although publicly-funded educational provision is expanding slowly, in general child care in Britain continues to be patchy and uneven, and is largely a matter of privately-funded services and informal care. Many parents put together 'packages' of care for their preschool children, using both statutory and voluntary sources, and family and friends. For lone parents, this seems to be considerably more difficult. Yet we know that this is precisely the group that is at risk of bringing up their children in poverty. It remains to be seen whether the voucher scheme announced by the government in 1995 will successfully tackle the inequities of the current situation as well as increase the total amount of provision available.

HEALTH CARE

The family provides care, it educates in health matters, and it mediates in the use of professional services. This renders the family sensitive to changes in health policy, a matter of particular relevance in Britain in recent years with its radical shift in policy. The emphasis today is less on what professionals can do for families, and more on what families, supported by voluntary efforts in the community, can do for themselves.

Families and Child Health

The family acts as an important transmitter of its children's health chances. The impact of the home environment on children's health is most noticeable among babies, with the sharpest class differences in mortality found in the post-neonatal period (28 days to 1 year). Rates of infant mortality and of low birthweight are highest among children of lone mothers; of mothers who have either many or no previous children; of younger and older mothers; and of mothers whose country of birth is not the UK (except when born in Australia, Canada, or New Zealand) (Graham, 1984; Blaxter, 1981). While infant mortality has declined steadily during the period under consideration, the persistence of the relationship between infant mortality and class remains a cause for concern (Cole-Hamilton, 1991).

Health Services

The majority of British women receive their antenatal and maternity care from the National Health Service (NHS). Within the NHS, there are a variety of providers of care including General Practitioners (GPs), hospitals, and community midwives. Antenatal treatment is aimed at monitoring progress, screening for abnormalities, and providing information to prospective parents. Childbirth has increasingly come to take place in a hospital setting. As a consequence, although birth rates have fallen during the period, spending on maternity health services has risen. In the British system, these services are generally regarded as being of good quality and accessibility.

Following the 1906 Education (Administrative Provision) Act, a School Medical Service was developed in Britain (later called the School Health Service). Routine school medicals have now been phased out, although sight and hearing tests and immunizations are still carried out on all school children. An early (1977) study of school nursing and medical services in London showed that over a third of children were diagnosed as having medical problems (Fry, Brooks, and McColl, 1984). Take-up rates of vaccines are associated with social class, as is the use of other preventive services such as dental check-ups.

The 1906 Act provided the basis for a school meals service. Until 1980, the Local Authority had a duty to supply school meals that provided one-third of a child's recommended daily intake of calories and met prescribed nutritional standards. The Education Act of 1980 released the Local Authority from this duty, and Local Authorities are now free to decide the form, content, and price of school meals. This has caused concern given the persisting relationship between dietary patterns in childhood and social class. For instance, a recent Department of Health report found that the contribution of chips (French fries) to a child's diet at least doubled between social classes 1 and 5.

A number of NHS services are available in the home. For newborn babies and small children, community midwives and health visitors administer health and developmental checks, as well as providing advice and support for new mothers. Visits by District Nurses may also be organized on the recommendation of the patient's GP in cases where the patient is immobile or the home is seen as the best care setting. Further services are available with some variability across NHS regions. These include night shared care, a night nursing scheme aimed to relieve the carers of acutely sick patients who need 24-hour nursing. Complementary care services for the chronically sick or severely disabled are available from the social services (again with variability among the regions in amount and quality of services), including home-help which provides non-medical domestic services to patients. Benefits, such as attendance allowance, are available to help meet the cost of paid care.

Families and Health Policy 1960–1990

Recent years have seen major reforms in the NHS, with possibly far-reaching consequences for health care provision, organization, and funding. The full impact of many reforms is yet to be recognized.

The organization of health care in Britain has been characterized by:

- the strong position of the NHS and marginal roles for private agencies in service delivery;
- the strong position of GPs within the NHS, in patient contact and as 'gatekeepers';
- centralized budget control and the comparatively low national cost of health care;
- quality and equity in service delivery;
- persistent problems in some aspects of efficiency, as seen in particular in long waiting times for some kinds of non-emergency treatments.

Because of the universal provision of health care, the family, or specific types of families, have not been central categories for the delivery of health care services, except for specific service for mothers and children, which have generally been good.

Current reforms are characterized by:

- internal reorganizations in the NHS, in particular the introduction of 'internal markets';
- increasing roles for private agencies in service delivery by opening up to private competition provisions previously monopolized by the NHS;
- the maintenance of the strong GP, but 'marketization' of relationships between GPs and other units of service delivery;
- certain forms of de-institutionalization and increasing reliance on community care;
- decentralization of budget control.

While many would identify the reforms exclusively with the Conservative governments of 1979 to 1997, the reform process had been set in place prior to 1979 with a comprehensive reorganization and review of management structures in 1974 that resulted in a reformed, three-tiered system of management. The various 'marketization' reforms, however, were not introduced until into the 1980s.

The aim of these reforms is to maintain quality and equity in service delivery while improving efficiency and cost control. As to whether this is being achieved, the jury is still out and opinion is sharply divided. Critics of the reforms warn about inequity, poorer cost control as a result of decentralization, some forms of 'new' inefficiencies, in particular in community care, and increasing bureaucracy: from 1989 to 1991, the number of managers in the NHS increased from 4,600 to 12,300 (Baggott, 1994). There is, however, broad agreement that some reorganization was needed to do something about 'old' inefficiencies (waiting times), but not about whether this is being achieved.

Are these reforms making the family more central in the consideration of the quality of health care in Britain? Yes and no. First, there are no signs that the quality and availability of antenatal and other maternity care are being eroded, or that the role of the NHS in the delivery of such service is being seriously reduced. Second, if 'marketization' within the NHS and the increasing role of private agencies were in effect to undermine the universality of access to health care, one might expect to see new social differentiations in access to and use of health care, and possibly in health itself, for example between well-to-do and poor families. Third, and possibly most important, the new emphasis on community care is reorganizing the delivery of certain services in ways which many families are feeling acutely. Hence, the consequences of recent reforms for families may so far be more noticeable in their capacities as care providers than as recipients of care.

The 1990 NHS and Community Care Act radically relocated responsibility for the care of large groups of patients and clients, including the elderly, mentally-handicapped adults and children, physically-handicapped adults and children, and the mentally ill. The institutions and long-stay hospitals which were traditionally the locus of care for these patients had long been criticized for poor conditions and inappropriate provisions. Lack of co-ordination between organizations providing care to the same individual often led to piecemeal and inadequate care, with no clear line of responsibility.

The new locus of care for these individuals is to be 'the community'. The principle of community care has in practice increased the responsibilities of families to provide care for needy members, in particular because of financial pressures on Local Authorities. The Equal Opportunities Commission has argued that the changes have had a particular impact on women: 'The Government's community care policy is . . . a euphemism for an underresourced system which places heavy burdens on individual members of the community, most of them women' (Stacey, 1988: 208).

Numerous concerns have been expressed about the Community Care legislation. First, while many of those already resident in institutions preserved their rights to stay there, considerable concern has been raised about the adequacy of future publicly-funded provisions, especially for the elderly. Second, there is concern about the mentally ill, many of whom are now resident in the community. Doubts have been raised as to whether these individuals are receiving adequate supervision outside of an institutional setting. Third, agencies dealing with drug and alcohol abuse have suffered cutbacks in funding as Local Authorities, faced with new responsibilities for community care, have lowered the funding priority of these agencies. Last, the legislation assumed that people had a home in which they could be cared for. Thus, few provisions were made for the re-housing of those affected by the Community Care legislation, and the Act has been held responsible for contributing to the increase in homelessness in recent years.

Public expenditure considerations have fuelled reforms to the NHS since its inception. The proportion of public spending on health rose from 11% of total spending in 1981 to 14% in 1990, with the NHS budget experiencing a 20% increase in real terms between 1980 and 1989. In international comparisons, however, Britain's expenditure on health care remains low.

The importance of private funding of health care has increased, albeit from a small initial base. In 1990, 11.6% of the UK population was estimated to be covered by private medical insurance; in 1960 this figure was less than 2% (Office of Health Economics, 1992). Private payments, including those made by insurance companies, represent 4% of all NHS income. This is a relatively minor contribution which nevertheless doubled in the period 1979–90. Private health expenditure as a percent of GDP rose from 0.6% in 1960 to 0.9% in 1990.

Abortion

Following long campaigns for the legalization of abortion, a 1967 Act made abortion available on social and health grounds, whereas it had previously been available on medical grounds alone. Two doctors are required to authorize an abortion. A 'conscience clause' means that doctors may, on moral grounds, refuse to conduct or authorize abortions, hence there is some variability in the ease with which abortions can be attained. Abortion is available free of charge on the NHS. Attempts have been made to curtail the abortion legislation, but they have met with public and medical resistance.

Infertility Treatment

The first child conceived in Britain through *in vitro* fertilization was born in 1978. The treatment became available through the NHS shortly afterwards, but the service has a limited availability and is rarely free of charge, with charges varying according to the region. The limited availability of fertility treatments means that now nine out of ten patients are receiving this treatment in the private sector (Stacey, 1988). Some infertility treatments have been removed from the list of treatments covered by private medical insurance, further limiting their accessibility.

HOUSING

Housing status is linked with other behaviour at the heart of the family, such as fertility, mortality, and family formation. This link is a two-way street: housing is both a determinant and a consequence of these behaviours. For instance, in Britain divorce and widowhood show strong associations with a move from owner-occupation to rented accommodation while fertility, marriage, and remarriage demonstrate associations in the opposite direction. More surprising, perhaps, is that housing status has been demonstrated to be a stronger predictor of such behaviours as fertility than the more commonly-used variable, social class (see Holmans, Nandy, and Brown, 1987; Murphy and Sullivan, 1985).

On the other side of the equation, family formation and fission is a key determinant of housing demand and household type. Upward pressure on housing demand has arisen from a number of long-term social trends. In 1962 the average household size was 3.09 persons. This figure has dropped steadily throughout the period, to 2.55 in 1991. Contributing factors include an increase in rates of divorce, a rise in the number of one-parent families, and an ageing population whose members are increasingly living alone.

Housing Provision for Families

The National Assistance Act of 1948 established a duty on Local Authorities to provide residential accommodation to those otherwise unable to attain it themselves and to provide temporary accommodation to those 'in urgent need . . . arising in circumstances which could not reasonably have been foreseen or in such other circumstances as the authority may in particular cases determine.'

The Housing (Homeless) Persons Act of 1977 (consolidated in the Housing Act of 1985) established a duty for Local Authorities to house those who are homeless, or threatened with homelessness, provided they are (1) in a priority need group—for instance, where a household member is pregnant or there are dependent children; (2) not intentionally homeless; and (3) connected in some way to the Local Authority.

The 1985 Act extended provision to include those made homeless by disasters such as fire or flood, and those who were vulnerable by virtue of old age, infirmity, and so on. The 1989 Children Act established a further duty to Local Authorities to accommodate 'any child in need who has reached the age of 16 and whose welfare that authority considers likely to be seriously prejudiced if they do not provide him with accommodation.'

Tenure Patterns

Britain has a high percentage of households in owner-occupation, standing at 68% of all households in 1993, and owner-occupation shows a younger profile in Britain than in some other countries (Council of Mortgage Lenders, 1993). The early occurrence of owner-occupation reflects the lack of viable alternatives in housing, with private and public rental largely concentrated in the poorer part of the housing market. As a result of high levels of owner-occupation and its young age profile, Britain shows unusually high ratios of loans to income, loans to property value, and debt to income. Britain has a comparatively small private rental sector (8% of all dwellings in 1989), but a large public rental sector, although that sector is gradually diminishing, having fallen from 27% of all dwellings in 1961 to 23% in 1989.

A breakdown of tenure by family type in 1992 and in 1973 is given in Table 3. The most marked shift over this period has been towards owner-occupation. The private rental market has shrunk in proportion, with the share of Local Authority housing remaining relatively stable. Housing Association housing has increased its share significantly, but remains a very small part of the housing market. This is reflected in the shifts in tenure patterns according to family type with all groups affected by the increase in home-ownership.

The changes in tenure patterns have created their own unique problems, with many more individuals becoming sensitive to changes in macroeconomic policy, particularly changes in the interest rate. The number of households experiencing problems of repossession and mortgage arrears has grown rapidly. The number of households with mortgage arrears of between 6 and 12 months rose from 15,530 in 1980 to 123,110 in 1990. In the same period the number of houses repossessed because of failure to make mortgage repayments increased from 3,480 to 43,890 properties (Joseph Rowntree Foundation, 1991).

In 1960, the influence of post-war housing policy was still strongly felt. The principle objectives of this post-war policy were (1) to provide a separate dwelling for each family, (2) to complete the slum-clearance programme, and (3) to improve the condition of housing. This policy resulted in an estimated 14.6 million dwellings being built between the end of World War II and 1960. A policy of construction and slum-clearance continued throughout the 1960s with Conservative and

TABLE 3. Tenure by household type, Great Britain 1973 and 1992 (in %)

Tenure	1 adult aged 16–59		2 adults aged 16–59		Small family		Large family		Large adult household		2 adults, 1 or both 60 or over		1 adult aged 60 or over		Total	
	1973	1992	1973	1992	1973	1992	1973	1992	1973	1992	1973	1992	1973	1992	1973	1992
Owner-occupied	33	57	52	78	60	67	47	63	48	76	48	71	38	47	49	67
Local Authority rental	28	20	26	10	26	22	44	26	38	15	31	20	36	38	32	21
Housing Association rental	1	5	1	2	0	3	0	4	0	2	1	3	1	7	1	4
Private rental	36	14	17	8	9	6	9	4	10	6	15	5	24	8	14	7
Other rental	3	3	5	2	6	2	4	2	4	2	2	1	1	0	4	2

Source: Office of Population Censuses and Surveys, 1976 and 1992.

Labour governments competing to build the greatest number of houses in their terms of office. Total completions peaked in 1968. Public-sector completions reached their highest point in the previous year, with 204,000 new dwellings built.

The period of cross-party consensus about the importance of public-sector construction for housing was not broken until 1979. Since then, public-sector construction has fallen rapidly and continues to fall in the 1990s. Despite the boom in private construction in the mid-1980s, private construction has been unable to compensate for this drop. Total output in 1992 was 168,000, with the private sector contributing 83% of the completion total.

A mix of policy objectives constitutes what might be termed the 'privatization of housing': increasing home-ownership; encouraging the renaissance of the private rental sector; and encouraging private finance and private management of public-sector and Housing Association housing.

The objective of increased owner-occupation found legislative form in the 1980 Housing Act. This Act (extended by the Housing and Building Control Act of 1984 and the Housing and Planning Act of 1986) reinforced and promoted the 'Right to Buy' whereby council tenants, by virtue of their stature as sitting secure tenants, were granted the right to purchase their homes at the market price, discounted by between a third and a half. Until then, council tenants could not oblige their Local Authorities to sell, although many had bought their homes at discounted prices before the Act. By 1990, over 1.5 million public sector dwellings had been sold. (The term 'council tenants' refers to tenants of social housing owned and managed by the Local Authority, as opposed to tenants of the alternative form of social housing—Housing Association housing.)

The 1988 Housing Act aimed to deregulate the private rental sector on the assumption that regulated tenancies and the imposition of fair rents had discouraged private landlords and investors. New tenancies taken out after 1989 were no longer regulated tenancies subject to rent control but assured tenancies or assured shorthold tenancies (of 6 months' duration) with rental set at the 'market value'.

The final objective of private finance and private management of public-sector and Housing Association housing was instituted in a number of Acts. The 1988 Housing Act introduced new financial arrangements for Housing Associations involving the greater use of private-sector funds. The Act also made provisions for the establishment of Housing Action Trusts which are designed to take over the worst council housing with the aim of renovating it and then passing its management into other hands. The 1986 Housing and Planning Act allowed for the block sale of council estates into the private sector. However, few successful transfers have been made under this provision.

Public expenditure on housing (as calculated in 1980/1 prices) decreased from £4.5 billion in 1980/1 to £1.4 billion in 1991/2 (Joseph Rowntree Foundation, 1991). This was heralded as the most successful of government attempts to control public expenditure. However, given the reorientation of expenditure on housing it is less clear what real savings have in fact been made. Two costs which do not show up directly in the calculation of expenditure on housing have grown significantly in the period: mortgage interest tax relief and Housing Benefit. The cost of mortgage tax relief increased strongly into the early 1990s, but has subsequently been cut back substantially.

Housing Standards

Generally, housing standards improved in the period from 1960 to 1990. For instance, while 22.4% of households lacked an inside bath in 1961, this fell to 1.9% by 1981. An alternative measure of housing quality—the mean number of persons per room—has dropped from 0.57 in 1972 to 0.49 in 1992. Other measures of housing standards suggest that although improvements have been made, they may not be consistent across all housing types. For instance, while the percentage of households with two or more bedrooms has increased overall, it has remained stable for Local Authority housing. In 1986 the number of dwellings 'that were unfit or in "serious" disrepair remained stubbornly high, standing at 1 million and 1.1 million properties respectively' (Joseph Rowntree Foundation, 1991: 26).

There has been continual concern about the standards of public housing. The Parker Morris Report of 1961 attempted to ensure minimum standards for the *internal* condition of public housing. Much public housing of the 1960s and 1970s was built to experimental designs that paid little attention to the infrastructure of shops and services essential for such high-density housing. Concern has not been quietened by the sell-off of council housing under the 'Right to Buy' scheme. As the most desirable properties have been the first to be sold off, Local Authorities risk becoming slum landlords. Given constraints on capital expenditure, they are forced to renovate what might otherwise be seen as inadequate stock, and suggest this might serve to further residualize council housing.

Homelessness

The definition of homelessness remains contentious. The statutory definition equates homelessness with rooflessness or threat of rooflessness. As with much legislation, there is wide scope for interpretation by Local Authorities, for instance in deciding who may have rendered themselves 'intentionally homeless'.

In 1979, 56,750 households were recognized as homeless under the 1977 Act (the majority being under 'threat of rooflessness'). This figure had risen to 117,550 by 1988, reaching 128,000 by June 1994. These figures refer to homeless households, not persons. Also of concern is the increase in the provision of temporary accommodation by Local Authorities. In 1983, 2,700 households were lodged in 'Bed and Breakfast' accommodation; by 1988, this number had risen to 10,970. Following government measures which favoured other forms of temporary accommodation, this figure had fallen to 4,830 in June 1994. The number of households in other forms of temporary accommodation increased from 9,840 in 1983 to 30,100 in 1988 and to 46,620 in 1994. Thus, in a period of just over ten years, the number of households accepted as homeless had more than doubled, and households in temporary accommodation had increased fourfold. Statistics on the numbers of children affected by homelessness are not available because official statistics do not include a record of household composition of those accepted as homeless. However in 1993, of those households accepted by Local Authorities for re-housing, 59% had a priority need because they had dependent children and 12% because a household member was pregnant (Department of the Environment, 1994).

The 'hidden homeless' consist of people who are not accepted under the statutory definition of homelessness. These people may not be eligible for Local Authority housing, falling outside the definition of those in priority need. A significant group not recognized as having priority needs is the single homeless without dependants. It has been suggested that the definition of priority need should be extended to include, at the very least, children leaving care and single women subject to or under threat of physical or sexual abuse (Greve, 1991).

Estimates of hidden homelessness are difficult to come by and often disputed. The London Working Party estimated all hidden homelessness in London alone to be between 64,500 and 78,000 persons while Niner has made national estimates of 180,000 hidden homeless (Niner, 1989).

CHILDREN IN NEED

The Children Act 1989 in England and Wales (implemented in 1991) endeavours to create a more equitable balance between the rights of parents to non-intervention into family life and the rights of the child to protection. Central to the legislation is a set of principles of how children should be treated under the law, including making the child's welfare paramount, ascertaining the wishes and feelings of the child concerned, upholding parental responsibility even when the child is looked after in public care, and presuming no order unless it is positively demonstrated that this is better for the child.

Under the Act, Local Authorities have two main responsibilities. The first responsibility is to identify and support children designated as 'in need' and to promote their upbringing in their families. If this is not consistent with the child's welfare, the second responsibility is to intervene to effect protection. The definition of a child 'in need' is designed to include not only those children who are disabled or at risk of abuse and neglect, but any child whose present and future health or welfare might be significantly impaired. A child is taken to be in need if:

1. he is unlikely to maintain or to have the opportunity of achieving or maintaining a reasonable standard of health or development without the provision for him of services by a Local Authority;
2. his health or development is likely to be significantly impaired, or further impaired, without the provision for him of services by a Local Authority; or
3. he is disabled.

A child is considered to be disabled if he is 'blind, deaf or dumb or suffers from mental disorder of any kind or is substantially and permanently handicapped by illness, injury or congenital deformity'. 'Development' includes physical, intellectual, emotional, social, or behavioural development and 'health' means physical or mental health. (The 'he' terminology is the terminology of the Act.)

The focus on children in need was intended to bring about a shift in policy from child rescue to family preservation, to reduce protective interventions through the courts, and to reinforce the responsibility of Local Authorities to provide preventive services. The Act, however, did not specify what was a 'reasonable standard' of health or development. A wide-ranging difference in the interpretation of this general Local Authority duty has been demonstrated (Aldgate, Tunstill, and McBeath, 1993). Where, however, a child was disabled, the Children Act is quite clear. The Local Authority has an unequivocal duty to provide services. The objective is to minimize the effect of a child's disabilities and to enable a child with disabilities to lead as normal a life as possible.

The Children and Young Persons' Act of 1963 took the first cautious step in the direction of family preservation by making Local Authority departments responsible for providing advice, guidance, and assistance in order to prevent children from coming into public care or before the Courts. These early efforts, however, were undermined by the 'rediscovery' of child abuse (by Henry Kempe) in the 1960s, and child rescue policies developed apace during the 1970s and early 1980s. An indirect result was a huge increase in the number of children and young people admitted into the public care, which reached a peak of nearly 100,000 by the end of the 1970s. Research commissioned by the Department of Health and Social Security and the Economic and Social Research Council into aspects of work with children in care revealed that, far from rescuing children, the State was inadvertently adding to their difficulties; family contact was lost (Millham et al., 1986); education needs were not met (Heath, Colton, and Aldgate, 1989, 1994); and on leaving care, young people were overrepresented among the homeless population (Randall, 1989).

The number of children and young people in public care has fallen since the implementation of the Children Act, and more children are now looked after under voluntary respite-care agreements. The expectation that the Children Act would result in lower levels of child protection court activity has been realized. However, the Children Act has not been successful in shifting the focus from child protection to prevention. Inspections of Local Authority services for children with disabilities have demonstrated that many Local Authorities are finding it difficult to move from a reactive child protection role to a pro-active partnership role with families (Social Services Inspectorate, 1994; Department of Health, 1994). Moves to support children in need have led to a re-emergence of the voluntary sector. For some children in need, such as children with disabilities, support by non-stigmatized voluntary associations is often preferred to support by social service departments. With the move towards 'marketization' in welfare, Local Authorities are increasingly buying services from the large national child care organizations. With the pressure on child protection services, some Local Authorities are being forced to buy in specialist child protection assessment and therapeutic services.

The Children Act 1989 only applies to England and Wales. The Children (Northern Ireland) Order 1995 (effective October 1996) will reform and consolidate most of the law relating to children into a single framework along the lines of the Children Act 1989 in England and Wales.

New legislation is also on the way in Scotland, but will be less closely related to the England and Wales Children Act 1989. In Scotland a rather different tradition of state intervention in children's lives has developed. In 1971, under the Social Work (Scotland) Act 1968, the 'Hearing system' took over from the courts most of the responsibilities for dealing with children under 16 who had offended or who were in need of care or protection. The principles underlying the Children's Hearings were based on the findings of the Kilbrandon Report of 1964. This committee found that children who came before the courts whether for offending and/or for care had common needs, and that the Juvenile Court, because of its association with criminality, was unsuited to respond to these needs. Today, children under 16 are only considered for prosecution in court where serious offences such as murder or assault are in question. Where children are prosecuted in court they may still be referred to the Children's Hearing. Referrals are made to a 'Reporter' who has the duty to decide whether or not to initiate a Hearing. At the Hearing are three Panel members, who are lay volunteers, as well as both parents and the child, and possibly other persons, such as a teacher with special knowledge of the child. Parents are legally obligated to attend. The Social Work Department provides a report. The Hearing's task is to decide on the measure of care which is in the best interest of the child. If the Children's Hearing thinks compulsory measures of care are appropriate, it will impose a supervision requirement or may decide that the child should live away from home. Families may appeal to the Sheriff and have access to free legal aid if necessary.

Under the Children (Scotland) Bill 1995 (implemented in 1996) the Children's Hearing system will remain a central pillar of the legislation. Although there are close links with the Children Act 1989, the Children (Scotland) Bill is less definitive about the specific needs of specific children and more inclusive of young offenders than the Children Act 1989. In England and Wales, young offenders largely come under the criminal justice legislation. In one sense, Scotland has been able to learn from the implementation of the Children Act 1989 and to build on the better concepts. In another sense, Scotland has fiercely maintained its independence in seeking to build on its own tradition of Children's Hearings and create its own legislation to meet the welfare needs of Scottish children and families.

CONCLUSION

The National Health Service has often been regarded as the jewel in the crown of the British welfare state, and it has provided good health care for families and children. Health care in Britain is currently under radical reorganization, and many fear that universal access to good quality health care may suffer. It is, however, too early to tell what the consequences of the new system will be in terms of equity, efficiency, and cost.

Like health policy, housing policy has undergone radical changes in the direction of 'privatization'. While the standard of housing has improved and home-ownership has increased, homelessness is a growing problem, as are financial difficulties for many (new) home-owners who bought at the top of a housing boom which subsequently collapsed.

The Children Act 1989 strengthened the rights of children and the duties of Local Authorities to provide services for 'children in need'. Otherwise, Britain remains a laggard in European comparison in the provision of non-educational childcare services, as it also does, as was seen in Chapter 2, in the provision of services for working mothers.

5

The Politics and Institutionalization of Family Policy

The family has always been a powerful rallying cry in politics, a litmus paper against which all policies can be measured, though a specific policy for the family has seldom found general approval. Family policy stands out as a key site of political and ideological differences and tends to mirror the core values of a society. As we approach the millennium, the key issue in family politics has become the obligation of family members to provide each other with both financial and physical support, instead of making demands upon the state or the community.

CONTEMPORARY CLEAVAGES

At the time of writing, the UK has been governed by the Conservative Party for sixteen years.[2] For most of that time the party had a large majority in the legislature and a strong leader with a clear personal view of the relationship between the family and the state. Since the mid-1970s the party has represented itself as the party of the family. (It is, of course, difficult to find a political party that does not.) This particular view rests upon three main assumptions (Coote, Harman, and Hewitt, 1990):

1. There is one true and natural family type, composed of a father who is the main breadwinner, a mother at home providing domestic care, and children. Other family types, with the possible exception of fit elderly households, are imperfect and problematic.
2. The family is an important site of social control through the exercise of strong paternal authority. Families without fathers are likely to lead to social problems and to be associated with juvenile delinquency.
3. The family is set against the state; it is the main defence of the freedom of the individual against the threat of collectivism. 'Traditional family values' can be relied upon to ensure that families take care of their members, and that the next generation grows up with proper values including respect for properly exercised authority.

Throughout the 1980s, traditional family values were seen as coming under pressure. Women, including women with young children, entered the labour market in increasing numbers. The dual-worker family was becoming an economic necessity. The number of lone-parent families was growing rapidly, and an increasing proportion of these were dependent on social security. The increasing numbers of elderly people, including a rapidly growing population of the frail old, needed care. The Conservative government faced a dilemma: to make public provision for these dependent members of society, particularly one-parent families and the frail elderly, ran counter to the political aim of decreasing collective provision and dismantling the bureaucratized apparatus of the 'nanny state'. But families appeared unable to maintain their traditional functions of caring for their members. If families were to maintain these tasks, they would have to be firmly encouraged to do so. And so, reluctantly and counter to their belief in the autonomy of the family, the government began to develop strategies for intervention. The most recent example is the child support legislation of 1991, concerned with assuring that absent parents, most often fathers, contribute to the costs of their children, instead of allowing this burden to fall on the state. Ironically, the party most reluctant to intervene in the private sphere of family life has developed some of the most intrusive and interventionist policies of the century in order to promote family self-sufficiency.

The policy represented by the Labour Party also includes a commitment to traditional Christian family values, but this commitment is combined with a more flexible attitude to changes in family structures and to supporting new family forms. Recent thinking has concentrated on defending established welfare-state family-support systems, particularly health and social security. While accepting the new role of women in the paid labour force, the Labour Party has attempted to identify and promote ways of reducing tension between the conflicting demands of home and work for both sexes. Lacking the clear call of the Conservative Party to defend traditional family values, Labour policies have a more pragmatic air, accepting a more complex relationship between family, individual, and the state.

PROGRAMMES AND ACTORS

The post-war welfare state enshrined the family as a private, self-contained unit, with the breadwinning father married to a non-employed caring mother of two children. Women from all classes were isolated at home with their children as their prime concern, supported by socialized systems of health care, education, and, to a lesser extent, housing.

When a Labour government followed nearly a decade of Tory rule in 1966, this consensus view began to be challenged by academics in the field of social policy who were able to make their views known as advisers to the Labour government of the day. Empirical work on poverty challenged the effectiveness of the new welfare state in banishing Beveridge's giants (Want, Disease, Ignorance, Squalor, and Idleness), and a steady stream of new problems appeared: poverty in large families, poor conditions in residential accommodation for the elderly, lone parenthood as a problem *per se*, poverty among the disabled. The political climate of the time encouraged discussion of each new subgroup discovered and the development of a policy solution. The problems of each newly-identified group were defined and publicized to great effect by specific pressure groups, e.g., Child Poverty Action Group, Help The Aged, National Council For One Parent Families, and the Disability Income Group. The impact of these sophisticated lobbyists has been considerable throughout the period of this study. Debate centred on strategies for promoting and supporting the self-respect of each problem group identified. It is difficult in the political climate of the 1990s to remember that in the 1960s, universality of service provision, as opposed to selectivity, was discussed in terms of avoiding stigmatizing recipients rather than in terms of limiting public expenditure. For example, school meals were free to children on benefit, but to avoid these children being identified as 'poor', teachers were encouraged to ask for dinner money to be handed over in envelopes so that no one in the classroom would know which children were unable to pay. Abel-Smith and Townsend defined and documented poverty, Titmus spoke of the social market and the benefits of altruism, of social justice and redistributing the burdens of the capitalist economic system, and Donnison documented the impact on families of the structure and funding of the housing market.

The relative affluence of the period, combined with the willingness of government to invest in public services and its optimism about the possibility of improving the lot of the citizen, made the degree of redistributive intervention the central policy issue. At the same time, however, we see the emergence of an anti-family ideology of the 1960s—e.g., in the work of R. D. Laing, *Bird of Paradise and Politics of Experience*, and David Cooper, *The Death of the Family*—which represented the family as a claustrophobic repression of individual development and the source of psychiatric illness. Alternative forms of more liberating social organization were discussed and tried, from the commune to the therapeutic community. Few have survived. And somewhere in the midst of this concern with the freedom of the individual came the ignition point for the women's movement.

The UK was accustomed to consensus politics, expecting a change of government to lead to a change of emphasis in social and economic policies, but within the context of an acceptance of the welfare state and a carefully-planned economy. This was not to be the case. For the first time since the war, the UK was to experience radicalism in politics, not as tradition would lead us to expect from the Left, but from the Right. Keith (later Lord) Joseph had said a little earlier that it was time to make a stand against the permissiveness of the 1960s and its ill effects on society as a whole. He singled out the case of single mothers, whose deviant condition, standing in contrast to normal family life, was both an effect and a cause of moral and social degeneracy. 'They are producing problem children, the future unmarried mothers, delinquents, denizens of our borstals, subnormal educational establishments, prisons and hostels for drifters' (quoted in Coote, Harman, and Hewitt, 1990: 10). The issue of the decline of the family came to the fore in the 1989 election. A prominent figure in the debate was Charles Murray, an American theorist who saw the formation in Britain, as in the US, of a new 'underclass'. A key predictor of the rate of formation of this new phenomenon was the rate of illegiti-macy, which had increased dramatically during the 1980s, with the increase strik-ingly concentrated in the lowest social class. What mattered to Murray was the failure to marry, for he identified marriage as having the virtue of civilizing men by turning them into economically productive members of society as they became family breadwinners. 'Men who do not support families find other ways to prove they are men, which tend to take destructive forms. As many have commented through the centuries, young men are essentially barbarians for whom marriage, meaning not just the wedding vows but the act of taking responsibility for a wife and children is an indispensable civilising force' (Murray, 1990). Adding Aristote-lian views on owning property, we have the Thatcherite recipe for a cohesive and economically productive society.

THE INSTITUTIONALIZATION OF FAMILY POLICY

This final heading indicates the international nature of this project and causes some difficulty to those reporting from the UK. We have no such institutionalization, only that in 1994, the Minister for Health was given special responsibility for fam-ily matters.

The two main political parties use the family in their policy statements, it is true, and clear differences of approach remain. The Conservative government continues to speak of traditional family values, placing the woman at the heart of the family with the chief responsibility for caring for both children and older family members. This responsibility is being put to the test as the policy of com-munity care for the disabled and frail elderly comes into operation, devolving care from the health service to Local Authorities in the community. At the same time there is some unease and lack of clarity about the role of women in paid employment. The emphasis for men is on accepting financial responsibility and providing family authority and discipline. The role of the state is to roll back, leaving the family as the most valued and efficient social unit for economic activ-ity, socialization, and social control.

In 1977, then Prime Minister James Callaghan claimed to put forward a national family policy, stating that 'the family is the most important unit in our community. That is why for the first time in our country our government is putting forward a national family policy. Our aim is straight forward: it is to strengthen the stability and quality of family life in Britain . . . to pay more attention to how industry organizes women's role at work, so that her influence as the centre of the family, and the woman is usually the centre of the family, is not weakened' (Coussins and Coote, 1981). A policy review in 1989 stressed the need for women to contribute to the economy, stating that Britain cannot afford to waste anyone's skills, and that women should have career breaks, every parent should have the right to six months' paid leave, and part-time members of the labour force, predominantly women, should also receive full rights. Turning to the role of men, the Left tends to stress not authority and breadwinning, but sharing parental responsibility and caring for children. 'It is essential to encourage men to play a greater role in caring for their families. Many young fathers want equal opportunities to enjoy parental leave, career breaks, and more flexible hours . . . a series of measures to assist women and men to combine family and work more fully' (Coussins and Coote, 1981).

Conclusion: The Profile of Family Policy

British governments have not sought to formulate explicit and institutionalized family policies. Nevertheless, across the spectrum of public and social policy range measures that influence, and are intended to influence, the living conditions of families and children. These measures add up to a policy with specific characteristics and profiles which make it possible and relevant to identify 'the British form of family policy', both in terms of current policies and policy trends over the last decades.

Governments enact policies in respect to the family when

- they identify *problems* in the family, either in performing what are seen as family functions in society or with respect to internal pressures and strains in families;
- pressures for government intervention are not overridden by what are considered to be *constraints* on the scope of government action;
- they believe it is in their *power* to intervene effectively with respect to the problems that are identified.

Current family policy in Britain can be characterized as reluctant. Family problems are defined as government responsibility less than in some other European countries. Prevailing ideology is prone to emphasize constraints on potential government action, including budgetary constraints, and regards the scope of effective government action as limited. In political rhetoric, the balance between government and family responsibility has shifted to a stronger emphasis on the responsibility of the family in society and of family members for each other. This profile of family policy, and the shift in ideological emphasis towards family responsibility, is entirely intentional. It is seen on one side of the political divide as desirable and rational, and on the other side as rolling back the values and practices of the welfare state.

The dominant theme of this overview of family policy in Britain from the 1960s to the 1990s has been the changing role of the state in relation to the family. Child care and employment are two examples. Other themes that have run consistently through the chapters are poverty as a mainspring for family policy; the debate between universal or selective services and the shift to greater 'targeting' of services on families seen as poor or needy; policy and gender (the strength of 'traditional' attitudes to working women is an example here); the residualization of policy areas such as housing; and the nature and form of the family itself.

Functions of Family Policy

In some European countries, concern over population developments, in particular recent low fertility, has been a basis for active family policies as a means to counteract the threat of population decline. In Britain, government concern over population has been conspicuously absent from the area of family policy (much to the credit of the British, many would say). One reason may be that fertility in Britain has remained relatively high by European comparison, but a more likely reason is that it would be alien to British family values for governments to adopt a specific policy of trying to influence families in their decisions about children. Governments in Britain have also been cautious in the area of family planning. They have taken initiatives on the study of population trends but have not shown any inclination towards the formulation of population policies. The exceptionally high rate of teenage childbearing—almost four times the Western European average—is often taken as evidence of a failure in sex education.

Public economic support for families in need has a long tradition that originated in the various poor law regimes and persists to this day. However, the earliest and most radical policy interventions in family life were in the form of compulsory education, which was enforced to prevent some parents from sending their children out to work. More recently, the duration of compulsory schooling has been extended, and enforcement may be more a matter of tackling the social and family problems that lie behind non-attendance. The education service's traditional social dimension (e.g., school health and meals services) has been reduced.

During the two world wars, and particularly World War II, governments intervened strongly in the family out of labour market concerns. In World War II, nursery places were provided for vast numbers of children in order to release their mothers for work in manufacturing and other war efforts. With the end of the war, however, the provision of nursery places was quickly reduced. Since then, it has not been government policy in Britain to encourage mothers (except for lone mothers) to work outside the family, nor to discourage mothers from so doing, although prevailing family values in the population may lean in the direction that at least mothers with small children ought not work.

In the field of housing, the main form of government support has traditionally been through the provision of public housing (council housing). During the last fifteen years or so, however, housing policy has undergone a radical shift: individual tenants have been encouraged to become owner-occupiers; Local Authority council estates have been transferred to Housing Associations, and subsidized rents in the remaining Local Authority housing have been phased out in favour of supporting poor tenants to meet market rents through means-tested Housing Benefit.

Like other European countries, Britain is experiencing great concern over law and order, including juvenile crime and deviance, and the possible decline of family cohesion and social control. This is the subject of strong political rhetoric but not of corresponding political action, probably because it is not easy to see what form such action might take.

Social Problems and the Family—'The Politics of Poverty'

One of the peculiarities of British social policy debate, which distinguishes it from the continental European or Scandinavian traditions, is the tendency to formulate social problems in the language of poverty. Problems that can be described persuasively as problems of poverty have had and continue to have considerable power in policy considerations, and 'the politics of poverty' are a battleground between Left and Right. During the 1960s and 1970s, the Left dominated this dialogue, and it was a period of social policy expansion in many areas, including income transfers and services for families. More recently, the Right has prevailed and to some degree held the poverty lobby at bay. The logic of poverty, however, remains a powerful policy influence behind the tendency to cut back on general policies to the family and to promote specific policies that can be directly related to poverty or need. Examples are the reduction in the relative value of state benefits (through the shift from wages to prices as the basis for uprating state benefits) and the increasing reliance on means-tested benefits. General problems in the family may well be recognized as facts, but do not constitute sufficient reason for policy action. For example, it may be broadly recognized that gender inequity in the division of labour both in the market and in the domestic sphere is a widespread problem, but there is little agreement that this should be an area of policy responsibility by the state. Instead, the strongly prevailing view appears to be that this is a private responsibility, either for families themselves or for employees and employers to sort out in contract arrangements and negotiations.

With respect to specific problems which are more or less clearly perceived as 'poverty' or 'needs', government recognizes its responsibility and often follows up with powerful policies. An example is income-testing of benefits, which is based on the notion of directing support where it is most needed, including to families and children in poverty. Another example is the central position of the concept of 'children in need' in the Children Act 1989. Through this Act, the rights of children generally were strengthened, and for 'children in need' in particular, rights were firmly established and Local Authorities' responsibilities specified. The power of this particular clause in the Act has been undermined, however, by ambiguities in interpretation and considerable Local Authority discretion.

In spite of the emphasis on policies intended to target poverty in families and children in need and to increase efficiency in the distribution of benefits, the British experience since the mid-1970s is one of sharply increasing (income) inequality. Since the 1970s, families with children, and children in particular, have found themselves on the losing end of a radical redistribution of living standards.

Constraints and the Role of the State

The privacy of the family is a traditional and firmly-established value in British culture. There is, as in other countries, disagreement about the role of public policy with respect to the family, but this disagreement is nevertheless contained within some shared perception of the value of privacy, autonomy, and responsibility in the family. Since 1979, Britain has seen a radical change in prevailing political ideology and policy practice. The shift towards the family taking more responsibility itself has its origins more in a different theory of the state than in a new theory of the family: it is not only that the family should do more, but also that the state should do less. This perceived constraint on government action is now visible most clearly in two areas that affect family policy.

First, it is currently not government policy in Britain to seek to equalize the overall distribution of income, consumption, or living standards, which has weakened general policies for the family. For example, the real value of the Child Benefit has been reduced, and income benefits have shifted sharply towards means-tested support. Families with children tend to be located towards the lower end of the overall income distribution and have for this reason suffered disproportionately in a period of increasing inequality. Available family support, income-tested or otherwise, has not compensated for this increased relative deprivation in standards of living for families with children.

Second, it is currently government policy in Britain to deregulate employment relations. Not only is government in Britain reluctant itself to provide child-care facilities as part of a policy of facilitating or encouraging mothers to work outside the family, it is also reluctant to legislate that employers should do so or to use financial or other incentives for this purpose, except in a minimal fashion. This partly explains the particular profile of child-care services in Britain, characterized by low levels of public provision, high levels of voluntary and private involvement, and great diversity of local child-care provisions—a system which may be described either as rich and pluralistic or as fragmentary and inadequate, depending on one's perspective. Services for children in Britain have been and remain strong in the field of education—children start school at five and increasingly at four—but weak in the field of non-educational child care. There is, however, strong public pressure for improved child-care facilities, as well as for more nursery education. It remains to be seen whether the preschool voucher scheme announced by the government in summer 1995 will produce a significant increase in provision. If so, it is likely to result in a further privatization of service.

British social policy between the 1960s and the 1990s has seen a reversal in thinking about the role and functions of the state and the provision of services. The first half of this period still fell within the post-war consensus of a strong welfare state, with a fair degree of support for redistributive policies and universal provision. The second half of the period, however, has seen a sharp 'rolling-back' of the state 'family responsibility', together with a residualization of state provision and rapid privatization of many services. At the time of writing, it is still unclear how the story line will develop throughout the 1990s and into the twenty-first century.

Notes

1 Those with main responsibility for each section are as follows:

Introduction: Anne Gauthier.

Chapter 1: Marriage, Divorce, and Births, and Household and Family Structure: David Coleman; Family Law: John Eekelaar; Family Values: Ann Buchanan and Teresa Smith.

Chapter 2: Paid and Household Work: Jay Gershuny and Stein Ringen; Labour Market Behaviour: Susan McRae and Joan Payne; Employment and Parenting Policies: Susan McRae.

Chapter 3: Patterns of Income: Stein Ringen and George Smith; Taxation: John Dewar; Family Benefits: John Dewar and Michael Noble.

Chapter 4: Child Care: Teresa Smith; Health Care: Katherine Rake and Stein Ringen; Housing: Katherine Rake; Children in Need: Ann Buchanan.

Chapter 5: Mavis Mclean; Conclusion: Michael Noble, Stein Ringen, and Teresa Smith.

2 The Labour Party has since won a majority in the 1997 elections; the implications for British family policy remain to be seen.

Appendix

LANDMARKS IN FAMILY POLICY

1870	Education Act
1895	Unpaid leave for childbirth
1902	Midwives' Act
1906	Free school meals
1907	Compulsory medical inspection in schools
1908	Old Age Pensions Act
1908	Children Act
1911	National Insurance Act (maternity benefits)
1914	Separation Allowance
1914	Matching funds for child and maternal welfare
1919	Maternity and Child Welfare Act
1925	Widows' and orphans' pensions
1942	Beveridge Report
1944	Family allowances
1946	National Health Service
1946	Maternity leave benefits
1967	Family Planning Act
1968	Abortion Act
1969	Divorce Reform Act
1969	Commission on One-Parent Families
1971	Family Income Supplement
1976	Single-Parent Benefit
1977	Child Benefit
1986	Income Support
1988	Family Credit
1989	Children Act
1991	Child Support Act

Family Change and Family Policies: Canada

Maureen Baker
Shelley Phipps

Introduction: Historical Roots
of Family Policy

Canada as a nation has never developed a comprehensive and explicit set of family policies, although the province of Quebec has taken this initiative since the late 1980s. Instead, policies affecting families with children are implicitly embedded within all social and economic policies. This means that any analysis of Canadian family policy must include a more general discussion of income security programmes, public health insurance, labour market policies, and income tax regulations.

Historically, Canadian social and economic policies favoured the traditional model of family life in which women and children were seen as dependants, but men were viewed as autonomous individuals (Baker, 1990). Furthermore, laws and policies have incorporated the values of self-reliance, individualism, and family privacy, and in recent years focused on employability and work incentives even for mothers with young children. Until the 1970s and 1980s when Canadian governments reformed family law, marital roles were considered complementary and of equal value to family and society. By law, men were required to provide financial support for their wives and children, and women were expected to maintain the household and care for the children. As more women entered the labour force from the 1960s to the 1990s, this traditional division of labour became less feasible and appropriate, providing new challenges for policy-makers. Furthermore, feminist researchers demonstrated that so-called complementary roles were not really treated as equal in court, especially after marriage breakdown (Morton, 1988). Although state involvement in family life has changed over the years, not all policies have kept pace with family trends, the needs of working parents, or the growing multicultural nature of the Canadian population.

In the constitution of 1867 which established Canada as a nation, jurisdiction for family policy was divided between federal and provincial governments. Despite several constitutional amendments and changes in the political and social climate over the years, family policy has remained a divided jurisdiction. Marriage law, child welfare legislation, the delivery and regulation of child-care services, employment legislation affecting maternity and parental leave (but not benefits), the enforcement of support orders after divorce, education, the delivery of health care, and social assistance all reside under provincial jurisdiction. On the other hand, divorce law, family benefits, old-age pensions, unemployment insurance, maternity and parental benefits, and services to status Indians living on reserves fall under federal jurisdiction. Provincial income tax concessions are federally administered except in Quebec, which has its own taxation department.

The federal government also funds a portion of post-secondary education, shares the cost of provincial social services with some guidelines for expenditures, and provides guiding principles and funding for health services, which are all programmes administered by the provinces. Because certain aspects of the constitution have never been clarified and new policy issues have arisen over the years, disputes over jurisdiction have typified Canadian social policy development.

Most of Canada's national social programmes (such as family allowances, unemployment insurance, maternity benefits, and Medicare) were introduced by Liberal governments. Yet the presence of the New Democratic Party and its predecessor (the Co-operative Commonwealth Federation) as an opposition party in Ottawa and as the government in several provinces has strongly influenced the development of the Canadian welfare state (Moscovitch and Drover, 1987). Canadian governments at the federal level have alternated between the Liberals and Conservatives, and unlike Britain and Australia, Canada has never voted a social democratic or left-wing government into power in Ottawa.

Alliances between trade unions and social democratic political parties, which have often been associated with the development of generous social programmes, have never been as strong in Canada as in Australia, Britain, or Sweden. In addition, trade union links with political parties appear to be weakening rather than strengthening. The rate of unionization in Canada has been relatively low (White, 1993) compared to countries such as Sweden or Australia, although it is twice as high as in the United States. Neither has there been a legal structure for the voices of labour to be heard in policy decisions, except their vote, petitions to Members of Parliament, and submissions to parliamentary committees.

Canada has always relied on immigration to help increase the population and expand the labour force. Although not all immigrants have stayed in this country, net immigration has accounted for about 20% of population growth in this century (Beaujot, 1991). Historically, the resource-based economy depended on foreign capital and markets, and many jobs have been seasonal and within primary industries. Urbanization and industrialization occurred later in Canada than in Europe, which delayed women's labour force participation and helped to postpone the decline of birth rates. Furthermore, after World War II, Canada experienced a 'baby boom' that was stronger than in Europe and kept the Canadian population relatively young (Beaujot, 1991). Conservative and patriarchal family values accompanied the high birth rates which continued until the early 1960s, especially in Quebec where the Catholic Church remained a powerful influence in social policy decisions as well as personal life. Consequently, the Canadian population has remained younger than most European nations and, until recently, has also been less preoccupied with fertility decline, resolving work/family conflicts, or financing future social programmes. Even now that Canadians are becoming concerned about the ageing population, people aged 65 and over make up less than 12% of the population compared to 20% in some European countries.

Canada is physically a large country, relatively sparsely populated with a diverse people from different cultural and racial backgrounds. It has two official languages (English and French) and two different legal systems. While nine provinces and two territories derive their legal system from English common law, Quebec's Civil Code developed from French law. The population has always been heterogeneous with strong regional and cultural concerns, and these differences continue to flourish with changing immigration patterns. While early immigrants came mainly from Europe and the United States, recent arrivals are mainly from Asia, Africa, and the Caribbean. Cultural and language differences, as well as regional inequalities, encourage varying ideas about appropriate social programmes. Diversity and controversy make any one point of view about reforming social policies less powerful in influencing government, especially when few formal structures enable the public to express their views.

Canadian governments are becoming concerned about low rates of economic growth, the rising deficit, and the increasing costs of social programmes. In Canada, unemployment rates have remained higher than in many other industrialized countries, resulting in greater demands on unemployment insurance and social assistance. Recently, more social programmes are being targeted to lower-income earners, including the former Family Allowance created as a universal programme in 1944–45. When the Liberal Party won the federal election in 1993, the Minister of Human Resources (Lloyd Axworthy) began a review of the cost and efficacy of social programmes, consulting widely among experts and advocacy groups across the country. Yet this review was truncated by the 1995 federal budget, which cut federal expenditures, phased out cost-sharing for social assistance programmes, and introduced block funding. Block funding provides lower levels of federal funds for provincial programmes but raises fewer spending restrictions. This reform was designed to appease demands for greater provincial autonomy (especially in Quebec) while reducing federal expenditures.

From the 1920s to the 1970s, the political lobby for improved family benefits and labour market equality was relatively weak. Now, the decline in birth rates, more women and mothers in the work-force, increasing rates of 'child poverty', growing cultural and lifestyle diversity, and the political organization of feminist, gay and lesbian, and anti-poverty groups, have all contributed to the development of stronger advocacy to reform family policies. Various groups have argued for an expanded definition of 'family', the elimination of inequality between benefits paid to different family configurations and between the roles and status of men and women, the reduction of child poverty, and help for parents to earn a living while caring for children.

At the same time, a strong lobby from conservative groups based in western Canada continues to promote 'family values', focusing on a 1950s-style family with a gendered division of labour. In addition, employers and financial organizations continue to press the government for deficit reduction, reduced government spending, more restrictive social programmes, and increased work incentives. In the mid-1990s, advocates of cut-backs to social programmes are making a greater impression on the government than those of 'progressive' reform.

1

The Formation of Families

Canada, like other industrialized countries, has experienced rapid changes in family structure, the labour force, and the economy since the Second World War. Family trends include smaller households, lower rates of legal marriage, declining fertility, more mothers in the labour force, rising divorce rates, an increase in births outside marriage, more one-parent households, and rising life expectancy. Family demography, laws, and values have tended to respond to economic, political, and social trends, but changes in lifestyle have also influenced social policy and public opinion.

Social policy and legislation are often developed or amended when people create advocacy groups and political alliances to resolve what they perceive to be 'social problems' arising from rapid demographic, economic, and social change. In order to comprehend pressures to change family policies in Canada, we need to understand the demographic, legal, and attitudinal trends of the past few decades. The first two sections will deal with family formation and family structure, including the reasons behind these trends and their implications for family policies. In the last two sections, we will discuss changes in family law and family values.

MARRIAGE, DIVORCE, AND CHILDBEARING

Marriage

Although conservatives sometimes lament the decline of family life in Canada, the current crude marriage rate (the number of marriages per 1,000 population) is similar to the rate of 75 years ago, though it has fluctuated considerably since then. At the end of the nineteenth century, marriage rates were relatively low. These low rates reflected the imbalance of the sex ratio, high rates of cohabitation in frontier areas, the lack of opportunity to meet partners in isolated regions, and inducements to forfeit marriage and enter religious institutions (especially in Quebec). In the late 1920s and 1930s the crude marriage rate declined to a low of 5.9 in 1932, reflecting the economic depression. But it rose again and peaked sharply during World War II at 10.9. Since then the rate has declined except for a brief period in the early 1970s when the 'baby boomers' reached marrying age. Although the rate of first marriages has declined steadily for the last forty years, more marriages today are remarriages (Vanier Institute of the Family, 1994: 37).

The mean age at marriage for both men and women gradually declined over the century until the mid-1960s and then slowly increased from the early 1970s until the present. While the mean age of first marriage was 22.6 for women and 25.0 for men in 1971 (Dumas and Péron, 1992: 118), it rose to 26.7 for women and 28.8 for men in 1991 (Statistics Canada, 1993c), reflecting the fact that many Canadian couples now live together before legal marriage. Furthermore, many marriages are remarriages for at least one partner. In 1967, only 12.3% of first marriages involved at least one partner who had been previously married; by 1992 this had risen to 32.5% reflecting the rising divorce rates over that period (Dumas and Bélanger, 1994: 28).

TABLE 1. Mean age at first marriage, Canada 1945–1991

Year	Men	Women
1945	27.3	24.3
1951	26.6	23.8
1961	25.3	22.6
1971	25.0	22.6
1981	25.9	23.7
1991	28.8	26.7

Source: Statistics Canada.

As the cohabitation rate has risen, the legal distinctions have been blurred between living in a permanent heterosexual relationship with or without legal marriage, and between the rights of children born inside or outside marriage. In the last thirty years, the number and proportion of babies born to women who are not legally married has increased. For example, 24% of all live births in 1990 were to women who were not legally married compared to 4% in 1960 (VIF, 1994: 58). Factors influencing this rise include the growing number of common-law relationships, increased financial independence of women, and the decreased stigma of birth outside marriage. Yet two-thirds of the women giving birth outside marriage are over 20 years old rather than adolescents, and many are cohabiting. Births to teenagers have declined both in numbers and proportion from 1961 to 1990 in Canada.

Divorce

The divorce rate rose almost consistently from 6.4 per 100,000 population in 1921 to 285.9 in 1982, but especially increased after 1968 and 1985 when the divorce laws were liberalized. After peaking at 355.1 in 1987, the rate declined to 280 in 1991 (compared to 470 in the US) (Dumas, 1994: 19). This decline reflects the economic recession, in which legal divorce was considered to be too expensive for many couples to contemplate, but also reflects the declining marriage rate and the rising average age of the population (as divorces tend to occur among younger couples). While Canada's divorce rate is considerably lower than that of the US, it is higher than in many European countries.

TABLE 2. Divorce statistics, Canada 1941–1991

Year	Divorce rate (per 100,000 population)	Remarriage rate of divorced persons (per 100 divorced persons)
1941	21.4	17.4
1951	37.6	26.5
1961	36.0	19.1
1971	137.6	17.0
1981	278.0	12.4
1991	273.9	8.4

Source: Statistics Canada.

After divorce, many Canadians remarry and re-establish two-parent families. In the mid-1980s, about three-quarters of divorced men and two-thirds of divorced women eventually remarried, although these figures have been declining in recent years with more common-law relationships (Adams and Nagnur, 1990). Further- more, the remarriage rates after divorce (and widowhood) remain lower in Canada than in the US.

Fertility

Since the mid-1800s, birth rates have been falling in most industrialized countries, and Canada is no exception. The crude birth rate has been falling since 1861, when it was 45 per 1,000 population. During World War II, it had declined to 22.4 but there was a substantial increase for twenty years after World War II known as the 'post-war baby boom'. After peaking at 27.2 in the 1950s, the birth rate fell again to 14.4 in 1987 before rising to 15.1 in 1991. The total fertility rate, or the average number of births per woman, has decreased from 3.84 in 1961 to 2.19 in 1970 to 1.66 in 1993, and is now lower than in the US but comparable to many European countries (United Nations, 1991).

Within Canada, there have been notable variations in fertility by province, reli- gion, and cultural background. Quebec fertility rates, which used to be the highest in Canada, have fallen dramatically since the 1960s. The total fertility rate in Que- bec, for example, fell from 4.0 children per woman in 1959 to 2.1 in 1970 (Le Bourdais and Marcil-Gratton, 1994). This decline has been attributed to the sweep- ing cultural changes of the 'Quiet Revolution' when the economy was modernized, English control was receding, the Catholic Church lost much of its authority, the education system was expanded and secularized, young people had more opportunity for occupational mobility, and young women played down their traditional role as mothers (Lachapelle and Henripin, 1982; Beaujot, 1991). By 1987, when fertility rates reached their lowest point in Canada, Quebec had a lower total fertility rate than the rest of the country (1.34 children per woman compared to 1.58). Although fertility rates in both Quebec and the rest of Canada have risen slightly since then, the Quebec rate (at 1.60) remains slightly below the Canadian average, which is about 1.66.

TABLE 3. Total fertility rate, Canada 1945–1993

Year	Total fertility rate
1945	3.0
1951	3.5
1961	3.8
1971	2.2
1981	1.7
1991	1.7
1993	1.7

Source: Statistics Canada.

The Northwest Territories, unlike Quebec, has experienced an extremely high birth rate in recent years. In 1990, there were 29.4 births per 1,000 population in the Northwest Territories (Strauss, 1992), compared to the Canadian average of 15.3. This situation has concerned social service workers, health practitioners, and politicians because a large percentage of lone mothers and poor families in the north require government assistance. Although fertility rates of Native people have been declining since the late 1960s and are becoming closer to the Canadian average, Native people still tend to produce larger families (Siggner, 1986). In 1991, the total fertility rate was 2.7 for registered or 'status' Indians, 3.4 for Inuits, and 2.3 for Métis and non-status Indians (Nault and Jenkins, 1993).[1] High birth rates and above-average infant mortality rates among Native people are associated with poverty and economic underdevelopment. Although Native people, especially those living in the north, tend to produce very large families, their numbers are too small to raise the Canadian average.

Contrary to popular myth, immigrants to Canada have traditionally had lower birth rates than Canadian-born women. Many immigrants come to Canada to improve their standard of living, and labour force participation rates among immigrant women have been above the Canadian average, which helps explain their lower birth rates. Furthermore, even those cultural groups that initially have high birth rates tend to adjust their lifestyle and expectations once they settle in Canada, and birth rates of subsequent generations become similar to the Canadian average.

Religious variations have also been evident in fertility rates, although they have diminished over the past generation. Traditionally, Roman Catholics produced larger families than Protestants although there were always substantial differences among Protestant denominations. Mennonites, Hutterites, and Mormons, for example, have also opposed birth control and encouraged large families. On the other hand, Jewish people (except Hasidic Jews) have generally had smaller families than other religious groups (Kalbach and McVey, 1979: 107). Although the fertility rates of Protestants and Catholics have become more similar, people from certain religious groups such as Orthodox Jews and Muslims continue to produce more children than others.

Not only have birth rates declined in Canada but more women are delaying childbirth. The average age of a mother at her first birth has risen from 23.5 in 1961 to 26.7 in 1991 (Statistics Canada, 1993a). The number of women in their thirties giving birth for the first time more than tripled from 1971 to 1988 (Wadhera and Millar, 1991). Reasons for delayed childbirth include the need to stay in school longer to find work, high unemployment rates, delayed marriage, and improvements in contraception.

Although Canadian fertility rates are now comparable to other industrialized countries, the decline has been relatively recent. Historically, women were encouraged to reproduce because families needed to compensate for high infant mortality and to create their own family work-force to make a living. The Canadian government wanted new citizens and workers to build the nation, and the Church considered the purpose of marriage to be procreation. Especially in Quebec, the Catholic Church reinforced this value by emphasizing the importance of reproduction to marriage and by forbidding artificial contraception. In addition, urbanization and industrialization occurred later in Canada than in Europe, which delayed women's participation in the labour force and postponed the decline of birth rates. Canada also experienced a baby boom after the Second World War which far outdid the post-war fertility increase in Europe (Beaujot, 1991). These factors kept Canadian birth rates above European ones until the 1970s and 1980s.

Quebec is the only provincial government which has expressed public concern and implemented new policies related to declining fertility, although other provinces (such as Ontario and British Columbia) are presently experiencing comparable birth rates. Quebec's initiatives originate from the extent and rapidity of fertility decline, as well as concern that the French language and culture will dwindle within Canada. While immigrants flood into Ontario and British Columbia, Quebec has been less successful in attracting and retaining immigrants or in persuading them to speak French once they settle in Quebec. Consequently, the Quebec government has developed a comprehensive set of family policies designed to raise the birth rate and a government structure to implement and enforce them. These initiatives include expanded parental leave and day-care spaces, interest-free housing loans for first-time home-owners with dependent children, and cash bonuses for parents at childbirth, which are worth up to $8,000 a child for third or subsequent children (Le Bourdais and Marcil-Gratton, 1994). Yet despite birth incentives, fertility rates have fallen slightly in Quebec as well as the rest of Canada in the last few years (La Novara, 1993: 13; Mackie, 1995).

Birth Control

The rapid decline in fertility rates is due in large part to the widespread use of contraceptives in Canada. The Canadian Fertility Survey (1984) found that about 80% of single women and 97% of ever-married women had used contraception at some point in their lives, with the most prevalent method being oral contraception. Among all Canadian women 18–49, 68% said that they were using a method of contraception at the time of the interview. A further 9% were pregnant, post-partum or seeking pregnancy, and 7% were non-contraceptively sterile. There were few differences based on education, but those who rarely attended religious services, Protestants, and native-born women were slightly overrepresented among contraceptive users (Balakrishnan, Lapierre-Adamczyk, and Krotki, 1993).

In 1969, the Canadian government legalized hospital abortions if a panel of physicians concluded that the health of the mother was at risk, and in 1988 the Supreme Court of Canada struck down the law which had made abortion a criminal offence if it did not coincide with the 1969 stipulations. From 1970 to 1993, Statistics Canada reported that the rate of therapeutic abortions per 100 live births rose from 3.0 to 26.9, mainly since the late 1980s. About 64% of the women having abortions in 1993 were single, and about 20% were under the age of 20. Although the Canadian rate has increased substantially, it is still far lower than in the US, where in 1992 the abortion rate per 100 live births was 37.9 (Mitchell, 1995a: A1).

HOUSEHOLD AND FAMILY STRUCTURES

Over the last century, the size of both families and households has declined in Canada. Marriage is no longer mandatory for all adults, more people are living outside families, and marriage has become less permanent. Fertility has fallen with improved contraception, changes in women's roles, and the rising costs of raising children (especially child-care services and higher education). Furthermore, fewer single people live at home or board with other families, as they can easily live in apartments, and live-in servants have long been too expensive for the vast majority of families to maintain. Despite the declining size of families and households, most Canadians continue to marry and spend at least part of their lives in nuclear families consisting of husband, wife, and their children.

Family Structures

Statistics Canada now defines a 'census family' as a married or common-law (heterosexual) couple living with or without never-married children, or a lone parent with at least one never-married child living in the same dwelling. While the vast majority of Canadians continue to live in families, the percentage has declined in the last twenty years. Of the 26.7 million people who lived in Canada in 1991, 84% lived in families while 16% lived in non-family households, compared to 1971 when 89% were in families and 11% were not. For the first time, the Canadian census showed in 1991 that a minority of families involved a married couple with children, as the percentage fell from 52% in 1986 to 48% in 1991 (Dumas, with Lavoie, 1992).

TABLE 4. Family composition, Canada 1991 (% distributions)

Family composition	1991
Married couples with children	48
Married couples without children	29
Lone parents	13
Common-law partners without children	6
Common-law partners with children	4

Source: Dumas, with Lavoie, 1992.

Since 1951, the number of children in Canadian families has declined. At the same time, the percentage of families containing only one child has risen from 32.3% in 1951 to 35.1% in 1991, and the percentage of families with only two children has risen from 23.5% to 26.4% (Statistics Canada, 1991b). However, the percentage of large families slowly decreased from 1961 until 1971 and then fell rapidly. In addition, the percentage of families with no children in the household has increased from 32.3% in 1951 to 35.1% in 1991, although there is considerable provincial variation. The highest percentage of families with no children living in the household occurred in British Columbia (40%), while the lowest occurred in Newfoundland (25%) (VIF, 1994).

Households

As families have become smaller, so have households. A 'household' is defined by Statistics Canada as a group of persons who occupy the same dwelling and do not have a usual place of residence elsewhere in Canada. In 1951, the average number of persons per household was 4.0 but this declined to 2.7 in 1991. The decline in household size has been influenced by lower birth rates, values of independence, the greater availability of apartment accommodation, and new services allowing people of all ages to live alone. Fewer Canadian families live with other relatives, boarders, or servants than in previous generations, and one-person households have significantly increased from 9.3% in 1961 to 22.9% in 1991 (Statistics Canada, 1993c).

Although some cultural groups were accustomed to living as an extended family, this arrangement was not considered ideal by most Euro-Canadians at any time during Canadian history (Nett, 1981). Extended family living has been more prevalent among certain cultural groups such as some Aboriginal people, Asians, Southern Europeans, Africans, or Caribbeans. Recently-married couples as well some-times share a residence with their parents for financial reasons, and many couples provide short-term accommodation for parents if they become widowed and frail. Statistics Canada collects data on the percentage of 'multi-family households', which approximates the concept of 'extended family'. Despite the fact that more immigrants are coming to Canada from countries in which people live in extended families, the percentage of such households declined from 6.7% in 1951 to only 1.1% in 1986 (Ram, 1990: 44). This decline can be explained by the fact that most Canadians now consider living alone more acceptable and feasible both for single persons and elderly widow(er)s. In addition, many immigrants alter their traditional practices after settling in Canada.

Cohabitation

A significant proportion of heterosexual couples now lives 'common-law' or co-habits without legal marriage, but as with other Canadian statistics, provincial variations are apparent. In 1990, Statistics Canada reported that 12% of all couples lived in common-law relationships compared to 6% in 1981 (Stout, 1991: 18). In Quebec, 19% of all couples lived common-law in 1991, but this rose to 61% among couples in which the woman was under 35 and there were no children. Furthermore, French-speaking Quebeckers are more than twice as likely to live common-law as English-speaking Quebeckers (Belliveau, Oderkirk, and Silver, 1994).

The vast majority of individuals living common-law are young and have never been legally married. More than half the women and 43% of the men who lived

TABLE 5. Percentage of couples living common-law,
Canada and Quebec 1981–1991

Year	All Canada	Quebec
1981	6.4	8
1986	8.3	—
1991	11.3	19

Sources: Stout, 1991; Belliveau, Oderkirk, and Silver, 1994.

common-law in 1986 were under 30, for example, but since then the median age of common-law partners has continued to rise. From 1984 to 1990, the proportion of Canadians aged 18 to 64 who had ever lived common-law nearly doubled, but among those aged 40 to 49, the proportion almost tripled (Stout, 1991). Statistics Canada's Family History Survey of 1984 found that 63% of first common-law unions end in marriage, while 35% end in separation and 2% with the death of one partner. A survey of married individuals in 1990 found that 17% had cohabited prior to marriage, but the percentage declines with age: while 37% of those between 20 and 29 had cohabited before marriage, only 4% of those over 50 had (Statistics Canada, 1990b). Because so many young people now cohabit before legal marriage, common-law living can be viewed as a new courtship pattern or trial marriage for a substantial number of people.

Although common-law relationships used to be considered temporary arrangements, legally and socially they are becoming more like traditional marriage. Yet statistically, there are still differences. Common-law relationships do not last as long as legal marriages. In fact, some researchers have found that marriages preceded by cohabitation have slightly higher rates of dissolution, although this may be diminishing as living together becomes more prevalent (Burch and Madan, 1986; Beaujot, 1990). Furthermore, fertility rates in common-law relationships tend to be lower than in legal marriage, suggesting that some couples marry only when they want to bear children. Yet in Quebec, where common-law relationships are more prevalent than in the rest of the country, 41% of these relationships include children living at home, either born to the partners or brought into the family from other unions (Belliveau, Oderkirk, and Silver, 1994).

One-Parent Families

Although the percentage of one-parent families has been rising since the 1960s as divorce rates have increased, it was just as high in the 1930s as it is now in the 1990s. The percentage of one-parent families declined considerably after World War II, but lone parents as a percentage of all families with children increased from 11% in 1961 to 20% in 1991 (Lindsay, 1992: 15). Eighty-two percent of lone parents are women (Statistics Canada, 1993a), but there have been changes in the

TABLE 6. Family structure, Canada 1931–1991 (% distributions)

Year	2-parent	1-parent
1931	86.4	13.6
1941	88.8	12.2
1951	90.1	9.9
1961	91.6	8.4
1971	90.6	9.4
1981	87.3	12.7
1991	87.0	13.0

Source: Statistics Canada.

paths to lone parenthood. Widowhood used to be the major life event leading to lone parenthood, as 66.5% of lone mothers were widowed in 1951. Today, the major route leading to lone parenthood is separation and divorce. Of all lone mothers in 1991, 32.5% were divorced, 24.6% were separated, 19.5% were never married, and only 23.4% were widowed (ibid.).

Raising a child in a one-parent family has become more socially acceptable and financially feasible for parents with full-time employment and/or adequate child support from the non-custodial parent. Consequently, the average number of years that children spend in lone-parent households is increasing. Yet this trend concerns policy-makers and social service workers because many lone mothers cannot find paid work, and when they work for pay, they cannot earn enough to support their children without child support or social assistance. According to Statistics Canada, 61% of lone mothers were living below the poverty line[2] in 1990 (Lindsay, 1992: 35). Using a standardized poverty line of 50% of median income adjusted for family size, the percentage of lone parents living below the poverty line in Canada is much higher than in some European countries but lower than in the US. Some of the factors affecting the poverty rates of lone mothers, such as poor enforcement of court-ordered child support, gender inequality in the labour force, lack of child-care services, and low rates of social assistance, will be discussed in the next section or subsequent chapters.

The increase in cohabitation and one-parent households has led to advocacy to re-examine family law and social assistance. Both laws and social programmes used to be based on the idea that legally-married partners had an obligation to each other but those without legal protection were disadvantaged. Now that so many children are living with unmarried parents, a new basis is needed to ensure their protection and support. In addition, high rates of separation and divorce are leading to growing controversies over the separation of marital property, child access, and child support.

In the next section, we will examine some recent changes in family law.

FAMILY LAW

Historical Background

The development of family policy in Canada has been influenced by the laws of the two European countries which originally colonized Canada (England and France) and the federal system, which results in divided and/or dual jurisdiction over family matters. When European settlers first came to Canada, they brought their marriage customs and legal traditions with them. In Quebec, the Civil Code, derived from French law, was based on guiding principles for judicial decisions. The rest of Canada adopted English common law that relied on the details of previous court cases as well as legislation. While Quebec maintained written regulations regarding issues of property, a difference from the common-law provinces, both systems supported the patriarchal family.

In both legal systems, the husband/father served as the intermediary between the family and the community, retained legal authority over his wife and children, controlled their property, and voted in elections as the family head. He was obligated by law to support his family and could expect his wife to provide sexual relations, children, and domestic services. The Married Women's Property Act, which began to be enacted by the Canadian provinces in 1872 (Dranoff, 1977: 48), was seen as a milestone by women's rights activists because it allowed women to retain their own wages, income, or property after marriage. Canadian women were granted the right to vote in federal elections in 1918 (but not in Quebec elections until 1940), and some provinces granted mothers the right to receive legal custody of their children as early as 1910.

For both men and women, marriage was an important economic and legal union. Without spouses, they could not normally survive on their own. Women could not always find paid work, and when they did, wages were too low to support a household. Men were expected to work long hours, had little time for household duties, and made insufficient wages to hire domestic help. Unmarried people generally lived with their immediate families or relatives or in some cases were provided board or basic accommodation by their employers. Consequently, legal marriage was viewed as the beginning of adult life, the first acceptable opportunity for sexual activity and reproduction, and one of the few ways to establish a household independent from family and relatives.

Marriage, Legitimacy, and Reproduction Laws

In Canada, the provinces have retained jurisdiction over who is permitted to marry and the minimum age of marriage. A legal marriage may take place between an unrelated[3] man and woman over the legal age who voluntarily agree to share a bed and their life. Although some gay men and lesbians consider themselves to be married, the law does not recognize their agreements and therefore they are not entitled to spousal benefits. Although women used to be permitted to marry at younger ages than men (as young as 12 in Quebec), the age is now 18 for both sexes in most provinces. Written parental consent is required for those between 16 and 18 (Bala and Clarke, 1981: 219).

Children born outside marriage used to be labelled 'illegitimate' which meant that they had no automatic right to financial support or inheritance from their father, and he had no right to make decisions about how they were raised. Illegitimate children took their mother's surname and she was their sole guardian (ibid.). Since law reform in the 1970s, however, most distinctions between legitimate and illegitimate children have been abolished. As of 1993, all distinctions regarding child status which are based on the marital status of the parents have been eliminated except in Nova Scotia and Alberta (Law Reform Commission of Nova Scotia, 1993: 26).

Laws and policies relating to reproduction remain controversial in Canada. Although the provinces administer and deliver health services, the federal government contributes to the funding of public health insurance. Consequently, the federal government imposes some conditions under the Canada Health Act (outlined in Chapter 4), and requires that all 'medically necessary' procedures be insured. Yet the provinces have some discretion to decide which services will be insured under their health insurance programmes, and some have argued that certain reproductive services (such as vasectomies and abortions) are not 'medically necessary'.

The federal government also influences reproductive policies through criminal law (Martin, 1989). Prior to 1969, the Criminal Code stated that the sale and dissemination of contraceptive information and devices were illegal and abortions could not be performed unless the life of the mother was in danger and the procedure took place in an accredited hospital. Throughout the 1960s, public pressure (especially from feminist groups) grew to reform abortion and contraception laws as rates of illegal abortion grew, the birth control pill was available, and attitudinal changes occurred among the Canadian population. In 1969, the Liberal government legalized the sale and dissemination of birth control devices.

In the common-law (English-speaking) provinces, adolescents under 16 have not always received contraceptive services because their ability to consent has been questioned. There is no legislation in English Canada and very little case law regarding youth consent (ibid.: 188). In contrast, Quebec clearly spells out rules of consent within its Civil Code, and physicians or health establishments must obtain parental consent before providing care and treatment to minors under 14 years of age (Campeau, 1992).

'Therapeutic abortions' were also legalized in 1969 although non-therapeutic abortions were still prohibited under the Criminal Code (Martin, 1989). A 'therapeutic abortion' could only be performed by a qualified medical practitioner in an accredited hospital after a positive decision by the hospital's abortion committee. This committee was composed of three doctors who had to conclude that the continuation of the pregnancy would, or would be likely to, endanger the life or 'health' of the woman. Moral opposition to abortion by some doctors and hospitals, and differences in the legal interpretation of the word 'health', resulted in unequal access to abortion across the country (Overall, 1993). In January 1988, the Supreme Court of Canada invalidated the federal law criminalizing non-therapeutic abortions because it was said to improperly infringe on women's right to equal access to health services under the Canadian Charter of Rights and Freedoms in the constitution (Martin, 1989). The court confirmed that the federal government could enact a new criminal law but had no obligation to re-criminalize abortion. The high degree of controversy and lack of consensus in Parliament and among advocacy groups has meant that no new law has been passed.

The absence of criminal law has allowed a wider range of choice in abortion policy, and provinces have taken very different stands. Some, like Ontario and Quebec, have promoted abortion as one of many services available in the health care system. Others have singled it out for special treatment and continue to impose conditions regarding where abortions can be performed, who can perform them, and the necessity of second opinions (Martin, 1989). Accessibility continues to be uneven and inequitable. Furthermore, the provinces may determine whether health services such as contraceptive counselling and sterilization are medically necessary and may establish the rate of compensation for physicians.

In 1989, the Law Reform Commission of Canada proposed a new category of crimes against the foetus. Since then, New Brunswick extended its child protection law to include the foetus in its definition of a 'child'. However, in Ontario, protection of the foetus has been attempted under child protection law with mixed results. The Children's Act in the Yukon allows a judge to order a pregnant woman to participate in supervision or counselling if the foetus is subject to serious risk of foetal alcohol syndrome or other injury resulting from the woman's use of addictive or intoxicating substances. Yet the court subsequently concluded that this section of the Act interfered with a pregnant woman's right to liberty under the Charter of Rights and Freedoms in the Canadian constitution (Royal Commission on New Reproductive Technologies, 1993).

Divorce, Custody, and Support

Divorce laws. In Canada, the federal government controls divorce law, which includes the legal right to remarry as well as those areas of corollary relief restricted to issues of child custody, access, and financial support. The provinces, however, control the implementation of divorce laws, the division of matrimonial property upon separation of spouses, and laws pertaining to child custody, access, child support, and spousal support (Syrtash, 1992).

From 1867 to 1968, the major ground for divorce was adultery, but divorce was so expensive, legally complex, and socially unacceptable that very few divorces were ever granted. Until 1925, divorce law contained a double standard allowing husbands to use adultery as a ground for divorce while wives were required to demonstrate that their husband had also committed an additional matrimonial fault, such as physical cruelty or bestiality. Women had to file for divorce in the province of their husband's domicile but as of 1930 they could apply for a divorce in their own province if they could demonstrate desertion (Peters, 1988). Before 1968, two provinces (Quebec and Newfoundland) had no court with jurisdiction over divorce decrees, and individuals in those provinces had to obtain a divorce through the federal Parliament. In all provinces, ex-husbands were expected to pay alimony or lifelong financial support to former wives, but only if the latter were shown to be 'without matrimonial fault'. Given the restricted grounds, cost, and lack of courts in certain provinces, legal divorce in Canada was rare before 1968.

Almost all Western countries modified their divorce laws during the post-World War II era, but Canada was relatively late in making these changes. Conservative religious-based groups criticized the easier divorce laws of some American states, viewing marriage for life as the most secure economic situation for women and children. Yet by the 1960s, backlogs in the divorce courts and pressure from the Canadian Bar Association, feminists, and social reform groups led to legal changes by the Liberal government. In 1968, the Divorce Act added a new ground for divorce: in addition to adultery and physical cruelty, divorces could be obtained because of 'marriage breakdown', which was strictly defined as separation for three years if both parties agreed or five years if the divorce action was unilateral.

After 1968, the divorce rate soared in Canada, and by the 1980s there was once again strong pressure for reform. In 1985, the Divorce Act was amended by the Conservative government to define marriage breakdown more liberally as a one-year separation without assigning fault to either partner. Although Canada moved toward a 'no-fault' divorce system with the 1985 reform, existing fault-based grounds were retained (Glendon, 1987).

Since the 1970s when family law was reformed, most provinces have amended their marriage and divorce laws to equalize the rights of husbands and wives. Typically, the family home and any property which spouses jointly use (called 'family assets' or 'matrimonial property') are divided equally between former spouses after divorce, and it may no longer matter whose name is on the deed of ownership. In addition, public pension credits may be split upon divorce.

The expectation of self-sufficiency after divorce is built into the 1985 divorce law and provincial support laws. Former wives are no longer awarded lifelong alimony based on moral conduct or domestic services provided during marriage. Instead, either spouse may be awarded temporary financial support based on need and principles of equity. Both partners are now expected to work to support themselves, although the new laws contain some judicial discretion with respect to spousal support, especially for older women and long-term home-makers. While the former laws were based on the principle that men were breadwinners and women were dependants, the amended laws tend to assume that both have equal opportunity to become self-supporting after marriage, even though considerable evidence exists to refute this assumption (Morton, 1988).

In 1989, Quebec introduced a new law on marital property which requires equal division of the 'family patrimony' when a marriage is ended by divorce, annulment, separation, or death. The category of assets to be divided, however, is relatively narrow and includes residences, furnishings, family cars, and pension rights. Yet the law also states that the court may divide assets unequally if equal division would result in injustice. Factors which are considered include the brevity of the marriage, the waste of certain property by one of the spouses, and/or bad faith by one of the spouses (Bala and Bailey, 1990–91).

Child custody and support laws. As divorce rates have increased, so has controversy over how child custody decisions are made and the amount of judicial discretion involved. Early in the twentieth century, custody of 'legitimate' children automatically went to the father but by the 1950s, this trend had reversed. Until the 1980s, one parent (usually the mother) was given sole custody or the legal right to make decisions concerning the child's upbringing, while the other was granted visiting rights or access. Some parents voluntarily shared parenting, but the courts did not necessarily sanction these private arrangements. Although joint custody was seldom awarded by Canadian courts prior to 1986, there has recently been a rise in joint custody and a slight decline in sole custody. In 1990, 73.2% of children in divorce cases were placed in the custody of their mothers, 12.3% with fathers, and 14.1% in joint custody (Statistics Canada, 1993b: 18). In Canada, joint custody means that both parents share decision-making about the child, even though the child may live with only one parent.

The federal Divorce Act 1985 contains two child support objectives. The first recognizes that both spouses have an obligation to support their child—in some provinces, this obligation extends to step-parents. The second is that child support should be divided between spouses according to their abilities, although property can substitute for regular support (Galarneau, 1992). Since 1987, provinces have been able to track defaulting parents using federal tax files and have been allowed to garnish federal money owed to the parent, such as income tax refunds (Morton, 1990). With this change, the amounts paid have increased slightly (Sev'er, 1992).

Traditionally, child support has been enforced privately through an adversarial court process (Richardson, 1988). Although federal law covers issues relating to divorce, custody, and support, the provinces are responsible for enforcing custody and support orders. Children are eligible for court-awarded support until age 16 or older if they are still financially dependent (Morton, 1990). Although enforcement procedures vary by province, officials have used their discretion to decide whether or not to enforce court-awarded child support, and no assessment formulae or periodic updating have been used (Garfinkel and Wong, 1990). When deciding on the award, judges consider any economic advantages or disadvantages arising from marriage breakdown, the financial consequences to the children, the length of the relationship, functions performed by the spouse during cohabitation, and any other order or agreement relating to the support of the child (Galarneau, 1992).

All provinces now have child support enforcement programmes, though these vary in scope, effectiveness, and jurisdiction. The majority fall under the jurisdiction of justice departments, but some are considered social service programmes. A few provinces (such as British Columbia) limit their programmes to welfare recipients, while others (such as Manitoba and Nova Scotia) monitor all child support orders in the province (VIF, 1993: 11). In 1995, a joint federal/provincial/territorial family law committee recommended a formula to standardize child support awards across Canada, as well as ways to address other weaknesses in the current system (Canada, F/P/T Family Law Committee, 1995).

Although the Canadian government has allowed non-custodial parents to receive an income tax deduction for both child and spousal support paid, support received is considered taxable income. These regulations were contested in the Federal Court of Appeal in 1994 and the Supreme Court of Canada in 1994 and 1995, with the case of Suzanne Thibaudeau, a lone mother from Quebec. In May 1995, the Supreme Court of Canada overruled the lower court decision, and concluded that asking custodial parents to pay income tax on child support received was not a violation of the Canadian Charter of Rights and Freedoms. Feminist groups strongly opposed this decision. In March 1996, the federal government eliminated both the deduction and the requirement to pay tax on child support for awards made after May 1997. National child support guidelines were also initiated.

In May 1995, the Supreme Court of Canada also decided that same-sex partners are not entitled to receive spousal benefits. Although gay and lesbian groups have been pressuring governments to redefine same-sex partners as 'spouses', there remains considerable public opposition to allowing them to receive the same government benefits available to heterosexual families.

Although fewer people are legally marrying, the distinctions are becoming blurred between legal and non-legal unions. Family law has undergone considerable reform since the 1970s, but not all laws have changed and not everyone agrees that the changes are improvements. Marriage is still a legal union between a man and a woman, and minimum age and incest laws remain virtually unchanged over the past twenty years. Yet the division of matrimonial property after divorce has been equalized and both partners are now required to support their children and become self-supporting after divorce. But feminists argue that women do not have equal opportunity to be self-supporting. Consequently, controversy continues over child access, custody, child support, and spousal support after divorce.

FAMILY VALUES

Despite the publicity given to rising divorce rates, family violence, and low marriage rates, Canadian opinion polls consistently report that respondents view family life as important. In 1994, 61% of respondents reported that they were generally happy with their family life, 75% said their families were full of love, and 83% of parents said having children made them happier (Nesmith, 1994). In a 1991 poll, 47% of respondents said that their greatest source of enjoyment was family and friends (Bozinoff and MacIntosh, 1991c). Among youth aged 15 to 24, 62% viewed family life as very important (Posterski and Bibby, 1988: 8). Depending on the poll, between 75% and 87% of respondents of all ages state that family is becoming more important in their lives (Wood, 1988; Gregg and Posner, 1990: 137).

Opinion polls also indicate that Canadians remain fairly traditional in their view of family. Faithfulness was considered to be a very important factor in a successful marriage by 94% of respondents to a Gallup poll in 1992 (Bozinoff and MacIntosh, 1992), and a 1994 poll found that 80% of respondents thought that an extra-marital affair was 'never okay' (Steele, 1994). In 1994, 68% of respondents agreed that the best type of family in which to raise children has two heterosexual parents with one at work and one at home, even though a shrinking minority of families actually fit this model. In the same poll, 67% thought same-sex couples raising children is negative for families and society (Nesmith, 1994).

Most Canadians (60%) opposed same-sex marriages in a 1994 Gallup poll, but 29% were in favour (Gallup Canada, 1994). As always, there were significant regional differences in these results, with more Quebec respondents favouring same-sex marriages and more in the Atlantic and Prairie provinces opposing. Polls also indicate that cohabitation is becoming more accepted as a family form, especially by those who enter into it. In 1994, 82% of those polled who are living with a common-law partner consider their living arrangement to be a family (Nesmith, 1994).

124   *Canada*

As fertility in Canada has declined, so has public perception of the ideal number of children for a family. In 1945, only 17% of respondents said that two or fewer children per family was the ideal, but in 1991, 59% gave this response (Bozinoff and MacIntosh, 1991a). Regional breakdowns in the 1991 poll indicate that those from Quebec, despite lower fertility rates than the rest of Canada, had a stronger preference for larger families, with only 49% viewing two or less children as ideal.

Abortion remains a divisive issue among Canadians and has been the subject of numerous opinion polls. While numbers fluctuate, polls repeatedly indicate that the majority of Canadians favour abortion, at least in certain circumstances, and that this opinion has increased somewhat since 1975. In 1993, 31% said that abortion should be legal under any circumstances, and an additional 56% said in certain circumstances. Among those who found abortion acceptable in certain circumstances, 81% said it was acceptable if the woman's health is endangered by the pregnancy, 70% said if conception is due to rape or incest, 64% said if there is a strong chance of serious defect in the baby, 42% said if agreed upon by the woman and her physician, but only 19% said abortion was acceptable if the family has a very low income. Ten percent of the sample felt that abortion should be illegal in all circumstances while 3% had no opinion (Hughes, 1993).

Recent Canadian polls reveal an increasing recognition of gender inequality. For example, when Gallup Poll asked: 'Do women get as good a break as men?', 60% answered 'no' in 1991 compared to 36% in 1971 (Bozinoff and MacIntosh, 1991b). In 1991, more people gave a negative answer in Quebec than in other provinces.

As the number of mothers with young children has increased in the Canadian labour force, public attitudes towards them have grown more positive. While 93% of respondents in 1960 thought that women with young children should stay at home (Boyd, 1984), only 35% responded this way in 1994 (Steele, 1994). In response to questions about child care, 74% of respondents in a 1987 study agreed that day-care services should be made available to anyone who wants them. Of these respondents, however, 59% thought that the cost should be borne chiefly by parents (Gregg and Posner, 1990).

Parents in the work-force are increasingly complaining about the shortage of time to meet work and family needs, called the 'time crunch'. In a 1994 poll commissioned for the International Year of the Family, only 36% of those who work 49 or more hours per week felt that they had achieved a good balance between their job and time with their family. On the other hand, 70% of parents who work 20 hours a week or less say they have been able to achieve this balance. Fifteen percent of parents felt dissatisfied with the amount of time they spend with their children, and 41% of these cited work pressures as the major reason (Nesmith, 1994).

Canadian polls indicate that most people grant considerable importance to their family life, but many also express concern about its quality. Of those adults in a 1989 poll who said that their job was less important than other aspects of life, 42% said they would like to spend more time with their family (Gregg and Posner, 1990: 137). A 1994 poll conducted for the Canada Committee for the International Year of the Family found that 63% felt that 'the family is in crisis' (Nesmith, 1994).

Interestingly, Canadians seem to feel that the 'crisis' is happening to someone else's family rather than their own. Perhaps the media, in their continual portrayal of the negative aspects of family life, are making Canadians feel that things are worse than they really are.

CONCLUSION

The declining birth rate, especially since the 1960s, has been the main contributor to population ageing, and over 11% of the Canadian population is now 65 or older. Yet relative to most European countries, Canada's population is moderately young. The national government has traditionally relied on immigration to help increase the population, and arrivals from developing countries have grown in recent years, making the society more heterogeneous in terms of culture, race, and religion. Yet the increased cultural diversity, as well as high unemployment and economic recession, have led to public concern over immigration targets and refugee claims.

Although legal marriage rates have recently declined in Canada, the rate of family formation remains as high as ever if we combine cohabiting and legally-married couples of all age groups. Yet family formation is declining among those under the age of 30, and marriages (broadly defined) tend to be less stable than a few decades ago. Furthermore, the size and structure of Canadian households and families have changed considerably since the Second World War. Families tend to be smaller and less stable units, marked by cohabitation, marriage, and repartnering.

Although family law is now based on the principles of gender equality and shared child support, court cases continue to be fought over perceived inequalities between the earnings and opportunities of former spouses after divorce. Although some family laws and social programmes have been reformed to acknowledge the participation of wives and mothers in the labour force, legislation still lags behind the need for reform. One area which remains very contentious is the enforcement of child support.

Most wives and mothers work full-time outside the home, although there is a growing gap between those with permanent work and those with insecure jobs. The income of wives helps maintain family income during difficult economic times but contributes to child-care problems and the 'time crunch'. Economic pressures and high expectations are placing greater stresses on marriage, raising divorce rates and the percentage of lone-parent families. Consequently, many more children than a generation ago now experience parental separation or divorce and live in mother-led families for at least a few years of their lives.

In the next chapter, we will outline and analyse those labour market trends that particularly influence family life, the impact of paid work on family, and the division of labour within the home.

2

Families and the Division of Labour: Employment and Family Work

As shown in Chapter 1, there have been major changes in Canadian demography over the past three decades: households are smaller, fertility rates are lower, divorces and remarriages are more common. There have been equally dramatic changes in patterns of paid and unpaid work. Labour force participation rates for women have increased from 24% in 1955 to 58% in 1990. The demographic changes outlined in Chapter 1 have facilitated this dramatic change in women's behaviour: it is easier to work outside the home when there are fewer children to care for, and it is more important to do so when there is a high risk of divorce. Higher levels of education, the women's rights movement, and growth in part-time and service-sector jobs have played an important role as well in encouraging this trend. Finally, many women have taken up paid employment because their families need the income, either because they are single parents or because deteriorating market conditions for men mean that many families are unable to survive on one income.

Increases in the labour market participation of mothers have had important implications for the day-to-day life of families. Although in most cases women continue to carry the major responsibility for household chores, they must now do housework after returning from the workplace, which creates time pressures as well as new potential sources of marital conflict since partners no longer have distinct responsibilities. Children are also affected as they spend more time in the care of adults other than their mothers.

The introduction of publicly-provided maternity benefits in 1971 was a clear response to increased labour force participation of women. The addition in 1990 of parental benefits, available to either father or mother, suggests a change in attitudes about gender roles, though the reality thus far appears to indicate that it is mainly mothers who take these benefits. Aside from these important policy developments, social institutions and workplaces have made little accommodation to acknowledge the changing work patterns of Canadian families.

DIVISION OF LABOUR AND ORGANIZATION OF TIME

As recently as 1970, men performed paid work outside the home and women performed unpaid work within the home in a significant majority (65%) of Canadian families. In 1991, following a dramatic increase in the labour force participation of wives, both partners worked outside the home in a majority (55%) of two-parent families (see Table 8). Despite increased labour force participation of wives, work within the home continues to be largely the responsibility of women. Women employed full-time outside the home have somewhat less responsibility for housework than do other women. Still, the majority of wives who are employed full-time have retained all or most of the responsibility for daily household tasks (defined as laundry, home repairs and maintenance, gardening, pet care, bill-paying, and travel to and from these household chores; Marshall, 1993). Sharing tends to be most prevalent among younger, well-educated couples with few or no children. The likelihood of shared responsibility also increases as the wife's income level rises (ibid.).

Large changes in the paid work patterns of women have not resulted in corresponding changes in the organization of domestic work. Thus, one important implication of the increase in women's labour force participation is that many women experience a 'double work day', as they return from the office to take up their responsibilities at home (e.g., McDaniel, 1993). Not only is this a strain in terms of long hours of work, but having to accommodate both home and workplace responsibilities can cause considerable stress. For example, the problem of caring for a sick child can create nightmares for mothers who work outside the home. The 'double work day' is also a problem for single mothers, a majority of whom work outside the home (63% in 1991; see Table 9). While there have been some policy responses (e.g., the introduction of paid maternity leaves in 1971), Canada still lags behind many European countries in this respect.

A second implication of increased labour market earnings of wives is the possible increase in women's bargaining power within families. Research on family decision-making indicates that wives with higher incomes tend to have more bargaining power in the relationship (see Phipps and Burton, 1993 for a survey). Why this is so is not entirely clear.

Sociologists (Blood and Wolfe, 1960) have argued that bargaining power increases with access to any personal resources, including higher education, social skills, youth, and physical beauty as well as income. The idea is that depending on the circumstances, decision-making power may shift from one spouse to the other. Economists have argued in terms of 'bargaining games'. For example, in 'divorce threat' bargaining games (e.g., McElroy and Horney, 1981), higher earnings make it more feasible for a wife to leave a bad relationship, making her threat of divorce more credible and hence increasing her bargaining power while married.

Regardless of which theory is correct, empirical evidence indicating that higher incomes increase women's power suggests that dramatic increases in labour market earnings of wives may have altered the pattern of decision-making within Canadian families. However, since it is still true that wives, on average, have incomes which are only 48% of those of their husbands (Phipps and Burton, 1995), these arguments do not suggest that women in general now have more power than men.

There is also empirical evidence indicating that women are more likely than men to spend income under their control in ways which benefit their children (Phipps and Burton, 1995). This idea has a long history in Canadian policy circles; making family allowances payable to mothers was regarded as a central feature of the original family allowance legislation. Thus, increases in mothers' market earnings may have increased the proportion of family resources devoted to children. On the other hand, growth in the labour force participation of parents has reduced parental time available for children.

Despite the physical distance which sometimes separates parents and grown-up children, the extended family continues to play an important social support role. Forty-nine per cent of Canadians provide unpaid help to family members living outside their household. Although support by grandparents is frequently overlooked and the elderly are often viewed as a population that requires service, 36% of seniors (65+) in Canada provide unpaid child-care services to family members living outside their households (Cohen, 1992).

LABOUR MARKET BEHAVIOUR[4]

Labour force participation among Canadian women has increased dramatically over the past thirty years, even more than in most other industrialized countries. In 1955, only 24% of women aged 15 years and over participated in the paid labour force; by 1993, this proportion had risen to 58% (see Table 7). Labour force participation rates for married women increased particularly rapidly so that rates of participation for married women are now roughly comparable (56%) to those for all women. The biggest changes in labour force participation occurred during the 1970s, although gains were still substantial during the 1980s. Interestingly, however, there has been a small reduction in female labour force participation between 1990 and 1993. This is attributable to significant reductions in participation rates for younger women (from 56% to 49% for women under 20 years of age; from 77% to 73% for women aged 20 to 24), which in turn have been associated with

TABLE 7. Labour force participation rates for women aged 15
and over, Canada 1955–1990 (% distributions)

Year	Participation rates
1955	23.9
1960	27.9
1965	31.3
1970	38.3
1975	44.4
1980	50.4
1985	54.6
1990	58.4

Sources: Statistics Canada, 1966 and 1991d.

deteriorating labour market conditions for youth in Canada (see Betcherman and Morissette, 1993).

The largest increases in labour force participation have occurred among women aged 35 to 44 (nearly 80% between 1970 and 1993[5]), but very substantial increases are also evident for those aged 25 to 34 (70%) and 45 to 54 (62%). Throughout the study period, labour force participation is lowest for women over 55 (very few women are labour force participants after age 65) and second-lowest for women under 20, many of whom are still in school. The most dramatic change is that women aged 25 to 34, in their prime childbearing years, had one of the lowest rates of labour force participation in 1970 but the highest in 1993.

Labour force participation among men has remained very constant for all but the older age groups (55+), among whom early retirement has become increasingly popular. Thus, there has been a convergence in male/female labour force participation for all age groups. Within each age group, however, male participation rates are still higher than those for females.

Such major changes in female labour force participation rates have, of course, resulted in new norms for the work patterns of Canadian parents. The 'father at office/factory and mother at home with children' model which prevailed during the 1960s and 1970s (65% of married couples families in 1971) has been replaced by the 'both mother and father at office/factory' model (55% in 1991; see Table 8).

TABLE 8. Employment patterns of married-couple families,
Canada 1971–1991 (% distributions)

Labour force status of parents	1971	1981	1991
both working	25.9	51.1	55.4
father only	64.7	42.4	27.7
mother only	1.7	1.6	8.6
both not working	7.7	4.9	8.4

Source: Luxemburg Income Study.

The *trend* towards increased labour force participation of mothers is evident regardless of the number of children in the family (see Table 10). For example, in 1971 28% of married mothers with three children were labour force participants; in 1991 64% were in the labour force. However, it remains true for both married and single mothers that participation is likely to fall as the number of children in the family increases, particularly when there are four or more children. In 1991, while 66% of mothers with one child were in the labour force, only 52% of those with four or more children were in the labour force. The cost of child care as well as the increased domestic work associated with larger families make it less and less likely that a mother with several children will take up paid employment. The fact that in most cases it is the mother who leaves the labour force in a two-parent family reflects the fact that it is still typically women who assume the major re-sponsibility for home and child care as well as the fact that women still typically earn much less than men.

Women with very young children are more likely to be out of the labour force than other mothers, but in 1991, it was nevertheless true that 41% of single mothers with a child less than three years of age were in the labour force; 64% of married mothers with very young children were in the labour force (see Table 9).

In the 1960s and 1970s, single mothers were generally more likely than married mothers to be in the labour force (see Table 10). In 1990, married mothers are more likely to be in the labour force. However, single mothers who work for pay are more likely to work full-time than are married mothers (see Table 9).

TABLE 9. Labour force characteristics of women with children, Canada 1991

| | Age of youngest child | | | Total, with children under 16 years |
	Under 3 years	3–5 years	6–15 years	
% employed				
lone parents	30.8	47.4	62.2	52.2
women in two-parent families	56.9	62.3	70.3	64.6
Unemployment rate				
lone parents	25.5	20.4	13.8	16.8
women in two-parent families	10.9	10.4	8.7	9.6
% not in labour force				
lone parents	58.6	40.7	28.0	37.4
women in two-parent families	36.1	30.1	23.1	28.5
% employed part-time, as a fraction of total employed				
lone parents	25.8	23.3	16.4	19.4
women in two-parent families	32.4	32.0	26.4	29.1

Source: Ghalam, 1993.

As women have entered the Canadian labour market, they have continued to enter traditionally 'female' sectors, so that despite large changes in the proportion of all employees who are women (from 31% in 1966 to 46% in 1993), the distribu-tion of women across broad industrial sectors is essentially unchanged. Since 1975, the vast majority of women (over 80%) have been employed in the service sector. Continued job growth in the service sector has, of course, facilitated increases in the labour force participation of women. Unfortunately, there has been a growing tendency for these new jobs to be 'bad jobs', with few hours, little security, and low pay (Economic Council of Canada, 1990).

Self-employment among Canadian women increased from 5% to 8% between 1975 and 1993. To date, there is insufficient evidence to conclude whether this is a positive trend towards increased entrepreneurship and independence for women, or whether the growth of self-employment is simply a way for employers to avoid paying some fringe benefits and making long-term commitments to workers (for example, by 'contracting out' tasks previously performed by regular employees).

TABLE 10. Labour force participation rates for women, Canada 1971–1991*

	1971	1981	1991
Married women			
no children	36.3	47.8	48.8
1 child	32.4	62.8	66.4
2 children	32.8	55.0	65.6
3 children	28.3	46.8	63.5
4 or more	22.1	41.6	52.4
Single/Other			
no children	43.9	50.7	49.1
1 child	42.4	62.4	61.4
2 children	41.3	58.6	59.9
3 children	31.6	54.8	51.6
4 or more	19.4	42.1	23.1

* As percentage of all women, by marital status and number of children under age 18.
Source: Luxemburg Income Study.

Part-time employment has always been extremely important for women in Canada and has become increasingly so since 1975. Part-time work accounted for 20% of female employment in 1975 and 26% in 1993. Roughly 70% of all part-time workers are women. While part-time employment offers women a way to engage in paid employment while continuing to fulfil their traditionally larger share of family responsibilities, part-time jobs are not typically 'good jobs' in Canada since employers can often offer lower rates of pay with limited fringe benefits. Moreover, some part-time workers are not eligible for unemployment insurance (which includes maternity leave in Canada).

While women's labour force participation has increased dramatically in Canada, their earnings as a fraction of male earnings have not changed correspondingly. While there has been improvement, in 1993 women, on average, earned only about 64% of what men earned; even women who work full-time, full-year earned only 72% of what their male equivalents earned. This compares with 46% and 58%, respectively, in 1967 (Statistics Canada, 1995b).

Increases in female labour force participation in Canada have occurred despite relatively non-supportive social policy (maternity leave is available, but is not particularly generous by international standards; day-care spaces are in chronically short supply; flexible working arrangements are rare). They have also occurred despite unfavourable macroeconomic conditions: unemployment rates for women have not fallen below 8% since 1975 (Statistics Canada, 1994b). In fact, it is likely that relatively hard economic times for husbands is one important reason for increased labour force participation among wives. Dooley (1989) demonstrates that without the large increases in mothers' labour force participation which we have observed over the past thirty years, poverty for children living in two-parent families would have been substantially higher.

Changes in female labour force participation, and particularly changes in the labour force participation of mothers, constitute a major change in the structure of Canadian society. The fact that a substantial majority of families do *not* have a parent at home full-time has not yet been adequately recognized by most Canadian policies and institutions. As examples, schools regularly schedule 'in-service' days for teacher training, leaving parents with paid jobs scrambling to find care for their children; some schools require children to go home for lunch; most visits to dentists or doctors must take place during working hours when a majority of parents are themselves at work; and there is no general legislation providing time off for parents to care for sick children. Coping with both home and workplace responsibilities thus places considerable strain on Canadian families, particularly mothers who work outside the home and yet typically retain primary responsibility for the care of their children.

EMPLOYMENT AND PARENTING POLICIES

In Canada, by far the most important parenting programmes are state-delivered cash maternity and parental benefits. These are designed as income replacement programmes for new parents with significant labour force attachment. The idea is that new parents will take a limited amount of time off to care for their infants, then return to the labour force. Maternity benefits are not viewed as a means of sharing the costs of infants among all members of society, since in Canada children are in general regarded as the private responsibility of their families. Thus, for example, there are no benefits for new parents without labour force connections, or with only very limited connections.

Since cash maternity/parental benefits are viewed as labour market programmes, they are administered through the Canadian Unemployment Insurance programme (UI). When UI was established in 1940, it contained no provisions for benefits payable to women taking time off work for maternity reasons. Of course, female labour force participation in the 1940s was much lower, so providing cash maternity benefits or job-protected leaves was not a priority at that time.

Rising female labour force participation in the post-war period prompted the introduction of compensated and job-protected maternity leaves in Canada. In 1971, the UI system was expanded to include cash maternity benefits; cash parental benefits did not become available until 1990. Although maternity benefits are administered through the UI system, the qualifying conditions for maternity benefits are slightly more stringent than for receipt of regular UI benefits. In order to collect UI for maternity reasons, a woman must have worked at least 20 weeks in the previous year. Claimants also must have worked for a minimum of 15 hours per week or had earnings above $163 (1994), 45% of average female wages. Self-employed women are ineligible for state-delivered maternity benefits. Unlike the qualifying conditions for maternity leave, which vary by province (see below), eligibility criteria for receipt of UI-delivered cash benefits are uniform across Canada. Benefits are payable for a maximum of 15 weeks.

Since maternity benefits are part of the regular Canadian UI system, they change when regular UI changes. Regular UI was made more generous in 1971 when maternity benefits were added to the programme. Since then, there has been concern that UI generates negative work incentives and increases unemployment. Thus, a variety of programme cut-backs have been made. For example, earlier benefit levels were relatively more generous than current levels: in 1971, replacement rates were 66.6%; in 1994, lower-income claimants (i.e., those earning less than $390 (1994) per week) receive 60% of insurable earnings, and others receive 55%. However, it is important to note that benefits are subject to a ceiling of $429 (1994), about 118% of average female wages, and higher-income recipients are also required to repay 30% of benefits received. Thus, higher-income women effectively receive much less than 55% of previous earnings. Finally, benefits are subject to regular income taxation. The federal government has recently proposed a series of changes to the UI programme which could reduce benefits for women having more than one baby within a five-year period, particularly if they have high earnings. Overall, maternity benefit levels in Canada are much lower than in other comparable countries. The average weekly before-tax maternity-related UI benefit received in 1992 was $273 (Routhier and Labowka, 1994).

Despite some flexibility in the start date of benefit receipt, a fairly rigid distinction is maintained between being on maternity leave and being in the paid labour force. Any earnings received during the benefit period are deducted dollar-for-dollar from maternity benefits. The Canadian approach, while assuming that new mothers will return to the paid labour force, does not accommodate the joint management of baby and job through a gradual return to paid employment such as is possible, for example, in Sweden.

In 1990, ten weeks of parental benefits were introduced. Eligibility conditions and benefit rates are the same as for maternity benefits. Either parent may claim the parental benefits or they can share the ten weeks at any time within the first year of the child's arrival into the home (Routhier and Labowka, 1994). An additional five weeks of benefits can be collected if the child requires special attention due to disability. Evidence shows that 98.9% of total beneficiaries of maternity/parental leave are women (Statistics Canada, 1995b).

Adoption benefits were introduced in 1984. Benefit levels and qualifying conditions for receipt of adoption benefits were the same as for regular maternity benefits. From 1984 to 1990, the duration of cash adoption benefits was 15 weeks, and the benefit could only be collected by one parent. Since 1990, adoptive parents are eligible for parental benefits (a reduction to ten weeks).

The UI programme, of which maternity and parental benefits are a very small part,[6] is administered by Human Resources Development Canada and is financed through employer and employee contributions.

There are at least two important implications of the Canadian rules for collection of cash maternity benefits. First, new mothers who already have children are less likely to qualify because they are more likely to have restricted labour force attachment. In this way, Canadian policy contrasts with that, for example, of France, where larger families receive more maternity benefits. Second, labour market trends toward more jobs with short hours and more self-employment, particularly for younger women, mean that a growing fraction of labour force participants who become new parents are ineligible for benefits. On the other hand, dramatic increases in the labour force participation of new mothers mean that maternity benefit recipients as a fraction of live births have increased from 19% in 1975 to 40% in 1991 (see Table 11). In 1987, 84.6% of women on maternity leave received cash

TABLE 11. Maternity benefits coverage, Canada 1971–1991[a]

	1971	1975	1980	1985	1991
Maternity[b]	2.8	19.5	29.0	35.1	40.0
Adoption[c]	—	—	—	0.1	4.3
Parental[d]	—	—	—	—	—
Total	2.8	19.5	29.0	35.2	44.3

[a] Annual number of initial claims filed for maternity benefits under the Unemployment Insurance Program, as a percentage of annual live births.

[b] Maternity benefits could be claimed under the Unemployment Insurance Program beginning in July, 1971.

[c] Adoption benefits were introduced in 1984.

[d] Parental benefits were introduced in 1990. Maternity benefits could only be claimed by the natural mother except in the case of her death or incapacitation; parental benefits could be claimed by either parent.

Sources: Statistics Canada 1985, 1992c, and 1995c.

benefits from the UI programme. This is a noticeable increase from 1980, when only 67.4% of women on maternity leave received UI, perhaps as a result of eliminating a rule stipulating that women be employed for ten weeks prior to conception (Moloney, 1989).

A small number of women have separate collective agreements with their employers to provide maternity benefits in addition to UI benefits: only 26% of women covered by a major collective agreement have provisions for cash benefits, in addition to UI, from their employers during a maternity leave (about 30% of paid female employees are unionized in Canada; Ghalam, 1993). However, this is a dramatic increase from only 6% in 1980 (Moloney, 1989). In 1987, 20% of women on maternity leave received financial benefits (either from their employers or from group insurance) other than UI (Moloney, 1989).

Conditions for taking maternity *leave* (as opposed to cash benefits) are governed by labour standards law and vary depending on the employer and the province. In all regions except the Northwest Territories, women have the right to an unpaid, job-protected maternity leave (Moloney, 1989), although the length of the leave varies and does not necessarily correspond to the duration of cash benefits. The average length of maternity leave is about 17–18 weeks (Canada, Human Resources and Labour, 1993), slightly longer than the 15 weeks of UI-delivered cash maternity benefits.

The qualifying conditions for unpaid maternity leave vary across regions and employers, although a specified period of work history is required in most provinces (except British Columbia, New Brunswick, and Quebec). For example, women in Nova Scotia are required to have 12 months of work history in the year prior to the leave, while women in Ontario must have 13 weeks to qualify for leave (Canada, Human Resources and Labour, 1993). A significant difference between leave and cash benefits eligibility criteria is that part-time workers in all jurisdictions are entitled to the same leave provisions as full-time workers (Labour Canada, 1985).

The conditions for parental leave also vary significantly across provinces. For example, no parental leave is available in Alberta or Saskatchewan. In Ontario, 18 weeks are available to each parent. In New Brunswick, 12 weeks may be shared between parents. In some cases, parental leave must be taken immediately following the maternity leave (e.g., British Columbia); in others it must begin within 52 weeks of the birth (e.g., Manitoba); while in others it must be finished within 52 weeks of the birth.

Some legislation in Canada provides short-term leave for other family responsibilities. For example, a majority of provinces allow from one to five days of leave (unpaid except in Quebec and Newfoundland) in the event of a death in the immediate family. Quebec also provides employees with one paid day off when they marry, or one unpaid day off to attend the wedding of an immediate family member. Quebec provides five days of unpaid leave for other family responsibilities as well (e.g., in case a child is ill) (Canada, Human Resources and Labour, 1993).

CONCLUSION

While women's paid work outside the home has increased dramatically, there has not yet been a corresponding increase in men's unpaid work within the home (though younger, more educated men are more likely than others to share household chores). Thus, increased labour force participation has generated a 'double work day' for many women. On the other hand, increases in women's market incomes may have increased their decision-making authority within the family. This, in turn, has probably increased the share of household resources devoted to children, since there is evidence that women are more likely to spend in ways which benefit children.

As Canadian mothers (both single and married) have entered the labour force in growing numbers, more and more young children spend long hours with a caregiver other than a parent. Increases in divorce rates have meant that a growing number of children have limited access to the time of one parent (usually the father). Offsetting these trends toward less parental time with children is the fact that average family size has fallen, reducing the need to divide parental time among children.

An important consequence of higher rates of labour force participation by women is that Canadian families have become increasingly dependent on the market. In earlier years, child care, most food (from growing to baking), nursing care, and clothing were all typically produced using family labour. Now, most of these things are purchased in the marketplace. Not only is this a major change in what families do, it means that families depend on market-generated incomes to carry on with life in the usual fashion.

And while families have come to be increasingly dependent on market incomes—in many cases wives' earnings hold two-earner couples above the poverty line (see Dooley, 1989)—a theme of Chapter 3 is that market opportunities have become much more limited during the 1980s, particularly for younger adults. Thus, while Canadian families experienced real growth in incomes (before and after tax) until the late 1970s, average real incomes have remained constant since then, despite continued increases in the labour force participation of wives.

Policy responses to these fundamental changes in the work patterns of Canadian families have been rather limited. Certainly the most important policy developments from the perspective of accommodating the new Canadian reality that most parents work outside the home were the introduction of paid maternity leaves in 1971 and paid parental leaves in 1990. However, since these programmes are part of the regular UI system, some changes have occurred which are somewhat 'haphazard' from the perspective of maternity/parental benefits policy. For example, benefit levels have been reduced as a result of concerns that regular UI generates negative work incentives.

Otherwise, many Canadian policies and institutions continue to operate as though the 1960s model of the family prevailed, and it is unlikely that there will be major new initiatives in the near future. New policy developments in Canada are severely restricted by the general feeling that 'we can't afford them'. This is a result of public acceptance of the right-wing orthodoxy that the public debt is too large and that generous social programmes will both reduce the incentive to work for pay and further increase the cost of government. Even given an easing of budgetary austerity, it is not clear what the right wing, which currently dominates policy debates in Canada, would propose in the way of labour-market-related family policies. Right-wing thinking in this area is somewhat contradictory, supporting, on the one hand, the traditional idea that the world of the family is a private place nurtured by stay-at-home mothers, and, on the other hand, the idea that all individuals, male or female, are responsible for providing for their own needs by working in the marketplace.

3

The Income of Families:
Earnings and Transfers

During the 1960s and early 1970s, Canadian families experienced real gains in income. However, despite continued increases in women's labour force participation through the end of the 1970s and during the 1980s, average real family income growth ended in the late 1970s (see Figure 1). Thus, for many families, increases in women's market work mainly served to prevent income losses during this period.

FIGURE 1. Average real disposable incomes, Canada 1971–1991
(in constant Canadian $)

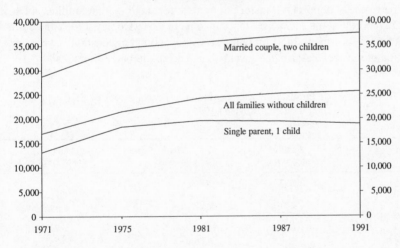

For most families with children, the most important sources of family income are labour market earnings and government transfers. Since 1975, the relative importance of labour market earnings has fallen while the relative importance of transfer income has increased. This is not because transfer programmes have been expanded—in fact, the reverse is generally true. Rather, the declining importance of labour market earnings reflects deteriorating labour market conditions in Canada. During the 1960s, unemployment averaged 5.2% while during the 1980s unemployment averaged 9.5% (Osberg, Erksoy, and Phipps, 1994a; Statistics Canada, 1975). Real wages increased until the mid-1970s and stagnated thereafter. Part-

Canada

time and short-term jobs grew as a fraction of total employment; self-employment became more prevalent. A major theme of Chapter 3 is the decline in economic opportunities for a large number of Canadian workers. Perhaps most importantly, younger Canadian workers have experienced increasing difficulties since the mid-1980s. Of course, some people have managed very well, so there is also growing inequality of earnings, though less marked than in the US.

While there have been cuts throughout the 1980s, it is nonetheless true that Canadian transfer programmes, particularly unemployment insurance, have managed to hold inequality of incomes relatively constant through a period of increased inequality of earnings. While not explicitly 'family policy'—indeed, Canada does not have an explicit family policy—the importance of Unemployment Insurance (UI) to families in Canada must be emphasized. For example, in 1991 26% of Canadian families with children experienced unemployment, and 75% of these families received UI (Osberg and Phipps, 1995). Cut-backs to UI during the 1980s and 1990s have meant increased reliance on social assistance. Since social assistance is a provincial responsibility (with partial federal sharing of costs) there is substantial variation in programmes offered across the country. However, one common theme is that, consistent with a Canadian concern with preserving incentives to paid employment, the level of assistance provided is very low. Social assistance is a particularly important transfer programme for single-parent families, 44% of whom reported some social assistance income in 1990 (Dooley, 1995). In contrast with the US, however, single individuals (without children) constitute a larger proportion of the social assistance caseload than do single-parent families.

TABLE 12. Average family allowance expenditures per child as % of GDP per capita, Canada 1945–1990

Year	Family allowance[a]	Youth allowance[b]	Family assistance[c]
1945	5.33	—	—
1950	5.46	—	—
1955	4.07	—	—
1960	3.79	—	—
1965	2.86	4.12	3.70
1970	2.00	2.83	2.47
1975	3.75	—	—
1980	2.14	—	—
1985	2.06	—	—
1990	1.68	—	—

[a] In 1993, the Child Tax Benefit replaced the family allowances, as well as the refundable child tax credits (RCTC) and the personal tax exemptions for dependent children.

[b] Introduced in 1964, the youth allowance was incorporated into the Family Allowance in 1973.

[c] Introduced in 1956, the family assistance benefit was incorporated into the Family Allowance in 1973. The number of children receiving family assistance, and therefore the average expenditure, is only available after 1963.

Sources: Canada, Health and Welfare (various years). *Inventory of Income Security Programs in Canada*; Canada, Health and Welfare, 1986.

Transfer programmes designed specifically for families have played only a small role in supporting family incomes. Although family allowances were available in Canada from 1945 until 1993, these benefits were always relatively small and were allowed to decline in value over time. In 1945, average family allowance expenditures per child were 5.3% of GDP per capita; in 1990, they had fallen to 1.7%, before income tax or clawbacks (see Table 12). Providing transfers specifically designed to assist all families with children is not particularly consistent with a pervasive Canadian attitude that children are the private responsibility of their parents unless the children are in need. Thus, an important theme in the recent history of family benefits in Canada has been a movement away from universality and toward benefits targeted on lower-income families. There has also been a movement away from benefits delivered through the transfer system and toward benefits delivered through the tax system. This latter policy shift was motivated by a perception, arguably incorrect, that delivering benefits through the tax system is administratively more efficient.

PATTERNS OF INCOME AND EXPENDITURES[7]

Historical Background

After a period of rapid growth during the 1960s and early 1970s, real incomes have stagnated and even fallen for some Canadian households (e.g., single-parent families). This pattern is true for families with and without children, using real income before tax, real income after tax, or real income after tax adjusted for family size. Three factors are particularly important in explaining these trends.

First, real wages increased during the 1960s and early 1970s, but levelled off thereafter (Osberg and Phipps, 1992). Second, unemployment rates averaged 5.2% during the 1960s, 6.7% through the 1970s, 9.5% through the 1980s and 10.2% for the period 1990–1993 (Osberg, Erksoy, and Phipps, 1994a; Statistics Canada, 1975). Moreover, the severity of cyclical fluctuations around these average levels has increased. In part, extremely high rates of unemployment reflect the economic hard times which have been experienced world-wide; they also reflect the macro-economic policy stance which has been adopted in Canada where fighting inflation has been the principal goal, regardless of the costs in terms of unemployment. Third, there has been significant growth in 'bad jobs': part-time employment, short-term employment, and self-employment of individuals who do not in turn have employees have grown to constitute nearly 30% of total employment (Economic Council, 1990).

Incomes and Standards of Living

Although average incomes have remained quite constant since 1975, some families have lost ground, while others have done very well. As in many other countries, earnings inequality has increased in Canada since the early 1980s, particularly for men (Beach and Slotsve, 1993). However, unlike the US, where polarization of hourly wages has been of key significance, in Canada, increases in earnings inequality have largely been driven by increased polarization of *hours* (Morissette, Myles, and Picot, 1994). Thus, changes in earnings inequality are linked to patterns of unemployment (Phipps, 1993).

When unemployment goes up, the Canadian UI system helps to stabilize household incomes, somewhat alleviating increases in *income* inequality which would otherwise occur. Although not explicitly family policy, unemployment insurance is a more important source of family income than in most other countries (Osberg and Phipps, 1995). While Canadian spending on social security transfers is low by international standards, unemployment insurance expenditures make up a relatively high percentage of the total (Osberg, Erksoy, and Phipps, 1994c). This helps to explain why income inequality has not increased as much in Canada as in many other similarly affluent countries despite similar demographic and labour market trends (Fritzell, 1992). In fact, aggregate income inequality has remained relatively constant over the past fifty years. The richest 20% of households have had access to over 40% of income in all years since 1951; the poorest 20% of households have had less than 5% of income (Phipps, 1993).

Single-parent families have historically experienced and continue to experience a lower standard of living than married-couple families or families without children. For example, the average equivalent income received by single parents with one child is about 75% of that received by married couples with one child and about 75% of that received by families without children. This ratio has been roughly constant since the early 1970s. There are at least three important reasons why single-parent families are less well-off than two-parent families. First, the family has only one adult income to rely on. Second, women still earn significantly less in the labour market than do men. Third, single-parent families are more likely to rely on social assistance than are two-parent families, and in Canada families who must depend on social assistance will be poor.

For both one- and two-parent families, average equivalent income falls as the number of children increases. For example, average equivalent income for married-couple families with three or more children has remained about 60% of that for married-couple families with one child, both because there are 'more mouths to feed' and because additional children increase work within the home, making labour force participation of both parents more difficult.

It is also true that some minority groups have experienced lower levels of income than the average for Canada. For example, the average annual income for all individuals with Aboriginal origins and/or Indian registration 15 years of age or older 'with income' is $17,000, compared to a national average of $24,000 (Statistics Canada, 1995a). This statistic reflects both very limited labour market opportunities for native peoples living on reserves as well as ongoing discrimination.

Immigrant families, on the other hand, are on average relatively affluent, given immigration laws which have tended to favour the relatively skilled. In 1990, average income for immigrant families ($46,000) was slightly higher than the national average ($41,000) (Akbari, 1995).

Younger workers have become increasingly disadvantaged relative to older workers over the past thirty years. Betcherman and Morissette (1993) document deteriorating labour market conditions for individuals aged 16 to 24 (the same patterns are evident to a slightly lesser degree for individuals under 35). In 1967, median wages and salaries for younger male workers (under 25) were 36% of those received by older male workers; in 1989, the equivalent figure was only 23%. Younger workers have been particularly affected by the growth of non-standard employment. Then, lack of access to 'good jobs' limits access to 'good transfer programmes' such as UI. Since nearly half of single mothers (48% in 1990) are less than 35 years old, deteriorating labour market conditions for young adults have had important consequences for the incomes of younger single mothers (Dooley, 1995).

Poverty Experiences

The poverty rate experienced by Canadian families with children has remained fairly constant at about 18% since the early 1970s.[8] This rate is roughly comparable to the UK and Australia, lower than in the US, but higher than in Sweden, Finland, Germany, or The Netherlands (Phipps, 1995). Of course, these figures assume income is shared equally within families. Since men typically have the higher incomes, if they do not share fully with other family members, then poverty rates for women and children are much higher than 18% (Phipps and Burton, 1995).

Childless families now experience lower rates of poverty than do families with children. This important change from earlier times is due to the successful reduction of poverty among elderly Canadians.

TABLE 13. Poverty of families, Canada 1971–1991 (% distributions)*

Family type	1971	1975	1981	1987	1991
All families with children	19	16	17	18	18
All families without children	42	21	16	14	13
All couples with children	15	12	13	13	12
Couples with one child	11	9	8	9	9
Couples with two children	11	8	11	12	10
Couples with three or more children	23	20	23	23	22
All single parents	63	47	43	46	45
Single parents with one child	55	34	35	37	38
Single parents with two children	55	49	45	50	45
Single parents with three or more children	82	70	66	80	69

* Definition of poverty: if gross equivalent family income < 50% median gross equivalent country income.

Source: Luxemburg Income Study.

One-parent families have always experienced higher rates of poverty (45% in 1991) than two-parent families (12% in 1991). Families with more children are more likely to be poor (69% and 22%, respectively, for one- and two-parent families with three or more children) (see Table 13). In part a reflection of poor labour market conditions for young adults, families with young heads are currently extremely vulnerable (Sharif and Phipps, 1994; Osberg, Erksoy, and Phipps, 1994b; Phipps, 1994). Aboriginal families with children are especially likely to be poor: 48% of registered Indian children living on-reserve live in poverty (Canada, House of Commons, 1991).

Finally, the incidence of poverty shows important regional differences (Phipps, 1993). While provincial poverty rates have converged since the 1970s, a gap of 14 percentage points remains between the province with the lowest incidence of poverty (British Columbia) and the provinces with the highest incidence of poverty (Newfoundland and Manitoba). This fact has played an important role in shaping many Canadian policies, including a system of equalizing transfers across the provinces to enable poorer regions to provide comparable standards of health and education, for example, without imposing an excessive tax burden on the local population. (Health and education are constitutionally provincial responsibilities.)

Sources of Income

Between 1975 and 1991, the composition of income for all Canadian families has changed relatively little. The contribution of wages and salaries to total income has fallen (from 68% to 59%), and the contribution of transfers has increased (from 22% to 26%). Since the Canadian unemployment rate increased from 6.9% in 1975 to 10.3% in 1991, it is perhaps surprising that changes have not been larger in the relative contributions of wages and salaries versus transfers to family income in the country. It is also true that the Canadian population is ageing, increasing the relative importance of transfers in the form of pension benefits.

However, the composition of family income differs significantly across family types. Single-parent families, on average, receive relatively less of their total incomes in the form of wages and salaries (about 50%), which has been generally true from 1975 until 1991. Means-tested cash transfers (including, most importantly, social assistance but also, after 1979, the income-tested refundable child tax credit) constitute the second most important source of income for single-parent families (22% in 1975; 30% in 1991). Other social security income (including UI and family allowances) is the third most important source of income for single-parent families (19% in 1975; 12% in 1991). The real value of family allowances has eroded over time. The reduction in the importance of UI is due to changes in UI legislation through the 1980s which have both made it harder to qualify and reduced the generosity of benefits. The increase in the importance of social assistance is linked with the decline in the importance of UI since individuals who do not qualify for or who run out of unemployment insurance typically must resort to social assistance.

For single-parent families, the relative importance of alternative sources of income changes substantially as the number of children in the family increases. Wages and salaries become less important while transfers, particularly means-tested transfers, become more important. Nevertheless, wages and salaries remain the most important source of income until there are three or more children in the household.

For married-couple families, roughly 80% of total income is derived from wages and salaries, although again the importance of this source of income has declined (from 82% in 1975 to 77% in 1991). Self-employment earnings have increased in importance for married-couple families and now constitute 6% of income. Transfers are much less important than for single-parent families. Among transfers, the most important is 'social security' (principally UI, but also family allowance payments).

TABLE 14. Household income by source as % of gross income, Canada 1971–1991

Income source	1975	1981	1987	1991
All families without children				
wages and salaries	60	58	58	54
self-employment income	2	3	4	4
investments	7	10	6	7
annuities and pensions	4	4	5	6
social security	20	19	19	21
other social security[a]	1	1	2	3
means-tested cash benefits	4	4	4	5
other income	1	1	1	1
Single-parent families				
wages and salaries	49	52	49	46
self-employment income	1	2	3	2
investments	4	4	2	2
annuities and pensions	1	1	1	1
social security	19	13	11	12
other social security[a]	2	2	3	3
means-tested cash benefits	22	21	25	30
other income	4	5	6	4
Married-couple families				
wages and salaries	82	81	80	77
self-employment income	3	6	6	6
investments	2	3	2	2
annuities and pensions	0	0	1	1
social security	8	6	7	8
other social security[a]	1	1	1	2
means-tested cash benefits	1	2	3	3
other income	0	0	1	1

[a] This category includes social retirement benefits, family allowance, and unemployment insurance.

Source: Luxemburg Income Study.

Again, the composition of income for married-couple families varies somewhat as the number of children increases, but this pattern is less marked than for single-parent families. There is no noticeable reduction in the contribution of wages and salaries until there are more than three children in the family.

Expenditure Patterns

Another approach to examining the material standard of living of Canadian families with children is in terms of expenditure patterns. It is interesting that there are not *major* differences in how various family types allocate expenditures. The share of the overall budget spent on food and clothing, for example, increases as family size increases; the shares of housing, transportation, and recreation fall. If we compare families in which the wife is employed full-time with families in which the wife is not in the labour force (which will be larger families), the proportion of the budget devoted to food increases while the proportion of the budget devoted to transportation falls. However, regardless of family type, the observed pattern of expenditures is roughly similar.

Likewise, no major changes in the way family budgets are allocated are discernible over time. The proportion of the budget devoted to the 'necessities' of food, clothing, and housing has remained fairly constant at about 50%, although the proportion of expenditures going to housing has increased from about 20% to 25% and the share of clothing has fallen from about 10% to about 6%.

FAMILIES, TAXATION, AND TRANSFERS IN CANADA

Attention to the family has never dominated discussion of either tax or social security reform in Canada. Thus, the effects of tax and transfer changes on families have often been somewhat haphazard. Given a growing preference for delivery of Canadian child benefits through the tax system as refundable credits, it is best to discuss tax relief and cash transfers in an integrated way.[9]

Historical Background

Provisions for the family first appeared through the tax rather than the transfer system. Income tax exemptions for dependent children (and spouses) were made available in 1918, with the rationale that it was inappropriate for a man (typically the principal breadwinner at that time) to pay tax on the basic income required to feed and clothe his children (and wife), though exemption levels were never as high as basic needs. Until 1945, tax exemptions were the major benefit available to families with children.

Prior to World War II, the prevailing attitude in Canada was that families were responsible for their own destinies; the 'Protestant work ethic' was widely accepted. A man unable to support himself and his family was viewed as a failure and had no option but private charity. Extremely high rates of unemployment during the Great Depression of the 1930s (e.g., over 19% in 1933) helped to create new attitudes in Canada about the appropriate role of government. With such high rates of unemployment, it was difficult to blame individuals who lost their jobs and hence lost the means of supporting their families. Keynesian ideas about a role for government in macroeconomic stabilization appeared as did preliminary thinking about the need for welfare programmes (expressed in the Marsh Report in Canada, which was strongly influenced by the British Beveridge Report). The Co-operative Commonwealth Federation (CCF, now New Democratic Party or NDP) emerged as an important left-wing political party during the 1930s, first coming to power as the provincial government in Saskatchewan in 1944. This also helped create an environment supportive of expanding social programmes.

Economic stabilization goals as well as concerns about social welfare were important factors leading to the establishment of universal family allowances in 1945.[10] In contrast with the earlier selective approach, all families with children were given the right to a cash transfer from the government. But while family allowances were established as a universal programme, older ideas had not disappeared. The history of Canadian family allowances until their eventual elimination in 1993 is a history of tension between a belief in the value of universal entitlements and the older attitude that only those 'in need' should receive 'handouts' from the government. Moreover, the history of child benefits in Canada since 1945 can be seen as a gradual return to the original exclusive use of the tax system to deliver financial assistance to families with children. Of course, the current system is vastly superior to the 1918 system in terms of vertical equity since the original tax exemptions granted larger absolute benefits to higher-income families while the current child tax benefit only provides benefits to lower-income families.

While operating with universal entitlement from 1945 until 1974, family allowances became less and less a truly universal transfer through the 1970s and 1980s as income taxes were imposed and clawbacks were instituted. Through the same period of time, the tax system became an increasingly important vehicle for the delivery of cash benefits to families with children (in the form of refundable credits), particularly lower-income families with children. Important reasons for the declining popularity of universal transfers include: a growing focus on the problem of child poverty; a growing concern with curtailing expenditures on social programmes; erosion of the real value of family allowances and hence diminished support by middle-class Canadian families. In an important sense, there has been a resurgence of the older Canadian tradition of viewing children as the private responsibility of their parents unless they are in need. After a number of smaller steps in the same direction, opposed by those on the left who still favour universal benefits, family allowances were completely replaced with child tax benefits in 1993. This gradual movement away from universal family allowances towards child tax benefits targeted on the poor and delivered through the tax system is an important theme in the history of Canadian family policy.

Tax Exemptions

In Canada, income taxes are paid to both the federal and provincial governments. The unit of taxation is the individual, although family income is now pooled for the purpose of determining eligibility for some refundable tax credits.

Taxation benefits for families with children in Canada can be traced back to 1918, when the government introduced a child tax exemption of $200 per child under 18 (Boadway and Kitchen, 1984). Personal, spousal, and child exemptions were intended to 'give a man sufficient to live on', although Kesselman (1979) notes that exemption levels were typically much lower than poverty income. Exemptions for spouses and children acknowledged the extra income needs of families relative to single individuals. The legislation implicitly recognized the social value of marriage and childbearing, as well as the government's obligation to support these activities. But offering assistance through a tax exemption was consistent with the *laissez-faire* attitudes of the time since exemptions meant government was *not* interfering with (i.e., taxing) private income. Tax exemptions were the major source of financial support for families with children for over twenty years.

Family Allowances

Family Allowances (FA), an exclusively federal programme, were first paid in Canada in 1945, at a time when several other industrialized countries were establishing programmes to assist families with the costs of children. The government hoped that family allowances would fulfil a Keynesian macroeconomic stabilization function as well. Unions first opposed the allowances as a back-door wage control measure; some English Canadians argued that family allowances would provide favourable treatment for larger Catholic families in Quebec. And it has been argued that the Liberal prime minister was feeling pressure from the left—the social democratic CCF had just been elected to form the government in Saskatchewan and the CCF had endorsed the idea of family allowances (Guest, 1980; Perry, 1989).

All Canadian families with children under 16 were eligible to receive benefits, financed from general revenue, though immigrant children had to wait three years to become eligible (Statistics Canada, 1982). In 1945, the average family allowance expenditure per child was about 5% of GDP per capita (see Table 12). By 1946, 92% of children under the age of 16 received FA (Guest, 1980). FA benefits were not subject to income taxation. Cheques were payable to the mother, if present, with the rationale that funds would then most likely be spent on the children. Benefits were not dependent on family income. Initially, families with five or more children received lower benefits for the fifth and subsequent children to placate concerns about undue benefit to Quebec, but that clause was eliminated in 1949 (Guest, 1980). Also in 1949, the three-year waiting period for immigrant children was reduced to one year.

In 1947, parents were allowed to claim a tax exemption of $100 per dependant on whose behalf family allowance benefits were received and $300 for dependants ineligible for family allowance benefits, that is, children aged 16–18 (Boadway and Kitchen, 1984).

Major Changes in 1974

This combination of family allowances and child exemptions remained in place for another twenty years, though in 1968 FA benefits were extended to children aged 16–18 attending school full-time (Guest, 1980). Child tax exemptions were increased periodically to reflect the rising cost of living, but were only indexed for inflation from 1974 to 1984 (Kesselman, 1993). The value of family allowances, never particularly high, was allowed to erode over time (see Table 12).

Canadians 'discovered' poverty in 1968 with the publication of the Economic Council of Canada's Fifth Annual Review, which adopted an approach to measuring poverty recently developed by Statistics Canada. Beginning in 1971, Statistics Canada began publishing estimates of the number of households with 'low incomes' (Ross, Shillington, and Lochhead, 1994). While not official poverty estimates, these reports carry substantial weight in Canada. With new attention to the problem of poverty, the idea of efficiently targeting expenditures on the poor again became popular—the early twentieth-century approach to social policy was given a new rationale. The majority Liberal government of the time attempted to replace the family allowance programme with a guaranteed-income-style programme, which encountered enormous public resistance. Moreover, an election replaced the majority with a minority government (still Liberal), with the balance of power held by the NDP, who favoured universal family allowances. Thus, family allowances were retained and tripled in value in gross terms in 1974, but at the same time they became subject to income tax—a very quiet way of moving away from strictly universal benefits since the net value of the transfer was reduced most for higher-income families (Perry, 1989; Guest, 1980).

Another important change to family allowances in 1974 was indexation to the Consumer Price Index (Canada, Minister of National Health and Welfare, 1974). However, indexation was temporarily suspended in 1976 for budgetary reasons (Statistics Canada, 1982) and full indexation was changed to partial indexation (i.e., indexation to inflation above 3% per year) in 1985 (Hess, 1992).

The 1974 Act also allowed for more flexibility with respect to the authority of the provinces in family allowance policy. Provinces were permitted to vary benefits according to the age of the child or the number of children, or both. The only restriction was that overall family allowance payments over a four-year period must be the same as the federal level of payments, and the minimum monthly payment per child must be at least 60% of the federal rate (Canada, Minister of National Health and Welfare, 1974). Two provinces, Alberta and Quebec, chose to exercise this right. Alberta varied the monthly family allowance payments according to the age of the children, while Quebec allowed variation with the age and number of children in the family.

Child Tax Credits

In 1977, to help compensate for the fact that tax exemptions provide a larger benefit to higher-income families, a small non-refundable child tax credit ($50) which could be claimed by families with incomes less than $26,000 was added to the child benefit package. Since the credit was non-refundable, it did nothing to benefit the lowest-income families whose taxable income was zero.

In 1979, another step towards the current targeted and tax-delivered system of child benefits occurred with the introduction of a $200 per child Refundable Child Tax Credit (RCTC), the elimination of the $50 non-refundable child tax credit, and a 23% reduction in family allowance payments to $20 per child per month. The full value of the RCTC was available when *family* income was less than $18,000 (1979); the credit was clawed back at a rate of 5% for higher-income families (Johnson, 1985). Families with no income tax owing received the credit as a cash benefit once a year (twice a year for very low-income families); others had the credit deducted from taxes owing. This infrequency of payment was criticized as a source of cash-flow difficulties for low-income families. The parent or guardian in receipt of family allowance payments (usually the mother) also received the RCTC. For a significant number of mothers, this involved filing an income tax return for the first time. Table 15 indicates that while the RCTC was a targeted benefit, it is still true that a majority of Canadian families (about 60% in 1990) received something from the programme. The average cash value per recipient family was about 4% of GDP per capita in 1990.

Although the RCTC increased significantly after the 1985 budget,[11] the partial de-indexing of FA benefits in 1985 offset the real cash benefits to families with children. One study concluded that the poorest families were no better off in 1991 than they were in 1984, due to the cancelling effect of the decline in real value of FA benefits against the increase in the RCTC (National Council of Welfare, 1987b).

Although the real value of tax exemptions had fallen over time (see Table 15) it was still, on average, worth as much per recipient family as the RCTC. But tax exemptions provide a larger absolute value for higher-income filers than for lower-income filers, given a progressive tax structure. The National Council of Welfare estimated that the top income quintile was receiving 50% of total tax savings from children's exemptions (National Council of Welfare, 1983). To improve the vertical equity of the system, child tax exemptions were replaced by a non-refundable Child Tax Credit in 1988, thus eliminating the relative advantage for higher-income families. In 1992, the flat-rate, partially-indexed credit was worth $71 per child under 18 per year; the third and each subsequent child qualified the parents for a credit of $142 per child (Canada, Department of National Health and Welfare, 1992). Of course, the non-refundable credits were only of value to families who owed income tax.

Continuing concerns about vertical equity led to a clawback on family allowance benefits for higher-income families in 1989. Families with net incomes exceeding $51,765 (1991) were required to repay a portion of benefits received, while families with net income greater than $57,192 (1991) had to repay the entire amount of family allowance benefits (Hess, 1992). The clawback marks another step away from universality in family allowance benefits. Nonetheless, all families with children under 18 still received a monthly cheque of $35 in the mail, an amount which is very low by international standards (Phipps, 1995).

TABLE 15. Family tax benefit expenditures, Canada 1980–1990

	1980	1985	1990
Personal tax exemptions for dependent children, average expenditure per taxfiler as % of GDP per capita	8.7	7.8	3.4
Number of taxfiler claimants as % of total number of families with dependent children	93.6	95.2	82.7
Child-care expense deductions, average expenditure per taxfiler as % of GDP per capita	7.3	8.4	9.3
Number of taxfiler claimants as % of total number of families with dependent children	10.8	15.1	17.1
Refundable child tax credits, average expenditure per taxfiler as % of GDP per capita	3.2˙	3.3	4.0
Number of taxfiler claimants as % of total number of families with dependent children	68.2	68.1	58.7

Sources: Revenue Canada, Taxation, 1982, 1987, and 1992.

By 1992, federal expenditures on the FA programme were $2.8 billion, although almost one-third of this sum returned to the government purse via clawbacks and income taxes.

Parents with paid employment are able to claim a portion of receipted child-care expenses on their income tax returns, partially recognizing an essential cost associated with earning a living. This benefit was introduced in 1972, at a time when the labour force participation of mothers was increasing rapidly. Since 1983, child-care expenses are to be claimed by the lower-income spouse, generally the mother (Boadway and Kitchen, 1984). In 1993, the ceiling on claimable child-care expenses was increased to a maximum of $5,000 annually per child under age seven, and $3,000 for children age 7–14, equalling 26% and 16% of average female earnings, respectively (Canada, Human Resources Development, 1995). The 1996 federal budget proposes increasing the age limit to 16 years and allowing parents who are students to claim child-care expenses. While claimed by a smaller percentage of families than other tax advantages (17% of families with children in 1990), the value of the child-care expense deduction is quite high (the average expenditure per claiming taxfiler was 9.3% of GDP per capita in 1990; see Table 15).

By 1992, the maximum RCTC benefit was $601 per child per year. The family income threshold was $25,921 (Canada, Department of National Health and Welfare, 1992). Families who did not claim child-care expenses were eligible for a supplement of $213 per child per year. This small supplement was granted after parents in one-income families complained that more tax concessions were being given to two-income families and that parents who cared for their own children at home were shortchanged by government benefits (Canada, Department of National Health and Welfare, 1992). Both the RCTC and the supplement were partially indexed for inflation in excess of 3% per year.

Lower-income Canadians with children became eligible for a refundable Goods and Services Tax (GST) credit of $105 (1993) per child, paid quarterly for eligible families applying at tax time. The GST is Canada's national sales tax. Provinces, except Alberta, also levy sales taxes, with exemptions which vary across provinces but which often include provisions to assist families (e.g., food, children's clothing). Parents with disabled children may be eligible to claim a disability credit.

Major Changes in 1993

In 1993, the entire system of tax credits and transfers was consolidated into a new income-tested Child Tax Benefit, which replaced Family Allowance benefits, Refundable Child Tax Credits, and non-refundable Child Tax Credits. The 1993 changes in the structure of benefits occurred in conjunction with an increase of $400 million (from $4.5 to $4.9 billion) in total federal funds allocated to child benefits (Canada, Department of National Health and Welfare, 1992). The major argument in favour of this policy change was again that funds should be targeted at child poverty. However, public response to the changes was rather different from the response to similar proposals in the early 1970s. First, many people agreed that higher-income families did not 'need' benefits and hence should not receive them. Second, as a result of the implementation of income taxation and clawbacks, as well as erosion of the value of family allowance payments, public opinion had come to disapprove of mailing out very small cheques to higher-income families when these funds would then largely disappear at tax time. Little account was taken of the administrative costs of income-testing benefits. Finally, given the decline in the value of the Family Allowance benefits, few middle-class families appeared to worry about the loss of these benefits.

The basic child benefit is $1,020 (in 1993 $) per child per year, clawed back at a rate of 5% on *family* net income above $25,921 for families with two or more children, or at a rate of 2.5% for families with one child. (High-income families no longer receive any benefits.) Child Tax Benefit (CTB), like the old family allowances and unlike the RCTC, is paid monthly, to the lower-income spouse (generally the mother). Net family income is based on the previous year's tax returns. The CTB, unlike Family Allowances, is non-taxable. In addition to the basic child benefit, an 'earned income supplement' (EIS) paid at a rate of 8% on family *earnings* over $3,750 to a maximum of $500 per year is also available. The EIS is clawed back at a rate of 10% on family net income over $20,921 and disappears entirely when the family net income exceeds $25,921.

There is no longer any general tax relief for families with children. The child-care expense deduction is all that remains for higher-income families with children. Single-parent families may also claim an 'equivalent-to-married' credit for their first child. Since credits for spouses are worth much more than those for children, this is an important advantage. Lower-income families also receive the refundable GST credit for each child.

The Canadian government claimed that the 1993 changes to the Canadian child benefit system would lead to improved 'targeting', 'fairness', 'efficiency', and 're-sponsiveness' (Canada, Department of National Health and Welfare, 1992). Critics have noted that the new CTB and EIS are unlikely to achieve these goals. First, since very low-income families are not eligible for the EIS, they are not the main beneficiaries of the programme change. In fact, some middle-income families gain more as a result of the switch from taxable family allowance to non-taxable child tax benefits (Wooley, 1994). Under the new Canadian child benefit regime, a higher-income family with two children, for example, could pay the same tax as a couple with the same income but no children. This constitutes 'unequal treatment of equals' and has thus been viewed as horizontally inequitable (Wooley, 1994; Kesselman, 1993).

The EIS component of the new child benefit system was introduced as a way of encouraging the labour force participation of parents. Encouraging labour force participation has been a major theme in Canadian policy debates in recent years. However, evidence (Phipps, 1995; Wooley, 1994) suggests that it is extremely unlikely that this hoped-for effect will occur, and the appropriateness of using *child* benefits to influence parents' behaviour has been questioned. Finally, the new system is unlikely to be more responsive to changes in family incomes since changes will only be noted when tax returns are filed, which could lead to adjustment lags of up to 18 months (Kesselman, 1993).

The treatment of marital status in Canadian family taxation has evolved throughout the years. Married couples file separate income tax returns in Canada, but since eligibility for the CTB and the EIS as well as the GST credit depend on combined income, there are growing links. Common-law couples with children often enjoyed greater tax savings than married couples prior to 1993 because they did not have to pool their incomes to determine the amount of the Refundable Child Tax Credit. However, the new Child Tax Benefit system now treats common-law parents in the same way as legally-married parents (Hess, 1992).

A final issue recently under debate in Canada was the tax treatment of child support payments. Until 1996, the person paying the child support (virtually always the father) could deduct the payment from taxable income. The recipient was required to claim the income and pay applicable income taxes. Since men generally earn more than women, the tax break was usually worth more to the father than the mother. The 1996 federal budget eliminated both the deduction and the requirement to pay tax on child support for awards made after May 1997.

152   *Canada*

FAMILY-RELATED CASH BENEFITS IN SOCIAL SECURITY

At the federal level, the most important explicit family-related cash transfer was Family Allowance and is now the Child Tax Benefit (CTB). Unemployment Insurance (UI) is also an extremely important federal transfer for Canadian families with children, but UI is not explicitly a family-related transfer. However, in the periods 1971–75 and 1994–96 there was a higher replacement rate for UI recipients with dependent children. It is proposed in the federal budget that, beginning in January 1997, unemployed individuals in low-income families receive a Family Income Supplement to UI benefits. The top-up will allow earnings replacement to reach a maximum of 65% (compared to 55% for most other UI claimants). There are no other federal cash transfers for families.

At the provincial level, social assistance (discussed in the next section) is, in general, the most important cash transfer for families. However, Quebec, the only province with an explicit family policy, offers a number of family-related cash benefits, such as birth grants and cash allowances supplemental to federal child benefits. It has been argued (e.g., Baker, 1994b) that these programmes in Quebec have been motivated by Quebec nationalism and a fear that declining birth rates in the provinces will eventually reduce Quebec's power in the federation. Some other provinces also offer small family-related cash transfers in addition to their basic social assistance programmes.

Family Income Support in Saskatchewan and Manitoba

Established in 1974, Saskatchewan's Family Income Plan (FIP) provides non-taxable monthly cash benefits to parents who satisfy asset and income tests, are residents of Saskatchewan, and are covered by the provincial health plan (Hess, 1992). In 1993, the maximum monthly benefit of $105 for each of the first three children and $95 for subsequent children was received by families whose annual net income was less than $8,700. Families on social assistance are eligible for the FIP, although FIP benefits are deducted from social assistance benefits.

Manitoba also administers a programme that supplements the income of needy families with children. The Child Related Income Support Programme (CRISP), which originated in 1981, provides non-taxable monthly cheques to low-income families who satisfy income and asset tests, hold a valid Manitoba health card, and receive the federal Child Tax Benefit. In 1991, a one-child family with income above $15,719 became ineligible for benefits (Hess, 1992). The maximum benefit of $30 per child per month is received by families whose annual net income is less than $14,187 for a one-child family; the threshold rises with additional children. In 1991, the average monthly benefit per family was about $62 (Hess, 1992).

Family Support Programmes in Quebec

Since 1988, the Quebec government has administered the Parental Wage Assistance Programme (PWA). The programme provides non-taxable monthly cash benefits to lower-income Quebec parents working outside the home, with children under age 18 (18 and over if the child attends school full-time), whose family income is above $100 per month and below a specified ceiling[12] and whose assets are limited (Hess, 1992). Additional features are partial reimbursement of child-care expenses and a housing allowance. The benefit level varies according to income from other sources, family type, duration of employment, number of children, child-care expenses, and accommodation costs (Hess, 1992). The average monthly benefit paid to eligible Quebec families in 1993 was $188 (National Council of Welfare, 1994a).

In addition to the PWA, Quebec offers cash benefits to families with children regardless of parents' labour force status. Since 1988, the Quebec government has provided the Allowance for Newborn Children, or 'baby bonus' grant to new parents. Initially, the grant was worth $500 for each of the first two children, and $3,000 each for the third and any subsequent children; in 1991, the bonuses were increased to $1,000 for the second child, and $7,500 for the third and subsequent children (Le Bourdais and Marcil-Gratton, 1994). In 1992, the Quebec government again increased the allowance for the third and subsequent children to $8,000 (Picard, 1992). Whether this programme is intended to provide income support to new parents or to increase the birth rate is open to debate (See Dandurand, Kempeneers, and Le Bourdais, in Le Bourdais and Marcil-Gratton, 1994).

Quebec also provides provincial family allowances (non-taxable since 1988) to families with children. There are two types: the Quebec Family Allowance and the Allowance for Young Children. Both are paid in addition to the federal benefit, and both vary according to the child's rank in the family. In 1990, the monthly benefits were $9.77 for the first child, $13.02 for the second child, $16.27 for the third child, and $19.49 for each subsequent child (Canada, Health and Welfare, 1991). The Allowance for Young Children offers a supplemental cash payment to families with children under six. This benefit was worth $8.75 per month in 1991 for the first child under six, while the second and third (and subsequent) children received $17.49 and $43.71, respectively (Canada, Health and Welfare, 1991).

Provincial Allowances for Disabled Children

Quebec, Newfoundland, and Ontario each offer cash benefits to parents with disabled children. In Quebec, all families with a disabled child either in the home or in a special care facility (where the parents pay the full cost) are eligible for a non-taxable Allowance for Handicapped Children. The monthly benefit was worth $106.73 in 1990 (Canada, Health and Welfare, 1991).

Newfoundland introduced a programme in 1982 which provides cash benefits for families with disabled children. The Special Child Welfare Allowance is non-taxable, and the amount depends on the family's income and the financial requirements of the child's disability. In 1990, the maximum monthly benefit per child was $415 (Canada, Health and Welfare, 1991). In Ontario, a family caring for a disabled child at home may receive the Handicapped Children's Benefit. The amount of the non-taxable cash benefit varies according to the child's needs, and in the event that the family does not receive Family Benefits, the benefit rate depends on the family's income. In 1990, the monthly benefit ranged between $25 and $325.

SOCIAL ASSISTANCE

Canadian social assistance is intended to provide financial assistance to all individuals and families in need, regardless of the cause of the hardship. There is no link with prior earnings, nor is there a limit on the duration of benefits. Over the past two decades, high rates of unemployment, deterioration in labour market conditions for youth, and cut-backs in the unemployment insurance programme have contributed to an increase of almost 120% in the number of social assistance recipients and a tripling of expenditures in real terms (Barrett and Cragg, 1995). In March 1993, three million Canadians, 40% of whom were children, received some social assistance benefits, up from 1.4 million in March 1981 (Canada, Human Resources Development, 1994a).

The majority (78%) of welfare recipients in Canada are potentially 'employable' (i.e., they could work if there were jobs), single (65%), and male (61%) (Barrett et al., 1994). There are important links between the Canadian social assistance and unemployment insurance systems. Almost 52% of all households with a UI claim needed social assistance while waiting for UI benefits to begin, 11% needed social assistance to supplement incomes while receiving UI, and 13% turned to social assistance when UI benefits were exhausted (Wong, 1994).

In 1990–91, single-parent families comprised only 25% of all individuals reporting social assistance income, *down* from 36% in the 1973–75 period (see Table 16). Thus the Canadian social assistance clientele differs significantly from that of the US, where single-parent families are the principal recipients of welfare. Nonetheless, social assistance is an important source of income for single mothers, about 40% of whom, on average, received some social assistance over the 1973–1991 period (Table 16). Social assistance has become increasingly important for younger single mothers as labour market conditions have deteriorated, though *less* important for single mothers over the age of 35 (Dooley, 1995; Table 16). Social assistance is particularly important for poor single mothers, almost 70% of whom received some benefits in 1992. While some poor two-parent families with children receive social assistance benefits, this is relatively less common (about 30%) (National Council of Welfare, 1994b).

Historical Origins

The origins of Canadian thinking about social assistance may be found in the British Poor Law of 1601. The distinction between employable and non-employable claimants appeared with that legislation and remains a central feature of social assistance programmes in Canada today (National Council of Welfare, 1987a).

TABLE 16. Social assistance, income, and lone mothers, Canada 1973–1991

	Period 1 1973 & 1975	Period 2 1979 & 1982	Period 3 1990 & 1991
% of lone mothers reporting SA* *income*			
aged <35	43	46	58
aged 35–59	37	32	31
total	40	39	44
% of SA reporters *who are lone mothers*			
aged <35	49	41	37
aged 35–59	30	22	16
total	36	29	25

* SA = Social assistance
Source: Dooley, 1995.

Until the 1920s, individuals with no other resources would apply to their munici-palities for financial aid and typically be referred on to some charitable organiza-tion. Applying for social assistance was a demeaning experience since it was inter-preted as an admission of personal failure.

Evolution of the Social Assistance System

Canada's present welfare system evolved from several pieces of legislation de-signed to provide means-tested cash benefits to needy persons, dating back to the Old Age Pension Act of 1927. The introduction of a number of different pro-grammes designed to assist needy families and individuals resulted in a piecemeal collection of income assistance arrangements in post-war Canada.

These were integrated into the Canada Assistance Plan (CAP) in 1966, intended as a comprehensive programme of federal/provincial cost-sharing for a variety of provincial welfare programmes, including social assistance. (The Constitution Act of 1867 gave the provinces responsibility for such programmes.) The CAP pro-vides for 50/50 cost-sharing between Ottawa and the provinces/territories in wel-fare payments, although the federal government is currently proposing to replace the 50/50 cost-sharing with a system of block funding called the Canada Health and Social Transfer (CHST), in which fixed sums will be transferred to the prov-inces to fund their welfare programmes. This change appears to be motivated by federal concerns about deficit reduction. Critics point out that since the CAP fi-nances Canadian programmes of 'last resort', it is not reasonable to deny individu-als in need access to benefits or to know in advance how many individuals will experience hardship as economic circumstances change (National Council of Wel-fare, 1994a).

In fact, there has already been a move away from 50/50 sharing of costs. Since 1990, Ottawa has capped its welfare payments to Alberta, British Columbia, and Ontario (the three most affluent provinces) in a federal effort to contain costs. Not surprisingly, this decision was not welcomed by the provinces affected. Ottawa now pays less than half the total welfare bill. For example, in 1992–93, the total cost of welfare in Canada was over $16 billion, of which Ottawa paid $7.4 billion (National Council of Welfare, 1995).

While costs are shared with the federal government, individual provinces and territories are responsible for the design and implementation of their own welfare programmes. The major restrictions imposed by the CAP are that provinces/territories provide benefits according to 'needs', do not impose residency requirements, and allow a process of appeal for anyone denied benefits. These restrictions will also disappear with the CHST.

Provincial Variations in Social Assistance

Since provinces design and administer their own social assistance programmes, rules and benefits vary substantially across the provinces, and relatively little data about these variations are publicly available (Dooley, 1995). While 'need' is supposed to be the only eligibility criterion, assessments of need are made differently in different provinces. Moreover, caseworkers are explicitly given discretion in working out itemized budgets for claimant households (e.g., for food, housing, clothing, medicine). Thus, families of the same size living in the same city may be awarded different social assistance benefits (Blank and Hanratty, 1993).

Available incomes and assets are compared with needs assessments to determine eligibility and benefit levels. Here again, provinces differ. For example, a single-parent family with $1,500 of liquid assets would not qualify for benefits in New Brunswick, but would qualify in Ontario (Allen, 1993). In all provinces, however, benefit eligibility is determined according to *family* income. Thus, women and children will be denied benefits on the basis of the husband/father's income even though, in some cases, they may have only limited access to his income (Phipps and Burton, 1995).

In general, average benefits received are lower in poorer provinces (see Table 17). For example, benefits received by a single mother with one child in New Brunswick are, on average, only 58% of benefits received in Ontario (National Council of Welfare, 1993b). However, it is also true that more conservative provincial governments in richer provinces may choose relatively low benefit levels.

Nova Scotia, Manitoba, and Ontario operate two-tiered social assistance programmes, in which some claimants qualify for aid from the provincial government while others rely on municipal sources. In these provinces, there are large variations in benefits within the province. The division of provincial/municipal responsibility is determined by the category of the claimant, but even this varies across provinces. Generally, persons in need of long-term assistance receive aid from the province, while short-term, emergency cases are referred to municipal authorities.

TABLE 17. Average social assistance benefits by type of household,
Canada 1993 (in 1,000 $)

Province	Single employable	Disabled person	Single parent, one child	Couple, two children
Newfoundland	4.3	6.8	11.3	12.2
Prince Edward Island	8.0	8.0	11.1	16.3
Nova Scotia	5.9	8.4	10.4	12.4
New Brunswick	3.1	6.2	8.5	9.5
Quebec	6.0	7.8	9.7	11.9
Ontario	7.9	11.1	14.6	18.9
Manitoba	6.3	7.2	9.7	15.6
Saskatchewan	5.8	7.5	10.4	14.6
Alberta	5.4	6.6	9.9	15.4
British Columbia	6.4	9.0	11.5	14.5
Yukon Territory	7.7	7.7	12.5	19.1
Northwest Territories	11.3	11.3	19.2	22.7

Source: National Council of Welfare (1994). *Welfare Incomes 1993.* Ottawa: Minister of Supply and Services Canada.

Current Issues and Problems

Despite significant differences across provinces, a few general points about social assistance in Canada can be made. The level of social assistance payments, while varying across provinces, is uniformly low. Presumably a reflection of Poor Law origins and present-day concerns that people not choose welfare over paid work, social assistance levels are set so that families relying primarily on this source of income live in poverty. For example, a couple with two children receive only 73% of poverty income in Ontario, and only 45% in New Brunswick (National Council of Welfare, 1994a). In keeping with a strong Canadian concern that work incentives be maintained, individuals deemed 'employable' receive significantly less than do other claimants. For example, a single individual who is unemployed but 'employable'[13] will receive benefits that are 50% of those received by a single disabled person in New Brunswick and 71% of those received by a single disabled person in Ontario (National Council of Welfare, 1993b). Able non-aged couples and single individuals are counted as employable. Single parents with young children are usually counted as non-employable, though this varies across provinces. In Alberta, for example, a single parent with a child aged six *months* or over is judged to be employable, while in British Columbia the child must be 12 *years* or older (National Council of Welfare, 1994b).

Cash benefits received through social assistance are non-taxable income, although they are counted in determining eligibility for the income-tested Child Tax Benefit. In general, social assistance benefits are not indexed for inflation. All provinces have schemes whereby social assistance paid to persons who are later deemed not entitled to welfare must be repaid to the government (Canada, Health and Welfare, 1991). There are generally no residency requirements for receipt of welfare benefits,[14] although a claimant is usually required to be physically present in the province in which the claim is made. There has been some ill will across provinces (particularly British Columbia and Alberta) concerning the 'export' of welfare clientele. British Columbia has recently instituted a three-month residency requirement for potential social assistance recipients. Since this requirement contravenes the conditions of CAP, the federal government is threatening to withhold its share of welfare payments. However, given the imminent replacement of CAP by the CHST (which places no restrictions on welfare requirements), it is unclear how seriously British Columbia regards the federal threat.

Most of the funds earmarked for welfare are paid out in the form of 'general assistance' cash benefits (National Council of Welfare, 1995). Families receiving general assistance have some discretionary spending power, although it is expected that the money will be spent on basic requirements, such as food, clothing, and shelter for the family. Social assistance programmes also administer and sponsor a variety of services and cover some child-care and health care expenses.

One criticism of social assistance programmes in Canada is that since some provinces and territories deduct as much as one dollar from the welfare benefits of recipients for every earned dollar past a token disregard (National Council of Welfare, 1993a), welfare recipients have little incentive to return to the paid labour force. Others point out that lack of available jobs may be an even greater problem (Phipps, 1994; Osberg, 1993).

The federal government is currently engaged in a large-scale 'self-sufficiency' project in British Columbia and New Brunswick. This social experiment is intended to assess the consequences of offering wage subsidies to single parents on social assistance who manage to find employment. The idea is that while a low-wage job would not initially provide adequate income to ensure self-sufficiency, the work experience may eventually lead to better employment and higher wages. Critics (e.g., Osberg, 1993) have demonstrated that few low-wage jobs offer significant promotion possibilities, particularly in the three-year time frame anticipated and given high rates of unemployment.

CONCLUSION

The 1960s and early 1970s were good years for family incomes in Canada. Labour markets were booming, so increased participation by women increased real family incomes. Good times persuaded people that social programmes were 'affordable', so important transfers such as UI and Family Allowances which had been established in the immediate post-war period were maintained, and UI was even significantly enriched in 1971. The Canada Assistance Plan (CAP), a comprehensive arrangement for federal/provincial cost-sharing of a variety of provincial welfare programmes, including social assistance, was set up in 1966.

But real family income growth ended in the mid-1970s, chiefly due to the deterioration of labour markets. Unemployment rose, real wages stagnated, and many of the new jobs created were 'bad jobs'—part-time, short-term, low-wage. Women continued to enter the labour force, but during the 1980s, increased labour force participation only served to keep family incomes constant. Families unable to supply an additional worker to the labour market, for example, single-parent families, lost ground.

A second important reason for family income stagnation during the 1980s and early 1990s was cuts in important transfer programmes. Poor economic conditions meant increased use of transfer programmes such as UI and social assistance and hence increased programme costs. Concern spread that a generous UI programme was leading workers to 'choose' unemployment, and a series of cut-backs in the name of economic efficiency followed through the late 1970s, 1980s, and early 1990s. Retrenchment of UI forced many unemployed workers to turn to social assistance. This was particularly true for younger workers who were the most severely affected by deterioration of the labour market. Shifting workers from UI to social assistance reduced federal expenditures at the expense of the provinces, generating ill will, which was further exacerbated in 1990 when the federal government, in a deficit reduction exercise, capped its contributions to the welfare costs of the three richest provinces and again in 1995 when proposals for block funding rather than cost-sharing of provincial welfare programmes were introduced.

Child allowances have never been sufficiently generous in Canada to constitute a major form of income support, particularly since their real net value was allowed to decline from the 1950 high of 5.5% of GDP per capita. Nevertheless, the monthly family allowance cheque received from 1945 until 1993 by all families with children was an income supplement that could be relied upon. All lower-income families with children in Canada still receive a monthly child tax benefit in the mail (the amount varies with family income), but the new benefit is a less effective source of income security since eligibility is dependent on last year's income, and adjustments to changed circumstances may thus occur with a substantial time lag. The fact that Canadian child benefits are now targeted rather than universal again reflects a concern with curtailing costs combined with the idea that families should only receive transfer income if they are in need. Despite substantial improvements to vertical equity, this policy is a return to the pre-war *laissez-faire* approach.

4

Families, Health Care, and
Social Services

Early in this century, voluntary organizations and municipal governments provided social services for low-income families and others unable to cope without assistance. Medical services delivered by physicians in private practice and hospitals were often unaffordable for the poor. By the 1930s, the cost of public welfare expenses was shared among three levels of government. After the 1930s Depression, when charities were stretched to the limit, municipalities went bankrupt paying unemployment benefits, and doctors worked without payment, many Canadians came to believe that the federal government had a larger role to play in funding health and social services.

By 1951, Canada had developed a universal old-age pension, a universal family allowance, and an unemployment insurance programme. Throughout the 1950s and 1960s when the economy grew and government bureaucracies expanded, attitudes about developing a 'social safety net' became more liberal. The federal government was pressured by the provinces, social democrats, and social reformers into sharing the cost of health and social service programmes established by the provinces.

During the 1960s and 1970s, social work became professionalized and provincial governments began to regulate or deliver social services. New income-security programmes were legislated and social housing was initiated in Canada. As more mothers entered the labour force in the 1970s and 1980s, public pressure grew for public child-care funding. Yet most family services remain targeted to low-income earners and abused or neglected children.

Historically, most social security programmes and welfare services in Canada have focused either on protecting children from parental abuse and neglect, or on supporting fathers as family 'breadwinners'. The needs of mothers as care providers or wage-earners have been downplayed until recently. In fact, feminist scholars argue that Canadian mothers were blamed for 'neglecting' their children when they worked for pay (Swift, 1995) and for failing to protect children from violence (Krane, 1994). Critics argue that family programmes continue to be reactive, focusing on protecting children from abuse after it has occurred, and to rely on unpaid child care by mothers (Wharf, 1993b; Callahan, 1993).

In this chapter, we will examine the development of programmes for child care, health, housing, and family services.

CHILD-CARE PROGRAMMES

Historical Background

In nineteenth-century Canada, the daytime care of children became a social issue when the number of 'neglected' and delinquent children noticeably increased in industrialized cities (Baker, 1993). Poor, deserted, and widowed women were often unable to care for their children because they needed to work or could not support their children on low incomes. Children from these families were temporarily placed in institutions or children's homes, cared for by relatives or friends, or left to fend for themselves while their mothers worked. As middle-class women seldom worked outside the home, child care for employed mothers was generally viewed as a welfare issue.

Orphanages and foundling homes, run by churches or charitable organizations, provided care for infants and children not looked after by their families. These institutions were financed through donations and volunteer labour. Furthermore, many poor and homeless children were brought from Britain to Canada at the turn of the century to find homes and to provide free labour for Canadian families in return for room and board. For example, the British philanthropist Thomas Barnardo organized the emigration of over 25,000 British children between 1882 and 1915 (Corbett, 1981).

The institutionalization of neglected and delinquent children declined considerably in Toronto in the early 1900s because experts concluded that children benefited from a home environment. The Toronto Children's Aid Society began to place children in foster homes whenever possible, and after 1920 children's institutions became less prevalent in Ontario, although many still operated across the country (Baker, 1993). Settlement houses or community welfare centres provided some daytime care for welfare children, as well as programmes to improve the health, 'morals', and education of the poor.

While child-care services in Canada originated from a welfare tradition, public kindergartens and nursery schools developed about the same time from educational philosophy. Child psychologists from Europe encouraged conscientious parents to provide their preschool children with disciplined but creative group play. The first public kindergarten opened in Ontario in 1883 (Sutherland, 1976), but it was not until the 1920s that kindergartens began to be accepted in Canada.

After World War I, birth rates declined but infant mortality and maternal death rates remained high in Canada compared to some European countries. Middle-class women's groups and health professionals expressed concern that mothers themselves were promoting child health problems by their lack of knowledge. Within this social and political environment, the Canadian government published pamphlets on pregnancy, breastfeeding, toilet training, and child discipline (Arnup, 1994), and educators began to develop nursery schools.

In 1925, nursery schools for children aged two to five were established as part of the child study programme at McGill University and the University of Toronto

(Strong-Boag, 1982). Children from middle-class families with educated parents attended programmes of creative play and 'scientific child care' grounded in behaviourist and Freudian psychology. Although the McGill experiment lasted only five years, the University of Toronto continued and became the model for settlement house and church nurseries. Opposition to nursery schools was always present, however. From the 1930s to the 1950s, research and theorizing on early childhood development emphasized the importance of the mother/child bond; some feared that nursery school children would be deprived of that bond and consequently would develop abnormally. Others believed that nursery schools would encourage married women to seek employment and to compete with male breadwinners, fearing the dissolution of the family (Pierson, 1977).

Despite opposition to married women's employment, their labour was needed during World War II in war industries and other positions vacated by men. As part of a plan to draw women into the work-force, Prime Minister Mackenzie King revised the Income Tax Act to allow husbands to claim their wives as dependants regardless of their earnings. In the middle of the war, he also offered federal cost-sharing to those provinces providing day-care centres for mothers working in war industries, which was extended to all working women towards the end of the war. Despite this offer, only Quebec and Ontario made use of the Dominion–Provincial Wartime Day Nurseries Act. Furthermore, all the day nurseries in Quebec and some in Ontario were closed after the war, and federal funding was discontinued until 1966 (Pierson, 1977).

In the 1950s, kindergarten programmes were integrated into the school system in some provinces. These programmes continued the nursery philosophy, providing half-day enrichment programmes for five-year-olds, and gradually some schools accepted four-year-olds. When educational theories emphasized creative play during the 1960s, private part-day preschools developed and parents established co-operatives to provide intellectual and social stimulation for preschoolers. Only when mothers' participation in the labour force rose in the 1970s were child-care centres established in significant numbers, and most were in Ontario (Friendly, 1994).

In the 1980s, the political importance of child care grew with the labour force participation of mothers and publicity granted to work/family conflicts. Government studies such as the Royal Commission on the Status of Women (1970) and the Royal Commission on Equality in Employment (Abella, 1984) gave considerable attention to the need for child-care services. A Task Force on Child Care, established by the Liberals and reporting to the Conservatives in 1986, recommended a comprehensive national child-care programme funded by taxes. Opposed to the high cost of this proposal, the Conservatives established a parliamentary committee on child care, reporting in 1987, that recommended improved services and increased government funding. After much lobbying, the Canadian National Child Care Survey was initiated in 1983 by university-based, federally-funded academics who gathered data in 1988 indicating the need for public child-care services (Powell, 1992).

Child-Care Funding

Although the administration of child-care services is provincial jurisdiction, the federal government made provision in 1966 to share the cost for low-income families under the Canada Assistance Plan (CAP). To receive federal contributions, provinces must first spend the money and then ask the federal government to match eligible expenditures. A limited number of families in financial need receives subsidized child care in day-care centres or regulated homes. Child-care expenditures per child under 13 years have varied considerably by province, from $15 in Newfoundland to $400 in the Yukon in 1991–92 (Mitchell, 1995b).

Child-care funding under CAP has provided neither a sufficient number of subsidies nor of licensed spaces. In 1991, 2.2 million children under 13 required care for at least 20 hours a week while their parents worked or studied. Yet only 333,000 licensed spaces were available for children of those ages, which suggests that only 15% would be served by licensed care (Lero and Johnson, 1994). Families whose income is above the provincial subsidy maximum must pay the full cost of care, which could be more than $10,000 per child for infant care or $6,500 for high-quality preschool in Ontario (Friendly, 1994). The shortage of regulated and subsidized spaces and the high cost causes most parents to rely on unregulated sitters to care for their preschool children.

As noted in Chapter 3, the federal government provides a tax deduction for child-care expenses of working parents. The federal government also offers child-care allowances for those in training programmes, and the Department of Indian and Northern Affairs funds child care on some reserves. Federal government expenditure on child-care services totals over $1 billion per year (Doherty et al., in press).

In 1987, the Conservative government announced a National Strategy on Child Care which contained increased tax deductions, research money, and a Child Care Act that would take funding out of welfare legislation (CAP). The first two parts of the Strategy were implemented, but the Act was not. Some provincial governments and most advocacy groups opposed it because it would have reduced federal contributions to child care in some provinces, would have funded for-profit facilities, and because it lacked national standards (Baker, 1995). Child care for families in financial need continued to be funded under CAP, but the Liberal government repealed this legislation in 1995, gradually replacing cost-sharing by block funding for social assistance, social services, Medicare, and post-secondary education.

Prevalence and Regulation of Child Care

When parents are employed or study full-time, they most frequently rely on unregulated care by relatives, neighbours, or hired sitters. Regulated child care in Canada tends to be centre-based, and although most centres are not-for-profit, this can vary considerably from province to province (Friendly, 1994). The National Child Care Study indicated that 3.2% of children under 18 months, 9.6% of children aged 18 to 35 months and 10.8% of children aged three to five who needed care were in day-care centres in 1988 (Statistics Canada, 1993f). Centres provide care for infants, preschool or school-aged children, and may be run by commercial ventures or not-for-profit organizations (Lero et al., 1992).

The only other form of regulated child care in Canada is family day care, which in 1989 comprised 12.7% of all licensed spaces (Goelman, 1992). Family day care, located in the caregiver's home and licensed in most provinces, is increasing faster than centre spaces because parents feel that it provides a more home-like environment (Ferguson, 1991).

Kindergartens are available for five-year-olds as part of the public education system in all provinces except Prince Edward Island and Alberta (Friendly, 1994). Half-day kindergarten for four-year-olds has been offered by the public schools in Ontario since the 1950s, and the former NDP government unsuccessfully attempted to expand this to full days. In Quebec, kindergarten for four-year-olds is available for some low-income families (ibid.). In 1988, 30% of Canadian children aged four to five attended kindergarten, almost always part-day (Statistics Canada, 1993f). Private preschools also offer early education programmes in most provinces, and before- and after-school programmes are available through community organizations and private operations, although these services are provided by school boards in Quebec (Ergas, 1990).

Provincial, territorial, and municipal governments fund and license services and enforce child-care regulations covering physical conditions, staff qualification, and staff/child ratios (Goelman, 1992). Many variations are apparent in the operation and regulation of services, and in the proportion of non-profit and for-profit spaces.

The quality and cost of child care continue to concern many parents. Although sitters are unregulated in all jurisdictions, regulations concerning the qualifications of centre employees are non-existent in some provinces. Sitters and child-care workers generally are paid the minimum wage or less, and these jobs have difficulty attracting and retaining trained workers. The quality of care received by most children can be monitored only by parents, who seldom have the time or opportunity to investigate conditions fully.

A number of advocacy groups have formed around child-care issues, and most have demanded increased federal funding for non-profit services and better training, working conditions, and pay for child-care workers. Furthermore, the provincial variations create a child-care system which lacks unity, consistency, and sometimes quality, yet is too expensive for some parents to afford. Many non-profit centres have long waiting lists, for the number of families who need care far outstrips the availability.

In 1992, the former Conservative government announced that no new child-care legislation would be introduced because limited resources were needed for child benefits and child abuse programmes. When in opposition, the Liberals promised a national child-care programme; once in the government, however, they introduced the new Canada Health and Social Transfer (CHST) in 1995, which will replace matched funding with lower block grants. Under the CHST, the provinces will acquire more discretion to create their own welfare programmes, which means that discrepancies among child-care systems will become more apparent. Although the possibility of creating a national child-care programme seemed remote after the CHST, the federal government promised in December 1995 to devote more money to provincial child-care programmes.

Researchers, policy analysts, and child-care advocates now argue that the shortage of reliable and affordable child care keeps mothers out of the labour force, counteracts employment equity programmes, raises welfare costs, and contributes to employee absenteeism, work/family conflicts, and reduced productivity (Friendly, 1994; Duxbury and Higgins, 1994; Baker and Lero, 1996). Despite government foot-dragging, child care remains an important policy issue in the minds of many Canadians. Educators view preschool as preparation for school readiness and a necessary part of child development. Feminists see preschool child care as a gender-equity issue, and anti-poverty activists see it as one way to reduce child poverty. Yet many conservatives still consider child care a private family matter.

Health care, on the other hand, has not been viewed as merely a family matter. Instead, hospital and medical services have been publicly funded since the 1950s and 1960s. In the next section, we will discuss some family health indicators and the development of public health services in Canada.

HEALTH CARE

Families as Health Guardians

Family members typically monitor one another's health and provide preventive health care, nutritional advice, nursing during illness, and attendant care for those with disabilities. Especially wives and mothers guard and maintain the health of their husbands, children, and relatives (Baines, Evans, and Neysmith, 1991). Parents usually decide when their children require professional medical attention and which treatment options they prefer. When hospital or medical care is needed, children are insured under provincial health programmes as dependants of their parents. In other words, families both provide health care and serve as intermediaries with the formal health care system.

Family and Child Health Indicators

Throughout this century, life expectancy at birth has gradually risen in Canada, as in other industrialized countries. In 1931, the average life expectancy at birth was 60 years for males and 62 for females (Dumas, 1992: 60), but by 1990 had reached 73.9 for males and 80.4 for females (Dumas, 1994: 104). According to the United Nations and the World Health Organization, Canada ranks eighth for male and fifth for female life expectancy at birth (ibid.: 42). As in other industrialized countries, life expectancy varies by social class and gender, with women from higher-income families living the longest.

The maternal death rate in Canada has fallen significantly in the last 50 years with improved nutrition, sanitation, and health care. In 1940, the number of maternal deaths per 100,000 births was 401, but this rate fell to 4 in 1990 (Statistics Canada, 1993i). Canada ranks favourably among other developed nations although all have very low maternal death rates.

The infant mortality rate (children under age one per 1,000 live births) also fell from 102.1 deaths in 1921 to 6.8 in 1990 (ibid.). As with maternal deaths, the decline in infant mortality can be attributed to improved nutrition, sanitation, housing, and health care (especially the invention of antibiotics and inoculations against contagious diseases). Canada's present rate ranks favourably among industrialized countries, and in 1990 Canada had the second lowest rate among the Group of Seven countries (Blomqvist and Brown, 1994: 80). Nevertheless, higher rates of infant mortality and injuries are apparent among children from low-income families and especially among Aboriginal children (CICH, 1994: 123).

Infant mortality remains significantly higher among Aboriginals than among the general population. Between 1982 and 1985 the Aboriginal stillbirth rate was three times higher than the general population, and the perinatal mortality rates (stillbirths and deaths in the first week of life per 1,000 total births) were 80% higher than the Canadian rate (CICH, 1989: 109). Although there have been recent improvements, death rates from accidents, suicide, and infectious diseases remain higher among Aboriginals than the general Canadian population (CICH, 1994: 143). Patterns of disease and death among Aboriginal people are closely linked to family poverty, cultural loss, and economic underdevelopment.

Concern continues in Canada over low-birthweight babies, defined as under 5.5 pounds or 2,500 grams. Despite major changes in other health indicators, the percentage of low-birthweight babies has decreased only marginally from 7.2% in 1961 to 5.5% in 1990 (Statistics Canada, 1993j). Furthermore, the rate of such births to teenage mothers is approximately 13% (Baumann and Connor, 1993). The best predictor of survival is weight at birth, and about 20% of premature low-birthweight babies suffer from long-term disabilities that are costly to families and governments (Fulton, 1994).

Health Services for Mothers and Children

Before the 1920s, most births in Canada occurred at home assisted by midwives. By the 1950s, hospitalization was seen as necessary for childbirth and today 98% of babies are born in hospitals. Yet hospital births are linked to higher health care costs and additional medical interventions, including anaesthetics, episiotomies, and Caesarean sections. In 1985, the Caesarean section rate was relatively high in Canada at 17 per 100 births, reaching a high of 20 in Ontario and Quebec, compared to an average of 15 in European countries (Hossie, 1985). In the last two decades, this rate has more than quadrupled in Canada and remains a source of controversy (Baumann and Connor, 1993).

Until recently, Canada was alone among industrialized countries in not providing a distinct legal status for practising midwives. In fact, midwives have been subject to criminal and civil charges in various provinces for offences such as criminal negligence and practising medicine without a licence (Burtch, 1994). Both Ontario and Alberta have now legalized midwifery to provide a wider range of birthing services and to reduce public health care costs, and Ontario has established a College of Midwifery. In 1990, Quebec agreed to study midwifery services within selected pilot projects in hospitals, but these projects experienced resistance from the medical profession (ibid.: 138).

Prenatal and postnatal health care is funded through government health insurance (Medicare), and information on nutrition, pregnancy, delivery, and infant care is often available in prenatal classes given by local hospitals, family planning clinics, public health services, or community groups. Most public health authorities also provide services such as well-baby clinics and child development information and education. Family planning and contraceptive information and services are available from medical practitioners under Medicare, but public health authorities and non-profit organizations also operate clinics, often targeting services to adolescents (McCall and Robertson, 1992).

Provincial social assistance programmes fund health care, institutional needs, and ancillary health-related benefits (such as prescription drugs, dental care, vision care, and prostheses) for social assistance recipients (Canada, Health and Welfare, 1991). Provision for medical and dental examination of all children is usually included in public health or education legislation (ibid.). In some provinces, the immunization of children is compulsory and free of charge; in others, the government strongly recommends vaccination but does not make it mandatory (Campeau, 1992).

Nutrition Programmes

Since the 1920s, the Canadian government has been publishing nutrition guidelines and health promotion material and initiating legislation on health and nutritional matters. For example, in 1989 the Food and Drug Act required specific ingredients and labelling for infant formulae (Knoppers, 1992).

For children of school age, promotion of proper nutrition is addressed in education legislation or ministries. In addition, boards of education in some jurisdictions provide food or milk to school children at nominal or no cost, especially in underprivileged areas (McCall and Robertson, 1992). In some provinces and cities, women on social assistance receive a supplementary food allowance during pregnancy and while nursing (National Council of Welfare, 1992a). Although the practice of breastfeeding babies has varied over the decades with changing professional advice, education and support programmes have recently increased the prevalence. While only 38% of newborns were breastfed in 1963, this rose to 80% in 1989 (Bernadi, 1992); breastfeeding remains most prevalent among higher-income mothers (Beaudry and Aucoin-Larade, 1989).

Since the 1980s, food banks have proliferated in Canada. These are centralized warehouses organized for collecting, storing, and distributing surplus food free to agencies providing food to the hungry (Riches, 1986). Most food banks are non-profit charities with roots in religious or non-government organizations, and most do not receive government funding. The first food bank was started in 1981; by 1991, 292 were operating with 40% of beneficiaries children under 18 (Oderkirk, 1992). The rapid growth of food banks has resulted from high unemployment and underemployment, low wages, and low levels of social assistance.

The donation of food for the hungry is not new in Canada, but the present level of organization and need has not been seen since the 1930s. Yet opposition to food banks is growing. They are said to reduce government responsibility for income security and for creating viable economic opportunities for citizens, as well as promoting powerlessness and social stigma (Hilton, 1993; Kerr, 1993; Riches, 1986). The recent proliferation of food banks suggests that social assistance levels are too low and that some needy persons are ineligible for government assistance.

Health Policy and the Development of Health Insurance

Although Medicare covers all Canadian residents, not just families, public insurance has enabled low-income families to access health services that were unaffordable when they had to pay cash. Pregnant women and children (along with very elderly persons) are major users of the health care system, and indicators of child and maternal health reveal substantial improvements since public insurance was introduced. For these reasons, we have included a brief history of Medicare in this document.

Since 1867, jurisdiction over health services has been divided, but the provision of health services is now considered a provincial responsibility. Indeed, the development of Medicare involved ten provincial and two territorial programmes, with cost-sharing and administrative principles from the federal government. Although public health insurance was discussed in Parliament as early as 1918 when it became part of the Liberal Party platform, no legislation was enacted until political pressure led the federal government to create such insurance.

Before Medicare, wealthier families used private insurance while poorer families were expected to pay cash for medical services. Public hospital insurance was pioneered in Saskatchewan in 1947 by the 'progressive' Co-operative Commonwealth Federation (CCF) government of Tommy Douglas; by 1955, government insurance plans were established in five provinces (McGilly, 1990). Escalating costs and disparities in provincial revenue led reform groups, unions, and provincial governments to pressure for funding assistance from the federal government.

In 1957 the Canadian government passed the Hospital Insurance and Diagnostic Services Act, promising to pay 50% of hospital-based medical expenses in provinces with public insurance programmes. By 1961 all provinces had agreed to provide such programmes, yet pressure continued for comprehensive health insurance. In 1966 the Medical Care Act created federal/provincial cost-sharing for physician services outside hospitals. To qualify for cost-sharing under both Acts, provincial health insurance programmes had to meet the following federal conditions: universal coverage, accessible services, portable benefits between provinces, comprehensive insurance for all 'medically necessary' services, and public administration. Medicare has been funded through taxes and, in some provinces, premiums. The total cost of all health services rose from $3.3 billion in 1965 to $66.7 billion in 1991, which was $2,500 per capita and 9.9% of GNP. Hospital costs account for 40% of expenditures (Blomqvist and Brown, 1994). Although total health services cost less in Canada than in the US, they are higher than in many European countries (Fulton, 1994).

Initially, the federal government lacked control over Medicare spending. Concern about rising expenditures led to the Federal–Provincial Fiscal Arrangements and Established Programs Financing Act in 1977, which ended 50/50 cost-sharing, limited federal expenditures, tied subsequent increases to growth of GNP, and shifted cost control to the provinces (Vayda and Debec, 1992: 129). Some provinces responded by introducing user fees for certain services, but the federal government passed the Canada Health Act in 1984 confirming the federal principles behind Medicare and introducing financial penalties for provinces allowing user fees or extra billing by physicians (Guest, 1985). Although all provinces eliminated these fees within three years (Taylor, 1987), they have recently been reappearing.

Hospitals and physicians negotiate their funding or fee schedules with provincial governments, although many physicians in Quebec practise in public clinics for a salary. Provincial health insurance may also cover other services such as ambulance, long-term care, dental, prosthetics, optometry, and chiropractic services (Vayda and Debec, 1992).

Health care expenditures now represent one-third of some provincial budgets and controversy continues over cost-control measures. As institutional and physician services absorb three-quarters of health expenditures, critics argue that the current system is based on the most expensive forms of health care: institution-based care and fee-for-service billing by physicians. They argue that Canada's health system could be reformed and services could be maintained if more emphasis were placed on prevention, community-based services, and paying doctors on salary (Evans, 1984; Fulton, 1994).

In 1995, the federal government began reducing health transfers to the provinces, forcing provincial governments to pay a greater share of health costs or to make facilities more cost-effective. Yet the federal cuts will augment the jurisdictional battles between the federal and provincial governments and the funding battles between medical institutions and community care services, and will place additional pressure on families (especially women) to provide unpaid care at home.

HOUSING

After World War II, when many people were forming new households, government programmes encouraged housing construction on a large scale (Silver and Van Diepen, 1995). Canadian housing policies have promoted home-ownership and boosted the building trades, but provided little social housing and few rental subsidies over the past forty years. Only a small minority of low-income families receive rent subsidies or social housing.

Gross family income kept pace with rising house prices throughout the 1950s and actually exceeded them in the 1960s. By the 1970s, however, family income fell behind soaring house prices, despite the labour force participation of wives (Adsett, 1995). Especially in Vancouver and Toronto, housing costs dramatically increased by the end of the 1980s, causing serious hardship for low-income families. The percentage of home-ownership is beginning to fall in some Canadian cities, although it has changed little over the past forty years. Fewer couples now share accommodation and more are renters.

Housing Standards

Although 64% of Canadian households own their own home, 72% of family households are owners and more families than single people live in single detached homes (Statistics Canada, 1993c). Mother-led families are more likely than others to rent and more likely to spend more than 30% of their income on accommodation. Nevertheless, only 11% of lone parents received housing subsidies in 1990 (Blakeney, 1992). City dwellers and residents of Quebec are more likely than others to be renters, with 42.1% of households renting in Toronto, 42.5% in Vancouver, 46.4% in Quebec City and 53.3% in Montreal (CMHC, 1993). Despite regional differences, the percentage of households renting has increased only slightly since 1951 (Silver and Van Diepen, 1995).

Although the quality of Canadian housing has improved substantially since the Second World War, Aboriginal families continue to live in homes that fall far below national standards. The *1991 Aboriginal Peoples Survey*, a national study of households with at least one person reporting Aboriginal status, found that 7% of Aboriginal households had no electricity, 6% no heating, 3% no bathroom, and 12% had no flush toilet (Statistics Canada, 1994a). Major repairs were needed in 20% of households and minor repairs in 29%. Twenty-one percent of residents reported that their needs were not adequately met by their housing; a typical requirement was the need for more space.

Statistics Canada designates housing as 'crowded' when the number of persons in a dwelling exceeds the number of rooms. The percentage of crowded households steadily declined from 1.6% in 1961 to 0.1% in 1991, reflecting the significant rise in one-person households, decline in average family size, increasing prosperity, and the relatively low cost of Canadian housing. Crowding and substandard housing, however, remain serious problems among low-income and Aboriginal families (CMHC, 1993).

Public Housing and Government Programmes

Although Canada was one of the last industrialized nations to fund public housing, three levels of government now support such programmes. In 1946, the federal government created the Canada Mortgage and Housing Corporation (CMHC), which now administers housing policy, partially covers operating costs and losses, provides subsidies, and funds research on housing. CMHC co-operates with provincial and municipal governments and the private sector to deliver social housing in Canada.

In 1971, the federal government began to provide direct grants to non-profit companies and co-operatives with 100% financing to build low-income housing. Co-operative units increased dramatically during the 1970s, yet they comprise only 0.6% of all housing units (Fung, 1992). Although this programme improved housing standards, public housing came under criticism for raising government expenditures and contributing to ghettos, stigmatization, and problems for surrounding neighbourhoods (Falls, 1993). Consequently, the federal government ended the public housing construction programme in 1978 (Fung, 1992), yet still spent over $3 million in 1993 maintaining existing public housing (CMHC, 1993).

In 1973, the federal government created the Residential Rehabilitation Assistance Program (RRAP) to provide one-time assistance to home-owners and landlords of sub-standard buildings to help them comply with minimum health and safety standards (CMHC, 1987). In 1986, however, eligibility was restricted to low-income households (CMHC, 1993).

In 1975, the provinces imposed rent control as part of national wage and price controls, but provincial variations are now considerable. British Columbia, Alberta, and New Brunswick have no rent control; Saskatchewan, Quebec, and Newfoundland developed moderate rent arbitration systems, while the remaining provinces have more stringent regulations. Most Canadian provinces also provide an income tax credit for home-owners, but several provinces limit this to low-income earners (Falls, 1993).

For families on social assistance, housing costs are factored into welfare payments, but most recipients must obtain private rental housing. Several provinces provide cash assistance for the housing needs of families with children. In the Parental Wage Assistance Program, Quebec includes a housing subsidy for low-income families with children. Manitoba offers a non-taxable monthly allowance to offset rental costs for these families (Canada, Health and Welfare, 1991).

Most Canadians spend less than a third of their income on shelter costs, but in 1991, 35% of all renting households paid more than this on housing (Lo and Gauthier, 1995). Only 5% of households received rent subsidies in 1990, mainly from government but also from employers or family members (Blakeney, 1992). Most of these subsidized households are headed by older women, but couples with children comprised 17% and lone mothers comprised 15%. The majority of subsidized household heads (64%) were not in the labour force.

During the 1960s and 1970s, federal housing policy was characterized by rapid programme growth, but rising costs and questionable outcomes contributed to downsizing. In recent years, the maintenance and narrowing of existing funding have replaced new initiatives. Consequently, many low-income families continue to spend a disproportionate amount of their income on housing.

OTHER SOCIAL SERVICES AND SUBSIDIES

Family Support Services

Numerous government and community programmes in addition to those mentioned above assist families in need. Family support services are usually provided through provincial social assistance or child welfare programmes. Services under social assistance are intended to enable parents to care for their children on a limited budget and to enter or return to paid work. Services provided under child welfare legislation attempt to protect children from abusive parents or to provide counselling, training, or supervision to parents experiencing difficulty raising their children (McCall and Robertson, 1992).

Some provinces, such as Ontario and Alberta, fund non-government organizations to provide family counselling and support. Quebec, on the other hand, has established a system of local community service centres (CLSCs) that are run by government and provide a range of health and social services. Several provinces offer parenting skills and early intervention programmes under health and social service ministries, and almost all provide divorce and custody mediation through social service or justice departments (VIF, 1993). However, most government funding for family services is targeted at child protection.

Protection from Child Abuse and Neglect

In the late nineteenth century, children's aid societies supported by religious organizations, benevolent societies, and middle-class volunteers were established in various municipalities to help orphaned, abandoned, and neglected children (Bala, 1991). In 1893, the Children's Protection Act in Ontario gave the children's aid societies broad powers including the right to remove neglected and abused children from their homes and become their legal guardians (ibid.). By the early twentieth century, agencies were established and child protection legislation was enacted in most provinces. Quebec did not enact legislation until 1951, however, reflecting the Catholic Church's role in social services and the view that family behaviour was private (Quebec Government, 1989).

In every Canadian jurisdiction, the provincial government or designated agency holds the legal responsibility to investigate reports of abuse and neglect and to protect children from ill-treatment. While legislation varies by jurisdiction, the law clearly presumes that parents are capable of raising their children without state interference and places the burden on agencies to establish the need for intervention. Child welfare agencies now receive most or all of their funding from provincial governments, and child protection workers are often government employees. These agencies may also provide family counselling, adoption services, and prevention programmes (Bala, 1991).

Child welfare agencies generally serve all children in the province, although some cater to specific religious or cultural populations. In Ontario, separate Children's Aid Society services have been available for Catholics and Protestants. In Manitoba and several other provinces, child welfare services for some First Nations people are now provided within their communities.[15]

In the last thirty years, an enormous growth and legalization of child welfare has taken place. Contributing factors include the identification of the battered child syndrome in the 1960s, the 'discovery' of child sexual abuse in the late 1970s and early 1980s, and the increasing concern over children's rights (Bala, 1991). The Canadian Charter of Rights and Freedoms (1982) increased the emphasis on individual rights and had a strong impact on child protection proceedings. The emphasis is now on due process, recognizing the rights of both parents and children, and placing greater controls on state intervention. Although rights are now better protected, the new procedures are time-consuming and costly.

Provincial legislation defines a child 'in need of protection' and many provinces include statements of basic philosophy. British Columbia and Prince Edward Island include short statements that decisions are to be based on 'the best interests of children'. Quebec, Manitoba, Alberta, New Brunswick, and Ontario include longer statements of principles which incorporate 'family autonomy', 'least disruptive or detrimental alternative', continuity, prevention, family support, and special considerations for Aboriginal families. These terms are not always clearly defined and are open to a wide range of interpretations (Barnhorst and Walter, 1991).

Two basic approaches to child protection are evident in Canada: the interventionist and the family autonomy approaches. The interventionist approach gives considerable discretion to social workers and judges by using relatively vague language focusing on home conditions and parental behaviour rather than harm to the child. The family autonomy approach more prevalent in Ontario and Alberta attempts to limit discretion and restrict intervention to well-defined situations. Harm to the child is linked to acts or omissions by parents, narrower grounds for state intervention are allowed, more specific definitions are included, and parental rights are emphasized (Bala, 1991).

All jurisdictions require reporting of physical and sexual abuse, while requirements vary concerning other types of harm. The reporter of child abuse is offered immunity from civil liability unless the report is made maliciously or without reasonable grounds. In addition, there is some degree of liability for failure to report; although lawsuits have been brought against child protection agencies for overzealous or incomplete investigations, none have succeeded (Vogl, 1991).

In all provinces, social service agencies retain the authority to apprehend children and place them in substitute care based on a social worker's assessment. In Ontario and Alberta, a social worker must obtain a judicial warrant and may apprehend without a warrant only if the child would be in 'substantial risk' (Barnhorst and Walter, 1991). The idea of independent legal status for the child has been accepted in Quebec and Ontario but acknowledged only in a few procedural ways in other jurisdictions (Vogl, 1991).

Child abuse registers, or centralized databanks of accused or convicted abusers, are in use in some provinces. Yet there have always been controversies about whether the names of convicted or accused persons should be entered in the register, who should have access to this information, how long names should remain in the register, and how the data should be used (Genereux, 1991).

Although child abuse is a criminal offence in Canada, family-based abuse is generally dealt with through civil proceedings (Bala, 1991). In 1988, however, the Criminal Code and the Canada Evidence Act were amended to abolish the corroboration requirement for children's testimony and to allow it to be screened from the accused or videotaped in advance. Also, cases could no longer be routinely diverted from the criminal justice system. Despite these legal changes, judicial discretion has led to uneven dispositions, lenient sentences, low conviction rates, and accusations that judges lack understanding of child sexual abuse (McGillivray, 1990).

The dramatic increase in child abuse allegations presents an important challenge to child welfare agencies. From 1971 to 1988, the Children's Aid Societies in Ontario saw a 160% increase in families served (Trocmé, 1991), while in Newfoundland, child protection service referrals increased 734% between 1984 and 1992 (Scarth, 1993). The cases of child sexual abuse causing the most public outrage took place in private day-care centres and in schools run by religious orders. Much of the increase in child abuse allegations can be attributed to growing public awareness and mandatory reporting laws.

Over the years, the percentage of children in substitute care has declined with the philosophy of family preservation (Barnhorst and Walter, 1991). Regulations state that children should not be removed from their homes unless parental care poses 'significant threat'. The rate of children in substitute care varies considerably by province, ranging from 4.3 per 1,000 children in Ontario to 20.2 in the Northwest Territories where higher rates reflect the overrepresentation of Aboriginal children in care (Scarth, 1993).

Child welfare services to Aboriginal people have been fraught with conflict over jurisdiction and lack of cultural understanding. After Confederation, responsibility for Aboriginal services was retained by the federal government, and residential schools provided education, substitute care, and the assimilation of Indian children into the dominant culture. In 1951, the Indian Act was amended to provide provincial health, welfare, and educational services on reserves under terms to be negotiated with the provinces. No additional funding accompanied this change, however, and only some provinces extended services (Armitage, 1993a). Until the 1960s, the federally-run residential school system was the central institution of child welfare policy for Indian children. Since then, however, these schools have been widely criticized as abusive, overly regimented, and biased against Native culture and language (Armitage, 1993a).

Ironically, provincial involvement with Aboriginal welfare dramatically increased the number of children in substitute care. By 1980, one in seven Indian children was in foster care and many were placed in non-Native homes. In recent years, First Nations' people have protested against residential schools, non-Native foster care, and the lack of cultural understanding which contributed to these practices. Some Native groups have negotiated tripartite agreements with the provincial and federal governments to allow control of their own child welfare and child-care services with money from both levels of government. Yet jurisdictional disputes remain and services vary widely.

Domestic Violence Against Women

As with child abuse, reports of domestic violence against women have increased dramatically in recent years. These incidents could have a lasting effect on the victims, their family life, and their children's development. Ninety-five percent of reported incidents of domestic violence involve a male perpetrator and a female victim. Typically, abuse is not an isolated event, as some women are assaulted and have sought help many times from neighbours, friends, social workers, and police (Johnson, 1990). Until recently, police did not seriously respond to these calls because they saw them as 'family matters' and perceived that women did not want charges laid or would later withdraw them (MacLeod, 1989). It is now nation-wide policy for police to charge men who batter. Research in 1980 estimated that one in ten women in Canada is psychologically, physically, or sexually battered by her intimate partner (MacLeod, 1980), even though many of these incidents are not reported to police. However, this figure is thought to be conservative by people working with battered women (MacLeod, 1989).

Although some researchers have tried to relate the apparent increase in domestic violence to changes in bargaining power within marriage, higher levels of unemployment, financial stress, and substance abuse, much of the apparent increase has been caused by legal reform and changing attitudes. Feminists in the shelter movement encouraged social workers to become more cognizant of the consequences of living in an abusive family and encouraged women to report abuse. Partners charged with violence are now more likely to be arrested and convicted than in the past when police and the courts saw such behaviour as private. Furthermore, the 1983 amendments to the Criminal Code removed spousal immunity from sexual assault charges. Reformed legislation and improved law enforcement have encouraged reporting and granted increased public visibility to family violence.

Although the feminist movement spearheaded the change, policy-makers, social service agencies, police, and researchers have developed new ways of dealing with violence against women. Many programmes involve crisis intervention with women and their children. When social workers intervene, the woman is usually encouraged to develop a protection plan that could involve hiring a lawyer, laying charges against her partner, finding transitional housing for herself and her children, and if necessary, acquiring social assistance to cover living costs. Either through individual counselling or group therapy, battered wives are helped to restructure their thinking and view violence as unacceptable regardless of their own behaviour (Baker, 1995).

Increasingly, male batterers are charged with an offence, but also provided with opportunities for counselling in order to learn to accept responsibility for the violence rather than blaming their partners, to control their emotions, develop better communication skills, and practise nonviolent behaviour. Controversy remains, however, over the use of scarce public resources. Feminists argue that women's shelters should receive most resources because women are usually the victims. Men's groups, some social workers, and many policy-makers argue that funding services for victims to the neglect of perpetrators deals only with symptoms and does not resolve the problem (Baker, 1995).

Action against family violence, including elder abuse as well as child and spousal abuse, has also involved public education for social workers, lawyers, and judges. For example, sensitization workshops are provided to increase knowledge of programme options and of the implications of domestic violence for women, their families, men who batter, and the wider society (MacLeod, 1989). In addition, limited support services have been provided for families perceived to be 'at risk' of violence because of stressful circumstances. Although all governments have voiced concern about family violence, lack of funding is the major barrier to new programmes. Until recently, many transition houses were funded by private donations, staffed by volunteers, and operated on the verge of closing from lack of funds. Governments are now providing limited operating grants, although recent cut-backs are evident in provinces such as Ontario. Follow-up therapy and counselling may also be necessary for the entire family, but these services also cost money to establish and maintain. Despite the serious nature of family violence, new programme funding is difficult to locate (Baker, 1995).

More women are leaving abusive relationships as divorce laws are liberalized, women are better able to earn a living, and child support laws are better enforced. Yet some battered women remain in abusive relationships for years, despite the emotional and physical risk to themselves and their children. For some, the risks of poverty, loneliness, and fear of reprisal are greater than living with abuse, and Canadian governments have offered these women and children few alternatives.

Services to Children With Special Needs

Support services for families with children having 'special needs' or disabilities are available, but access, service, and benefit levels vary significantly among provinces. All provinces (except the territories) provide some programme to help families pay for special equipment and respite care, but the amount paid and items covered vary substantially. Further, funding has been eroded by recent cut-backs.

Most jurisdictions provide grants and subsidies to day-care facilities to cover the extra equipment and staffing required for children with disabilities. Most provinces also assist parents with the extra costs required to maintain a child with disabilities in day care. In British Columbia, families whose child is designated as having 'special needs' are not required to take an income test nor to pay for care. Until recently, the Ontario government covered 87% of costs of approved child-care programmes for children under five with disabilities. Integrated child care appears to be the goal of most provincial programmes, but no provincial government requires day-care centres to accept children with disabilities. Consequently, inadequate access to child care is a great concern for families with special-needs children (Roeher Institute, 1993).

The federal government also provides a non-refundable tax credit for taxfilers with physical or mental disabilities that markedly restrict their daily activities. A tax deduction is also available for part-time attendant care for employees with disabilities. The attendant, however, cannot be a family member (Hess, 1992).

CONCLUSION

Although health services and basic education are provided for all Canadian children, the provinces have targeted family services to low-income families or those experiencing some family crisis. Children and adolescents from lone-parent, visible minority, and low-income families are overrepresented in the child welfare system, yet few policies focus on reducing family poverty, stress, or cultural and racial discrimination. Instead, policies and programmes concentrate on resolving the symptoms of abuse and delinquency on the assumption that clients are experiencing mainly psychological or interpersonal problems.

Although Canadian family laws give equal responsibility to mothers and fathers to provide daily care and protection for their children, social service workers and societal attitudes typically place more responsibility on mothers. Low-income mothers with family problems are taught home-making and child-rearing skills, but their employment and financial needs are not always adequately addressed through social assistance or labour-market programmes.

In comparison to health and education, family services are vastly underfunded, but social agencies are increasingly expected to provide more services with less money. Most social services have been funded by the Canada Assistance Plan (CAP) which used to provide for 50/50 cost-sharing between federal and provincial governments. In 1990, however, the federal government limited CAP contributions paid to the three 'fiscally-strong' provinces of Ontario, Alberta, and British Columbia. With the 'cap on CAP', the federal share of income assistance dropped to 28% in Ontario and 34% in British Columbia, creating an outcry from these provinces (Torjman, 1994b). Furthermore, provincial governments argued that the federal government placed too many restrictions on eligible services funded under CAP. In response, the federal government announced its unwillingness to continue open-ended funding after 1995 and its intention to provide reduced block funding for social assistance, post-secondary education, and Medicare.

While Canada signed the UN Convention on the Rights of the Child in 1991 and the former Prime Minister publicly committed the government to reducing child poverty and family violence, more effort has gone into child protection than solutions to family poverty. In comparison to some European nations, Canada's social and welfare services for children appear ungenerous and reactive, though public education and health services compare more favourably (Baker, 1995).

5

The Politics and Institutionalization
of Family Policies

Over the past century, the fight for policies and programmes for families has been closely linked to debates over social programmes in general. Broadly speaking, this debate continues to rage between groups on the left of the political spectrum (labour, feminist groups, anti-poverty groups, and the New Democratic Party) and the political right (representatives of employers' and financial organizations, conservative politicians, and the neo-conservative 'pro-family' movement). While the left has attempted to protect and expand social programmes, the right has argued that we can no longer afford programmes designed during the prosperous 1960s. At the same time, regional political differences, antagonisms, and unequal prosperity have created varying ideas about social needs. And finally, jurisdictional disputes between the federal and provincial governments continue to influence programme development. In this chapter, we examine which interest groups have pressed for policies affecting families, the ideological positions of Canada's political parties concerning the role of the state in family life, and the institutionalization of family policies.

Canada is presently restructuring all social programmes. Federal/provincial cost-sharing for social assistance is being replaced by lower federal grants to the provinces with fewer federal restrictions. In addition, the federal government is transferring money for social assistance, social services, health, and post-secondary education in one block grant, and the Unemployment Insurance programme has been redesigned. The Liberal government argues that this restructuring is a modernizing process designed to make social programmes more consistent with new labour market trends and economic globalization, as well as more cost-effective. Critics claim that the changes are really designed to reduce federal expenditures and to provide more programme autonomy to the provinces. Furthermore, this restructuring has occurred within the political context of Quebec's 1995 sovereignty referendum and a growing call for more provincial autonomy. Consequently, it is not possible to discuss family policy without referring to this political climate and these more general policy issues.

INTEREST GROUPS AND FAMILY POLICY

Historical Background

In the late nineteenth century, interest groups mobilized around various social issues, including urban poverty, juvenile delinquency, a shorter working week, equal rights for women, child welfare issues, and family income assistance. The urban reform movement in the 1880s was one of the first organizations to urge collective solutions to social problems, and its establishment signalled a weakening of the *laissez-faire* ideology predominant in nineteenth-century Canada (Guest, 1985: 31).

With industrialization, children and working-class women began to work alongside men in shops and factories, and reformers became concerned about health and safety. Their efforts eventually resulted in protective legislation and the abolition of child labour, but the fight for political rights for women continued. The Ontario Married Women's Property Act of 1872 was seen as a milestone by activists because it enabled women to control their earnings, bank accounts, and property after marriage. The other provinces soon created similar legislation.

In the 1890s, Protestant religions began to apply Christian doctrine to social problems such as child labour, prostitution, gambling, and low wages to create the social gospel movement. The churches in this movement allied with labour unions to form the Moral and Social Reform Council of Canada, which in 1906 successfully lobbied the government to reduce the length of the working week. Over the years, the renamed Social Service Council advocated income support for dependants, improved housing and health, and social insurance against accidents, sickness, unemployment, and old age (Allen, 1971). The Council successfully lobbied for the first Mother's Allowance programme in Manitoba in 1916 and the federal Old Age Assistance Act in 1927. Furthermore, many 'progressive' politicians established their roots in the social gospel movement.

From the late nineteenth century until about 1920, the provinces developed compulsory education laws requiring parents to send their children to school until the age of 12 or 14 (later 16). The lobby for compulsory education came from educational reformers as well as from those concerned with the potential consequences of 'idle youth' on social unrest in the growing cities. Furthermore, employers wanted a labour force that was literate, disciplined, punctual, and eager to learn new skills. Yet compulsory education laws were frequently ignored by parents who needed their children's income or labour.

From 1910 to 1923, social reformers and women's rights activists persuaded provincial governments to allow mothers as well as fathers to gain legal custody of their children during and after marriage. In 1918, after a long struggle, women gained the right to vote in federal elections although they could not vote in Quebec elections until 1940. Until then, men as family heads voted on behalf of their wives or adult unmarried daughters.

In 1920, the Canadian Council on Social Development (CCSD) was established (originally called the Canadian Council on Social Welfare). This voluntary agency, supported by federal subsidies, advised the government on child and family welfare issues and by 1930 became the most influential voice in social welfare. Yet the traditional view that poverty reflected family disorganization initially permeated CCSD, which did not support the movement towards government benefits for low-income families (Guest, 1985).

The common link among the diverse reform groups which proliferated at the turn of the century was a consistent pro-family, pro-natalist, and patriarchal thrust (Ursel, 1992). As secular social work became more firmly established in the 1920s, the social gospel movement declined in influence, but the goal of pushing the state into a more active interventionist role and laying the groundwork for the welfare state had already been accomplished.

Gender-Based Advocacy Groups

Since the 1900s, Canadian women's groups have remained strong and consistent voices for reforming or creating policies influencing marriage, child support, divorce, and employment equity. At the turn of the century, several women's groups were actively involved in social reform, but the most influential was the National Council of Women of Canada (NCWC).

Founded in 1893, NCWC was established by middle-class women who believed that women's mothering and nurturing within the home could be transferred to the public sphere, resulting in more humane and progressive social policies. This ideology has been labelled 'maternal feminism'. Canada's high infant mortality rate especially concerned NCWC, which helped to establish well-baby clinics, sponsored health talks, and organized home visits to mothers (Strong-Boag, 1976). NCWC also lobbied for children's aid societies, mother's pensions, minimum age-of-work legislation, and curfew and truancy acts as strategies to reduce juvenile delinquency. Although members campaigned for jobs for women in social work, teaching, nursing, recreation, and police work, they undercut the same professional advances by insisting that women's most natural place was at home (ibid.).

Numerous other women's groups began in the early years of the twentieth century. For example, the Young Women's Christian Association (YWCA) focused on providing a safe place for young urban working women to live, and has continued to provide accommodation, community activities, and support groups for women and their families up to the present. The Women's Christian Temperance Union (WCTU) promoted child protection legislation and reformatories for juvenile delinquents, as well as fighting for the prohibition of alcohol which was viewed as detrimental to family life (MacIntyre, 1993). The Canadian Federation of Women's Labour Leagues, established in the early 1900s as a vehicle for working-class participation in the women's suffrage movement, also focused on concrete reforms of working conditions such as maternity leave and equal pay for equal work (Ball, 1988). Women's groups flourished during the first half of the twentieth century, although most accepted the patriarchal family and worked within the tradition of volunteerism.

During the 1960s, however, a new feminist movement developed that opposed the inequalities of the patriarchal family and competitiveness of capitalist society (Cohen, 1993a). These groups pressed for gender equality in all aspects of life, forming small consciousness-raising groups as well as mass protests. Reproductive rights and access to abortion became a central focus for the early feminist movement in Canada.

In 1970, the Abortion Caravan crossed the country to Ottawa accumulating support for further changes to the federal abortion law. The activists wanted to remove abortion from the Criminal Code, to provide free and safe birth control, and to allow the development of community-controlled abortion clinics (Pierson, 1993). In 1974, the Canadian Abortion Rights Action League also formed to decriminalize abortion, establishing the Abortion Information and Referral Service in 1980. The strong and steady pressure for unrestricted access to abortion contributed to the development of clinics outside accredited hospitals in some provinces.

In 1967, the Committee for the Equality of Women, a coalition of 33 groups, successfully pressed for the Royal Commission on the Status of Women, which reported in 1970. As a result, in 1973 the federal government appointed a Minister Responsible for the Status of Women and a government department (Status of Women Canada) to co-ordinate efforts to promote the advancement of women. Because women are closely aligned with children and family, numerous family policy issues have been promoted.

In the same year, the federal government established the Canadian Advisory Council on the Status of Women (CACSW), a para-governmental organization to advise government and inform the public through research and education (Cohen, 1993a). For over twenty years, the CACSW researched and analysed numerous issues relating to family policy, such as reproduction, family law, child care, and employment leave for family responsibilities. After the 1995 cut-backs, however, the CACSW was dissolved and some of its functions merged with government. Throughout the 1970s and 1980s, provincial advisory councils also monitored women's status and provided research and information on family issues.

The National Action Committee on the Status of Women (NAC), a non-governmental organization established in 1972, has been the most influential feminist group in Canada (Cohen, 1993a). NAC continues to lobby for numerous family policy issues including access to contraception and abortion, employment equity, a national child-care policy, family benefits for same-sex couples, and a commission to study new reproductive technologies. Several other non-governmental organizations have been established to improve the legal status of women and in doing so have had an impact on family law. The most influential is the Women's Legal Education and Action Fund (LEAF), which promotes equality through legal action and public education and sponsors test cases to challenge discrimination against women in court. LEAF has successfully intervened in cases involving domestic violence, sexual assault, and equal property division between spouses (LEAF, 1992).

Feminist groups have also initiated and developed important family services at the local level, especially transition houses for women and their children fleeing from abusive homes. While the shelter movement began as a feminist alternative to mainstream social services, many transition houses now receive government funding. By the mid-1980s, however, women's groups focused more on preventing the erosion of social programmes than on pushing for new ones, with greater public concern over government spending and a backlash against feminism (Cohen, 1993b).

Since 1983, the conservative group REAL Women of Canada (Real, Equal and Active for Life) has argued that the state is undermining the traditional family by responding to alternative lifestyles and by funding 'interest' groups such as NAC. REAL Women, with roots in the western Canada anti-abortion or 'pro-life' movement and in fundamentalist Christianity, promotes stronger government support for home-makers but opposes abortion, liberal divorce laws, pay equity, and universal day care (REAL Women, 1986).

Men's rights groups (such as Fathers for Justice) have argued that fathers are treated unfairly in the divorce courts with respect to child custody, access and support, and the division of matrimonial property (Bertoia and Drakich, 1993). In 1987, a number of men's groups joined together to form the Canadian Council for Family Rights (Crean, 1988). These groups have lobbied for paternity benefits, joint custody, and more liberal access by divorced fathers to their children, arguing that lack of access inhibits fathers' willingness to pay child support (Crean, 1988). Yet the government's own research has failed to support these alleged inequalities in the law. Furthermore, men's rights groups have not curbed the widespread reform of support enforcement legislation, and child custody laws have not been changed, although joint custody is now awarded more often.

Over the past century, Canadian women's groups have made a strong impact on family legislative and policy reform. They fought for and helped win numerous changes in family and labour laws before the Second World War, family allowances in 1945, maternity benefits in 1971, the liberalization of abortion and contraceptive laws in 1969, divorce reform in 1968 and 1985, employment equity legislation in 1984, and provincial pay equity legislation, and successfully lobbied for royal commissions on the status of women and on new reproductive technologies. Although women's groups have experienced less success with other issues such as child care, they helped achieve greater visibility for these issues on the policy agenda (Vickers, Rankin, and Appelle, 1993).

The early maternal feminists, the 'pro-family' movement, and the fathers' rights movement have all viewed the (patriarchal) family as the basic unit of society, worthy of government support. In contrast, present-day feminists have argued that the individual, not 'the family', should be the unit of reform. For these feminists, the very concept of 'family policy' is associated with right-wing efforts to bolster the heterosexual patriarchal family and to reduce freedom of choice in personal life.

Child and Family Welfare Groups

Although several voluntary organizations have exclusively focused on family issues, other groups have fought hard for social programmes in general. Because all family policies are embedded within social programmes, we must briefly note the efforts of these organizations as well as the specific family-related ones.

The Canadian Council on Social Development (CCSD) has promoted 'progressive' social policies for 75 years through research, public education, consultation, and advocacy. CCSD has organized conferences on day care and sponsored books on poverty, the homeless, housing, and Aboriginal child welfare (CCSD, 1993). During the 1960s and 1970s, several new groups formed to strengthen family life and to advocate more comprehensive family programmes. Since 1965, the Vanier Institute of the Family has funded research, lobbied Parliament, and published monographs and a quarterly magazine on family life. The Family Services Association has also urged governments to develop consistent family policies and programmes. The National Council of Welfare has served as an advisory body to the federal government since 1969, adopting an advocacy stance usually found in client rights organizations (Wharf, 1993b). Their insightful reports have dealt with income security programmes, women in poverty, employment policy, child benefits, child care, and welfare reform.

Since 1971, the National Anti-Poverty Organization (NAPO) has used public awareness, community organizing, and advocacy to try to reduce poverty, especially among lone mothers (NAPO, 1989). The Canadian Institute of Child Health focuses on injury prevention and health promotion for infants, children, adolescents, and mothers, producing statistical monographs and briefs to the government. Since 1982, the Child Care Advocacy Association of Canada has lobbied for an affordable, comprehensive, high-quality, and non-profit child-care system that is supported by public funds and accessible to all parents (Friendly, 1994: 148).

Since 1985, a coalition called the Child Poverty Action Group has produced a series of reports on child poverty. In 1989, this group formed a new coalition called Campaign 2000, a national movement to build awareness and support for the 1989 House of Commons resolution to end child poverty by the year 2000. They continue to advocate:

1. national strategies to generate sustaining employment, such as a living minimum wage, work-sharing, and redefining work to include financial recognition of the social value of caring for children;
2. a supportive social security system which includes a progressive children's benefit system, a child support assurance system, a federally-financed, comprehensive child-care system, and a comprehensive employment insurance system to protect periods of transition; and
3. a responsive community support system to include health education throughout the life cycle, pre- and postnatal care and nutrition programmes, and child-care and family resource programmes (Campaign 2000, 1994).

In addition to national organizations, many provincial groups have been providing advocacy and service on family issues for years. For example, since 1912 the Ontario Association of Children's Aid Societies has provided education and training, and advocates for increased funding in child welfare (Wharf, 1993b).

184   *Canada*

While many organizations are concerned with the welfare of families, women, and children, their influence on government has been limited. One reason is that they represent the interests of the less powerful and must compete with employers' groups and bond market raters for the government's ear. Second, they are underfunded and cannot afford much research and advocacy work. And finally, they have tended to act in isolation from one another and from the provincial ministries providing services. Yet Campaign 2000 may be a reflection of a growing and unified movement to reform child welfare and to reduce family poverty (Wharf, 1993b).

Other Interest Groups

In addition to the above groups, we should mention the involvement of labour unions, professional associations, and 'think-tanks' in current debates over social and family policies.

Over the years, the Canadian labour movement has fought hard and successfully for the right to organize trade unions, for higher wages, a shorter work week, statutory holidays, and even protective legislation for women and children. Yet social welfare reform, family policy, and women's equality have not been central concerns of the labour movement in Canada as they have been in other countries (Baker and Robeson, 1986; Armitage, 1988). Furthermore, the recent decline in private-sector unionization has limited the movement's influence, although unionization in Canada has not experienced the recent declines seen in the United States and Britain (Armitage, 1988). As the number of women workers has increased, however, unions have taken stands on family policy issues. In 1980, for example, the Ontario Federation of Labour adopted a policy advocating universal day care and the extension of maternity and paternity leave (Colley, 1983).

Professional associations, such as the Canadian Medical Association and the Canadian Association of Schools of Social Work, have consistently submitted briefs to government on health and social issues. The Canadian Bar Association has long been concerned with promoting uniformity of legislation and has pressured for law reform commissions (Hurlburt, 1986). These commissions have initiated many reforms in family and divorce law, as discussed in Chapter 1, including equalizing the division of matrimonial property, considering 'the best interest of the child' in custody decisions, and requiring stronger child support enforcement.

Several conservative think-tanks have been very influential in shaping public opinion and encouraging governments to cut social programmes and rely more on family resources. In fact, their influence extends beyond that of the 'progressive' voluntary organizations lobbying for family programmes. Since 1958, the C. D. Howe Institute has published neo-conservative studies on monetary policy, taxation levels, government spending, and social programmes (Ernst, 1992). Since 1974 the western-based Fraser Institute has advocated lower taxes, less government involvement, and cuts to social programmes, receiving widespread attention by the media and the Reform Party of Canada (Sillars, 1994). On the other hand, the Canadian Centre for Policy Alternatives (CCPA), one of the few national organizations addressing economic policy from the political left, has been far less influential (Muszynski, 1988).

In the 1990s, several new research organizations have attempted to influence family policy. The National Forum on Family Security, established in 1991 with private funding to commission policy papers and to conduct seminars, has argued that economic and social insecurity now permeate middle-class as well as poor families and that policy must shift from remedial measures to prevention (National Forum on Family Security, 1993). Since 1992, the privately-funded Caledon Institute of Social Policy has been influential in policy discussions through organizing consultations for government and preparing publications based on rigorous research. In 1995, the Caledon Institute proposed a new way to fight child poverty by developing a stronger federal income security programme for children, combining existing federal and provincial money now spent on children (Battle and Muszynski, 1995). So far, the federal government has not acted upon this recommendation.

Although many organizations advocate changes in family and social policies, their voices are not always heard in Ottawa. In recent years, conservative groups pressing for deficit reduction, cuts to government expenditures, and the tightening of work incentives have been given more credence by both Liberal and Conservative governments than have the voices of social democracy. The Liberal government has widely consulted on initiatives to reduce child poverty and to create a national child-care programme, but has not yet created any new programmes. This inaction is partly ideological, but also relates to the fact that creating these programmes would be costly and would require difficult federal/provincial negotiations over jurisdiction.

PARTY POLITICS AND PROGRAMMES

In order to understand why Canadian governments have listened to some lobby groups and ignored others, we need to say more about party politics and the structure of government. Canada is an independent, self-governing democracy with a constitutional monarchy. Because it has a single-member plurality electoral system as opposed to proportional representation, the strongest parties receive a larger proportion of seats than votes and the total number of effective parties is constrained. Unlike most countries with a single-member plurality electoral system, Canada has not been a two-party system at the federal level since the 1920s. Concentration of support for third parties in certain regions has given them seats in the national Parliament (Blake, 1991). Nevertheless, since Confederation in 1867, Canadians have elected either Liberal or Conservative governments to Ottawa, but the Liberals have formed the government for most of those years.

The Liberal Party of Canada

Historically, the Liberal party has been in government when most social welfare legislation was passed, but it has also exhibited periods of neglect and disinterest

186   *Canada*

(Armitage, 1988: 92). Provincial Liberal governments have also shown varying attitudes toward social legislation. In 1919, the federal Liberal Party platform included social insurance against unemployment, sickness, and dependence in old age, as well as widows' pensions and maternity benefits (Guest, 1985: 66). Yet legislation was not enacted for old-age assistance until 1927 and for unemployment insurance until 1940, partly because both national programmes required constitutional amendments. In 1944, the universal family allowance was introduced by the Liberals.

During the 1950s, the commitment of the post-war Liberal government to a comprehensive system of social security was shallow, with considerable 'foot-dragging' (ibid.: 142), although they were responsible for the Old Age Security Act (1951) which made pensions universal, the Unemployment Assistance Act (1956), and the Hospital Insurance and Diagnostic Services Act (1957). The election of Liberal governments in 1962 and 1965 was influenced by pledges to introduce the Canada Pension Plan and Medicare (Armitage, 1988: 23), and legislation was enacted shortly after each election. The Liberal government was also responsible for the Canada Assistance Plan (1966) which extended federal cost-sharing to provincial social welfare programmes, though the same party was responsible for its demise in 1995. Legislation reforming divorce in 1968 and legalizing contraception, hospital abortions, and homosexuality between consenting adults in 1969 was also enacted by the Liberals.

Although the Liberals gave rhetorical support to welfare ideals in the 1970s, they bureaucratized welfare functions rather than expanding services (Armitage, 1988: 92). Before the 1984 election, the Liberal government passed the Canada Health Act, prohibiting user fees in health care, and the Employment Equity Act, targeting several groups for fairer employment practices. In 1993, after a nine-year absence from power, the Liberals made a commitment to providing a national child-care programme and to modernizing social programmes. After cutting funding to all social programmes, they promised to match provincial child-care funding in December 1995.

The Progressive Conservative Party

The Conservative Party, renamed the Progressive Conservative Party (PC) in 1942, has had less opportunity to legislate social programmes because it has formed the government for fewer years. Ideologically, the PCs have focused more on fighting inflation and reducing the deficit than on creating or reinforcing social programmes. A Conservative government attempted to create unemployment insurance before the 1935 election, but the legislation was later declared unconstitutional because employment programmes were provincial jurisdictions (Guest, 1985: 88). Yet PC governments laid the foundation for some reforms by appointing royal commissions, such as the Hall Commission recommending Medicare (1961).

Although Brian Mulroney's PC government was not known for its progressive social policy platform, they created fundamental policy changes with lasting consequences (Rice and Prince, 1993). From 1984 to 1993, the Mulroney government cut federal cash transfers to the provinces, created more stringent regulations for unemployment insurance with lower benefits, and eliminated the universal family allowance. Yet the PC government was responsible for liberalizing divorce legislation in 1985 and for the unsuccessful proposal to remove child-care funding from welfare legislation in 1988. Following the 1993 election, the PC Party's influence was drastically reduced with only two seats in the House of Commons.

Provincial PC governments in power for extended periods, such as in Ontario and Alberta, have tended to reduce social expenditures and cut social programmes for families. For example, the Alberta (Klein) government abolished public kindergarten, and the new Ontario (Harris) government has just reduced spending on child care, junior kindergarten, women's shelters, and social assistance.

The CCF/NDP

The Canadian political party that has most consistently argued for strong social programmes is the New Democratic Party (ibid.: 91). The NDP has its roots in the Co-operative Commonwealth Federation (CCF), founded in 1932, which was a social democratic party advocating increased state involvement in income security (Avakumovic, 1978: 56). Federally, the CCF was most successful in the 1945 election, winning 28 seats in Parliament compared to eight in 1940 (ibid.: 132). The significant growth of the CCF in the 1940s influenced the federal Liberal government, which released ten studies or inquiries on welfare during that period (Ursel, 1992: 207). During the 1950s, however, CCF popularity waned.

In the 1960s, the CCF was reorganized into the New Democratic Party. From 1963 to 1968, the NDP held the balance of power in Ottawa, a period in which the Liberal government was forced to legislate many social reforms, including Medicare. Between 1972 and 1974, the NDP held the balance of power in the minority Liberal government and helped reduce the impact of inflation on the poor (Avakumovic, 1978: 221). In the 1980s, the NDP became more successful, winning 43 seats in Parliament in the 1988 federal election.

The NDP has also formed provincial governments in Saskatchewan, Manitoba, British Columbia, and Ontario. The CCF/NDP formed the government in Saskatchewan from 1944 to 1964, pioneering government hospital insurance in 1947 and medical insurance in 1962 (ibid.: 174). The implementation of these provincial programmes placed pressure on the federal government to enact national legislation. Manitoba and Saskatchewan NDP governments abolished Medicare premiums, and in the 1970s the three western provinces with NDP governments redistributed income by raising taxes on corporations and the rich (ibid.: 255–6).

The NDP has supported the welfare ideal of redistributing income, wealth, and power more clearly than other parties. The CCF/NDP was the first party to raise in Parliament the need for such programmes as pensions, Medicare, public housing, and income guarantees, which had a significant influence on the development of the Canadian welfare state (Armitage, 1988: 91). The NDP is formally and structurally linked to organized labour, with representatives from trade unions on most policy-making bodies of the party (Archer, 1991). Yet the alliance between the NDP and Canadian unions has never been as solid as the link between socialist parties and labour in many other countries, which reduces their power base.

In recent years, the federal NDP has often been in the position of defending the status quo from government-initiated reform, and the objectives of the party have been challenged by its members (ibid.). Consequently, the NDP experienced a significant reduction of Parliamentary seats in the 1993 election, from 43 in 1988 to nine in 1993, which sharply reduced its influence at the federal level.

Other Political Parties

Other political parties have influenced family and social policy, including the Social Credit Party in Alberta and British Columbia, and the Union Nationale and the Creditistes in Quebec. These parties developed from regional interests or protest movements, adopting right-wing agendas. In 1987, the Reform Party was created in western Canada with a neo-conservative platform focusing on government cutbacks and policies strengthening the patriarchal family. The Reform Party aims to reduce the size of the federal bureaucracy, transfer jurisdiction over social programmes to the provinces, and use voluntary organizations and families to replace government services (Laycock, 1994; Sigurdson, 1994). In the 1993 federal election, Reform made significant gains, especially in Alberta.

The Parti Québécois (PQ), which formed the provincial government in Quebec from 1976 to 1985 and was re-elected in 1994, is an exception to the right-wing focus of the other third parties. In addition to its goal of sovereignty for Quebec, the PQ's platform includes progressive social policy objectives similar to the NDP's, although in recent years it has been seen to move away from its traditional social democratic focus. Another Quebec-based federal party, the Bloc Québécois (BQ), gained enough seats in the 1993 federal election to form the official opposition in Ottawa where it continues to pursue its sovereignty agenda for Quebec. Ironically, the BQ has become the main voice in Canada's Parliament for the maintenance of social programmes (Roy, 1994).

Canadian politics are dominated by the party system and party discipline, which forces elected members to adhere to the party platform. Only occasionally will members from different parties unite over an issue, such as when female members united to defeat a restrictive abortion bill in Parliament (Lynas, 1993).

Royal Commissions and Other Significant Reports

Historically, Canadian governments have relied on royal commissions to investigate controversial policy issues and to recommend action to Parliament. These commissions have sometimes provided blueprints for social programmes but have also led to inaction or continued controversy. In this section, we will highlight a few government or parliamentary reports that have influenced family policies.

The Royal Commission on Dominion–Provincial Relations (1937–40) was appointed to resolve the jurisdictional disputes over the creation of a national unemployment insurance programme. The report recognized that certain income maintenance functions, such as insurance for unemployment and old age, were best performed on a national basis, but recommended that other social services remain provincial responsibility. The Commission emphasized that provincial revenues could not handle the new expectations for social welfare, recommended a national minimum of social services, and argued that federal cost-sharing would help achieve that minimum (Guest, 1985: 91–2). The Unemployment Insurance Act was passed in 1940, immediately after the Commission's report, and maternity benefits were added to this legislation in 1971.

The Report on Social Security for Canada (1943), chaired by Leonard Marsh, formed the groundwork for the Canadian welfare state. Heavily influenced by the British Beveridge Report (1942), the Marsh Report recommended a two-part social welfare system: social insurance to cover wages lost through unemployment, sickness, disability, or maternity, and flat-rate benefits for old age, permanent disability, and death of a breadwinner. The Marsh Report also recommended policies to ensure full employment, a universal child allowance rather than a family wage, and a strong federal role in co-ordinating programmes and setting national standards (Marsh, 1943). This report encouraged the implementation of several national programmes, including Family Allowances, Unemployment Insurance, and the universal old-age pension.

Several royal commissions were initiated on public health insurance. The Heagarty Commission reported in 1943, calling for an insurance programme administered by the provinces but with federal funding and standards (Guest, 1985: 138). The Royal Commission on Health Services or the Hall Report (1961–4) echoed the recommendations of the Marsh and Heagarty Reports in advocating universal health insurance (ibid.: 162). Hospital insurance had already been initiated in 1957 but the Medical Care Act was passed in 1966, largely as a result of the Hall Report.

After strong pressure from women's groups, the Royal Commission on the Status of Women (1967–70) examined a variety of issues relating to family, including gender stereotyping, women's role as mothers, and state responsibility for children (Bégin, 1992). Among the recommendations that were implemented were equal minimum wages for men and women, paid maternity leave, strategies for fair hiring and promotion practices, the removal of ceilings on maintenance orders, and freer access to abortion. The Report also recommended a national child-care programme and a guaranteed annual income that were never implemented.

The Special Senate Committee on Poverty, or the Croll Report (1968–71), criticized low levels of social assistance, noted wide variations among provinces, and recommended a guaranteed annual income programme, to be financed and administered by the federal government (Canada, Senate, 1971: xv). The report affirmed the goal of full employment and recommended the separation of income maintenance and social services, pay equity legislation, indexed minimum wages, and the expansion and development of child-care services.

The Dennis Report (1969–72), a federal task force on housing and urban development, was the first full-scale review of housing policy since 1944 (Guest, 1985: 164). It recommended a guaranteed annual income or a shelter allowance to ensure adequate income for housing, a large-scale social housing rehabilitation programme, and the provision of community services and facilities to low-income neighbourhoods (Dennis and Fish, 1972: 15–17). The report, which formed the blueprint for federal policy, focused on the need for government housing policy while relying on the free market to provide housing.

In the 1960s and 1970s, the federal government and most provincial governments established law reform commissions as neither common law nor statute law had kept pace with changing social conditions. Ontario was the first province to establish an ongoing law reform commission in 1964, and the federal government established a national commission in 1971. These commissions recommended changes in divorce, support enforcement, and children's rights, and many recommendations have been legislated. The Canada Law Reform Commission was instrumental in the creation of unified family courts in several provinces (Hurlburt, 1986).

The Royal Commission on Equality in Employment, or the Abella Commission (1983–4), recommended that all federally-regulated employers be required to implement employment equity, including equal pay for work of equal value. The absence of affordable and quality child care was seen as a major barrier to women's equality in the workplace. The Abella Report recommended that the federal government, in co-operation with the provinces, develop an appropriate funding mechanism for a universal and publicly-funded child-care system (Abella, 1984). As a result of this commission, the government legislated the federal Employment Equity Act in 1984.

In response to child-care concerns, the Task Force on Child Care (chaired by K. Cooke) was appointed in 1984 by the Liberals and reported to the Conservatives in 1986. The Cooke Report concluded that Canada lagged far behind most western industrialized countries in the provision of child care and recommended a new cost-sharing arrangement. In addition, Cooke urged all levels of government to work together to develop complementary systems of parental leave and child care, and argued that the new child-care system should be as comprehensive and accessible as health care and education (Canada, Status of Women, 1986: 279). The government responded by appointing a special parliamentary committee on child care chaired by the Conservatives, which recommended less costly measures.

In December 1987, the Conservative government proposed a national Child Care Strategy with legislation to take child-care funding out of welfare legislation, improve child-care tax deductions for working parents, and develop a research fund. Although the legislation was not passed, the tax deductions and the fund were implemented. One of the fund's first projects was the Canadian National Child Care Study, intended to provide comprehensive data on child-care needs and patterns of use, and to examine the relationships among family, work, and child-care variables (Statistics Canada, 1992a: 19). The study involved two components: a

1988 survey of over 24,000 families and a review of policy and programmes in each jurisdiction (ibid.: 23). The study has yielded a wealth of information and underscored the need for a comprehensive government strategy.

After much lobbying by feminist groups, the Royal Commission on New Reproductive Technologies was appointed in 1989 and reported in 1993, after considerable controversy. The report recommended legislation to prohibit with criminal sanctions several aspects of new reproductive technologies, such as the sale of eggs, sperm, zygotes, and surrogacy. It also recommended a regulatory licensing body for new technologies (Royal Commission on New Reproductive Technologies, 1993).

In 1992, the federal government announced the National Longitudinal Survey on Children. Beginning in 1994–95, a sample of 25,000 children under age 12 was surveyed, to be repeated at two-year intervals as they grow to adulthood. In addition, the children's parents and school personnel will be interviewed. The survey's purpose is to develop information for policy analysis and programme development on critical factors affecting the development of children (Canada, Government of, 1994).

Increasingly, taxpayers and advocacy groups are complaining about the high cost of government-sponsored studies and the way this research seems to be used to defer political action. Activists argue that new social programmes are needed rather than more research, and that the money spent on these studies could easily fund programme innovations. Yet royal commissions have been an important decision-making tool for Canadian governments, as well as an exercise in the appearance of democracy and a way to delay difficult decisions.

THE INSTITUTIONALIZATION OF FAMILY POLICIES

National Efforts to Integrate Family Policy

At the national level, family policy has been implicit and embedded in all social and economic policies. As we have seen, royal commissions and government advisory committees have played an important role in designing national programmes and highlighting the need for policy change. In addition, non-governmental organizations such as the Vanier Institute of the Family (VIF) continue to focus on the implications of government policies on families and to highlight the need for 'family-friendly' policies.

Most federal social programmes affecting families used to be the responsibility of Health and Welfare Canada. In November 1993, however, the new Liberal government reorganized departments to create Human Resources Development Canada, which is now responsible for income security programmes, education, and employment-related programmes. Health Canada deals with health-related programmes. Revenue Canada oversees the Child Tax Benefit and other taxation matters (except personal income tax in Quebec), as well as contributions to the Canada

Pension Plan and Unemployment Insurance (Canada Communication Group, 1994). The federal Department of Justice retains jurisdiction over the Criminal Code and divorce, and has recently established the Family Law Enforcement Program which assists provincial governments or agencies to enforce child support. Information from federal databanks is used to locate individuals and to garnish federal monies from those in default of support orders (VIF, 1993: 9). Yet because of the piecemeal way in which legislation was created and because of divided jurisdiction, family programmes are sometimes inconsistent among jurisdictions.

Provincial Efforts to Integrate Family Policy

Quebec is the only province to make explicit and continuing efforts to integrate family concerns into government policy. In 1981, the government formed a working group to identify family problems and to develop family policy (Sarrasin, 1994: 10). The *Regroupement inter-organismes pour une politique familiale au Québec* was founded in 1983, comprised of key family-related non-government organizations. The government created a Secretariat in 1984 to develop and integrate family policy, and appointed a Minister of the Family in 1985. Furthermore, the *Conseil de la famille* was established in 1988 to advise government. The first three-year plan of action regarding family policy, including 58 measures, was introduced in 1989 while the second plan, including 88 measures, was introduced in 1992 (ibid.). The Secretariat was instrumental in amending the Labour Standards Act in 1990, which increased unpaid parental leave following birth of a child and allowed an additional five days of unpaid parental leave for activities related to child care, health, and education (Le Bourdais and Marcil-Gratton, 1994). Quebec family policy is largely pro-natalist, although it has not tackled the important issue of income replacement for parents on parental leave (ibid.: 113).

In the late 1980s, Saskatchewan identified 'the family' as a primary focus for policy development and created the Family Foundation to oversee family policy issues across government departments. This unit has since been reintegrated into existing government departments (VIF, 1993: 153). In 1989, Alberta created a Premier's Council in Support of Alberta Families to advise on relevant programmes, policies, and services (Gunter, 1992), but this council was abolished in recent cutbacks. The British Columbia Council for the Family, a non-governmental organization with government funding, promotes family unity and prosperity, produces resource material, and helps integrate groups working with families (VIF, 1993: 41). In addition, several provinces have integrated their courts so that issues relating to divorce, custody, child support, child welfare, and young offenders are decided in Unified Family Courts (ibid.).

The provinces administer most family-related programmes. Ministries of Social and Community Services typically deal with child welfare, day care, family support, and social assistance. Some provinces have combined health and social services under one ministry. Provincial Ministries of Justice oversee laws related to marriage, child support, and child welfare while maternity and parental leave fall under Labour Departments. (Maternity and parental benefits continue to be provided by the federal government under Unemployment Insurance.) Housing programmes tend to be delivered through provincial departments of Community or Municipal Affairs (VIF, 1993).

Financing Family Programmes

Canadian programmes for families are funded in different ways. The Child Tax Benefit is funded by the federal government from general revenue. Maternity/parental benefits are part of the Unemployment Insurance programme funded by employee and employer contributions. While the cost of social services and social assistance used to be shared by the federal and provincial governments, it will be financed through block grants from the federal to provincial governments, along with health and post-secondary education.

Federal regulations about how the provinces should spend federal transfers have always been contentious. For example, the Canada Assistance Plan (CAP) specified that funds must be spent on families 'in need', that there be no residence requirements for those eligible for social assistance, that workfare not be permitted, and that government funds be used in regulated non-profit agencies (Friendly, 1994: 73). Furthermore, the Canada Health Act (1984) requires that provinces abide by the five principles noted in Chapter 4 and prohibits user fees and extra billing. Aside from these basic requirements, provincial governments have been free to develop and administer their own health and social programmes.

In recent years, several provincial governments have voiced concerns about federal requirements on cost-shared programmes such as CAP. Some provinces have already implemented or wish to develop new programmes that do not conform to federal regulations. Provincial complaints about 'rigid' spending restrictions, as well as federal attempts to limit spending and reduce the deficit, have led to major policy changes in 1995. The federal Liberal government has passed legislation to phase out CAP and the funding arrangements for health and post-secondary education, and replace them with lower levels of block funding with fewer restrictions to allow more provincial experimentation and autonomy in social welfare programmes.

Critics of block funding for social programmes argue that the federal government has offloaded to the provinces difficult decisions about how to reduce expenditures. In addition, they argue that funding for social assistance will no longer be based on need but on a complex formula relating to population and tax entitlements. Critics also fear that Canada Health and Social Transfer (CHST) will eliminate future possibilities to create new programmes with national standards. Furthermore, they say that one block grant for health, social assistance, social services, and post-secondary education will especially augment funding competition among health organizations, universities, and social agencies. Critics are also concerned that discrepancies in social services among the provinces will grow, to the detriment of national unity. Yet this policy of block funding appears to be designed to promote national unity by allowing more provincial autonomy.

POLITICAL DIVISIONS AND FAMILY VALUES

Disagreement Over Social Spending

In recent years, the cleavage has widened between groups that support high levels of social spending and further development of the 'social safety net', and groups that want lower government funding on social programmes. Those who support stable or higher spending include feminist groups, child advocacy and anti-poverty groups, trade unions, the New Democratic Party and, more recently, the Bloc Québécois (BQ). Using principles of equality and justice, these groups argue that government should play an important role in helping people find work and providing programmes to enable them to earn a living while caring for their families. They argue that high rates of child poverty, sole-support mothers, and unemployment demand supportive social programmes to ensure equality of outcome, and that we cannot afford to ignore the problems of child poverty and work/family conflicts. Essentially, they believe that social programmes could be financed through shifts in spending priorities and income tax reform, especially fewer tax breaks for business and wealthier Canadians.

Groups opposing present government funding for social programmes and families include the Reform Party, the 'pro-life' movement, REAL Women of Canada, employers' organizations, the financial community, and conservative think-tanks. These organizations argue that taxes and social spending are out of control and must be curbed. Reducing the deficit and remaining competitive in global markets are more important than maintaining social services, which have become too generous. When government programmes exist, they argue, they should strengthen traditional families instead of encouraging divorce and lone parents. Further, family members should be encouraged to care for one another with the assistance of voluntary organizations or the private sector. Existing welfare programmes have been ineffective in reducing poverty or unemployment, they claim, because the programmes lack work incentives, are too generous, and encourage dependency.

Canadian opinion polls have recently shown strong support for the traditional nuclear family and the widespread belief that lone parents and same-sex couples raising children are undesirable for society (Nesmith, 1994). Focusing on the belief that many of the poor do not deserve public support, conservatives throughout North America have been able to cut social programmes and promote greater reliance on 'family values'.

Changing Values

Values are changing on most family-related issues, but conflicting values are sometimes used as a rationale by governments for policy inaction. Although more Canadians now feel that the employment of mothers is both necessary and acceptable, most Canadians do not support a comprehensive public child-care programme despite the shortage of regulated child care.

Abortion also remains a divisive issue. While the majority of Canadians (56%) believe that abortion should be permitted only in certain circumstances, those circumstances vary widely, and significant percentages believe in either free access or complete prohibition. Considering this lack of consensus, the federal government has enacted no new law concerning abortion, and provincial access remains unequal.

Although religious organizations continue to advocate family policy reforms, their voice was stronger in former decades. At the turn of the century, Protestant denominations played a key role in the social reform movement, and both Catholic and Protestant churches were involved in the development and delivery of child welfare services. The Catholic Church in Quebec retained a strong political influence, delaying the development of state-based social programmes. Since World War II, however, religious organizations have played a declining role in the development of family policy. Yet groups such as the United Church of Canada and the Canadian Council of Catholic Bishops continue to release policy papers and attempt to influence legislation. Furthermore, the 'Protestant work ethic' has recently enjoyed a revival in the philosophy of the Reform Party, especially in western Canada. Conservative groups in rural areas and in the west continue to argue for 'family values', emphasizing the heterosexual family with a breadwinner father and caregiver mother, who work hard to raise their children with minimal government support.

Since the 1930s, the locus of family programmes has shifted from municipal government and voluntary organizations to provincial and federal governments. Health care, social services, child care, and employment programmes remained under provincial jurisdiction, but the federal government gradually became more involved by creating national programmes through cost-sharing or federal grants to the provinces. National programmes were created because the voluntary organizations, municipalities, and provinces could not keep pace with the growing programme needs created by industrialization, urbanization, and changing family structures.

A significant cleavage remains in Canada between those who expect a strong central government to maintain national programmes to support families and those who want more provincial, voluntary agency, and family involvement. In recent years, regionalism has grown and the federal government has been unable to gain the necessary provincial consent to make constitutional changes or create national programmes. After the 1993 election, two major parties promoting decentralization gained seats in Parliament: the Reform Party and the Bloc Québécois. Although both advocate greater provincial autonomy, the BQ supports the sovereignty of Quebec and strong state intervention in an independent Quebec, while the Reform Party advocates less government and major cut-backs to the welfare state. These issues continue to influence the political context of family policy reform and inhibit change.

In 1995, the federal government introduced a new way of funding health and social programmes in Canada: the Canada Health and Social Transfer. This block grant will reduce the amount of federal funding to provincial programmes but will also reduce federal restrictions on how the money is spent. Although advocacy groups on the right support this reform, the political left remains strongly critical because they value national programme standards and do not want federal funding reduced.

Conclusion

As the Canadian government has created no explicit 'family policy', policies affecting families are embedded within the legislation or regulations of broader social or economic programmes. This means that any change to family policies necessarily requires reform to many economic and social programmes, including laws, taxation systems, and employment programmes. Like all public policies, the development and reform of policies affecting families have been influenced by changes in ideology, the efforts of various advocacy groups, and the structure of decision-making in Canada.

Family policies especially reflect changing ideologies concerning gender roles, the rights of parents and children, and who deserves government support. In early family policies, the patriarchal family was explicitly recognized as the basic institution of society, with all other family structures considered 'deviant'. Canadian law and policies have increasingly come to view marriage as an equal partnership between husband and wife, both of whom have equal responsibility for their children. Yet gender differences in socio-economic status and parental roles continue to influence parents' ability to support their children. While more mothers have entered the labour force in recent decades, they typically retain primary responsibility for home and child care, which influences their opportunities to earn a living.

Throughout the decades, children have gained greater protection from parental abuse and neglect, though Canadian governments have seen most family matters as outside government control. Within marriage, governments have usually viewed spousal support, childbirth, and child-rearing as private family responsibilities, although they have always regulated marriage, recorded births, marriages, divorces, and deaths, and protected children from severe physical abuse. Since World War II, governments have provided income assistance to families with children and to the elderly, but most social services for families have been targeted to those in need of protection or those unable to cope without assistance.

Since the 1980s, this targeting of family benefits and programmes has increased. The federal government is now focusing scarce resources on child poverty and abuse rather than on the well-being of all children, and on employability rather than job creation or improvements to income security programmes. The emphasis on efficiency, cost-effectiveness, and reliance on the market to create jobs continues despite a change in government from Conservative to Liberal.

In recent years, the political and moral right has encouraged the government to reduce the deficit, cut social programmes, tighten up work incentives, and renew support for 'family values'. The 'pro-family movement' has used the concept of 'family values' to express disapproval of legalized abortion, contraception, sex education, benefits for same-sex couples, and public child-care services. On the other hand, feminists and social reformers from the political left have viewed appeals to family values as contrary to gender equality and lifestyle choice.

The political left continues to argue that reducing high rates of unemployment is one of the most important family policy issues, as children are poor because their parents are underpaid, unemployed, or underemployed. Unemployment, low wages, and child poverty necessitate increased public expenditures on social programmes and reduce tax revenue. For this reason, governments retain an economic interest in assisting the poor and unemployed, as well as a moral obligation to reduce child and family poverty.

Feminists and reformers from the left have cautioned governments not to create *a* family policy, but rather social policies which view the individual rather than the family as the unit of society. Furthermore, they argue that there is no one type of family that the government should promote through policy. They note that most Canadians no longer live in nuclear families with husbands as breadwinners and wives as home-makers, and argue for policies that treat all family configurations equally and respect differences in the experiences of women and men (McDaniel, 1990). Feminists also argue that using gender-neutral language in policy must not mask the different social realities of men and women or confuse policy initiatives. Using the concept of 'lone-parent family', for example, could obscure the fact that most lone parents are mothers and that substantial socio-economic differences exist between lone fathers and lone mothers, as well as among lone-parent families created through widowhood, separation, divorce, or births outside marriage.

Because most family policy concerns fall under provincial jurisdiction, creating national programmes was always a complicated process, even requiring constitutional amendments in several cases in Canadian history. Since the 1980s, however, developing national programmes has become even more contentious with continuing disputes over jurisdiction and strong voices for decentralization. In fact, on some policy issues, provincial and federal governments are now working at cross-purposes. For example, while Quebec has been elaborating its family benefits to make them more generous for all parents, the federal government has been targeting benefits to middle- and lower-income families.

The Canadian government and several provincial governments have verbalized the importance of family as the basic institution in society. Politicians have reiterated that children should be viewed as a future resource to be preserved by eradicating poverty, abuse, and neglect. Governments across the country have ensured children's access to education and health care. They have reformed child welfare law and family law to ensure due process and equal responsibility by mothers and fathers in child custody and support. We cannot deny that serious attention has been paid to some aspects of family policy, yet governments have spent less effort and money improving leave for family responsibilities, providing child-care services, preventing family violence, creating jobs, or raising the incomes of poor families through tax benefits or transfer payments.

In comparison to certain European countries, many Canadian programmes for families with children are less generous (Baker, 1995; Phipps, 1995). In 1993, for example, Canada abolished the universal Family Allowance, which had been allowed to decline in value for years, and combined the funds with the child tax benefits to create a new targeted benefit. Canada's maternity benefits have strict eligibility requirements and replace less than 60% of previous wages compared to 80%–100% in many European countries.

Canada's child-care services are subsidized for low-income parents, but subsidized spaces are in short supply; many parents with higher incomes also need financial assistance with child care. The federal government allows working parents to deduct a portion of child-care expenses from their income tax if they obtain official receipts, but this tax deduction benefits only those using non-family caregivers who declare their earnings to the tax department, and benefits mainly those parents with higher incomes. Furthermore, parents are required to locate child-care services themselves. We know that lack of affordable child care keeps some parents out of the work-force and on welfare; for those who do have work, lack of adequate child care reduces their employment productivity and promotional opportunities. We also know that lack of access to early-childhood education may reduce the future opportunities of children. Yet the availability and quality of preschool education in Canada falls behind most European countries.

Until recently, child support enforcement procedures in most Canadian provinces left the onus and cost on custodial mothers and offered little assistance in locating the father and securing payment. A majority of fathers defaulted on their court-ordered support payments within a year after divorce, and almost half of lone mothers lived below the poverty line. Although the federal and provincial governments have been discussing enforcement procedures and support guidelines for several years, only a few provinces have implemented new procedures, and considerable judicial discretion continues in support awards. Because child support enforcement is provincial jurisdiction, the federal government cannot create a national system or even force the provinces to create their own.

Provincial child welfare systems tend to be reactive to complaints and overburdened with cases of child abuse. Most clients are living in poverty, and many are lone mothers caring for their children with minimal support from fathers or governments. Some of these mothers are victims of abuse themselves, but child welfare systems in some provinces are mandated to deal only with children rather than the entire family. Even when the entire family is an agency concern, scarce resources limit intervention. Although we know that pro-active community-based services are more effective in reducing family crises and poverty (Wharf, 1993b), Canadians have been unwilling to pay for them in higher taxes or by shifting spending priorities.

Federal expenditures on social programmes for families have certainly increased over the years. Expenditures on Family Allowances increased from $172.6 million when it began in 1945 to $2.65 billion in 1989–90. Federal expenditures on all cash benefits for children were over $5 billion in 1989–90, nearly double the amount from ten years before. Federal maternity benefits reached $657.5 million in 1989–90, while the Quebec newborn allowance cost $110 million. Federal contributions to provincial welfare services amounted to $1.2 billion in 1989–90, up from $22 million in 1968–69, while contributions for child care increased from $4 million in 1971–72 to $290.7 million in 1991–92.

Yet social spending as a percentage of gross domestic product has not increased so dramatically. Social spending, including health care, unemployment insurance, family transfers, disability pensions and services, and old-age pensions (but excluding education) in 1981 comprised 15.3% of GDP (Kerans, 1990), but by 1990 had reached 18.8% of GDP (Smith, 1994: A6).

Explaining the Development of Canadian Family Policies

In searching for explanations for the 'chilly climate' of child-rearing and family life in Canada, we cannot focus solely on economic trends such as the cost of social programmes or the need for global competitiveness. Other countries have also experienced increases in social expenditures and changing labour market trends, yet have maintained a more 'child-friendly' climate. Instead, we must turn to a combination of political, demographic, and economic factors to explain the development of Canadian family policies.

Despite the fact that the Co-operative Commonwealth Federation/New Democratic Party (CCF/NDP) has been most supportive of strong social programmes, Canadians have never given this political party a majority at the federal level. Instead, they have elected relatively conservative governments which have not emphasized the importance of a redistribution of wealth, gender equality, or improved child and family services. The trade union movement has been relatively weak in Canada and has not created an effective alliance with any political party that has ever won a federal election. In addition, Canada's political structures, especially federalism and the division of powers between federal and provincial governments, have not encouraged rapid policy change. Instead, they have led to disputes, protracted negotiations, and limited reform. Canadian decision-making structures have sidelined many of the interest groups which support improved family policies.

Because Canada has been divided by regional, language, and cultural issues, finding consensus on social policy has been challenging. Further, Canadian women have been less involved in political decision-making than have women in countries such as Sweden and The Netherlands. Only now that women have become more involved in Canadian public life (including the labour force, unions, and government) have policy options for child care, family leave, and child support enforcement been discussed seriously in a public forum. Yet the legal system still emphasizes individual rights rather than group rights or collective responsibility.

Canadians, like their neighbours to the south, have been unwilling to pay taxes as high as Europeans have been paying in return for better social programmes and services. Yet Canadians have paid higher income taxes than Americans and have developed social insurance programmes patterned after Britain's. Economic ties with the US remain strong, however, which creates strong pressure for comparable wages, interest rates, and employment conditions. Unemployment in Canada has historically surpassed the rate in the US, however, and Canada's relatively high unemployment has counteracted the effect of government programmes to keep families out of poverty.

Demographic trends can also help to explain the lack of explicit family policy in Canada. After the Second World War, Canada's substantial baby boom averted any concerns over population decline, as were felt overseas. In addition, the population has remained young through immigration, while Europe has experienced considerable emigration, especially among young people. These trends inhibited the formation of advocacy groups pushing for pro-natalist policies to encourage child-bearing and family formation. Consequently, Canada has never adopted an explicit population policy except through relatively high immigration targets.

Social changes are apparent in Canada that are leading to increased political pressure to reform family policies. Women's labour force participation has grown, especially among mothers with young children. Numerous lobby groups have formed to advocate extensions to parental leave, the development of statutory leave for family responsibilities, and improved child-care facilities. These groups have increased government awareness of the conflicts, especially for mothers, between earning a living and raising children. They have also enjoyed some success in influencing policies.

A larger percentage of women now graduate from universities and have entered professions such as politics, economics, law, policy research, and government administration, providing articulate leadership for the feminist movement, especially for groups focusing on legal changes. At the same time, however, the conservative pro-family and fathers' rights movements have also been effective in their lobbying efforts.

The birth rate has been declining for years, and at least one provincial government has responded with more government supports for families raising children. Yet family policy reform in Quebec has been motivated largely by nationalism and the fear that a decline in the Francophone population will reduce Quebec's power in the federation.

The rising cost of family poverty, especially within lone-mother families, is now placing economic and political pressure on all levels of government. Instead of dealing with adult poverty, however, the federal government has targeted 'child poverty' for its policy initiatives. This focus on children allows for greater public sympathy and for programmes to be centred on children's services rather than the parents' low wages, unemployment, and underemployment. In addition, the Canadian government continues to focus on the concept of 'employability' in social assistance and labour force programmes, which sidelines any discussion of job creation or improvements to income security. Child welfare and anti-poverty groups have united to improve income security, social services, and the well-being of all families with children. Although this coalition is becoming more powerful, lobbying remains strong from employers' groups and the political right to reduce government spending.

Canada

Despite the growing pressures to formalize family policies, different groups are pushing governments in opposite directions. The strongest voices appear to be those arguing for reduced taxes, smaller government, social spending cuts, more work incentives, and greater provincial autonomy. Although unemployment rates remain high, income security and social benefits are already becoming more restricted. The unemployed are encouraged to accept low-paid temporary jobs or are forced to move onto provincial social assistance. At the same time, provincial governments are tightening eligibility rules for their programmes.

In the future, Canada will continue to support programmes for families with children, but these programmes will probably be targeted at lower-income groups or at those experiencing more serious family problems. As Canada becomes more decentralized, the possibility of creating new national programmes for children will diminish. Instead, provincial programmes will become even more divergent, and some programmes that used to be offered by government will be provided by voluntary organizations or families.

Notes

1. A status Indian is an indigenous person registered by the Canadian government under the Indian Act and subject to the responsibilities and benefits of that legislation. A Métis is part French-Canadian and part indigenous, and a non-status Indian is unregistered and not covered by the Indian Act.

2. The poverty line is defined by Statistics Canada's Low Income Cut-Offs (LICOs), which vary by community and family size as well as average income.

3. As in most countries, incest laws prevent marriages between members of a nuclear family, including step-family members.

4. Unless otherwise noted, all figures cited in this section are based on authors' calculations using the Luxemburg Income Study.

5. Throughout the text, trends are described for the longest period, post-1960, for which data are available.

6. For example, in 1992, UI maternity benefits comprised about 4.3% of total UI benefits, parental benefits were 2.6%, and adoption benefits were less than 0.03% of total UI benefits paid in Canada (Human Resources and Development Canada, 1993, cited in Routhier and Labowka, 1994, Appendix D).

7. Unless otherwise noted, all figures cited in this section are authors' calculations using the Luxemburg Income Study.

8. Families are counted as poor if gross equivalent family income is less than 50% of median equivalent family income. This approach differs slightly from the methodology employed in the Statistics Canada Low Income Cut-Offs, but the two measures give qualitatively similar estimates (see Sharif and Phipps, 1994).

9. Thus, the Canadian report differs slightly from the format followed for other countries.

10. This period of time was extremely important for establishing the foundations of the Canadian welfare state since family allowances followed shortly after the establishment of a national UI programme, which has historically been very important for Canadian families.

11. For example, the credit rose from $384 per child in 1985, to $454 in 1986, to $489 in 1987, and to $524 in 1988 (National Council of Welfare, 1987b: 14).

12. The ceiling depends on the number of children in the family. For example, in 1991, a single parent with one child was eligible as long as employment income did not exceed $18,897. The ceiling also varies with child-care expenses claimed. See Hess, 1992.

13. An individual can be classified as employable even when unemployment rates are so high that there are actually no jobs available.

14. Exceptions to this are found in Manitoba, Nova Scotia, and Ontario, the provinces in which a 'two-tiered' welfare programme is in place. A claimant's residency status determines the municipality to which he or she applies for assistance.

15. The term 'First Nations' is typically used for groups of Aboriginal persons who feel that they are capable of self-government.

Appendix A

CHRONOLOGY OF LEGAL CHANGES RELATING TO FAMILIES

1872   Married Women's Property Act (Ontario) allows women to retain their earnings and property after marriage.

1884   Factories Act (Ontario) provides health and safety regulations and restrictions on female and child labour.

1891   First Children's Aid Society is established in Canada (Toronto).

1893   Children's Protection Act in Ontario.

1910   British Columbia grants mothers equal rights to custody over children.

1918   Income Tax Act creates deductions for taxpayers with dependent spouses and children.

1918   Women win right to vote in federal elections.

1925   Grounds for divorce are equalized for men and women.

1940   Unemployment Insurance Program is created.

1945   Family Allowance first paid to mothers with children under 16.

1964   Quebec is the last province to allow mothers equal child custody rights.

1966   The Canada Assistance Plan allows for federal/provincial cost-sharing of social assistance and social services (including child-care subsidies for low-income parents).

1968   Divorce Act, 1968, expands grounds for divorce, adding 'marital separation'.

1969   'Therapeutic' abortions, contraception, and homosexuality between consenting adults are legalized.

1971   Maternity Benefits first paid through the Unemployment Insurance Program.

1971   Child Care Expenses Deduction (from federal income tax) is created.

1985   Adoptive parents gain Adoption Benefits under the Unemployment Insurance Program.

1985   Divorce Act, 1985, reduces time period to one year to obtain a 'no-fault' divorce.

1988   The Child Care Act, which would have removed child-care funding from welfare legislation, fails to pass in Parliament.

1989   Members of Parliament resolve to eliminate child poverty by year 2000.

1990   Parental Benefits are added to Unemployment Insurance Benefits.

1993   The Child Tax Benefit is created by combining money from Family Allowance and the child tax credits.

1995   The Supreme Court of Canada rules in the Thibaudeau case that asking custodial parents to pay income tax on child support received is not a violation of the Canadian Charter of Rights and Freedoms.

1996   The Finance Minister announces that parents paying child support will no longer receive a tax deduction, and parents receiving child support will not be required to pay income tax on this support. The new ruling applies only to new court awards or agreements effective May 1997.

Appendix B

1918   Income Tax Act introduces tax exemptions for families with children.

1943   Marsh Report outlines recommendations for social security in Canada.

1944   Family Allowances (FA) Act passed, granting universal cash benefits to all Canadian families with children under 16.

1945   FA Act comes into effect; first FA cheques mailed to Canadian families with children in July 1945.

1947   Child Tax Deduction for families with children.

1949   Government repeals clause which provided lower benefits for fifth and subsequent children. Waiting period for immigrant families to receive benefits reduced from three years to one year.

1956   Introduction of Family Assistance Program to aid immigrant families with child expenses; in effect until 1973.

1964   Youth Allowances Act passed, extending eligibility for receipt of family allowance benefits to children under 18 in school attendance.

1972   Child Care Expense Deduction introduced.

1973   Family Allowances Act passed; major restructuring of programme: monthly benefits increased, extended eligibility by eliminating stipulation on school attendance, more authority given to provinces in formulation of family allowance policy, family allowance benefits become taxable, family allowance benefits indexed annually to account for inflation. Immigrant children generally eligible until landed immigrant status granted.

1974   Family Allowances Act comes into effect.

1977   Introduction of $50 income-tested non-refundable Child Tax Credit. Families with income less than $26,000 eligible.

1978   Major reforms to Family Allowance Program in an effort to achieve distributive goals: monthly benefits slashed by 23%, replacement of $50 non-refundable Child Tax Credit by $200 income-tested Refundable Child Tax Credit. Parents who do not claim child-care expenses eligible for supplement to tax credit.

1979   Reforms of 1978 come into effect.

1982   Full indexation of family allowances eliminated; only inflation over 3% per year is accounted for.

1988   Replacement of child tax exemptions by credits. Introduction of new Non-Refundable Child Tax Credit and Equivalent-to-Married Credit, which can be claimed by single parents.

1989   Clawback of family allowance benefits to higher-income families.

1993   New Child Tax Benefit implemented; amalgamates family allowances and tax credits. No tax credits for families with children, except for the child-care expense deduction, and Equivalent-to-Married credit for single parents. Eliminates monthly family allowance cheques, ends universality in the Canadian system of income security for families. Intended to target lower-income families, consolidate benefits system, and supplement earned income.

Family Change and Family Policies: New Zealand

Ian Shirley
Peggy Koopman-Boyden
Ian Pool
Susan St. John

Introduction: An Historical Review

Over the last century across the developed western countries, patterns of family formation have undergone radical changes, above all in terms of levels of fertility. This shift in family formation has accompanied major changes in the organization and structures of core and extended families. Moreover, the links to the broader society, particularly through the need to support families, have been a central concern of social policy. New Zealand has escaped none of these trends. In fact in many ways its patterns and values fit closely with those of the other 'neo-Europes' (Crosby, 1986), particularly Anglophone Canada and Australia.

In other respects New Zealand's population of 3.5 million persons has followed a distinctive path, in part a function of its very different post-colonial history. The starting point for any analysis of New Zealand society is that all New Zealanders are 'boat people'. The first arrivals from the Pacific, the Maori, were followed centuries later by a wave of migrants primarily from Europe, particularly after New Zealand's cession to the British Crown through the Treaty of Waitangi in 1840. More recently these major groups have been joined by 'plane people', drawn predominantly from Polynesia and Asia. By the 1991 census, 80% of New Zealanders were of European descent (called Pakeha), 13% were Maori, 5% Pacific Island Polynesians, and most of the rest Asian, particularly from the east and southeast. Most New Zealanders are Christian, although a significant and growing minority report no religious affiliation. Among Christians, most are Protestant, while the proportion that is Catholic falls far below the levels recorded in Australia and Canada.

Family policy in New Zealand must therefore deal with two major and several minor socio-cultural traditions of family formation and organization, which have confronted each other since first Maori/Pakeha contact in the late eighteenth century (Koopman-Boyden and Scott, 1984). Pakeha voyagers to this country encountered a complex set of indigenous Maori structures and traditions, the central principle of which was genealogy. These cultural practices were reinforced by complex ambilateral patterns of inheritance, adoption, and kinship, details of which were registered through highly formalized oral traditions. This form of organization did not wither under the impact of European settlement. It was sustained in the face of colonialism, a high level of intermarriage, and the imposition of a completely alien system of formal organizations, structures, norms, and social policies. Moreover, it was maintained in spite of the absence of native reservations of the form seen in North America, which had the effect of isolating indigenous people from the wider society.

Even in the early colonial period, Maori had access to services such as colonial hospitals (Thomson, 1859) and in legislative terms they were granted full rights of

210   *New Zealand*

citizenship. In 1867 Maori men received the full franchise before Pakeha males, the first men anywhere to achieve this right, and in 1893 Maori women joined Pakeha in gaining universal suffrage. Apart from the alienation of land, there was never a policy of formal, systematic discrimination against Maori (although there was discrimination against Asians, similar in form to that in Australia, Canada, and the United States).

From colonization until World War II, the Maori population was clustered mainly in remote rural areas in the northern third of the country. Their economic base during this time shifted gradually from semi-subsistence and unskilled or seasonal jobs to pastoral farming, on which the country's exports depended. The situation of the Maori changed rapidly with very accelerated rural migration in the 1950s and 1960s, one of the more rapid such movements on record (Pool, 1991). Today three-quarters of Maori are urban, yet even in the 1990s, the distinct traditions of *whanau* (family), sub-tribal, and tribal organizations (*hapu* and *iwi*) still play a major role in the transactions between the state and many groups within the Maori population. This is as true for broader political questions, such as compensation for land alienated since 1840, as it is in terms of family policies and services.

FIGURE 1. Maori and non-Maori total fertility rates, New Zealand 1843–1992*

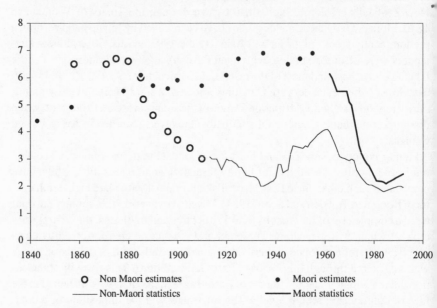

O Non Maori estimates			• Maori estimates	
—— Non-Maori statistics			—— Maori statistics	

* Non-Maori rates estimated for census years; for 1858 and 1878 estimates made for this report using Rele's technique, see Pool, op. cit., passim, adjusting age groups by linear interpolation, assuming e(o)=40 years and 50 years. Maori rates estimated for various years.

Sources: Gibson, C. (1971). *Demographic History of New Zealand.* Berkeley: University of California (Unpublished doctoral thesis), 199. Pool, I. (1991). *Te Iwi Maori.* Auckland: Auckland University Press, Tables 5.3, 6.2.

The most significant change to Maori families has been their recent reproductive revolution, as shown in Figure 1. From first colonization in 1840, Maori family sizes (as measured by total fertility rates) appear to have increased a little, for what were specific biosocial reasons, and then to have remained high until the 1960s. At that stage a decrease commenced and then accelerated, becoming in the 1970s the most rapid decline for a population anywhere (Pool, 1991). Today levels of Maori reproduction are just above replacement. Although Maori teenage and young adult fertility has decreased, the declines at older ages (25+) have been so radical that much of childbearing is at younger ages, a factor which affects all other aspects of family dynamics and structures. Family policies, even in recent times, have failed to address this demographic reality (Jackson and Pool, in press).

The social system, which after contact and particularly after colonization was to become the dominant form for much of New Zealand's legislation and policy, drew its values and structures from British society of that time. From the outset of its colonial history a persistent element of social policy has been the recruitment and settlement of waves of immigrants (Oliver, 1988) with inflows reaching their highest level, both relatively and absolutely, in the Vogel Ministry in the 1870s, when the settlement of land acquired from Maori and 'public works' such as road construction and forest clearance were the key policy instruments. Favoured migrants were respectable working-class and middle-class families or marriageable single persons. Their Victorian and Protestant values, mainly of British origin (infused by Northern Europeans during the Vogel period), have affected both popular attitudes and public policy over much of the period since then. These 'European' migrants established small rural settlements modelled on the nineteenth-century English village and based on the colony's natural resources of coal, timber, kauri gum, and gold. As native bush was cleared from the land, grassland farming was established and the foundations were laid for New Zealand's highly productive and scientific approach to pastoral farming (Shirley, 1982). As a result, for much of its post-colonial history New Zealand has been dependent on pastoral sector exports, yet paradoxically it is an urban culture based around low-density suburbs, even today composed of detached single-family houses on large allotments.

From the first phase of colonization, major differences emerged between Pakeha family life and that of their cousins in the United Kingdom. Above all, these differences were manifested in the most favourable levels of life expectation reported at that time, and in particularly high levels of fertility (Figure 1), two births per woman more than that recorded for Great Britain. This differential was produced by a number of factors, but most notably the early and almost universal marriage of the colonists, a behaviour pattern which differed from the British. The high levels of reproduction in that early period, reinforced by those of the baby boom after World War II, laid down the pro-natalist, child-orientated values of Pakeha society (Sceats, 1988a) and the ethos of family services which followed (see Chapter 4). A rapid switch between 1875 and 1900 to British nuptial patterns (late marriage and significant levels of spinsterhood) resulted in a very rapid decline in fertility to three births per woman. This was associated with further rapid decreases in mortality, particularly among children, a trend that occurred in the absence of effective bio-medical practices or an adequate health system (Pool, 1994). The decrease further strengthened the prevalent attitude that, by comparison with urban industrial Europe, New Zealand was 'a great place to raise children'. The increasing use of barrier contraceptives within marriage saw fertility decline more slowly to reach replacement in the 1930s.

From 1943, Pakeha New Zealanders, like other western populations, threw themselves into a baby boom, which was to endure longer (thirty years), to reach higher levels, and to be more intense in terms of the spacing of births than in any of the other countries in this volume (Sceats, 1981). The very high incidence of early marriage mirrored what had occurred in the pioneer period a century earlier, but in the baby boom it was frequently precipitated by premarital conception or followed immediately by post-marital pregnancy. The timing of first births, particularly the historically high levels of teenage pregnancy peaking at the end of the boom in 1971, was also noteworthy.

Viewed over the period since 1875, the baby boom seems an aberrant phenomenon, yet it has had two major residual effects. Firstly, the precipitate marriages at young ages of this era were more likely than others to be dissolved. Secondly, the current crop of policy-makers were parents of the baby boom, particularly at the end when teenage pregnancy and precipitate marriage rates were so high. Their views about reproduction, notably concerns over apparent declines in the frequency of two-parent families or recent trends of sub-replacement fertility, were probably shaped by their own experiences in that peculiar period—yet it is the behavioural norms of that era which are often held up as a desirable model (Pool, in press).

In the 1970s, in common with most western developed countries, total fertility rates dropped to sub-replacement levels, which was associated with a major shift upwards in the peak ages of childbearing. In New Zealand the family formation patterns of the current group of new parents closely resembles that of the most conservative maternal cohort this century, the parents of the 1920s/30s economic depression. These changes in fertility patterns have taken place alongside shifts away from the family structure prevalent in the baby boom. Changes include, most notably, a decline in the proportion of families with two parents and increases in non-parenting households and mother-only families. These shifts are often portrayed as indicators of a decay in family life and even as potentially threatening the foundations of society. In reality, these changes are more a function of other demographic changes, particularly the shifts in family formation just noted, than of societal dysfunction.

FAMILY POLICY

Given these demographic realities, one of the central questions which this study aims to address is how well family policy has responded to a changing environment. In the first place, the *ad hoc* services that evolved from the early colonial period dealt mainly, but not exclusively, with the Pakeha family. For the most part these policy provisions and services shared certain common features with the Northern European tradition. One of its first manifestations was the 1877 Education Act which paralleled developments in other countries and facilitated access to primary and secondary education for the vast majority of Maori and Pakeha children. But by the turn of the century New Zealand had developed its own distinctive set of economic and social policies which were fashioned less by ideology than by pragmatism and serendipity (Shirley, 1991). As a 'new' society New Zealand had no established aristocracy or landless peasantry, and as a result the working class sought tangible benefits from the state in the form of wage and employment security. Similarly, small-business interests such as farmers and manufacturers relied on the state for economic security which took the form of protection from overseas competition and regular adjustments to the labour market by means of controlled immigration. It was this distinctive approach to social policy which led Lord Asquith, the English Liberal leader, to describe the country as a social laboratory 'made for the information and instruction of the older countries of the world' (Sinclair, 1980: 187). Based essentially on three major periods of radical policy formation, New Zealand's reputation as a social laboratory has endured to the present day.

In the nineteenth century, the radical policy initiatives centred on legislation such as the 1893 Act granting universal suffrage to women (the first country in the world to do so) and the 1894 Industrial Conciliation and Arbitration Act, which attracted overseas scholars to these shores to study the concept of a basic minimum wage. Four years later the New Zealand parliament passed the world's first Old Age Pensions Act, and in 1900, spurred by the threat of bubonic plague in neighbouring Australia, the Public Health Act set down a comprehensive health system that was to endure until the late 1980s. These policy changes had direct and indirect impacts on society, as for example in reinforcing New Zealand's already favoured position in terms of life expectation (Pool, 1993).

The second phase of radical policy formation was initiated by the first Labour government in the wake of the Great Depression. At the centre of Labour's innovative programme in the 1930s was the 1938 Social Security Act which established the most comprehensive social security system in the world at that time (International Labour Office (ILO), 1949). The concept of a social wage underpinned the various provisions of the Act, and thus policy initiatives in areas such as health were not limited to the treatment of the sick, but rather to the creation of a social environment in which individuals and families might live healthy and productive lives (Hanson, 1980). This broader integrated approach to economic and social policy established one of the most successful welfare states of the post-war period with an unparalleled record of full employment and one of the highest living standards in the industrialized world. It was a record that was maintained for more than three decades (Shirley, 1993).

Subsequent social policy initiatives followed this general philosophy thereby reinforcing the country's reputation for innovation. The 1958 and 1964 Family Benefits (Home Ownership) Acts, provided 'family benefits [which could] be capitalised and paid in advance to assist parents with the erection or purchase of house properties', (Department of Statistics, 1980: 154). In the event, this seemingly pro-natalist legislation was inversely related to fertility levels, suggesting, at least in the New Zealand context, that incentives to increase fertility are not likely to have a significant impact. In the 1970s, the introduction of Accident Compensation leg-islation was lauded as 'a landmark in the development of the welfare state' (Bryn Mawr, 1978) and was followed by a series of important acts which were to have a major impact on family policy. These acts encompassed the status of children born ex-nuptially (eliminating illegitimacy as a status); guardianship and custody; mar-riage and divorce; matrimonial property; support for sole parents; equal pay for women; and abortion, contraception, and sterilization (Cartwright, 1985).

Since 1985, New Zealand has once again been promoted as a model for the industrialized world, but the radical changes of this period are very different from their antecedents. The earlier accolades were based on New Zealand's reputation for domestic compensation (Castles, 1988), but today they stem from the acceler-ated programme of economic liberalization introduced in the 1980s and followed in the 1990s by an overt set of policies aimed at 'dismantling' the welfare state. These programmes have had a major impact on the well-being of many families, as will be shown in later chapters. As a consequence, economic restructuring has overshadowed other interesting, sometimes innovative, legislative changes in a number of areas pertinent to this study, such as sex education in schools and the care and protection of children.

These dramatic shifts in economic and social policy have often been misinter-preted, largely because those both prescribing and reviewing public policy have failed to understand the distinctive nature of New Zealand's welfare state arrange-ments (Castles, 1985; Shirley, 1993). Whereas the Western European and Scandinavian countries based their welfare states on extensive systems of income maintenance and social insurance, the organizing principles of the New Zealand system centred on the industrial court that arbitrated between employer and em-ployee and established wage rates that would give the worker a decent living ac-cording to the colonial standard. The wage structure, and in particular the concept of a 'fair wage', enabled a man 'to maintain a wife and three children in a fair and reasonable standard of comfort' (Woods, 1963). This concept of a 'family wage' was at the centre of New Zealand's post-war development, and in that sense it comes closest to what might be defined as family policy.

The family wage not only established a minimum income for the majority of households, it also protected wage rates and conditions and included provisions for sickness leave and overtime. As these provisions were extended by the first Labour government in the 1930s, the family wage was complemented by the state in the provision of generally free primary and secondary education, a community-based preventive health scheme, a salaried medical service, a free public hospital system, and a state housing programme for those who could not afford a home of their own. Those outside the wage structure (or with special needs) had access to a selective benefit system accompanied often, it should be said, by moral judgements distinguishing between the 'deserving' and 'undeserving' poor. While the components of the family wage were extensive by any international measure, New Zealand's approach to 'undeserving' beneficiaries has always been rather punitive, and this is particularly true of the current political environment. For a large part of the post-war period, however, the country maintained an exceptional record of full employment, and thus until the last decade or so there were few so-called 'undeserving beneficiaries'.

NEW ZEALAND FAMILY AND SOCIAL POLICY IN THE 1990s

These, then, have been some of the longer-term changes in family structure and social policy which have moulded the contemporary situation. By adopting an historical approach, it is possible to establish the philosophy, conditions, and forces that have shaped patterns of family policy over time. Whereas the earlier patterns that promoted New Zealand's international reputation as a social laboratory were driven by the pragmatic concerns of a small society on the periphery of the global economy, the radical reforms of the past two decades have been dominated by the imported ideology of the New Right. These initiatives were often imposed without accurate consideration of longer-term demographic trends and realities. Social policy reforms were often implemented without consultation and on occasion in apparent ignorance of the social and cultural context into which they were being injected.

The most graphic illustration of this form of policy-making can be found in the sweeping social reforms of 1991, which were introduced in a one-hour budget speech, the contents of which had been protected by the secrecy of the budgetary process. Although some of these initiatives proved to be unworkable even in the short term, they were passed into law on budget night without any effective opposition. The reason for this lies in New Zealand's unicameral Parliament: in contrast to other social democracies, which maintain checks and balances on the policy process, the first past-the-post electoral system operating in this country effectively gives the state executive sweeping powers. These powers are likely to be modified in the near future with the introduction of proportional representation, but until such time as that occurs the state executive will continue to dominate the policy process.

A second issue arising out of recent reforms concerns the population on which restructuring was imposed. Whereas small Western European states have been able to combine economic liberalization and domestic compensation (Katzenstein, 1985), New Zealand has effectively abandoned the form of family policy which made it so successful during the post-war period. To some extent the political choices made were conditioned by the pressures of the global economy and New Zealand's economic vulnerability; in other respects, domestic factors have been persuasive, both in shaping the post-war consensus and in detaching New Zealand from that consensus in the late 1980s (see Chapter 5).

For some individuals, the reforms of the past decade have created new freedoms as well as greater choices and opportunities, but for others, income and living standards have declined significantly. In contrast to the principles of 'belonging' and 'participating' as articulated by the 1972 Royal Commission on Social Security, the devaluation of the family wage has increased social inequities and effectively disenfranchised a significant section of the population. Within this second tier of society, families with children have become particularly vulnerable. The following analysis will trace these developments, beginning with the demographic patterns that have evolved since the advent of 'European' settlement in the nineteenth century.

1

The Formation of Families

Over the last 150 years, the most extensive changes to the family have come from demographic transitions in fertility and family formation. These produced the shift, shown in Figure 1, from the large families of the past to the small families of today. Accompanying changes in size and in strategies of family formation were shifts in family and household structures, some a direct consequence of the wider demographic transitions of New Zealand's major ethnic groups, which will be briefly described below.

Others resulted, however, from changes in societal norms relating to family organization, particularly as these govern the roles, forms, and functions of conjugal unions and families of procreation: for example, the relationships between reproduction and nuptiality, or between the legal status and the cultural legitimacy of conjugal unions. Thus this chapter looks in detail at changes in family size and structure as well as associated demographic and social factors.

We cannot attempt to explain these changes or to comment on the matrix of values and attitudes within which they have taken place. This is because, in contrast to colleagues in Australia, North America, and Western Europe, the New Zealand researcher is handicapped by the lack of micro-sociological information (Pool, 1992). New Zealand has few data beyond the conventional official sources, the census and vital statistics, and no national surveys. Most official information is of a high quality, some such as statistics on abortion extraordinarily so, but all are restricted in terms of content. For example, the major source, the quinquennial census, which covers families and households, asked questions on fertility only in 1911, 1945 ('married' Maori women only), 1971, and 1981. Analysts using data on families and households face varying and major conceptual and interpretational problems. All these statistics are subject to problems relating to the definitions of ethnicity, and these difficulties interact with those encountered with family/household data. That said, New Zealand researchers have conducted detailed reviews of the sources and quality of these data.

THE DEMOGRAPHIC CONTEXT OF FAMILY STRUCTURAL CHANGES

At the time of contact with Europeans, Maori were 'an isolated and relatively diseaseless people', and thus probably had levels of life expectancy at birth exceeding those of most 'Europeans, perhaps the least isolated people on earth'

(Crosby, 1986: 232; Pool, 1991). Expectancies then declined to very low levels, particularly after the Treaty of Waitangi (1840), so that by 1890 their numbers had decreased to 40% of the pre-contact size. The Treaty opened the way for land alienation, through confiscation during the Land Wars of the 1840s and 1860s and more importantly through purchase. This permitted the accelerated spread of European settlement and thus the exposure of Maori to new diseases and the breakdown of their traditional social order. Fears that 'the race' might disappear were frequently expressed at that time, and the need to procreate so as to restore the demographic balance (a sort of 'revenge of the cradles' as this attitude used to be called in Quebec), is still occasionally commented on today when numbers are ten times what they were in 1900. The view among some Victorian Pakeha (New Zealanders of European descent) that Maori 'had lost the will to procreate' was demographically incorrect, for fertility rates appear to have edged up after contact. The reasons are complex, but most notably it seems that because of new protein-rich dietary sources, foetal survivorship could improve, once Maori had also spontaneously gained some degree of immunity against newly-introduced, and thus virulent, strains of the common venereal diseases, particularly gonorrhoea.

From the Maori 'renaissance' of the 1890s, primarily generated by Sir James Carroll, a Maori who was a minister in the Liberal Cabinet, the population decline halted and recuperation set in. By the end of the nineteenth century total fertility rates had reached six births per woman. Between then and 1960 this rate gradually increased to just under seven births.

From levels of life expectancy in the range 20–25 years at birth at the end of the nineteenth century, there was a significant improvement to 30–35 years early in this century, mainly because of a primary health-care programme in which Maori medical graduates played an important role. The level gradually moved up to around 48 years at the end of the Second World War, and from 1945 until 1961, the implementation of an efficient health policy saw Maori life expectancy increase very significantly. A major factor (contributing 50% of the decrease) was the successful programme against tuberculosis.

Over the period during which estimates can be made (the 1840s until 1960), Maori fertility remained relatively high. Many of the props for this were very much as might be expected: low levels of infant and childhood survivorship, little resort to birth control and abortion, and early and almost universal marriage. Unions were legitimated according to customary practices and often involved a church wedding, but equally often may not have been registered. Thus throughout the period for which data are available, a high proportion of Maori babies (1990, 73%) were born 'ex-nuptially' in a strictly legal sense, even to women near the end of their reproductive span who would have been in long-standing unions, but this in no way indicated a lack of legitimacy in the eyes of the Maori community. All of these behaviour patterns were reinforced by a value system that saw children as the means of sustaining extended families (*whanau*) and lineage groups (*hapu*). Child-adoption was easily and informally realized and strongly encouraged for a wide range of reasons, but did not involve the total separation of the child from its biological parents. Indeed, most remarkably, pro-natalist cultural values were retained in the face of both very high levels of intermarriage with the lower-fertility Pakeha population, and, from the late nineteenth century, free and compulsory attendance in a school system which primarily instilled Pakeha norms. In the last two decades, as will be elaborated below, this picture has changed dramatically. Maori fertility has dropped almost to replacement, and Maori family structures have changed radically, with Maori families seemingly overrepresented among sole parents. These historical trends are of major importance for family structures today, for Maori couples in their forties or older were parents when fertility was much higher, yet see their own children now bearing only two or three children. Moreover, the frame of reference of senior Maori policy-makers is to a large degree derived from their own experiences before fertility declines were well under way.

Pakeha demographic patterns deviated from those of their British antecedents almost immediately after colonization (Cameron, 1990; Gibson, 1971; Jackson and Pool, 1994; Khawaja, 1985; Koopman-Boyden and Scott, 1984; O'Neill, 1985; Pool, 1985; Sceats, 1981 and 1988a; Sceats and Pool, 1985a and b). The high masculinity ratios among the settlers encouraged very early and almost universal marriage among Pakeha women, and thus high natality rates. These nuptiality patterns were also facilitated by the availability of land for farming, which meant that rules of primogeniture were no longer necessary. As the settlers were overwhelmingly Protestant, escape into celibate female religious orders was also not an option. Thus, until late in the century, whereas British women were having around five children, the 'New Zealanders' were having between six and seven (see Figure 1). Moreover, the first available life-tables show that Pakeha early achieved high levels of survivorship: the first-ever national population to reach 60 years' life expectancy at birth were Pakeha women (1901).

In the late nineteenth century Pakeha reproduction went through a very significant decline, from a total fertility rate of just under seven live births per woman in the 1870s to just over three at the start of the twentieth century. The mechanisms involved were primarily a shift upwards in the age at marriage and an increase in the proportion of women remaining celibate, but by the 1890s resort to barrier contraception and abortion to limit births within marriage may have become more widespread. An interesting side-effect of the accelerated fertility decline in the late nineteenth century was a rapid decrease in infant and childhood mortality well before the founding of a voluntary agency dedicated to this purpose, and before the introduction of systematic public measures to improve child survivorship (for example, the 1900 Public Health Act).

The declines in Pakeha fertility continued at a slower pace in the early twentieth century, mainly because of fertility regulation within marriages. By the depression years of the 1930s reproduction was just at replacement, and childbearing was delayed, being concentrated at ages 25–34, exactly the same conservative family formation strategy being followed by the generation of young New Zealanders at peak childbearing ages in the 1990s. Nevertheless, unlike some of their European peers, so far this century every New Zealand generation has replaced itself. Mortality declines continued in the twentieth century, but in a decelerated way, so that Pakeha New Zealanders gradually ceded rank in terms of life expectancy to European welfare states.

It is also worth noting that the period from just before World War I until the 1930s saw another aspect of family formation which was to disappear in the baby boom: women and couples achieved a wide range of family sizes, from celibacy (typically women who opted to stay in the labour force) and no children, to the larger families that are selectively remembered by present generations.

From about 1943, and through the heyday of the welfare state to the early 1970s, Pakeha New Zealand enthusiastically underwent its 'baby boom', which, as was true elsewhere in developed countries, was as much a 'marriage boom' as a baby boom. In New Zealand's case it took the form of a radical re-adoption of pioneer patterns of family formation: early and almost universal marriage and childbearing for women. Most fertile couples had one or two children, so that there were very low levels of childlessness by comparison with previous generations, and once again the society was dominated by strongly pro-natalist and pro-familist values and by a cult of domesticity that depended on gendered divisions of labour. The Pakeha baby boom was distinguished from those of many other western countries by higher-parity childbearing, producing a peak baby-boom total fertility rate (around 1960) of above four births per woman, and even a completed family size for the leading baby-boom maternal cohorts (born around 1931) above 3.5 births.

Levels of teenage fertility also reached historic highs in this era, very frequently taking the form of premarital conception followed by a precipitated marriage and a nuptial birth, then another pregnancy soon thereafter. By 1971, when adolescent fertility levels peaked, ex-nuptial conception was increasingly being followed by a birth outside registered marriage. Finally, both timing of first pregnancy and spacing between it and subsequent ones were more accelerated and intense than in Canada or Australia.

For Pakeha, therefore, the very large nuclear family of pioneer days, often cut off by the process of migration from kin in Europe, had ceded place to the smaller family of the inter-war years, then switched back to the somewhat larger nuclear unit of the baby boom. Throughout all these years reproduction was overwhelmingly within registered marriage, so that entry to marriage was itself a key means of fertility regulation. Thus fertility was higher when marriage was universal and at younger ages, in the pioneer period and during the baby boom, as against the decades between these epochs and since the baby boom, when fertility declined or was lower because couples married at older ages and celibacy was a significant factor.

Trends in family formation as far back as the 1920s continue to have an impact on family structures and organization today in several different ways. These include the size of generations at various ages, the structure of broader family groupings (e.g., siblings and their nuclear families), and the age gaps between cohorts. These differ as a function of the timing and spacing strategies employed for family formation by past parental generations (Sceats, 1988b). They also have implications in terms of questions such as sibling support at older ages (McPherson, 1992).

Reproductive Changes Since 1960

As is clear in Figure 1, family formation has undergone dramatic socio-demographic changes over the last three decades (Pool, 1992, puts the New Zealand transitions into a cross-comparative context). Pakeha fertility declined gradually through the 1960s, but in the latter part of the 1970s dropped rapidly to reach sub-replacement levels, so that New Zealand joined in what some European demographers (e.g., van de Kaa, 1987) call the 'Second Demographic Transition'. In the 1970s, Maori fertility underwent the most accelerated decrease on record for any population anywhere, and their total fertility rate converged with that of Pakeha.

About 1990, total fertility rates temporarily edged up to reach replacement, bringing New Zealand slightly above Sweden and the United States, the other two developed countries to share this trend. Contrary to the experience in Sweden (Hoem, 1990), family policy does not seem to be a factor because this increase in fertility occurred when what should have been disincentives to reproduction were being introduced. In New Zealand's case the key factors were purely demographic.

Over recent years teenage fertility has declined significantly for both Maori and Pakeha, a trend associated with an upward shift in ages of marriage and childbearing, to such an extent that age-specific fertility patterns are totally different from those in the baby boom. It is thus somewhat curious that policy concerns about this phenomenon, verging on moral panic, have reached a crescendo in the 1990s when rates are much lower than in the baby boom, the peak period of adolescent childbearing. Known conceptions (abortions and births) at ages 15–19 have remained almost unchanged, so that either the young are less exposed to intercourse at younger ages than were their elders, or they are better contraceptors.

Figure 1 graphs a summary measure and does not show the single most significant recent trend in New Zealand family formation: the change in the age patterns of Pakeha reproduction, related to the declines in teenage fertility just noted. In the late 1970s a shift in timing to a higher age was occurring, and couples who would have had a birth at a younger age were 'delaying' this until they reached later reproductive ages, when the birth would then, as it were, be 'recuperated'. This pattern of delay and recuperation happened to coincide with the arrival at mid-reproductive span of the large parental cohorts born about 1960, thereby producing the short-term return to exact replacement about 1990.

Figure 2 shows the repositioning of the peak single-year age of childbearing for Pakeha cohorts this century. This vividly demonstrates the shifts that have taken place, and the same trends are reflected also in the maternal ages at which first births are occurring. Young Pakeha couples have gone back to the patterns of childbearing which characterized their grandparents in the 1930s, and thus are following radically different parenting strategies from those seen in the baby boom, an era that stands out in Figure 2 as aberrant. Consequently, from the mid-1970s there have been increases in age-specific fertility at all ages over 27 years, even at 40–49, and marked decreases in fertility at younger ages. In short, Pakeha fertility has achieved a reprise of past patterns by a repositioning to older ages.

FIGURE 2. Maternal age at which non-Maori age-specific fertility rate has peaked for cohorts born 1910–1964, New Zealand

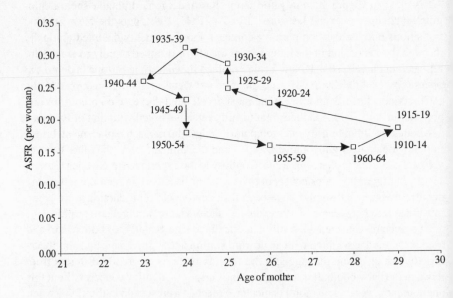

For Maori, rates dropped at all ages, with the steepest declines occurring at the mid- and later parts of the reproductive span. At ages 25–34 Maori fertility has been below Pakeha since the late 1970s, but recently has started to edge back upwards.

In New Zealand, as in the United Kingdom and United States, many commentators and policy-makers confuse adolescent with ex-nuptial fertility. Moreover, the misleading and inexact ratio (ex-nuptial births to nuptial, or total births) is often used in this discourse. It is inexact because it does not reflect ex-nuptial conception followed by nuptial birth (the baby-boom pattern) and thus merely measures relativity, not volume. That said, it is clear that ex-nuptial fertility in general has increased, from 8% of all births in 1962 to 36% in 1991. In contrast, the rate (ex-nuptial births per 1,000 unmarried women aged 15–49) increased more modestly, from 24 in 1961 to 51 in 1990 (Department of Statistics, 1961–95).

Looking at these figures more critically, it can be seen that increases have been most marked at older ages, with four separate factors operating to produce this trend. What has almost disappeared is the baby-boom phenomenon of ex-nuptial conception, precipitated marriage, and nuptial birth, the overwhelming pattern then at younger maternal ages, at which most first births occurred. Secondly, patterns of ex-nuptial fertility have followed the general upward shift in reproduction, so that today this form of childbearing is more the prerogative of older couples than of teenagers. In 1976, the ratio between ex-nuptial births at 25 and over and those at less than 20 years was 0.71 to 1.00; and between ex-nuptial births at 25+ years and all teenage births, 0.27. By 1991, the two ratios had shifted radically to 2.35 (25+) to 1.00 (adolescence) and 2.22 (ex-nuptial births, 25+) to 1.00 (all teenage births) respectively.

It is not difficult to speculate about the more proximate explanatory factors for recent shifts in reproduction. Most important has been the availability, for the first time in history, of efficient means of contraception which has produced in New Zealand (as across the developed countries) a 'weakening of the link between marriage and childbearing' (Santow, 1989). Across the developed world this has occurred within the context of major shifts in societal values, evidence of which can be supported in New Zealand's case only by anecdotal data (which concur with those in values surveys overseas, as in Lesthaeghe, 1991), and in jurisprudential changes (for New Zealand, see later in this chapter; also Cartwright, 1985). Together, these shifting values have the effect of separating societal legitimation of conjugal unions, particularly those within which reproduction is taking place, from the registration of marriages.

The immediate mechanisms for changes in reproduction obviously were the adoption by New Zealand couples of the armoury of efficient means of fertility regulation, which became available in their modern form in the 1960s and 1970s: the pill, tubal ligation and vasectomy, the modern IUD, injectable hormonals, and modern condoms. The fragmentary data available suggest that current prevalence rates, particularly for the first two of these, match the levels found in North America and other 'developed' countries. Overall, induced abortion has played a minor role, although at some ages (20–24 years) and for some migrant minority groups (Asians, Pacific Islanders) levels are higher. More importantly, except among Pacific Islanders, abortion tends to be employed at younger ages, among the unmarried as a back-up when contraception has failed or intercourse has been unprotected, rather than for higher-parity married couples at older ages as a prime means of fertility regulation (Sceats and Parr, 1995).

Nuptiality (Registered Marriages) and Marital Status

Historically, marriage trends for Pakeha have paralleled fertility trends. Early and almost universal marriage has traditionally been related to higher fertility, as in the baby boom, and later marriage with higher levels of celibacy associated with lower fertility. But since the 1970s the relationship between marriage and fertility has increasingly weakened, as the registration of marriage has become increasingly a rite indicating publicly and formally the start of a union, regardless of the procreative achievements or intentions of the couple concerned. For Maori, community legitimation had always been far more important than formal registration (Pool and Sceats, 1981).

The following commentary on recent patterns generally relates to women only in the total population; unless otherwise noted, male rates are parallel. There are no recent data on marriage registrations by ethnicity, but as Pakeha are the majority population the data presented here will mainly reflect their experience.

Two very recent trends in nuptiality are evident in New Zealand. Firstly, at all reproductive ages there have been declines in marriage rates, with the most radical decreases at the youngest ages. At 16–19 years (16 is the legal age for marriage), the rate for women in 1991 was 10% of what it was around twenty years earlier when marriage at that age had reached its twentieth-century peak. This had been achieved to a considerable degree, as noted above, by prenuptial conception and precipitated marriage.

Secondly, age at marriage (from all marital statuses) has increased, with the mode shifting from 20–24 years to 25–29; the mean age at first marriage in 1971 was 21.7, but by 1992 was back up to the level it had been in 1935 (25.5). Recently, moreover, there have been gradual increases in first marriage rates at age 30–34 years (women) and 35–44 (men), which may indicate that some of the much-publicized decline in marriage as an institution is a function instead of the 'delay' and 'recuperation', or 'repositioning' taking place independently of a parallel trend in reproduction. This trend in registered marriages is apparently being reinforced by patterns of cohabitation, for which there are virtually no data available, although Carmichael (1984) showed that at least half of New Zealand brides and grooms reported the same residence on marriage registers.

An issue of policy concern is divorce, which in New Zealand as well as in other developed countries has increased in recent years, although this trend appears to have peaked (McPherson, 1995). Undoubtedly, there have been changes in values and norms relating to the preconditions for formal marital termination, on which there are virtually no data, but the changes are also a function of both prior demographic forces and of jurisprudential changes. The precocious marriages of the baby boom, often precipitated because of pregnancy, were more likely to end in divorce, regardless of marriage duration, than were those of more mature couples (Carmichael, 1982). New Zealand is still feeling the effects of this even though the couples concerned represent what would by today's standards be the 'tail end of the distribution' of 'early starters'. The impact of this factor was exaggerated by law changes, which came into effect in 1981, resulting initially in a doubling of divorces in the first year it was in operation, and then gradually declining to about two-thirds of its peak once the 'backlog' had been cleared.

Conventional divorce rates (divorces/married women), even age-specific indices, give a misleading impression of trends. They are not only affected by the population at risk, consisting of persons who have married some time in the past at a younger age, but also by the number of married women in the age group for which the divorces are being measured. As marriage rates have declined, the situation has arisen where the numbers of both marriages and divorces at any age are low and decreasing, yet the divorce rates, coming from marriages to a minority of the age group years before, are increasing. When, instead of married women, the population by age is employed as the denominator, the proportion undergoing divorce is shown to be low and declining over recent years. For example, where 1.5% of women aged 30–34 years (the peak age group) divorced in 1986, this had declined to 1.3% by 1991. Using a population-based synthetic rate (5 x sum of the

Age-Specific Divorce Rates), the probability that a woman would have a divorce between 16 and 59 years edged down from .39 in 1986 to .38 in 1991.

The proportion of all marriages which are remarriages, mostly of divorced persons, is increasing, with first marriages down from 83% of the total in 1976 to 75% in 1991. Age and gender patterns of nuptiality have also changed, notably by a shift upwards. For example, only 41% of marriages of women at 30–34 years were first marriages in 1981, but this had shifted to 62% in 1991. This change merely reflects the whole repositioning of reproduction and nuptiality. Overall, women are more likely than men to enter a first marriage, or to remarry as widows, while men are more likely than women to remarry when divorced. Of interest is that these gender differences are decreasing for first marriage and divorce, but increasing for widow(er)hood.

Above 25 years, males of all conjugal statuses are more likely to marry than their female counterparts, but this is largely a function of the fact that men typically marry women two to three years younger than themselves. At 35 years and over, divorced men were more likely than divorced women to remarry, but the opposite is true for widow/ers, except at the oldest ages.

In sum, levels of adolescent fertility and reproduction at young adult ages have declined radically. At least for Pakeha, both fertility, nuptial and ex-nuptial, and marriage have undergone a significant repositioning to older ages. Divorce rates are still being affected by the young marriages precipitated by ex-nuptial conceptions of the baby-boom years as well as by divorce law changes. For Maori, even though fertility rates have declined, the rate of reproduction is still greatest at younger ages. These factors, as well as changes in social attitudes and behaviours, affect the demographic aspects of family structures to which we now turn.

FAMILY AND HOUSEHOLD STRUCTURES

Much of the attention of family policy is directed towards what are perceived to be 'dysfunctional' families, with a great deal of the focus, particularly ideological, directed towards mother-only families. In New Zealand, as in the United Kingdom and North America, some politicians and pressure groups, using very simple and frequently misleading indices, express deep concern over the apparent demise of the two-parent family and the growth of 'sole-parenting', as this is termed statistically and popularly in New Zealand (Pool, in press).

In discussing this very complex issue, however, several general methodological and substantive points must be taken into consideration. This analysis is based on census data, and thus the 'families' it covers are not necessarily in registered marriages. We also need to distinguish between household data, which relate to the living arrangements of people regardless of emotional or kinship ties, and family data, which cover persons interrelated and co-residing, and who may form a subset of a household. Unfortunately, New Zealand has drawn on European statistical practices based on the classic 'nuclear family', which does not capture satisfactorily the structures found in present-day New Zealand, not just among non-European ethnic minorities but—as also is the case in Britain (Murphy, in press) and perhaps elsewhere—even for the majority population. Related to this is the need to distinguish between parenting and non-parenting households and families. Because of these problems, unless otherwise noted, this chapter uses household data in order to be able to refer to wider households, which play a very important role in New Zealand family life (Jackson, 1994a).

At a more technical level, the choice of denominator for rates has important implications for policy analyses. The use of households/families, as against a population base, produces very different perceptions of structures, particularly for sole-parenting. To take a critical case, using data on sole-parent families (instead of households) conjures up the perception of a woman and her child(ren) living in an independent household. In reality, many are not in sole-parent households, but live in multi-family households with other adults, very often the mother's own parents and wider family. This has connotations both ethnically and by age: one-quarter of Pakeha, one-third of Maori, and almost half the Pacific Island sole-parent families are not in sole-parent households (i.e., they are not isolated, but instead there are other related or non-related adult-headed families present in the household). For mother-only families at 15–19 years there were twice as many Pakeha sole-parent families as sole-parent households. For 15–19-year-old Maori and Pacific Islanders the level is more than three times, and remains above 1.5 for Maori and 2.0 for Pacific Islanders at every other age.

In 1991, 19% of all parenting households were sole-parent, while 42% of the household category parents-plus others included sole parents and their children, and a further 5% had two or more sole parents. Some 27% of sole-parent families were thus part of an extended household, while 73% of sole parents live alone with their children. Only 64% of sole parents are recipients of benefits. Most (79%) sole-parent families are headed by a woman, and 90% of beneficiaries are women. Data are not available on the marital status of sole parents.

These conceptual/methodological questions are not the only ones having an impact on policy-makers' perceptions of family structures. The demographic changes in reproduction and nuptiality noted earlier have had a major effect, not the least of which is the general shift upwards in the attainment by Pakeha of the family life-cycle phase at which different structures are likely to become more or less prevalent. Different demographic forces are operating for Maori: the fusing together of a generally younger overall age structure with their family formation pattern of early childbearing. This means, for example, that, all other things being equal, Maori will be at risk of sole-parenthood at a younger age than Pakeha, but are more likely to live with other families.

The Demographic Squeeze

The prototypical two-parent family or household, particularly Pakeha, is undoubtedly undergoing changes in structure, which will be documented below, but perceptions of the prevalence of this type of family are often misinformed by a failure to take into account a number of demographic factors. The exact composition of these varies from decade to decade, from generation to generation, and between ethnic groups.

Most importantly, because of the delays in reproduction noted above, by the 1990s young Pakeha (15–30 years) were staying in non-parenting households longer than was the case in the baby boom: living in units composed of non-related persons, or alone, or as a couple without children (couple family). At the post-reproductive ages there were couple families at an empty-nest stage plus people in single-person households, most commonly widows. In 1966, 18% of private households were composed of non-related persons or persons living alone; by 1976 this was 21%; and by 1991, 26%, an increasing proportion of whom were single persons. Among 'family households', in 1966 21% were couple families; in 1976 this was 26%; and by 1991 this had reached 32%. We will call these effects a 'demographic squeeze'.

Squeezed between younger and older non-parenting households were the parenting families. They are defined in New Zealand censuses as those with one or more co-resident child(ren) aged less than 17 years, or a child aged 16–18 still in school, although many families had dependent offspring aged more than 18 years. This statistical unit no longer fits with social policy definitions of parental obligations towards their offspring. The upward boundaries of social dependency have increased since the 1991 census because the budget that year tightened eligibility for unemployment benefits and tertiary educational allowances, in effect making many families responsible for support of the unemployed and full-time student members up to 25 years of age.

The impact of the demographic squeeze is illustrated in Table 1, which summarizes the end-effects of shift-shares between household types. It also demonstrates the ethnic differences which confound family policy formulation. By 1991, the majority of Pakeha and of all households were non-parenting, as defined here. This is a short-term phenomenon affected by the peculiar conjunction of the delayed reproduction of younger couples and the early childbearing and thus early 'empty nesting' of their parents, many of whom are still in their forties and early fifties, yet who bore their last child over twenty to thirty years ago. They will be followed by a generation of parents who have started later and thus will be much older at an 'empty-nest' stage. For Maori this change had not proceeded very far, while for Pacific Islanders, lagging behind Maori and Pakeha in terms of their fertility transition, there was virtually no change, and the levels were much lower. It should be added that ethnic groups with higher fertility had a wider spread of ages for their dependants, and also were more likely to face unemployment among both the caregiver (parental) generation and among their youth aged less than 25 years. This structural issue is of particular importance when family incomes are discussed in Chapter 2.

New Zealand

TABLE 1. Non-parenting households by ethnic group,
New Zealand 1976 and 1991 (in %)

Year	Pakeha	Maori	Pacific Islander	Total
1976	43	22	18	42
1991	54	28	17	50

Source: Summarized from Jackson and Pool, 1994.

Parenting Households

Parenting households do not divide simply into two groups, two- and sole-parent. Instead there is a third very important category termed in New Zealand 'parents-plus others' (called parents-plus here). Data on parenting are given in Table 2. Once again both time and ethnic differences as well as shift-shares in household type are shown. The growth of the sole-parent category is evident, although it should be noted that the shift to this category involved a loss from the parents-plus group as well as from the two-parent, particularly in the case of Pacific Island families.

TABLE 2. Parents-plus, two-parent, and sole-parent households by
ethnic group, New Zealand 1976 and 1991 (in %)

	Pakeha	Maori	Pacific Islander	Total
1976				
parents +	15	29	43	17
2-parent	76	62	51	74
1-parent	9	10	6	9
1991				
parents +	17	25	34	15
2-parent	72	46	47	67
1-parent	11	29	19	19
Total	*100*	*100*	*100*	*100*

Source: Summarized from Jackson and Pool, 1994.

These data should be put into perspective. When looking at the number of children in the different types of parenting households as a proportion of all dependent children, the impact of these shift-shares is less than might be expected. In 1991, 85% of children were living in two-parent or parents-plus households, that is, in a unit with two or more adults to care for them. Moreover, and contrary to popular perceptions, a more detailed analysis has shown that by 1991, the nation's children were more likely to be cared for by mature parents (30–44 years) than by young parents (15–29), than had earlier been the case (Pool, in press). This fits with the upward shift in reproduction.

For each ethnic group the proportion of the population by age in two-parent households follows a bell-shaped curve with peaks at 25–54 years. More than 50% of the Pakeha population at these ages are in such households. For both Maori and Pakeha this peak dropped in level between 1976 and 1991.

The parents-plus category follows a different trajectory, as it increased by age, peaking from about 30 years on to about 60 years, but without a distinct pattern. More than 20% of Maori men and women are in this sort of household at ages between 40 and 65, while for Pacific Islanders 25–35% of the population between 25 and 65 years are in these multi-family households. The older population in these households will often be co-residing with younger families, two-parent and sole-parent.

Sole-Parenting

Much of the policy concern in New Zealand, as elsewhere, revolves around sole-parenting. But the popular images of sole-parenting, as frequently relayed by policy-makers, are shaped by information which is often based on misleading indices. For example, the Newsletter of the Committee for the International Year of the Family (1994) reported that 25% of New Zealand families (and 25% of the entire population) lived in sole-parent families. The latter figure received wide coverage in the popular media, associated in radio talkback shows with a great deal of invective against 'solo-mothers'. Neither statistic was correct: only 2% of adult males, 7% of adult females, and 15% of children live in sole-parent families. But more importantly, this incident raises the methodological question of whether policy analyses should be centered more on family structures, or on the population living in different sorts of units.

It is thus important to be very clear about the situation in New Zealand, which does not fit closely with the popular image of seemingly profligate childbearing and isolated teenage sole parents. Firstly, as already noted, adolescent fertility has declined radically since the baby boom. Secondly, using the most widely cited, yet imprecise statistic, the proportion of babies born 'out of wedlock', ex-nuptial childbearing most definitely increased. But as was shown above, today this is more and more being concentrated at exactly those ages at which the rest of childbearing is taking place for Pakeha, at 25+ years: the peak rates for this and for all childbearing are in fact at 25–29 years. Thirdly, as referred to earlier, the young sole parent, and even sole parents at other ages, is two to three times as likely to be living in a multi-family household than alone, and even at older ages the majority are in an extended family situation. Fourthly, we do not have data on family careers, but anecdotal evidence confirms what is known from overseas, that sole-parenting is a

230　　　　　　　　　　　　　*New Zealand*

FIGURE 3. Female sole-parent families, by ethnic group, by age of mother,
New Zealand*

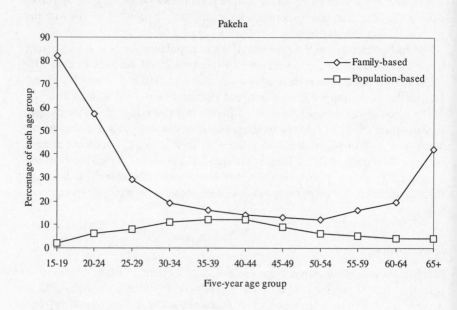

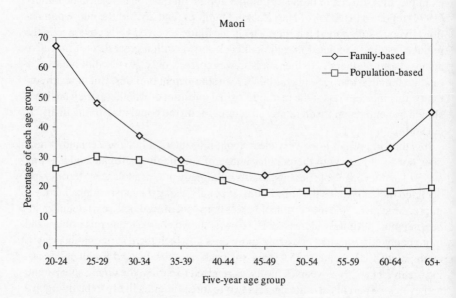

* (i) as a percent of the female population by age (population-based), and (ii) as a percent of one-
and two-parent families with 'occupiers' of the same age (family-based).

situation, not a status, in and out of which people (mainly women) move as families split and new reconstituted families are formed. Finally, the image of sole-parenting as the prerogative of teenagers is also untrue.

In conventional analyses the data on family or household types are computed as a percentage of all families/households, but this provides in particular a very misleading view of the age specificity of sole-parenting. This is seen in Figure 3 on sole-parent families (recalling that many of these will be a component of a multi-family household), which compares (1) a population-based measure (i.e., the percent of the female population by age in the figure; the methodology for these population-based indices was developed and elaborated in Davies et al., 1993; and Pool et al., 1993) with (2) the conventional index. The population-based measure shows that only a minority of women are in this situation at any time. Moreover, it demonstrates that female Pakeha sole-parenting is clustered at ages 25–49 years, especially 30–44, while Maori sole-parenting is skewed more towards younger ages. In contrast, the conventional index implies that sole-parenting is very much a phenomenon of young women. At those ages at which the incidence for the formation of parenting families is low (below 25 years), those units formed are likely to be sole-parent households. At late middle ages widowhood adds to divorce as a cause. For male sole parents, the age groups are older, and the distribution is generally skewed upwards.

FAMILY VALUES

The structures outlined above operate within a complex attitudinal and normative framework. Much of this can be inferred from our earlier discussion. For example, in behavioural terms New Zealanders of all ethnic groups seem to be pro-natalist (Sceats, 1988a), as fertility levels have not dropped to the levels of sub-replacement seen even in neighbouring Australia. Moreover, it has been shown that fertility increased around 1990 at the very time when social policy props for procreation (e.g., family benefits, support for adolescent unmarried mothers), factors claimed to be the determinant of a similar rise in Sweden, were being removed.

At the same time, changes in patterns of fertility and the resort to efficient means of family planning have undoubtedly taken place in a context in which modern methods are no longer perceived simply as contraceptive technologies. They have permeated and form an essential part of the matrix of norms, values, and knowledge about reproduction, or, to use Murphy's term, they constitute a form of 'macro-contraception' as opposed to 'micro-contraception' (the techniques themselves) (1993). An indirect indication of the effects of macro-contraception was the very rapid adoption of the pill by New Zealand women in the 1960s and the widespread use of sterilization by the late 1970s.

Moreover, there are significant differences in the ways in which the different ethnic groups reproduce and organize their family lives. This implies marked differences in some familism values, as was demonstrated for Maori and Pakeha in a pilot study carried out in the early 1980s on behalf of the United Nations Economic and Social Commission for Asia and the Pacific (ESCAP, 1986).

What has not been discussed earlier and is worth stressing here is the fact that New Zealand family values' systems have been far from immune from the recent somewhat diffused form of 'moral panic' about the family that is spreading across North America and Great Britain. As the earlier text has shown, much of this panic is based on misleading indices, but also has been fuelled by those who see the family failing in its fiscal responsibilities. These commentators argue that the state has sapped self-reliance and see the slashing of welfare as a prime mechanism for reducing government expenditures. They focus on sole-parenting, which is frequently linked to ex-nuptial childbearing, which in turn is often wrongly seen as being concentrated among adolescents. In the public discourse on families, as in the United States and United Kingdom, these behaviours are linked together as exemplifying 'welfare burdens' (e.g., the Republican Contract With America; see British Social Security Secretary Lilley, as quoted in the *Daily Telegraph*, 31 March 1995; for New Zealand see, for example, Gibbs, 1994). In some cases there are even calls for counter-measures verging on the punitive, especially towards adolescent mothers (for New Zealand see Richardson, 1995, which echoes the Republican Contract With America).

All the various elements of international panic can be detected: concern over sub-replacement fertility, divorce rates, abortion, ex-nuptial childbearing, cohabitation, and the alleged demise of the two-parent family. Some even see in these trends the portents for the decline of western civilization. Associated with these extravagant notions is the potentially harmful and nebulous set of views which carry undertones similar to those that fuelled the inter-war eugenics movements, more particularly the Social Darwinistic idea that the wrong people breed, while the more desirable do not. In contemporary New Zealand such ideas arise from the fact that to such observers a minority of women, usually younger and poorer, often Maori or Pacific Islander, seem to procreate with ease but then keep their babies. Other well-established older couples have difficulties conceiving, and yet there is a shortage of babies available for adoption. One must stress that this is not New Zealand's first such panic; indeed, it is an historical curiosity that the present one echoes that associated with the last rapid decrease in Pakeha fertility at the end of the nineteenth century (Pool, in press; Condran and Furstenburg, 1994).

FAMILY LAW

The norms, values, and traditions of society, providing the context for changing family patterns and trends, are frequently codified in what is defined as 'family law'. Much of the corpus of family law in New Zealand derives from British common law and yet there is no coherent body of family law any more than there is a clearly-defined set of family policies. Family law has developed in a piecemeal way over the past 150 years with Acts of Parliament being passed at different times for different purposes.

Although family law is recognized as a specialist area of legal practice based on legislation such as the Marriage Act (1955), the Guardianship Act (1968), the Matrimonial Property Act (1976), the Family Proceedings Act (1980), the Family Courts Act (1980), the Domestic Protection Act (1982), and the Children, Young Persons and Their Families Act (1989), there is no explicit definition of family in this legislation. As Henaghan and Tapp (1992) conclude from their review of legislation over the period 1863 to 1992, only nine Acts attempt to define the term 'family', with another six Acts specifying aspects of family life and responsibilities. These definitions range from the open-ended approach of the Local Government Amendment Act (1979) wherein the definition of family includes 'one person living alone', to the Children, Young Persons and Their Families Act (1989) which refers to the 'family group' rather than the nuclear or biological family. The emphasis in this latter definition is on connection with the child, with the relationship being defined in biological, legal, and psychological terms or by reference to one's *whanau* (extended family) or cultural group.

Three major themes can be identified from the way in which legislation defines 'family' in New Zealand (Henaghan and Tapp, 1992). Firstly, there is an assumption that marriage is an essential prerequisite for the definition of a family. Terms such as wife and husband are consistently used to define one's family connection, and for more than a hundred years husbands have been generally cast as the 'head of the household' with the responsibility to provide for and protect 'dependants'. This gendered construction of familial roles has changed in more recent times as evidenced in labour legislation, where there has been a shift from protecting women (based upon historically-specific and outmoded views about the role of women and their occupational 'capacities') to an emphasis on equal opportunities and 'sameness' with men (Galtry and Callister, 1995). This shift in emphasis is embodied in legislation such as the Equal Pay Act (1972) and the Human Rights Act (1993). Yet despite this shift in emphasis, legislation such as the Parental Leave and Employment Protection Act (1987) continues to distinguish between parents on the basis of gender.

A second theme to emerge from the legal definitions of family concerns financial accountability. Those Acts which define family tend to be associated with policies and practices in which the state is providing economic assistance. This assistance can be classified either as private maintenance provisions or as public law. The legislation concerned with private maintenance has been historically linked with matrimonial property, and in these cases the law has been preoccupied with the orderly devolution of property and the stability of the family unit. In the case of public law, which has its genesis in the Elizabethan poor laws, the aim has centred on saving public funds by enforcing familial responsibility.

The third theme that emerges from historical definitions of family in law concerns the Eurocentric nature of New Zealand legislation. In the nineteenth century, the government passed a Native Lands Act which was interpreted by one colonial authority as having two major objectives. The first was to bring the bulk of land belonging to the Maori within the reach of colonization, while the second was the 'detribalisation of the natives—to destroy if it were possible the principle of communism which ran through the whole of their institutions, upon which their social system was based, and which stood as a barrier in the way of all attempts to amalgamate the native race into our own social and political system' (Sewell, 1870). The annexation of land was followed by a policy of assimilation which was maintained through to the 1950s, although after the publication of the Hunn Report in 1961, assimilation was replaced with integration. From the 1970s on, there were significant changes in the public consciousness with regard to alternative cultural traditions and practices, and these changes were reflected in the passing of that body of legislation referred to today as 'family law'. However, some Maori viewed integration as a synonym for assimilation, as was evident in the constitution of the seven 'family' statutes. Six of these statutes endorse assimilation, largely by ignoring Maori social policies and objectives, while the seventh, the Children, Young Persons and Their Families Act, in its vocabulary and provisions, recognizes the existence of *hapu* (lineage groups) and *iwi* (tribal organizations).

Both the content of family law and the system for resolving family disputes have been subjected to major reforms over the past 15 years. In 1980, a series of legislative reforms such as the Family Courts Act, the Family Proceedings Act, the Guardianship Amendment Act, and the Social Security Amendment Act represented a major commitment to improving the system for resolving family disputes. The Family Courts Act created a new division of the District Court with its own specialized services and personnel selected to deal exclusively with family cases, whereas the Family Proceedings Act placed emphasis on counselling, conciliation, and mediation in resolving family disputes. This latter piece of legislation also simplified the law of divorce by adopting a no-fault basis for the legal termination of marriage. Similarly, the Guardianship Amendment Act was designed to ensure a more personalized legal resolution to custody and access disputes, while the Social Security Amendment Act set down the financial obligations resulting from the dissolution of a family in the form of the liable parent contribution scheme. This Act has since been updated by the Child Support Act 1991 (Atkin, 1992). Wide legal powers aimed at protection are also in place in the form of the Domestic Protection Act (1982) and the Domestic Protection Rules (1983). These Acts were designed to protect those who are victimized by violence and molestation in their homes; they extend to unmarried cohabitants as well as spouses and ex-spouses.

One area which has added a new dimension to family law concerns modern birth technologies which potentially involve three sets of parents: the commissioning parents, the donors, and the surrogate and her partner. The Status of Children Amendment Act (1987) was designed to address this issue by clarifying the legal status of children conceived by the use of donated sperm, ova, or embryos, and by the use of techniques such as artificial insemination, *in vitro* fertilization, and gamete intra-fallopian transfer. While the aim of the Act is to endorse the social parents as legal parents, thereby removing parental status and liability from the donor parents, the Act did not address the wider issues of access and use of new birth techniques, access to information by children born as a result of such techniques, or the storage of, and experimentation with, embryos (Butterworths, 1993).

Similar deficiencies are apparent in legislation dealing with the dispersion of property, where the equal division of existing assets has not produced an equal financial result between parties when the marriage has ended. Research in New Zealand (Maxwell and Robertson, 1990) indicates that the non-earning spouse (in most cases the woman) is financially vulnerable, particularly if that spouse is left with the care of children. Whereas the non-earning spouse experiences a drop in living standards following the termination of the relationship, the earning spouse tends to have fewer liabilities and generally experiences a higher standard of living. Comprehensive legislation addressing these issues and the particular situation faced by *de facto* couples in the dispersion of assets is well overdue (Parker, 1995).

In general terms family law has developed in a piecemeal fashion with each Act reflecting the particular concerns of the time. Historically speaking, however, the legal relevance of fault in family proceedings has declined, and the system has moved away from the superficial attachment of blame. Attempts have also been made to simplify family law both in its legal complexities and in its application. Children have been given greater protection and awarded greater status, and at the same time the protective aspects of family law have been extended beyond the legal construction of marriage. Likewise, the concept of family as defined in law has been broadened, although there is still some way to go before those living in different types of relationships experience equal opportunities and equal results.

CONCLUSION

This chapter has described the increasingly complex structures, values, and laws, as well as the underlying demographic changes characterizing the contemporary New Zealand family. It was to this entity, in all its many varieties, that the government turned when initiating the reformation of the welfare state in 1991. The problem government faced was simple: if the state is no longer to be responsible for the welfare of its citizens, then there must be something with which to replace it. Unfortunately, the 'family' construct which the government designed was not based on empirical data, but rather drew its inspiration from a nostalgic view of the family which probably never existed and which was clearly out of step with demographic realities. They called it a 'Core Family' and saw it taking on 'collective responsibility' for the social, emotional, and financial needs of its members, thereby permitting these persons to gain 'self-reliance' while 'throw[ing] off the burden of welfare' (Shipley et al., 1991). This simplistic concept immediately ran into major definitional problems, and as later chapters will show it has since undermined the economic and social well-being of families with children. While Chapter 2 focuses on family income generated through the labour market, Chapter 3 will address the issue of financial assistance as provided by the state.

2

The Family and the Labour Market

THE LABOUR MARKET AND THE SOCIAL WAGE

The major transaction between the family and society has to do with the way in which the family can or cannot provide its own sustenance through labour market participation. Thus a central issue for family policy concerns the income-generating capacity of family members. Success in this regard will ensure that the family has little need for social policy support, at least with respect to income maintenance. Limited access to the labour market, either because members are unemployed, or because family status, health, or other factors render them unable to work for remuneration, means that income may well be below the average. Beyond this, the more mouths to feed, the less likely that any given family income will adequately meet the family's needs (Easting and Fleming, 1994; Rainwater, 1994). Moreover, in a multicultural society, groups have differential access to the labour market, varying family sizes, and different earning capacities.

The underlying questions to be analysed here come from research on family and household income in New Zealand (Martin, 1995; Mowbray, 1993a; Mowbray and Dayal, 1994; New Zealand Planning Council, 1990) and other countries (Barclay and Hills, 1995; Karoly, 1993; Oppenheimer, 1994). This research has shown a consistent trend of declining economic well-being alongside increasing inequity between different family and household types (Martin, 1995; Saunders, Hobbes, and Stott, 1989). Furthermore, differences are apparent even within each family type (Rochford et al., 1992; Rochford, 1993).

This chapter begins with a brief historical analysis of labour force participation, particularly of women. The balance between the self-generation of the family wage and the need for outside support is not a simple dichotomy. In each period it has varied because of the way in which family members, particularly wives, have had access to the labour market. The chapter then focuses on the period for which detailed family income data are available (namely, since 1981), by first undertaking a review of differentials in family income. This part of the analysis controls for labour force status (employment income being the most important component of New Zealand income as recorded by the Department of Statistics, 1991) and the average number of dependent children (the poor are most likely to be found among families with growing children: Crean, 1982; Easton, 1994b). The chapter concludes by providing a synthesis: it determines whether certain families are more vulnerable than others to changes within the labour market, and it identifies the types of families concerned.

A Methodological Comment

The historical analysis in this chapter is based on one major macro-level source (Davies and Jackson, 1993), with the balance drawn primarily from an empirical analysis of a custom-designed set of data, carried out especially for the present study. A more detailed discussion of the methodology and major findings is documented elsewhere (Johnstone and Pool, 1995), but several key points are germane to the present analysis.

The main data source for recent family analyses in New Zealand is the quinquennial census of population and dwellings, for the years 1981, 1986, and 1991. Hence Statistics New Zealand definitions of family must be employed in this chapter, while the time-series analysis does not extend beyond 1991. Problems with definitions were discussed in the previous chapter. It is important also to note that a family is defined as either a couple (married or *de facto*) with or without dependent children (defined statistically as any children in that family under 16 years of age or 16–18 years and still in education), or one parent, usually co-resident in a household. A census family therefore does not include adult children, albeit that new rules of eligibility for benefits may extend dependency to 25 years (see Chapter 3). The present chapter concerns the following 'family' types: couple-only (without children); two-parent; and sole-parent (male or female). It also makes a distinction between couple families (with or without children) and sole-parent families, the important point being whether there are two potential income earners.

The census is also the only systematic longer-term source of information on family incomes, permitting controls for the range of socio-economic correlates to be analysed in this chapter. It does not, however, distinguish between sources of family income (market and non-market), and thus provides merely an overall view of family well-being. The shorter-run set of data drawn from the Household Expenditure and Income Survey, to be used in the next chapter, are more precise for financial details but permit only limited analyses of associated social variables.

Four labour force status categories are available from recent New Zealand census data: full-time labour force (30 hours or more per week); part-time labour force (1–29 hours per week); unemployed and seeking full-time or part-time work; and not in the labour force. For couple families an hierarchical arrangement was used to aggregate and classify labour force status as follows:

1. both partners in full-time employment;
2. one partner in full-time employment, one in part-time employment;
3. one partner in full-time employment, one unemployed or non-labour force;
4. both partners in part-time employment;
5. one partner in part-time employment, one unemployed or non-labour force;
6. both partners unemployed or non-labour force.

Although persons unemployed and not in the labour force have been grouped together for couple families, the same rationale was not applied to sole-parent families. The reason is twofold: firstly, the number of variables is reduced when there is only one parent. Secondly, the income characteristics of unemployed and non-labour force sole parents are likely to differ more significantly for sole parents than for couples, due to the eligibility criteria for state benefits. Where there are joint caregivers with one in employment, assessment on joint income means state support of any type is less likely to be received, regardless of whether the second partner is unemployed or not in the labour force (St. John, 1994). The categories used for sole-parent families are as follows:

A. full-time employment
B. non-labour force
C. part-time employment
D. unemployed

Standard methodologies are used for the calculation of the average number of children (Jackson and Pool, 1994) and median income (Martin, 1995). In order to take account of families of different size, the Whiteford Scale has been used to calculate equivalent median income (Johnstone and Pool, 1995; Mitchell and Harding, 1993; New Zealand Planning Council, 1990).

Analysis focuses on three broad age groups: 15–29 years, 30–44 years, and 45–59 years. These age groups capture key stages of the life cycle although no attempt has been made to show movement between each group (reflected in the exclusion of those aged 60 years or more). The ensuing discussion refers to the two major population groups of New Zealand, the Maori population and the Pakeha, and not to Pacific Islanders or Asians, for whom small numbers in cross-tabulations produce inconsistent and unreliable results.

Given the high degree of intermarriage (Pool, 1977; Rochford, 1993) New Zealand families are likely to have members of more than one ethnicity. But for families a single reference is needed, and here it was arbitrarily decided to use the ethnicity of the father to determine family ethnicity (except in the case of female sole-parent families). Less problematic is the use of the father's age to classify the family, for age differences between spouses are minor in New Zealand (O'Neill, 1985).

HISTORICAL TRENDS IN LABOUR MARKET ACCESS

By the late nineteenth century, Pakeha New Zealand had become a society based on small businesses, typically family-run, of which the efficient owner-operated pastoral farm was the most noteworthy example (Davies and Jackson, 1993). Wives (and daughters) played a major role in the enterprises, though this was not recognized statistically. From the late nineteenth century up to World War II, the Maori economy was primarily rural and based on family-centred subsistence. Limited access to market incomes for men came from seasonal labour, mainly in primary export industries (e.g., shearing, abattoirs) while casual employment centred on roads and other public works. The casual employment of women was primarily confined to seasonal work (e.g., assisting the shearers, fruit picking) and domestic service jobs (Pool, 1991).

In 1891, women made up only 18% of the reported Pakeha labour force (no data were available at that date for Maori), although a large number of women who had signed the petition preceding the gaining of the vote designated themselves as farmers or in some other occupation. By 1991, 37% of all workers were women (the evolution of this increase and its correlates are shown in Table 3).

Over the twentieth century, other major related social and economic changes took place. By 1900, almost 50% of New Zealand's population was already urban, and by 1990 this had gone up another 30 percentage points to 80%. The rapid postwar urbanization of Maori, from about 10% of the population in 1936 to more than three-quarters today, had seen men and women enter manufacturing, and women the urban service industries. Many Maori men also took up forestry jobs in the large exotic plantations and mills coming into production in the 1950s. For Pakeha, urban-based industries, first manufacturing and then the tertiary sector, displaced primary industries as the major employers, although women who reported themselves in the labour force had historically been concentrated in service industries.

By 1956, two-fifths of male workers as well as a majority of women were in the tertiary sector; by 1991 half of the men and 80% of women in the labour force were in service-sector industries. Although a minority of workers remained in the traditional family farm/small business sector, most were now in large-scale formal enterprises, a majority of which were in the tertiary sector. It should be noted in passing that changes to laws governing taxation, equal pay, and matrimonial property in the 1970s and 1980s saw increasing numbers of women in family businesses report themselves as employed on a wage or salary, as against 'relative assisting, unpaid' or outside the labour force. Moreover, a growing proportion of farm families depended on the non-farm earning of one of the partners, typically the wife.

Throughout this century male labour force participation by age followed a simple pattern: rates were low at adolescence, but higher at each successive age to plateau from the early adult to the late middle ages, then to become lower at each older age. Changes came from the older attainment of the plateau, a function of prolonged tertiary study, and a younger fall-off in rates because of a trend to earlier retirement.

For women, however, as is shown in Table 3, age-specific patterns of employment as defined statistically have varied significantly over time. At first, a key factor was a combination of social pressures and discrimination, even legislation, which forced married women to leave the paid labour force, particularly if they were parents. Pay inequities and both formal and informal job segregation reinforced these pressures. Over time the legislation was amended, although in practice full pay equity has never been achieved.

The higher fertility of the baby boom and its attendant social attitudes saw a cult of domesticity reach a peak, with marked gender differences both in the division of tasks and in social relationships: the women stayed at home; the men went to work

TABLE 3. Women's labour force participation, New Zealand 1893–1993

	Pre-war era: Phase 1			Post-war era: Phase 2		Contemporary era: Phase 3	
	1893–1926	1926–36	1936–45	1945–61	1961–71	1971–81	1981–93
Key social and economic events	Women win right to vote World War I	Depression High unemployment	World War II Major social policy changes National register of manpower	Baby boom Economic expansion	Economic expansion Labour shortages Emergence of part-time work Second wave of feminism	Fertility declines Economic downturn Emergence of unemployment Women's Liberation Movement	Economic restructuring Large-scale unemployment
Key legislation	PSA adopts equal pay policy 1927	Unemployment Act 1930	Minimum Wage Act 1936 Revised 1945	Apprentice Act 1948	Public Sector Pay Equity 1960	Equal Pay Act 1972 Matrimonial Property Act 1976 Human Rights Commission Act 1977	Income Tax Amendment Act 1983 Parental Leave & Employment Protection Act 1987 Employment Equity Act passed and repealed 1990 Employment Contracts Act 1991
Non-Maori women's participation	Increase to 1921 Decrease to 1926	Gradual declines	Rapid increases	Slight declines	Increases marked from 1961	Full-time employment growth slows, part-time growth continues	1981–86 stalled 1986–91 declines Female unemployment grows
Maori women's participation	No data	Declines	Increases commence	Increases	Marked increases from 1951	Continued increases	Declines Severe unemployment
Women's participation by age	Work after marriage uncommon	Work after marriage uncommon		Work after marriage more common	Incipient 'M'-shaped curve	'M'-shaped curve more clearly defined	Transformation of 'M'-shaped curve

Source: Davies, 1993, Figure 3.2.

(see Chapter 5). Since then, the age-specific pattern of female labour force participation has taken the form of an increasingly shallow 'M'-shape. By the 1960s most women were working before their first pregnancy, and many after the children gained a degree of independence. Since then the pattern has become more extended, so that the 'M'-shape is converging towards the plateau-like pattern of the male work-force. Moreover, the delayed childbearing described in the last chapter has seen higher participation rates by women in their later twenties, whereas prolonged tertiary education is now reducing adolescent and early adult levels; more and more women are opting for maternity leave and then returning to work after the first and subsequent births; more and more women are also returning or staying in the labour force at the older working ages. In 1976, 57% of female workers aged 15–59 were married; by 1991 this figure had risen to 62%. By contrast, in 1976, 35% of female workers had never been married; this declined to 29% in 1991.

Although women have always made up a high proportion of the part-time labour force (over 80% until the 1980s and just below this in 1991) they represented only between 29% (1976) and 36% (1991) of full-time workers. The female part-time labour force grew far more rapidly than the female full-time work-force over this period. Since 1986 the female full-time work-force has started to contract, while the entry of men into part-time employment has led to a decline in the proportion of part-time workers who are women. As elsewhere in western countries, casualization and the increasing concentration of young women workers in lower-paid service jobs is also a feature of the New Zealand labour market. Maori and Pacific Island men have been particularly affected by the restructuring and 'downsizing' of manufacturing and forestry industries.

Employment and Parenting Policies

Maternity and parental leaves are often cited in the international literature as indices of employer or governmental responsiveness to the needs of working parents. New Zealand women were first protected from dismissal due to pregnancy in 1980 by the Maternity Leave and Employment Protection Act 1980, which was superseded by the Parental Leave and Employment Protection Act 1987 prohibiting dismissal by reason of pregnancy or state of health during pregnancy, or because an employee chooses to take parental leave. Paid maternity or parental leave is not part of New Zealand law or practice.

The parental leave legislation allows for fathers as well as mothers to take leave at the time of birth or adoption of a baby. Parental leave is only available if the parent-to-be has worked for the same employer for at least 12 months before the expected date of delivery/adoption and has been employed at least ten hours per week. There are three kinds of parental leave: maternity leave available to women for 14 weeks over the time the baby is due, which may be started six weeks before the baby is due and in some cases earlier; paternity leave of up to two weeks for male parents-to-be at the time of birth/adoption; and extended leave of up to 52 weeks (including maternity leave) for either or both parents to care for the child.

As noted, none of this leave is paid. The jobs of those on parental leave must be kept open for leave of less than four weeks; thereafter, the onus is on the employer to prove that the job cannot be kept open longer. If the job cannot be kept open, the employer must offer a preference period of six months after the leave ends, during which time the parent on leave must be offered any job similar to their old job which becomes vacant. Time on parental leaves counts as unbroken service. Parental leave rights may be enforced through the Employment Tribunal.

Historically, therefore, the patterns of labour force participation followed in New Zealand provided a counterpoint to the main thrust of family policy. It operated through a fairly well-defined sexual division of labour, with the function of child-raising shored up by the state through the various provisions of the social wage. Where a family's access to the labour market failed to provide sufficient income security, social policy was pragmatically directed to fill any gap. By the 1970s, however, exogenous demographic, economic, and social forces were collectively operating to erode this symbiotic relationship (see Table 3), and in the late 1980s, through radical policy shifts to be discussed in Chapters 3–5, this process of gradual erosion was transformed into a major reformation. One of the central concerns for this chapter is to record the way in which the family wage was affected by recent changes in labour force participation and income generation.

The Decade 1981–91

Incomes for all family types, for all ethnic groups in New Zealand showed declines between 1981 and 1991 (Martin, 1995). Furthermore, inequities between family types and between ethnic groups increased, and the gap between those with the highest incomes and those with the lowest widened. When disaggregated by labour force status, income relativities are further exacerbated: those in employment earn significantly more than those out of employment (non-labour force or unemployed). It is this latter group, comprised of families receiving low incomes, however, which had shown increases in real income between 1981 and 1986. This was true for sole parents and the partners of couple families in each age group for all those unemployed or not in the labour force. Income also increased over this five-year period for male sole parents in part-time employment. This rise in income during the early 1980s for those with low incomes was followed, however, by income declines between 1986 and 1991.

The increases seen for families with parents/partners in these particular labour force status groups and declines for all other groups are consistent for all families, regardless of ethnicity. Although the trend line has been similar, ethnic income differentials are in evidence. Firstly, income for Maori families is, on the whole, less than that of Pakeha families. Secondly, and more recently, in some cases, Maori income as a percentage of Pakeha income declined between 1981 and 1991 (Johnstone and Pool, 1995).

These differentials can be seen as a direct result of the different types of employment in which Pakeha and Maori are found. Maori are underrepresented in the financing, insurance, and real estate industries where wages and salaries tend to be higher than in manufacturing, where a high percentage of Maori find employment (Brosnan and Rea, 1992). This pattern was most noticeable for Maori sole parents in full-time employment and for older Maori couple families where at least one partner was in full-time employment. The same Maori families whose income declined as a percentage of Pakeha income also experienced the greatest percentage decline in income between 1981 and 1991. For example, Maori couple families with both partners employed showed an income decline between 2.4% and 9% greater than the decline experienced by Pakeha couple families.

The income decline seen during the 1980s in New Zealand was not, however, monotonic in nature, as some significant shorter-term effects were taking place because of wage and price levels and income maintenance policies. Two points are of significance here. Firstly, for those families where the parent/partner was unemployed or not in the labour force, income in 1991 was higher than in 1981, despite declines in income between 1986 and 1991. This was because of a second and more important issue, the timing of the income decline throughout the 1980s. For those families with a parent/partner in full-time employment, most of the decline occurred over the 1981–86 period, while for families with a parent/partner not in employment, or employed part-time, most of the decline took place during the 1986–91 period. The effect of the wage and price freeze imposed by the National government between June 1982 and July 1984 must be acknowledged for its impact on full-time workers, who, as a result, experienced consistently high income declines for the early 1980s. Data from this period show that wages remained more permanently stable than prices and that following the removal of the ban, prices were much quicker to inflate than wages and salaries (Boston, 1984).

Labour force status was certainly an important factor influencing incomes at this time. During the 1980s families with full-time workers retained higher real incomes than all other families. Despite high incomes these families with at least one worker in full-time employment also experienced the greatest percentage decline in income between 1981 and 1991, with the severest decline being experienced by Maori male sole parents. Among couple families the severest drop in real income was seen where both parents/partners were in full-time employment.

Some important age differences were also in evidence throughout the 1980s and these are discussed for each family type below. The trends discussed here hold generally, but not entirely, true for both Pakeha and Maori families. For male sole parents, it was the older age groups which had the highest incomes throughout the 1980s, while the younger age group experienced the greatest income declines. Female sole parents in employment (either full-time or part-time) experienced the sharpest income decline at ages 15–29, while for those not employed it was mothers aged 30–44 years who experienced the greatest decline. It was this middle-aged group, however, which retained the highest income of all age groups for all labour force statuses in each census year.

No clear pattern is evident for couple-only families, although it appears that those young families in employment experienced a greater percentage decline in income than older families with the same employment status. It was the oldest age group (45–59 years) who were not in employment (and probably receiving benefits) who experienced the greatest percentage decline in income. Of all couple-only families receiving benefits, it was, however, this oldest age group who had the highest income. For all other couple-only families, it was those aged 30–44 years who had the highest incomes.

Among two-parent families, it was the older families who had two full-time workers, or one full-time and one part-time worker, who consistently earned the highest incomes throughout the 1980s. This is in contrast to other two-parent families with differing labour force participation patterns, where those aged 30–44 had the higher incomes.

In sum, young families were worse off than older families, and although those families with at least one full-time employed person received the highest real incomes, they also experienced the largest percentage decline in income over the 1980s. It is sole-parent families where the parent is unemployed or not in the labour force who have consistently received the lowest incomes. This is especially true for young sole parents not in employment, who at each census have shown lower incomes than any other family type (for each age group and for each labour force status). Young families are in a more vulnerable position in terms of income levels, which reflects the inability of younger workers to find and retain employment as well as command a high income when compared to older, more experienced workers. It is also a result of younger workers belonging to New Zealand's largest-ever birth cohort reaching the labour market at the same time and competing for jobs. This exactly coincided with the radical economic restructuring of the late 1980s under the fourth Labour government, which resulted in growing unemployment.

RECENT LABOUR FORCE PARTICIPATION TRENDS

A description of income changes must be set in context if the results are to be meaningful. The fact that female sole-parent families where the mother is not in employment have the lowest incomes of all families has little significance unless we know how many people fall within that family category.

As was noted in Chapter 1, two-parent families as a percentage of all families have declined over the 1980s while all other types have increased, yet two-parent families remain the most common form (see Table 4). This general trend, however, does not apply to all labour force categories within each family. For example, there has been a steady increase in the percentage of families that are two-parent families with neither parent in full-time employment.

Of greater interest, however, is the distribution of families within each family type and for each age group according to labour force status. Because we already know the income levels of different families of different ages, in order to understand a family's potential for earning it is necessary to know whether they are more likely to be in or out of employment once in a particular family. For example, are couples aged 15–29 more likely to be found in full-time or part-time employment?

Among male sole-parent families some important shifts are taking place, highlighting important ethnic differentials. Most Pakeha male sole parents are still likely to be in full-time employment, and this is more likely the older they are, despite the fact that over the 1980s full-time employment declined. In 1981, most Maori sole fathers were in full-time employment, but by 1991 they were more likely to be outside the labour force. This decline was more significant for younger Maori male sole parents than for older ones. All male sole parents were significantly affected by rising unemployment throughout the 1980s, so that by 1991 their economic situation more closely resembled that of female sole parents.

Most of the decline in full-time employment for male sole parents resulted in increases in the percentage of sole fathers out of employment: they were less likely to find both full-time and part-time work. Ethnic differentials were once again in evidence, as an increasing percentage of Pakeha sole fathers became unemployed but remained in the labour force, while Maori sole fathers were more likely to be excluded from the labour force. In other words, Pakeha sole fathers were more likely to expect paid employment, as well as fulfilling the parental role, while Maori sole fathers tended to be engaged as full-time parents. Some of the declines in full-time employment were countered by increases in sole fathers working part-time, especially among Pakeha men. Again Pakeha sole-fathers coupled parenthood with paid employment, while Maori were more likely to concentrate on parenting.

Female sole-parent families show a different and far less complex pattern. They remained, overwhelmingly, in the non-labour force category right throughout the 1980s, with a higher predominance of this among younger mothers. Most women therefore who were fulfilling the parenthood role on their own did not couple this with paid employment—whether through choice or circumstance is beyond the scope of this analysis. For female sole parents in the labour force, there was a significant decline in both full-time and part-time employment over the 1980s (i.e., an increase in those who were unemployed), these changes being, in general, more severe for Maori than Pakeha. This difference can partly be attributed to the effects of economic restructuring during the 1980s which reduced employment opportunities in the manufacturing and service industries, industries where women were heavily represented (Brosnan and Rea, 1992). For Pakeha, the largest percentage increase in sole-parent unemployment was in the youngest age group, while for Maori it was for those aged 30 to 44 years.

Among two-parent families, the patterns seen for Maori and Pakeha are quite diverse and need to be considered separately. The only common trend across all ages at each census is the predominance of families with one parent in full-time employment and one not in employment. This decreases with age and over time: young two-parent families are likely to have one parent employed and the other at home, but as the children grow up, some diverse employment patterns emerge.

For the 1981–91 period, Pakeha two-parent families saw declines in the percentage of families with one parent employed full-time and the other not employed, and from 1986 there were also decreases in the percentage of two-parent families with one parent in full-time employment and one in part-time employment. Conversely, there were significant increases in the percentage of families where neither parent was in full-time employment, with these shifts having the most impact on families with younger parents. Young two-parent Pakeha families, the family form most resembling the stereotypical structure favoured by moralists, are likely to be struggling because of the parents' employment difficulties.

A smaller percentage of Maori two-parent families had a parent in full-time employment in 1991 than in 1981. Like Pakeha two-parent families, Maori two-· parent families are increasingly likely to have parents out of employment. In their case, however, the trend is marked at all ages, not only at young ages.

The most common labour force status among couple-only families is for both partners to be in full-time employment, although fewer Maori than Pakeha couples tend to have both partners in full-time employment. For both Pakeha and Maori couple-only families there was an increase during the early 1980s in the percentage of families where both partners were employed full-time, but this was followed by declines between 1986 and 1991, resulting in overall declines for the 1981–91 period. Furthermore, these declines were more noticeable for the younger age groups. This decline in employment was also seen among couples where one partner was in full-time employment and the other not employed.

As with the other family types, a decline in the percentage of couples with one or either partner in full-time employment has been accompanied by an increase in the percentage of couples who are not employed. Such an increase has been much more dramatic for Maori couple families than for Pakeha couple families. For Pakeha couples the rise in couples out of employment has most affected those at the younger ages, while for Maori couples it is those aged 30 to 44 years.

In summary, then, we see that for those people identified as belonging to one of the four family types under discussion in this chapter, there has been an increasing trend over the 1981 to 1991 period towards parents and partners not being in employment. This is by no means a straightforward trend, however, as the overall patterns mask some highly complicated changes. During the early 1980s, the only consistent pattern that emerges is an increase in part-time employment which does not noticeably carry through to the late 1980s. By the late 1980s, there was a clear trend of declining full-time employment and increasing unemployment.

The Recent Period: The Effects of Dependent Children

The preceding section showed that, in general, families' ability to generate income through full-time employment in 1991 was more limited than in 1981. In terms of family vulnerability, however, these results have little meaning unless we know the demand placed on that income. The average number of children provides a summary measure of family size and thus an indication of demand placed on income.

With some minor exceptions, all families have declined in size. Female sole parents who were unemployed showed a slight deviation from this pattern between

1981 and 1986 when there was an increase in the average number of children for Maori and Pakeha mothers.

As is to be expected, given age-specific fertility patterns for New Zealand, the largest families are those where the parents are between 30 and 44 years old. Furthermore, Maori families consistently have a higher average number of children than Pakeha, regardless of age group, family type, or labour force status. Moreover, two-parent families have more children than sole-parent families (Johnstone and Pool, 1995).

When looking at the average number of children by labour force status, parents out of employment generally have larger families than those in employment. This means that families receiving the lowest incomes face greater demands. This is certainly the case for Pakeha sole parents and Maori female sole parents. (Rates for Maori male sole parents show statistical perturbations attributable to small cell sizes.) This pattern is echoed for Maori two-parent families, as the highest average number of children is found in those families where neither parent is in full-time employment. Moreover, a shift has occurred whereby in 1981 the largest families had at least one parent in part-time employment, but by 1991 often both parents were unemployed. For young Pakeha two-parent families this pattern was applicable and occasionally true for the middle ages. For older two-parent families the largest average number of children was found where one parent was employed full-time and the other part-time.

In terms of average number of children per family and demand placed on income, it is clear that not only do different family types have differing needs, but that labour force status will also have an influence—although the differences are not always significant.

The Recent Period: Who is Vulnerable?

The evidence shows that there has been a decline in real income, with families with parents or partners out of employment earning the lowest incomes. Additionally, more and more families have parents or partners in this position. It is also these families that generally have the highest average number of children. Although it is useful to have a detailed understanding of these variables, it is their interaction that is of greater relevance when determining family vulnerability. This section therefore looks at the interaction of income levels, labour force status, and the number of children using equivalent median real gross income as the main unit of analysis (referred to hereafter merely as equivalent income for the sake of simplicity).

When equivalent incomes are graphed for Maori and Pakeha families at ages 30–34 years, covering the central family life cycle period (see Figure 4), three factors are immediately apparent:

1. Income levels differ significantly between family types, particularly where there is at least one full-time worker.
2. There are significant differences by ethnicity, with Pakeha earning the highest incomes.

FIGURE 4. Equivalent median gross income (inflated to 1991 levels) for families with parents or partners aged 30 to 44 years, New Zealand 1981, 1986, and 1991*

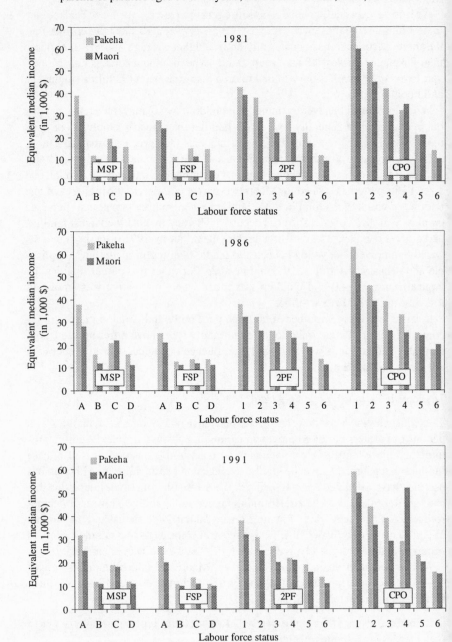

* MSP = male single-parent family, FSP = female single-parent family, 2PF = two-parent family, CPO = couple-only family. For categories 1–6 and A–D see pp. 237 f.

3. Labour force status has a significant impact on income levels, as is most clearly illustrated by couple-only families.

What is less noticeable in Figure 4 is the general pattern of overall decline between 1981 and 1991. This decline mainly occurred in the five-year period 1986–91, when it often outweighed gains made in the period 1981–86. Once family size has been controlled for similar income patterns, those families with parents or partners who were unemployed or not in the labour force (and presumably receiving state benefits) experienced a rise in equivalent income between 1981 and 1986, while all other families experienced equivalent income declines. Between 1986 and 1991, however, there were declines for all families, with one or two minor exceptions. During the later 1980s, the greatest percentage decline in equivalent income was seen among families with a parent or partner who was not in employment. Almost all families therefore experienced a decline in equivalent income during the late 1980s. For those in employment this decline had started earlier. The continuation of this decline in the late 1980s, coupled with the decline in income for those on low wages following increases during the early 1980s, indicates that policies centred on a free market economy were influencing the standard of living in New Zealand at that time.

The overall pattern of decline seen between 1981 and 1991 shows that those families with a parent or partner in full-time employment experienced the largest percentage decline in equivalent income of all families. Furthermore, declines in equivalent income during this period were greater for Pakeha families than for Maori families.

By using equivalent income as the main unit of comparison, it is possible to determine the characteristics of families who were most at risk during the 1980s. In 1981 and 1991, those families with the lowest equivalent income were predominantly Maori sole parents aged 15 to 29 years who were unemployed or not in the labour force. Conversely, the highest equivalent incomes for that period were found in Pakeha couple-only families at the older ages with both partners in employment (at least one of these being full-time). By ranking all equivalent incomes at each census and dividing them into five groups, the key characteristics of high- to low-income families have been identified (summarized in Table 4). It is clear that, although ethnicity is important when discussing family income levels, the family type and the labour force status of parents and/or partners are also very important. Sole-parent families and those families with parents/partners who are unemployed or not in the labour force are much more likely to have lower rather than higher equivalent incomes. It is these families therefore who can be viewed as being most vulnerable.

Although Table 4 shows remarkable consistency throughout the 1980s in terms of the ethnicity, age, and labour force status of those receiving the highest and lowest incomes, one very important shift can be seen. By 1991, two-parent families were among those earning the lower incomes, while in 1981 they had been among the highest income earners. As is clear from the lower panel of Table 4,

TABLE 4. Key characteristics of families by equivalent median gross real income
ranking (inflated to 1991 levels), New Zealand 1981 and 1991[1]

Income quintiles	Year	Ethnicity	Age[2]	Labour force status	Family type
1 (highest)	1981	Even distribution	Old	Two full-time workers	Couple-only families
	1991	Pakeha	Old	Two full-time workers	Couple-only families
2	1981	Even distribution	Even distribution	At least one full-time worker	Couple-only & two-parent families
	1991	Even distribution	Even distribution	At least one full-time worker	Couple-only families
3	1981	Even distribution	Young to middle	Part-time employ-ment, some full-time	Two-parent & couple-only families
	1991	Even distribution	Young to middle	Part-time employ-ment	Couple-only families
4	1981	Pakeha	Middle to old	Not employed, (some part-time)	Sole-parent families
	1991	Pakeha	Middle to old	Not employed (some part-time)	Male sole-parent & two-parent families
5 (lowest)	1981	Maori	Young	Not employed	Sole-parent families
	1991	Maori	Young	Not employed	Sole-parent families

[1] Key and % distributions at each census.
[2] Old = 45–59 years, middle = 30–44 years, young = 15–29 years.

two-parent families are the most common family type and account for half of all families, thus a significant number of people have been affected by the income declines seen throughout the 1980s.

It is instructive to note that it is the well-being of the family type favoured by the moralists that has been adversely affected by the income shifts of the 1980s. This makes nonsense of the argument advanced by some commentators in New Zealand (Gibbs, 1994) and abroad (for example, in the Republican Contract With America) that the problems poor families face are due to the demise of the two-parent family, rather than to economic change.

Further, a detailed cohort analysis of family vulnerability, indexed by employment, family size, and family type, showed that some groups had faced disadvantage continuously from 1976. Moreover, it is also evident that in the same family, unemployment could be suffered simultaneously by the caregiver generation (say fathers around age 40) and their offspring at young labour force ages. Ethnic differences were significant, with this factor most marked among Maori and Pacific Islanders (Jackson, 1994b). It is not clear that the new targeted policy initiatives adequately cater for such multiple risks.

TOWARDS A CONCLUSION

Throughout much of this century, New Zealand couples depended on the income of the sole breadwinner in the family, which in turn relied on a strict sexual division of labour to guarantee the husband's access to the labour market. The state provided a safety net when labour market wages were insufficient. This balance was best achieved during the baby boom, but since then a number of props have been removed with the restructuring of the labour market and a reduction in state supplements to the family wage.

In terms of income levels, some families are more disadvantaged than others and therefore more vulnerable, as evidenced by the increasing inequities of the past decade and the concomitant rise in the prevalence of poverty. Furthermore, it is the same families, already on low incomes, who have suffered most by decreasing participation in full-time employment and who may consequently be seen as more vulnerable to changing economic circumstances at the national level. A number of variables have been shown to be indicative of income levels and hence vulnerability, but their interactions are complex.

What is clear is that family size is an important factor when looking at family income. Age is still important for the highest- and lowest-income earners, but is less relevant for those earning in the middle ranges.

The labour force status of the family providers is also an important indicator of vulnerability. The increasing percentage of families with neither parent or partner in full-time employment indicates a growth in families who are in a position of vulnerability. These families with poor employment patterns also have the largest number of children.

The timing of the income declines seen over the 1980s highlights the differential effect of economic policy on family income. Those families with parents/partners in full-time employment experienced continuous erosion of their real income throughout the 1980s, with the severest declines between 1981 and 1986. Those persons unemployed, employed part-time, or not in the labour force (and hence receiving low incomes, predominantly in the form of state benefits) experienced an increase in real income between 1981 and 1986, which was followed between 1986 and 1991 by declines attributed to the benefit reforms that accompanied economic restructuring (Martin, 1995; St. John, 1994).

The results presented in this chapter raise a number of important policy issues. For those families identified as vulnerable, the issues revolve around the problem of raising children with limited resources. Added to this is the passing of increasing responsibility for welfare needs from the state to the 'family' (Jackson, 1994a). Not only income, but also changes in fertility timing and levels will determine a family's ability to meet the demands made on its resources (McPherson, 1992). Underlying demographic changes mean, therefore, that the interaction of different-sized birth cohorts (both at an inter- and intrafamily level) will also affect a family's vulnerability. While financial assistance policies could have played an important role in reducing vulnerability, as the next chapter will show, the overall trend of policy was in the opposite direction.

3

Financial Assistance to Families

Throughout most of the post-war era it is possible to see some continuity in the financial assistance provided for families with children, with incremental improvements reflecting changing demographic patterns and needs. In recent years, however, this momentum appears to have been lost, with policy changes responding to fiscal concerns, and policy design based on an implicit view of how the family ought to be. Meanwhile the pace of economic and technological change has not abated, and many families face an uncertain future.

In the early post-war period there were few policy debates over the definition of 'the family' or the nature of 'dependency'. Until the 1980s, the standard family norm was still a male breadwinner, 'his' wife who stayed home, and their children, considered to be 'his' dependants. The age at which children achieved 'independence' was not a major issue during a period of full employment and highly-subsidized tertiary education. But by the mid-1980s, economic priorities had changed, with full employment no longer the primary goal of macroeconomic policy (Shirley et al., 1990). Since then many elements of the 'social wage' have been eroded.

Given these changes, it is reasonable to question whether or not the redistributive mechanisms now in place for families are appropriate. Historically, family income assistance has taken a variety of forms. Earlier in this century, state regulations ensured that wages paid to the male breadwinner were sufficient to maintain a wife and several dependants in a reasonable standard of comfort. As these regulations lost favour, cash supplements, special tax exemptions and rebates, and health and housing subsidies evolved to supplant them. These mechanisms have their own problems, but they do not significantly distort market wages and with care can be tailored to individual family characteristics such as income and family structure.

Income supplements for families with dependent children involve *universal* payments that implicitly recognize the social contribution families make to the rearing of the next generation, and *targeted* payments that are directed at low-income families with the principal objective of alleviating or preventing poverty. Either form of assistance may be in cash, or in-kind (e.g., subsidies for health, housing, and education). This chapter focuses on cash supplements, while the next covers in-kind family support.

The rationale for direct financial assistance has changed over the years to reflect changing attitudes and dominant ideologies. Since 1990, the balance between tar-

geted and universal provision has shifted dramatically in favour of full targeting
and a lowered safety net of welfare provision for those outside the labour market
Along with the loss of universal cash supplements, in-kind assistance for the bet
ter-off has been reduced.

The current ideology as expressed in recent government reports (Richardson
1990; Shipley et al., 1991; Department of Social Welfare, 1995) asserts that 'wel
fare' traps individuals in poverty by encouraging state dependency. Lower welfare
benefits and tighter targeting are recommended to improve the incentive to find
work, with economic growth viewed as the primary means to reduce poverty.

While the idea of targeting is that limited resources should go where they are
most needed, there is a tendency for targeted systems to become less generous over
time (and in comparison to more universal systems). In the case of New Zealand
the welfare system has become much less generous since 1991, and direct family
assistance, at least since 1986, has been seriously eroded. Whereas many other
OECD countries are willing to offset the additional costs of children by means of
tax-generated funding, financial assistance to New Zealand families is small. A
Stephens and Bradshaw (1996) observe, total direct family assistance in this coun
try fell from 1.4% of the gross domestic product (GDP) in 1984 to 0.8% of GDP by
1993. In the case of families with three or four children, New Zealand appears
towards the bottom of the league table in terms of generosity.

HISTORY OF FINANCIAL ASSISTANCE FOR FAMILIES

At the beginning of this century the state accepted some role in alleviating poverty
Financial assistance to families was highly selective, tending to focus on large
families rather than all families with children. Selectivity was ensured by an in
come test that also took some account of assets, which discouraged many Maori
from applying. Tax exemptions were eventually made less selective, and a Family
Allowance was introduced in 1927 for low-income families. The income threshold
was reduced twice as the government came under increasing financial pressure
during the 1930s economic depression, and the level was not restored until 1936
when it became possible for either parent to apply for the benefit. It was generally
paid to the mother, at 20 pence for each child under 15 after the second child.

The Social Security Act (1938) introduced new benefits, virtually free health
and education, and state-funded maternity benefits giving entitlement to free pre-
peri-, and postnatal care for all, regardless of income. The Family Benefit replaced
the Family Allowance, and alien, Asiatic, and 'illegitimate' children (who had for
merly been ineligible) now qualified. In 1940, the Family Benefit became payable
for the second child and was then extended to all in 1941. Some adjustments were
made in the following three years, but the payment remained selective until 1946
when the means test was entirely removed, the sole requirement being the sighting
of the child's birth certificate. The elimination of bureaucratic procedures made
Maori feel free to apply, and it had the incidental benefit of ensuring full birth

TABLE 5. Chronology of major direct cash assistance and tax measures affecting
family well-being, New Zealand 1927–1990

Direct cash assistance	
927	Family Allowance introduced, targeted to low-income families
938	Social Security Act: provides universal superannuation to all over age 65, complete range of means-tested benefits including Family Benefit, made universal in 1946, and generally free national health service for all New Zealand residents
973	Domestic Purposes Benefit for sole-parent families
984	Family Care, targeted to low-income families
991	Social security cuts across the board; Family Benefit and Family Support amalgamated
Tax measures	
976–1982	Series of rebates introduced for low-income families
Early 1980s	Tax flattening in a series of steps
986	Goods and Services Tax (GST) introduced with no consumer items exempted; Family Support, a refundable tax credit, introduced; concept of a guaranteed minimum family income advanced but not introduced; tax flattened further and tax loopholes plugged
987	Flat tax rate proposed but rejected
988	Shift to two-tiered tax rate
990	Family Benefit and Family Support amalgamated

registration and the late registration of children born back as far as 1932 (Pool,
1991). By the end of the Second World War, the stringent targeting of the Family
Benefit and tax exemptions for spouses had been relaxed. The Family Benefit was
eventually enjoyed by households of all sizes and all income levels. In 1946 it
became fully universal, was not taxed, and was paid at the rate of 10 shillings a
week per child. For a woman with two children, this was the equivalent of at least
a full day's pay for a labourer (Beaglehole, 1993).

In the post-war period the Family Benefit was not indexed, and as a consequence
its purchasing power was not maintained. Relative to average wages, its value declined from around 8% at the end of the war to about 3% by 1983. In 1958, the
Family Benefit was increased from 10 shillings to the equivalent of $1.50, and in
1972, following the Report of the Royal Commission on Social Security, it was
raised to $3, when the tax exemption per dependent child under 18 years was abol-
ished. In 1979 the Family Benefit was raised to $6. This was the last inflationary
adjustment before the abolition of the benefit in 1991.

In the 1970s tax exemptions for the breadwinner's children and 'his' dependent
spouse fell out of favour. They were of greatest value to the highest-income taxpayers, so that reliance on them was an inappropriate way to deliver assistance
fairly to all families. From 1976 to 1982 the National government introduced various tax rebates designed to help low-income families with children. Rebates were
paid to the principal income earner; because they were a fixed amount, they were

more progressive than tax exemptions. These rebates were generally targeted so that they declined in value as family income increased.

By the 1980s assumptions about the family on which the rebates were based were becoming less appropriate. Some adjustments were inevitable, and in 1982 the 'Family Rebate' was introduced to take their place. The Family Rebate targeted assistance to low-income families, but it had certain disadvantages: it was not available either to beneficiaries or to very low-income earners who paid no tax, and it was only available in part to those who paid less tax than the total rebate. It was paid to the main income earner so that it may not have been accessed by the primary caregiver. Most significantly, it took no account of family size, and larger families were relatively disadvantaged as a result.

Along with changes to family rebates, the tax system itself was transformed in the 1980s by a series of tax flattening and broadening exercises. Adopting the McCaw Committee (1982) recommendations, a long flat tax bracket was established at the rate of 31% for salaries between $6,000 and $24,000. The highest-income earners were the clear beneficiaries of this move, at least in the short run.

In 1984 a $10 per week, per child, targeted payment called 'Family Care' was introduced. Unlike the Family Rebate which was targeted solely at low-income families, Family Care was abated only after reaching the income level at which the Family Rebate was completely eliminated. Families on benefits, such as the sickness or unemployment benefit, were ineligible for Family Care and the Family Rebate, but they were paid a supplement for children of $10 a week in addition to the Family Benefit. Thus beneficiaries and other low-income families were treated differently with the type of assistance based on the cause of low parental income. In 1986 a refundable tax credit called 'Family Support' replaced the Family Benefit, the Family Rebate, Family Care, and the child supplement, so that from then on all families with children would be treated the same. This change was facilitated by the grossing up of social security benefits so that they became taxable income. In the case of married couples, tax rebates or concessions were traditionally received by the male as the main income earner. The new family rebate (Family Support) was equally divided between parents, thereby overcoming this problem and reinforcing the view that parenting was not the domain of one individual.

In the late 1980s, the two instruments (Family Benefit and Family Support) came under scrutiny as concern about low family incomes mounted. A Royal Commission on Social Policy strongly supported the retention of an increased Family Benefit and its indexation (Royal Commission on Social Policy, 1988), but these recommendations and others advanced by the Commission were largely ignored.

TAXATION

Major changes to the tax system in New Zealand occurred in the mid-1980s, particularly in 1986. In October of that year a direct tax/indirect tax trade-off was made by further flattening the tax scale and introducing a comprehensive Goods and Services Tax (GST). The top rate was reduced from 66% to 48%, mostly benefiting high-income earners who had suffered most from fiscal drag in a period of high inflation. At the same time, many high earners did not actually pay as much tax as the scale implied, due to avoidance and evasion, as well as tax exemptions of various kinds. Tax reform during the 1980s consistently brought more income into the tax net by broadening the base and closing many loopholes. Nevertheless, one of the difficulties associated with tax flattening and the switch to a comprehensive indirect tax is that the burden of taxation shifts to the disadvantage of the poor. In other countries some of the adverse impact on families is reduced by exempting items such as food and children's clothing. After some debate in this country, it was argued that the complexities introduced by these special treatments were not justified. Exemptions from GST would benefit the better-off most and require a high overall rate of tax to achieve the same revenue. They would also significantly complicate the administration of a value-added tax. To alleviate the burden, especially for families, a transitional income tax rebate was introduced and the family assistance package was broadened with the introduction of Family Support and a Guaranteed Minimum Family Income (GMFI).

Other more extreme proposals were advanced by the Minister of Finance in 1987, but were abandoned following strong opposition, including opposition from within his own party. The Minister had announced that New Zealand would lead the world by introducing a flat rate of tax, estimated to be about 23%. In recognition that such a change would most disadvantage those on low incomes, a 'top-up' was proposed so that every 'working family' would have an income considerably above the level of benefits. Families with children were to be rewarded if they were in the full-time work-force, while others would have a subsistence benefit only.

In 1988 a 'watered-down' version of the flat tax proposal was introduced and two statutory rates of tax (24% up to $30,875 and 33% above that) were adopted. A low-income earners' rebate effectively changed this to a three-rate system (15% up to $9,500, 28% between $9,501–$30,875 with 33% above $30,875). The Family Support/Family Benefit combination that had been put in place in 1986 was reaffirmed and the original GMFI was also retained, but as before, it affected few families.

In 1990, the Labour government initiated a wide-ranging review of the social security system and in the budget of that year proposed a Universal Benefit based on the principle that the standard unit for benefits should be the individual. Thus the benefit of a couple would be twice the benefit of an individual who would have an add-on if he or she lived alone. The election of the National government later in the year saw the Labour proposals abandoned; then, in a controversial move, in December 1990, it was announced that social security benefits would be cut starting 1 April 1991. Families with children on benefits, such as unemployment, had a decrease of between $25 and $27 a week, representing a severe decline in disposable income. The Family Benefit was amalgamated with Family Support and the entire amount made subject to abatement. The threshold and abatement rates were not adjusted, with the effect that abatement at 30 cents in the dollar extended further into the $30,000s income range, especially for large families. In 1993 and 1994 some adjustments were announced, and in late 1994, the Labour opposition formulated its plans to increase Family Support, in case it became the next govern ment. By this time it is fair to say that both major political parties had accepted that Family Support was the way to assist low-income families. The tax system re mained neutral to marriage and there were no special exemptions for married per sons or dependent children, either within the income tax system or GST.

FAMILY ASSISTANCE SINCE 1986

The Real Value of Financial Assistance 1986–94

The introduction of Family Support in 1986 was an important supplement for large families on low incomes. Since then, the real purchasing power of family assist ance has declined, despite some adjustments. Families experienced lower incomes in the severe recession of the early 1990s, and more families applied for benefits. Moreover, 'user-pays' policies for education, health, and housing further dimin ished the living standards of many middle-income families. In the early 1990s some reduction in interest rates helped offset the impact of these changes, but by late 1994, real interest rates were at an historic high. Many families were facing a substantial increase in their mortgage interest payments at a time when gains from the appreciation of residential property seemed unlikely.

It is difficult to assess overall how families are faring when tax policies and social assistance, as well as market-driven costs, are changing. In particular, it is not appropriate to look at policies such as child allowances in isolation from the tax treatment of families or other family subsidies, as changes in one may be traded off for changes in the other. Nominal values are also unsatisfactory as they do not allow for changes in purchasing power over time. However, since 1986 tax poli cies directed at families have not been altered, so that the value of cash assistance for a family on a given income is simply the annual amount received in the form of Family Support and the Family Benefit. While not the full story, it is a relatively simple matter to compare the financial assistance provided over this period. Real assistance has fallen, both because *ad hoc* adjustments to the level of maximum assistance have not fully compensated for inflation, and because as wages rise with inflation, entitlement to Family Support is lost.

These features are demonstrated in Table 6 which shows the changes in the real value of family assistance from 1 October 1986 to the 1993/4 financial year for a typical low-income family. This could be either a sole-parent or two-parent family where the income is earned by only one partner. It is assumed that the family's income rises in line with movements in the average wage, as measured by Average Total Weekly Earnings (AWE). Table 6 takes into account the timing of any changes to either the amount of Family Support or the threshold for abatement, which usu ally take effect from 1 October rather than the beginning of the financial year. The 1994/95 year is also forecast using the announcements of the 1994 budget.

TABLE 6. One- and three-child families on Average Weekly Earnings,
New Zealand 1986–1995[1]

	Financial years			
	1986/87	1993/94	1994/95[2]	1986–95 (% change)
One-child family, 0.75 Average Weekly Earnings maximum amount of assistance includes				
Family Benefit (in $ per week)	42	42	42	-29.0
average consumer price index (Dec. 1993 quarter = 1,000)	716	998	1,008	40.8
average total weekly earnings (in $)	412	587	596	44.7
income threshold for abatement (in $)	14,000	17,500	18,750	33.9
annual income for low-income family (in $)	16,070	22,877	23,259	44.7
family's weekly Family Assistance (in $)	35	23.4	26.40	—
Family Assistance (in 1994/95 $)	49.3	—	26.40	-46.0
Three-child family, 1.0 Average Weekly Earnings maximum amount of assistance includes				
Family Benefit (in $ per week)	86	88	93	8.1
average consumer price index (Dec. 1993 quarter = 1,000)	716	998	1,008	40.8
average total weekly earnings (in $)	412	587	596	44.7
income threshold for abatement (in $)	14,000	17,500	18,750	33.9
annual income for low-income family (in $)	21,424	30,524	30,992	44.7
family's weekly Family Assistance (in $)	60.30	32.80	41.40	—
Family Assistance (in 1994/95 $)	84.90	—	41.40	-51.0
Three-child family, 1.5 Average Weekly Earnings maximum amount of assistance includes				
Family Benefit (in $ per week)	86	88	93	8.1
average consumer price index (Dec. 1993 quarter = 1,000)	716	998	1,008	40.8
average total weekly earnings (in $)	412	587	596	44.7
income threshold for abatement (in $)	14,000	17,500	18,750	33.9
annual income for family (in $)	32,136	45,786	46,488	44.7
family's weekly Family Assistance (in $)	23.20	0	0	—
Family Assistance (in 1994/95 $)	32.00	0	0	-100.0

[1] All children under 13 years.   [2] Estimates.
Source: St. John, 1994.

The analysis shows that a one-child family on 0.75 of Average Weekly Earnings (AWE) would need another $25.40 a week (or $1,320 a year) to have the same real value of family assistance in 1993/4 as in 1986. The threshold in 1993/4 would need to be $19,514, and the maximum family support $58.50, to restore the 1986 value. The deterioration in the value of this assistance is cumulative in its effects. If the real value had been protected, the low-income family whose income is a steady 0.75 AWE would have received around an extra $4,500 (1993/94 dollars) over the seven-year period. In the 1994 budget some adjustments were made to the threshold, but as Table 6 shows this has nowhere near restored Family Support in 1994/ 95 to its real 1986 level. The percentage loss in the annual value of support in 1994/95 dollars since 1986 is estimated to be 46%.

While the one-child family did not receive a boost when Family Support was first introduced in 1986, the larger family did gain at this time. Family Support for second and subsequent children was also increased in 1993 and 1994, even if only from 1 October in each year. Those families with older children may also have fared better as the amount for a second child aged 13 or over was significantly increased in 1993. Nevertheless, as Table 6 shows, a three-child family with all children under 13 on AWE has also suffered a severe erosion in the purchasing power of family assistance since 1986. The effect is even more marked for the middle-income family on 1.5 AWE because of the loss of Family Benefit and the increased targeting of the assistance for incomes above $27,000.

In summary, family assistance has fallen sharply since 1986 when same-size families on incomes that bear the same relativity to average earnings are compared. If income distribution had remained the same and family incomes had moved up in line with average wages, the effect would be startling enough. But beyond this, retrenchment in the labour market and a decline in real after-tax incomes for low- and middle-income groups have made the impact even more serious. Reductions in housing assistance and in the value of social security benefits, discussed in the next section, also have a severe impact on families with lower incomes.

While there were improvements in Family Support in 1993 and 1994, especially for those with older children, the younger, smaller family gained very little. In particular, those on benefits who were already getting the maximum rates did not gain from the lifting of the abatement threshold. The changes announced in 1994 took effect only from 1 October, so that the full impact was not experienced until the 1995/6 financial year. In the meantime the cumulative losses for low-income families have been large, contributing, no doubt, to a deterioration in the net wealth of many families from which it will be difficult to recover.

FAMILIES ON BENEFITS

The Post-War Social Security System

The post-war welfare state in New Zealand evolved from the comprehensive foundation of the 1938 Social Security Act. The aim of this Act was simply stated as 'safeguard[ing] the people of New Zealand' by providing medical treatment and benefits in order 'to maintain and promote the health and general welfare of the community' (New Zealand Social Security Act 1938). Thirty years later the Royal Commission on Social Security (RCSS) (1972) reiterated the basic principles of the 1938 Act, with particular emphasis on the ideals of community responsibility for the relief of need through flat-rate benefits paid for by taxation. The overriding aim was 'to ensure . . . that everyone is able to enjoy a standard of living much like that of the rest of the community, and thus is able to feel a sense of participation in, and belonging to, the community' (RCSS, 1972: 65). In the wake of this 1972 report, flat-rate, income-tested social security benefits were extended and the Domestic Purposes Benefit (DPB) for sole parents was introduced. As frictional unemployment increased, spending on welfare benefits rose, and their role and structure were increasingly questioned.

In 1985, a budget task force focused on the interface between the taxation and benefit systems, reflecting concerns that beneficiaries face high marginal tax rates when they undertake part-time work. The report concluded that the income exemption was too low, and that the joint income test for couples was particularly harsh. These issues were not fully resolved, but the 1986 budget announced that the income exemption would double, with an extra $10 for those with children. Benefits were grossed up and made taxable to improve equity among low-income earners. Beneficiaries also became eligible for the tax credit Family Support on the same basis as other low-income families.

A further attempt to resolve these intractable issues was undertaken by the Royal Commission on Social Policy. In its 1988 report, the Commission reviewed the major income maintenance schemes of Accident Compensation and National Superannuation, alongside existing social security transfers. It concluded that the systems as a whole reflected conflicting objectives and principles. The Commission identified problems such as: the differential treatment of those with similar needs; the lack of simplicity, transparency, and certainty, particularly within the income maintenance system; the inadequacies of joint income testing for all benefits (except National Superannuation) which failed to reflect ongoing social change and to account for the growing participation of women in the work-force; and the disincentive effects of the income support system which was becoming an impediment to work and a disincentive to individuals in providing for the future. Associated issues were the poverty trap and the replacement ratio (that is, the ratio of income when out of work to income when in work); and the lower priority awarded family assistance by comparison with income support for the elderly.

Few changes were actually made to the benefit system following the Royal Commission's report in 1988. Instead, the December 1990 Statement of Economic and Social Initiative (Richardson, 1990) expressed concern over low growth levels in the New Zealand economy, high fiscal deficits, high interest rates, inflation, and unemployment. A 'stiff medicine' of wage restraint and measures 'to arrest the drift from work to welfare' was prescribed, with more 'user-pays' in health, housing, and education. The Statement contained four new principles that significantly departed from those of the 1988 Royal Commission:

- fairness, interpreted as adequate access to government assistance for those with a genuine need;
- self-reliance, meaning that government programmes should not foster state

dependency, but increase the ability of individuals to take care of themselves;
- efficiency in the provision of social services so as to ensure the highest possible value from each tax dollar spent; and
- personal choice, through fostering alternative providers to the state in areas such as health, education, housing, and welfare services.

Despite the benefit reforms of the early 1990s, the numbers of New Zealanders supported by benefits (excluding those on National Superannuation) continued to increase (Department of Social Welfare, 1985–95). Department of Social Welfare data show that on 3 July 1994, around one-quarter of all dependent children were in households supported by benefits (excluding Family Support). This figure of 261,697 children excludes any adult children who may also be partially or fully dependent on parents and may still live at home. The majority of these dependent children (65%) are in sole-parent households receiving the Domestic Purposes Benefit (DPB) or Widows Benefit, with a further 26% in families on Unemployment or Training Benefits.

Most recipients of the DPB are female with small families. Just over half of all DPB beneficiaries with children have only one child, while only 5% have more than three children. Growth in the numbers of families on the DPB and the Unemployment Benefit appeared to flatten out after the benefit cuts in 1991, but interpretation of the data requires caution as those on the Sickness and Invalids benefits continued to show a strong increase. Eligibility appears to have tightened as the number of rejected applications for the DPB more than doubled from 1990 to 1994 (Department of Social Welfare, 1985–95).

As core benefits declined in value, applications for supplementary assistance in the form of Special Benefits and Special Needs Grants increased. The criteria for such grants were tightened in 1990, but after an initial decline, the numbers continued to grow because of increasing demand and a policy change that permitted more than one grant application per year. In 1993 around three-quarters of recoverable grants (e.g., clothing and bedding, accommodation, power, furniture, and education) and non-recoverable grants (e.g., medical costs and re-establishment costs) were paid to those on the Unemployment Benefit and the DPB. The switch to an Accommodation Supplement was expected to diminish the number receiving special benefits and one-off grants, but the monthly data in 1994 show that these special benefits were used as much as before.

Increased Targeting of Social Assistance

Along with reductions in core benefits and the tightening of eligibility for special benefits and grants, many other social payments and subsidies also became targeted. Housing assistance was rationalized into one cash-based Accommodation Supplement from 1 July 1993, for which all low-income people are eligible, not just those on benefits. This was accompanied by a shift to charging market rents for all state houses, and later to privatizing state mortgages through their sale to Mortgage Corporation.

Until 1992, subsidized state housing was allocated through a points system which ranked applicants according to 'need'. Recent housing reforms are designed to treat everyone the same, by reducing the subsidy for state tenants and transferring additional funding to those in private-sector accommodation. Underlying this policy is the principle of 'matched' accommodation: the accommodation supplement is paid according to the number of bedrooms required. Those with extra bedrooms are not subsidized on the full market rent so as to encourage them to relocate to smaller accommodation.

User-pays policies were also extended to selected aspects of tertiary education, child care, and health. Tertiary study grants became fully targeted on parental income for unmarried students under 25, and students' loans were introduced, repayable above a threshold of income as an additional marginal tax. Payments by noncustodial parents in the case of marriage breakdown were rationalized in the Child Support Act 1993 which provided that even those on benefits would pay a minimum of $10 per week. Most health care is paid for by the state, but token attempts to move to a user-pays regime were introduced: patients could now be charged varying amounts for pharmaceuticals, general practitioner and public hospital outpatient services, and a small percentage of the first few days of hospital 'hotel costs'. Low-income, child, and retired patients were allocated a 'Community Services Card' permitting them to receive all or some of these services free of charge. These targeted changes have extended to low-income workers the poverty trap already experienced by beneficiaries of social assistance. The cumulative effects can result in effective marginal tax rates (EMTRs) well above 70% and even above 100% for low income ranges (St. John and Heynes, 1993).

High EMTRs affect many men, but may be particularly adverse for women who are more likely to be the secondary earners in families with children. For example, above $27,000 of joint parental income, Family Support abates at 30 cents in the dollar. Thus a contribution in the way of part-time work by a secondary earner may seem scarcely worthwhile if as a result, 15 or 28 cents is paid in tax, then 30 cents of Family Support and maybe 25 cents of the Accommodation Supplement is lost. If the woman concerned is also a student with a loan to repay, the combined loss may be between 80 and 93 cents for every additional dollar earned. Losses can also be extended to child-care subsidies and the Community Services Card.

A low tax policy has necessitated a stringent user-pays approach to social assistance, which in turn has imposed high dead-weight losses through the impact of abatement on the EMTR of lower- and middle-income families. Perversely, concern about the efficiency or dead-weight losses associated with high marginal tax rates has helped keep the top personal and company tax rate in New Zealand at a low 33 cents in the dollar.

Problems at the interface between benefits, taxes, and other forms of social assistance remain acute, both for those on benefits and those on low to middle incomes. The income exemption for benefit abatement for those in receipt of benefits has not been altered since 1986. The cumulative effect of these problems became evident in the early 1990s, when a series of reports prepared by groups critical of the direction of social policy confirmed the experience of serious deprivation and suffering among a significant minority of New Zealand families. There was evidence of long hours, low pay, and child labour in the retail sector; a deterioration in the position of most women workers; an association between the benefit cuts and increasing stress on family relationships and intrafamily conflict; and indications that the scale of the benefit cuts was linked to relative poverty and increasing destitution (Second New Zealand Sweating Commission, 1990; People's Select Committee, 1992; Family Centre and BERL, 1991).

The economy began to show signs of a recovery in late 1992, but the benefits for families were not apparent. In a report on family and child poverty, the New Zealand Council of Christian Social Services expressed grave concern about the stress of financial hardship on New Zealand families (Jackman, 1993). Problems identified included overcrowding, inadequate diet, inadequate clothing, lack of medical attention, behavioural problems, and child abuse. The report concluded that social disintegration was increasing and the policy of reducing welfare provisions had created a social deficit that would remain for generations. The Council commissioned a further report by an economist who disputed the view that there had been no alternatives to the benefit cuts of 1991, arguing that these cuts were in effect, a 'tax on the poor' (Dalziel, 1993).

The 1991 cuts in social welfare benefits were especially severe when considered in conjunction with the radical changes in housing policy. One study showed that some households had to pay more than 40% of their income in rent, and single people living alone on basic benefits could be paying more than 50%. Most people pay their rent and power first, then other essentials, with food purchased out of the remainder which is often insufficient to meet basic needs (Labour Caucus, 1994).

In 1994, reports from voluntary agencies in the welfare field, such as food banks, continued to confirm that the recovery was not effectively reducing hardship. Many argued that they were over-stretched in meeting demands for their services. Evidence of increasing stress on low-income families led to a relaxing of criteria for Special Needs Grants just before Christmas 1994. Between Christmas and New Year, government grants for food totalled over six times the amount in the same period the year before, while these and other special-needs grants tripled in number.

Poverty in New Zealand

Chapter 2 has identified vulnerable families, taking as its base an analysis of census data on trends and differentials in income and labour force participation, controlling for family size and type. This provides a context for the present review of poverty based on data from the Household Expenditure and Income Survey (HEIS). The HEIS gives precise information on income, but it is somewhat restricted in its range of socio-economic variables. While it is difficult to establish precisely the numbers experiencing poverty and the depth of that poverty and trends over time, it is clear that relative poverty and deprivation disproportionately affect children and their parents. This conclusion is supported by analysing the proportion of all dependent children in each quintile of disposable household income (adjusted for household size using equivalence scales).

It is a little difficult to interpret the results in Table 7 particularly given the high numbers in 1992/3 in the lowest quintile. They could be seen as confirming the income shifts by age, labour force status, family size, and ethnicity as identified in Chapter 2 (e.g., the decline in incomes of two-parent families). However, in both periods, nearly 50% of all children are located in the bottom two quintiles.

TABLE 7. Quintiles of equivalent disposable household income by numbers of dependent children, New Zealand 1987/88 and 1992/93

Income quintiles	1987/88		1992/93	
	No. of children	%	No. of children	%
Bottom	202,017	22.2	308,838	32.1
2nd bottom	236,340	26.0	152,919	15.8
Middle	232,999	25.6	208,267	21.6
2nd top	160,923	17.7	182,250	18.9
Top	77,877	8.5	111,694	11.6
Total	*910,156*	*100.0*	*962,968*	*100.0*

Source: Unpublished analysis of HEIS. Social Policy Agency 1994.

Between 1987/8 and 1992/3 the boundaries between quintiles (1993 dollar values) fell systematically (upper panel, Table 8). Against that, the mean income for the lowest quintile has dropped, while that for the highest has increased by about 9%. Thus while there is some uncertainty surrounding the figures for HEIS in 1992/93, they do suggest that the gap in equivalent disposable income (after benefits, tax, and Family Support) has widened significantly, mainly because of gains at the top end. The largest groups in the bottom quintile are two-adult households with three or more children, one adult with one or more children, and two-adult households with two children. The first two family types have their modal groups in the bottom quintile (Easton, 1994b).

The size of the benefit cuts in 1991 was apparently based on formal research by Treasury (Brashares, 1993), which attempted to determine income adequacy by setting various, if somewhat arbitrary, poverty lines. Among the most controversial of these was the food share standard, based on the costs of food converted by a multiplier to give a minimum income level. The cost of food was variously determined, with one measure taken as the average cost of feeding a prisoner at $27.09 per week. Multipliers of various food standards of 3, 4, and 5 were considered, with 4 favoured as 3 was felt to be 'too stringent'.

The same paper also used a relative measure expressing the poverty line as some multiple of median disposable income, but the choice of the multiplier appears equally arbitrary. Other researchers (e.g., Stephens, 1992) have also used various relative poverty lines, but such research provides no objective answer to the question of what constitutes poverty for a given family. Trends over time are also disputed (Easton, 1994b; Stephens, 1994b). While researchers disagree on methodology, it is widely agreed that poverty among families has worsened in the 1990s. Easton (1993) concluded that the benefits of economic growth would not significantly 'trickle down' to the poor and that we may be seeing the beginning of a permanent 'two nations' New Zealand, with one nation prospering, rich, and skilled, and the other stagnating, poor, unskilled, and largely unemployed.

TABLE 8. Quintile boundaries of equivalent disposable household income, New Zealand, 1987/88 and 1992/93 (1993 $)

Income quintiles	1987/88	1992/93
Quintile boundaries		
bottom and second bottom	16,994	15,019
second top and top	39,299	37,531
difference	22,305	22,512
Mean income of quintiles		
bottom quintile	11,334	11,132
top quintile	51,028	55,483
difference	39,694	44,351

Source: Unpublished analysis of HEIS. Social Policy Agency 1994.

An Analysis of Family Support

If it is true, as some economists argue (St. John, 1994), that improving family assistance is an important way to address family poverty, then there is a dearth of research into the design of such assistance and even of debate about its nature. Family assistance has evolved from a selective approach in the first part of this century to a universal approach in the early post-war period, to one that is now tightly targeted through family income testing. The loss of the Family Benefit and universal subsidies for certain areas of health care has signalled the demise in the 1990s of the notion of community responsibility for all children. It has been replaced with the notion of community responsibility for children in low-income families and as such it contrasts with the situation in Western European countries. In the UK, for example, universal child allowances have been retained and indexed, but recent proposals include an increase in the child allowance funded by taxing higher-income families (but, significantly, not means-testing it). In Australia, while means tests have been levied on the family allowance, they do not apply until very high levels of assets and income are reached.

There has been very little debate about whether Family Support is a suitable mechanism for redistribution, and little research is available on how it is perceived by recipients. It is currently allocated by the Department of Social Welfare to beneficiaries and by the Inland Revenue Department through the tax system to income earners. A major study (Fleming and Easting, 1994) on how couples share their income hardly mentions Family Support. While it is distributed to the primary caregiver (in most cases the woman), the women interviewed did not mention Family Support as an identifiable amount of money over which they had control. In that respect it was in no way different from the overall pattern of financial control in the household. Another micro-level study (West Auckland Women's Centre, 1994) had little to say about Family Support, in spite of a high level of financial difficulty being noted by respondents.

In essence, Family Support reduces the parents' tax liability on account of their dependent children (up to 18 if still at school). It is a tax credit, rather than a rebate, as it can result in a payment from the Inland Revenue Department (IRD) if tax liability is too low for the rebate to cancel out all the tax due. In any case, the usual method of payment is in the form of a direct cash credit to the primary caregiver's account. The amount of tax credit is a function of the joint gross income of the two parents, or that of the custodial caregiver in a sole-parent family. The basis of the joint income test is the income of the caregiver and his/her partner if he or she is resident in the same house. The income of a separated or divorced parent is ignored. For those who receive benefits the procedure is a little different: the Department of Social Welfare pays Family Support, and the primary benefit for recipient families is that they are able to recover this amount by billing the IRD.

Although the concept of Family Support has become widely accepted, family structures and circumstances have changed. Families are extremely diverse and face uncertainty in employment as well as income insecurity, so that increasing numbers receive a benefit for part of a year. Complex custody situations and blended families frequently create situations in which the income of one partner is not necessarily available to the children of the other. In addition, older teenagers who have left school and cannot access the unemployment benefit increasingly depend on state support, as do families facing growing demands to support adult children and dependent family members in the case of sickness or infirmity. Many families who might be described as vulnerable are exposed to multiple and simultaneous social risk, such as unemployment among both caregiving and younger dependent members of the same household (see Chapter 2).

Moreover, many of the mechanisms of Family Support are unwieldy and complex. It is calibrated on a current income basis, so that it is reconciled at the end of the year when some portion of Family Support may have to be repaid. (This is more likely in a recovering economy, especially for those who have come off benefits.) There is also a potential for conflict over who should repay any excess family support with no guarantee that the partner who pays will be compensated. The reliance by many families on end-of-year adjustments means that many women are not receiving this money on a regular basis and may indeed not receive it at all. Furthermore, many families will now be affected by higher rates of abatement as the top threshold remains unadjusted.

Family Support is poorly integrated with other targeted provisions that have tended to be added on top. The cumulative impact of taxes, the abatement of Family Support, the Accommodation Supplement, and the repayment of student loans could easily take the effective tax rate to 70–98 cents in the dollar, depending on who earns the extra family income. Other targeted amounts may also be affected, such as child-care subsidies, the Community Services Card, and Child Support payments. Moreover, families on benefits for part of the year face two different departments, while some targeted provisions such as the Accommodation Supplement are dealt with by other agencies. Uptake is constrained because the application form is very complicated and there is widespread ignorance and apprehension about the agencies involved. Time costs for families trying to ascertain their entitlements are also significant.

CONCLUSION

This chapter casts doubt on the adequacy of income support for New Zealand families. Overall state spending on financial assistance for families on account of their children has declined, as spending has become more targeted. Moreover, this has not meant that higher-income families get less, while those at the lower end have been protected. Real family assistance for low-income families has fallen since 1986; when coupled with core benefit reductions, this decline in assistance has resulted in a rapid rise in the number of those in need. Major problems arise from the imbalance between targeted and universal provision, and from the inappropriateness of Family Support as a major means of redistribution to families.

Social welfare benefits, Family Support, the Accommodation Supplement, the Community Services Card, child-care subsidies, and student allowances are all determined on the basis of family income. Moreover, the impact of targeting all social provisions, with the associated high effective marginal tax rates, is exacerbated by the insistence on the couple as the unit of assessment. For women who are frequently the secondary earners, targeting on the basis of joint incomes results in high effective marginal tax rates, thereby providing a considerable work disincentive.

Although an analysis of the impact of joint income testing and possible reforms lies outside the scope of this study, a few comments are appropriate. In the case of beneficiaries, using the couple as the assessment unit is manifest in both the lower benefits paid to couples as compared to two single people (who may also live together) and the severe joint income test that applies when either partner earns extra income. This form of targeting assumes a high degree of intrafamily dependence and support which may not occur in modern families. It is true that families may share with other family members, but it is doubtful whether policies made on the presumption that this happens are effective in promoting this behaviour. From a fiscal viewpoint, couple-based targeting superficially appears to save money, but rapid social change and more fluidity in family structures make this form of targetng difficult and expensive to administer. As targeting treats married or *de facto* couples more harshly than single people, anecdotal evidence suggests that it is an additional pressure on families to separate.

Another of the unattractive features of today's targeted welfare state is that the separate targeting arrangements are not integrated. The result is that New Zealand has a clumsy, costly, inefficient set of overlapping provisions with different measures of income, different units of assessment, different rates of abatement that become cumulative, and different departments involved in each targeting provision. On the other hand it is clear that an integrated system such as the one proposed in the 1991 budget, using 'smart card' technology, would be both unworkable and unfair. Such an arrangement would not solve the problem of high effective marginal tax rates, but would extend targeting so that practically all families were captured in the targeting net. The combination of Family Support, other targeted social provisions, low top marginal tax rates, and user-pays policies has clearly shifted the problem of high marginal tax rates from rich to poor and middle incomes. It is difficult to see how any amelioration can occur unless the doctrine of targeting the poor' is effectively challenged. In some quarters it has been suggested that a basic income be provided for all, with a relatively high marginal tax applying to the first dollar earned (Rankin, 1991). While this may seem a radical concept, in many respects it is based on the same broad assumptions which underpinned the provision of a 'family wage'.

4

Families and Social Services

The main provisions of the 'family wage' in New Zealand's post-war economy centred on the activities of the industrial court and the participation of wage-earners in the labour market (see Chapter 5). The wage itself was not limited to income but included social components, such as predominantly free access to health and education, the widespread availability of housing and housing finance, and a comprehensive range of welfare services. The history of these services has been dominated by the changing responsibilities of central government, voluntary organizations, and to a lesser extent, private-sector agencies.

In the case of health care, a hybrid system evolved from the merging of private, voluntary, and public services (local and central government). While central government was initially a reluctant participant, almost 80% of health care today is publicly funded. Similarly, in education, the predominantly state system of primary and secondary schooling is available to all children between the ages of five and 19, with attendance at school compulsory until the age of 16. Early-childhood education is also widely available to children under six years of age through a comprehensive range of services primarily administered by voluntary agencies with financial assistance from government.

One of the consequences of comparatively high wage rates in New Zealand (Castles, 1985; Davidson, 1989) has been the extremely high level of home-ownership encouraging New Zealand families to regard the costs of purchasing a house both as a normal cost of living and as a form of social security in retirement (the possession of a mortgage-free home). Access to home-ownership was facilitated by state finance at low interest rates; where families could not afford their own home, the New Zealand government (especially after the passing of the 1938 Social Security Act) developed a state housing programme based on single-family rental homes. The significance of government support for private home-ownership is graphically illustrated by the lending policies of the 1920s, when the definition of a 'worker' was broadened to include most white-collar workers, and home purchasers were able to borrow up to 95% of the cost price of a home. By the end of the 1920s, the state was directly or indirectly financing almost half the houses being built in New Zealand at that time.

By contrast, in the provision of 'welfare' services, the state appeared more ambivalent. During the colonial period considerable emphasis was placed on individual responsibility, with support services limited to 'near relatives' or private charities. Government had no mandate to 'interfere' either in the workplace or the ome, and when children were neglected through parental destitution or desertion, hey could be sold, traded, or farmed out as domestic servants and unpaid appren-ices. It was not until the latter years of the nineteenth century that social problems, uch as child neglect and exploitation, prompted the establishment of a number of vomen's organizations aimed at protecting and rescuing children from 'unworthy')arents (Tennant, 1989). Welfare services since that time have vacillated between)revention and treatment, and while services today are conceptually divided into levelopmental, remedial, and rehabilitative categories, in practice they exhibit dual unctions of reform and control.

EARLY-CHILDHOOD SERVICES

Nowhere are these conflicting aims better exemplified than in the development ınd provision of early-childhood services. The earliest attempts to provide child-ıood services for infants were largely confined to the voluntary philanthropic ac-ivities of well-to-do women providing care for the unsupervised children of poor vomen in paid employment. These early child-care activities were followed by a nore socially 'respectable' service to 'educate' the children of affluent parents, hereby prompting the ambivalence between 'education' and 'care' which has domi-ıated the history of early-childhood services to the present day. While the child vas at the centre of these disparate developments, the needs of women in paid ımployment were either systematically opposed or conveniently ignored. House-ıolds generally supported the gendered division of labour and the domestication)f women, and government policies were aimed at discouraging women's access o the paid work-force. Early-childhood policies through to the 1970s simply re-`lected these broader societal attitudes and practices.

The 1970s saw a gradual shift, first in thinking and attitudes, and then in policy, ıs the women's movement among others called for alternatives for the care of :hildren, so that women might achieve some occupational choice as well as greater :ontrol over their own lives. The Select Committee on Women's Rights (1975) identified child care as the most important factor in enhancing opportunities for women, but there was still considerable resistance to the notion of child care out-side the immediate or extended family. Despite this resistance, the availability and ıse of child-care services rapidly expanded with a sevenfold increase in participa-:ion rates between 1976 and 1987. In 1987, over 100,000 children were enrolled in ₴arly-childhood education, representing two-thirds of the children in that age group, attending at least 26 different types of facilities.

In 1989 early-childhood care and education services were brought together with funding and regulations applied across the sector as a whole. The diversity of the system was retained with a high degree of autonomy for a wide range of providers, within a centrally-controlled regulatory framework that included the Education Act (1989) and the Education Amendment Act (1990). These regulations required early-childhood centres in receipt of government funding to be licensed and char-

TABLE 9. Children enrolled in early-childhood services at 1 July 1995, New Zealand

Service	No. of children enrolled
Licensed services (total)	*141,115*
kindergartens	47,208
playcentres	19,108
child care (regular)	53,769
child care (home-based)	6,114
correspondence school	901
Kohanga Reo	14,015
Unlicensed/developing services (total)	*18,287*
funded playgroups	14,155
Pacific Islander early-childhood centres	3,709
developing *Kohanga Reo*	248
unlicensed playcentres	175
All services	*159,402*

Source: Ministry of Education Data Management Unit.

tered. Licensing was designed to ensure the maintenance of basic standards in the provision of premises and staffing, whereas the development of charters established a framework for quality assurance.

Today, more than 90% of all four-year-olds and over 70% of three-year-olds are enrolled in a formal early-childhood service. The participation rates for under-ones, one-year-olds, and two-year-olds are 11%, 22%, and 37% respectively. The main providers are free kindergartens, playcentres, Pacific Island language groups, child-care centres, home-based services, and *Kohanga Reo* (Maori language groups). These services depend on voluntary contributions of both time and money by primary caregivers (and, to a lesser extent, other family members). Over 90% of primary caregivers of children under five are women, and 98% of those employed in the early-childhood sector are women.

A 1993 survey of primary caregivers found that only 35% of preschool children were outside formal or informal early-childhood services. Twenty-eight percent of children were cared for in unlicensed premises, with lower-income households (having at least one adult employed) the most likely users of informal care arrangements. The use of child-care centres tends to rise in accordance with socio-economic status.

Over the decade 1983–93, the number of Maori children enrolled in early childhood education more than doubled from 12,516 to 28,503. *Kohanga Reo*, where Maori language is the medium of learning and instruction, are the single most popular form of early-childhood education for Maori families today, followed by kindergartens and child-care centres. Despite the improvement in Maori participation rates, they have not kept pace with the non-Maori participation rate. One of the main reasons for this difference is the cost of early-childhood services, which remains a significant barrier to many low-income families, especially those of Maori and Pacific Island origins. It seems evident that the child-care subsidy is not fully meeting its objective in making early-childhood care and education affordable for those on low incomes. This problem has been exacerbated by 1994 regulations limiting eligibility to those parents who are employed or engaged in education or training. Significant users of the child-care subsidy are on the Domestic Purposes or Unemployment Benefit. In the case of *Kohanga Reo*, it is estimated that 90% of the 5,000 subsidy-users will lose access to financial assistance because of the 1994 regulations, which in turn is likely to have a significant impact on the provision of *Kohanga Reo* services.

TABLE 10. Early-childhood services: government expenditure (in million $), New Zealand 1990–1995

	1990/91	1991/92	1992/93	1993/94	1994/95
Type of service					
child care	57.7	55.7	65.8	73.3	80.6
kindergarten	56.4	58.9	59.2	60.2	61.4
playcentre	10.4	10.1	10.4	10.5	10.3
home-based	6.0	6.2	9.9	12.8	11.3
Kohanga Reo	19.9	37.5	40.5	41.5	45.6

Source: Ministry of Education Data Management Unit.

Chartered services receive $2.25 per hour of government bulk funding for up to 30 hours a week for each child over two years of age; $4.50 is payable for under-two-year-olds and a notional rate of $2.86 per hour applies to kindergartens. Non-chartered and developing *Kohanga Reo*, Pacific Island language nests, and playgroups receive a lower level of funding. Child-care centres, home-based care, and *Kohanga Reo* can also receive a child-care subsidy with up to 30 hours allocated to families who meet the income criteria and who are employed or engaged in education or training programmes approved by the New Zealand Income Support Service, and up to nine hours a week for those not in employment or training.

Subsidy funding is paid to early-childhood services based on the number of children enrolled and the period over which they are enrolled. As funding is demand-driven, government expenditure increases in accordance with the level of participation. From 1 March 1992, kindergarten teachers' salaries were included with sessional funding, allowing kindergartens to generate more funding by expanding their services. Funding for *Kohanga Reo* was not fully financed by the government's education budget until 1991/92, but from that time on funding has been available on the same basis as for other types of services. Although the conceptual integration of child care and education has taken place at an administrative level, some historical inequalities, notably access to funding, still remain. Kindergarten teachers, for example, work fewer hours for much higher pay than child-care work ers, even though they do the same work and receive essentially the same training Despite these inconsistencies, education remains a significant factor in the compo sition of the family wage even though the wage itself has been fundamentally al tered since the mid-1980s.

HEALTH SERVICES

A second component in the constitution of the family wage concerned the develop ment and spread of health services. The government was involved in the provision of health services starting in the early colonial period, although the main feature of the present system originated with the 1938 Social Security Act. Free hospita services and free medicines were introduced in 1939, and a maternity benefit schem followed shortly afterwards. The first Labour government also proposed to offer free general medical services, but this proposal was strenuously opposed by the Medical Association of the time; as a consequence, the private practices of genera practitioners today are subsidized by the state.

The government has some involvement in financing all major types of health service in the country, although the relative size of its contribution varies greatly Public and environmental health services are carried out almost exclusively by means of government funding, as are teaching and medical research. In the provi sion of hospital care, state funding predominates, though the private sector plays a significant role. The principal source of public funding for health, as well as for other social services, is general taxation levied on private income (see Figure 5).

Although the state dominates the provision of health services in terms of aggre gate expenditure on health (i.e., public and private), it is difficult to argue that New Zealand is overspending by international standards. In 1990, New Zealand spent 7.3% of gross domestic product (GDP) on health, compared with an average of 7.6% for the OECD countries (McKendry and Muthummala, 1993; Bowie and Shirley, 1994). Only a handful of OECD countries, and notably some of the poor est ones, spend a significantly lower proportion of their GDP on health care. Fur ther, unlike the experience of various other countries, such as the USA, Canada, Australia, Germany, and France, New Zealand's total spending on health as a per centage of GDP has remained stable since 1980, as has real per capita spending on health (Easton and Bowie, 1993).

In 1980, public funding was 88% of total health expenditure (public and pri vate). By 1992 it had been pegged back to 78.9% as successive governments shifted the cost of health care from the public purse to the individual. Between 1980 and 1992, private health insurance increased from 1.1% of total health expenditure to 4.8%, and the amount paid directly by individuals increased from 10.4% to 16% The cost shifting of health expenditure has been driven by a belief in the efficacy of competition when the international evidence to support this view is far from com pelling.

FIGURE 5. Sources of health funding, New Zealand 1990–1991

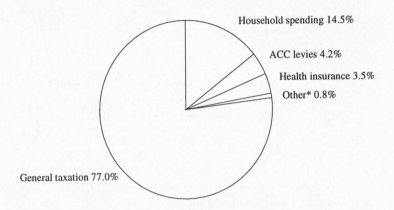

* Other comprises 0.5% local bodies and 0.3% voluntary organizations.
Source: McKendry and Muthummala, 1993.

FIGURE 6. Distribution of health funding, New Zealand 1990–1991

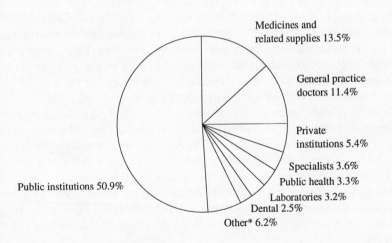

* Other comprises physiotherapy (1.5%), diagnostic services, including X-rays (1.5%), teaching (2%), and research (1.2%).
Source: McKendry and Muthummala, 1993.

New Zealand

FIGURE 7. Health spending in relation to the life cycle, New Zealand 1989–1990

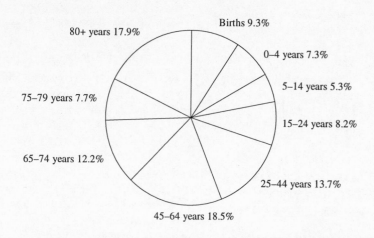

Source: Morris, 1991.

The impact of cost shifting, however, has significant ramifications for certain sectors and groups when considered in relation to the life cycle. There are differences between men and women in the quantity and type of health services they use: women are the majority users of primary and secondary care, particularly for life events such as pregnancy, childbirth, and contraception. Pregnancy and childbirth account for a high proportion of hospital admissions. Furthermore, women interact with the health services more than men on behalf of others in their care, such as children and elderly dependants. Whereas women use the health services more for non-communicable diseases, men are more likely to be admitted to hospital as a result of an accident in every age group under 65 years.

The range of child health services provided in New Zealand includes newborn screening, parenting support, vision and hearing screening for children aged 0–4 years, and immunization programmes. The majority of child health services are provided by Crown Health Enterprises (previously Area Health Boards) and the Plunket Society, a major voluntary agency which, like other voluntary organizations in the health sector, is now heavily subsidized by the government. The immunization of children against a range of diseases is free and is usually performed by general practitioners, although some immunizations are administered by public health nurses.

One of the most pertinent barometers of child health services in New Zealand is health camps (Tennant, 1994), which were established in the early twentieth century to cater for malnourished children or for those who had been exposed to tuberculosis. These camps initially catered for Pakeha children, with school and district nurses providing a link between home and school. With the economic depression of the 1930s, short-term, intensive 'holiday' camps for disadvantaged children mushroomed, and in 1936 a Federation of Health Camps was established.

During the second phase of the Health Camp movement, the promotion and development of permanent health camps was linked with the Department of Health. Although the medical model of health was always particularly prominent, by the 1950s and 1960s children were also being sent to health camps for emotional and behavioural reasons. This broader interpretation of child health continues to the present day, although over the past decade increasing numbers of children have been referred to the camps for malnutrition, which was characteristic of the movement's formative years. The increasing incidence today of malnutrition and communicable diseases such as tuberculosis can be associated with an increase in relative poverty and a significant decline in the health component of the family wage.

HOUSING

Another significant element in the range of in-kind support services for families is the provision of housing assistance for low-income families, which formed a major part of government policy during the post-war period. New Zealanders have always placed a high value on home-ownership (71% in 1983), with government policies offering low-interest loans for the purchase of a home, as well as state-provided low-rental accommodation. As in other areas of family assistance, government policy in the 1960s and 1970s was forced to adapt to the diversity of family forms by providing a wider variety of programmes encompassing low-rental homes or low-interest loans, with few constraining criteria apart from low income. In the early 1980s priority was given to first-home seekers irrespective of factors such as family size, marital status, or dependants. Since then, however, assistance has become far more targeted, and in the 1990s government policies have been dominated by market rentals and commercial practices.

The increasing demand for housing in the early 1980s was initially prompted by factors such as a change in the geographical distribution of the population (e.g., large population gains in the north of the North Island), the increasing number of young adults, and significant growth in the numbers of smaller families (single-person households and incomplete family households). A growing disparity between the housing supply and demand became a major issue. Changing economic circumstances and escalating unemployment particularly affected Maori, who found it increasingly difficult to secure mortgage finance and affordable housing. This problem was further accentuated by the demographic youthfulness of the Maori population and was one of the trends highlighted by the National Housing Commission in its 1988 report. The Commission identified a serious housing need among households with children in central and southern parts of the Auckland region, with Maori and Pacific Island families, low-income households, unemployed single people, sole-parent households, and ex-psychiatric patients identified as the groups with the most pressing housing requirements.

As far as older families are concerned, a number of policy initiatives (such as the Homeswap Scheme, Home Equity Conversion, and the provision of relocatable or 'granny' flats) have been developed to enable elderly people to be housed on a relative's or friend's property, with the sponsoring organization leasing the units to the home-owner. Initially there was widespread interest in the provision of 'granny flats', but this scheme had a low take-up rate, partly because of the heterogeneity of the elderly population and older New Zealanders' preference to live independently in their own homes. Often the equity of the larger house is insufficient to purchase a smaller home, yet the cost of maintaining the larger home is beyond the income of an elderly home-owner.

Government has also provided assistance for disabled adults and their families in the form of grants for alterations to homes, suspensory loans for motor cars, expenses to attend treatment, and salary subsidies for carers in day-care centres. However, the extent of government support has been criticized as inadequate in the context of 'de-institutionalization', which shifts the costs of community care to family members, especially women. Although housing was once a key determinant in the egalitarian ethos of the welfare state, today it is increasingly portrayed as an indicator of socio-economic and ethnic inequality.

WELFARE SERVICES

Whereas education, health, and housing services have historical significance as in-kind support provided for families and households as components of the 'social' wage, welfare has generally been viewed as a remedial or rehabilitative service for dysfunctional individuals and families. The first piece of child welfare legislation was the Neglected and Criminal Children Act of 1867, which led to the establishment of industrial schools. Conditions were harsh, and children were often kept so long that they became thoroughly institutionalized. When the Education Department assumed responsibility for these schools in 1880, it developed a range of child welfare services impinging on family life through the work of truancy officers, school nurses, infant life protection officers, and juvenile probation officers. These early services established a pattern of central state involvement which remains to the present day.

The need to cater for differing family practices among Maori and Pakeha was evident early in the settlement period. One such example relates to adoptions, which have always been undertaken in New Zealand under a separate statute administered by the Department of Justice. The first adoption bill was passed in 1881 to encourage couples to care for children other than their own. Contrary to the official view that adoption required the separation of ties with birth parents, the Maori customs described in Chapter 1 were accepted by government authorities as convenient, although there was no state investment in the Maori system of caring.

From 1920 to 1940, in any one year the child welfare system was involved with about 1 in 50 New Zealand children, of whom the majority were in the direct care of the child welfare division, principally in orphanages or children's homes. These numbers decreased in the 1950s to 1 in 100 with the majority being under supervision in their own homes, but from the early 1960s the number of children either under supervision or in care increased substantially, partly because of increments in the number of Maori children with whom the department was working.

The 1925 Child Welfare Act recognized the importance of children and extended the philosophy of child care beyond physical and moral well-being to include psychological adjustment. Church, voluntary, and state agencies combined in the provision of institutional care for children, with the state becoming more dominant in the post-World War II period in building family homes and secure units for 'problem' children. The Act allowed for the appointment of child welfare officers, placing increasing emphasis on foster care and providing for separate children's courts. In practice, magistrates and the police often failed to acknowledge the spirit of the Act, but it was nonetheless the major law governing child welfare in New Zealand until the 1970s. Child Welfare Officers themselves were a sign of the growing bureaucratization of social work.

From the 1950s, a preventive and educational approach gradually became more prominent, as in the case of the Child Welfare Division, which had a statutory role encompassing the supervision of 'illegitimate' children. There were growing links with the schools and co-operation with school nurses and visiting teachers. As the focus extended beyond the physical and moral well-being of children to include psychological adjustment, the Education Department established a psychological service, and in the 1950s guidance counsellors were appointed to a number of secondary schools. However, this preventive role often came into conflict with the more traditional controlling approach of other state officers, such as Child Welfare Officers. At the same time the Department of Social Welfare was becoming less interested in keeping unwanted children in large residential homes. Between 1950 and 1981, the Department established over 150 family homes catering for children and young persons on both a short- and long-term basis. These homes were for children or young persons who had not settled into foster care and yet did not require the specialized resource of a residential facility. Family homes were located in small centres as well as cities, thereby enabling children to be kept within their local communities and, where desirable, close to their families. Other children were catered for within families of adoption, as adoption in its modern form, with an emphasis on secrecy, adoption in infancy and by strangers, became significant as a primary means of catering for unwanted ex-nuptial children in the post-war period.

The 1950s and 1960s were relatively stable decades, in effect the heyday of the welfare state. Full employment was maintained and universal services in health and education were important elements in subsidizing the family's budget. As a consequence, social services were either associated with the voluntary activities of church groups or organizations dealing with specific needs (such as the Organization for Intellectually Handicapped Children) or with state activities primarily concerned with the protection of children or the control of juvenile offenders.

The 1970s and 1980s saw major legislative and attitudinal changes in the area of child welfare. The amalgamation of the Child Welfare Division of the Department of Education with the Department of Social Security ensured that the financial means of family support (such as benefits) were linked with other family support services in one department. The introduction of the Domestic Purposes Benefit in 1975 made it easier for single parents to keep their children, and the 1974 Children and Young Persons Act provided legal aid for children under the same provisions as those available to adults.

The growth in the number of children living in sole-parent or reconstituted families had implications for their financial, social, and psychological support throughout this period. While a large number of voluntary organizations were involved in helping to support such families, the state was increasingly expected to give assistance. Child welfare policies placed more emphasis than before on the resolution of family problems rather than the removal of children from the home. Where children were removed, there was an emphasis on maintaining links with the biological family or *whanau*. Growing awareness of family violence (including sexual abuse) and of the role of males in perpetrating much of this violence led to attempts to implement preventive and educational programmes.

Thus the state's involvement in family and child welfare focused increasingly on the family, rather than the child, and on preventive as well as rehabilitative programmes. At the same time, a significant shift from institutional to community or family care was prompted by a growing concern over the costs of institutional care and by the large number of Maori in family homes and juvenile institutions.

Adoptions were widespread during the 1960s, but from the 1970s on the practice of adoption was in continuing decline as a result of more effective contraceptive practices and the availability of abortion, along with better income support for sole parents. Along with these changes came an increasing interest in more open adoptions and greater access of adopted children and adults to their birth parents. The Adult Adoption Act 1985 allowed adopted adults to gain copies of their original birth certificates through the Registrar General. It also allowed the birth parents of adopted adults access to information about their birth child through the Department of Social Welfare. Both adopted adults and birth parents were able to place a veto of ten years to prevent the access of information directly related to themselves, although more recently, children have been adopted with all parties knowing each other and in many cases establishing a form of extended family.

Similar changes towards a more open policy were also introduced in the foster care of children. In 1980, a research study of 654 children in care between 1971 and 1976 (McKay, 1981) highlighted the instability of foster placements and the strong bias toward foster care as a type of pseudo-adoption in the New Zealand system since the introduction of the 1925 Child Welfare Act. The study showed that the key problems with foster care arose from the very high failure rate of foster placements: over the five-year period from 1971 to 1976, children averaged 6.5

placements each, and 40% of long-term placements actually ended within a year. Children growing up as members of foster families did not maintain links with their natural family, and yet they were not eligible to be adopted. The object of placement in a foster home was to remove certain children from what was perceived to be the bad influence of their parents.

Over the years this policy was gradually reversed. By the 1970s it was accepted that children maintaining close ties with their natural families had a better chance of growing up well-adjusted and secure. However, this made the foster parents' task much harder: they had to be parents when parents were needed, yet retain a kind of professional detachment in helping the child come to terms with the birth family and its problems, and with the difficulties of growing up in two households.

A similar reversal of policy took place with residential services. In 1980 the Department of Social Welfare operated 23 institutions, some with over 100 residents. The residents (young offenders and young people with behavioural problems) were predominantly Maori, many of whom stayed in the residence for over a year. A decade later, only four residential institutions remained, with the largest catering for approximately 20 residents. Today, the focus on young offenders has been maintained, and while some young people on remand for serious offences stay for several months, most residents stay for less than three.

The dramatic reduction in the scale and scope of residential services was the result of three major factors: a small reduction in the size of the eligible population; changed patterns of dealing with young offenders with a greater emphasis on community-based programmes; and changed Departmental policies, in particular the decision not to place young people in institutions outside of the region if at all possible and not to use residential care as an option for children. In keeping with the findings of *Puao-Te-Ata-Tu* (the Report of the Ministerial Advisory Committee on a Maori Perspective for the Department of Social Welfare, 1986), the Department moved away from the institutional care of pre-adolescent children in favour of alternative community and *iwi-* (tribal) based programmes.

Young Persons (18–25 Years)

The 1980s saw a much greater cognizance of Maori tribal and *whanau* (family) links and of the need to empower families to take more responsibility for their children. *Maatua Whangi* was established in 1983 as a Maori family initiative to strengthen the lines of tribal, cultural group, and extended-family connections, so that responsibilities for family members would be recognized. This method of thinking was completely different from the concept of individual therapeutic services being provided anonymously from a professional bureaucracy. The concept of *Maatua Whangi* was supported by the Department of Social Welfare as a means of finding placements for its most difficult cases, and in that respect it operated as a diversionary programme.

The most important piece of welfare legislation to affect families in the 1980s was the Children, Young Persons and Their Families Act (CYPF Act, 1989) which clearly denoted a shift in emphasis from a child welfare perspective to a family group perspective. The Act defined the family in its various forms as the social unit most suited to the needs of children and young people. It was based on a belief that children and young people need a sense of continuity, identity, and stability, which can best be provided within the child's immediate or extended family. It was also seen as an effective way to reduce the costs of caring for abused and neglected children by placing responsibility on the wider family.

The CYPF Act legally recognized the wider family of the child and thus the reality of Maori and Pacific Island family structures. It established the family group conference as the primary means of dispute resolution, involving the family network, the social worker, and other relevant expertise. The removal of children from their families was to occur only in extreme situations, with the interests of the child or young person being paramount.

In the Act's implementation, problems of finding suitable service providers, obtaining approval of the new programmes, funding the programmes, and ensuring accountability have delayed developments, especially among *iwi* authorities for services to Maori people. The empowerment of families depends on resources and support services, but the expectation of family responsibility can all too readily lead to an unrealistic reduction in support from the state sector.

The CYPF Act also made a clear distinction between processes appropriate for dealing with children and young persons needing care and protection, and processes for dealing with young people who offend against the law. The Act holds young people (those between 14 and 17 years of age) accountable when they commit offences, and it assures them of the same rights as an adult in a court of law. The Youth Justice Section of the CYPF Act emphasizes 'restorative justice' to heal the break in social harmony by bringing the victim and offender together in a process of reconciliation. Since the Act came into force, the number of arrests as well as the number of matters dealt with in court have fallen by over two-thirds.

PARENTS, CAREGIVERS, AND DEPENDANTS IN THE FAMILY

The 1980s and 1990s saw the further liberalization of the divorce law, the increasing tendency for couples to live in a *de facto* relationship rather than get married, and a growing number of step-families, with the result that family forms became increasingly diverse in their functions and needs. The lower birth rate meant that there were fewer young dependants, but this was compensated for by the rise in the numbers of dependants who were either disabled or elderly. Public awareness began to query the level of assistance available for these persons in comparison with that available for children, and considerable debate ensued about their relative costs and appropriateness. As with the government policies for children, there were major changes in focus and delivery for parents, caregivers, and dependants.

One notable new programme illustrating this change was the Parents as First Teachers Programme introduced to New Zealand in 1992. The programme emphasizes the empowerment of parents so that they might become more confident in their parenting role and thereby participate more effectively in the development and education of their children. The programme has a strong education and health focus and was designed to provide sustained ongoing professional support for parents from before the birth of the child until the age of three years.

In New Zealand law the parent-child relationship is maintained through parents having a right to control the upbringing of their children and by placing a duty on parents to nurture children to the stage where they become independent of their parents. Corporal punishment by parents and schools is outlawed, and adoption, custody, access, guardianship, and care and protection proceedings all make provision for the child's view to be taken into account.

The establishment of the Family Courts in 1980–81 put the administration of family law in New Zealand on a new footing with a major departure from the traditional role of a court and the court system in both philosophy and style. A major function of the Family Courts' work is to facilitate the resolution of family difficulties and disputes through conciliation and through consultation with families by counsellors, social workers, mental health professionals, and specially-trained lawyers. In this way 90% or more of custody and access cases are settled, and detailed arrangements for children in need of care and protection are agreed upon. These agreements require the approval of the court without the need for a defended hearing.

During the 1980s, social services for parents and caregivers included the provision of courses and counselling in preparation for marriage, family relationships, family planning, parent education, and communication. While some counselling services existed in the public sector (e.g., the family health counselling services provided by the hospital boards in the early 1980s), most services were largely the domain of community organizations (e.g., Marriage Guidance). With the passage of the Family Proceedings Act (1980), these organizations became conduits of the justice system, undertaking counselling services for the Family Courts. Directing couples into counselling and mediation by the Family Courts was seen as a positive development, in that often a high level of agreement was attained between couples without recourse to the stress and acrimony of defended hearings.

In the early 1980s, Marriage Guidance regarded family-building and the prevention of marital dissolution as its first priority, but by the late 1980s had noticeably shifted emphasis away from marital reconciliation in favour of considering the parental roles of the parties after the dissolution of the marriage relationship. It increasingly recognized various forms of relationships, even those outside traditional marriage, and intervened in relationship difficulties at an earlier stage (represented in a name change from 'Marriage Guidance' to 'Relationship Services'). Such changes reflected an evolving system of justice, especially marked by the establishment of the Family Courts (1981), which recognized the provision of mediation as a complement, if not an alternative, to adversarial court procedures.

Community groups have also been heavily involved in aspects of parent education and relationship counselling. While Relationship Services is the largest national organization, other groups such as Lifeline, Presbyterian Support, and Parent Line have also played an important role. A nation-wide network of budget advisory services was established to provide families with budgeting assistance. More recently, national networks of women's refuges and rape-crisis and sexual-abuse services have evolved in response to the increasing incidence and public awareness of family violence and rape (both in and out of marriage).

While education programmes and parental services became more varied in recognition of increasingly diverse relationships, so did the delivery of such services. For example, a network of Maori and Pacific Island groups and counsellors was established by the Department of Justice in 1987/88 to provide appropriate services for the resolution of family and extended family disputes among these groups, and the Te Korowai Aroha Association was established in 1990 as a professional Maori counselling agency providing education and training to an emerging range of *iwi*-based social services.

CONCLUSION

The provision of social services for families has changed significantly over the past two decades, conditioned by state restructuring and by a deterioration in New Zealand's policy environment. There was little impetus for change in the 1960s given the relative affluence of the country, but during the 1970s the welfare state was criticized for failing to eradicate poverty, for the higher rate of juveniles and adults in custodial institutions, and for the monocultural bias of its social service provisions. Government responded to these criticisms by extending support to voluntary organizations through grants and subsidies. In particular, a wide range of self-help groups and programmes providing developmental or preventive services were assisted by the state. As frictional unemployment increased in the late 1970s, this funding was extended in support of community-based 'work' and education programmes.

In the 1980s, these activities, and indeed the activities of the social service sector as a whole, came under greater scrutiny. Motivated by reports portraying mental institutions and child welfare homes as oppressive structures, and encouraged by voluntary groups and families (particularly Maori) wanting community rather than institutional care, a systematic de-institutionalization programme was put in place. By the late 1980s, most social welfare homes had been closed and the number of children in care had markedly declined. Child advocacy notably gained ground through the 1970s and 1980s with official endorsement through agencies such as the Human Rights Commission and the Office of the Commissioner for Children.

As the economic depression deepened in the 1980s, the demand for remedial social services increased. Structural unemployment, increasing relative poverty, and major social problems associated with escalating rates of youth suicide, child abuse, and violence in general were the manifestations of a society experiencing serious social dislocation (Shirley, 1992). The demands for social service support

ncreased, but the state distanced itself more and more from the direct provision of
ocial services, preferring instead to subsidize private agencies and voluntary or-
;anizations. At the same time, funding criteria were tightened in accordance with
he government's emphasis on targeting and user-pays. Even those services pro-
'ided under the Children, Young Persons and Their Families Act (1989), regarded
nternationally as an enlightened approach to the care and protection of children,
·ontinue to suffer today from funding limitations.

In the delivery of family services the concerns of the 1970s, 1980s, and 1990s
vere not too dissimilar from those which existed in the liberal period of the last
.entury—namely, increasing expenditure and the appropriate targeting of that ex-
>enditure; the need to mobilize volunteers and encourage self-reliance and self-
letermination; the appropriate balance between the interests of taxpayers and the
teeds of social service recipients; and the devolution of services to the community,
·ssentially increasing family responsibilities. While the nineteenth-century system
•f charitable aid survives only in a residual form today, the values and attitudes
issociated with terms such as 'discipline, benevolence and the deserving poor'
·Oliver, 1977) continue to dominate public perceptions of welfare services. When
·oupled with the systematic reduction of in-kind support in providing services such
.s education, health, and housing, the quality of family life for substantial sectors
•f the population has significantly declined over the past decade. At the centre of
hese changing circumstances is a decline in the value of the family wage, and it is
o this distinctive feature of family policy in New Zealand that we now turn.

5

Family Policy and Political Economy

THE 'FAMILY' WAGE

In the early twentieth century, New Zealand commentators wrote of a 'theory of fair wages . . . sufficient to give the worker a decent living according to the colonial standard' (Le Rossignol and Stewart, 1910: 239). Since the average 'worker' of the time was male and since 'normal needs' encompassed domestic responsibilities, the 'fair wage' was soon defined as being a family wage sufficient to support a wife and two or three children. With the election of the first Labour government in 1935, the family wage was enshrined in legislation. Government established base wage rates for adult male workers to enable a man 'to maintain a wife, and three children in a fair and reasonable standard of comfort' (Woods, 1963).

The provision of a family wage based on male employment led to a distinctive set of welfare arrangements which established New Zealand as one of the leading welfare states of the post-World War II period. In contrast to those European and Scandinavian countries that based their welfare states on extensive systems of income maintenance and social insurance, New Zealand used wage regulation as the primary instrument of social protection. It was a form of domestic compensation forged in the 1890s in the wake of an economic depression that had threatened the security of the country during the 1880s. The major source of New Zealand's depression was the decline in export receipts for primary products for the British market. When unemployment dramatically increased, the working class turned to democratic political action in their 'quest for security' (Sutch, 1966).

At the heart of this reformist activity was the notion of compulsory conciliation and arbitration. In 1894, an arbitration court was established to resolve industrial disputes by mediating between companies and their employees, and by making compulsory awards as to wages and conditions. The aim was to regulate industrial conflict by transferring the battle of capital and labour to the courts. This mechanism achieved two ends: it set parameters for wage determination, and in that respect it met the demands of the working class; and it regulated wage adjustment problems in a country subject to fluctuating export prices. The outcome was the establishment of a wage-fixing system influenced by forces other than those of the market. At the same time social policy criteria were directly introduced into the wage-fixing procedures of the state.

These procedures were extended and developed over a period of almost eighty years, with the most significant developments occurring in the wake of the 1930.

depression. The first Labour government elected in 1935 insulated the domestic economy from overseas influences by establishing protective tariffs, imposing import licences, and creating marketing agencies for New Zealand's primary exporters. Within New Zealand itself, government concentrated on maintaining the viability of small-scale farming and manufacturing by means of price stabilization and by linking wages to prevailing economic conditions through the rulings of the arbitration court.

If the regulation of wages was a cornerstone of New Zealand's welfare state arrangements, then a second fundamental element was full employment. Conceived as 'the fulcrum of the welfare state' (Rosenberg, 1977) in the post-war period, 'full employment' represented an historic compromise (Davidson, 1989) forged in response to the depression, when measured unemployment rose to 12% of the labour force. The substance of the 'compromise' was encapsulated in the Labour government's 1935 electoral strategy based on the concept of 'insulation': insulation of the economy through protective measures, such as tight controls on immigration, so that employers could provide the requisite number of jobs to accommodate all eligible male workers, and insulation of the 'family wage' by establishing base wage rates, which would enable a man 'to maintain a wife and three children in a fair and reasonable standard of comfort'.

Both the assumptions on which the family wage was based, and the complex system of awards and conditions which governed its continuing viability, effectively avoided the traditional practices of welfare states in Europe, which were dominated by public expenditure programmes and the state taxation system as the primary means of income distribution.

In New Zealand the combination of male employment and wage regulation ensured a high standard of living for the majority of the population, with those 'outside' the waged majority protected by a selective benefit system. Benefits could be residual rather than universal because they were only required by those with no labour market connections—they could be flat-rate rather than earnings-related because they merely provided a safety net below stipulated minimum wages—and they could be more appropriately financed by Treasury rather than through wage-earners' contributions. These would have implied a right to welfare assistance, whereas the only right within the New Zealand system was the right to a 'fair wage' (Castles and Shirley, 1996). It was a right nevertheless that encompassed general wage increases and conditions, including hours worked, penalty rates for overtime, and special provisions for sickness leave. The means-tested and selective system of social benefits only came into play when the wage award procedures were not applicable. Even in these cases, however, the notion of fairness was particularly persuasive, in that beneficiaries outside the wages system received a similar amount from progressive income taxes imposed on those earning higher incomes. It was an egalitarian ethos which drove the philosophical assumptions, if not always the practices, of successive governments throughout most of the post-war period.

The combination of a family wage and full employment distinguished and dominated the development of the New Zealand welfare state for almost fifty years. The basic minimum wage was supplemented by government in the form of a National Health Service (with limited fees for primary medical consultations), access to free primary and secondary education, a state housing programme for those who could not afford a home of their own, and a comprehensive, although largely selective, system of social benefits.

Home-ownership was particularly significant, both as a stabilizing influence and as a central element in a family's economic and social security. Within the context of the family wage, it attached a 'man' firmly to a job, to a piece of land, and to a social group; it established a base for 'his' family, and so to a network of neighbourhood institutions, such as church, school, and voluntary society (Oliver, 1978). In national terms, the high wage rates, made possible by the relative affluence of the country, led to high levels of private home-ownership, with mortgage repayments serving in effect as a major form of retirement security.

By any standards, the level of welfare achieved in the immediate post-war period was exceedingly high; the increasing affluence of the population was reflected in New Zealand's consistent rating among the top five of the world's wealthiest nations. The country was socially and politically stable and for over thirty years maintained a remarkable record of full employment. The illusion of consensus generated by this stable environment was interpreted by some as an extension of the colonial dream:

a specially favoured place . . . where race did not matter in any harmful way, where class divisions did not exist as barriers, where the old and the young were equally looked after, and where the family and women as its cornerstone were kept secure and protected (Oliver, 1978: 52).

The evidence to support the illusion was impressive, but by the 1970s the veneer of consensus on which this illusion was based had clearly fractured. The visibility and strength of a second Maori Renaissance; the changing parameters of the labour market as women sought paid employment as an alternative to domesticity; the rediscovery of relative poverty despite the achievements of the welfare state; and overt political conflict between different interest groups demanding action on a range of social and moral issues—these cultural and social divisions revealed a society no longer able to insulate itself from the rest of the world or disguise its internal contradictions (Shirley, 1991). Beyond this, as noted in earlier chapters, major changes were occurring in the demography and structure of New Zealand families.

Economic Vulnerability and Decline

At the heart of these contradictions lay New Zealand's vulnerability as a trading nation. New Zealand exports were dominated by agricultural products intended predominantly for the British market, but it became an increasingly restricted market as Britain established closer economic relations with Europe. The value of foreign trade declined, and the increasing gap between export receipts and import prices was further exacerbated by the oil crisis of 1973 and the actions of overseas governments who sought to protect their productive sectors. In response to this changing international environment, the New Zealand economy was slowly opened up to overseas competition by the dismantling of some import controls and by means of incentives designed to strengthen the export potential of both the agricultural and manufacturing sectors. As a diversification strategy supported by government policies in taxation and investment, the restructuring programme of the 1960s and 1970s was relatively successful. It not only widened the base of the New Zealand economy, but it also expanded the labour market during a period in which jobs were being replaced by new technology, industrial restructuring, and resource depletion (Easton, 1993). It also markedly reduced the trading importance of Europe which was replaced by Asia, Australia, and the Middle East.

This trend toward economic liberalization was reversed for a short period when the National government embarked on a capital-intensive development programme based on industries such as petro-chemical production, electricity generation, aluminium, steel, and forestry. Euphemistically referred to as 'think big', the programme was ill-conceived in that the partnership between private companies and the state resulted in companies being relatively immune from risk, while the New Zealand taxpayer was forced to bear a disproportionately large share of any subsequent deficit (Van Moeseke, 1980; Shirley, 1982). While these projects did generate limited employment opportunities and provide scarce foreign exchange through import and export substitution, they significantly increased the country's indebtedness. Even when combined with the wage and price freeze of the early 1980s, these initiatives could not revitalize the lagging New Zealand economy. They merely postponed the implementation of economic reforms more in tune with the increasing globalization of the world economy. The 1970s had cast doubts on the ability of traditional Keynesian policies to manage the twin problems of stagnant economic growth and rising inflation; thus, when the major international currencies moved to a regime of floating exchange rates, monetarism became more attractive.

While economic imperatives were at the centre of New Zealand's drive toward economic liberalization, other factors were also significant. Although the constellation of forces that came together in the mid-1980s is sometimes described as 'classical liberalism', it embraced factions of both the Left and the Right. It enveloped those members of the middle class who articulated a highly individualistic liberal philosophy concerned with individual as opposed to social well-being, and it encompassed individuals who had been engaged in the protest movements of the 1960s and 1970s. In contrast to previous working-class movements that concentrated on issues of political economy, the liberal politics of the 1960s and 1970s focused on foreign policy issues such as the Vietnam War and moral issues such as apartheid and abortion. The politics of classical liberalism celebrated diversity, self-determination, personal choice, and individual responsibility. It simultaneously undermined the notion of a universal moral code and inevitably challenged the social conservatism and traditional moral attitudes associated with the post-war consensus.

The Sexual Division of Labour and the Cult of Domesticity

In social terms the most significant impetus for change emanated from a decline in the family wage, the sexual division of labour, and the 'cult of domesticity'. Throughout the 1950s and 1960s the family wage largely determined the status and lifestyle of the household. The labour market, rather than the family or the state, was the mechanism through which resources were distributed. Men were the primary income-earners, as reflected in the rulings of the arbitration court, which set female base wage rates at around half the male rate on the ground that women were generally not responsible for supporting dependants. This legal construction of female dependency ensured limited female participation in the labour force and reinforced the role of women as defined by a set of familial responsibilities.

The gendered division of the labour market was mirrored by the way in which domestic responsibilities were allocated within the home. Whereas the care of children, coupled with domestic activities such as cooking and cleaning, dominated the tasks performed by women, men's domestic production was dominated by gardening, household renovations, and car maintenance. It was a form of role differentiation that was reinforced by government policies aimed at strengthening the purchasing power of the family wage and endorsing 'man' as the head of the household. The latter endorsement was evident in the assignment of property rights and in the preferential treatment accorded men in the labour market.

This cult of domesticity was supported, even 'jealously guarded', by women themselves (Saville-Smith et al., 1994). Research conducted by the Society for Research on Women in 1967–68 illustrated that there was considerable resistance to the notion of child care outside the home, while a study by James (1985) during the early 1980s concluded that women had a strong commitment to the sexual division of labour and that they too, strongly resisted non-familial child care.

The undermining of the family wage began in the 1950s with the significant decline in New Zealand's terms of trade, the sharpest fall occurring in the 1960s through to the mid-1970s. This decline was accompanied by a sharp fall in production and, given the nature of New Zealand's dependency on agriculture, it affected the whole community (Chatterjee and Michelini, 1983; Easton, 1990). Not only did the spending power of the community decline, but increasing prices for both imported and domestic goods, as well as the rising costs of land and property, significantly reduced the purchasing power of the family wage.

Households responded to the decline in the value of the family wage by expanding their total income through multiple jobs and part-time employment. Women entered the labour market in increasing numbers, moved by a desire to protect and expand household income (Haines, 1989). Multiple jobs and part-time work were seen primarily as a material requirement for many families trying to maintain a normative standard of living. A study by the New Zealand Institute for Social Research and Development identifies the changing relationship between the family and the market originating at this time (rather than in the mid-1980s) as households and markets adapted to the new economic environment (Saville-Smith et al., 1994)

The women's movement in the 1960s and 1970s was clearly a significant factor in these changing relationships. The success of the women's movement was reflected in a series of legal reforms such as the Equal Pay Act 1972 (guaranteeing gender equality in setting wage rates); the Matrimonial Property Act 1976 (establishing equal entitlements to matrimonial property and recognizing the contribution of unpaid work); and the Human Rights Commission Act 1977 (prohibiting discrimination against access to employment, housing, and other goods and services on a variety of grounds, including sex and marital status). In political terms the women's movement increased awareness of the contribution of unpaid work to the national economy (Waring, 1988) and alerted the wider community to the impediments facing women in the labour market. These campaigns demonstrated the 'double load' being carried by women as they entered the paid work-force and reinforced the case for parental and family leave, both to accommodate women workers and to ensure that men accepted a greater share of family responsibilities.

Government policy throughout this period remained focused on the nuclear family and was primarily concerned with maintaining household income. When economic instability increased along with a rise in frictional unemployment, government extended its role, both as an employer in its own right and in providing temporary employment programmes for those actively seeking a job. The New Zealand government has long assumed a significant role in production and distribution, and this role was extended to the provision of services which were free (or heavily subsidized) for New Zealand families. Services provided by the government through to the early 1980s ranged from electricity generation, forestry, and telecommunications, to public schools, hospitals, and social services. Many of these services, as well as the trading activities of the state, operated at a loss, but such losses were explicitly regarded as components of the social wage.

The taxation system was central to the viability of the social wage. Not only was it the means by which government funded the income maintenance system of benefits, but it was also used to subsidize the routine costs of family life for wage- and salary-earners. Subsidies to the family wage included rebates for low-income families and a capitalization scheme based on the family benefit which provided access to affordable housing. These two domains of the taxation system catered for different constituencies, who in turn received differential treatment. Subsidizing families (i.e., nuclear families) was strongly endorsed by government who saw the family unit as 'the bastion of society'. For similar reasons, services such as health and education were supported, as were subsidies to primary exporters and manufacturers. But subsidizing beneficiaries, especially sole-parent beneficiaries, created problems for conservative governments. The support of sole parents might be seen as encouraging women to leave their husbands, and without an adequate income these women would inevitably compete with men for jobs at a time when the labour market was finding it increasingly difficult to accommodate the eligible male work-force. The government eventually succumbed to the changing household demography of the 1970s by supporting sole-parent beneficiaries, but it was a most reluctant commitment.

Although the welfare state achieved notable success in the immediate post-war period, by 1976 a significant section of the population could be described as relatively poor (Easton, 1976); within that classification, families with dependent children and those on aged benefits were identified as being most vulnerable. Some Maori were particularly disadvantaged: at the time of the 1971 census the average Maori male income was $1,109 compared to an average male income of $2,067. Even when adjusted for the difference in age distribution, the average Maori income was only 72.3% of the national average. In education, 74% of young Maori men and 36% of young Maori women left the education system without any national academic qualifications, and after leaving school 25.9% of all Maori workers went into unskilled occupations, compared with 6.5% of the non-Maori population. Similar inequalities were evident in housing and health. Although the government encouraged the integration of Maori with its 'pepper-potting' housing policies of the 1950s and 1960s, most Maori could not afford to live outside areas of cheap rental housing, thus by the 1970s state housing areas on the periphery of the large urban centres had become symbols of class and ethnic disadvantage.

As disparities increased, various sector groups became more strident, each demanding policy initiatives to counter the perceived decline in social and economic conditions. Unions sought compensation for the escalation in prices and the relative decline of the social wage, and employers agitated for greater profitability and an end to what was described as 'over full employment'. These demands brought the state directly into wage determination as it attempted to control prices and wages. However, this task proved to be extremely difficult because production slowed considerably, and thus by the early 1980s, even conventional Keynesian economists were advocating increasing economic liberalization.

ECONOMIC RATIONALIZATION AND STRUCTURAL UNEMPLOYMENT

Events of the late 1980s and early 1990s radically changed the relations between work, family, and state that had prevailed throughout most of the post-war period. The forces and conditions that produced economic rationalization in New Zealand were similar in many respects to the circumstances that produced 'Thatcherism' and 'Reaganomics'. But whereas the pursuit of market forces in Britain and North America was led by traditional conservative governments, the New Zealand experiment was carried out by a social democratic party that had established the welfare state. The changing international environment created the conditions for economic liberalization, but domestic factors were equally significant. While there was widespread support for a shift in the relationship between state and market in favour of increasing liberalization, the fourth Labour government took New Zealand within a few years from being the most regulated, to the most deregulated, economy of all the OECD countries (Castles, Gerritsen, and Vowles, 1996).

At the change of government in 1984 the New Zealand currency was devalued by 20%. By early 1985 the dollar was floated, and the regulatory structure in place when the Labour government took office was almost completely dismantled. Interest rate controls were removed and restrictions were lifted on the flow of money into and out of New Zealand. The economy was opened up to competition from imports, and foreign companies were given greater access to the New Zealand market. Agricultural subsidies were phased out, and the protective shield was removed from manufacturing. Government departments were reorganized along commercial lines and then selectively privatized. At the same time monetary and fiscal policies were tightened in order to reduce inflation.

In the early phase of restructuring, the government focused mainly on economic reform, using social policy to maintain existing levels of social protection. The underlying philosophy attacked the assumptions, as well as the mechanisms, on which the post-war consensus had been built. Social factors were artificially separated from economic policy, as a residual role was prescribed for the state in facilitating the process of restructuring and in 'targeting' assistance to individuals in 'exceptional' circumstances. Unemployment was treated as an 'adjustment problem' with one of the major impediments to employment being identified as the lack of labour market flexibility.

The process by which the programme of economic liberalization was implemented and then extended by successive governments has been examined by a range of studies (Bollard and Buckle, 1987; Boston and Dalziel, 1992; Chatterjee, 1992; Collins, 1987; Easton, 1989; Jesson, 1987 and 1989; Shirley, 1990 and 1991). The impact of this programme has also been studied, although there are wide discrepancies when it comes to evaluating the reforms as a whole. Clearly the microeconomic reforms did produce a number of benefits. These reforms were designed to confront production units with a more competitive environment in order to ensure a more efficient allocation of resources. In areas such as electricity generation, telecommunications, transportation, and government trading activities, there have been obvious benefits to the national economy. But a recent comparative study of the New Zealand and Australian economies over the period 1985–92 concludes that despite 'a more favourable external environment New Zealand did worse'. While in some areas 'New Zealand's economic performance was a little better than Australia's; much was worse, especially for GDP growth and employment' (Easton and Gerritsen, 1996).

One of the more contentious initiatives of the programme of economic reform was the government's target of 0–2% inflation, a goal that has been achieved using the tight monetary controls of the statutorily-independent Reserve Bank. Some commentators maintain that the costs of achieving this inflationary target have been too high (Whitwell, 1989). When the disinflationary programme was first introduced, the combined effect of sustained fiscal deficits and a tight monetary policy forced up domestic interest rates; higher interest rates in turn attracted considerable injections of foreign capital. Pressures generated by foreign investors seeking New Zealand dollars forced up the exchange rate, which meant that it was more profitable to import than to export. These policies directed spending flows away from production and into speculation. As it became more difficult to compete in the international marketplace, firms reduced production and employment, and the economy moved into a deep recession (Shirley et al., 1990).

The cumulative impact of these policies over a period of more than two and a half years was severe damage to the tradeable sector. Profits, employment, and investment were all affected, and at the same time export growth sharply diminished. In the farming sector production levels dropped, confidence declined, and many farmers who had borrowed unwisely for expansion during the years of government subsidies and high land values found themselves operating uneconomic units. There was also a substantial change in New Zealand's industrial pattern with labour-intensive industries, such as clothing and furniture, suffering large declines in exports, while imports were allowed into a depressed domestic market. Factory closures in these industries produced a significant increase in unemployment, with investment in New Zealand manufacturing falling by almost 50% between 1985 and 1989. The restructuring of the state sector alone added at least 40,000 people to the pool of unemployed, while major employment areas such as forestry and manufacturing declined by 67% and 21% respectively. Within 18 months of implementing the programme of economic liberalization, unemployment trebled, and by 1991 registered unemployment represented 11% of the total labour force. In particular, long-term unemployment became a serious social problem; because of the segmented nature of both employment and unemployment, the social problem had racial overtones. An estimated 20% of the Maori working-age population lost their jobs in the two years from March 1987 to March 1989. Two years later the unemployment rate for non-Maori aged 15–24 years was nearly 20%, while for Maori it was approaching 40%.

Exclusion from the paid work-force placed increasing pressure on immediate and extended families. Where families were unable to support or sustain this dependency, the state became the primary means of income support. As a consequence, government faced relatively high levels of welfare expenditure. In 1981 (apart from National Superannuation and Family Benefit) almost 115,000 people were receiving a welfare benefit. By 1985, that figure more than doubled, and by 1992, it had almost trebled (Department of Statistics, 1961–1995). In 1993 just over one-quarter of all dependent children were in households supported by benefits.

The increasing dependency of families on the state, for either income support or social welfare benefits, was a consequence of increasing structural unemployment and a marked decline in disposable incomes. Throughout the post-war period, the primary source of income was the family wage. As the purchasing power of the family declined in the 1970s and early 1980s, households expanded their income by extending their employment options, but these options were severely restricted in the 1980s as the labour market contracted and unemployment rapidly increased. Government became directly involved in altering the parameters of the family wage, using a combination of tax adjustments, income supplements, and benefits. In 1986 a comprehensive Goods and Services Tax (GST) was introduced, personal income tax rates were flattened, and Family Support (a refundable tax credit) was introduced. The proportion of income from government transfers increased markedly, from approximately 12% in 1982 to 17.6% in 1992.

As state expenditure increased, government sought to target its expenditure by narrowing the criteria for benefit eligibility and reducing state-funded services such as education, health, and housing. In 1988, the unemployment benefit for young (under 18) childless beneficiaries was reduced, and in 1989 school leavers were given a 27-week stand-down period before claiming the unemployment benefit. These measures, along with the termination of Family Benefit once a child reached 18 years of age, effectively increased the number of 15–19-year-olds living in dependent circumstances. Between 1981 and 1991, the proportion of young people aged 15 to 24 living with their parents increased from 51% to 57%, while the number of families with adult children increased by 24% (Department of Statistics, 1994). At the same time, government sought contributions from non-custodial parents under the Liable Parent Contribution Scheme, and, when these contributions were not forthcoming, the law was strengthened in order to enforce payment.

The targeting of state services in major social policy areas such as health, housing, and education was somewhat more difficult to achieve. Although the parameters of the 'welfare state' had already changed when full employment ceased to be government's top priority (Shirley et al., 1990), the Labour administration continued to assert that the role of state in social policy would not be substantially altered. There was clearly some disjunction between the government's official line and the realities of the reform process. Traditional social policy departments such as health, education, justice, and social welfare were subjected to a series of task-force reviews, with working parties dominated by private-sector entrepreneurs and committed devotees of the Chicago School. While little empirical research existed to support the conclusions reached by the review teams, they generally advocated a reduced role for the state and a concomitant affirmation of market forces as a means of increasing efficiency and accountability.

In areas such as education, this meant devolving certain state responsibilities to the 'consumers' of the service, by involving parents directly in school administration. Primary and secondary schools were to be administered by parent-elected boards of trustees operating under charters that were essentially written contracts between the 'community', the school, and the state. In this way, government's role in education was changed by devolving both responsibility and liability for the service to parents and teachers, while the state retained control of education policy and ultimately the ability to determine resource allocation. Similar strategies were used in social welfare with the Department of Social Welfare being divided into three business units, while some services previously provided by government were delegated to community groups. The concept of local control coincided with the interests of the voluntary social services, especially Maori, whose traditional structures were based on tribal forms rather than national or centralized control.

Housing policy also changed with the development of a systematic targeting regime based on income and housing need. The Housing Corporation initially offered subsidized home loans for first-home buyers on the basis of a family's ability to pay and later introduced a points system in order to prioritize those with a serious housing need who were waiting for a state home. Those in serious housing need included people living in overcrowded conditions or in temporary accommodation, those compelled to share housing with other families, and those who could not afford to buy a home of their own. State support for first-home buyers was extended to single-parent families and people with disabilities, groups that had not specifically been identified in previous assistance provisions. Loans on existing homes were also expanded in order to increase the financial flexibility of home buyers, but these provisions were tightened as New Zealand entered the 1990s. While the increased emphasis on targeting social services did not extend to the introduction of vouchers, as proposed by the Treasury, the reforms of the late 1980s cleared the way for the systematic 'dismantling' of the welfare state under the National government following its election in 1990.

'DISMANTLING' THE WELFARE STATE

Increasing state dependency was one of the major concerns identified by the new administration, determined to address 'the crushing burden of government spending' (Richardson, 1990). The National Party indicated that it was intent on arresting 'the drift from work to welfare'; some months later, in conjunction with the 1991 budget, it introduced a series of measures focusing specifically on social policy. Whereas the previous government had attempted to draw an artificial distinction between economic and social policy by concentrating their reforms essentially in the economic domain, National extended the same commercial principles and practices to social policy in general and to health, industrial relations, and social welfare in particular.

The changes proposed for the health system included the following: an interim targeting regime with those on lower incomes eligible for a Community Services Card (for the purpose of tightly-targeted subsidies); in-patient and out-patient hospital charges; a social insurance scheme allowing government to charge individuals and families based on their expected share of health system costs; the separation of the purchasing and provision roles of the former area health boards (elected boards abolished by National in 1991); the establishment of an advisory committee on core health and disability services; and the creation of a public health commission. Many of these proposals, which were advanced without any form of public consultation, were later reversed: hospital in-patient charges were abolished after 12 months; the social insurance proposal was abandoned; the activities of the core health advisory committee were altered; and the public health commission was disbanded. However, at least in the political discourse the overall emphasis on the commercialization of health care continued, with the public hospital expected 'to operate as a successful business'. Not only did these reforms represent a major shift in New Zealand's health policy (Bowie and Shirley, 1994), but they directly undermined a significant component of the social wage by shifting substantial costs from the tax-funded public health system to individuals and families, especially households with children. A similar strategy involving cost-shifting to individuals and families occurred with the introduction of market rentals for state housing.

One of the most far-reaching policy initiatives introduced by the National administration was the April 1991 welfare benefit cuts which widened income differentials and effectively redefined poverty in absolute terms. Benefit levels were set with reference to a minimum budget required for subsistence; as a consequence, social welfare benefits no longer relate to the standard of living experienced by the rest of the community (Stephens, 1992). Mounting evidence indicates that these cuts increased the level of hardship for many families, yet at the same time the government established the most punitive set of measures adopted by any OECD country designed to make claiming benefits less attractive (Gough, 1995). In general terms, tax and benefit cuts (along with the introduction of user-pays) favour those in full-time employment over those on benefits, the healthy over the sick, childless households over households with children, and those with accumulated wealth over those with few assets.

Prior to these changes, social security benefits were generally assessed on the basis of a household's joint income, in contrast to retirement income and accident compensation, where the individual was the unit of assessment. Although government retained the individual as the unit of assessment for taxation purposes, in 1991 it proposed the 'core family' as the means of assessing all forms of social assistance (St. John, 1991). The concept of the core family was based essentially 'on the "norm" of the nuclear family, with specific variations to recognise situations where that type of family [had] not formed or [had] broken down' (Angus and Gray, 1995). It was advanced by the Treasury (Prebble et al., 1991) as a means of devising a comprehensive targeted regime which would be a cheaper option for government than that prescribed by using the individual as the unit of assessment. In the context of changing demographic patterns it was an extremely narrow definition that proved to be unworkable and—like many other initiatives outlined in the 1991 budget—it was ultimately abandoned. The benefit cuts, however, were not abandoned; thus in place of a coherent system of domestic compensation New Zealand has inherited a 'welfare mess' that seems to be preoccupied with benefit fraud and the excessive targeting of public expenditure.

Another area in which recent policy changes have had a radical impact on family life is employment. Like the other essential components of the family wage, namely industrial conciliation and arbitration, employment has been radically altered. Government policy initiatives in the mid-1980s were intended to create a more competitive environment, which in turn led to increasing demands for a more flexible labour market. The 1987 Labour Relations Act moved industrial relations toward decentralized bargaining, followed in 1988 by the State Sector Act, which radically changed the *modus operandi* of government departments. In 1990, the notion of labour market flexibility was taken to its inevitable conclusion: the Employment Contracts Act removed the bargaining rights of unions and effectively dismantled the award system, which was replaced by a radically decentralized framework based on the concept of individual bargaining between employer and employee. The state was not to be involved, except through the employment court, and collective bargaining (where it existed) was decentralized to the enterprise level. As Harbridge (1993) illustrates, union membership dramatically declined. The state withdrew from labour market regulation, and power shifted toward employers and away from employees.

This change of policy in New Zealand is significant for the way in which it altered the parameters of the family wage. As previously outlined, industrial relations provided the mechanism for ensuring that workers had access to employment and 'fair wages'—the pivotal elements in the development of the family wage. One of these elements disappeared when employment ceased to be government's main economic priority; the second went with the passage of the Employment Contracts Act. Having thus done away with the 'family wage' that was the core of family policy in the post-war period, New Zealand has essentially abandoned any coherent form of domestic compensation.

CONCLUSION

The radical shifts in policy which have dominated New Zealand life over the past two decades (but more specifically since 1984) have completely reversed the distinctive set of arrangements that identified this country as one of the leading welfare states in the post-war period. During the early phase of economic restructuring the state continued to support the family wage by various forms of domestic compensation. Some of these initiatives were consistent with the resourceful European states of Katzenstein's study (1985), which combined economic openness (or liberalization) with a form of democratic corporatism. But this approach was abandoned in New Zealand in the 1980s as the political executive of consecutive governments implemented radical reforms effectively bypassing the normal conventions of public consultation. In contrast to countries such as Australia, which went through a similar transformation using a gradualist approach and a 'consensual' form of government, the New Zealand reform process has been characterized as 'crash through or crash' (Castles, Gerritsen, and Vowles, 1996). By 1993, the New Zealand electorate was no longer prepared to tolerate this form of executive power, opting instead for a proportional system of electoral government.

While the new political structure is likely to curb the wild fluctuations which have dominated the policy-making process in New Zealand over recent years, it will not necessarily address the changing patterns of familial life or the demise of the family wage. Changes to the family wage were inevitable given its gendered construction, while the insulated economic framework that had provided high levels of protection for primary producers and industry in the early post-war period was no longer a feasible option for a dependent and vulnerable economy on the periphery of the world. Nor was it realistic to persist with policies reinforcing the rigid demarcation of male and female roles within the household and the labour market. The New Zealand family began adapting to these changing circumstances long before the radical policy reforms of the 1980s and 1990s. Women became increasingly involved in the formal economy and men (with somewhat less enthusiasm) were drawn into the domestic sphere of the household and the informal economy. The family was not simply a casualty of economic change: it not only adapted to a changing world but also played a significant role in shaping the market economy of the 1980s and 1990s.

The broad configurations of family, state, and market have changed, as has the nature of dependency. In the early decades of the post-war period the family wage established a pattern of familial and working life which reinforced the dependency of women and children on male employment. The 'male wage-earners' welfare state' was characterized by full employment and by the provision and maintenance of a household income that included the state provision of education and health services, a high level of private home-ownership, and a selective system of benefits for those outside the labour market. When these provisions began to decline, the state became increasingly involved in protecting the family's welfare through sometimes contradictory measures including the promotion of equal employment opportunities, the care and protection of children, and a substantial increase in state expenditure in order to provide protection for individuals and families as frictional unemployment increased and the viability of the family wage declined. The nature of dependency shifted from male employment to the support of a strongly interventionist state. With the advent of economic rationalization, the unfettered market became the major reference point for family, as well as for national, well-being.

For some individuals these changing relations between family, state, and market have provided new freedoms and new opportunities. Others have experienced a significant decline in income and in their standard of living. Whereas the family wage ensured that the majority of New Zealanders in the immediate post-war period were able to enjoy a standard of living much like the rest of the community (and in that sense they participated in and belonged to society), the new environment of the 1990s has effectively disenfranchised a significant sector of the population. The parameters of the welfare state have changed, and in the process, the family wage has been replaced by an incoherent set of policies which neither recognize the demographic patterns of family today, nor provide an effective framework for the maintenance of family and national well-being.

Conclusion

Like the other nations included in this volume of country studies, New Zealand does not have a coherent set of family policies that adequately address the changing demographic patterns of the post-war period or the new policy environment of the 1990s. While the concept of the 'family wage' distinguished New Zealand's welfare state arrangements in the wake of the 1930s depression, the family was narrowly conceived as a nuclear household with clearly-defined domestic and employment responsibilities. It is doubtful whether this approach was ever entirely appropriate to the needs of Maori. Moreover, since that time, the demographic patterns of familial life have changed and so too have the broad configurations of family, state, and market.

The changing familial patterns and structures which provide the framework for government economic and social policies are markedly different from the idealized family that tends to dominate public discourse. While the New Zealand pattern broadly resembles the changing familial trends evident in other Western societies, it has many distinctive elements, most notably its need to accommodate Maori and Pakeha, as well as Asian and Pacific Island traditions. The key features of changing family patterns in New Zealand include:

- major shifts in household types, with non-parenting families becoming very important mainly due to demographic changes, particularly the large numbers of young people in couple-only families, or households composed of non-related persons, and at the other end of the age distribution, empty-nest middle-aged couples and widowed elderly in single-person households;
- within the parenting family category, an increase in sole-parent families and a decrease in two-parent households;
- a significant rise in the number of children born ex-nuptially, particularly to couples at the mid-childbearing ages;
- declines in the rate of formally-registered marriages;
- an incipient shift away from a period in which divorce rates had increased to historically high levels, particularly among parent-couples who married precipitately at young ages following a pre-marital conception;
- a decline in the average family size and a significant shift away from early to late parenting, whether nuptial or ex-nuptial;
- a trend to later childbearing;
- a decline in the market economic resources of families, especially families with children.

The fact that these changes were not uniform, but vary significantly between ethnic groups, has major implications for policy formation. To take two examples:

the earlier chapters pointed to tempo and quantum differences in childbearing and to differentials in the likelihood of a sole mother being part of an extended family. Such variations require refined policy formation, yet there is little evidence to suggest that policy initiatives over the past two decades have understood, let alone been in sympathy with, the demographic changes that have occurred in the post-war period. Family law continues to be based on the married two-parent family, with the one major exception being the Children, Young Persons and Their Families Act 1989. Legislation aimed at regulating families is publicly criticized for failing to distribute reciprocal rights and responsibilities, while the clumsy, costly, and inefficient set of income-support measures that have been introduced tend to trap families who are already disadvantaged.

Today, there are different measures of income, different units of assessment, different rates of abatement, and different state departments involved in each targeting provision. Many of these design problems, lying at the interface between cash transfers and tax exemptions, are based on unsustainable assumptions about the family. Moreover, changes made to the delivery of family social services place increasing demands on the family at a time when both household income and state support are in decline.

Of course there were limitations to the welfare state arrangements underpinning family policy in New Zealand during the post-war period. The gendered construction of the family and the labour market neither explicitly recognized the significance of unpaid work nor the rights of women in the paid work-force. While it may have attached a man firmly to a job, a piece of land, and a social group, it defined women and children in accordance with their 'family roles' and 'responsibilities'. The labour market, rather than the family or the state, was the mechanism through which resources were distributed; within this market, men were the primary income-earners with overall responsibility for 'their dependants'. It was a relationship, defined in law, which was based on three important assumptions:

1. that male employment was a primary economic and social goal aimed at ensuring the income security of the household;
2. that men required a 'fair wage' in order to maintain a family in a reasonable standard of comfort; and
3. that the role of women was primarily prescribed by their marital status and by the nurturing requirements of motherhood. As a consequence, the level of remuneration for labour market participation was a secondary (and indeed undesirable) consideration.

Setting aside these limitations of familial dependency (reinforced, it should be said, by male and female alike), the family wage ensured a high degree of economic and social security for over three decades. Today much of that security is gone. While changes to the family wage were inevitable, given the high level of domestic insulation and protection afforded both the family and the economy in the post-war period, the extreme shifts in policy which have occurred since 1984 have undermined social policy in general and family policy in particular.

The conditions that changed the parameters of the welfare state had both globa and domestic origins. In the international context, New Zealand's economic vu nerability prompted a market-driven programme of diversification which widene the base of the economy and altered the country's trading relationships. In th domestic sphere women became increasingly involved in the paid work-force, an the family actively exploited the increasing liberalization of the market, both a producers and consumers. These trends were evident long before the programm of economic rationalization was introduced in the mid-1980s. What was distinc tive about this earlier period of liberalization, both in terms of domestic and ecc nomic relations, was the way in which the 'historic compromise' forged in th post-war period was maintained. Employment continued to be the New Zealan government's primary economic and social objective, and when frictional unem ployment occurred in the 1970s, the state became actively involved in expandin employment opportunities and in providing temporary programmes for those ou of work. Similarly, when the value of the social wage declined, considerable pres sure was applied to government in order to maintain the country's standard o living. The thinking behind this strategy was articulated by the Royal Commissio on Social Security in its 1972 report emphasizing the importance of work in secur ing economic and social security.

At one level, changes in the configuration of family, state, and market were botl inevitable and easily understood. Many countries went through similar adjustments although it might be argued that no other country adopted such an extreme 'about face' as New Zealand. The major policy shifts in New Zealand are significant fo the way in which policy changes were predicated on clearly deficient informatio sources and data. New Zealand is probably the most disadvantaged country in thi cross-national study when databases are compared, due to three major factors Firstly, traditions of intellectual and scientific enquiry found, say, in the Unitec States, are less developed in New Zealand (Pool, 1987). Secondly, the framewor within which social policy developed from the 1890s, and more particularly in the immediate post-war period, were driven by pragmatic, political concerns rathe than imported ideologies, such as those that have dominated more recent reforms And thirdly, the post-war welfare state's high degree of economic and social secu rity meant that few demands were made of social scientists or the data sets witl which they worked. The major policy reforms of the past ten years really require sound policy models based on accurate data, but these were not available, or i available, were not consulted. In this vacuum, models were created which had n empirical substance or credibility. The concept of the 'core family' discussed ear lier is one such example.

In the process of reform the major principles and assumptions on which New Zealand's distinctive 'welfare state' arrangements had been based were radicall redrawn. Full employment, one of the central elements in the provision of a famil wage, has gone, as has the process for regulating wages which provided 'the fam ily' with 'its' economic security. At the same time, other components of the socia wage, such as health, housing, and education, have been increasingly targeted; i ertain critical areas these services have been subjected to market forces and user-ays. By removing the two central elements of family policy and by undermining e universal provisions of the family wage, New Zealand has effectively aban-oned any coherent form of domestic compensation. Unlike Western European nd Scandinavian welfare states, which have long had extensive systems of income aintenance and social insurance, New Zealand has always had a very selective nd residual benefit system. It was never designed to be a universal system—it was erely provided as a safety net for those outside the waged majority. By changing e core of New Zealand's welfare state arrangements, the country is left with a iecemeal system of 'Family Support' which is incapable of providing an effective amework for the maintenance of family well-being. It is therefore not surprising at establishing a new pattern of domestic compensation to provide economic and ocial security, especially for families with children, is one of the major challenges cing New Zealand society at the turn of the century.

Notes

1 Comment by a Vietnamese senior official to one of the co-authors.
2 Following New Zealand conventions, this study uses the term 'ex-nuptial' rather than 'out of wedlock'.
3 All amounts given are in New Zealand dollars (NZ$).
4 The threshold for abatement was $17,500 with abatement at 18 cents in the dollar, to $27,000, from which it was 30 cents in the dollar.

Family Change and Family Policies: United States

Sheila B. Kamerman
Alfred J. Kahn

Introduction: Themes in the American Tradition

The United States has no explicit national, comprehensive family or child policy, nor has there been any such policy or cluster of policies in the past. Nonetheless, over the past century, even as European welfare states were being shaped, the US too developed many of the institutional supports and commitments to what in Europe would be called a welfare state (or in Germany, a social market). Among these, from time to time, were measures directed at children or families with children. These enactments were in considerable part concentrated in several 'bursts' during periods of reform: the Progressive Era (approximately 1895–1920), the New Deal and its aftermaths (1932–54), the War on Poverty and the Great Society (1960–74). A hundred years after the Progressive Era, at the beginning of the Clinton Administration, there were new child and family initiatives, but by the middle of his term a wave of conservative reaction had begun to dismantle a sixty-year history of increasing social entitlements.

Thus, to the extent that the US has had implicit child/family policies, they can be identified and assessed only in the context of social policy more broadly defined; and they can be understood only with reference to a tradition that has included several major elements:

- Natural-rights individualism as reflected in the Declaration of Independence and the Constitution, which spelled out protection of the individual and limitations on the potential tyranny of the state *vis-à-vis* the individual.
- The separation of Church and State in order to be receptive to diverse religions and ensure their freedom. This is often interpreted to mean that government must avoid interference with family matters, a major concern to religion.
- Puritanism and related Protestant religious streams that stressed that one could legislate to prevent evil but that 'goodness' had to be voluntary. As a result, voluntarism as opposed to statutory enactment was favoured for social welfare.
- Social Darwinism, a mid-nineteenth-century 'scientific' buttressing of Puritanism, without its religious conscience, which emphasized that survival of the fittest was the 'natural' order and that societal intervention into the process was counter-productive.
- A history of slavery followed by 'emancipation' after the Civil War (1865); this 'emancipation' was rapidly subverted by a doctrine of 'separate but equal', which did not establish equality. A second more complete reform followed the civil rights movement and landmark legislation in the 1960s, but strong strains of racism and major tasks of implementation remain.

- A strict work ethic as central to the value system guiding all of the above.
- A relatively open immigration policy which created population growth while reducing, perhaps eliminating, any case for pro-natalist policies.
- A limited role for the federal government, which was deprived of all powers not specifically authorized and, until late in the nineteenth century, was no believed to have responsibilities in what is now thought of as the social sector which was considered to be the province of the states.
- *Laissez-faire* economic and social policy ('liberalism' in the European sense) as the dominant ideology that would bring a society growth and prosperity: nothing in charity, welfare, or labour policy should interfere with work motivation or the success of the market.
- The late development of a civil service and government bureaucracy, which limited the national government's capacity for social policy and raised doubts about the quality of states' efforts.
- An ambivalence after World War II regarding women's roles, in particular whether public policy should take a position of supporting or encouraging women with young children to remain at home, providing care for their children, or to enter the work-force, helping to sustain family income.

Historically, these themes have played out in various ways as economic, social, and political contexts changed with the settlement of the continent and the evolution of the economy through the industrial revolution to a post-industrial society, and as demographic and social change wrought major shifts in the family.

Within this context, social policies affecting children and their families focused first on the unfortunate, the handicapped, and the most severely deprived; and second, on the poor. Except for free and compulsory public education, a development in which the US was among the leaders internationally, the US was late in its development of social policy for children generally. Overall, it has placed a heavy emphasis on services and other in-kind benefits for the vulnerable and poor. As for improving the economic situation of families with children, the policy has been largely one of ending almost all taxation of the poor except for social security payroll taxes, offering modest and inconsistent cash benefits to some low-income families and tax benefits to the middle and upper classes.

The point of departure was poor law. For present purposes we note the evolution of a strong and important voluntary middle-class charitable movement in the nineteenth century, compensating for the limitations of poor law and aiding those considered more 'helpable' and 'deserving'. This movement built on private charities and church activities of the eighteenth century. At various times between the late eighteenth and late nineteenth centuries, national movements developed in several fields covering: children's institutions for the dependent and handicapped; boys' and girls' clubs; early foster home care (Children's Aid Societies and State Children's Home Societies); family guidance and related financial aid (societies for prevention of pauperism, associations for the improvement of the conditions of the poor, charity organization societies); services encouraging integration, socialization, and mobilization of urban settlers and immigrants (settlement houses); child protection (Society for the Prevention of Cruelty to Children); programmes and homes promoting socialization and protection of young adults in urban settings (Young Men's Christian Association, Young Women's Christian Association).

Characteristically, these were private, voluntary developments, some with Protestant origins but 'non-sectarian', and others active affiliates of religious groups. Except for those organizations providing residential care for children, most did not receive public funds. Indeed, until the 1960s, most private child welfare agencies, settlement houses, family service agencies and similar organizations, through their national associations, refused public funds as a matter of principle. However, during the economic depressions of 1894 and the 1930s the need to co-operate with government in getting food to large numbers of people did lead to emergency actions as agents of government by many voluntary agencies.

The US Civil War (1861–65) constituted an important turning point. Cities had become larger and more impersonal. Immigrants arrived from new and different areas. Social Darwinism was strong in the *laissez-faire* economic context, and objections to any governmental social welfare programmes in other than the spirit of poor law were further buttressed by government corruption and inefficiency during the rapid industrial and population growth of the post-Civil War Gilded Age.

Educated middle-class women became important in voluntary charity, including Charity Organization Societies, State Charities Aid, hospitals, and medical and educational services for freedmen during and after the Civil War. Later in the century, the new leisure of a bourgeois class that increasingly separated work from home gave rise to the concept of women's 'special place'. Mothers were to create a family haven, rear and educate children, and enrich family life. Women also would bring their moral values to the public household (mostly local government).

The shift that was to lead to the launching of the American welfare state by the New Deal, from 1933 to World War II, in fact began at the close of the nineteenth century, after the 1894 depression and during the Progressive Era. A 'responsible' wealthy and patrician class took the lead in seeking to create honest and efficient state and local government as a vehicle to meet the needs of an urban industrial society and a complex industrial economy. Programmes of 'social welfare' (today's term) began in more progressive states. New leaders understood the need for regulatory activity by the central government. Various groups of citizens began to advocate for some broader federal programmes in health, labour regulation, and welfare, to be implemented by the states. The movement for equal rights and the vote for women reflected changes in education and the family. In some states organized labour began to have some political impact. At the same time crusading journalists, novelists, clergymen, and social surveys publicized the problems of child labour and urban housing conditions and the realities of poverty, including the strong evidence that more than individual moral failure was involved.

Most important for our purpose, the reformers of the Progressive period converted the late nineteenth and early twentieth century into a major era of child reform. Child reform in fact was paradigmatic for the Progressive Era: kindergartens, Juvenile Court, maternal and child health, the US Children's Bureau, child labour regulation, the child guidance clinic movement, and the beginnings of mothers' or widows' pensions were all developments of the time. At the state level, there were such developments as the establishment of workers' compensation, unemployment legislation, and systems of free, public, and compulsory education. Educated young people, many with religious motivations and some who were secular idealists, became the 'professional altruists' and the early settlement house residents who created social work. Women played a particularly strong leadership role, and the emphasis on children's issues reflected their special concerns.

By the time of the Great Depression (1930–39), extensive precedent for social reform, social service, and government regulatory activity had been established—even though the country as a whole needed several years to begin to absorb the lessons. In responding to the crisis of the early 1930s, the federal government began to create an economic safety net that was eventually to have work and food relief, medical, social service, and housing ramifications. The federal government assumed new power *vis-à-vis* the weak and impoverished states. The economic and industrial requirements of World War II were to strengthen this process considerably as fiscal and monetary policy also became institutionalized as legitimate concerns of government. Also, as noted recently by Skocpol (1992) and others, the country began to develop on the national level the bureaucratic capacity needed to mount large and expensive cash benefit programmes.

The New Deal and its aftermath created the foundation of a minimalist welfare state that included federal social insurance programmes for old-age pensions, survivors' benefits, unemployment insurance, and a partial safety net for the poor elderly, the blind (later the poor disabled as well), and dependent children. In contrast to much of Europe, however, World War II did not lead to major new social policy initiatives except for a dramatic expansion of access to higher education for demobilized members of the military.

The next major developments in social policy, including several of great importance to children, were left to the decade of the 1960s and the 'Great Society' of President Lyndon Johnson. From the mid-1960s through the early 1970s, the American welfare state took a great leap forward. Equal opportunity, racial justice, economic aid, and compensatory education were the primary new focus. Depth, range, coverage, and expenditures for social welfare all increased. The civil rights movement and the War on Poverty broadened and specified the definitions of the problem and required a larger response that included both federal and local governments. Social welfare clients and consumers, not just professionals, private philanthropists, and public administrators were involved.

The particular configurations of state politics and the ethnic/racial politics of the big cities, in their interaction with voluntary social welfare agencies and federations in the 1960s and 1970s, changed the dominant philosophy regarding public funding of the voluntary sector. Before the end of the 1970s, much of the old voluntary sector and almost all new grassroots social service programmes in the localities were publicly funded. Nearly the entire enormous expansion of public social services took place through such funding. The process only gained in complexity in the 1980s and 1990s, leaving serious problems of fragmentation, categorization, lack of co-ordination, and high administrative overhead. By the mid-1980s, a very large infusion of foundation funds for family and children's services was divided between support for innovation and programme initiatives and support to find ways to co-ordinate and integrate fragmented categorical initiatives.

Some of the federal oversight and leadership capacity that developed with the New Deal and the Great Society was deliberately dismantled in the Reagan–Bush era, and state operations became more important once again until stymied by economic problems, resource shortages, and cuts in federal support in the early 1990s.

What of the trade unions? Their strongest days were from the 1930s through the 1970s, but even then their influence never matched that of organized labour in many European countries. Like their counterparts in other countries, unions in the United States have preferred to deliver benefits gained for their members through collective bargaining. However, facing the limits of that process and as part of the New Deal coalition, unions eventually supported the creation of the American welfare state infrastructure and its elaboration. Currently much weakened, the trade union movement must hope for expanded public programmes as the only major prospect for most purposes. Only among public employees has union membership increased, while unionization in the private sector has declined to about 11% of that sector's workers. Recently, women have become a growing source of trade unions' limited membership, making so-called 'women's issues' (child and family issues) of greater concern to organized labour. Unfortunately, this development comes at a time when unions are weaker and far less influential politically.

The feminist movement began having its second significant impact in the 1970s, concentrating much of its energies on workplace discrimination, equal rights, and abortion. It gave relatively limited attention to child- and family-related issues such as parental leave and child care until late in the 1980s (the Bush years) and the start of the Clinton era. Results are thus far modest.

When, in 1994, a conservative populism, strongly backed by fundamentalist, right-wing Protestant churches, swept Republicans into control of the Congress with a pledge to undo many of the social foundations established by the New Deal and the Great Society and to 'remoralize' America, it could be seen as a possible continuity with the Reagan–Bush era after a two-year Clinton interruption. The new reformers sought to re-establish the states' dominance over Washington in social policy, to cut the means-tested safety nets for the poor, and to cut social expenditures generally. Such cuts were justified as a method of encouraging work and more 'moral' behaviour, such as less out-of-wedlock childbearing. The consequences would be largely felt by poor single mothers in particular and working mothers generally—and their young children.

As indicated in the following chapters, it is too soon to judge whether this shift will be a brief detour or a fundamental change of direction for American child and family policies and for social policy generally, now possibly pointed back to an era believed long past.

1

The Formation of Families

Since the early 1970s, both popular and scholarly literature in the United States have highlighted issues of family change. Although the debate has been couched in terms of whether the family is failing as society's primary institution of child socialization, it was stimulated by the growing awareness of significant changes occurring within families. That the family has changed, in particular over the last three decades, is a subject of general agreement. That the major changes have to do with the declining significance of 'traditional' families—two-parent, husband/wife families with children, in which the husband works outside the home in the paid labour force and the wife works inside the home as an unpaid family worker—is also a source of general agreement. Debate centres on the following questions:

1. whether the changes have positive as well as negative consequences;
2. whether the family is dying or declining, or whether it remains in changed form and will once again emerge as a powerful institution; and
3. whether these family changes have generated new and responsive social policies toward children and their families and/or whether the policy developments have shaped some of the family changes, and what the implications of these developments might be.

The main theme of what follows is that all of these family changes have their roots in developments that began at least one or two centuries ago, that the overall trends were either interrupted in the post-World War II period and the baby-boom years or have fluctuated somewhat over time, and that over the last thirty years these changes have finally reached a critical mass in the population: instead of encompassing a small minority of families and family members, they now affect a large minority or even the majority. Public policies by and large have lagged in their apparent responses to these changes and, once in place, have sometimes facilitated them, but did not by themselves generate radical new trends.

A second theme is that US population diversity—religious, ethnic, and racial—as well as the presence of large infusions of new immigrants throughout the nineteenth and early twentieth centuries and again in the 1970s and 1980s contributed certain distinctive patterns of family formation. For example, rising rates of single parenthood and out-of-wedlock births, although characteristic of family change generally, began earlier as a significant family form and characterized a larger portion of families with children among blacks than in the population at large. Adolescent unwed parenting is more significant among blacks and, in recent years,

Hispanics. Total fertility rates, although converging for all groups, are still somewhat higher for blacks and significantly higher for Hispanics, among whom are many recent immigrants. Because new immigrants in general tend to be younger than the rest of the population and are more likely to have their children at earlier ages, they are also more likely to have more children, thus offsetting some of the overall trend toward fertility decline. Finally, as we shall see in Chapter 2, blacks were also forerunners in the development of dual-earner families.

In this chapter, we focus primarily on the changes in family formation, structure, and composition that occurred between 1960 and 1990, while placing them in a larger historical context. We also look at how the changes are linked to or reflected in developments in family law and in public attitudes toward and values about family change. Other changes are discussed subsequently.

MARRIAGE, DIVORCE, AND CHILDBEARING

Our starting point is what Andrew Cherlin, family sociologist and demographer, states as a more accurate if clumsy title for his influential monograph, *Marriage, Divorce, and Remarriage*: 'cohabitation, marriage, divorce, more cohabitation, and probably remarriage' (Cherlin, 1992: vii).

Marriage

Marriage remains the most common means of family formation in the US. Marriage rates are higher in the US than in almost every other advanced industrialized country. The institution of marriage has changed dramatically, however, especially during the last three decades, and is still changing: marriages now tend to be briefer and encompass a smaller portion of adults' lives; age at first marriage has increased; first-marriage rates have declined and now plateaued; divorce rates have increased and plateaued at a high level. Remarriage rates have varied: rising when divorce rates rose dramatically in the late 1960s, then declining in parallel with first-marriage rates. More people are forgoing marriage entirely, and far more are cohabiting before marriage and between marriages, if not yet instead of marriage (at least not in significant numbers). Some of these developments began as far back as the nineteenth century while others are more recent.

Although marriage remains the dominant experience for most adults, and the number of marriages that occurred during the 1980s was at an all-time high, marriages have a far shorter average lifespan in the 1990s than they did in the 1960s. Despite adults' increased longevity and in part because adults are getting married later, marriage encompasses a smaller part of an individual's lifetime than previously.

The age of first marriage has fluctuated over the last two centuries. It increased significantly in the eighteenth and nineteenth centuries (Wells, 1973), then declined during the first half of the twentieth century, only to rise again beginning with the 1960s. Median age at first marriage reached a low of 22.5 years for men and 20.1 years for women in 1956, remaining roughly at that level until 1970. Over the last two decades, median age at first marriage has increased by more than three years for both men and women, remaining level since the late 1980s. In recent years, women have had the highest age at first marriage (23.9) since data were first collected on this topic in 1890 (Norton and Miller, 1992). For men, the median age at first marriage in 1990 (26.1) was the same as in 1890. An expanding economy and high employment rates may have encouraged many young couples in the 1950s to marry early, but clearly a contracting economy and changes in social attitudes contributed to a sharp rise in median age of first marriage since then, as did the general trend toward extending education (Sweet and Bumpass, 1987).

While Americans may be delaying entry into marriage, until now almost all adults eventually got married at least once. However, this pattern may be changing too. The highest probability of marriage occurs for young adults in their twenties. Sweet and Bumpass (1987) point out that although marriage rates have also declined for older persons, most of the decline in marriage rates is accounted for by the decline in marriage among 18–24-year-olds. In 1990, 63% of women aged 20–24 had never married, compared to 28% in 1960; for men the comparative rates were 79% in 1990 vs. 53% in 1960.

Racial patterns in marriage have also changed, with growing differences between white and black women. Before World War II, marriage rates were similar for both groups of women, and blacks tended to marry at earlier ages than whites. Today that pattern is reversed: Norton and Miller (1992) point out that by 1990 the percentage of white women aged 30–34 who were married had fallen from 94% in 1975 to 86%, while the percentage of married black women had fallen from 87% to 61%. Assuming stability in the marriage rates for both groups over the age of 40, current projections are that less than three out of four black women will eventually marry, compared with about nine out of ten white.

Divorce

Divorce rates in the US are among the highest in the advanced industrialized countries. Divorce rates have increased since at least 1860, the earliest year for which data are available (Cherlin, 1992), reaching a first peak in 1945–47, then steadily rising, with a sharp increase from the early 1960s to the late 1970s and levelling off since the mid-1980s. From 1948 to 1966 the divorce rate was about 16 per 1,000 married women 15–44 years of age. Between 1966 and 1977, the rate increased from 17 to 37; it peaked in 1980 at 40 and has stabilized at around 37 since the mid-1980s (Norton and Miller, 1992).

In 1990, 2.4 million marriages and 1.2 million divorces took place. The Census Bureau estimates that half of all marriages occurring since 1970 will end in divorce, but that the majority of the divorced persons are likely to remarry. Younger people are more likely to divorce and to remarry after divorce than older persons. Divorce rates are relatively similar across religions. There are some racial differences, however: among white and Hispanic women at the end of the 1980s, over one-third had divorced, while for black women, the rate was almost 50%.

Economic factors as well as attitudinal and legal changes are seen as contributing to the rise in divorce. The legal and attitudinal changes will be discussed later in this chapter, while the economic factors will be addressed in Chapter 3. Women's entry into the labour force brought them more economic independence, which meant that for many women it was no longer necessary to remain in an unsatisfactory marriage. Similarly, rising divorce rates left many women with the view that marriage was no longer a lifetime contract. Given the growing sense of marriage as fragile, more and more women sought paid employment as a form of personal insurance against the negative economic consequences of a (probable) divorce, reinforcing the pattern of obtaining some economic independence—leading to greater marriage fragility—leading to greater need for economic independence.

The general patterns of divorce after first marriage differ for white, black, and Hispanic women (data for the last category are available only since 1980). Norton and Miller (1992) point out that, overall, black women have higher divorce rates than white or Hispanic women, and Hispanic women are likely to have the lowest divorce rates.

Remarriage

Remarriage in the US has become a relatively common life course event (Cherlin, 1992; Norton and Miller, 1992; US Bureau of the Census, 1990; Sweet and Bumpass, 1987). Almost half of all marriages in the US in 1990 involved a remarriage for the bride, groom, or both. One-quarter of all first marriages are now to a previously-married spouse. Rates of remarriage were at their low during the Depression (along with rates of first marriages) but rose steadily, paralleling the increase in first-marriage and divorce rates, to peak in the immediate post-World War II years. Remarriages then declined until the early 1960s, when remarriage rates rose along with the increase in divorces, only to decline again and later exceed the downward trend for first marriages. Remarriage rates for women whose first marriages ended in divorce declined for all age groups between the late 1970s and the late 1980s (Norton and Miller, 1992).

Racial differences regarding remarriage are significant. White women were far more likely to remarry than black or Hispanic women; when added to much lower first-marriage rates among blacks, this tendency further contributes to the increase in black mother-only families.

Cohabitation

Cohabitation (unmarried partners living together) became an accepted pattern during the 1970s and 1980s, in particular as a prelude to marriage, albeit nowhere near as common as in many European countries. Cohabitation was rare among couples born before 1940 and was largely confined to those with limited education. Cherlin

316   *United States*

(1992) points out that, beginning with those born in 1940, cohabitation began to increase among young adults regardless of their level of education. However, despite a sharp rise in cohabitation among college graduates in the 1970s, rates of cohabitation were higher among the less-educated throughout the 1970s.

According to data from the National Survey of Families and Households, only 11% of persons who married between 1965 and 1974 cohabited before marriage, while 32% of those married between 1975 and 1979 did so, as did 44% of those who married between 1980 and 1984. Cherlin (1992) and Bumpass and Raley (1995) estimate that more than half of those marrying in the 1990s will have cohabited before marriage. Given this pattern, young adults are as likely to be living with another adult of the opposite sex in the 1990s as they were in 1970; however, now they are likely to be cohabiting rather than legally married. Between 1970 and 1985 the rise in cohabitation compensated for 59% of the decline in marriage among men and 76% of the decline for women (Cherlin, 1992). Cohabitation is even more prevalent among the previously-married than among the never-married.

Evidence suggests that for the majority of adults in the US, 'cohabitation is not a lifelong alternative to marriage but rather a stage of intimacy that precedes (or sometimes follows) marriage' (Cherlin, 1992: 14). Cherlin refers to a Bumpass and Sweet study in which the authors estimate that about half of all cohabiting couples either marry or break up within one and a half years and 90% within five years, with most of them marrying. However, marriages that follow cohabitation are more likely to break up than other marriages. As Bumpass and Raley (1995) point out, ignoring the dramatic rise in cohabitation in the 1990s leads to exaggerated reporting of single-parent families due to the classification of unmarried two-parent families as lone-parent families. Nonetheless, cohabiting couples are far less likely to have children than married couples.

Despite increases in cohabitation, later marriage, and divorce, marriage is clearly not on its way out. Some may remain unmarried, but for the vast majority, certainly for white women, marriage remains the basis of family formation. In contrast,

Black women . . . are less likely to marry, stay married, and remarry. Those who marry do so at an older age than do whites. The differences between blacks and whites in the timing of marriage, the lifetime chance of ever marrying, and the chance of a divorced women ever remarrying are greater than they were a generation ago. As a result, black women spend far less of their life in a marriage than do white women. . . . Marriage has become just a temporary stage of life for blacks . . . For blacks, even more so than for whites, a long, stable marriage is the exception rather than the rule. (Cherlin, 1992: 95.)

Children and Fertility

Children have always been viewed as central to American families, although in the last thirty years their significance has clearly declined. Indeed, the greatest change in American households has been the decline in the presence of children, from 48.6% of American households in 1960 and 45.3% in 1970 to 38.4% in 1980 and

4.6% in 1990 (Lugaila, 1992). Some of this diminishing importance of children
1 US households is due to the growth in one-person households and households of
lderly couples, but much is due as well to changes within those households that
istorically have included children. Fewer families include children now, as com-
ared to the 1960s, because childbearing has been delayed, fertility rates have
eclined, and families are having fewer children; there are fewer married-couple
amilies because divorce has increased, more births are occurring outside of mar-
iage, and a disproportionately large number of births is occurring to unmarried
dolescent females.

A census report on historical trends and perspectives on American fertility be-
ins by stating that 'the sustained decline in the birth rate from the earliest period
1 our nation's history to the Great Depression of the 1930s is the dominant charac-
ristic of the course of fertility in the United States. . . . the crude birth rate . . . may
ave been about 50 in 1800 as compared with the current [1978] rate of about 15'
US Bureau of the Census, 1978). Thus, fertility in the United States was probably
igher than in any Western European country at the beginning of the nineteenth
entury. Although the birth rate had fallen to approximately 45 by the 1850s, it was
till considerably higher than in most contemporary European nations. It was not
ntil the late 1800s that the birth rate for the white population in the United States
ell to levels comparable with those recorded in Western Europe (US Bureau of the
'ensus, 1978: 1).

Despite the larger number of children in the eighteenth-century American fam-
y, the importance of children in the life of families has steadily declined from the
itter half of the eighteenth century to the 1990s. Eighteenth-century Quaker women
re estimated to have spent more than 17 years bearing children; the median age of
iothers at the birth of their last child was 37.9 years (Wells, 1973). Women born in
ie 1930s spent a median of about eight years in childbearing, and the median age
f mothers at the birth of their last child was 30. As a result, women now spend
orrespondingly fewer years in child-rearing, too.

Beginning in the late eighteenth century, American fertility experienced a long-
erm decline, which accelerated sharply during the nineteenth and early twentieth
enturies. This decline was interrupted by the baby-boom years 1947–63 and then
ontinued, though a slight increase in fertility emerged at the end of the 1980s. At
ie beginning of the nineteenth century, American families tended to be large, with
vomen typically having about seven children (Ahlburg and De Vita, 1992). A
undred years later, the average number of children per woman had dropped to
bout 3.6; by the mid-1930s, the average had dropped still further, to 2.1. The
ost-World War II baby boom reversed this trend dramatically, but after 1960, the
otal fertility rate (TFR) declined sharply to a low of 1.8 in 1974. From 1974 to
990, the rate fluctuated between 1.8 and 2.1, where it was in 1990. Because women
iorn during the baby boom constitute such a large cohort, the number of births rose
teadily from 1977 through 1990, but has declined since then. Women can still
xpect to have on average two children, a family size that has been a consistent
iorm for the last thirty years.

As we saw earlier, the age at first marriage is higher now than at any point since the end of the nineteenth century. Given that about 70% of all live births are to women in their twenties, deferring age of marriage and postponing the birth of a first child after marriage have major consequences for women's total fertility rates. Birth rates have increased among 30-year-olds, though not enough to make up for the decline among those in their twenties.

Theories accounting for deferred childbearing include Easterlin's explanation (1980) that poor employment prospects for men in large cohorts have influenced the timing of births; and Butz's and Ward's (1978) theory that higher labour force participation and higher wages lead women to defer childbearing until the opportunity costs are lower. Others argue that women's recognition of the pay-off from more education has led them to postpone having children until after completing their education and getting a start in their careers.

Although the overall fertility patterns are similar among black and white women, black fertility has remained somewhat higher than white, never going below replacement. The gap between the two rates has shrunk since the early 1960s. Since 1985, both groups have increased fertility, but rates for blacks have risen more than those for whites.

Minority births also constitute a larger portion of total births in recent years as a result of the growth in immigration since 1965. Immigration usually brings a younger population, more apt to be concentrated in the childbearing years. Moreover, women have constituted a higher proportion of the recent waves of immigrants. Minority births accounted for one in five in 1989 as compared with one in seven in 1960 (Ahlburg and De Vita, 1992).

Childlessness has increased significantly over the last two decades, especially for women over 25. Women aged 40–44 in 1990, which includes the forefront of the baby-boom generation, will complete their childbearing years with childlessness rates of 16% as compared with 10% in 1976 and 1980 for earlier cohorts (US Bureau of the Census, 1991a). Despite a significant increase in childbearing among women in their thirties, 15–20% of the women who were born during the 1950s (the peak years of the baby boom) are likely to be childless—possibly the highest rates of childlessness ever recorded in the US.

Changing patterns in adolescent pregnancy and parenting made these issues of concern on the US public agenda in the early 1970s. Before 1970, most births to adolescents were to married teens or to those whose pregnancy led to marriage; the number of births to younger adolescents (15–17-year-olds) declined in the 1960s and those teens who had babies out of wedlock relinquished their babies for adoption. Beginning in the 1970s, the pattern was for young mothers to keep their children. Numbers of births to teenagers increased steadily between 1955 and the early 1970s, then declined through the mid-1980s, to rise again in the late 1980s and decline in the early 1990s (Hofferth and Hayes, 1987; Moore, 1994). The teenage fertility rate declined throughout most of this period: from 89 births per 1,000 women aged 15–19 in 1960, to 53 per 1,000 in 1982, with a low of 50 per 1,000 in 1986. The rate then began to rise, reaching 62 per 1,000 in 1991, then declined again through the early 1990s. Teenage fertility outside of marriage has been rising: in 1992, 71% of the births to mothers 19 or younger occurred to unmarried mothers, compared with 30% in 1970. Overall, however, the percentage of out-of-wedlock teen births declined as a portion of all out-of-wedlock births, from 50% in 1970 to 30% in 1991.

Teen fertility rates vary by race and ethnicity. The rate is highest among black teens, rising by 10% between 1980 and 1991 (from 105 to 118 per 1,000 females aged 15–19). The rate for Hispanics, which had been significantly lower than that for blacks, rose by more than 25% during the same years (82 to 107), while rates for white teens remained relatively stable (41 to 43). Most of the recent increase in teen fertility rates is attributable to the rise in rates for Hispanic teens, now almost as high as for blacks.

The public concern with teenage pregnancy and childbirth is understandable: very young mothers are less likely to receive timely and adequate prenatal care; they are more likely to give birth to low-birthweight babies; more likely to be poor; more likely to be reported for incidents of child abuse; more likely to receive public or social assistance during their twenties and to be long-term recipients; and their daughters are more likely to have babies as teens themselves (Moore, 1994).

In contrast to most continental European countries, adolescent out-of-wedlock fertility is clearly considered a major problem in the US and has dominated the debate about social assistance reform for the past decades (see Chapter 3). Yet the pattern needs to be seen in the larger context of the growth in out-of-wedlock births generally. Births to unmarried women of all ages more than tripled over the past three decades, increasing from about 700,000 in 1960–64 to 2.2 million in 1985–89 (Lugaila, 1992). In 1960, only 5% of all births were to unmarried women, while by 1992, the share had increased to 30%, a rate not unlike Canada's (29%), the UK's (31%), and France's (33%), while significantly lower than Denmark's (46%) and Sweden's (50%) (US Bureau of the Census, 1995). With birth rates declining overall and out-of-wedlock birth rates increasing, the proportion of all births constituted by out-of-wedlock births is ever larger. About one-third of all children born in 1994 were born to unmarried mothers.

Since 1960, out-of-wedlock births have been more common among blacks and Hispanics than among non-Hispanic whites. However, among white women, the rate of out-of-wedlock births more than doubled between 1964 and 1989: for all white women aged 15–34 who had a first birth between 1960–64, the rate of out-of-wedlock births was 8.5%; between 1985–89, the rate was 21.6%. For Hispanics, the rate during the same periods almost doubled, from 19.2% to 37.5%. Among blacks, the rate increased by a smaller amount, about 66%, but from a much higher base: from 42.4% in 1960–64 to 70.3% in 1985–89. Given the greater decline of marriage rates among blacks than whites and the greater decline of marital fertility rates, the rate of out-of-wedlock births to blacks has assumed dramatic proportions. Two-thirds of all births to black women in 1992 were out of wedlock.

HOUSEHOLD AND FAMILY STRUCTURES

The focus here is on families with children under 18 and how they have changed. Over the last three decades, households have become smaller; family households have become smaller in size as well as a smaller proportion of all households; family households have become less likely to include children; and those that do are less likely to include two parents. In effect, because there are fewer children per family, more one-parent families, and a growing number of persons living alone, the average size of households and families has declined. Because there is more divorce, more out-of-wedlock childbearing, and more remarriage, family composition and structure are changing also. The results include changes in the nuclear and the extended family: cohabiting couples (a small but growing component); one-parent families, largely female-headed (an increasingly large component); reconstituted or 'merged' families (a very large and growing component). We now have a decrease in husband/wife families (the 'traditional' family type). These changes have obvious consequences for how children are reared and how they experience growing up, and do not yet take account of the gender-role changes discussed in the next chapter.

The trend toward smaller families and households began in the nineteenth century, was interrupted during the baby boom, and has accelerated since the mid-1960s. In 1960 the average number of persons in a household was 3.3, and average family size was 3.7 persons; in 1990 the comparable figures were 2.6 persons per household and 3.2 per family. Most households are still family households, but this household type has steadily decreased as a portion of all households, from 87% in 1960 to 70% in 1990.

Changes have occurred within family households as well. Family households with children have declined as a portion of all households from 48.6% in 1960 to 34.6% in 1990. Married-couple family households with children have declined dramatically, from 44.2% of all households in 1960 to 26.3% in 1990, and from 52% of all families with children in 1960 to 37% in 1990.

Numbers of children per family have also declined. Among families with children, those with three or more children decreased from 36% to 20%, while those with one child grew from 32% to 42%, and those with two children from 31.5% to 38%. Until the late 1970s, the average number of own children under 18 was about the same for both one- and two-parent families; since then, married couples have been somewhat more likely to have more children. The two-child family has been the norm for the past thirty years and had begun to evolve even earlier.

The most dramatic changes in family structure are the decline in two-parent families with children and the increase in one-parent families, in particular, female-headed families. Between 1970 and 1992, two-parent families declined as a portion of all families with children for whites, blacks, and Hispanics from 87% to 70% (US Bureau of the Census, 1993a). Paralleling this decline, the portion of all families with children headed by a lone parent increased from 13% to 30%, and the absolute number of one-parent families grew from 3.8 million to 10.5 million.

TABLE 1. One-parent family groups, by race, Hispanic origin, sex, and marital status of householder or reference person, United States 1970–1992 (in 1,000 and % distributions)

Subject	1970 no.	1970 %	1980 no.	1980 %	1990 no.	1990 %	1992 no.	1992 %
All races								
One-parent family groups[a]	3,808	100.0	6,920	100.0	9,749	100.0	10,499	100.0
Maintained by mother	3,415	89.7	6,230	90.0	8,398	86.1	9,028	86.0
never married	248	6.5	1,063	15.4	2,775	28.5	3,284	31.3
married, spouse absent[b]	1,377	36.2	1,743	25.2	1,836	18.8	1,947	18.5
separated	962	25.3	1,483	21.4	1,557	16.0	1,658	15.8
divorced	1,109	29.1	2,721	39.3	3,194	32.8	3,349	31.9
widowed	682	17.9	703	10.2	593	6.1	448	4.3
Maintained by father	393	10.3	690	10.0	1,351	13.9	1,472	14.0
never married	22	0.6	63	0.9	345	3.5	400	3.8
married, spouse absent[b]	247	6.5	181	2.6	217	2.2	308	2.9
widowed	124	3.3	107	1.5	89	0.9	100	1.0
White								
One-parent family groups[a]	2,638	100.0	4,664	100.0	6,389	100.0	6,938	100.0
Maintained by mother	2,330	88.3	4,122	88.4	5,310	83.1	5,753	82.9
never married	73	2.8	379	8.1	1,139	17.8	1,391	20.0
married, spouse absent[b]	796	30.2	1,033	22.1	1,206	18.9	1,341	19.3
separated	477	18.1	840	18.0	1,015	15.9	1,146	16.5
divorced	930	35.3	2,201	47.2	2,553	40.0	2,692	38.8
widowed	531	20.1	511	11.0	411	6.4	328	4.7
Maintained by father	307	11.6	542	11.6	1,079	16.9	1,186	17.1
never married	18	0.7	32	0.7	253	4.0	292	4.2
married, spouse absent[a]	196	7.4	141	3.0	169	2.6	239	3.4
divorced	—	—	288	6.2	591	9.3	581	8.4
widowed	93	3.5	82	1.8	65	1.0	73	1.1
Black								
One-parent family groups[a]	1,148	100.0	2,114	100.0	3,081	100.0	3,216	100.0
Maintained by mother	1,063	92.6	1,984	93.9	2,860	92.8	2,994	93.1
never married	173	15.1	665	31.5	1,572	51.0	1,799	55.9
married, spouse absent[b]	570	49.7	667	31.6	570	18.5	548	17.0
separated	479	41.7	616	29.1	502	16.3	482	15.0
widowed	148	12.9	174	8.2	144	4.7	97	3.0
Maintained by father	85	7.4	129	6.1	221	7.2	222	6.9
never married	4	0.3	30	1.4	74	2.4	83	2.6
married, spouse absent[b]	50	4.4	37	1.8	38	1.2	45	1.4
divorced	—	—	43	2.0	93	3.0	68	2.1
widowed	30	2.6	19	0.9	18	0.6	25	0.8
Hispanic[c]								
One-parent family groups[a]	—	—	568	100.0	1,140	100.0	1,298	100.0
Maintained by mother	—	—	526	92.6	1,003	88.0	1,112	85.7
never married	—	—	120	21.1	361	31.7	407	31.4
married, spouse absent[b]	—	—	199	35.0	314	27.5	321	24.7
separated	—	—	170	29.9	249	21.8	259	20.0
divorced	—	—	162	28.5	266	23.3	318	24.5
widowed	—	—	46	8.1	62	5.4	65	5.0
Maintained by father	—	—	42	7.4	138	12.1	186	14.3
never married	—	—	7	1.2	62	5.4	74	5.7
married, spouse absent[b]	—	—	13	2.3	26	2.3	41	3.2
divorced	—	—	13	2.3	40	3.5	55	4.2
widowed	—	—	8	1.4	9	0.8	15	1.2

[a] Family groups comprise family households, related subfamilies, and unrelated subfamilies.
[b] Data for 1970 include divorced fathers.   [c] Persons of Hispanic origin may be of any race.

Source: US Bureau of the Census (1993), *Household and Family Characteristics: March 1992*, Current Population Reports, P20–467, Washington, DC: US Government Printing Office, xvi, Table H.

Although the percentage of male-headed, single-parent families with children has more than tripled since 1970 (from 1.3% in 1960 to 4.2% in 1992), women are overwhelmingly more likely to head a family alone than men (25.5% in 1992) (US Bureau of the Census, 1993a). Racial and ethnic differences in single-parent families are almost as dramatic as the gender differences. The number of white single parents is more than double the number of black single parents, but the portion of black families with children headed by a lone parent (62%) is far greater than the comparable portion of white families (24%).

Lone-parent families also differ by marital status. In the nineteenth and early twentieth centuries, most mother-only families were headed by a widow, whereas divorced and separated women became the dominant group in the twentieth century. The proportion of single-parent families with children headed by widows declined still further between 1970 and 1992, dropping from 18% to 4%, while separated and divorced women remained the largest group of lone parents, the proportions remaining relatively stable during this period: 54% in 1960 and 48% in 1992. The most dramatic change has been the increase among the never-married, rising from 6.5% of all lone-parent families in 1970 to 31.3% in 1992 (US Bureau of the Census, 1993a). Though some of these may be cohabiting unmarried couples, as Bumpass and Raley (1995) point out, most by far are not.

There are significant differences in single-parent marital status by race: divorced mothers are the dominant type among white lone-parent families throughout the last two decades, despite a more than sevenfold increase of the never-marrieds from 2.8% to 20% between 1970 and 1992. Among blacks, the rate of increase was less but the base much higher: never-married mothers constituted 56% of black lone mothers in 1992 as compared with 15% in 1970. Hispanic rates of growth were lower, with the proportion of never-married mothers rising from 21% to 31% of Hispanic single mothers during the same years.

As family structure and composition have changed, the living arrangements of children have changed dramatically as well. The percentage of children living with two parents was relatively stable between 1940 and the late 1960s, when the proportion of children living in single-parent families began to rise sharply along with the growth in mother-only families. Recent estimates suggest that 60% of all children born in the 1980s are likely to live in a single-parent family for at least some time before their 18th birthday (Sweet and Bumpass, 1987). Despite the increase in cohabitation, the proportion of children reported as living with cohabiting parents was less than 2% in 1990.[1]

The proportion of children living with one parent increased from 12% to 27% between 1970 and 1992, with the vast majority living with their mothers. Here, too, rates differ significantly by race: despite the rates for white children more than doubling, from 8.7% in 1970 to 20.9% in 1992, white children are far less likely to live in single-parent families than are Hispanics (32%) or blacks (57%) (US Bureau of the Census, 1993b).

Although most children living with one parent were living with a divorced or separated parent, this type declined from 73% of lone-parent families in 1970 to

TABLE 2. Living arrangements of children, by race and Hispanic origin,
United States 1970, 1980, and 1992 (in 1,000 and % distributions)

Living arrangements	1970 no.[a]	1970 %	1980 no.[a]	1980 %	1992 no.[a]	1992 %
All races						
Children under 18 years	69,162	100.0	63,427	100.0	65,965	100.0
Living with:						
two parents	58,939	85.2	48,624	76.7	46,638	70.7
one parent	8,199	11.9	12,466	19.7	17,578	26.6
mother only	7,452	10.8	11,406	18.0	15,396	23.3
father only	748	1.1	1,060	1.7	2,182	3.3
other relatives	1,547	2.2	1,949	3.1	1,334	2.0
non-relatives only	477	0.7	388	0.6	415	0.6
White						
Children under 18 years	58,790	100.0	52,242	100.0	52,493	100.0
Living with:						
two parents	52,624	89.5	43,200	82.7	40,635	77.4
one parent	5,109	8.7	7,901	15.1	10,971	20.9
mother only	4,581	7.8	7,059	13.5	9,250	17.6
father only	528	0.9	842	1.6	1,721	3.3
other relatives	696	1.2	887	1.7	643	1.2
non-relatives only	362	0.6	254	0.5	243	0.5
Black						
Children under 18 years	9,422	100.0	9,375	100.0	10,427	100.0
Living with:						
two parents	5,508	58.5	3,956	42.2	3,714	35.6
one parent	2,996	31.8	4,297	45.8	5,934	56.9
mother only	2,783	29.5	4,117	43.9	5,607	53.8
father only	213	2.3	180	1.9	327	3.1
other relatives	820	8.7	999	10.7	625	6.0
non-relatives only	97	1.0	123	1.3	154	1.5
Hispanic origin[b]						
Children under 18 years	4,006[c]	100.0	5,459	100.0	7,619	100.0
Living with:						
two parents	3,111	77.7	4,116	75.4	4,935	64.8
one parent	—	—	1,152	21.1	2,447	32.1
mother only	—	—	1,069	19.6	2,168	28.5
father only	—	—	83	1.5	279	3.7
other relatives	—	—	183	3.4	196	2.6
non-relatives only	—	—	8	0.1	41	0.5

[a] Excludes persons under 18 years old who were maintaining household or family groups.   [b] Persons of Hispanic origin may be of any race.   [c] All persons under 18 years.

Sources: US Bureau of the Census (1992), *Marital Status and Living Arrangements: March 1992*, Current Population Reports, P20–486, Washington, DC: US Government Printing Office, xii, Table G. Hispanic data for 1970: *Persons of Spanish Origin,* 1970 Census of Population, PC(2)–1C.

2% in 1990. Similarly, the percentage living with a widowed mother declined from 20% to 7% during those years. The proportion living with a never-married mother increased from 7% in 1970 to 31% in 1990, a more than fourfold increase.

An obvious question is to what extent grandparents or other relatives in the home have acted to fill the gap left by absent parents. Hernandez (1993a) points out that, although grandparents have played an important compensatory role for children in lone-parent families, only a minority of these children had a grandparent in the home: about 10% of white children on average between 1960 and 1990, and 20–35% of black children, for a total of 20–27% of all children in one-parent families. Despite the increase in single parenthood, children are far less likely now to live with a grandparent and *neither* of their own parents (43% in 1960 and 27% in 1990), but they are somewhat more likely to live with a grandparent and their mother (3.2% in 1960 and 5% in 1991). In 1991, 8.0 million children, 12.5% of all children under 18, lived in an extended family household, with black and Hispanic children far more likely to live in such families (22% and 25%, respectively) than white children (10%) (US Bureau of the Census, 1994). Children in one-parent families are far more likely to live in an extended family (30%) than those with two parents (7%). Of those children living in an extended family, about half live with a grandparent, overwhelmingly a grandmother.

Clearly, families are changing: they are smaller, with fewer children. One consequence is that resources—both time and money—can be shared among smaller numbers. Does this mean that parents are able to invest more time and money in their children? More families are headed by lone mothers, and, as we shall see in subsequent chapters, women are spending less time in childbearing and child-rearing and more time in labour market activities. More couples are cohabiting outside of legal marriage.

Concern about these changes is understandable. The growth in lone-parent, mother-only families, in particular those formed by divorce, is correlated with negative outcomes for both mothers and children (McLanahan and Sandefur, 1994). However, for most children in divorced families, these consequences are not severe and are unlikely to last for any sustained period. Recent research suggests similar patterns for children born out of wedlock or living in reconstituted families. However, the consequences of adolescent childbearing are likely to be negative for both the young mothers and their children. Those children who do live in two-parent families are increasingly likely to be living in 'reconstituted' or 'merged' step-families, regardless of race. It is estimated that about one-quarter of all children today will live with a step-parent before their 16th birthday (Zill and Rogers, 1988). Growing up in step-families is also associated with negative outcomes similar to those experienced by children in one-parent families.

We know that two-parent families are more likely to break up if the father is unemployed, the family is poor, the couple is young, and/or both parents work full-time. Although mother-only families are more likely to be poor than either husband/wife families or father-headed families, women heading such families alone are more likely to have begun their families while poor than the others (Hernandez, 1992 and 1993a).

We turn next to family law, to see how it has changed and how this family policy domain has related to family changes. We then turn to a review of public attitudes toward these changes and what their implications might be.

FAMILY LAW

Family law[2] matters have traditionally fallen under state rather than federal control.[3] While state law retains supremacy, the trend over the last thirty years is toward national convergence and some uniformity in family law matters. State sovereignty has been eroded in three ways: first, the United States Supreme Court has entered the arena of family law and established constitutional protections in a number of key areas previously left to the states (Krause, 1989). As a result, the Court has raised issues in family law to a constitutional level, thus superseding state regulation. The rights of individuals have been recognized and protected as primary, with the state interest in the family unit left as a secondary concern. To the extent that these decisions overruled any prior inconsistent state decisions, the Court has created 'national' law and set the legal parameters for all subsequent decisions.

Second, there is a growing trend toward uniformity in enacted family law legislation among states and greater co-ordination and co-operation between states in enforcing individual state law. For example, several model statutes having to do with marriage, divorce, child custody, and child support have been drafted by the National Conference of Commissioners on Uniform State Laws and proposed for adoption in all states. Although these proposed acts have met with varying receptions in different states, they are symbolic of the trend toward a unified, if not comprehensive, set of family laws.

Third, federal social and tax legislation has increasingly touched, both directly and indirectly, on matters concerning the family, with a resulting impact on family law. By providing and withholding benefits on the basis of marital status or dependency, federal legislation affects many aspects of family behaviour (Krause, 1986). Furthermore, federal funding to states is frequently conditional upon enactment of laws that follow federal specifications, thereby also creating greater uniformity in family law and making it more national in scope.

With regard to marriage and divorce: prior to the enactment of the first no-fault divorce legislation, divorce was based on a traditional view of marriage that incorporated several important assumptions. Marriage, a monogamous, heterosexual union for the purpose of procreation, involved a lifelong commitment and was based on a strict division of labour (Weitzman, 1985). Traditional sex-based roles designated the husband as primary financial provider for the family unit, while the wife was obligated to perform domestic and child-care services. Once married, a woman lost her capacity to contract, to manage her own property, to sue or to be sued in her own name, and to earn and manage her own wages (Glendon, 1977 and 1989). Since marriage was viewed as permanent, its breakdown must necessarily be the result of wrongdoing by one of the parties. All divorce law rested on a foundation of attributing fault to one of the spouses. Fault allowed the courts to reward 'innocent victims' and punish transgressors. Alimony, custody, and visitation rights were determined by being filtered through the lens of attributed fault.

In 1969, California enacted the first legislation in the US which permitted no-fault divorce, based on 'irreconcilable differences' causing the 'irremediable breakdown' of a marriage. In doing so, it initiated a trend that changed the nature and function of marriage as both a legal and social institution.[4] By 1985, when South Dakota became the last state to add 'irreconcilable differences' to its list of grounds for divorce, all 50 states had legislation permitting the legal dissolution of marriage without attributing fault to one of the parties.

The effect of recharacterizing the nature of marital breakdown precipitated a search for new theoretical doctrine from which to assess family relationships. Writes one scholar, 'legal norms which had remained relatively undisturbed for centuries were discarded or radically altered in the areas of marriage, divorce, family support obligations, inheritance, the relationship of parent and child, and the status of children born outside marriage' (Glendon, 1977: 1). In the aftermath of no-fault divorce, it has taken the last 25 years for the legal system to develop a relatively consistent approach to some core issues.

In searching for a new theoretical framework from which to evaluate the terms of dissolution, the legal system turned to the closest analogy it could find: small-business or partnership law. Courts shifted the focus of the divorce process away from moral questions and replaced them with ones of equity and economics (Weitzman, 1985). The job of the court in divorce proceedings was now to guarantee that the partners left the marriage with an equal share of the family business.

Assessment of marital dissolution, using partnership principles, necessitated shifting the underlying assumptions about the nature of the marital relationship. It placed a heavier emphasis on the contractual, rather than the status, nature of marriage. It required viewing the partners as equal and autonomous individuals, not as a single merged identity. It blurred the distinctions between marriage and other forms of cohabitation (Glendon, 1989). Finally, it placed children in the uncomfortable position of being left both outside the partnership agreement and without caretakers whose responsibilities were clearly defined by tradition.

Traditional divorce law linked the financial terms of divorce settlement to fault. Modern support law rests on the foundations created by no-fault divorce. The concept of autonomous partners replaced the home-maker/breadwinner paradigm.

To complicate matters further, these changes spilled over into areas of law not generally considered within the family domain, including public assistance, employment, social security, and taxation (Glendon, 1977). Family matters which were previously in the province of state law were soon to be regulated by federal legislation based on national interests.

During the first decade of the no-fault trend, maintenance was primarily seen as 'rehabilitative', and awards were both temporary and transitional in nature. Gender-neutral terms such as 'maintenance', 'allowance', 'recovery', or 'spousal support' replaced 'alimony'. The new terms emphasized the irrelevance of both fault and gender. The new expectation was that women would become independent and self-sufficient after divorce (Weitzman, 1985). They were expected to mitigate damages and to reduce their economic dependency by taking steps to become financially independent. Permanent awards, which had been based on the premise of the wife's continued dependency, were replaced by time-limited transitional awards.

The second decade of reform revealed the draconian effect of limited awards, and courts began to find reasons for more significant and longer-term support orders.

The current focus is not on assuring that each spouse maintain an equal standard of living in the post-divorce future but rather that they equally divide what they have at the time of divorce. The effect of this change is to penalize the wife. More often than not the husband's potential earning capacity is considerably higher, both because he tends to have the advanced training or experience and because women face lower wages in the market. In addition, the wife frequently retains custody of the children, adding another layer of emotional and financial strain potentially lessening her earning capacity.

Although some have argued that the development of no-fault divorce accelerated the trend toward more single-parent families, it is difficult to find evidence for this, given that divorce rates began to increase in the US in the mid-nineteenth century, peaked first soon after World War II, and then began to rise rapidly again beginning in the early 1960s. One could argue as readily that the legislative developments at the close of the 1960s emerged in response to the rapid increase in divorce and the growing demand for making divorce easier. The no-fault divorce developments may have just reinforced an already-existing tendency rather than instigated it. One consequence may have been to make serial marriages and a complex array of reconstituted families more prevalent, but it did not create these trends in marriage and family formation. These developments were well under way in any case.

Family law has struggled to keep up with the changes that we described earlier. Historically, family law dealt most comfortably with dichotomous situations: couples were either married or unmarried, and children were either born in wedlock or outside it. Legal protections, or the lack thereof, flowed from identifying the appropriate relationship status. Some consequences of the blurring of these distinctions follow below.

Court-ordered alimony or spouse maintenance is deductible from income for income tax purposes for the payor, counts as taxable income to the payee, and terminates upon death or remarriage. Child support (see Chapter 3) is not tax-deductible for the payor and is not part of taxable income for the payee, and continues after remarriage (but not after death). Property division, however, has less clear tax consequences: recent legislative and judicial trends have been toward 'equitable distribution' of property, a principle which subjects all marital property to judicial distribution upon divorce, regardless of whether it was accumulated during the marriage or originated from other sources, such as inheritance (Weyrauch and Katz, 1983). Equitable determinations necessarily rely heavily on judicial discretion. Factors affecting distribution decisions include: duration of marriage, prior marriage, antenuptial agreements, age, health, occupation, amount and sources of income, vocational skills, employability, liabilities, and needs (Glendon, 1989). In the 1970s, pensions were recognized as marital property while professional licenses and advanced degrees were sometimes recognized and sometimes not. In the 1980s, the right of spouses to share in pension entitlements was guaranteed.

As the courts began to base regulation of marital relationships on contractual theory, it became increasingly difficult not to extend contractual principles to parties outside a formal marriage relationship. Virtually all jurisdictions have found arguments giving rise to 'marriage-like' treatment of cohabitants when equity seems to demand it.

Child Custody and Support

Up to the late nineteenth century, fathers were the presumed custodial parents. Then the traditional marital role of wife-as-caretaker was reinforced in child custody proceedings through the use of the 'tender years doctrine' which created a legal presumption that, for children under six, the better caretaker was the mother. This gender bias created a higher legal standard of proof for fathers seeking custody. Not unpredictably, equality arguments affected custody determinations. There is currently a norm of gender neutrality in child custody cases which is rooted in constitutional law. In virtually all states, by statute, men and women have an equal legal right to custody of their children. The standard for determining custody between natural parents is an assessment of the child's best interest.

In the 1980s, joint custody statutes proliferated. California led the way with one of the most extreme examples which 'creates a presumption favoring joint custody where both parties agree to it', based on an explicit public policy finding that joint custody supports 'the child's best interests to have frequent, continuing and meaningful access to both parents who divorce or separate' (Freed and Foster, 1983: 291). A Uniform Child Custody Act (UCCJA), approved by the American Bar Association in 1968, has now been enacted in varying forms by every state. It requires that the state with the closest ties to the child provide the forum for custody litigation.

Divorce is likely to have severe economic consequences for the resulting female-headed families with children. Several contributing factors were commonly identified: courts often failed to order child support, and when ordered, child support awards customarily were low, typically covering less than half the costs of raising a child and representing only about 13% of the non-custodial parent's (usually the father's) income (Glendon, 1977). Even adequate initial awards were typically not modified with sufficient regularity or rigour to cover cost-of-living increases over time or other increased child-rearing expenses (Garfinkel and Melli, 1990), and support orders at any level were difficult to collect. Judicial discretion led to inequity in child support awards: orders varied among people with similar economic situations and family circumstances (Thoennes, Tjaden, and Pearson, 1991). Another major factor was that welfare in the US was, to a significant extent, a problem of the non-support of children by their absent parents.

The solutions to most of these issues came in a series of federal legislative responses beginning in 1975 when the child support enforcement programme was added to the Social Security Act (Title IV–D) (see Chapter 3) and when normative standards of child support began to be applied.

'Illegitimacy' and Paternity

Under common law, an out-of-wedlock child was not afforded any of the rights guaranteed legitimate children, nor were his/her parents held responsible for the normal legal duties imposed on parents of legitimate children. For example, such children were disqualified from inheriting property from either parent (Friedman, 1992).[5] A number of factors have converged to pave the way for more civilized treatment of children born out of wedlock. Perhaps most important was the recognition that births outside marriage are highly correlated with poverty. Second, the increased autonomy of individuals in marital and non-marital situations blurred the historic dichotomy between legitimate and illegitimate children and made legal distinctions between the two appear arbitrary. Third, the increased sensitivity to equality between the sexes has generated an interest in paternal rights. Last, medical technology has developed to the point where disputed paternity can be resolved through testing. In a series of decisions beginning in 1968, the United States Supreme Court has held that nearly all laws discriminating against children born outside marriage violate the equal protection clause of the 14th Amendment to the Constitution.

Abortion

Abortion continues to be an area of hotly debated and evolving law. *Roe v. Wade* (410 US 113, 1973), the landmark Supreme Court case in legalizing abortion in the US, held that the state had no interest in regulating abortion during the first trimester of pregnancy, and that the state's interest in prohibiting abortion occurred in roughly the third trimester when the foetus became 'viable'. Subsequent challenges have as yet unsuccessfully threatened women's access to abortion during the first trimester. However, protests, demonstrations, and anti-clinic violence have expanded on a large scale over the last fifteen years, and expenditure of government funds to pay for abortion has been outlawed in many places; as a result, the availability of abortion services has decreased significantly. The conflict over abortion is one of the most visible and heated aspects of the current US family policy debate.

Conclusion

Although changes in US family law have been dramatic over the past three decades, these changes have largely followed rather than led demographic and social developments regarding families; for example, no-fault divorce legislation followed many years in which divorce and separation rates were rising. Perhaps the most important consequence of the change was to reduce the separation rate by making divorce easier. A second may have been to change people's perceptions of the barriers to divorce, and thus make more permissible what had been more burdensome. Changes in laws regarding illegitimacy and abortion also followed changes in society, attitudes, and relevant technology. Changes in child support laws are clearly linked to changes in gender roles (resulting in the decline in the use of alimony at the end of the twentieth century) and to the growing recognition of the severe economic deprivation of women and their children after divorce, as well as to the growing concern regarding the public burden of providing such support (albeit, some would say, at an inadequate level). Changes in child custody law also paralleled social change: growing emphasis on gender equity led to a more neutral position regarding custody. With the rise of autonomous marriage partners came an increasing recognition of the separate rights of children and adolescents, initially with regard to dependency, delinquency and status offences (uncontrollable problem behaviour which is not delinquency), but now increasingly in other areas as well.

Of particular importance is the general trend toward a uniform national family law. Although states remain primary, Supreme Court decisions, federal laws, and a general tendency among the states are defining a national pattern of family law which reflects and shapes the legal response to family change.

FAMILY VALUES

Here we turn to American attitudes towards the family and family relationships. How have these changed along with changes in family formation and household and family structure, and how do American attitudes toward these developments compare with those in other countries?

Results of the International Values Surveys for 1981–83 and 1990–93 suggest the difficulty of gaining a clear and coherent picture of American values regarding family relationships and the family as an institution. For example, most Americans, along with most of those living in the western OECD countries, are increasingly convinced that it is important to share similar values with one's partner and with one's parents. Indeed, Americans felt more strongly about this in the early 1990s than a decade earlier and more strongly than did those in other comparable countries. Yet at the same time, Americans continue to marry increasingly across ethnic and religious lines.

Most Americans believe that children are needed for a marriage to be successful. More Americans were convinced of this in 1991 than in 1981, and more Americans support this statement than do those in other countries. Yet families with children continued to decline as a share of all families during these years.

An even larger majority of Americans believe that parents must always be loved and respected by their children, that it is the duty of parents to do their best for their children, and that children need both their fathers and their mothers to develop well. Similarly, only about 34% of Americans in 1981–83 believed that divorce was justified—but over two-thirds believed divorce was justified if the spouses no longer loved one another! Despite these strongly-held values, Americans continued to divorce in record numbers and to lead the industrialized world in lone parenting.

TABLE 3. Family attitudes, United States 1981–83 and 1990–93 (% distributions)[a]

Item	1981–83			1990–93		
	USA	Total average[b]	Specific average[c]	USA	Total average[b]	Specific average[c]
Divorce[d]						
divorce is justified	34.2	35.6[e]	36.1	—	—	—
divorce is justified because 'cease of love'	66.6	59.1[e]	68.4	—	—	—
Abortion						
abortion is justified	49.8	56.8[e]	53.8	48.8	58.8	53.8
abortion is justified because child not wanted	24.8	35.9[e]	28.3	25.7	38.3	31.2
Family model						
'child needs both father and mother'	60.9	71.8[f]	65.5	71.9	83.4	73.3
'single women may have children'	32.4	38.5	33.7	36.5	37.9	35.9
Closeness of relationships[d]						
respondent very close to mother	56.3	53.7	55.0	—	—	—
respondent very close to father	39.9	42.5	41.6	—	—	—
parents very close to each other	47.3	48.3	48.5	—	—	—
Common attitudes						
share attitudes with partner	54.3	53.1[e]	56.2	64.1	54.3	60.9
share attitudes with parents	60.8	49.4[e]	58.4	63.7	51.4	58.4
Obligations						
'parents must always be loved and respected'	72.1	58.5	64.6	70.5	61.1	67.6
'parents' duty is to do their best for children'	69.8	62.9	68.0	72.8	65.3	70.6
Child orientation						
'need children for a successful marriage'	59.9	54.6[e]	60.8	65.2	60.6	63.6
'woman needs children to be fulfilled'	17.8	39.2[e]	36.0	20.7	37.8	21.5

[a] Sample: France, Britain, West Germany, Italy, Netherlands, Denmark, Belgium, Spain, Ireland, United States, Canada, Hungary, Norway, Sweden, Finland. [b] Unweighted average of the countries in the sample. [c] Specific average includes Australia, Canada, Great Britain, and the United States (in 1990 without Australia). [d] Not asked in 1990 survey. [e] Without Finland. [f] Without Hungary.

Source: International Value Surveys 1981–83 and 1990–93. Calculated by Benno Burkhart.

Americans overwhelmingly rejected the concept that a woman needs children to be fulfilled, with only 18% supporting that position in 1981 and 21% in 1991, as compared with twice those rates in the other countries. Acceptance for a woman having a child while single is supported fairly consistently over time and cross-nationally, with between 32% and 37% of respondents in the US and elsewhere supporting this position, and with support increasing slightly over the last decade.

The dramatic growth in out-of-wedlock parenting in all the industrialized countries, including the US, during the 1980s suggests that the real growth in this family structure is much greater than any increase in popular support.

About half the Americans and about 60% of those in other countries believe that abortion is justified, but only about 26% of Americans and 38% of those in other countries give complete support for abortion under all circumstances.

According to a 1980 Lou Harris survey, 80% of Americans said that their families were either the most or one of the most important elements in their lives, and over 90% were very satisfied or mostly satisfied with their family lives; 45% thought family life had worsened in the last 15 years, while about one-third expected family life to get worse in the future (Lou Harris and Associates, 1981). A 1990 survey reaffirmed these findings (National Commission on Children, 1991). However, it also revealed parents' growing concerns about their adequacy as parents, especially with regard to the economic and time constraints they faced; at the same time, they continued to stress the centrality of children to their lives. In addition, most of the baby-boom generation of Americans appear to regard the changes occurring to families over the last couple of decades as a breakdown of the family and at the heart of America's social problems.

In 1980, Americans believed that providing 'health care assistance for the elderly living at home or with their families, providing assistance to poor families, and taking families into account when enacting laws and making regulations are three priority choices for governmental action to help families' (Lou Harris and Associates, 1981). Similar positions continue to be reflected in surveys in the 1990s.

'Family values' emerged as a code term for the conservative/liberal debate about social and family change in the early 1990s. Although the roots of the debate go back to the eighteenth and nineteenth centuries, a national debate around family change emerged early in the 1970s. The 1970 White House Conference on Children identified a number of changes and problems occurring in children's lives. Some of these were addressed in proposed federal legislation which then failed to be enacted (e.g., the Child Development Act and the Family Assistance Plan of 1970). The first Congressional hearing on children and families was held under the sponsorship of the Senate Sub-Committee on Children and Youth, which itself was created to implement the recommendations of the 1970 Conference (Committee on Labor and Public Welfare, 1974). In many ways, this hearing helped launch a national debate which intensified over the next two decades (see Chapter 5).

The 1992 presidential campaign exploded in a debate on 'family values'. The political right views family values 'as a chance to assert themselves as the moral guardians of the past, a world of two-parent families and heterosexuality' (Shalit, 1993: 13). The political left defines the issues in terms of gender equity and support for alternative family patterns. Because the US is a very pluralistic society, responses to surveys on the family are often contradictory, and the debate continues as it has for the past twenty years. Is the American family going through a difficult transition, needing and deserving public support as the process unfolds? Or is the family becoming weaker, falling apart, and thus failing drastically in its child-rearing function, its disintegration helped along (some would say) by inappropriate and permissive public policies? While the debate rages, families are changing and policies are enacted. Assessing whether the latter are responsive to the former is one of the tasks of this study. In the next chapter we look at the division of labour between home and market and within the family, and in the third and fourth chapters, at social policy developments.

CONCLUSION

The twentieth century has clearly brought changes in the family. Most of these changes began in the previous century, though the pace of change has accelerated since the 1960s. Marriage rates have declined, divorce and cohabitation have increased, one-parent families (headed largely by women) have become more common, fertility has declined, and more children are being born out of wedlock. Family law, the component of family policies dealing most directly with these developments, has also changed significantly, but changes in family law have trailed the changes occurring in families, not preceded them. Revisions in family law may have confirmed or facilitated further change, but did not cause it. Attitudes of the American public toward these developments have also changed; significantly, their attitudes reveal contradictions, inconsistencies, and differences, reflect ambivalence and ignorance regarding the new realities, and offer insight into why the debate remains heated.

2

Families and the Division of Labour: Employment and Family Work

Whether referred to as a 'subtle revolution' or as the most significant social change of the twentieth century, changes in gender roles have had enormous implications for families. In particular, women's entry into the labour force and their continued attachment to it have had a major impact on the household and family economy, the lifestyle of husbands and wives, the viability of single-parent families, and the ways that children are reared and cared for. Of particular importance have been the increased labour force participation of married mothers, especially those with young children; the sustained labour force attachment of women regardless of pregnancy, maternity, and child-rearing; and the rise in full-time, year-round work by married women with children.

For this dramatic change to occur, other developments were needed to create the 'push' and 'pull' leading to more women entering the labour force. The development of compulsory education for children gave women more time for employment outside the home. The changes in family structure and composition discussed in the last chapter—fewer children and higher risk of divorce (as both cause and effect)—led to women having both more time available and greater anxiety about their economic futures. Changes in the economy led to an increase in the availability of paid employment and the types of jobs women could qualify for. Increased education led to higher opportunity costs for women remaining at home. Trends in wages and family income, to be discussed in Chapter 3, also helped shape women's decisions to enter the labour force. All of these changes affected how work was and is shared both in and out of the home.

THE FAMILY DIVISION OF LABOUR AND THE ORGANIZATION OF TIME

Hernandez (1993a) points out that the rise in compulsory education and the enactment of child labour laws were important factors in changing the allocation of parental time and the division of labour in and outside the home. The need for mothers to spend time in child care decreased both because of the dramatic decline in the numbers of children women were rearing (see Chapter 1) and the amount of time children were spending in supervised arrangements outside of the home. As a result, by 1930, mothers of school-aged children needed much less time to care for their children, making this time available for paid employment. Between 1940 and 1990, mothers of school-aged children increased their labour force participation rates from 26% to 74%.

Labour force participation rates for mothers of preschool-aged children increased even more dramatically during these years, from 10% to 60%, despite only limited growth in non-parental care. (Child-care policies and programmes will be discussed in Chapter 4.) Here, it is fathers who have played an increasingly important role (O'Connell, 1993). Between 1977 (the first year for which there are comparable data) and 1991, fathers increased as a proportion of all primary child-care providers by almost 50%, from 14% to 20%. Among married couples, O'Connell found that during these years fathers provided child care equal to or greater than that provided by grandparents, rising from 17% to 23% of the care provided children while their mothers were at work. By 1991, one out of every five children under age five was cared for by a father while the mother worked.

US time-use studies carried out in the 1960s and 1970s provide some indication of initial changes in the division of family work, as women increasingly shared market work responsibilities with their husbands. Pleck characterized the central question as: 'Do husbands do more in the family in absolute terms when their wives are employed, and how does the total workload of employed wives and their husbands (that is, the sum of their time at their separate jobs in housework and child care) compare to each other?' (Pleck, 1985: 29). Pleck concluded that by the late 1970s employed wives continued to put in significantly more time in market work and family work combined than their husbands. The overload was largely due to wives' spending more time with their children, not more time in housework. Husbands of employed wives spent more time on family work, in particular 19 minutes per day in child-related activities, but husbands of non-employed wives also increased their investment in family work. All wives, not just employed wives, were decreasing time spent in housework. Over time, the result was a somewhat smaller amount of overload for employed wives and a greater involvement with their children by fathers generally.

A survey carried out in the early 1980s found that fathers' time investment in their children did not seem to be significantly affected by whether the mothers worked (Timmer, Eccles, and O'Brien, 1985). What was affected was working mothers' time: employed mothers spent less time with their children, less time on housework, less time in eating and sleeping, and less time on recreation. Employed mothers are also less likely to have preschool-aged children, which may account for some of the differences, especially with regard to time spent with children. Gershuny and Robinson (1989) reported that mothers' time invested in child care (for preschoolers) as a primary activity declined by about 20–25% between 1965 and 1985 largely because of their increased employment outside the home. Working mothers were able to devote only about half as much time to child care as a primary activity as did at-home mothers, but since women were having fewer children, the net decline in time per child was less. Moreover, fathers appear to have increased their primary child-care activity during these same years by a modest

15–20%, to about one half-hour a day, about half or one-third of the time mothers spent in child care.[6]

Bianchi notes that employed mothers in two-parent families with preschoolers spend less time than at-home mothers 'in play and educational activities with their children on weekdays (14 minutes less, on average), less time "having fun" (about an hour less), less time providing physical care (almost 40 minutes less), [and] less time at meals with their children (12 minutes less)', while fathers in these families 'compensate for this by spending considerably more time on the weekend with preschool-age children than do fathers who are the sole breadwinners' (Bianchi, 1990: 20–1).

Although there are relatively few data on time use by single parents, women heading such families spend more time in market work and appear to invest more time in their children than married women (often watching television with their children, for example). Given that there is only one parent, however, the overall parental time investment is lower. In effect, single-parent families are dually disadvantaged, in that they lack both money (see Chapter 3) and time. Since after divorce most fathers have limited contact with their children and because of the dramatic increase in lone-mother families, fathers generally are spending less time with their children. Thus, fathers in two-parent families may be devoting more time to their children, but children in mother-only families are dually deprived, both economically and in time spent with fathers (McLanahan and Sandefur, 1994).

LABOUR MARKET BEHAVIOUR

The pattern here is similar to that described in the previous chapter. Labour force participation rates (LFPR) of married women have increased steadily since the late nineteenth century, with each US decennial census revealing a steady rise: from 5.6% in 1900, almost doubling to 10.7% in 1910, to 11.7% in 1930, and 15.2% in 1940 (Chafe, 1972). The rates jumped to 21.6% during the 1940s, when World War II increased the demand for women in the labour force. Despite a brief reversal of the trend immediately after the war, the proportion of wives working continued to rise at an accelerated pace. By 1950, women's LFPR were higher than during the war, rising to 30.5% in 1960, 40.8% in 1970, 50.1% in 1980, and 58% in 1990.

Women as a proportion of the labour force also rose rapidly during the 1940s, going on to reach 29.6% in 1950 and 45% in 1990. During the same years, male LFPR slowly but steadily declined, with the movement accelerating somewhat during the 1970s and 1980s, largely as a consequence of earlier retirements among men in their late 50s and early 60s. In addition, labour force participation of prime-age male workers during the 1980s declined significantly, largely as a consequence of the declining growth in manufacturing, construction, and transportation jobs traditionally held by less-educated men. A 1994 article reported that in the 1970s, 80% of men aged 22–58 worked full-time year-round in at least eight out of ten years,

Families and the Division of Labour   337

TABLE 4. Women's labour force participation rates, by presence and age of youngest child, United States 1947–1992 (% distributions)

Year	No children under 18	With children under 18				
		Total	Age 6–17 only	Under 6		
				Total	Under 3	Under 2
April 1947	29.8	18.6	27.3	12.0	—	—
April 1950	31.4	21.6	32.8	13.6	—	—
April 1955	33.9	27.0	38.4	18.2	—	—
March 1960	35.0	30.4	42.5	20.2	—	—
March 1965	36.5	35.0	45.7	25.3	21.4	—
March 1970	42.8	42.4	51.6	32.2	27.3	—
March 1975	45.1	47.3	54.8	38.8	34.1	31.5
March 1980	48.1	56.6	64.3	46.8	41.9	39.2
March 1985	50.4	62.1	69.9	53.5	49.5	48.0
March 1990	52.3	66.7	74.7	58.2	53.6	52.1
March 1992	52.3	67.2	75.9	58.0	54.5	54.3

Source: Committee on Ways and Means, US House of Representatives (1993), The Green Book: Overview of Entitlement Programs, Washington, DC: US Government Printing Office, 973, Table 1.

while in the 1980s only 70% did (Nasar, 1994). During the same years, women with comparable education have been working more.

In 1992, married mothers constituted about 30% of the labour force; two-thirds of US families with children were headed by these women and their husbands. In contrast, single mothers made up about 10% of workers and headed a little more than one-quarter of families with children.

Although the trend actually began in the late nineteenth and early twentieth centuries, the pace of change accelerated following World War II, with each decade seeing a younger group of wives, with younger children, entering the work-force. In the last quarter of the twentieth century, women became increasingly likely to remain in the work-force regardless of childbearing and child-rearing. The increased labour force participation of wives with young children has had especially important implications for family policy.

Despite these dramatic changes, however, policy responses have been slow to develop and limited in scope and significance. State policy is primary in many relevant areas, and developments have been slow, sparse, and relatively diverse. Federal policy responses, where they developed, emerged only recently, often in the 1980s and early 1990s. The paucity, indeed inadequacy, of federal policies continues to reflect a public preference for market and voluntary solutions and an emphasis, where public provision has emerged, on the poor and deprived.

Hayghe (1990) points out that 1940 was a watershed year for statistics on the family, because it was the first time that concepts of the family and of the labour force that are still in use today were incorporated into a decennial census. Of all working women in 1940, 30% were married and living with their husbands, 16% maintained their own families, and the remaining 54% were single. By 1970 this pattern had changed dramatically: 59% were married (husbands present), 19% headed their own families and about 22% were single. This pattern has remained relatively stable since then; by 1990 the proportion of married women had declined slightly (to 55%) while the portion heading families alone had increased to almost one-quarter.

The most dramatic changes occurred among married women with children, especially those with young children. LFPR of married women with *no* children rose from 30.3% in 1950 and 34.7% in 1960 to 42.2% in 1970, 46.0% in 1980, and 51.3% in 1990. LFPR of women *with* children under age 18 rose from 18.4% in 1950 to 27.6% in 1960, 39.7% in 1970, 54.1% in 1980, and 66.3% in 1990.

The 1970s and 1980s were especially important decades with regard to LFPR of married women with children under age six. These rates rose from 11.9% in 1950 and 18.6% in 1960 to 30.3% in 1970, 45.1% in 1980, and 58.9% in 1990. Labour force participation for women with children under age three rose from 25.8% in 1970 to 32.5% in 1975, 41.5% in 1980, and 57.3% in 1990. Labour force participation of wives with children aged one and under also increased steadily since 1970, from 24% in 1970 to 39% in 1980 and 53.4% in 1990. In 1986 half of all women with children under age three were in the labour force, and by 1987 half of those with children aged one and under were.

Labour force participation of lone mothers has historically exceeded that of married mothers and continued to do so during the initial period of dramatic growth in this family type in the 1970s. By 1990, however, the rates had largely converged. LFPR of lone mothers were 59% in 1970 as compared with 40% for married mothers. About two-thirds of lone mothers have been in the labour force since the early 1980s, by which time the rate for married mothers had increased to 62%. The pattern for lone-mother families with very young children has begun to change, however. Since the late 1980s, the LFPR for lone mothers with preschool-aged children have lagged behind the rates for married mothers, despite much higher rates among divorced mothers, primarily because the rates for never-married mothers (especially the very young) are very low, and this family type has become an increasingly large component of lone-mother families.

Rates have varied by race and ethnicity, with black mothers (especially married mothers) significantly more likely to be in the labour force than whites, and Hispanic mothers less so. But the gap between black and white mothers has closed from ten percentage points in 1975 (and 17 points for married mothers) to four points in 1985 (and nine points for married mothers) and slightly less in 1990.

As much as marriage, divorce, and fertility patterns have changed patterns of family formation, the increase in labour force participation by married women with children has created major changes in how families function and how children are reared. Family structure has been transformed not only by the increase in lone-parent families, but also by changes in husband/wife families as more wives have

TABLE 5. Women's labour force participation by marital status, age, and presence of children, United States 1975–1990[a] (% distributions)

Year and marital status	Total	No children under 18	With children under 18						
			Total	Age 6–17 only			Under 6		
				Total	14–17 years	6–13 years	Total	3–5 years	Under 3 years
Total									
1975	45.9	45.1	47.3	54.8	56.2	54.3	38.8	44.9	34.1
1980	51.1	48.1	56.6	64.3	63.1	64.9	46.8	54.5	41.9
1985	54.5	50.4	62.1	69.9	69.8	69.9	53.5	59.5	49.5
1990	57.2	52.9	66.7	74.7	75.8	74.3	58.2	65.3	53.6
Married									
1975	44.4	43.9	44.8	52.3	53.5	51.8	36.6	42.0	32.5
1980	50.1	46.0	54.1	61.7	60.4	62.4	45.1	51.6	41.3
1985	54.2	48.2	60.8	67.8	67.0	68.2	53.4	58.4	50.5
1990	58.2	51.3	66.3	73.6	75.1	73.0	58.9	64.1	55.6
Divorced									
1975	72.1	69.7	74.8	80.1	81.5	79.6	65.8	68.0	61.1
1980	74.5	71.4	78.2	82.3	84.0	81.6	68.3	74.4	56.8
1985	75.0	72.1	79.1	83.4	85.5	82.4	67.5	75.1	52.2
1990	75.5	72.2	81.3	85.9	87.2	85.4	69.8	78.4	57.6
Never married									
1975	56.8	57.5	41.7	61.1	B	58.7	36.3	48.8	30.5
1980	61.5	62.1	52.0	67.6	B	70.3	44.1	48.8	41.7
1985	65.2	66.9	51.6	64.1	67.0	63.4	46.5	53.9	42.2
1990	66.4	68.1	55.2	69.7	67.8	70.2	48.7	62.4	41.9
Separated									
1975	55.2	56.9	53.9	59.1	64.3	57.6	49.4	54.0	46.0
1980	59.4	58.9	60.0	66.3	67.2	65.9	52.2	65.4	42.4
1985	61.3	60.0	62.6	70.9	76.4	68.5	53.2	58.3	48.9
1990	63.6	59.2	67.6	75.0	73.2	75.7	59.3	69.9	51.6
Widowed									
1975	23.9	21.5	51.2	53.8	59.7	48.6	36.1	B	B
1980	22.5	20.0	58.4	60.7	60.7	60.8	44.7	B	B
1985	20.6	18.6	59.4	62.9	61.4	64.6	45.7	B	B
1990	19.5	17.6	56.1	58.0	59.5	56.6	50.1	51.1	48.8

[a] Data collected in March.   B= Base is less than 75,000.

Sources: US Department of Labor, Bureau of Labor Statistics (1986), *News*, Washington, DC: US Government Printing Office, Table 1. 1990 data from Bureau of Labor Statistics, unpublished.

entered the labour force. Dual-earner husband/wife families have steadily increased, further reducing the numbers of traditional, one-earner two-parent families. In 1975, 43.4% of all two-parent families had both husbands and wives in the labour force. In 1980, the proportion was 52.5%, and in 1992, 60%.

Hayghe and Bianchi (1994) point out that although most mothers today are in the labour force, more work part-time, part-year, or stay at home than work full-time, all year. Nonetheless, the most dramatic of the changes in family work patterns is the increase in the proportion of families with children in which both parents work full-time (35 hours a week or more), all year. The proportion of married mothers following this pattern rose from 16% in 1970 to 37% in 1992, including 43% of mothers of school-aged children and 31% of those with preschool-aged children. Labour force participation and work experience rates (employment at some time during the year) rose dramatically for married mothers, almost converging regardless of the age of the youngest child and becoming much closer between blacks and whites. However, racial differences have remained for full-time, year-round work, with 36% of white mothers working full-time, all year in 1992 (as compared with 15% in 1970), and 49% of black mothers (as compared with 27% in 1970). Comparable rates for those with children under age six are 29% for white mothers in 1992 (as against 8% in 1970) and 45% for black mothers in 1992 (as against 21% in 1970). Part-time LFPR of these women remained remarkably stable during these years, rising only slightly for white mothers while declining significantly among black married mothers regardless of the age of their children.

Hayghe and Bianchi (1994) emphasize how this rise in full-time, year-round work by married mothers changed family work patterns. In only one out of eight husband/wife families in 1970 did both parents work full-time all year (Hayghe and Bianchi, 1994: 29, Table 6). The proportion more than doubled by 1992 to 30%. The change was even more dramatic among families with children under age six: the rate more than tripled during these years, from 7.3% in 1970 to 24.3% in 1992. At the same time, traditional families with a father working full-time all year and a mother at home declined by about 50%.

Later marriage rates and later age at first birth made it possible for women to develop stronger labour market ties before pregnancy and a greater likelihood of remaining in the labour force throughout their adult lives. Growth in the service sector of the economy expanded the demand for women workers while slow wage growth for men, higher rates of inflation and unemployment, and higher female wages (the result of greater access to higher education by females and higher demand for female labour) increased both the pressure on women to enter and remain in the work-force and the opportunity costs of remaining at home.

The experiences of children growing up have also changed significantly as more and more now have a mother in the work-force. It took from 1840 until 1930 to show a rise in the number of non-farm breadwinner/home-maker families, and in only five censuses during that period did at least a majority of children live in such families (Hernandez, 1993a). In contrast, the number of dual-earner and one-parent, sole-earner families went from about one-fifth to nearly three-fifths of families with children between 1950 and 1980. Today, children are overwhelmingly likely to live in working one- or two-parent families, for all or some of their early years. The rates were and still are persistently higher for black children.

Thirty-nine percent of all children (37.6% of those in husband/wife families and 53.2% of those in mother-only families) lived in families with working mothers in 1970; 53% (51.7% in husband/wife families and 62.4% in mother-only families) in 1980; and 62% in 1992 (65% in husband/wife families and 62% in mother-only families). In 1970, 29% of children under six (27.6% of those in husband/wife families and 40.4% of those in mother-only families) had working mothers. The rates were 43% in 1980 (42.1% in husband/wife families and 50.1% in mother-only families) and 54% in 1992 (57% in husband/wife families and 50% in mother-only families).

Child care, once an at-home activity of parents, thus underwent two revolutions: the first, in the late nineteenth and early twentieth centuries with regard to compulsory schooling for children aged six and older, and the second, in the latter part of the twentieth century with regard to preschool (Hernandez, 1993a: 136). Given the period in focus, it is the latter which is of particular interest, and which we will address in Chapter 4.

EMPLOYMENT AND PARENTING POLICIES

The term 'family-friendly' was coined in the late 1970s to describe workplace policies responsive to the needs of employed parents, especially those with young children. To the extent that they exist in the US, family-friendly employment policies are largely the result of voluntary efforts on the part of employers and, in recent years, of collective bargaining agreements. Any federal role is limited and very recent: the first federal legislation to acknowledge the problem of pregnancy and maternity for working women, the Family and Medical Leave Act, was enacted in 1993. This legislation provides for an *unpaid* but job-protected leave for employed parents or caregivers of dependent or elderly family members, thus acknowledging the burden of caregiving generally for working women. No national or federal legislation mandates that employers provide their workers with sick leave (short-term, non-job-related disability or invalidity leave), vacations, personal leaves, or related cash benefits. Some modest developments have occurred as a result of federal and state policies.

Maternity and Parenting Policies

Maternity or parenting benefits are policies that provide for job- and seniority-protected leaves at the time of childbirth, and often adoption as well; some also provide a cash benefit to replace all or part of wages forgone while on leave. No such statutory policies existed in 1960 or in 1970, although some private-sector policies did exist, and the roots of current policies go back to these years. The Family and Medical Leave Act enacted in 1993 was the result of 15 years of intense efforts, especially impassioned during the six years prior to passage. Before 1987 no state had such legislation; the only federal/national or state maternity policy was an equal rights and anti-discrimination policy dating from 1964 that was amended in 1978 to require that pregnancy and maternity be treated the same way as any other disability. Thus, if employers provided a disability leave for any reason, they would have to make it available to women at the time of childbirth; but employers were under no obligation to provide such disability protection.

The first legislation enacted in the US that provided a kind of paid maternity leave—but not necessarily a job-protected leave—were five state Temporary Disability Insurance (TDI) laws, enacted in California, New Jersey, New York, and Rhode Island in the 1940s and in Hawaii in 1969. These laws originally protected workers against loss of income in case of short-term, non-occupational disabilities but did not cover pregnancy or childbirth. In 1978, as a result of an amendment to Title VII of the 1964 Civil Rights Act, these TDI laws were required to provide income protection for working women at the time of pregnancy and childbirth.

The 1964 law states that it is unlawful to discriminate with respect to 'compensation, terms, conditions, or privileges of employment because of sex' (Kamerman, Kahn, and Kingston, 1983). Although Title VII of the law explicitly banned sex discrimination, there was no record concerning Congressional intent as to whether childbirth and pregnancy-related disabilities were meant to be included. Despite a significant number of court decisions stating that to deny pregnant women workers benefits available to other employees was a form of discrimination based on sex, in 1976 the Supreme Court held in *Gilbert v. General Electric Corp.* that the exclusion of pregnancy-related disabilities from a company's disability insurance programme was *not* discrimination. State TDI plans, therefore, were not required to cover women at the time of pregnancy and childbirth, nor were private employee health insurance or disability plans required to do so.

A coalition of women's organizations, civil rights organizations, and labour unions responded by mobilizing in support of legislative reform. In 1978 Congress enacted the Pregnancy Discrimination Act which amended the wording of Title VII to specify that 'discrimination on the basis of sex included, but was not limited to, discrimination with regard to pregnancy, childbirth, or related conditions' (Kamerman, Kahn, and Kingston, 1983). Within a short time, health insurance, disability insurance, and sick-pay policies were modified to cover pregnancy and maternity as well. The law required pregnant women to be treated the same as all other employees, but did not require employers to provide such protection.

By the late 1980s, about 25% of working women nationally were protected through the five state TDI plans with a paid leave at the time of childbirth, and another 20–25% through voluntary plans. Typically, these state policies protected women against loss of income for about four to six weeks before childbirth and six to eight weeks after, a period defined as 'maternity disability'. The cash benefit, financed as a social insurance benefit, was worth about half of the employee's wage, an amount roughly equal to the benefit provided through unemployment insurance. The maximum duration of the benefit for a normal pregnancy was 10–12 weeks.

Following enactment of this amendment to the Civil Rights Act, growing pressure emerged for some form of federal parental leave legislation (not just a maternity disability leave). Beginning in 1985, Congress began to consider federal legislation that would provide for job-protected parental, family, and personal disability leave. Legislation was introduced in Congress in 1985, re-introduced in

TABLE 6. Full-time employees participating in employer-provided benefit plans, United States 1980–1991 (% distributions)

Item	Medium and large private firms[a]						Small private firms[b]	State and local govt.[c]
	1980	1985	1986	1988	1989	1991	1990	1990
Time-off plans								
Participants with:								
paid lunch time	10	10	10	11	10	8	8	11
avg. minutes/day	—	27	27	29	26	30	37	36
paid rest time	75	72	72	72	71	67	48	56
avg. minutes/day	—	26	26	26	26	26	27	29
paid funeral leave	—	88	88	85	84	80	47	63
avg. days/occurrence	—	3.2	3.2	3.2	3.3	3.3	2.9	3.7
paid holidays	99	98	99	96	97	92	84	74
avg. days/year	10.1	10.1	10.0	9.4	9.2	10.2	9.5	13.6
paid personal leave	20	26	25	24	22	21	11	39
avg. days/year	—	3.7	3.7	3.3	3.1	3.3	2.8	2.9
paid vacations	100	99	100	98	97	96	88	67
paid sick leave	62	67	70	69	68	67	47	95
unpaid maternity leave	—	—	—	33	37	37	17	51
unpaid paternity leave	—	—	—	16	18	26	8	33
Insurance plans								
Participants in medical care plans	97	96	95	90	92	83	69	93
Particip. with coverage for:								
home health care	—	56	66	76	75	81	79	82
extended care facilities	58	67	70	79	80	80	83	79
mental health care	98	99	99	98	97	98	98	99
alcohol abuse treatment	—	68	70	80	97	97	97	99
drug abuse treatment	—	61	66	74	96	96	94	98
Participants with employee contribution required for:								
self coverage	26	36	43	44	47	51	42	38
average monthly contribution (in $)	—	12.1	12.8	19.3	25.3	26.6	25.1	25.5
family coverage	46	56	63	64	66	69	67	65
average monthly contribution[d](in $)	—	38.3	41.4	60.1	72.1	70	109.3	117.6
Participants in life insurance plans	96	96	96	92	94	94	64	88
Participants with:								
accidental death/dismemberment insurance	69	73	72	76	71	71	78	67
survivor income benefits	—	13	10	8	7	6	1	1
retiree protection	—	62	59	49	42	44	19	45
Participants in long-term disability insurance plans	40	48	48	42	45	40	19	27
Participants in sickness/accident insurance plans	54	52	49	46	43	45	26	21

(continued)

TABLE 6. (continued)

	Medium and large private firms[a]						Small private firms[b]	State and local govt.[c]
	1980	1985	1986	1988	1989	1991	1990	1990
Retirement plans								
Participants in defined-benefit pension plans[e]	84	80	76	63	63	59	20	90
Participants with:								
normal retirement prior to age 65	55	67	64	59	62	55	54	89
early retirement available	98	97	98	98	97	98	95	88
ad hoc pension increase in last 5 years	—	41	35	26	22	7	7	16
terminal earnings formula	53	57	57	55	64	56	58	100
benefit co-ordinated with Social Security	45	61	62	62	63	54	49	8
Participants in defined contribution plans	—	53[f]	60[f]	45	48	48	31	9
Participants in plans with tax-deferred savings option	—	26	33	36	41	44	17	45
Other benefits								
Employees eligible for:								
flexible benefits plans	—	—	2	5	9	10	1	5
reimbursement acounts	—	—	5	12	23	36	8	31

[a] From 1979 to 1986, data were collected in private-sector establishments with a minimum employment varying from 50 to 250 employees, depending upon industry. In addition, coverage in service industries was limited. Beginning in 1988, data were collected in all private-sector establishments employing 100 workers or more in all industries.

[b] Includes private-sector establishments with fewer than 100 workers.

[c] In 1987, coverage excluded local governments employing fewer than 50 workers. In 1990, coverage included all state and local governments.

[d] Data for 1983 refer to the average monthly employee contribution for dependant coverage, excluding the employee. Beginning in 1984, data refer to the average monthly employee contribution for family coverage, which includes the employee.

[e] Prior to 1985, data on participation in defined-benefit pension plans included a small percentage of workers participating in money-purchase pension plans. Beginning in 1985, these workers were classified as participating in defined contribution plans.

[f] Includes employees who participated in payroll-based Employee Stock Ownership Plans. Beginning in 1987, these plans were no longer available.

Source: US Department of Labor, Bureau of Labor Statistics (1993), *Monthly Labor Review* (April), Washington, DC: US Government Printing Office, 81, Table 25.

1987, passed by Congress and then vetoed by President Bush in 1990, re-introduced and passed again in 1991 and 1992 and once again vetoed by President Bush. In early 1993, the Family and Medical Leave Act was re-introduced once more, passed by Congress and signed into law by President Clinton. It was viewed by advocates for women and children as a significant development. By international standards, it is very modest legislation that provides public employees and private employees in firms with 50 or more workers with the right to take up to 12 weeks of unpaid leave each year to care for a newborn child, a newly-adopted child, or one just entering foster care; to care for a seriously ill child, spouse, or parent; or to care for an employee's own serious health condition. Employees are eligible if they have worked for the same employer for at least 12 months or 1,250 hours at the time of claiming the leave. Employers can refuse job protection to 'key' employees, those in the top 10% of the work-force.

Paralleling this process at the federal level, states began in 1987 to enact policies providing for an unpaid but job-protected parental leave. Between 1987 and 1992 almost half the states enacted such laws, applicable to firms of different sizes and providing leaves of varying duration, depending on the state. The US was rapidly on the way to enacting such policies in all states by the time the federal government finally passed such a law.

Through a combination of civil rights law, anti-discrimination policies, and fair labour standards law, working parents earned some modicum of protection. Finally, by 1993 most working women—and parents—had job, benefit, and seniority protection while away from work at the time of childbirth (or serious family or personal illness). Nonetheless, less than half of all working women have income protection while out on maternity disability or parental leave, and almost no fathers have such a benefit. Some evidence suggests that collective bargaining agreements are including more extensive provision, as are some employers, voluntarily, but these affect only a small minority of working women/parents.

Tax Policy

A federal tax policy was established in 1982 creating an incentive for employers to provide or pay for dependant care (the care of a child under age 13, or of a physically- or mentally-incapacitated child or spouse) in order to enable the taxpayer or the taxpayer's spouse to work (Congressional Research Service, 1990). The Internal Revenue Code Section 129 (Dependent Care Assistance Program) permits employers to provide or pay for dependant care up to a maximum of $5,000 (or the earnings level of the taxpayer or spouse, if lower) without it being counted as taxable income to the employee. The programme, which is separate and distinct from the Dependent Care Tax Credit described in Chapter 4, was first established in 1982. In fiscal year 1984, tax expenditures for this benefit (taxes forgone) were $5 million; in FY 1989, expenditures were $120 million.

Employee Benefits

Employee benefits regarding work and family life emerged in collective bargaining agreements for the first time in the 1980s. According to a Bureau of Labor Statistics report, three categories of work and family provisions were identified (US Department of Labor, Bureau of Labor Statistics, 1992):

TABLE 7. Employee benefits in medium and large firms, 1989, and small firms, 1990, United States (% distributions)[a]

	Medium and large firms, 1989				Small firms, 1990			
	all employees	professional, administrative	technical, clerical	production, services	all employees	professional, technical[b]	clerical, sales	production, services
Paid:								
vacations	97	98	99	95	88	94	93	83
holidays	97	97	96	97	84	95	91	75
jury duty leave	90	95	92	87	54	72	62	43
funeral leave	84	87	86	80	47	57	54	38
rest time	71	57	69	80	48	42	46	51
military leave	53	61	57	45	21	29	26	15
sick leave	68	93	87	44	47	70	61	29
personal leave	22	28	30	14	11	17	13	7
lunch time	10	4	4	16	8	7	7	8
maternity leave	3	4	2	3	2	3	3	1
paternity leave	1	2	1	1	0	0	0	0
Unpaid:								
maternity leave	37	39	37	35	17	26	20	12
paternity leave	18	20	17	17	8	13	8	5
Insurance plans:								
medical care	92	93	91	93	69	82	75	60
non-contributory	48	45	41	54	40	46	40	37
hospital/room and board	90	91	89	91	69	82	75	60
in-patient surgery	90	91	89	91	69	82	75	60
mental health care	89	91	88	90	68	80	74	59
private duty nursing	79	82	80	78	66	77	72	58
dental	66	69	66	65	30	38	35	24
extended care facility	74	75	74	74	57	66	63	49
home health care	69	74	72	65	55	66	62	45
hospice care	39	46	43	33	35	40	40	30
vision	32	33	33	33	8	7	8	8
in HMOs	16	20	18	11	10	12	8	9
alcohol abuse treatment	89	90	88	89	—	—	—	—
in-patient detoxification	—	—	—	—	67	80	73	58
in-patient rehabilitation	—	—	—	—	54	64	58	47
out-patient	88	90	87	89	50	60	54	43
drug abuse treatment	—	—	—	—	—	—	—	—

	Col 1	Col 2	Col 3	Col 4	Col 5	Col 6	Col 7	Col 8
in-patient detoxification	—	—	—	—	65	77	71	56
in-patient rehabilitation	—	—	—	—	50	60	55	44
out-patient	—	—	—	—	47	55	51	41
life	94	95	94	93	64	79	70	55
non-contributory	82	82	81	83	53	69	60	43
accident/sickness	43	29	29	58	26	25	24	27
non-contributory	36	22	22	51	17	14	15	19
long-term disability	45	65	57	27	19	36	25	9
non-contributory	35	50	43	23	16	30	21	8
Retirement and savings plans:								
defined benefit pension	63	64	63	63	20	20	23	18
earnings-based formula[c]	47	59	54	38	14	17	19	9
defined contribution	48	59	52	40	31	40	36	24
savings and thrift	30	41	35	21	10	16	15	5
stock ownership	3	4	3	3	1	1	1	0
deferred profit sharing	15	13	13	16	15	17	17	13
money purchase pension	5	8	6	3	6	9	6	6
Additional benefits:								
parking	90	85	86	94	86	84	85	88
educational assistance	69	81	75	59	39	58	46	30
travel accident insurance	53	69	60	39	15	24	19	9
severance pay	39	54	46	27	19	30	26	12
relocation allowance	36	68	29	21	12	22	15	6
recreation facilities	28	36	26	24	6	12	6	4
non-prod. bonuses, cash	27	26	28	28	45	42	47	44
child care	5	6	6	3	1	2	2	1
flexible benefits plans	9	14	15	3	1	3	2	1
reimbursement accounts[d]	23	36	31	11	8	13	9	4
elder care	3	4	3	2	2	5	1	1
long-term care insurance	3	3	3	2	1	0	1	1
wellness programs	23	30	25	19	6	10	8	4
employee assistance programs	49	57	50	44	15	21	17	11

[a] Full-time employees in private industry. Medium and large firms: more than 100 workers, executive and travelling operating employees; not Alaska or Hawaii. Small firms: less than 100 employees. Covers only employer-paid (in part or in full) benefits, except unpaid parental leave and long-term care insurance. Based on a sample survey of establishments. [b] And related occupations. [c] Pay a percent of employee's annual earnings per year of service. [d] Account used throughout the year to pay for plan premiums or reimburse employee for benefit-related expenses; may be financed by employer, employee, or both.

Sources: *Statistical Abstract, 1993*, US Bureau of Labor Statistics; *Employee Benefits in Medium and Large Firms, 1989*, Bulletin 2363; and *Employee Benefits in Small Private Establishments, 1990*, Bulletin 2388, Washington, DC: US Government Printing Office, 1993, 417, Table 662.

- those concerned with 'conventional areas of interest, including maternity and parental leave, adoption, child care, elder care, leave for family illness, and employee assistance programs';
- 'provisions not among the conventional areas of interest but open to interpretation by the parties to accommodate family needs', including personal time off, flexible work schedules; and
- 'miscellaneous clauses touching on matters affecting the family' including tuition assistance, parental loan programmes, and financial counselling.

According to the Bureau of Labor Statistics report, in line with changes in the work-force, the family, and society at large, collective bargaining agreements are now showing a trend toward a package approach to work and family issues that concentrates relevant benefits in one place in the contract (US Department of Labor, Bureau of Labor Statistics, 1992). The report states that in doing this, unions and management have signalled that work and family issues are really on a par with traditional contract concerns such as wages and hours of work. An analysis of 452 agreements covering 5.7 million workers (about 5% of the civilian work force), found that more than 50% included at least one conventional work and family benefit. More than four-fifths of the workers affected were in the manufacturing sector, where women are less likely to be working; the next most significant groups affected were in the retail trade, communications, utilities, and other service industries where women are most likely to be working.

In short, although the trend toward family-friendly benefits provided voluntarily or in collective agreements has clearly increased in recent years, only a very small proportion of the work-force receives them (see Tables 6 and 7). Less than 15% of the labour force is unionized, including less than 11% in the private sector; few employers have moved voluntarily to establish significant policies. Only where statutory benefits are required of employers is coverage likely to be adequate; as we have seen, statutory provision is very modest.

CONCLUSION

The division of labour within the family has changed significantly since 1960, and the change is nowhere more dramatic than in the division of family labour in the marketplace. As was first pointed out in the 1950s by Klein and Myrdal (1956), women continue to carry two jobs: primary responsibility for child care and child-rearing, and paid employment outside the home. In recent years it has been suggested that in fact women carry three jobs, with the frequent addition of primary responsibility for the care of an elderly parent or parent-in-law. Husbands of employed wives now play a more active role in family work than earlier, especially with regard to children, but primary responsibility remains with wives. Married mothers' investment in paid employment has increased enormously during these same years while single mothers' labour force participation rates have not increased significantly. LFPR of very young never-married mothers have in fact declined,

:ading to a near convergence of labour force participation for married and single 1others. Despite a decline in labour force participation of older men, the LFPR for athers of children under 18 remain much higher than that of their wives, and more kely to be full-time (although less so than earlier). The combined burden of fam- y and market work is becoming more similar for both mothers and fathers, but the alance between the two types of work still varies by gender. When unemployment ccurs, however, women are now likely to have lower rates than men, a reversal of 1e earlier pattern.

For children, especially preschool-aged children, the change has been dramatic. :hildren are far more likely now to have both parents or their sole parent away rom home and at the workplace during the work day, with the percentage of reschoolers with working mothers more than doubling since 1960 and doubling gain since 1970.

Public policies designed to respond to these changes have emerged only recently nd have been modest at best. Some tax benefits have been established, as have a imited unpaid parental leave for working parents and some public funding and rovision of child care (see Chapter 4). Voluntary initiatives and market responses ontinue to be stressed over statutory provision.

3

The Income of Families: Earnings and Transfers

The economic situation of families with children is largely contingent on five factors: the rate of employment; the level of wages; the number of earners in the family; and the size and the composition of the family, i.e., the number of children and whether the family is headed by one or two parents. Government income transfers can offset some of the consequences of the other four factors, but in the US such transfers have been modest.

Except during the 1930s, the gross domestic product (GDP) rose steadily from the beginning of the twentieth century. Per capita real GDP increased by about two-thirds between World War II and 1974 but only by about one-fourth between 1974 and 1992. Families' standard of living improved steadily between World War II and 1974 but later stagnated, with different consequences for different types of families. The mid-1970s may be thought of as the post-World War II watershed in the economic situation of families. The slowdown in economic growth following the first world-wide oil shortage had significant consequences for family economic well-being. Family income inequality increased during the latter period, with shares in family income rising only for the highest quintile, declining for the three lowest, and remaining stable for the fourth (US Bureau of the Census, 1992). The economic situation of the poor also worsened during these years.

Despite periodic rises in unemployment, the percentage of the adult population in the labour force increased steadily during both periods, as discussed in the last chapter. The average number of earners per family decreased slightly overall (from 1.39 in 1973 to 1.28 in 1991), but varied significantly by family type. Husband/wife families experienced a jump in the number of earners per family; this rise was offset by the dramatic increase in the proportion of families headed by single women and therefore with no earners or only a sole earner.

Real wages rose dramatically from the end of World War II to 1975, then stagnated (Levy and Michel, 1991). Median family income in constant dollars doubled between 1947 (the first year the Census Bureau began to report family income on a regular basis) and 1970, then increased only by about 10% between 1970 and 1991. This increase was sustained largely by the growing contribution of working wives to their families' economies. White families did better than blacks and Hispanics, in part because they were more likely to be two-parent families and in part because of wage and employment discrimination. Children's economic well eing improved up to 1970 largely through the rising wages of their fathers and, ater, the increased contributions of their employed mothers. This trend was re-ersed after 1970 when children emerged as the age group most likely to be poor Smolensky, Danziger, and Gottschalk, 1988).

Demography clearly played a role in the economic situation of families: the rise n female labour force participation protected against a deteriorating situation in wo-parent families; the growth in lone-mother families exacerbated already nega-ive trends for this family type; and the decline in fertility protected per capita amily income. But macroeconomic developments and government income trans-er policies were also factors.

Aid to Families with Dependent Children (AFDC), the paradigmatic US family olicy, was established during the Great Depression of the 1930s, a time of severe conomic crisis for families with children. AFDC's major growth was during the 960s, a decade of both extraordinary economic growth and social upheaval. Most f the constraints and heated debate regarding AFDC occurred during the 1970s nd 1980s, following a rise in the numbers of lone-mother families, especially hose headed by never-married mothers, and a failed effort in 1971 to establish a uaranteed minimum income for poor families with children. Despite this failure, fforts to protect the poor continued between the late 1960s and early 1970s, with ederal investment in in-kind benefits and services increasing significantly. It took nother two decades before significant attention was paid to protecting the eco-omic situation of the working poor, which was achieved largely through the use of ax policy and subsidies for child-care and health care services (see Chapter 4). By he mid-1990s, it seemed as if the poor were being relegated to the bottom of the ational policy agenda while the situation of the middle class assumed greater isibility. Indeed, the pressure to allocate a greater share of a smaller pie to the niddle class appeared to be leading to more punitive policies toward the poor.

Demography clearly is an underlying dynamic in AFDC policy even though it oes not take the form of an effort to counter low fertility, as in some European ountries. On the other hand, the virtual 'explosion' in the numbers of single-par-nt families, resulting from divorce, separation, and out-of-wedlock childbirth, along vith the much increased labour force participation of all mothers, has influenced oth the size of the AFDC programme and its policy directions. In the mid-1990s lemography—in the form of the continued high and rising rates of out-of-wedlock hildbirth and the declining rates of labour force participation among single moth-rs with young children—continued to be a factor in the rejection of AFDC and the doption of new policy directions.

PATTERNS OF INCOME AND EXPENDITURES

A central theme in Levy's and Michel's (1991) study of the economic situation of American families is that real wages increased steadily and significantly from the nd of World War II to 1973, the year of the first world-wide oil shortage, and have

TABLE 8. Money income of families by type of family and income level, United States 1991

Type of family	No. of families (in 1,000)	Number of families by income level								Median income ($)
		Under $9,999	$10,000–14,999	$15,000–19,999	$20,000–24,999	$25,000–34,999	$35,000–49,999	$50,000–74,999	$75,000 and over	
All families	67,173	6,521	4,844	5,192	5,553	10,502	13,116	12,661	8,785	35,939
Married-couple families	52,457	2,349	3,030	3,557	4,116	8,343	11,139	11,574	8,350	40,995
wife in paid labour force	30,923	518	840	1,239	1,723	4,621	7,310	8,587	6,086	48,169
wife not in paid labour force	21,534	1,830	2,189	2,318	2,392	3,723	3,828	2,987	2,264	30,075
Male householder[a]	3,025	370	274	312	335	559	575	396	204	28,351
Female householder[a]	11,692	3,803	1,540	1,323	1,102	1,599	1,403	691	231	16,692
With own children[b]	34,861	4,613	2,429	2,581	2,536	5,274	6,952	6,535	3,940	34,990
married couple	25,357	1,049	1,202	1,480	1,652	4,093	5,969	6,124	3,787	42,514
female householder[a]	7,991	3,308	1,075	908	711	918	742	255	75	13,012

[a] No spouse present.
[b] Children under 18 years old. Includes male householders not shown separately.

TABLE 9. Median money income of families and unrelated individuals,
United States 1970–1990 (in current and constant (1991) $)[a]

	1970	1980[b]	1985[c]	1990
Money income in current dollars				
Families[d]				
married-couple families	10,516	23,141	31,100	39,895
wife in paid labour force	12,276	26,879	36,431	46,777
wife not in paid labour force	9,304	18,972	24,556	30,265
male householder, no wife present	9,012	17,519	22,622	29,046
female householder, no husband present	5,093	10,408	13,660	16,932
Unrelated individuals				
male	4,540	10,939	14,921	17,927
female	2,483	6,668	9,865	12,450
Money income in constant (1991) dollars				
Families[c]				
married-couple families	34,680	38,297	39,366	41,574
wife in paid labour force	40,484	44,483	46,114	48,745
wife not in paid labour force	30,683	31,397	31,083	31,539
male householder, no wife present	29,720	28,993	28,635	30,268
female householder, no husband present	16,796	17,224	17,291	17,645
Unrelated individuals				
male	14,972	18,103	18,887	18,681
female	8,188	11,035	12,487	12,974

[a] Constant dollars based on CPI–U–X1 deflator. Unrelated individuals are persons not living with any relatives. See also US Bureau of the Census (1975), *Historical Statistics of the United States: Colonial Times to 1970*, Series G 179–188.

[b] Beginning 1983, data based on revised Hispanic population controls and not directly comparable with prior years.

[c] Beginning 1987, data based on revised processing procedures and not directly comparable with prior years.

[d] Beginning 1980, based on householder concept. Restricted to primary families, see source.

Source: United States Statistical Abstract (1993), Washington, DC: US Government Printing Office 465, Table 727.

stagnated since then. For example, the average 50-year-old man working full-time, all year had income (in constant dollars) of $15,257 in 1946 (the first year for which there are published data) and $30,578 in 1973, while in 1986 his income was only $32,960.

According to the US Bureau of the Census (1975), real median income for all families almost doubled between 1947 and 1970; for black families, it rose by still more (133%). A Congressional Budget Office report (1988) adds to this picture by analysing Census Bureau data on trends in family income between 1970 and 1986. Pointing out that median family income continued to increase in the 1970s and 1980s, the report stresses that this growth was at a much slower pace and that it varied significantly by family type, leading to greater income inequality among families with children.

354 United States

Before the 1970s the incomes of married-couple families and lone-mother families grew at about the same rate. With the growth in the numbers of lone-mother families and the proportion of all families with children that they constituted, and the parallel rise in husband/wife families with two wage-earners, the income patterns of these two family types diverged. This divergence is especially apparent among black families, where husband/wife families experienced significant growth in median family income while the dramatic rise in lone-mother families overwhelmed the income picture for black families generally. Underscoring the importance of working wives' contribution to family income, real median income of families with wives in the paid labour force rose by about 25% between 1970 and 1991, while median income for families whose wives were not in the labour force declined slightly.

Family income also varied by the age of the family head (with those under 25 likely to have low earnings), by the age of the youngest child (usually associated with young family heads), and by family size (with larger families more likely to have low incomes because mothers in these families are less likely to be in the labour force and because the division of income among more family members means lower per capita income).

Income sources also changed in these years by family type, with low-income, single-mother families more likely to depend on transfer income, middle-class husband/wife families more dependent on the earnings of wives, and middle-class lone-mother families more dependent on earnings alone.

The Danzigers (1993) note that although child poverty declined significantly between 1949 and 1973, largely because of rising wages and employment rates, and was stable in the 1970s, it increased in the 1980s and early 1990s. Only the most advantaged families experienced rising incomes after the mid-1970s as their market incomes increased and their taxes decreased, while both market incomes and government benefits decreased for the poor.

Referring to an 'absolute' Census Bureau poverty line based on a market basket of items whose value is adjusted each year to reflect changes in the cost of living, the history of income distribution and poverty since 1959 is a story of progress and backsliding. The current child poverty rate (22.7% of all children in 1993) is about the same as in 1965, when President Johnson first launched the War on Poverty. Child poverty cases are concentrated disproportionately in female-headed families and in black and Hispanic families. Rates are higher for families with three or four children than for those with one or two, and higher for children under age six than for those older (in 1992, 26% as compared to 20% for those aged 6–17). Poverty rates among the elderly exceeded those for children until the mid-1970s when transfers for the elderly improved and those for children began to decline. Female-headed families have constituted about half of all poor families with children since the mid-1970s; children under 18 are about 40% of the poor, and those over age 65 make up about 11%.

The several analyses based on the Luxemburg Income Study (LIS) database also show US child poverty statistics in the 1980s and early 1990s leading the major

The Income of Families 355

TABLE 10. Composition of poverty population for selected demographic groups, United States 1959–1990 (% of poverty population)[a]

	1959	1966	1975	1985	1990[b]
Aged	13.9	17.9	12.8	10.5	10.9
Children	43.6	42.6	42.1	38.8	39.5
Non-aged adults	42.5	39.5	45.1	50.7	49.7
Individuals in female-headed families[c]	26.3	36.0	47.4	49.5	53.4
Individuals in all other families[c]	73.7	64.0	52.6	50.5	46.6
Blacks	25.1	31.1	29.2	27.0	29.3
Whites	72.1	67.7	68.7	69.1	66.5
Other races	2.8	1.2	2.1	3.9	4.2
Hispanic origin[d]	—	—	11.6	15.8	17.9
Individuals in families with children[e]	—	—	—	—	68.0
male present	—	—	—	—	30.7
female-headed	—	—	—	—	37.2
Individuals in all other families	—	—	—	—	32.0

[a] Data are for March of the following year.
[b] 1990 estimates are not comparable to prior years due to processing changes in the Current Population Survey. 1959–1985 estimates based on data from 'Money Income and Poverty Status of Families and Persons in the United States 1985,' P-60 No. 154 and No. 157. 1986–1990 data from 'March Current Population Survey.' Table prepared by Congressional Research Service.
[c] Includes unrelated or single individuals.
[d] Hispanic origin may be of any race; therefore numbers add to more than 100%.
[e] Family includes related children under 18.

Source: Committee on Ways and Means, US House of Representatives (1993), The Green Book: Overview of Entitlement Programs, Washington, DC: US Government Printing Office, 1315, Table 5.

industrialized countries by far, whether for poverty in single-parent families, poverty in two-parent families, or poverty among all children (Committee on Ways and Means, 1993; Rainwater and Smeeding, 1995).

The relative impacts of wages, transfer income, and taxes on single- and two-adult families with varied amounts of earnings and different numbers of children are displayed in Tables 11–13 (National Commission on Children, 1991). Looking first at two-parent families with any children at all (Table 11), one notes that families with no wage-earner were all in poverty, and that in the one-earner families, a minimum wage plus Food Stamps (discussed below) kept only one-child families at about the poverty line, even with the supplementation of the Earned Income Tax Credit (EITC), to be discussed below. Families with one worker earning the current statutory minimum wage and more than one child were all below the poverty line. In two-parent families in which both parents earned a minimum wage, those with one or two children remained above the poverty line on the basis of earnings plus the EITC, despite a fairly heavy tax burden and lack of eligibility for Food Stamps; the income tax burden was more manageable for them. But when such

TABLE 11. Effect of current system on family income, two-parent families, United States 1991 (in 1991 $)

	Two parents' income								
	Unemployed			One employed minimum wage			Both employed minimum wage		
Source of income	1 child	2 children	4 children	1 child	2 children	4 children	1 child	2 children	4 children
Wages	0	0	0	8,500	8,500	8,500	17,000	17,000	17,000
Exemptions				[6,540]	[8,600]	[5,700]	[6,450]	[8,600]	[12,900]
Standard deduction				[5,700]	[5,700]	[5,700]	[5,700]	[5,700]	[5,700]
Insured child support benefit	...	...	...	...	...	...	...	...	...
AFDC	4,404	5,184	6,924						
Food Stamps	2,762	3,428	4,706	2,043	2,943	4,743	0	0	2,703
Taxable income	0	0	0	0	0	0	[4,850]	[2,700]	0
Income taxes	0	0	0	0	0	0	-728	-405	0
Social Security taxes	0	0	0	-650	-650	-650	-1,301	-1,301	-1,301
Work expenses				-1,000	-1,000	-1,000	-1,250	-1,250	-1,250
Refundable child tax credit	0	0	0	0	0	0	0	0	0
Earned Income Tax Credit	0	0	0	1,192	1,235	1,235	506	524	524
Net income	7,166	8,612	11,630	10,085	11,028	12,828	14,227	14,568	17,676
Poverty guidelines	10,932	14,018	18,714	10,932	14,018	18,714	10,932	14,018	18,714

Source: National Commission on Children (1991), Beyond Rhetoric: A New American Agenda for Children and Families, Washington, DC: US Government Printing Office, 446, Table A–4.

TABLE 12. Effect of current system on family income, two-parent families,
United States 1991 (in 1991 $)

| | Two parents' income | | | | | |
| | One employed median income | | | Both employed median income | | |
Source of income	1 child	2 children	4 children	1 child	2 children	4 children
Wages	35,000	35,000	35,000	70,000	70,000	70,000
Exemptions	[6,450]	[8,600]	[12,900]	[6,450]	[8,600]	[12,900]
Standard deduction	[5,700]	[5,700]	[5,700]	[5,700]	[5,700]	[5,700]
Insured child support benefit	...	...	...	...	...	...
AFDC	0	0	0	0	0	0
Food Stamps	0	0	0	0	0	0
Taxable income	[22,850]	[20,700]	[16,400]	[57,850]	[55,700]	[51,400]
Income taxes	-3,428	-3,105	-2,460	-11,778	-11,176	-9,972
Social Security taxes	-2,678	-2,768	-2,768	-5,355	-5,355	-5,355
Work expenses	-1,000	-1,000	-1,000	-1,250	-1,250	-1,250
Refundable child tax credit	0	0	0	0	0	0
Earned Income Tax Credit	0	0	0	0	0	0
Net income	27,894	28,127	28,772	51,617	52,219	53,423
Poverty guidelines	10,932	14,018	18,714	10,932	14,018	18,714

Source: National Commission on Children (1991), *Beyond Rhetoric: A New American Agenda for Children and Families*, Washington, DC: US Government Printing Office, 446, Table A–4.

families had four children, they fell into poverty despite Food Stamp eligibility and relief from income taxes.

At the median earnings level, however, both one-earner and two-earner two-parent families did relatively well, despite lack of any special transfer payments, in the sense that all avoided poverty or near-poverty. However, in neither one-earner nor in two-earner families with median earnings was there a significant margin to take account of child-cost burdens.

What of the single parent? Only wages offer any possibility of protection against poverty. If the single-parent earner has a minimum-wage job, he or she is ineligible for AFDC but eligible for Food Stamps. That and the EITC will place the parent with one child just about at the poverty line, but it is insufficient if there are two or more children in the family. The median-income single parent does better, helped a little by the child tax exemptions.

What of the impact of income transfers? A US Congressional report (Committee on Ways and Means, 1993: 1368) found that 'between 1979 and 1989 . . . almost two-thirds of the child poverty increase was due to changes in governmental policy', more specifically: a major erosion in the real value of public assistance (AFDC) benefits.

Analyses that take account of the entire income transfer system (cash benefits and taxes) and assign cash value to Food Stamps and to housing benefits have been

TABLE 13. Effect of current system on family income, single parents, United States 1991 (in 1991 $)

	Single parent's income								
	Unemployed			Employed minimum wage			Employed median income		
Source of income	1 child	2 children	4 children	1 child	2 children	4 children	1 child	2 children	4 children
Wages	0	0	0	8,500	8,500	8,500	35,000	35,000	35,000
Exemptions	...	...	...	[4,300]	[6,450]	[10,750]	[4,300]	[6,450]	[10,750]
Standard deduction	...	...	...	[5,000]	[5,000]	[5,000]	[5,000]	[5,000]	[5,000]
Insured child support benefit	...	0	0	0	0	0	0	0	0
AFDC	3,540	4,404	6,072	0	0	0	0	0	0
Food Stamps	2,013	2,762	3,953	1,035	2,043	3,735	0	0	0
Taxable income	0	0	0	0	0	0	[25,700]	[23,550]	19,250]
Income taxes	0	0	0	0	0	0	-3,855	-3,533	-2,888
Social Security taxes	0	0	0	-650	-650	-650	-2,678	-2,678	-2,678
Work expenses	...	...	...	-1,250	-1,250	-1,250	-1,250	-1,250	-1,250
Refundable child tax credit	0	0	0	0	0	0	0	0	0
Earned Income Tax Credit	0	0	0	1,192	1,235	1,235	0	0	0
Net income	5,553	7,166	10,025	8,827	9,878	11,570	27,217	27,539	28,184
Poverty guidelines	8,932	10,932	16,578	8,932	10,932	16,578	8,932	10,932	16,578

Source: National Commission on Children (1991), *Beyond Rhetoric: A New American Agenda for Children and Families*, Washington, DC: US Government Printing Office, 446, Table A–4.

carried out systematically over the years, most recently covering 1979–92 (Committee on Ways and Means, 1993, 1994; US Bureau of the Census, 1993c). Forgoing detail, we note the consistent finding that with regard to single-parent families with children under age 18, transfers and tax policies reduced the total 1992 poverty gap by 61.6% (the poverty gap being the distance between each family's income and its poverty threshold cumulated for the entire group). This left a poverty *rate* of 38.5%, high but not the 51.6% that would have existed without means-tested cash transfers, food and housing benefits, social insurance, and tax credits. A similar analysis, focused on married-couple families with children, showed that taxes and transfers reduced the poverty gap by 57.6% but left a poverty rate of 8.5%. For both family types the outcomes were better in 1992 than a decade earlier, but less satisfactory than in 1979.

Although AFDC plus Food Stamps by themselves do not take any families above the poverty line, means-tested programmes had an overwhelming impact on reducing the poverty gap for single-parent families. For married couples, both means-tested programmes and social insurance programmes (old-age, disability, and unemployment insurance) had significant impact. Tax policy was not a major factor.

How does all of this affect consumption? While some analytic work is under way, there are no recent comprehensive analyses of benefit impacts (or poverty impacts) on standard of living in sufficient detail to suit our purposes. A recent study reports as follows: 'food expenditures of poor households were about $2,500 less than those of their non-poor counterparts. Poor households also had a higher average household size. There is some evidence that lower food spending puts people at nutritional risk' (Lino, 1996: 12).

We turn now to the specific tax policies and public transfers already mentioned and offer a brief historical background, an overview of policy and programme developments, and an analysis of each programme's current status. We stress here that US tax and transfer programmes are not targeted at reducing the gap between those at the top and bottom ends of the income distribution or at equalizing consumption. Nonetheless, the situation of the dependent poor or the working poor has at times received special attention, whether as a political strategy or as a matter of social philosophy.

Jobs and earnings remain the main factors in income and expenditures except for those removed from the marketplace by age, retirement, or disability and eligible for Social Security and perhaps supplementary private pensions. Their survivors and dependants also receive aid. Without regular jobs and adequate wages, families with children are likely to remain poor; the public transfer that they most rely on is social assistance, which offers low levels of help. Income transfer policy since the 1960s has moved increasingly and ever more aggressively toward an emphasis on training and work for the 'welfare' poor and toward modest income supplementation for the working poor (EITC), both strategies with long traditions in the US. But these initiatives, only partially realized, may be superseded or drastically revised even as we complete this report.

TAXATION

The personal income tax and Social Security payroll tax are the major sources of federal revenue (67% in 1993). The personal income tax system components with the greatest influence on families are the alternative filing statuses, personal exemptions, and standard deductions. Also critical are the recognition of child-care expenses as part of the costs of earning income, the treatment of divorce, and the tax treatment of families in or near poverty. In the section that follows, we will briefly touch on filing status, personal exemptions, taxation of the poor, and the Earned Income Tax Credit (EITC), intended as an income supplement for low-income, working families with children. The tax treatment of divorce, the tax-exempt status of employer-provided or -financed child care, and the tax credit for child-care costs are discussed in Chapters 1, 2, and 4.

The history of personal income tax policy since its enactment in 1913 is one of often disjointed incremental action, with occasional episodes involving major efforts to reshape or direct new policy thrusts (as in 1986). The manifest goals may be adequate revenue, macroeconomic policy, fairness, or efficiency. Interest groups compete heavily for favourable treatment, and the stakes and political complexities are such that even the major reforms are never comprehensive or completely realized. Family policy is not the central concern in most tax reform and often struggles even for modest consideration. Some inequities should probably be attributed, as tax policy expert Steuerle (1991) suggests, to 'inattention'.

In an international context, US total tax burdens are below European Union (EU) and Organization for Economic Co-operation and Development (OECD) averages, as are US government expenditures as a portion of GDP (OECD, 1994). However, the US personal income tax burdens are above EU and OECD averages. Single persons in the US end up with more disposable income as a percentage of gross pay than do average EU and OECD single workers, whereas a married couple with two children has lower disposable income than those averages (OECD, 1992). When transfers are added to the equation, the US single worker is a bit below the median in take-home pay, and the couple is still worse off.

Filing Status

The filing status of an income unit, and thus the tax rate schedule determining how much is to be paid, allows four possibilities. Beyond the very lowest income groups, whose filing status matters little, the highest rate schedule is assigned to married individuals filing a separate return. The lowest rate is assigned to those married and filing a joint return (or a widow/widower with a dependent child), and an intermediate rate is assigned to those who are single or heads of households. The head-of-household status is for unmarried individuals who provide a home for certain other persons, and for certain married persons who live apart. A single mother with one or more children files as head of household. There is a long history of efforts to create and maintain equity among these categories. These fine balancing acts cannot by their nature ever satisfy all parties, and each attempt often creates the new alleged inequities that follow.

Exemptions for Dependants

The taxpayer has the choice of taking personal exemptions for self, spouse, and dependants (those for whom the taxpayer provides over half the support) or of using a standard deduction ('zero bracket amount') that varies by filing status. The two are seen by policy-makers as related and are alternative ways of being sensitive to families, although, in general, higher-income families are likely to itemize (i.e., to list expenditures and other factors justifying deductions from income liable to taxation) and to use exemptions, while lower-income families elect standard deductions. Campaigns for improved personal exemptions thus often have the higher-income 'itemizers' in mind.

Early in the history of the income tax, exemptions were reduced, then increased, in accord with revenue needs. Dependant (largely child) exemptions were low compared to those for heads of families. Only since 1944 have these exemptions been equal for all on a per capita basis. The 1948 dependant exemption equalled 42% of per capita personal income. There was no change in exemptions ($600 per capita) between 1948 and 1970, thus their value eroded dramatically, to 7.6% of per capita personal income. Indexing for inflation was enacted in 1981, to go into effect in 1985. The dependency exemption was equal to 11% of per capita income in 1991.

Family advocates who focus on intact middle-class families in particular call for an increase in exemptions for dependent children from $2,450 (1994) to something like $8,000–9,000 to restore the 1948 situation, taking account both of inflation and the growth in real per capita income (Bauer, 1991). Other analysts (see below) favour a refundable child tax credit as a more equitable mechanism, since the exemption has its highest values for high-income taxpayers in the top marginal tax rate brackets. All are agreed that despite the 1986 correction, dependant exemptions are still eroded and Social Security taxes are high. For those above the earned income tax credit band, the tax burden remains high and has grown. For example, federal, state, local, and Social Security taxes claimed 14% of median family income in 1960, 23% in 1970, and 25% in 1990. In mid-1996, in an effort once again to aid middle-class families, Congress seemed likely to enact a $500 child tax credit. Although not available to the highest-income families, it also would provide no benefit to families with incomes below the tax threshold.

It should be noted that the definition of dependency has broadened over this period, going well beyond minor children, so that it now encompasses all closely-related people for whom the taxpayer provides more than half the financial support. Extended family obligations which are not legally binding are recognized.

The Poor

In 1986, tax reform raised tax thresholds and removed six million poor taxpayers from the tax rolls, including many families with children. This was a by-product of a major tax reform aimed at simplification, fairness, efficiency, and economic stimulus. The new tax system, now indexed to inflation, should continue to protect from taxation people with incomes below the poverty threshold. There was no such protection before 1986. However, rising payroll taxes have undone some of the improvements in income taxes. High Social Security payroll deductions, which take no account of family status, require many families with poverty-level earnings to pay significant taxes. Families with children in the lowest income quintile are well below the poverty line, further below now than in 1977. Local and state sales taxes do not differentiate by individual income status and remain regressive.

Earned Income Tax Credit (EITC)

The EITC was enacted in 1975 at the time of a considerable increase in the payroll tax for Social Security. It was seen as a way to give some relief to low-income working taxpayers *with children*. In effect, it was a tax credit as compensation but—and this was an innovation—it was made refundable (non-wasteable). If the tax credit due was greater than the tax liability, payment would be made. Initially, the maximum credit was a modest $400, 10% of $4,000 of earned income. The credit began to be phased out for earned income or adjusted gross income (AGI) over $4,000 and was entirely phased out for an AGI of $8,000 or more. There were several subsequent increases in the credit and in the income levels at which it was phased out. In the context of the tax reform of 1986, all the dollar amounts were increased and indexed for inflation.

In changes effective in 1991, the maximum amount of the basic credit was substantially increased, and, for the first time, an adjustment that partially reflected family size was added: a higher credit would be paid if a family had two or more children. Now the rationale was to help and encourage the 'working' (non-welfare) poor. In 1993, additional relief was given to this group (Leonard and Greenstein, 1991). In the context of a Presidential objective to 'make work pay' even if it is minimum-wage work, this legislation, partially effective in 1994 and fully effective in 1996, would supplement earnings in the $8,425–$11,000 band by 40% of $8,425 (i.e., $3,370) in families with two or more children. The credit is lower for earners above and below the band, with gradual phasing in and out; the maximum credit in a one-child family would be $2,040. However, before this significant enhancement became fully effective, a budget-cutting Congress, ignoring the objective of encouraging the working poor, eliminated the final increase; efforts at further cutbacks were initiated but blocked in the legislative struggles of 1996.

From 1975 to 1986, between 5 and 7.5 million families received the EITC in any one year. The number rose to over 18 million for 1994, after the enhancements. To sum up: EITC is income supplementation for the working poor with children. The EITC enactment and enhancements signify heightened consciousness of the potential of taxes in an income transfer strategy. Those who favour family allowances for the US, for example, now talk increasingly of a child tax credit (National Commission on Children, 1991).

Tax Expenditures

Tax expenditures affecting families and children have a long history in the US but are not included in social welfare expenditure data series. They have been regularly, if separately, reported by legislative mandate. For the most part it is not possible to disaggregate those to families with children among those important tax expenditures available to a larger public: deductions of interest on home mortgages from gross income before federal tax rates are applied; deduction of state and local property taxes; deductions of high medical costs above a threshold. On the other hand, much of the dependant-care tax credit is used for child care, as discussed in Chapter 4, and we have described the EITC (a portion of which is a tax expenditure) as an important benefit for families with children: in 1994, it involved, in direct outlays plus tax expenditures, federal expenditures at a level almost equal to the social assistance for (largely) single-parent families with children. In addition, dependant exemptions may also be regarded as tax expenditures. For example, the estimated 1991 cost in revenues for child exemptions was $21 billion, approximately the combined federal/state costs for AFDC, as discussed in the next section.

FAMILY BENEFITS

Early in the twentieth century many states enacted provisions for mothers' or widows' pensions, intended to keep children of widows (and some other single mothers) with their mothers as an alternative to foster homes, institutions, and child labour. Later, this 'targeted' early 'family allowance' was to become a social assistance programme for single-parent, mother-only families, or Aid to Families with Dependent Children (AFDC). By the 1950s, the social insurance system had added dependants and survivor wives to the recipients of significant insurance coverage. In the 1970s an important federalization of social assistance for the aged, blind, and disabled (always the 'worthy poor') included children with handicaps, allowing a very important targeted benefit for some children (discussed in Chapter 4). Because AFDC, a state-implemented programme, offers limited benefits that vary across states, a unique Food Stamp programme established during the 1960s has supplemented cash grants with 'cash equivalents' for food. School meals have also been available, free to low-income children and at reduced fees to others.

In 1996, in a conservative move to cut social spending and end what were seen as incentives to unwed motherhood, especially for adolescents, the Congress voted to abolish AFDC and to provide 'block grants' (a fixed sum of money regardless of any increase in the number of claims for assistance). States are given considerable flexibility in designing and determining eligibility for the assistance programme that replaces AFDC. The new legislation ends both the states' 'entitlement' to federal funds to match their AFDC expenditures by set ratios, whatever the caseload, and clients' entitlement to aid if they met the state's eligibility criteria.

This almost-complete list of developments, to be elaborated in what follows, reflects not coherent national policy or integrated plans, but rather the succession of national concerns in periods of crisis, interest group pressures and political bargaining around specific issues, periods of focus on children (the Progressive Era), on poverty, hunger, welfare, and health reform (in the 1960s), on taxes, and on building voter constituencies.

The US does not have a child and family allowance system. Even though many union leaders and others early in this century set their sights on wage levels which might have been considered a 'family wage', there have been no large family wage campaigns or any such enactments. The two European motivations for child allowances—to provide an alternative to general wage increases and to encourage fertility—have not entered into policy discussion. When child allowances were proposed in the 1950s and 1960s as anti-poverty measures, they were opposed by many economists as less efficient than alternatives (the negative income tax) or were rejected as offering undesirable encouragement (first to Catholics and later, to blacks) to have babies in a country that has not considered itself as having a deficient birth rate. Since the late 1980s, child allowances in the form of tax credits have been suggested from several points on the political spectrum as measures to cope with child poverty and to encourage low-wage earners to work (National Commission on Children, 1991), as have the higher personal exemptions mentioned in the previous section. A tax credit of $500 per child, proposed by both the Congress and the President in 1995 and 1996, in a drive to aid the 'middle class', would not be available to those below the tax threshold. This credit remains under active discussion.

Aid to Families with Dependent Children (AFDC)

Although it will be considerably changed over the next several years as the 1996 devolution and block grants go into effect, AFDC was the major US child and family policy from 1935 to 1996. A review of the programme reveals much about changing policy currents. We use the present tense because the programme remains as we go to press, although it is to be phased out. Over the past several years many of the states have received permission to experiment with various work and training incentives, behavioural rules, and administrative changes. These reflect diverse objectives.

AFDC, popularly referred to as 'welfare', is a child-conditioned social assistance programme.[7] It serves children and their caretakers, overwhelmingly in single-parent female-headed families, but occasionally in families with two parents, one of them unemployed and with a sharply-defined qualifying recent employment history. In some cases, the caretaker is not a biological parent. AFDC began as a widows' pension and became a nationally-enacted social assistance benefit. Subsequently, and for almost 25 years, AFDC slowly evolved into a transitional support programme for most of its adult recipients. Under this concept it now offers job search, educational, and training experiences as preparation for labour market ntry and support. This and strict enforcement of child support orders are the current policy thrust, enacted in 1988, although results are modest thus far. AFDC contrasts sharply with European family allowances and with Australian and British nationally-uniform means-tested assistance programmes.

The history, to be briefly reviewed here, offers an instructive US family policy case study, clarifying thinking at several AFDC transition points since its 1935 beginnings and explaining why advocates of universal child or family transfers have currently selected another route (Kamerman and Kahn, 1988). Although Aid to Dependent Children (ADC) was enacted as one provision (Title IV–A) of the original Social Security Act, it is best understood against an earlier backdrop which includes poor law, nineteenth-century humanitarian charities, children's institutions under public and voluntary auspices, 'missions' to street children in large cities, and the free foster home movement.

The early twentieth-century invention of mothers' or widows' pensions was tied to the notion of preserving families and sustaining women at home. First established in 1911, they were soon developed in 20 states, existed in 40 states by 1921 and in all but three states by 1935. The grants were small, availability depended on the locality, blacks were generally excluded, and most recipients were widows. The 'pension' concept was hardly pure, yet this was not the stigmatized social assistance which it was to become. In a few places divorced or separated women and their children received help, but practically never unwed mothers, who gave up their children or laboured to support them and remained as invisible as possible. These pensions carried a 'suitable home' requirement; no one doubted that 'immoral' or 'inefficient' (i.e., incompetent) homes called for other kinds of intervention—such as removal of the children.

These pensions helped some poor women, mostly widows, to do what many middle-class women had been doing since late in the nineteenth century: stay at home and make home into a haven and a place for secure child-rearing. That, at least, was the theory; aid often was inadequate, insecure, sporadic, and was provided only for the children, not the mothers.

The pension titles of the 1935 Social Security Act added dependent and survivor spouses and children in 1939. Gradually, widows left the ADC rolls, and the character of the ADC caseload changed as did the public attitude toward it. ADC added 'caretakers' (mothers) as recipients in 1950 and was renamed AFDC as part of a family intervention thrust in the 1960s.

The history of AFDC reflects varied objectives, none fully realized: protecting children; offering a minimum, means-tested family allowance; supporting an at-home role for widows (and for some divorced women, in an era of lower divorce rates). By the 1960s, however, a new and major dimension was added: AFDC was to encourage a mother's work in the labour market when children reached school age. While not articulated clearly at the time, this change paralleled the major shift to labour force participation by married mothers.

However, much else was going on which would change the AFDC caseload and affect public perceptions and, eventually, policy. A revolution in cotton technology

accelerated the southern black migration to northern cities. The civil rights movement, the War on Poverty, legal advocacy, and a poor people's movement encouraged AFDC applications. A large number of the new applicants were unmarried
mothers, disproportionately black. Southern exclusion of blacks from AFDC on
the grounds that their homes were unsuitable was decreased by a federal policy
stating that if AFDC-eligible children were found to be in unsuitable homes, action
to protect the children was essential, and AFDC would pay for their foster care and
social services.

The AFDC revolution which ensued expanded the rolls and added many divorced, separated, and unmarried mothers and many blacks. The positive case for
alternatives to AFDC was buttressed by a punitive case as well: a series of 'work
incentive programmes' was enacted; AFDC's stigma effect was increased and the
programme became increasingly unpopular with the general public even among
those sympathetic to the poor.

By the time the civil rights revolution and the War on Poverty had increased
access to AFDC, public support for a programme to allow all AFDC-receiving
single mothers to stay at home to rear their children until age 16 had faded significantly. Mothers of young children not receiving AFDC were entering the labour
force, and a philosophy that preferred work for AFDC mothers when the children
reached compulsory school age (usually age six) took over. Actual implementation
was to move slowly beginning in 1967, taking the form of financial incentives to
work, child-care support, and gradually-increasing work requirements. The latter
were elaborated in the Family Support Act of 1988 which defined a single mother
with children over age three (age one or older, at state option) as employable and
specified employment quotas and targets for states. The work/education/training
programmes were reinforced by a year of transitional Medicaid (health assistance
for the poor) and child-care support after employment and leaving the AFDC rolls
(see Chapter 4).

States all developed Job Opportunities and Basic Skills (JOBS) programs with
federal help, but implementation, recruitment, and job placement were limited in
most places despite moderately favourable evaluations of the programmes. The
recession of the late 1980s and early 1990s both curtailed work opportunities and
constricted state budgets; lacking adequate matching funds, states were not able to
draw fully on federal offerings. President Clinton's original proposed reform would
have built on the 1988 reform, stressing time limits for cash support and creating
strong work requirements. However, public jobs were to be made available if private sector work was not. This programme failed in Congress because the budgetary situation and Congressional budget rules did not offer a viable financing option
for public job creation. And by 1993–94, some states were experimenting with
more radical, punitive proposals (see below).

Today AFDC is a means-tested (income- and asset-tested), stigmatized, cash
benefit programme available to some poor children under 18 years of age (to age
19 if a full-time student and completing a course) and their caretaker parents or
certain other caretakers. As seen in Table 14, caseloads essentially reflected popu-

lation growth in the 1970s and 1980s but exploded with the economic problems of
the early 1990s. Between 1993 and 1996, with an improved economy, the caseload
declined from its peak of 14 million recipients to less than 13 million.

AFDC recipients have constituted between 4.1 and 5.2% of the US population
since 1970; the rate remained well below 5% until the 1990s, then reached an all-
time high of 5.34% in 1992. Some analysts, including the Congressional Budget
Office, stressed the recession of the late 1980s as the major factor in the recent
increase, but others focused on the growing population of mother-only families.
The all-time high of 14% of the total child population as AFDC recipients in 1992
certainly reflects both need and greater readiness to ask for the aid. Overall, the
AFDC population as a percentage of the total population and AFDC child recipients as a percentage of the total child population had been remarkably stable over
two decades before the explosion of the 1990s. AFDC also covered a smaller percentage of the poverty population during the significant increase in child poverty
from the late 1970s through the early 1990s.

AFDC carries automatic eligibility for Medicaid and Food Stamps (see below).
Income criteria for eligibility as well as need standards (and thus benefit levels)
vary from state to state and in some states from county to county. The programme
is financed by federal and state (and in some states, local) governments, and the
federal share ranges from 50–83% of total expenditures (54% on average), with
the higher shares allocated to states with lower per capita incomes.

Lone mothers must co-operate with AFDC officials in establishing the paternity
of their children and must assign their child support rights to the state. AFDC is
paid monthly by cheque or bank deposit to the claimant, usually the mother. A
small amount of earnings is excluded from income subjected to the means test, as
is a modest amount of child-care and work-related expenses. These policies are
designed to encourage work, though only a small minority of recipients holds jobs.

States are not required to offer the AFDC programme, but all have chosen to do
so. They are required to comply with federal guidelines, as stated in the Social
Security Act, assuring a recipient or applicant fair treatment. Unlike Old Age, Survivors, and Disability Insurance, however, the amount of the grant is not justiciable.
Although AFDC remains largely a single-mother family programme, in 1988 federal legislation required the states to cover qualified two-parent families as well.

Monthly AFDC benefits vary considerably from one state to another: from a
$923 monthly maximum for a two-child family in Alaska to $120 for a two-child
family in Mississippi (1993). The national median maximum for a family this size
was $366. Benefits are not indexed. Except for Alaska and Hawaii, two states with
high living costs, no state offers current benefits which, when combined with Food
Stamps, constitute above-poverty incomes. This weak result is in part the consequence of benefit erosion during the 1970s and 1980s, so that on average, in constant dollars, the median state's income benefit for a four-person family with no
other income fell 47% between 1970 and 1993. A stable (indexed) Food Stamp
programme, which provides *more* to families with lower earned or public assistance incomes, partially offset the decline, making the effective drop approximately

TABLE 14. Number of AFDC recipients, and recipients as a percentage of various population groups, United States 1970–1992 (in 1,000 and % distributions)

Calendar year	Total AFDC recipients[a]	AFDC child recipients[a]	Total populations ages 0–17[b]	AFDC recipients as % of total populations[b]	AFDC child recipients as % of total child population	AFDC recipients as % of pre-welfare poverty population[c]	AFDC child recipients as % of children in poverty[d]
1970	8,303	6,104	69,759	4.07	8.75	—	58.5
1975	11,131	7,952	67,164	5.17	11.84	—	71.6
1980	10,599	7,295	63,684	4.66	11.45	49.2	63.2
1985	10,672	7,074	62,624	4.49	11.30	45.0	54.4
1990	11,699	7,922	64,185	4.69	12.34	48.0	59.0
1992	13,623[e]	9,224[e]	66,163	5.34	13.94	—	63.1

[a] Annual numbers. In calculating the number of AFDC recipients, data for Guam, Puerto Rico, and the Virgin Islands were subtracted from the total AFDC population. Data for these territories were not available for 1970–76, so an estimate was used based on the ratio in later years (1977–87) of the number of recipients in these areas to the total number of recipients.

[b] Population numbers represent US resident population, not including Armed Forces overseas.

[c] Poverty population is determined by the number of people whose income (cash income plus social insurance plus social security before taxes and means-tested transfers) falls below the appropriate poverty threshold. This information can be found in *The Green Book* (1992), Appendix J, Table 20.

[d] This information can be found in *The Green Book* (1992), Appendix J, Table 2.

[e] Recipient estimates assume the same number of AFDC recipients in Guam, Puerto Rico, and Virgin Islands in 1992 as existed in 1991.

Source: Committee on Ways and Means, US House of Representatives (1993), *The Green Book: Overview of Entitlement Programs*, Washington, DC: US Government Printing Office, 399, Table 10–26.

!7% over this period. Expenditures for direct benefits are quite low as compared with social insurance: 1–2% of total social expenditures and well under 1% of JDP in recent years. The combined worth of the AFDC grant plus Food Stamps in the median state for January 1992 was equal to 29% of an average male production worker's wage and 44% of the average female production worker's wage.

Expert estimates placed AFDC participation at 62–72%, and Food Stamp participation at 54–66%, of those eligible in 1986–1987. The caseloads, as noted, are now the highest ever, but growth appeared to stop in 1994 for reasons not yet clear. Many poor families do not benefit from AFDC either because their income is not low enough to meet state standards, or because the stigma attached to the programme keeps them from applying.

What are the characteristics of AFDC recipients and how have they changed over time (Table 15)? First, this is a caseload of households without fathers (90%). Yet since the early 1970s, fewer than 5% of the children have been orphans; since the early 1980s, fewer than 2%. Second, divorce or separation, the leading cause of family breakup through the late 1970s, remains a major factor, but unwed childbearing has been more important since the early 1980s and is now implicated in over half the cases. Other causes are minor: unemployment is the problem in slightly more than 8% of cases. Given current demographic trends, significant numbers of children in the US are likely to become AFDC beneficiaries for these same reasons—divorce, separation, or out-of-wedlock birth—at some point before they become independent.

What of race? AFDC has been condemned both directly and implicitly as a minority, especially a black, programme. Hostility to a programme said to encourage or sustain the very high rate of black unwed motherhood has hindered reform efforts to increase benefit levels or to enact a child or family allowance; hostility has clearly been some of the motivation to use work requirements punitively. Racial data on a systematic basis are available from the late 1960s onward: whites (referring usually to mothers) have constituted 38–42% of the caseload since the early 1970s, while blacks have declined from 46% in 1973 to 37% in 1992, falling below the white rate of 39% for that year for the first time in two decades. However, the Hispanic portion has increased gradually from 13% to 18% over the same period. Thus the total minority proportion of the caseload was 56% in 1990 and 55% in 1992. Native American and Asian totals are very small.

Many welfare 'spells' are brief: half of those with accepted cases will be gone within two years, whereas 17% will continue for eight or more years. A cross-sectional view of those receiving AFDC at a given point and who have used it more than once shows that 65% have been receiving aid for eight or more years. Advocates stress the considerable use of AFDC as a one- to two-year transition; critics point to the costs of long-term welfare dependency and its negative effects on children. Reformers wish to strengthen laws and policies to ensure that AFDC will in fact be used as a transition benefit.

An increasingly important component of the AFDC programme since the mid-1970s is the Child Support Enforcement Program (Title IV–D of the Social Secu-

TABLE 15. AFDC characteristics, United States 1969–1992 (% distributions)

	May 1969	May 1975	March 1979	1986[a]	1990[a]	1992[a]
Average family size (persons)	4.0	3.2	3.0	3.0	2.9	2.9
Number of child recipients (% AFDC cases)						
one	26.6	37.9	42.3	42.7	42.2	42.5
two	23.0	26.0	28.1	30.8	30.3	30.2
three	17.7	16.1	15.6	15.9	15.8	15.5
four or more	32.5	20.0	13.9	9.8	9.9	10.1
unknown	—	—	—	0.8	1.4	0.7
Basis for eligibility (% children)						
Parents present:						
incapacitated	11.7[b]	7.7	5.3	3.2	3.6	4.1
unemployed	4.6[b]	3.7	4.1	7.4	6.4	8.2
Parents absent:						
death	5.5[b]	3.7	2.2	1.9	1.6	1.6
divorce or separation	43.3[b]	48.3	44.7	36.3	32.9	30.0
no marriage tie	27.9[b]	31.0	37.8	48.9	54.0	53.1
other reason	3.5[b]	4.0	5.9	2.4	1.9	2.0
unknown	—	—	—	—	—	0.9
Mother's education (% mothers)[c]						
8th grade or less	29.4	16.7	9.5	4.8	5.8	4.9
1–3 years of HS	30.7	31.7	20.8	14.3	16.5	18.8
high school degree	16.0	23.7	18.8	17.3	19.3	22.4
some college	2.0	3.9	2.7	3.4	5.7	6.8
college graduate	0.2	0.7	0.4	0.5	0.4	0.5
unknown	21.6	23.3	47.8	59.7	52.3	46.6
Age of mother (% mothers)[c]						
under 20	6.6	8.3	4.1[d]	3.3[d]	7.9	7.6
20–24	16.7	([e])	28.0[f]	33.6[g]	23.8	24.5
25–29	17.6	([e])	21.4	20.0[h]	24.6	23.3
30–39	30.4	27.9	27.2	30.1	32.0	32.7
40 or over	25.0	17.6	15.4	13.0	11.7	11.8
unknown	3.6	3.0	4.0	—	—	0.1
Ages of children (% recipient children)						
under 3	14.9	16.5	18.9	21.9	24.2	24.6
3–5	17.6	18.1	17.5	21.1	21.5	21.7
6–11	36.5	33.7	33.0	32.4	27.5	32.4
12 and over	31.0	30.9	29.8	24.3	71.3	21.2
unknown	—	0.8	0.9	0.1	0.0	0.0
Mother's employment status (%)[c]						
full-time job	8.2	10.4	8.7	1.6	2.5	2.2
part-time job	6.3	5.7	5.4	4.2	4.2	4.2
Presence of income (% families)						
with earnings	—	14.6	12.8	7.5	8.2	7.4
no non-AFDC income	56.0	71.1	80.6[j]	81.3[j]	80.1[j]	78.9[j]

(continued)

TABLE 15. (continued)

	May 1969	May 1975	March 1979	1986[a]	1990[a]	1992[a]
Median months on AFDC						
since most recent opening	*23.0*	*31.0*	*29.0*	*27.0*	*23.0*	*22.5*
Race (% parents)[k]						
white	—	39.9	40.4	39.7	38.1	38.9
black	45.2	44.3	43.1	40.7	39.7	37.2
Hispanic	—	12.2	13.6	14.4	16.6	17.8
Native American	1.3	1.1	1.4	1.3	1.3	1.4
Asian	—	0.5	1.0	2.3	2.8	2.8
other and unknown	4.8	2.0	1.4	1.4	1.5	2.0
Incidence of households (%)						
living in public housing	12.8	14.6	—	9.6	9.6	9.2
participating in Food Stamps	52.9	75.1	75.1	80.7	85.6	87.3
or donated food program						
including non-recipient members	33.1	34.8	—	36.7	37.7	38.9
Father's relationship to						
youngest child (%)						
no father	—	—	84.7	91.2	92.0	89.4
natural father	—	—	9.6	—	—	—
adoptive father	—	—	0.0	—	—	—
stepfather	—	—	5.6	—	—	—

[a] Data are for the federal fiscal year October through September. All percentages are based on the average monthly caseload during the year. Hawaii and the territories are not included in 1983. Data for 1986 include Hawaii, but not the territories. Data after 1986 include the territories and Hawaii. [b] Calculated on the basis of the total number of families. [c] For years after 1983, data are for adult female recipients. [d] Under age 19. [e] The percentage for 20–29-year-olds was 43.1. [f] Ages were 19–24 in 1979, 1983, and 1990. [g] In 1986 and 1988 this age group was 19–25. [h] In 1986 and 1988 this age group was 26–29. [j] States began collecting child support directly in 1975, removing one source of non-AFDC income. [k] For 1983, 12.6 percentage points where race was unknown were allocated across all categories.

Source: Committee on Ways and Means, US House of Representatives (1994), *The Green Book: Overview of Entitlement Programs*, Washington, DC: US Government Printing Office, 402, Table 10–27.

ity Act). Strengthened once in the early 1980s and then again substantially in 1988, this programme is available to non-AFDC mothers as well for a small fee. As a result of a succession of reforms, the US is attempting to ensure that: (1) each child's paternity is established; (2) absent parents are located; (3) courts order regular support contributions by the non-resident parent; (4) the support level is made adequate, when feasible, by presuming that a state-established payment rate (percentage of wages or salary) be followed; and (5) collection rates improve by virtue of better collection mechanisms, interstate co-operation, wage and other income withholding, and related measures.

As of the early 1990s, the philosophy and preoccupation of AFDC was defined by an emphasis on job training and employment along with enforcement of child

United States

support obligations of the non-custodial parent. AFDC remained a stigmatized social assistance programme, highly categorical, available mostly to single mothers and their children, with a growing caseload and modest turnover. Nor had there been adequate discussion of policy for families with infants and toddlers, almost half the caseload, whose mothers are not required to participate in training or educational activities—nor of policy for the many poorly-educated and unskilled long-term AFDC recipients whose prospects for financial independence are not encouraging.

Talk of 'reform' included what some saw as regressive and punitive 'new' themes. Provisions for federal 'waivers' of AFDC requirements, enacted in the early 1980s, resulted in a multiplicity of initiatives in the Bush and Clinton years. In the midst of a Republican call for 'devolution' of responsibility and power to the states by ending entitlements and enacting block grants for 'welfare', the Clinton Administration began to approve most waiver applications made by state governments, many for policies and practices contrary to long-established AFDC philosophy. These new initiatives involved various punitive or constricting measures: for example, not permitting a baby conceived while parents were receiving AFDC to be added to the budget; limiting the duration of a family's AFDC benefits to two years, after which the family head would be expected either to have a job in the private sector, or to earn the benefit by performing public service, or be left without any support at all; not permitting grants to mothers under a certain age (18, 19, or 20); cutting grants if children did not attend school regularly. In place in over 35 states by late 1995, these waivers clearly had become ways to change the programme on a state level, often justified by what opponents considered pseudo-research rationales.

As the Republican Party gained the majority in Congress in 1995, these were the elements out of which a new welfare 'reform' was being shaped. The alternative they proposed was block grants to the states (a fixed lump sum to be granted to each state); an end to entitlement, the principle whereby all eligibles receive grants and states automatically receive federal appropriations; and states' freedom from most federal regulations. AFDC policy appeared to be taking a new turn, motivated not by the desire to improve the lives of the dependent-child recipients for whom the law was passed in 1935, but by a conservative movement attempting to reverse the trends in family change (out-of-wedlock childbirth in particular) within the context of a movement to cut the federal budget, decrease taxes, reduce the size and role of the federal government, and eliminate the federal safety net. Not, in short, a comprehensive family policy move, although some of the actions were motivated by a reaction against adolescent unwed motherhood (responsible for only a small part of the AFDC load).

A political compromise led to 1996 legislation limiting the duration of benefits, requiring recipients to work, and devolving authority to the states, which now may exercise many options regarding eligibility, benefits, work programmes, child care, and Food Stamps, among others. This legislation reflects many motivations, from dissatisfaction with AFDC, to racial bias, strong condemnation of unwed motherhood, and the belief that what is needed is not income support but a job transition programme. The impact on future family policies remains unclear.

An Emergency Assistance programme, enacted in 1967 and clearly linked to AFDC, allows aid for up to 30 days in any year to prevent destitution of children under 21. Families may be covered, except in cases of refusal without good cause to accept work or training for employment. Caseloads have gradually increased to a monthly average of about 56,000 families in 1990. Federal financial participation is similar to that for the regular AFDC programme. In recent years this programme has been very important to localities coping with homeless families. However, it has now been eliminated and absorbed into the new 'welfare reform'.

Dependants' Allowances Under Social Insurance Programmes

Social insurance programmes in the US, like those in most other countries, provide for dependants and survivors: spouses, children, and divorced spouses. In the US, these programmes display no unusual features comparatively; they were enacted incrementally over the years as problems were noted and proposals made, often without controversy, for reasons of equity. They are universal, unstigmatized, and more generous than the means-tested programmes described above. We summarize only briefly.

An overview of dependant/survivor coverage and costs shows a 3.7 million child total for 1994, compared with almost 9 million AFDC child recipients at the same time. Average benefits for survivors and dependants are far more generous than for social assistance. At state discretion, dependants receive supplements to the basic unemployment insurance benefit; these benefits are available in only ten states, however, and compare very unfavourably with European provisions. State workers' compensation programmes (occupational disability insurance) pay to the survivors of workers who die from on-the-job injuries benefits that are keyed to worker wages. Special programmes are available to military veterans and their families.

Food Stamps

The Food Stamp programme is in some senses the US's 'guaranteed income'. Food Stamps are vouchers treated as cash for food purchases. Not found in any other country, Food Stamps have a long history in the US linked to the use of surplus farm products to help needy families. The programme took its present, important form after the defeat of the so-called 'guaranteed-income' legislation in the 1970s. Food Stamps are available to households in which all members are participating in AFDC or Supplemental Security Income (SSI) programmes (see Chapter 4), having met the respective income and asset tests. In addition, other households are eligible if their total income is less than 130% of the poverty level for their family size-type and their income after deductions is less than 100% of the poverty level. Households with elderly and disabled members need not meet the total income test but must meet an assets test: countable assets for all families of no more than

United States

TABLE 16. Food Stamps: number of persons participating, value of bonus coupons, and average bonus per person, United States, fiscal years 1962–1993[a]

Fiscal year	Persons participating, average during year (in 1,000)	Annual bonus value of coupons (in 1,000 $)	Annual average monthly bonus[b] per person (in $)
1962	143	13,153	7.66
1966	864	64,781	6.25
1970	4,340	550,806	10.58
1975	17,063	4,386,144	21.42
1980	21,077	8,685,521	34.34
1985[c]	19,910	10,744,200	44.99
1990	20,038	14,184,028	59.01
1993	26,983	22,840,989	68.01

[a] Between 1974 and 1979, Supplemental Security Income (SSI) recipients were made ineligible for Food Stamps in Massachusetts, Wisconsin, California, and selected counties in New York and Virginia because those areas supplemented SSI payments in amounts that included the value of Food Stamps. As of 1983 and 1992, SSI recipients were returned to the Food Stamp Program in Massachusetts and Wisconsin, respectively, when these states chose to stop including a value for Food Stamps in the SSI supplement.

[b] The portion of the Food Stamp allotment, before the purchase requirement was eliminated, representing the government's share of total Food Stamps received. Since January 1979, participants receive only the bonus portion of the total Food Stamp allotment.

[c] Excludes participants and benefits under the Puerto Rico Nutrition Assistance Program after July 1, 1982.

Source: Social Security Administration (1994), *Annual Statistical Supplement to the Social Security Bulletin*, Washington, DC: US Government Printing Office, 346, Table 9.H1.

$2,000 ($3,000 if there is an elderly member). Adult household members must also fulfil work-related requirements ('workfare') imposed by state agencies. Some categories of persons—most college students, for example—are not eligible.

Food Stamps are an important addition to AFDC benefits, although it may be argued that, since the amount of Food Stamps received depends on income, including public assistance, they permit some of the states to continue with their low AFDC benefit levels. They also create significant, if lesser, improvement in SSI benefits. In December 1992, 10.4% of the US population, some 26.6 million persons, were receiving Food Stamps at an annual cost of $24 billion. Average per-person monthly benefits were $68.50. Since, at the end of 1992, the AFDC caseload totals were about 13.5 million and the SSI totals were about 5.1 million, the importance of the broader eligibility conditions for Food Stamps is apparent. The federal government meets all Food Stamp costs out of general revenues but states share administrative costs. A survey by the Department of Agriculture released in 1994 found that in the summer of 1993, Food Stamp recipients averaged 27.3 million in 11 million households; of those in the programme, 51.4% were children. The stamps constituted about one-fourth of a family's total income, or $170 (Select Committee on Children, Youth and Families, 1992b).

After steady growth in the 1970s, the programme remained on a caseload and cost plateau in the 1980s, indeed showed a small decline, and then exploded during the recent recession and rise in unemployment, stabilizing again in 1994. Take-up in the early 1990s was 50–60%. Some efforts have been made to understand the failure of even larger numbers to apply for Food Stamps, given the numbers of potential eligibles estimated in computer simulations.

The Food Stamp programme has maintained strong support and resisted efforts to convert the expenditures into increased cash benefits for the eligible, or 'cashing out'. Food Stamps meet the objectives of those who want to get money designated for food purchases to the poor and are not successful at reforming the cash assistance programmes; in this sense they are welcomed by needy recipients. Some research evidence exists to indicate that 'cashing out' cuts the amount and nutritional value of the food actually purchased, though it reduces administrative costs as well as social stigma. Food Stamps would also appear to satisfy those conservatives not prepared to trust the poor with too much cash ('they'll use it for liquor and tobacco'), but who know that the hungry must be fed. And the programme has been favoured by the political alliance of convenience between those who would feed the poor and farmers who want to dispose of their surplus or who simply appreciate the enlarged market. Food Stamps are a cash-equivalent supplement to other inadequate income transfers and—as suggested above—in some sense a federally-administered, national income guarantee.

By mid-1996 the Food Stamp caseload was down to 25.6 million, in part reflecting the decline in the AFDC caseload. The legislation that abolished AFDC made some families ineligible and decreased grants to others, resulting in some budgetary savings. There is no clear policy message in these cuts to what had been viewed as the ultimate safety net.

CONCLUSION

The United States has an episodically, incrementally developed system of family benefits in the tax and cash transfer systems. The social insurance system most resembles that of other countries, protecting spouses and dependent children against standard risks, reflecting traditional family obligations, and, since the 1960s, increasingly conscious of gender-equity concerns. The tax system's responsiveness to families is limited, in the sense that dependency burdens have only modest attention; but it has played an increasingly important role in the income transfer system since the 1980s. During these same years the poor have been largely spared income tax burdens, though not the social insurance payroll tax. An EITC offers an income supplement to the 'working poor', part of an effort to decrease the need for social assistance and to 'make work pay'.

Begun as a pension for widows, social assistance for single mothers and children has developed to meet a demographic trend, the increased number of lone-mother families. At the very moment that the civil rights movement and the War on Poverty led to its broader availability in the 1960s, however, the large-scale entry of married mothers into the paid work-force (paralleled by the growing number of unmarried mothers claiming AFDC) initiated a gradual shift in emphasis from AFDC as a programme of income support for at-home mothers to AFDC as a transitional programme of aid during job search and training. The programme has a strong aura of stigma, and real benefit levels have been substantially eroded since 1970. As we write, measures to revert federal support for poor children and their families to pre-1935 state responsibility, end entitlements, and punish unwed adolescent and other single mothers (in the name of morality, family values, and an emphasis on work) are about to be implemented as the result of 1996 legislation.

4

Families and Social Services

Responsiveness to family change requires more than attention to income, workplace adaptations, and family law. It also requires a wider range of supports for improved quality of life (health care, child care, and housing) and special help for families and children with special needs (Supplemental Security Income, child welfare, and nutrition). The programmes grouped in this chapter make little claim for coherence, but they do constitute a significant and distinctive component of family policy. Historically, these programmes were in the province of state and local government and private agencies but since the mid-1960s have increasingly involved the federal government, usually though not always working through or sharing with the lower tiers.

Despite its pioneering role in public education, the US is a laggard in providing public support for early-childhood care and preschool education. The US is a laggard as well in health care and in its response to the housing needs of lower-income families. Personal social services[8] are well developed, perhaps overdeveloped in a country that does less with regard to child-related income transfers and tends to believe that much poverty and many family difficulties are to be attributed to personal defects that must be remedied. Child nutrition programmes provide needed help, avoiding what some regard as potential parental misuse of resources if 'cashed out', and efficiently contribute to child well-being where the specific nutritional content is important.

CHILD-CARE POLICIES AND PROGRAMMES

Child-care services are here defined as including all types of out-of-home, non-relative care of children under compulsory school age whether in schools, centres, or homes. In the US, the major functions of child-care services are providing care for the children of welfare-dependent and low-income mothers so as to facilitate movement off social or public assistance and into the work-force; providing care for the children of working mothers generally; providing compensatory education and socialization experiences for deprived and disadvantaged children; and providing an opportunity for early-childhood education and development. Over time, federal policies have emphasized one or another of these goals.

Most child-care developments occur at the state and local governmental levels. Unfortunately, state-level data are largely unavailable, so we are dependent on the population census and occasional special surveys for data about users and coverage. Whereas the federal government covers only 8% of expenditures for public education, it is the major public funder of child care. However, it is hard to draw the total and precise picture of federal financial assistance for child care, and supply, usage, and expenditure data integrating pre-primary school programmes with social welfare child care are simply not available in systematic fashion over time.

The major federal child-care policies, most of which date from the 1960s, stress the financing of child care rather than direct public provision. They include funding for child care for Aid to Families with Dependent Children (AFDC) beneficiaries and low-income working families, compensatory education programmes, and child-care tax credits which primarily benefit the middle and upper classes. State and local government funding goes toward some child-care services and most pre-primary education. A large part of child care is a market service and as such is heavily paid for by parents themselves—and to some extent by the tax credits.

What follows is a brief history of federal child-care policies and programmes in the US focused primarily on the years since 1960, including a brief mention of coverage and expenditures (Kamerman and Kahn, 1976; Kahn and Kamerman, 1988; Gettis and Vinovskis, 1992; Vinovskis, 1983; Cahan, 1989).

Child-care services began in the US in the 1820s as 'infant schools': early-childhood education programmes designed on the one hand to provide moral improvement to poor city children, and on the other, to offer early educational opportunities to the very young children of affluent families. This split focus launched a two-tiered pattern of development which has continued into the present, modified only to the extent that in recent years the needs of working mothers have played a growing role in shaping the child-care system and that new research findings have attenuated public fears about the consequences of non-parental care.

Except for some day nurseries for the children of working mothers following the Civil War, the first federal child-care initiatives occurred during the Great Depression of the 1930s with the establishment of nursery schools for two- to five-year-olds under the auspices of the Works Progress Administration (WPA). Concern for the children of working mothers emerged again in the 1940s with the rapid growth in the numbers of employed mothers during World War II. The Lanham Act was passed by Congress in 1942 to provide funding for the establishment of day-care centres in areas where war industry was concentrated. At the end of the war most of these centres were closed: public ideology supported the idea that women belonged at home, where their children were best cared for, and their jobs were needed by returning, discharged soldiers.

Beginning in the 1960s a confluence of dramatic demographic and social changes, in particular an explosion in the rates of labour force entry for mothers, led to the first significant sustained expansion of child-care services as a result of federal policies. The two-tiered pattern of social welfare day care for the poor and preschool nursery education for the middle class continued, but findings from new research on child development led to the recognition that early-childhood education can markedly enhance children's subsequent learning abilities. As a consequence, President Lyndon Johnson's War on Poverty included early-childhood education as an important strategy for attacking poverty by compensating for early deprivation.

Head Start was launched in 1965 with the objective of bringing poor children the educational advantages of good nursery school education, supplemented by other essential social services such as health care and counselling. In effect, Head Start established a comprehensive compensatory education programme for poor children. But because it was largely a part-day programme and demanded heavy parental participation, it did not really answer the child-care needs of poor working parents. Nor, because of limitations in funding, did it reach more than a small proportion of all poor children.

During these same years federal support of day-care centres continued to increase as part of the initial efforts to reduce welfare use and increase the employability of AFDC mothers. Amendments to the Social Security Act in 1962 and 1967 provided for limited federal matching funds to states for the development of licensed day-care centres to serve current and potential welfare beneficiaries. At the initiative of parents and local governments, attendance of children aged three to five in private nursery schools and public pre-primary programmes increased dramatically from 3.2 million children in 1964 to 4.2 million in 1973 (Kamerman and Kahn, 1976).

The 1970s saw intense debates about the federal role in expanding child-care services: whether the federal government should have such a role and indeed, whether group child care was a good idea. In 1971 a comprehensive national child development programme was enacted by the Congress but vetoed by President Richard Nixon, whose veto message reflected the conservatives' fears that subsidized child care was a move toward 'communalizing' child-rearing and would undermine parental authority. A second attempt at enacting such a programme was made in 1975 but failed to achieve even Congressional support. However, funding for social welfare child care was increased when Title XX of the Social Security Act was enacted in 1975, adding significantly to the available social services funds that states could spend on child care for the children of low-income working mothers or children in families with problems, among other service options. A tax credit for all working families with children was established in the mid-1970s, creating for the first time a new and significant form of federal child-care financial assistance to middle- and upper-income working families. In providing this 'demand subsidy', the federal government in effect avoided taking a position on the type of care used, leaving it up to parents to choose. At the same time, however, it showed its acceptance of market care by subsidizing it. By the mid-1980s, this was the single largest federal child-care expenditure, important mostly to the tax-paying middle class. In the early 1990s, significant federal child-care legislation was enacted, targeted largely at children from low-income working families; by the middle of the decade, however, that legislation was threatened.

In short, the federal role in child care increased steadily between the mid-1960s and early 1990s. It has tended to focus on three components of child care: (1)

compensatory early-childhood education (Head Start), which grew significantly in the 1980s and early 1990s; (2) child care for low-income and AFDC beneficiaries which was increasingly intended to facilitate work by these women; it also emerged during the 1960s and grew through the end of the 1980s up to 1990; and (3) child care for the children of working parents, which emerged in the mid-1970s in the form of a tax credit and was increased in the mid-1980s.

Pre-primary education for three- to five-year-olds increased as well under state and local government initiatives. Both direct and indirect federal child-care subsidies increased during these years, as did the numbers of child-care places and of young children in out-of-home child care of all types. There is full coverage for the five-year-olds and about 75% coverage for the four-year-olds, but only about one-third of the three-year-olds have places in child care, and most are part-day. Despite significant increases in the last decade, infant and toddler care remains scarce in relation to the proportion of children this age with working mothers.

Despite the dramatic growth in labour force participation rates of women with young children and the significant rise in full-time, year-round work by mothers, the child-care public policy response has been very limited at best. The two major streams of programme growth, pre-primary school education and social services, continue, now formally supported by federal policy. The two federal policies laid down in the 1960s and 1970s continue now as well: direct financial support for child-care services for children in poor, dependent, deprived, dysfunctional families; and indirect financial support (through the tax system) of private for-profit and non-profit care. The former is the primary current focus of federal policy and sustains the historical preference for selective rather than universal programmes. The latter is driven primarily by the needs and preferences of middle-class parents in the labour force, for whom child care is a necessity if they are to work, and those who are increasingly convinced that a group educational and socialization experience is essential if their children are to develop well and be adequately prepared for primary school.

US child-care policy reflects the historical preference for market or voluntary solutions rather than public provision. State responsibility for education has made the growth of pre-primary school programmes haphazard and *ad hoc*, while the limited development of infant and toddler care reflects continued ambivalence on the part of the public regarding women's roles at home and in the workplace. The sum total is a non-system of very uneven and often poor quality, part-day service where full-day coverage is needed, inadequate provision for infants and toddlers, and no public commitment to improving the system.

Table 17 attempts to present overall national child-care expenditures. It concludes that the total of direct expenditure in 1993 was $6.2 billion (about one-tenth of 1% of GDP), in effect almost triple pre-1990 federal expenditures. The tax credit adds another $2.4 billion, and the total constitutes $8.6 billion, or 0.14 of 1% of GDP. Despite this significant growth, funding is nowhere near sufficient to provide coverage comparable to what exists in many European countries.

TABLE 17. Federal expenditures for child care, United States,
fiscal years 1980, 1986, 1990, 1993 (current $)

Programmes	Expenditures in million $			
	1980	1986	1990	1993
Title XX (SSBG)	600[a]	387[a]	400	400
Head Start	766[b]	1,040	1,200	2,776
AFDC (Title IV–A; including transitional benefits in 1993)	120[c]	35	350	596
Child Care Food Program	239[a]	501[a]	670	1,200
Title IV–C (WIN)	115[d]	(165)[e]	216[a]	NA
Child Care Development Block Grant	...	...	...	893
At-risk child care	...	...	...	308
ARC (Appalachian Regional Commission) child development	11[b]	1	732[b]	NA
Employer-provided child care	...	110[c]	32[f]	32[f]
Dependent Care Tax Credit	956[a]	3,410[a]	2,800	2,450
Total	*2,807*	*5,649*	*6,370*	*8,655*
Total without tax credit	1,851	2,239	3,570	6,205

[a] ACYF estimate provided by Patricia Divine Hawkins.   [b] J. Gasper (1984), testimony, in
Child Care: Beginning a National Initiative, Washington, DC: Government Printing Office.
[c] E. Duval et al., 'AFDC: Characteristics of Recipients in 1979', *Social Security Bulletin* 45(4): 4–19.
[d] Congressional Budget Office (CBO).   [e] Estimated.   [f] CBO, based on Joint Tax Committee estimates.

Source: Congressional Research Service and *The Green Book*.

MATERNAL AND CHILD HEALTH CARE

National health insurance or a health service is one of the two major components missing from the US welfare state, the other being family allowances. A major effort at enacting national health insurance was proposed, debated, and rejected during the first half of the Clinton Administration. It is not clear at this writing whether any changes will be enacted in the near future. Nonetheless, the federal government does play a significant role in health care.

The federal role in child health services began in 1921 with the Maternity and Infancy (Sheppard–Towner) Act, a state/federal partnership designed to provide services to children and pregnant women. This legislation was passed at the end of a reform era in which women played a major national leadership role and children's issues were emphasized. The programme was allowed to die in 1929 when the legislation was not re-authorized, but its principles were incorporated into the second federal initiative, Title V of the 1935 Social Security Act, Maternal and Child Health and Crippled Children's Services (MCH). This legislation established one of the three pillars on which child health care still stands: maternal and child health services; health assistance/health care for the poor; and the tax expenditure subsidy of health insurance for the employed.

Title V of the Social Security Act is the only federal programme concerned exclusively with the health of mothers and children (Klerman, 1991). It provides federal support to the states to enhance their ability to 'promote, improve, and deliver' maternal and child health care and handicapped children's services, particularly in rural and poor areas. The Act's goal was to build a maternal and child health care delivery system. It was enacted in part to respond to the dramatic rise in infant mortality rates that occurred following the demise of Sheppard–Towner and the onset of the Great Depression. From its inception the programme was universal, requiring no means test for service users, although targeting its services primarily at low-income women and children and those with limited access to health care. At a time when health insurance was not available to ordinary families, Title V represented the only source of public funding for health care for many children.

Except for a modest and temporary programme established during World War II, no significant new federal child health legislation was enacted until the mid-1960s. However, federal developments that encouraged employers to provide private health insurance as an employee benefit, although not specifically addressed to children, nevertheless had important consequences for children's access to health care. Health insurance benefits provided by employers were defined as a tax-free benefit by the Internal Revenue Service in 1939. The number of employers providing such benefits increased rapidly over the next three decades as a result of two other important developments: (1) federal policy permitted labour/management bargaining for employee benefits while maintaining a wage freeze during World War II and again during the Korean War; and (2) the National Labor Relations Board ruled in 1947 that benefits could be included as a collective bargaining issue. As a result, between 1950 and 1970 health insurance coverage for workers and their dependants increased dramatically: by the mid-1970s almost 80% of children under age 18 were covered under private health insurance (about two-thirds under workplace plans). During the 1980s, however, this proportion declined, and by 1991 less than 70% of children were covered under private health insurance (US Bureau of the Census, 1992). This continuing decline was one of the factors that led to the pressure for health care reform in the 1990s. It reflected the decline of unionization and the high cost of health insurance for employers and for those without employer coverage.

In the 1960s, the decade of the War on Poverty and the Great Society programmes, the federal role in child health care increased greatly. Title V was expanded, neighbourhood health centres were established in poor communities, and, of particular importance, in 1965 Medicaid was enacted as Title XIX of the Social Security Act to provide health assistance for the poor. Although it, too, was not specifically designed as a programme for children, Medicaid rapidly became the largest single public medical programme for children and their families and soon emerged as the third leg on which the child health care delivery system was to stand, clearly much stronger than Title V.

Financed in the same way as AFDC, with the federal contribution ranging from 50% to 83%, with a state's reimbursement inversely related to the state's per capita income, Medicaid covers all AFDC, AFDC-eligible, and Supplemental Security Income (SSI) beneficiaries as well as the 'medically needy' in some states. 'Medically needy' are the non-AFDC or SSI beneficiaries whose income falls below a particular state-determined level and who have high medical expenses. Medicaid is, in effect, 50 different programmes, with eligibility varying from state to state. Nonetheless, it pays for comprehensive medical care in a state-defined programme with some federal mandates.

Initially, Medicaid was expected to provide access to health care for all poor children. This did not occur because it was left to the states (which must share costs) to determine eligibility levels, and these may be well below the poverty line. Not all poor children were—or are—in AFDC families or within the medically-needy category as defined by states; as a result, only about half of all poor children were covered between 1979 and 1988, as compared with 60% in 1990, including 70.5% of those under age 6, following significant expansion of Medicaid coverage for poor children in the late 1980s. This last figure is a higher portion of poor children than the percentage covered under AFDC.

In 1967, the Early and Periodic Screening, Diagnosis, and Treatment (EPSDT) programme was enacted in amendments to both Title V and to Medicaid, requiring states to provide preventive health services for poor children under age 21. For a variety of reasons the law was not implemented until 1973, when only half the states implemented it.

The 1960s set the pattern for the federal role in maternal and child health policy. The stress was to be on increasing access to health care for poor and disadvantaged children, largely by financing health care for poor children and their families and leaving the development of a delivery system to the states. Title V expanded its scope, received increased funds, and was influential at the state level, but at no point did it create a state-wide, much less national, maternal and child health delivery system. Medicaid, an entitlement programme with seemingly open-ended funding, expanded dramatically and soon emerged as the dominant programme. The 'welfare' philosophy of Medicaid prevailed over the universal philosophy of maternal and child health.

All these developments were solidified in the 1970s, only to be confronted with resource constraints followed by political attacks in the 1980s. In 1981, Title V was folded into the Maternal and Child Health Block Grant (MCHBG) with eight other small, categorical child health programmes. The goals of the MCHBG continued the mission of the original Title V; however, funding was cut substantially and Medicaid eligibility was curtailed for AFDC beneficiaries. In 1987, funding in constant dollars was still below 1970s levels.

By the middle of the 1980s, however, policy was reversed: sub-standard health performance, as seen in comparisons between child health indicators in the US and poorer, less-developed countries, was widely publicized—as were data about the cost-effectiveness of prevention. In reaction, Congress enacted a series of expan-

TABLE 18. Medicaid coverage of poor children under age 18,
United States, 1979–1992*

Year	Number of poor children (in 1,000)	Poor children with Medicaid coverage	
		in 1,000	%
1979	10,111	4,907	48.5
1980	11,764	5,525	47.0
1985	13,010	6,569	50.5
1988	12,455	6,514	52.3
1990	13,900	8,500	61.2
1992	14,617	9,877	67.6

* Table based on one prepared by Congressional Research Service. These estimates of Medicaid coverage of poor children are based on Current Population Survey data collected annually by the Bureau of the Census. Poverty status is based on total cash income, including transfer income. Medicaid eligibility is based on income prior to receipt of transfers. The CPS totals do not include children in institutions.

Source: Current Population Survey (CPS), Annual March Income Supplements. Committee on Ways and Means, US House of Representatives (1991, 1992, 1994), *The Green Book: Overview of Entitlement Programs,* Washington, DC: Government Printing Office.

sions in Medicaid eligibility. Beginning in 1986, states have been required to cover pregnant women and children under age six with family incomes less than 133% of poverty. Since July 1991, states have been required to cover all children under age 19 who were born after 30 September 1983 and whose family income is below the poverty threshold. This means that by the year 2002 all poor children aged 18 and younger would be covered under Medicaid. States were also permitted to cover children under age one and pregnant women in families with incomes between 133% and 185% of the poverty level. Administrative directives mandated treatment of conditions detected in the EPSDT even where it is not part of a state's usual treatment offerings. Thus while the MCHBG became significantly less important and certainly never assumed its expected leadership role, Medicaid has become increasingly important as a child health service. And despite its curtailment in the 1980s, employer-provided health insurance remained very important.

Over 90% of all children under age 18 were covered by some kind of health insurance in 1991: 70% by private insurance, 20% by Medicaid, and 4% by a federal health plan covering civilian dependants of the military. Nonetheless, some of the coverage is for very limited service.

One result of US federal child health policy is the lack of a real, universally-available maternal and child health care system as found in many industrial societies. By 1990, 6% of pregnant women were receiving either late or no prenatal care, down from 8% in 1970; 7.3% of live births were low-birthweight babies, down only slightly from 1960 and 1970 rates; infant mortality rates in 1993 were 8.4 per 1,000, down significantly from 26 in 1960 and 20 in 1970, but still far higher than in 21 other industrialized countries; and one-third of all children under age two were still not immunized against the standard childhood diseases, whereas most industrial countries have 85–90% coverage.

Family planning services, including information, advice, and contraceptives, are critical to the health and well-being of women and children and their families. The first significant federal family planning initiatives were enacted in the mid-1960s, supplemented by several significant Supreme Court decisions. The major federal funding streams for these services include Titles V (MCH) and XX (Social Services) of the Social Security Act and Title X of the Public Health Act, which provide funds for state governments to allocate for family planning services, and Title XIX (Medicaid) of the Social Security Act, which provides funds to reimburse providers for services to Medicaid-eligible clients. Since 1980, Public Health, MCH, and Social Services funds have been curtailed, though Medicaid funding (open-ended entitlement funding) has increased significantly. Recent federal policies have also increased pregnant women's access to prenatal care but severely curtailed access to family planning services and abortion. As in the case of AFDC, however, the Medicaid entitlement could end in 1996, to be replaced by block grants to the states, involving significant cuts and few, if any, service mandates.

HOUSING

Although the federal government has periodically undertaken what were conceived of as major initiatives in housing, including building public housing and supporting some 'new towns', it has never made an explicit and systematic large-scale housing effort on behalf of families and children. The most important federal housing policy, which began after World War II, was income tax concessions for interest on home mortgages and for local real estate taxes, resulting in federal subsidization of home-ownership and the large-scale development of suburbs. The ensuing process has changed the character of urban America, contributing to the deterioration of the inner city and to the development of racial and ethnic ghettos. This housing policy also did much to shape a pattern of suburban middle-class family life which began to change only in the 1970s with the large-scale entry of mothers of young children into the labour force. This series of tax concessions was and continues to be the main manifestation of a family orientation in housing policy. Since the relevant data are compiled as tax expenditure reports, it is not possible to disaggregate the portion assignable to families with children. And since tax expenditures for mortgage payments and real estate taxes are available to people of all ages, existing data offer no basis for an estimate relevant to families and children.

Apart from tax expenditures available to potential consumers, the instruments used in public housing policy since World War II have included: subsidies for builders or owners to reduce land costs, subsidies to owners to reduce rental costs, housing allowances or vouchers for tenants, and favourable tax treatment of investment losses. To suggest the limited investment in housing, however, we note that in 1987, when 71% of the poor received Food Stamps and 42% were covered by Medicaid, only 29% of renter households with incomes below the poverty line either lived in public housing or received some kind of federal, state, or local housing subsidy. Despite encouraging research results in the 1970s and favourable views of housing allowances for low-income renters, the scale of the federal programme depends on annual appropriations and remains very modest. There has been no significant advocacy of a housing allowance entitlement similar to what is known in such countries as Sweden, France, or Britain.

As of 1991, of $113 billion in federal housing benefits annually, 69% went to *home-owners*, 14% went for subsidized rental housing for the poor, and 1.8% went for public housing. Those in the top quintile of the income distribution received 58% of all benefits, and those in the lowest quintile received 13%.

The dominance of the market in a field in which economic trends leave many below-average earners unable to command decent housing at market prices leaves a policy gap that exacts a toll on families and children, though the specifics are unknown. Homelessness, doubling-up among families in single-family residences, excessive expenditures on housing, and living in substandard housing are all part of the price paid.

POLICIES FOR FAMILIES AND CHILDREN WITH SPECIAL NEEDS

In this section, we begin with an income transfer programme, Supplemental Security Income, insofar as it covers children with disabilities. We then turn to the major special social service supports for children with handicaps and those with special needs. Last, we examine programmes and funding streams covering social services for troubled families and children, especially the major child welfare services under the Social Security Act and the more general social service funds available for or categorically assigned to child welfare. The last two sections demonstrate that if the United States lags behind comparable nations with regard to income transfers for families with children, health care, and child care, it does make a major investment in treatment-orientated services. This situation is consistent with an ethic that worries about dependency and work motivation with regard to general social assistance for the able-bodied, but cares about people who need personal help and wants to control certain types of deviance. Individualized rather than structural interventions are preferred—since the ethic also tends to be biased toward psychological and moral definitions of family and personal problems.

Supplemental Security Income

Almost by chance, the Supplemental Security Income (SSI) programme, administered by the federal government, offers unstigmatized social assistance to children with handicaps, including infants, toddlers, preschoolers, and school-aged children. SSI was not conceived as a programme for children or for families with children. Instead, it was a federalization and consolidation, effective in 1974, of state-operated, means-tested programmes known as Old Age Assistance, Aid to the Blind, and Aid to the Permanently and Totally Disabled (APTD). Except for the last, these programmes were the counterparts of AFDC in the 1935 Social Security Act and followed a similar financing (federal/state matching) and administrative pattern (state/local delivery), but provided somewhat more generous grants. Similar federalization would have cured some of the very same problems that existed in AFDC, but AFDC, an unpopular programme, was not included.

The SSI programme established a uniform national eligibility standard, a single (and less onerous) asset test, and uniform, indexed national benefits for individuals and couples. States already providing higher benefits were required to maintain current efforts via supplementation of the federal grants and could add further supplements in the future. The programme is administered by the Social Security Administration, a fact which in itself decreased stigma associated with predecessor programmes.

Children entered SSI through incorporation of APTD, the last categorical assistance programme added to the Social Security Act (1950). Although many of the state APTD programmes had not covered children, the House of Representatives Committee on Ways and Means included them specifically in the course of drafting SSI legislation because such children, when in low-income households, were 'certainly among the most disadvantaged of all Americans' (Trout and Mattson, 1984: 5). The result was an increasingly important means-tested programme providing income assistance to handicapped and disabled children. In most states, SSI offers entry to Medicaid as well.

Adjusting for inflation, the Social Security Administration annually sets a monthly SSI benefit rate for individuals at about 75% of the current poverty line (between 71% and 77% of the poverty line since 1974). In all but two states, SSI recipients receive Food Stamps, raising the benefits somewhat. SSI child recipients may not be included in the AFDC assistance unit, and their income and resources are not counted for AFDC income-eligibility purposes. AFDC eligibility workers at the state and local level give precedence to potential SSI eligibility since the federal government pays for SSI (except for possible state supplementation), and in most of the country, levels of benefits and allowable assets are higher than for AFDC.

Initially, the blind or disabled child was accepted for SSI only if he/she had an impairment of a type expected of a qualifying adult, and only modest numbers qualified. In a 1990 decision, the US Supreme Court determined that the Social Security Administration was improperly deciding eligibility of disabled children for the SSI programme (*Sullivan v. Zebley*). A child-specific functional assessment now being developed. As a result of more open access for new applicants and an ongoing review of cases rejected since 1980, the numbers of child beneficiaries exploded: the total SSI caseload, which began below 4 million in 1974 and was at 4.1 million in 1980, reached 4.8 million in 1990 and rose to 5.6 million recipients by early 1992, an all-time high. Children made up 9% of the total, or 527,000; by the end of 1994, the child total was 900,000.

The child component of SSI has become largely an income support programme for poor mentally-retarded and mentally-disordered children, those children with diseases of the nervous system, and children born with congenital abnormalities. By chance, SSI was in place to help meet financial needs of families with low-birthweight babies who would not have survived before recent advances in medical technology and services. When parents have inadequate or no health insurance these situations would create financial and emotional catastrophes but for the current SSI ruling that very low-birthweight babies automatically meet the definition of disability until they are at least a year old. If income and resources are limited, eligibility continues following the return home.

SSI thus fills an important income maintenance gap in the US system and, unlike AFDC, exemplifies federal assumption of the major economic burden. The coverage of disabled children, clearly a poor group, was a fortunate by-product of a reform targeted at adults. However, the story is not over yet: in a move to cut the federal budget, and in reaction to the use of SSI for large numbers of alcoholic and chemically-dependent adults, Congress began to tighten SSI rules in the late 1980s. The 1996 legislation that ended the AFDC entitlement also tightened eligibility rules for children (only medically-specified conditions will qualify as child disability, and functional assessments will cease) and for immigrants. The full effects on caseloads will be seen over the next few years, but more than 300,000 children could lose eligibility.

Social Services for Children with Special Needs

In 1975 Congress passed the Education of All Handicapped Children Act (P. L. 94–142), which specified that handicapped children aged five to 18 were to be assessed and offered 'free, appropriate' educational services, including development of an 'individualized educational program' with the involvement of their parents. The Act also specified that schools were to provide 'related services' to enable a child to benefit from special education. 'Handicapped' is defined as including both physical handicaps and severe emotional disturbance. The policy favours programmes in the 'least restrictive environment commensurate with the children's needs.' The programme is federally funded and has been implemented in a variety of ways; it usually involves a professional who uses varied resources to determine the child's needs and then co-ordinates the contributions of experts in making a service and treatment plan, with active parental participation. This or another professional integrates the implementation, often called 'case management'.

In 1986, new legislation guaranteed handicapped children aged three to five access to an educational programme (preschool), something not assured for non-handicapped three- to five-year-olds. In the words of the responsible Congressional committee, this same legislation also created 'a new federal discretionary program to assist states to develop and implement a program of early intervention services for handicapped infants, toddlers, and their families' (Part H of P. L. 99–457). In short, what is an educational commitment for the older children became a guarantee, at state discretion, of early intervention services (health, education, social services) to promote development.

The legislation now known as the Individuals With Disabilities Education Act (IDEA) is federally financed. In fiscal year 1992, it covered 4.6 million school-aged children and 372,000 preschoolers; the infant programme, still being phased in, served 194,000 children. Including discretionary grants of $240.8 million for research, training, education, and technical assistance, the expenditure was $2.7 billion. While there are as yet no comprehensive evaluations, both outstanding achievements and poor implementation have been reported.

Child Welfare Services

Child welfare services developed in the voluntary, non-profit sector in the nineteenth century, beginning with the creation of specialized children's residential institutions and followed in mid-century with the development of what was to become modern foster-home care. These approaches were supplemented by the appearance later in the century of child protective agencies to find and deal with neglect and abuse. Although the states were involved to some extent in financing, particularly of institutional care, this whole domain was regarded as more appropriate for philanthropy, churches, and localities. Much of this thinking persists today despite the considerable expansion of state financing and involvement and, since the 1960s, of federal funding. In recent decades, the federal government has begun to have a significant impact on policy as its portion of the funding burden has expanded and as national-level advocacy groups and Congressional committees have successfully targeted the federal government and helped shape its policy. The overall trend has been from institutional provision to foster family care and now, increasingly, to an emphasis on 'preventive' care provided to children and families in their own homes.

The first federal child welfare legislation was a title of the 1935 Social Security Act which provided modest funding to the states for social services; earlier, most funding was state and voluntary. The modern pattern began in the 1960s when the federal government began to reimburse states for part of the costs of foster care services, the core of child welfare. Washington set a new child welfare philosophy under 1980 federal legislation which guides much of the programme emphasis today: a focus on protecting and re-establishing the child's family in order to avoid foster care.

Another development created a separate programme initiative, which, while very modestly funded, was to have a major impact on all of child welfare: federal child abuse legislation. While child protective programmes had begun a century earlier, in the 1970s suggestions that the traditional child welfare apparatus was missing many serious cases of physical abuse of children led to new federal legislation, many new programmes, and what may be described as a social movement. While mainstream child welfare programmes had started converting to an effort to protect or restore the child's home or to get him/her into a new home quickly, the child abuse programme emphasized protection of children by removing them from dangerous homes quickly. The tension between these two goals has characterized the child welfare policy debate for the past two decades.

The story of child welfare policy and programmes is complex, but the direction is clear: despite much talk about prevention, child welfare remains a foster care programme, responding to dependency, neglect, abuse, and out-of-control behaviour as it did in the nineteenth century. It was then and is today essentially a state, local, and voluntary-sector effort. Nonetheless, the states no longer carry the burden alone. The current federal role began modestly in 1935 with the passage of the Social Security Act and expanded considerably in the 1960s as a result of Social Security Act amendments intended to protect some children, especially minority children, on the AFDC rolls.

In the 1970s, in response to an explosion of cases and evidence that children were being 'lost in the system', child welfare professionals, advocates, public officials, media attention, Congressional hearings, and leadership initiatives in some states urged the federal government to make funding available for prevention and permanent adoption services as well as foster care. The federal government joined the campaign in 1980 and soon led it, hoping to decrease foster care and maintain children in their own homes. As a result, the Adoption Assistance and Child Welfare Act was enacted in 1980 (P. L. 96–272), which (with subsequent amendments) defines current policy and funding streams. 'Permanency planning' expresses the philosophy. The legislation provides payments to people who adopt a child with special needs involving high medical costs, special tutoring or rehabilitation, etc. Low-income parents may have their adoption subsidized through federal payments. Subsequent amendments also created and later expanded a transition programme, 'independent living', to help children aged 16 and over move out of foster care.

All of these efforts coincided with a new explosion of reported child abuse and a variety of social problems including crack cocaine. Foster care declined only briefly since 1980 and has now increased. Federal financial and policy involvement today is considerable; the states are still the major child welfare funders, but Washington is fast catching up: 40% of the foster care load, the federal part, is from AFDC families.

Legislation enacted in 1993 has added new federal funds and funding flexibility to encourage states to develop new family preservation programmes that avoid child placement and provide support to families before they experience serious difficulties. The states, in turn, will work through localities and the voluntary sector. But even these programmes are targeted at problem populations and problem areas: US child welfare does not fund universal programmes or basic prevention. To the extent that such programmes exist, they are funded and operated by the voluntary sector.

Public child welfare expenditure growth was modest until the 1960s; 90% came from states and localities and only 10% was federal. From 1965 to 1980, federal child welfare payments under the Social Security Act grew from $354.3 million in 1965, to $585.3 million in 1970, to $800 million in 1980. Beginning in 1981, reporting of total expenditures was no longer required, the result of the Reagan Administration's dismantling of the federal child welfare statistical system. Since then, a voluntary reporting system estimates that the federal share of all child welfare and foster care costs in 1990 was 43%, and the total federal and state cost was $3.5 billion (Committee on Ways and Means, 1993).

National foster care caseload totals were in the 300,000 range in the 1960s. Rapid growth appeared in the late 1980s with increasing publicity of and concern over physical and sexual abuse of children and the consequences of an epidemic of crack cocaine. Close to 630,000 children are estimated to have been served by the system in 1991. Even larger numbers received community-based child welfare and adoption services (*VCIS Research Notes*, 1993). The estimated foster care ratios grew from about 3.9 per 1,000 children in 1962 to 5.9 per 1,000 in 1990.

While the majority of children in foster care is white, black and Hispanic children are by far disproportionately represented. Almost half of all children are placed for 'protection', almost a quarter because of parental condition or absence, and over 10% as delinquent or status offenders (displaying uncontrollable behaviour that is not delinquency). Most foster care children (71.4%) are in foster care homes or non-finalized adoptive homes, and 18.6% are in group homes, residential treatment, or emergency shelter. The pressure for 'permanency' creates many short-term placements (most under two years), considerable 'churning' (i.e., leaving foster care, only to return prematurely), and a core group of long-termers who eventually 'age-out'. The high placement rates for infants and toddlers and the tendency for these children to remain in placement longer, in contrast to the earlier predominance of older children in the caseloads, have also created alarm.

To conclude, we mention briefly the Social Services Block Grant (SSBG), the other major funding stream for child welfare and related social services. The SSBG was originally enacted in 1974 as Title XX of the Social Security Act. Before this, social services funds had been a by-product of the funding for administration of the categorical public (social) assistance programmes. Title XX was the first social services title of the Social Security Act; it encompassed an effort to encourage state planning and creation of a social services infrastructure, a requirement for public participation in the planning at the state and local levels, and a broad view of social services, all with special attention to children and the elderly.

A significant federal appropriation of $2.5 billion was to be divided among the states in accord with population sizes. These funds were significantly reduced in 1981 when the Reagan Administration converted Title XX to the SSBG with few mandates to the states, and without planning, participation, or reporting requirements. Funding was cut and declined further in real value between 1975 and 1990. Nonetheless, about half of these funds went for children's services, still a significant amount.

The lack of any federal data collection except for lists about what states said they intended to do in the 'pre-expenditure' periods leaves only lists of categorical services provided. There are no data on what actually was done, on what scale, and for whom. A variety of other very modest, categorical grant-in-aid federal programmes is also part of this picture.

Child Nutrition Programmes

The child nutrition programmes trace their origins to the Great Depression and an Agricultural Adjustment Act intended to assist a depressed farm economy through government purchase of surpluses. In conjunction with federal, state, and local programmes, this surplus was channelled to relief programmes for families and to schools and related agencies. Later, with still more surplus available, what became the National School Lunch Program began. School districts and health officials added their political support to that of the farm lobbies.

The increased awareness of hunger early in the Kennedy Administration found a receptive attitude in the agricultural sector towards 'programs specifically directed to disadvantaged groups'. The advocacy movement reflected a growing coalition of school interests and anti-poverty and anti-hunger groups (Hayes, 1982: 16). Congressional support grew further after 1967–68 hunger exposés. What began as the Great Society's Child Nutrition Act of 1966 grew into programmes providing school breakfasts and improved school lunches, the Special Supplemental Food Program for Women, Infants, and Children (WIC), and modified commodity, school milk, and summer food programmes. It also influenced the evolution of the Food Stamp Program. But whereas the other child nutrition programmes were completely dominated by the preference to aid the needy through 'in-kind' benefits or services, Food Stamps, as we have seen, became cash-equivalent vouchers at a moment when the civil rights movement and the anti-poverty campaign converged to shift public sentiments somewhat and the farm surplus lobby joined the urban poverty bloc in an effective Congressional coalition.

Programmes suffered in the Reagan era as financial support was curtailed and participation decreased. A variety of other small federal programmes provides nutritional assistance to children as well. The only one of real significance, the WIC programme, was created in the midst of the War on Poverty as a component of the Child Nutrition Act of 1966. Responding to concerns about hunger and the publicized medical research about the effects of malnutrition on foetal and infant development, the Johnson Administration inaugurated a small supplemental food programme. Despite mixed evidence of effectiveness, popular support grew steadily. Like Head Start, WIC is protected as 'obviously' beneficial by the Congress and by a strong public constituency.

The programme is designed to provide nutritious supplemental foods to pregnant and postpartum women, infants, and children through age four who are deemed to have inadequate income and to be at 'nutritional risk'. Beneficiaries receive monthly food packages or vouchers that may be used in retail stores for actual purchase of specific food items. Income standards for eligibility are set at 185% of the federal poverty line.

In 1991, the annual cost per participant was $497, of which 24% was for administration. WIC is federally funded and thus more attractive to states than AFDC and other programmes requiring state and/or locality fund-matching. Participation rates and expenditures have grown steadily. In 1991, about 56% of those eligible benefited from the programme, and 73% had incomes at or below the poverty level; thus, 'higher-income' eligibles were being rejected in the face of limited federal appropriations (Hayes, 1982; Committee on Ways and Means, 1993). Despite current proposals to cut various children's programmes, Congressional and public support of nutritional care for pregnant women, infants, and toddlers seems firm. Although school lunch and breakfast programmes were included in the proposed conservative 'reforms' early in 1995, many interests rallied behind them, and they will apparently survive with curtailed funding.

CONCLUSION

The programmes described in this chapter are not part of an integrated system and do not reflect a holistic strategy. Instead, they reflect problem-solving at various times and in different arenas and the particular problems having attracted specific constituencies and coalitions. Nonetheless, these are important programmes. Despite the political and value conflicts alluded to throughout this chapter, the American welfare state has responded incrementally to child and family issues. This response is far from universal and does not even cover all poor families with children in need. Poverty, handicap, and personal problems are the major triggers for action; family structure *per se* does not occasion programmes—as in the instance of single parenthood, for example. But child-care developments do reflect some response to changing gender roles.

5

The Politics and Institutionalization
of Family Policy

It is no surprise that a country with the belief systems and political tendencies listed in the historical introduction has not developed a holistic and national family policy. The doctrine of separation of Church and State and the strong commitments to states' rights, individualism, voluntarism, and family privacy have precluded contrary initiatives. Presidents, leaders in all walks of life, and citizens responding to public opinion polls routinely and fluently affirm that the family is the 'cornerstone of society' but—with few exceptions and with regard to most circumstances—do not advocate that it be interfered with or even strongly supported if that might create the possibility of interference.

Government *per se* remained a secondary actor in US social welfare until well into the twentieth century. The states were involved first in the nineteenth century. Only after the 1935 Social Security Act did the federal government become a major provider of cash benefits and a facilitator and partial funder of services at the state level. The real expansion of the federal government's social role came only relatively recently with the Great Society programmes of the 1960s and 1970s.

As documented in the earlier chapters, specific needs have led to some public responses to some families, and some actions taken by government in reaction to varied interests and concerns have had clear, if not necessarily intended, impact on families. Although many of these concerns involve policies relegated to the states, we also have seen a tendency in state law toward convergence, described in earlier chapters. None of this negates one American scholar's view of the process:

Characteristically the American reformer has not attacked the American resistance to government head-on. He justifies particular actions of government by pointing to particular needs and builds piece by piece a welfare state without trying to build a theoretical underpinning about the relationship of human beings and the potential role of government.

Despite all of this . . . Americans have shown themselves able to do more for social justice than their language and heritage might suggest (Miller, 1977: 25).

In concluding, similarly, at about the same time as Miller that the United States does not have an explicit national family policy, we underscored the existence of what we characterized as *implicit* family policy and significant—if not systematically integrated or comprehensive—family *policies* (Kamerman and Kahn, 1978). Both Steiner (1976) and Grubb and Lazerson (1982) add the insight that, despite a continued stress on the privacy of the family, Americans have a strong sense of the need to maintain public responsibility for families in crisis and especially to care for children and assume responsibility for their development when parents cannot. Finally, specific initiatives or issues have at times placed the family at the centre of policy-making in a given field, employed the family as a vehicle for policy objectives, or made family well-being a criterion for social policy.

INTEREST GROUPS

The United States has never had family associations as known in a number of European countries, organizations that advocate for *all* families. The closest that the country has come to a nation-wide 'movement' on behalf of all women and children were the efforts of various women's groups to bring about child-orientated social reforms in the late nineteenth and early twentieth centuries (Skocpol, 1992; Rothman, 1978). They created support for the state mothers' pension laws and were active in shaping the first White House Conference on Children and the US Children's Bureau. By the 1920s, their energies were otherwise deployed after women gained the vote and presumably had access to mainstream politics.

Specialized interest group organizations—largely either problem-focused or client-group-focused—have played an important role in child and family policy developments, especially since World War II. Two of the major overviews of these developments (Steiner, 1976; Grubb and Lazerson, 1982) report on day care, child care, child nutrition programmes, child health, public education, youth policy, public assistance policy, and parent education. There are specialized analyses of other measures such as child abuse legislation (Nelson, 1984). Each of the accounts discusses leading interest groups, often including churches, relevant provider associations or professional membership groups, general 'social altruists' (Steiner's term), and—in some instances—major *ad hoc* or semi-permanent coalitions of organizations, parent-users, and unions. While such 'permanent' organizations as the National Catholic Welfare Conference or the Child Welfare League of America may be active on a number of issues, no major 'family policy' interest groups have maintained ongoing activity on the American scene in the period 1960–90.

In a society in which it is generally assumed that adequate parents provide their children with good schools, health care, child care, and recreation, interest group advocacy often focuses on adequate funding of programmes for the less advantaged or on creating programmes to deal effectively with specific problems, such as delinquency, abuse, neglect, or school failure. Interest groups are not always successful, however. For some twenty-five years, contending groups have attempted with increasing intensity but only modest success to get society on the national level to come to grips with a problem affecting large parts of the population: the need for adequate child-care resources to meet the needs of children with working parents. A similar effort on behalf of maternity/parental leaves took over a decade.

Much of the national income transfer debate is about Aid to Families with Dependent Children (AFDC), a programme largely for poor single parents and their children. Several active interest groups are advocating with regard to this programme, ranging from unions to professional associations to churches to the anti-poverty lobbies. Although recipient families did mobilize around 'welfare rights' in the 1960s, they have not constituted a significant voice in the last two decades. Most ordinary non-recipient families do not consider themselves involved. Much of the data for the debate come from scholars and think-tanks (see below) or are generated by Congressional hearings and investigative journalists.

In this environment it is possible to chronicle the activity, importance, and disappearance of interest groups, topic by topic, over the period 1960–90 (Steiner, 1976 and 1981; Grubb and Lazerson, 1982). Organizations focused on children's issues are among the most influential groups with a history of ongoing involvement. Playing an important but somewhat lesser role are women's organizations and the feminist movement, expert groups, trade unions, and religious groups.

The Child Welfare League of America, an association of voluntary and public social agencies active on behalf of child welfare services, has been a strong advocate for children since its founding in 1920. Its successes are based on appearance before Congressional committees and the ability to lobby the Congress with local-level social agency support.

Perhaps the most visible and effective advocate for poor and minority children is the nationally-recognized Children's Defense Fund (CDF), based in Washington, DC. Founded in 1973 as an offshoot of the Washington Research Project, with origins in the grassroots Mississippi Head Start Program of the War on Poverty era, the CDF is probably the most influential children's lobby in the country. Led by the very effective and charismatic Marion Edelman, who was trained as a lawyer, the CDF became visible nationally in the child-care debate of the 1970s. Since then it has worked on children's issues across the board, especially issues with great impact on poor and minority children. Over the years it has developed a strong grassroots constituency out of the tradition of Head Start parent participation; it has also won the respect and ongoing financial support of major foundations and corporations. The CDF has strong programmes of research, data collection, lobbying, regional and state organization, and public education. If any one organization has a right to credit for the important child-care legislation of 1990, it is the CDF, which organized and led a major coalition. Its current slogan urges that the country 'Leave No Child Behind', and it highlights child care, health, child nutrition, and teen pregnancy. It has developed close ties to the Democratic White House of President Clinton (but has criticized the President for waivering on basic principles) and has urged an active campaign to combat the various attacks on children's entitlements and related measures in the 1995–96 Republican legislative agenda known as the 'Contract With America'. It has not come out in favour of a family policy *per se*.

Although some of the more traditional women's groups have consistently played an important role in advocating children's issues, feminist organizations have entered the arena only recently. Feminism's main agenda since the 1960s has been equal opportunity, pay equity, equitable treatment under the social security and tax systems, and abortion rights; the movement's specifics and tactics have varied over the years. Only in the 1980s, as one branch of feminism adopted a broader pro-family agenda, did feminist groups, along with religious groups and social welfare organizations, become visible in the campaign for federal legislation for maternity/parental leaves and child care. In the 1990s some feminist groups began addressing policies affecting poor women and their children, especially single mothers.

What of the unions? During the period under consideration, 1960–90, unionism in the United States has been in decline, so that currently only a small minority of workers—about 11% of the private-sector labour force and about 15% overall—is organized. Labour's original view, gradually discarded by the 1930s, was that social benefits should come out of collective bargaining, not legislation. Currently more interested in legislation, labour must choose its priorities from a variety of issues. Such issues as child care and parental leaves were not visible to most union members until the Coalition of Labor Union Women was formed in the 1970s and more women became active in the ranks and even leadership of labour in the 1980s. Issues such as affirmative action, equal rights, and comparable worth dominated the trade union women's agenda until the 1980s when a 'family responsiveness' agenda—child care, flexible benefits and flextime, parental leaves, etc.—began to appear as well, though it was stressed only by a few unions with large female memberships. Some of these unions bargained successfully for workplace child-care programmes and maternity leaves. Where unions negotiated short-term disability insurance as part of the fringe benefits package, maternity leaves were insured as well after a 1978 amendment to the equal opportunity legislation. In general, however, while many nation-wide unions have been part of pro-child care and pro-parental leave coalitions, they have not been in the lead.

Industry has been split on the issue, with large companies generally willing to bargain for some elements of a family responsiveness agenda or initiating benefits themselves even without union contracts, although the extent or scale should not be overstated (see Chapter 2; also Kamerman and Kahn, 1987). On the other hand, small industry, as represented by the National Federation of Independent Business and the US Chamber of Commerce, has been a leading *opponent* of federal parental leave legislation in the 1980s and 1990s on the grounds that the costs would be ruinous.

Expert groups have also played an important role, first with regard to public education and later, and to a lesser extent, with regard to legislative enactments. We discuss blue-ribbon panels and commissions below.) Here one sees more attention to family policies: for example, in the 1970s, responding to the family changes which many interpreted as family breakdown, a series of groups tried to point to a broader concept and a more coherent structure for family policy. In response to a government request and grant, the prestigious National Research Council/National Academy of Sciences assembled a high-status expert group whose ultimate report, *Toward a National Policy for Children and Families*, could unfortunately not claim important results. It did form the basis for a subsequent, very useful research-analytic and forum group, the Committee on Child Development Research and Public Policy, currently the Board for Children and Families. The National Conference on Social Welfare, also with a federal grant, produced its own family policy report in the form of an analysis of family demographic and legal trends and an inventory of issues about family policy. Its contribution may have been to educate and to clarify thinking, but it had no visible action outcomes (National Conference on Social Welfare, 1977).

Religious groups have played a less visible role in advocating for or shaping family policy than might have been expected, but they are now emerging as a powerful interest group. While national Catholic Church leadership, especially the National Conference of Catholic Bishops, has been outspoken about and active with reference to family needs since World War II, even urging child allowances in the 1950s and 1960s, interest in the family in Catholic and Protestant churches has not been channelled into a systematic legislative-issue agenda. Whether acting on their own or in coalitions, many religious groups became active around specific issues such as day care, child nutrition, parental leave, or abortion, but have not addressed a more holistic agenda. Some religious leaders joined with some behavioural scientists and philosophers in the 1980s to voice their alarm about divorce rates, cohabitation, and sexual permissiveness as undermining traditional family values and causing crime, the drug culture, out-of-wedlock births, and a decline in cultural values and civility (Select Committee on Children, Youth and Families, 1986 and 1992a; Subcommittee on Family and Human Services, 1983). They have begun to generate a new and active traditionalist pro-family movement, much of it emerging out of the more fundamentalist wings of the Protestant churches and associated with an activist campaign to outlaw abortion.

In effect a strongly traditionalist family policy ethos has now appeared, not yet manifest in a comprehensive family policy agenda but increasingly visible (Aldous and Dumon, 1980; Peden and Glahe, 1986). Groups representing this traditionalist position first appeared on the national scene in the late 1970s at Congressional hearings and at the 1980 White House Conference on Families (see below) attacking liberals' acceptance of a diversity of family forms as inevitable responses to modernization, industrialization, and social change. They were also active in a series of Congressional conflicts over child-care legislation in the 1970s, 1980s, and 1990s, first rejecting federal support for out-of-home child-care services as 'communalizing' child-rearing, then withdrawing from that position but insisting on the right of church-based child-care facilities to public support and opposing federal imposition of mandated standards. In recent years some have advocated channelling funds to help one-earner families with at-home mothers. Some opposed parental leave legislation on the grounds that government should not favour at-work over at-home mothers. Some urged major increases in per-child tax exemptions to make things more manageable for families with several children; some also backed child tax credits—all from a broader perspective of supporting the 'traditional' family. These groups lined up with the anti-abortion movement in some instances; in others, while of similar derivation, they remained apart, since anti-abortion groups tend toward 'single issue' activism.

In the 1990s, all these conservative groups have begun to converge into a several-stream 'pro-traditional family via family policy' lobby. A well-organized, multistate, grassroots organization at the right wing of the Republican Party heavily influenced by a fundamentalist Protestant movement was very visible in the 1994 election of a conservative Congress and dominated the 1996 nominating convention. For family policy it represents an attack on basic safety net social programmes for children and their families in favour of a block-grant devolution strategy that will remove most federal mandates and standards, turn programmes and policies over to the states, and undo much of the post-1935 federal assumption of leadership and responsibility. The states, in turn, are expected to adopt measures they believe will decrease out-of-wedlock births and compel mothers to work, rather than depend on public assistance. The 1996 legislation includes time limits for assistance and work quotas to be met by the states.

In brief, the interest groups supportive of specific child and family policy measures have been 'specialized' and have usually operated in issue-specific coalitions. No broadly representative and influential groups have carried a 'family policy' banner. Nonetheless, at various times the Congress and the Administration have been responsive, for better or worse, to interest group influences (either additive or in coalitions created for a given legislative objective) in dealing with child nutrition, child care, Food Stamps, AFDC programmes, or the initial and/or expanded legislation for children with handicaps (IDEA; see Chapter 4), as well as abuse/neglect and child welfare programmes. The results of interest group activism derived from diverse concepts of the role of government and of the federal government are mixed. As seen in previous chapters, results in many fields have been modest. America remains a laggard.

PARTY POLITICS

The American political scene is dominated by two parties, each of which is in itself a rather broad coalition. While party platforms for the presidential election every four years invariably refer to the family and to family 'values' as societal cornerstones, the parties do not develop comprehensive family policies. Where consensus is possible, they may express themselves on specific issues such as public assistance, Food Stamps, family leave, or abortion. The presidential candidate may say more or less than the platform, but always proclaims the family's primacy.

In the absence of a disciplined parliamentary system of governance, the platform of the victorious party does not become a programme to be enacted by government. Therefore, unlike the situation in much of Europe, an analysis of party platforms is not a productive enterprise. It is not that differences between parties do not exist: Democratic party platforms in general endorse or advocate the safety net, equal opportunity, gender equity, and less restrictive abortion measures, while

Republican platforms usually support a minimalist governmental social policy role and are more responsive to the social welfare expenditure conservatism of business. In the recent past, as already noted, the Republican party has largely been taken over by a 'traditional family conservatism' and a 'radical Christian right' that may be said to espouse a relatively broad family policy.

The very proliferation and dispersion of interest groups tends to make political parties and their platforms less decisive in policy-making. Parties and individual candidates tend to depend on interest groups for resources and grassroots mobilization, and the parties reflect interest group pressures as they decide when and how to act. Or, more precisely, the individual senator or congressman responds to such pressures, often as much or more so than to the party. For—in a process both complex and gradual—in the very years when family policy might have called for more holistic perspectives and enactments beyond the historical American incrementalism, patterns of campaigning (particularly on television), fundraising, and 'reformed' nomination procedures have weakened political parties and their capacity to plan and implement programmes. Candidates in nominating primary elections and general elections to the Congress often run as individuals, depending more on their own personal appeal and on interest groups than on parties. Vulnerable families, children, and many social welfare institutions are politically weak and powerless in this environment.

THINK-TANKS, FOUNDATIONS, NON-GOVERNMENTAL COMMISSIONS, AND OTHER INSTRUMENTS

The institution of 'blue-ribbon' citizen panels, created to investigate public or private programmes or institutions or specific problems, has a long and distinguished history in the US. Started in the nineteenth century, the institution moved to the national level early in the twentieth century, with regard to child labour and child health, precursors to federal legislation; but it began to assume its current scale, range, and sophistication after the New Deal and especially during the Great Society era, when national social legislation had become more common and the media were available to disseminate findings to the public.

Some major US philanthropic foundations with special programme interest in families and their children have supported citizen panels to investigate and suggest solutions to important national problems. Several Ford Foundation efforts contributed to the anti-poverty and welfare policy debates and programme initiatives from the 1960s to the 1990s, some with more impact than others. Two Carnegie Corporation panels generated considerable public focus on education reform and on adolescents, with generally positive impact. A Grant Foundation panel developed proposals for education for non-college-bound youth, for vocational education, and for school/workplace co-operation. Several ambitious projects of the Edna McConnell Clark Foundation played a major role in shaping federal child welfare legislation in 1980 and again in 1993. These are only a few of many illustrations.

In the early 1970s, among widespread discovery of the family policy concept as a way to support increased and improved social provision for families, the Carnegie Corporation created a Council on Children. After a five-year inquiry which produced a series of reports and a major book, the Council outlined a comprehensive family policy anchored in 'universal entitlement' (Kenniston, 1977). The report generated considerable discussion but no visible legislative impact, despite many quite specific recommendations. A more recent and ambitious Carnegie panel report, intended to create action on behalf of children under age three, is currently attempting to find a pathway to implementation.

Like many governments, the US government often creates blue-ribbon committees to deal with crises (the ghetto riots of the 1960s), complex problems requiring political compromise away from the spotlight of partisan political debate (Social Security reform, tax reform), or public concerns that need deliberate exploration (the evidence that many children—especially poor, handicapped, and minority children—are not doing well). In lieu of a series of detailed case studies, we offer here a generalized conclusion with which most published analyses would agree: the crises which must be solved tend to be solved, e.g., Social Security and tax reform. The solutions may go well beyond the prevalent incrementalism into the realm of the comprehensive. But the explorations of major complex problems absent a current crisis tend to yield analyses, some of them superb, like the Kerner Commission Report (National Advisory Commission on Civil Disorders, 1981), but are not necessarily able to generate action. The fate of proposals from such panels is completely dependent on the political context in which they appear.

The most recent and immediately relevant illustration is the report of the statutory, bipartisan National Commission on Children, *Beyond Rhetoric* (1991), which analysed the status of children in changing American families and, without *explicitly* formulating a family policy, developed comprehensive, research-based recommendations for income security, health services, and education, as well as social services for the vulnerable. The report offers detailed cost estimates and proposes methods of financing. Despite prestigious membership, expert staff, a respected senator as chair, and more than adequate platforms for dissemination, a shifting political environment left the well-researched report behind as a valuable reference source but with no immediate impact on policy.

These are the blue-ribbon panels of incrementalism: most take on specific problems, some are more ambitious, and a few have urged broader family policy. Their achievements are usually modest but they remain useful instruments in the environment in which they operate. They have no societal mandate to do more.

Think-tanks offer a parallel case, which will not be examined here in detail. Rare in the 1960s, their numbers grew in the 1970s and exploded in the 1980s. They are funded by foundations, government, or universities and conduct both basic and policy-orientated fact-finding, research, and evaluation on almost all the topics covered in this report. They have ambitious publication programmes, span the political spectrum, and rise and fall in public visibility with the changing political landscape. Most deal with broader social policy than children's programmes alone.

Currently the most visible such group to the left of the political centre is the Center for Budget and Policy Priorities. It has an active, high-quality programme of research and reporting on poverty, social assistance, nutrition, medical care programmes, housing, tax policy, federalism, and the federal budget. It is foundation-supported, as is the influential American Enterprise Institute, which is a bit to the right of centre, particularly visible as we write on teenage sexuality, single-mother families, child welfare, and child care. Neither takes a 'family policy' perspective *per se*, although each asks frequently about family well-being as it analyses proposals and programmes. A similar stance is found in the extraordinarily productive Urban Institute whose many studies cover much of the full range of contemporary social policy and social programming. The Cato Institute, the Manhattan Institute, and the Heritage Foundation buttress the conservative surge with their reports. These research centres, relatively unimportant in the past, are currently attended to in the Congress and are visible in the media as well.

In a category between the blue-ribbon panel and the think-tank is the National Academy of Sciences' (NAS) Commission on Behavioral and Social Sciences and Education. This congressionally-chartered voluntary group undertakes study of public policy issues at the request of government or the voluntary sector (usually foundations). The relevant operating group concerned with children and families, the Board on Children and Families (originally the Committee on Child Development Research and Public Policy) appoints an expert advisory panel which guides a highly qualified research staff. Reports undergo review at several levels before receiving the Academy imprint. Studies of child care, adolescent pregnancy, and special education policy, for example, make substantial contributions to basic public and professional knowledge but, given the auspice, seldom lead to immediate and specific legislative actions. The Institute of Medicine of the NAS functions in a similar fashion in the health sphere; its report on prenatal care may be cited as an influential and authoritative contribution to a reform debate which eventually influenced the Medicaid enhancement legislation (see Chapter 4) and provided a rationale to a governmental commission dedicated to improved prenatal care.

In the last three decades it has become almost a tradition that new governmental initiatives carry mandates for evaluation and related funding. This is the case for the many experiments and demonstration projects funded by private foundations in response to major social problems, including those affecting children and their families, adolescents, young mothers and their children, and AFDC. The evaluations are conducted by university-based scholars, think-tanks, and large private consulting organizations specializing in evaluation. The latter include Abt Associates, Westat, and the Manpower Development Research Corporation (MDRC). To illustrate, MDRC has developed an outstanding record as a reliable evaluator of experimental efforts with teenage mothers, of work-transition programmes associated with AFDC, and of drug treatment, and played an important role in the 1988 welfare 'reform' legislation.

Without further elaboration, we note again that incrementalism, by its nature, requires and generates categorical and somewhat fragmented initiatives, and that such initiatives (including policy and programme evaluations) can be and have been very influential in helping chart the next policy increments.

THE 'INSTITUTIONALIZATION' OF FAMILY POLICIES?

The proper heading for this section is 'the *non*-institutionalization of family policy'. The United States has never assigned to any place in government broad or powerful mandates regarding the family. In 1912, it created a centre of leadership to deal with troubled or disadvantaged children, the US Children's Bureau, in part a product of the women's social reform movement of that era, but gave it only a limited mandate.[9] The Bureau was essentially a fact-finding agency; under strong leadership, however, it also acted as an advocate to create awareness of children's circumstances and influence the federal passage of child labour legislation and a maternal child health programme, both short-lived but subsequently revived in other ways. From the 1930s through the 1960s, the influence of the Children's Bureau rose and fell as it became important in the administration of the federal child welfare and child health efforts and in developing programmes and staffing standards.

Since the 1970s the Children's Bureau has had a quite secondary programme administration role in the more complex structure of the Department of Health and Human Services (DHHS) (originally the Department of Health, Education, and Welfare, established in 1953 and renamed in the 1970s). This department is the national locus of family concerns. Within it, the Surgeon General has been visible over the years on child health issues, and a commissioner leads on Social Security. (The Social Security Administration became an independent agency in 1995.) Since the 1960s an Administration for Children, Youth and Families, or a similar unit within the department has carried responsibility for Head Start, child welfare, youth, and handicapped children. The same or related units have dealt with AFDC and the maternal and child health block grant. In an interesting departure, the Carter Administration gave this administration a somewhat more universal mandate, but the Reagan Administration stressed dealing with poor children and their families—in the established tradition.

Family issues are dealt with in many different government departments: taxes in Treasury; housing in Housing and Urban Development; preschools in Education; juvenile delinquency in Justice; family leaves and work-related benefits in Labor; military child care and family policy in Defense, and so forth. A chart of the distribution of children's issues (or, for that matter, issues of the elderly) within the Executive Branch or Congress would be extraordinarily complex; thus, not only is there no one locus for policy-making, but even efforts to achieve better operational co-ordination and services integration at the local level are often frustrated by federal legislative roles, mandates, and prerogatives. The states, in turn, develop their own structures with little more coherence than the federal government.

The consequence of this fragmentation is that special devices are required to create federal government overviews of the child/family situation and to mobilize for co-ordinated action. Over the years, this role has been performed by decennial White House Conferences on Children, building on the tradition established by a very influential meeting in 1909. The second conference in 1919 remained small, but conferences grew thereafter in scope and size of delegations. All specialists, interest groups, parent organizations, religious bodies, and others concerned with children wanted to be present and have their interests attended to. But despite excellent documentation, preparatory sessions, and research reports, meetings of thousands of delegates cannot deliberate policy issues and choose among alternatives. Steiner (1976) concludes that the White House Conference on Children clearly is not a device for 'formulating a workable policy program'. A kinder observer might conclude that most conferences have contributed to public education, influenced professional associations, led to exchange of experience which has affected actions in some cities and states or private agencies, and often produced useful data and research reports. They have not, however, provided an 'engine' for family policy developments over the succeeding decades.

At first consideration, the White House Conference device can be appealing. In 1980 an effort to move further in clarifying national government's strategies *vis-à-vis* what was conceived of as a changing and increasingly troubled family was focused on a White House Conference on Families. The Conference grew out of a promise made by Jimmy Carter during the 1976 presidential campaign, following considerable interest in and discussion of family policy from the mid-1960s on. But from the time of the Carter inauguration the family conference was troubled. Steiner (1981) has described the political problems: after many delays and concerns and White House loss of enthusiasm, the Conference became three regional meetings which, despite all possible precautions, were overwhelmed by sharp conflicts about the definition of family and attacks on out-of-wedlock births, homosexuality, abortion, and on those whose response to family change was to propose supportive programmes and benefits. While the conference process was brought to a civil conclusion and reports followed, there were no significant follow-ups.

Special committees in the Congress constitute still another device. In 1973, the Senate Subcommittee on Children and Youth highlighted child and family problems, queried whether—and which—government policies helped or hurt families and inquired about 'the kinds of support services [that] should be available' (Subcommittee on Children and Youth, 1973). The hearings listened to Census Bureau demographers, leading psychologists, psychiatrists, sociologists, child development experts, tax experts, parents, social welfare leaders, civic leaders, and religious leaders. These hearings proved to be the launching of a family policy discussion in the US (Kamerman and Kahn, 1978; Steiner, 1981; Aldous and Dumon, 1980; Rice, 1977). During the 1970s the meaning of 'family policy' was debated, European experiences were explored, demographic trends were subjected to careful analysis and consideration, and the history of the family in the US and the world received major attention.

Given the visible interest in the family policy cause and a readiness to attract support for various social policy initiatives by underscoring their potential for strengthening family life, each of the branches of Congress created or renamed a committee to suggest dedication to (or concern with) the family. In 1982, the Democratic House established a Select Committee on Children, Youth and Families which, prior to its abolition in an economy sweep in 1993, was to hold dozens of hearings on the problems of children and families, on demographic trends, and on exemplary programmes. While its documentation was excellent and its reports well used, it lacked a legislative mandate, and the Senate subcommittee which could have had one undertook few legislative initiatives.

To complete the discussion, two other policy development vehicles deserve attention: 'family impact analysis' and the child social indicators movement, both public and private. The idea of reviewing ongoing and proposed new governmental actions for potential 'family impact' was mentioned by several social scientists at the 1973 hearings of the Subcommittee on Children and Youth. This idea had considerable appeal and was subsequently expanded and offered as a parallel to environmental impact statements. After some exploration (Kamerman, 1976), a foundation-supported Family Impact Seminar, led by a former Congressional aide for family issues, convened in Washington, carried out a diversity of explorations over more than three years, produced an illustrative 'impact' statement and made family policy somewhat more visible, though it became cautious as it gained insights into family diversity and value pluralism in US society. Other efforts to study family impact followed, along with many new family policy research endeavours.

The several White House Conferences on Children adopted pre-conference data collection and research as a planning platform. President Herbert Hoover gave a large boost to public reporting and to ongoing governmental statistical work with the very important compilation, *Recent Social Trends* (1935). It was clear to many that data were a foundation for programme and policy development.

During the Great Society era, advocates of more systematic social planning offered proposals for public social accounting as a component, and the Department of Health, Education, and Welfare published 'Toward a Social Report' in 1969 as a pilot effort. The Russell Sage Foundation supported and published pioneering work on social indicators, and the Social Science Research Council (SSRC) developed (and later dropped) a major social indicators programme activity. One result of all this was the development of a child social indicators research programme based in Washington. While not a formal part of a social planning activity, this centre, Child Trends, is one of several drawn upon by governmental and non-governmental users, social scientists, and advocates in work on child and family policy.

The city or state 'state-of-the-child' report is a related initiative, visible in social surveys and needs studies from the turn of the century, and improved as a result of interest in local community planning in recent decades. Social indicator research and census data are reduced to the geographic area of interest and circulated to the media, social welfare agencies, governments, and advocates, who regard them as highly useful. Currently, the Annie Casey Foundation publishes *Kids Count* annually. This child social indicator report, organized by state, is compiled with the help of state teams funded by the foundation. An exemplary city effort, organized by neighbourhoods, is *Keeping Track of New York City's Children*, from the Citizens' Committee for Children.

The United States lacks a comprehensive, explicit family policy, and it lacks a focused governmental centre for family policy. These two facts are of course interrelated. Instead, the US adopts small and large measures and creates governmental instruments in a pattern of interest group incrementalism, occasionally broken by farther-reaching thrusts. The focus is far more likely to be on individual family members than the family unit. The dominant objectives of these measures reflect the political balances of the time.

The last two decades have led to increasingly heated debate between left-of-centre 'liberals', in the New Deal and Great Society sense, who raised the family policy banner in support of enriched programme offerings and supports for families with employed parents, for single-mother families, or for poor children and their families; and conservative, radical right, and Christian fundamentalists who invoked family policy in support of traditional families and gender roles, a more visible role for religion, rejection of diversity in family types, and rejection of the right to abortion.

The Congressional elections of 1994 have led to the most recent episode in the country's family policy story: the new House of Representatives' leadership put together a plan of action, called the Contract With America, to weaken or dismantle much of the social welfare edifice of the New Deal and the Great Society. A conservative religious coalition followed with a proposed Contract With the Family, proposing more family-related tax concessions, school prayer, stricter control on abortions, and further devolution of educational policy to the local level.

Conservatives have not proposed a family policy *per se*, but the undercurrent of the new Republican activism has been a campaign by conservative scholars and the religious right to 'remoralize America' by attacking much that national government does, promoting devolution from Washington to the states and from the states to civil society (Himmelfarb, 1995). En route they could be undermining some or much of the safety net on which poor and vulnerable children and their families rely. Conservatives argue that incentives to out-of-wedlock births and long-term dependence could thus be removed and more desirable behaviour encouraged. One can easily foresee suffering and alienation, but little scientific evidence indicates that the family changes and moral reforms sought would follow. It is ironic that despite earlier conservative criticism of the concept of family policy as a mask for the liberal social agenda (Carlson, 1980), conservatives have now managed to usurp the 'pro-family' label; the political approach to family policy most potent and visible now seems to be that of the far right.

Conclusion

The pace of family change in the United States has accelerated rapidly since the 1960s. Marriage rates have declined, while divorces and out-of-wedlock births have become more common. The number of lone-parent—overwhelmingly lone-mother—families with children has grown dramatically. Labour force participation rates of women, in particular married mothers with young children, have also increased dramatically in conjunction with a variety of factors: women's levels of education have increased; with help from improved contraceptive technologies women have chosen to have fewer children and to bear those they do have later; and job opportunities for women have expanded and wages risen while job opportunities and wage levels for men have declined. Two powerful trends—the rise in lone-mother families and the rise in employment rates of wives—have acted on each other as both cause and effect: greater economic independence for women has led to higher numbers of lone mothers, and the growth in divorce rates and out-of-wedlock births has led to a greater need for economic independence for women.

Just as the trends in family change differ by race, so do the causes of these changes. Not changes in family law or policies, but economic independence, both the drive for it and the consequences of it, is the dominant factor in white women's decision to defer or forgo marriage. Thus, McLanahan and Casper (1995: 41) found that, among white women, increased labour force participation can account for over 70% of the decline in marriage rates between 1970 and 1990, whereas declines in men's employment and earnings can account for only 8%. The decline in male employment explains about 12% of the decline in marriage among blacks; however, in contrast to whites, the rise in labour force participation among black women, high to begin with, is not a significant factor in higher rates of lone parenthood among these women.

Did family policies create these trends? Apparently not: changes in marital and fertility behaviour began long before the changes in family law first occurred largely in the 1970s. The changes in law may have facilitated some subsequent family changes but clearly did not cause them. In effect, family law acknowledged and accepted the growing diversity of family forms. Indeed, this acceptance may be reflected as well in the law's recently increasing acceptance of such diverse family forms as cohabiting couples, gay and lesbian families, and families created as a consequence of new forms of reproductive technology; these family forms are now more likely to be recognized in family law than to be targeted in public policy or counted in the census. Nor can other social/family policies be found responsible for these family changes. Between 1970 and 1990, when the rise in the rate of lone mothers was most dramatic, the real value of Aid to Families with Dependent Children (AFDC) benefits and the AFDC/Food Stamp package declined significantly. Tax policies were only marginally facilitating.

McLanahan and Casper (1995) conclude that there is still no clear answer as to why black marriage rates declined so dramatically during these years. They suggest that changes in attitudes and values may have made out-of-wedlock births, divorce, and lone-parent status far more acceptable in the black community than earlier, although they do not find these changed attitudes to have had a significant effect on white women. Of particular importance, their findings suggest that understanding which factors shape family change requires acknowledging the diversity among lone mothers and disaggregating the diverse forms of lone-parent and married-couple families by marital status, educational level of parents, employment status, and wage levels, as well as racial and ethnic status. These factors apparently play a far more important role in accounting for family change than do family policies.

Clearly, neither child poverty nor family income inequality can be understood without recognizing the importance of family structure and parental employment (Hogan and Lichter, 1995, among others). Nonetheless, neither a return to the traditional family (a married couple with husband as breadwinner and wife at home) nor a move toward the non-traditional employment pattern (dual earners) would solve these problems alone, without acknowledging differences in wages and benefits, inadequacies in income supplementation policies, and racial prejudice in the labour market. Moreover, when there are young children in the family, full-time work can be managed only if child care is adequate, affordable, and available. Relatives are increasingly unavailable to provide this care as grandparents, too, enter or remain in the labour force.

Changes in the economy have made the rise in labour force participation rates of wives a necessity whether to protect families' standards of living or women's economic independence. A public policy response is needed even for two-parent families who may experience low earnings, unemployment or underemployment, time pressures, and a need for child care; at least an equivalent response is needed for lone mothers who are likely to experience all of the above problems as well as the lack of financial support from the absent parent and an even greater time crunch. For parents, the costs of rearing a child continue to be an additional economic and time burden; and children face the consequences of poverty and low family income, family disruption, and parental time constraints.

If family policies have not *caused* these family changes, what then has been the policy *response* to the increased challenges these changes pose? Family law has recognized the diversity of family types in the late twentieth century. Only with regard to abortion is there still an obvious gap between public policy and current family realities. However, despite public acceptance of family change, public attitudes and values regarding these changes reveal inconsistency and ambivalence. Family policies in domains other than family law mirror these value conflicts and problematic attitudes. Husbands of employed women now play a more active role in family work than before, especially in child care, but the primary burden of family work is still carried by women, a fact of which women contemplating marriage and childbearing are aware. Public policies designed to respond to family developments have emerged only recently and are very modest: some subsidies for child care have been developed, but not nearly enough to assure easy access for all who need or want help with child care. After long delay, the US enacted legislation to provide brief and unpaid parental leave. The result of such lacks is clearly a stressful situation for parents and one that is potentially harmful for children.

Given children's increased vulnerability to growing up in poverty as a result of differences in family structure, numbers of wage-earners, and wage levels, the existing policy response is meager, fragmented, and inadequate. The US provides no child or family allowance; families with children have only limited economic protection at a level significantly lower than the country's low absolute poverty threshold, let alone at the international standard of 50%—or even 40%—of median family income. For several years US family policy did respond to the growth in lone-mother families by expanding AFDC, but benefits declined in value, and even that stigmatized system was repealed in 1996 and replaced by 50 different state programmes offering no guaranteed right to assistance and designed to discourage unwed motherhood and promote work, even for parents of very young children.

Nor has there ever been adequate support for poor husband/wife families with children. Support of working poor families has recently been expanded modestly through income supplementation and child-care reform; but that, too, may be under attack in the near future. Children in lone-mother families have no assurance that they will receive support from their absent living parent, although efforts to locate these parents and require them to make maintenance payments are increasing. Unlike many countries, the US does not offer a governmental child support guarantee (advance maintenance). Increasingly, the policy focus is on short-term support for poor single-mother families, with the expectation that the mothers in these families will enter paid employment. But the supports needed to make sure that jobs are available, to facilitate work when jobs are available, and to make it possible for parents to take jobs without negative consequences for their children, are either inadequate or non-existent.

Finally, responsiveness to family change requires more than attention to marital status, employment status, and income. It also calls for a wider range of basic service supports for improved quality of life, and special help for children and families with problems and special needs. The US has never developed a universal health care system comparable to those of the other major industrial societies, nor has it managed to establish a universal maternal and child health care system. Here, too, policy has focused on services to poor young children and still does not attend to all children or even all poor children. Indeed, Medicaid for the poor is currently facing devolution and cuts. Only with regard to provision of personal social services for special-needs situations has the US clearly responded. Poverty, handicap, and personal problems, not family structure, are the major triggers for action.

How then would we characterize the US family policy regime? We begin by restating our opening sentence: the US has no explicit national family policy, nor does it have an implicit but comprehensive or coherent family policy. It does have some of the major policies characteristic of welfare states, but not all: it lacks national health insurance, child or family allowances, maternity or parental insurance, and sickness benefits. The result is a truncated welfare state. Despite these limitations, the US has had a series of discrete, sometimes contradictory social policies affecting children or families with children. In recent years, this cluster of social policies has increasingly come to be called US 'family policy' or 'family policies'.

As noted in the introduction, these policies can be understood only in the context of US social policy more broadly defined and the US historical and political context, with its emphasis on individualism, the constitutional separation of Church and State, family privacy, a strict work ethic, a limited role for government generally and for the federal government in particular, a stress on the private sector in economic and social policy, an openness to immigration, a history of slavery followed by continuing racism, and ambivalence in recent years regarding women's roles. All of these elements are visible in this profile of US family policies.

More specifically, the profile of US family policy includes the core elements:

- implicit rather than explicit family policy;
- a minimalist public social protection system with large holes in the social infrastructure (no national health insurance or health service, no family or child allowance, no maternity or parenting insurance, no sickness benefits, no housing allowance, no universal preschool);
- fragmented and categorical rather than holistic policies, targeted at specific population groups (lone-mother families; dependent children) or problem groups (handicapped, abused, or neglected children);
- selective and targeted rather than universal policies, directed toward poor children and their families rather than all children and their families, and carried out by means-testing for benefits and services (AFDC; Food Stamps; Earned Income Tax Credit; Medicaid), leading to a reduction in the poverty gap experienced by low-income families but not a lower poverty rate;
- a system of family law that accepts great diversity among family types, in contrast to a system of family policies in other domains that accepts diversity only among middle- and upper-class families, rejecting it for families needing more direct support from the state;
- continuing ambivalence about gender roles, in particular the role of women, with inconsistent, often inadequate and even conflicting responses to women's changed behaviour in the workplace and in the home;
- non-interference with most families and social control of those with problems as the primary family policy objective rather than sustaining and buttressing families as in countries with explicit, universal family policy.

Drawn from a report of public child expenditures between 1960 and 1995 (Clark and Berkowitz, 1995), the data in Tables 19 and 20 underscore much of our analysis with the economic facts. Although in absolute amounts, state expenditures for children increased by about one-third more than federal expenditures between 1960 and 1995, the rate of growth in federal expenditures was more than twice the rate of increase in state and local child expenditures: federal expenditures rose by a factor of eight while state and local expenditures close to quadrupled. Public investment in children became most significant when the federal role in child policy increased, during the Great Society years 1965–75 and again during the Clinton Administration in the early 1990s. Except for public education, which is the responsibility of state and local governments, social spending for children and their families has been overwhelmingly targeted at the poor. AFDC has never been as significant a programme for children and their families as have other programmes. AFDC expenditures peaked in 1975 and, despite increases in the 1980s and 1990s, never achieved that level again. Thus the continuing public anger and frustration about the programme seem more a matter of ideology or symbolism than of real concern about expenditures. More recently, the US has stressed the use of tax policy as an instrument of social policy, demonstrated in the first half of the 1990s by making the Earned Income Tax Credit (EITC) the single largest federal programme for children and their families. The tax benefit package for low-income working families with children almost doubled in value between 1985 and 1990, from about $7 to $13 billion, then doubled again between 1990 and 1995 to $26 billion. Medicaid and Food Stamps followed in importance at about half that rate of spending growth, while AFDC trailed well behind. Indeed, total federal spending for children's personal social services exceeded federal spending for AFDC. Apart from public education and a tax benefit, the US has established little in the way of universal child and family policies.

It appears doubtful that the near future will see family policy responses in the United States more in line with progressive European welfare state traditions. While many advocate such changes, the political party currently dominant includes and is often responsive to conservative elements who would further constrain or outlaw abortion, introduce prayer in the public schools, weaken public education and support religious education, make divorce more difficult, and use public assistance programmes in an attempt to control personal morality. Joined to an ideology that would cut taxes, weaken central government, and assign more prerogatives to states and the private sector, such tendencies would preclude the responsive family policy that family changes would appear to justify.

TABLE 19. Total federal expenditures for children and per-child expenditures for major areas, United States 1960–1995 (in constant 1995 $)

	1960	1965	1970	1975	1980	1985	1990	1993	1995
	Total Expenditures								
Total expenditures (in million $)	89,403	125,115	191,234	239,694	244,053	266,869	334,881	385,177	410,129
Total federal expenditures	18,119	22,922	42,086	65,116	74,964	77,932	94,442	124,102	142,755
income security	14,061	16,943	22,631	28,506	26,780	24,138	22,788	27,433	29,466
nutrition	1,173	1,341	2,579	10,993	15,926	15,306	16,700	22,403	24,841
housing	293	442	676	1,723	3,987	8,877	9,365	10,693	10,138
tax credits	0	0	0	0	5,199	7,052	13,260	17,544	26,310
health	174	692	3,052	4,315	4,427	5,733	14,307	21,683	24,041
social services	0	526	2,277	4,558	4,585	4,608	5,513	9,008	11,422
education	2,417	2,978	10,471	11,717	12,261	10,029	10,615	13,328	14,857
training	0	0	399	3,304	1,799	2,189	1,894	2,012	1,680
State and local expenditures	71,284	102,193	149,149	174,578	169,089	188,938	240,439	261,075	267,374
Federal dollars as % of total	20.3	18.3	22.0	27.2	30.7	29.2	28.2	32.2	34.8
	Per-Child Expenditures								
No. of children 0–18 (in 1,000)	67,138	73,536	73,474	70,496	67,939	66,613	67,528	70,489	72,416
Total expenditures (in $)	1,331.64	1,701.41	2,602.75	3,400.10	3,592.24	4,006.27	4,959.14	5,464.36	5,663.52
Federal expenditures	269.88	311.71	572.79	923.68	1,103.40	1,169.91	1,398.56	1,760.59	1,971.33
income security	209.43	230.40	308.01	404.37	394.18	362.36	337.46	389.17	406.90
nutrition	17.48	18.24	35.10	155.93	234.41	229.78	247.31	317.83	343.04
housing	4.36	6.02	9.20	24.44	58.69	133.26	138.69	151.69	140.00
tax credit	0.00	0.00	0.00	0.00	76.53	105.86	196.36	248.89	363.32
health	2.60	9.41	41.54	61.21	65.16	86.06	211.86	307.60	331.98
social services	0.00	7.15	30.99	64.66	67.49	69.18	81.64	127.79	157.72
education	36.01	40.50	142.52	166.20	180.46	150.56	157.20	189.07	205.16
training	0.00	0.00	5.43	46.87	26.47	32.86	28.05	28.54	23.20
State and local expenditures	1,061.76	1,389.70	2,029.96	2,476.42	2,488.84	2,836.35	3,560.58	3,703.77	3,692.19

Source: R. Clark and R. Berkowitz (1995), *Federal Expenditures on Children*, Washington, DC: The Urban Institute.

TABLE 20. Federal and state expenditures for children for major areas, United States 1960–1995 (in million $, constant 1995 $, based on Consumer Price Index)

	1960	1965	1970	1975	1980	1985	1990	1993	1995
Total expenditures	*89,403*	*125,115*	*191,234*	*239,694*	*244,053*	*266,869*	*334,881*	*385,177*	*410,129*
Total federal expenditures	*18,119*	*22,922*	*42,086*	*65,116*	*74,964*	*77,932*	*94,442*	*124,102*	*142,755*
Income security	*14,061*	*16,943*	*22,631*	*28,506*	*26,780*	*24,138*	*22,788*	*27,433*	*29,466*
Social Security									
Old Age and Survivors' Trust Fund	5,203	6,290	8,211	10,074	9,626	9,221	7,726	7,970	8,395
Disability Trust Fund	255	952	1,387	2,370	2,738	2,281	2,905	2,681	3,105
Aid to Families with Dependent Children									
administrative and benefits expenditures	3,745	5,625	7,872	10,319	9,033	8,027	8,919	9,634	9,725
reimbursement from child support enforcement	…	…	…	…	-309	-314	-413	-543	-620
Child support enforcement	…	…	…	…	438	527	822	1,060	1,321
Emergency Assistance	…	…	17	85	64	70	128	141	581
Supplemental Security Income	…	…	…	473	816	1,109	1,333	4,165	4,762
Railroad Retirement	643	486	451	417	289	175	135	130	70
Veterans' Benefits									
compensation and DIC	2,580	1,621	2,767	2,814	2,147	1,467	927	899	878
disability	1,634	1,968	1,925	1,925	1,909	1,553	281	1,265	1,219
Black Lung Disability									
Part B	…	…	0	28	20	15	19	19	19
Part C	…	…	…	0	8	7	6	12	11
Nutrition	*1,173*	*1,341*	*2,579*	*10,993*	*15,926*	*15,306*	*16,700*	*22,403*	*24,841*
Food Stamp Program	…	81	1,102	6,334	8,199	8,053	8,496	12,555	13,649
Child nutrition	1,173	849	1,154	4,041	6,135	5,098	5,701	6,834	7,627
Special milk	in child nutr.	412	323	342	289	22	21	16	18
Special Supplemental Food for Women, Infants and Children	…	…	…	275	1,266	2,080	2,430	2,949	3,500
Commodity supplemental food	…	…	…	in WIC	36	53	52	50	47

TABLE 20. (continued)

	1960	1965	1970	1975	1980	1985	1990	1993	1995
Housing	293	442	676	1,723	3,987	8,877	9,365	10,693	10,138
Low Income Home Energy Assistance	…	…	…	…	…	1,490	692	575	797
Low-rent public housing	293	442	647	1,119	1,023	1,269	1,024	1,611	1,842
Section 8 low-income housing assistance	…	…	…	…	2,319	5,754	7,351	8,247	7,225
Rent supplement	…	…	28	186	189	35	22	8	22
Rental housing assistance	…	…	1	418	457	330	276	252	253
Tax credits	0	0	0	0	5,199	7,052	13,260	17,544	26,310
Earned Income Tax Credit	…	…	…	…	…	…	…	…	…
Refundable portion	…	…	…	…	2,317	1,530	4,987	9,097	16,845
Non-refundable portion	…	…	…	…	1,308	480	2,428	4,393	5,680
Dependent Care credit	…	…	…	…	1,575	5,041	5,844	3,247	3,785
Credit for child medical insurance premiums	…	…	…	…	…	…	…	808	…
Health	174	692	3,052	4,315	4,427	5,733	14,307	21,683	24,041
Medicaid	…	…	1,669	3,296	3,397	3,709	6,605	10,604	12,408
children	…	…	…	…	…	…	1,961	2,973	3,349
disabled children	…	…	…	…	…	914	4,464	6,541	6,541
pregnancy and delivery	…	…	…	…	…	…	…	…	…
Maternal and Child Health (block grant)	169	522	1,053	648	660	621	540	573	609
Immunization	5	38	62	17	55	76	214	353	465
Fluoridation	—	—	—	—	10	1	0	0	0
NICHD	…	132	269	354	298	396	508	560	558
Sudden Infant Death Syndrome	…	…	…	…	5	…	…	…	…
Healthy Start	…	…	…	…	…	…	…	68	98
Emergency medical services for children	…	…	…	…	…	3	4	5	9
Adolescent Family Life	…	…	…	…	2	13	9	4	3
Social services	0	526	2,277	4,558	4,585	4,608	5,513	9,008	11,422
Social Services Block Grant	…	…	946	2,810	2,314	1,798	1,523	1,345	1,551
Community services block grant	…	…	…	…	…	15	15	23	24

Table 20. (continued)

	1960	1965	1970	1975	1980	1985	1990	1993	1995
Children and families services programs	—	20	—	362	388	256	353	531	525
Head Start	...	458	1,316	1,232	1,474	1,430	1,493	2,693	3,405
Child welfare services	—	—	—	130	108	271	260	286	281
Child welfare training	—	—	—	23	15	5	4	4	4
Child welfare research	...	...	...	...	...	16	6	6	6
Violent crime reduction programs									10
Foster care	...	—	—	in AFDC	in AFDC	700	1,578	2,405	3,108
Adoption Assistance	...	...	...	...	...	48	164	260	397
Independent Living	...	...	...	...	...	...	66	66	70
Child Care and Development Block Grant	...	...	...	...	...	...	...	426	900
AFDC child care	...	...	...	...	...	...	...	487	542
Transitional child care	...	...	...	...	...	...	...	117	154
At-risk child care	...	...	...	...	285	...	...	282	300
Juvenile justice	...	47	16	—		70	48	68	69
missing children	...	...	...	...		0	3	10	9
Family Preservation and Support	...	...	...	...				...	67
Education	*2,417*	*2,978*	*10,471*	*11,717*	*12,261*	*10,029*	*10,615*	*13,328*	*14,857*
Educationally deprived/economic opportunity	239								
Supporting services	323								
Dependents' schools abroad	166								
Public lands revenue for schools	207								
Assistance in special areas	51								
Other	23								
Impact aid	1,306	1,662	2,532	1,722	1,254	901	935	448	1,088
Vocational (and adult) education	103	387	800	911	821	511	773	626	767
Grants for the disadvantaged	...	...	5,166	5,215	5,822	5,853	5,147	6,853	7,032
School improvement	...	344	1,112	1,949	1,433	732	1,362	2,106	1,592
Indian education	...	...	...	...	...	...	...	...	...
Department of Education	...	...	...	111	170	115	80	104	83

TABLE 20. (continued)

	1960	1965	1970	1975	1980	1985	1990	1993	1995
Bureau of Indian Affairs Schools	—	440	370	392	324	247	221	382	407
Johnson–O'Malley Assistance	—	74	62	62	51	36	29	24	24
Bilingual and immigrant education	...	...	82	258	308	219	216	129	251
Education for the handicapped	...	66	305	421	1,493	1,416	1,852	2,656	3,612
Emergency school assistance (civil rights)	...	6	41	675	585	...	...	...	...
Training	*0*	*0*	*399*	*3,304*	*1,799*	*2,189*	*1,894*	*2,012*	*1,680*
JTPA/CETA	...	...	...	2,201	1,271	824	723	676	491
Job Corps	...	...	382	274	491	484	516	556	536
Summer youth employment	...	...	...	785	in CETA	861	639	741	606
JOBS/WIN participants who are minors	...	...	17	45	37	20	15	39	48
State and local expenditures	*71,284*	*102,193*	*149,149*	*174,578*	*169,089*	*188,938*	*240,439*	*261,075*	*267,374*
State elementary & secondary education	29,172	42,767	61,974	75,716	82,387	93,449	112,520	119,312	122,087
Local elementary & secondary education	42,113	59,426	80,964	87,434	76,356	84,896	110,887	118,162	118,351
Aid to Families with Dependent Children									
administrative and benefits expenditures	—	—	4,648	8,603	7,827	7,054	7,513	8,003	8,130
reimbursement from Child Support Enforcement	...	...	...	...	-434	-516	-681	-829	-995
Child support enforcement	...	...	...	...	147	224	423	506	662
Emergency Assistance	...	...	23	54	73	74	165	408	1,681
AFDC child care	...	...	...	...	...	...	...	352	387
Transitional child care	...	...	...	...	...	...	...	83	110
Medicaid									
children	...	...	1,540	2,772	2,734	3,015	4,810	7,938	9,486
disabled children	...	...	...	...	...	...	1,428	2,225	2,561
pregnancy and delivery	...	...	...	...	...	742	3,374	4,914	4,914

Note: Medicaid pregnancy and delivery expenditures were not available for 1995, so 1993 charges are used.

Source: R. Clark and R. Berkowitz (1995), *Federal Expenditures on Children*, Washington, DC: The Urban Institute.

Notes

1 This figure is likely to be somewhat larger in reality since some cohabiting couples with children appear as married couples in census data.

2 This section was prepared with the assistance of Karen Staller, J. D.

3 The Tenth Amendment says that 'the powers not delegated to the United States by the Constitution, nor prohibited by it to the States, are reserved to the States respectively, or to the people.'

4 No-fault divorce recognized and legitimized existing social conditions. Judges and lawyers had complained for years that divorce based on fault created a situation where litigants routinely perpetrated fraud on the judicial system by requiring sworn testimony that was primarily manufactured for the purpose of dissolving an unhappy marriage. It was argued that this incentive to commit fraud degraded the judicial system.

5 By now, the term 'illegitimate' is not used except by those who would deliberately emphasize stigma or promote punitive measures. The preferred term is 'born out of wedlock'.

6 Although Haveman and Wolfe (1994) state that the number of hours that children spend with their parents has declined by about half between 1965 and the late 1980s (from 30 hours per week to 17), the research suggests that the decline has been less, albeit still significant.

7 In late 1996 AFDC was replaced by Temporary Assistance to Needy Families, or TANF.

8 Personal social services include child welfare services, social services for adolescents or the elderly, residential treatment, etc.

9 In 1920, the Department of Labor created a parallel fact-finding and monitoring agency, its Women's Bureau—which over the years has risen and declined in visibility and influence on issues such as job discrimination, equal opportunity, child care, family leave, and workplace safety.

Appendix: Legislative Chronologies

CHAPTER 1

1967: Children's rights regarding delinquency and status offences. In *Re: Gault*, extended due process protection to juvenile court proceedings.

1968: Uniform Child Custody and Jurisdiction Act (UCCJA).

1968–83: Rights of illegitimate children defined incrementally by the US Supreme Court, on a case-by-case basis, largely during these years.

1969: California enacts first no-fault divorce legislation.

1973: *Roe v. Wade* legalized abortion. In *Webster v. Reproductive Health Services*, the Supreme Court permitted a state statutory ban on public employees and facilities performing abortions.

1975, 1984, 1988: Amendments (Title IV–D) to the Social Security Act regarding child support.

1977: *Marvin v. Marvin* upheld the right of unmarried couples to enter into express and implied contracts governing property distribution following the dissolution of a relationship.

1988: South Dakota last state to enact no-fault divorce legislation.

CHAPTER 2

Maternity and Parenting Policies

1949–69: State Temporary Disability Insurance Laws in California, Hawaii, New Jersey, New York, and Rhode Island, enacted between 1949 (New York) and 1969 (Hawaii). These laws were required to cover pregnancy and maternity (including convalescence following childbirth) in 1978.

1964, 1972: Title VII of the Civil Rights Act of 1964, as amended in 1972 and 1978.

1993: Family and Medical Leave Act.

CHAPTER 3

Child-Conditioned Social Assistance

1911–21: Mothers' and widows' pension laws in 40 states (45 by 1935).

1935: Aid to Dependent Children (ADC) as Title IV of the Social Security Act, covering children under age 16 and including a formula for federal matching of expenditures under approved state plans.

1950: ADC amended to include caretaker benefits: one needy relative with whom the dependent child was living.

1961: Optional 'unemployed father' programme added.

1962: Renamed 'Aid to Families with Dependent Children' (AFDC) as part of a broader thrust. Separate formula to allow higher federal match for social services to current, former, and potential AFDC families.

1967:	Emergency assistance programme added. Income disregard provisions added as incentive for parent to seek work. WIN programme of work incentives added.
1975:	Child Support Enforcement provisions added. A $50 'disregard' from monthly absent parent payments added as an incentive (1984). Further strengthened (1988).
1981:	Work incentives reduced. States allowed option of requiring that recipient work to match value of grants at minimum wage rate.
1988:	Family Support Act of 1988 replaced WIN and other work programmes with a comprehensive Job Opportunities and Basic Skills (JOBS) programme, mandating participation of caretakers of children over age 3 (or 1, at state option), setting participation-rate quotas for states, and providing transition supports for parents who leave rolls for employment (Medicaid and child care). States required to offer programme for unemployed parents (AFDC-U) but may limit coverage to six months each year.
1996:	The Personal Responsibility and Work Opportunity Reconciliation Act of 1996 abolishes AFDC and the JOBS programme, eliminates any individual entitlement to assistance, limits receipt of aid to a lifetime maximum of 5 years, and requires participation in work (paid or voluntary) within two years of claiming the new assistance benefit (Temporary Assistance to Needy Families (TANF)). Also curtails SSI benefits for functionally-disabled children, cuts maximum Food Stamp benefits, and severely limits the right of legal immigrants to receive benefits. States given considerable flexibility in specifics of programme design.

Food Stamps

1964:	Food Stamp Act designed to enable eligible low-income households to buy a nutritionally-adequate low-cost diet. Provided coupons (vouchers) that could be purchased at a reduced price by qualified individuals, worth up to 30% of poverty threshold income. As amended subsequently.
1974:	Amendments mandated the programme on the states.
1977:	Eliminated the requirement that individuals purchase the stamps. If qualified, individuals were now *given* stamps with the same value. Some constraints on eligibility were also imposed.

Earned Income Tax Credit (EITC)

1978:	A tax credit equal to a specified percentage of wages up to a maximum awarded to low-income working families with children. If the credit exceeds the taxpayer's federal income tax liability, the excess is payable to the taxpayer as a direct transfer payment, thus, a 'refundable tax credit'.
1987:	Credit indexed for inflation.
1990–93:	Credit significantly increased and adjusted for families with two or more children.

CHAPTER 4

Child Care

1946:	Child Care Food Program authorized under the National School Lunch Act of 1946. Provides federal financial assistance for breakfasts, lunches, suppers, and snacks served to children in licensed child-care centres and family or group day-care homes. The vast majority of children served is aged 3–5.

1962, 1967, 1988, 1990: Title IV–A of the Social Security Act (SSA) as amended. Title IV–A of the SSA, under which the AFDC programme is established, authorizes four different child-care programmes, three of which fund child care for poor children: (1) child care for AFDC families; (2) child care for those leaving AFDC for jobs ('transitional' child care, 1988); (3) child care for families who are 'at risk' of becoming eligible for AFDC (Omnibus Budget Reconciliation Act (OBRA), 1990). The fourth is aimed at improving quality (1990).

Since 1962, amendments to Title IV–A have been designed to encourage state departments of public (social) welfare to develop child-care services for children of past, present, and potential AFDC beneficiaries as a strategy for helping these women end their use of public assistance. The state agencies can provide child care directly, arrange for care with providers through contract or vouchers, reimburse families, or use other arrangements.

1964:   Head Start enacted as part of the Economic Opportunity Act of 1964 that launched the Johnson Administration's War on Poverty. It was designed as a compensatory education programme for poor children (up to 10% may come from families with higher incomes) as well as to increase parental involvement with children and provide necessary health, nutrition, and social services to them and their families. At least 10% of the children enrolled must also be handicapped.

1965:   Title I of the Elementary and Secondary Education Act enacted; like Head Start, it is also a compensatory education programme. Provides federal funds for programmes to meet the needs of educationally-disadvantaged children including preschoolers.

1975, 1981: Title XX (later the Social Services Block Grant (SSBG)) of the SSA, authorized grants to states for providing social services for individuals with incomes up to 115% of the national (or state, if lower) median income. A significant portion of Title XX funds (which have ranged from $2.5 billion in 1975 to $3 billion in 1979–80 and $2.8 billion in 1990) has gone to child-care services for low- and moderate-income working families.

1976:   Child and Dependent Care Tax Credit expanded. Originated in 1954, the benefit is a non-refundable tax credit for taxpayers who work or are seeking work and have at least one child under age 13. Expansion in 1976 transformed it into a 20% tax credit on child-care-related expenses up to $2,000 for one dependant and $4,000 for two or more.

Note: Although participation includes care of the elderly and the disabled, the overwhelming majority of the credit is used for child care.

1990:   Child Care and Development Block Grant (OBRA, 1990) targeted on childcare services for low-income families (with up to 75% of the state's median income) and the supply and quality of child-care services generally.

Child Health

1935:   Title V of the SSA, 1935, as amended. Title V authorized the federal government to provide funds to states to extend and improve (especially in rural areas and in areas suffering from severe economic distress) (1) services for reducing infant mortality and otherwise promoting the health of mothers and children; and (2) services for 'locating crippled children and for medical, surgical, corrective, and other services and care for and facilities for diagnosis, hospitalization, and aftercare for, children who are crippled or who are suffering from conditions leading to crippling.'

1965:   Title XIX (Medicaid) of the SSA. Medicaid is a federal/state matching programme providing medical assistance for certain low-income persons. Each state designs and administers its own programme within broad federal guidelines. As a result, there is substantial variation among states in groups covered, services offered, and amount of payment for services. The programme is administered by the US Department of Health and Human Services and by the relevant state agencies. Eligibility is restricted to AFDC beneficiaries, those eligible for AFDC but not receiving it, Supplementary Security Income beneficiaries, and most poor children and pregnant women.

1970:   Public Health Services Act, as amended.

Community Health Centers (Section 330). Grants to public or non-profit organizations to plan, develop, or operate community health centres in medically-underserved areas.

Childhood Immunizations, Section 317. Grants for planning, organizing, and conducting immunization programmes and for purchasing vaccines.

Childhood Lead Poisoning Prevention Program, Section 317. Grants to initiate and expand state- and community-based lead poisoning prevention programmes.

Family Planning Services, Title X. Support for family planning clinics, personnel, training, and services.

Preventive Health and Health Services Block Grant, Title XIX of the Public Health Service Act.

1981:   Maternal and Child Health Block Grant. The current form of Title V, SSA. Eight programmes were collapsed into this block grant which provides funds for services that are free to poor families, though fees may be charged for those with higher incomes. (Although the states are not required to set an income ceiling or to charge fees to higher-income families, most states now use 185% of poverty as their cut-off point for services.)

Child Welfare and Related Social Services

1961, 1962, 1967, 1975, 1980: Titles IV–B of the SSA as amended in 1961, 1962, 1967, 1980; Title XX, 1975 and 1981; Title IV–E (1980). All provide federal funds for foster care for children in AFDC-eligible families and for 'preventive' services. Title XX covers all types of personal social services.

1972:   Supplemental Security Income (SSI), implemented 1974. SSI is a means-tested (income- and asset-tested) federally-administered public (social) assistance programme, authorized under Title XVI of the SSA as amended in 1972. Provides nationally-uniform monthly cash benefits in accordance with nationally-uniform eligibility requirements to poor aged, blind, and disabled persons, replacing the earlier categorical assistance programmes established in the original SSA in 1935. SSI pays benefits to poor blind or disabled children. As a result of a 1990 Supreme Court decision, the number of children who qualified for SSI on the basis of disability increased dramatically.

1974:   Child Abuse and Neglect Prevention Act providing funds for demonstration and research.

Bibliography

INTRODUCTION

Baker, M. (1995). *Canadian Family Policies: Cross National Comparisons.* Toronto: University of Toronto Press.

Bradshaw, J., et al. (1995). *Social Assistance in OECD Countries.* London: HMSO.

Castles, F., ed. (1993). *Families and Nations: Patterns of Public Policy in Western Democracies.* Brookfield, Vermont: Dartmouth Publishing Co.

Ditch, J., et al. (1995). *A Synthesis of National Family Policies.* York, England: University of York.

Eardley, T., et al. (1995). *Social Assistance in OECD Countries*: Vol. I, Synthesis Report. London: HMSO.

Esping-Anderson, G. (1990). *Three Worlds of Welfare Capitalism.* Princeton, New Jersey: Princeton University Press.

Flora, P. ed. (1985, 1986). 'Introduction'. *Growth To Limits: The Western Welfare States Since World War II.* Berlin: Walter de Gruyter.

Kahn, A., and S. Kamerman (1983). *Income Transfers for Families With Children: An Eight-Country Study.* Philadelphia: Temple University Press.

Kamerman, S., and A. Kahn (1978). *Government and Families in Fourteen Countries.* New York: Columbia University Press, 489.

——, and A. Kahn (1981). *Child Care, Family Benefits, and Working Parents.* New York: Columbia University Press.

——, and A. Kahn (forthcoming). 'Investing in Children'. In Cornia, G., and S. Danziger, eds. Children in Poverty in Industrialized Countries. Oxford: Oxford University Press. (Revised version of a working paper issued by the Innocenti Centre. Florence, Italy: UNICEF, 1991.)

Kuusi, P. (1964). *Social Policy for the Sixties.* Helsinki: Finnish Social Policy Association.

Levine, D. (1988). *Poverty and Society.* New Brunswick, New Jersey: Rutgers University Press.

Mishra, R. (1990). *The Welfare State in Capitalist Society.* Toronto: University of Toronto Press.

Mitchell, D. (1991). *Income Transfers in the Welfare State.* Brookfield, Vermont: Gower Publishing Co.

Mitterauer, M., and R. Sieder (1982). *The European Family.* Oxford: Basil Blackwell.

Myrdal, A. (1941). Nation and Family: *The Swedish Experiment in Democratic Family and Population Policy.* New York: Harper and Brothers.

Pampel, F., and P. Adams (1992). 'The Effects of Demographic Change and Political Structures on Family Allowances'. *Social Service Review* 66(4): 524–46.

——, and J.Williamson (1988). 'Welfare Spending in Advanced Industrial Democracies, 1950–1980'. *American Journal of Sociology* 93(6): 1424–56.

Pierson, C. (1991). *Beyond the Welfare State.* University Park, Pennsylvania: Pennsylvania State University Press.

Rainwater, L., and T. Smeeding (1995). *Doing Poorly: The Real Income of American*

Children in a Comparative Perspective. Luxemburg: Luxemburg Income Study Working Paper No. 127.

Ringen, S. (1987). *The Possibility of Politics.* Oxford: Oxford University Press.

Rose, R., and R. Shiratori, eds. (1986). *The Welfare State East and West.* New York: Oxford University Press.

Wilensky, H. (1975). *The Welfare State and Equality.* Berkeley, California: University of California Press.

Wynn, M. (1970). *Family Policy.* London: Michael Joseph.

GREAT BRITAIN

Abel-Smith, B., and P. Townsend (1965). *The Poor and the Poorest.* London: Bell.

Aldgate, J., J. Tunstill, and G. McBeath (1993). *Implementing Section 17 of the Children Act: The First 18 Months.* Oxford: Department of Applied Social Studies and Social Research.

Anderson, M. (1971). *Family Structure in Nineteenth Century Lancashire.* Cambridge: Cambridge University Press.

—— (1983). *What is New about the Modern Family? An Historical Perspective.* The Family OPCS Occasional Papers 31. London: OPCS.

Atkinson, A. (1983). *What is Happening to the Distribution of Income in the UK?* London: LSE Welfare State Programme.

Baggott, R. (1994). *Health and Health Care in Britain.* London: Macmillan.

Ball, C. (1994). *Start Right: The Importance of Early Learning.* London: Royal Society for the Encouragement of Arts, Manufactures and Commerce.

Barrington, I., et al. (1977). *The Matrimonial Jurisdiction of Registrars.* Oxford: Centre for Socio-Legal Studies.

Blackburn, C. (1991). *Poverty and Health: Working with Families.* Milton Keynes: Open University Press.

Blaxter, M. (1981). *The Health of the Children: A Review of Research on the Place of Health in Cycles of Disadvantage.* London: Heinemann.

Bock, G., and P. Thane, eds. (1991). *Maternity and Gender Policies.* London: Routledge.

Bone, M. (1977). *Preschool Children and the Need for Day Care.* OPCS. London: HMSO.

Bradshaw, J. (1990). *Child Poverty and Deprivation in the UK.* London: National Children's Bureau.

—— (1993). *Household Budgets and Living Standards.* York: Joseph Rowntree Foundation.

——, and J. Millar (1991). *Lone Parent Families in the UK.* DSS Research Report 6. London: HMSO.

Brannen, J., et al. (1995). *Employment and Family Life: A Review of the Research in the UK.* London: Employment Department Research Series No. 41.

——, and P. Moss (1988). *New Mothers at Work.* London: Unwin Hyman.

Bridgewood, A., and D. Savage (1993). *General Household Survey 1991.* OPCS. London: HMSO.

Butler Sloss, E. (1988). *Report of the Inquiry into Child Abuse in Cleveland.* London: HMSO.

Central Advisory Council for Education (1967). *Children and their Primary Schools.* The Plowden Report. London: HMSO.

Central Policy Review Staff (1973). *Report of the Population Panel* (Cmnd. 5258). London: HMSO.

Coale, A., and S. Watkins (1986). *The Decline of Fertility in Europe.* Princeton, New Jersey: Princeton University Press.

Cohen, B. (1988). 'Caring for Children: Services and Policies for Childcare and Equal Opportunities in the United Kingdom'. Report for the European Commission's Childcare Network. Commission of the European Communities.

—— (1990). *Caring for Children: Report for the EC Childcare Network.* London: Family Policy Studies Centre.

——, and F. Fraser (1991). *Childcare in a Modern Welfare System: Towards a New National Policy.* London: Institute for Public Policy Research.

Cole-Hamilton, I. (1991). *Poverty Can Seriously Damage Your Health.* London: Child Poverty Action Group.

Coleman, D., and J. Salt (1992). *The British Population: Patterns, Trends and Processes.* Oxford: Oxford University Press.

Commission on Social Justice (1994). *Social Justice: Strategies for National Renewal.* London: Vintage.

Cooper, D. (1971). *The Death of the Family.* Penguin.

Coote, A., H. Harman, and P. Hewitt (1990). *The Family Way: A New Approach to Policy Making.* London: Institute for Public Policy Research.

Coulter, F., F. Cowell, and S. Jenkins (1993). 'Family Fortunes in the 1970s and 1980s'. In Blundell, R., I. Preston, and I. Walker, eds. *The Measurement of Household Welfare.* Cambridge: Cambridge University Press.

Council of Mortgage Lenders (1993). *Housing in Britain.* 3rd ed. London: Council of Mortgage Lenders.

Coussins, J., and A. Coote (1981). 'Family in the Firing Line.' NCCL/CPAG Poverty Pamphlet, March 1981.

Daniel, W. (1980). *Maternity Rights: The Experience of Women.* London: PSI.

Davis, G., and M. Murch (1988). *Grounds for Divorce.* Oxford: Oxford University Press.

De'Ath, E., and G. Pugh, eds. (1985, 1986). *Partnership Papers.* London: National Children's Bureau.

Department for Education (1994). Statistical Bulletin 6/94. London: DFE.

Department of Health (1994). *Children Act Report 1993.* London: HMSO.

Department of Health and Social Services (1993). *Proposal for a Draft Children (Northern Ireland) Order 1982.* Explanatory Document. Belfast: DHSS.

Department of Social Security (1993). *Households Below Average Income: A Statistical Analysis 1979–1990/1.* London: HMSO.

—— (1994). *Annual Statistical Enquiry.* London: HMSO.

Department of the Environment (1994). *Information Bulletin 517.* London: Government Statistical Service.

Eekelaar, J. (1991). *Regulating Divorce.* Oxford: Oxford University Press.

—, and M. Maclean (1986). *Maintenance after Divorce.* Oxford: Oxford University Press.

Emmerich, M., and J. Lewis (1991). *Unemployment in Oxfordshire.* Manchester: CLES European Research Network.

Ermisch, J. (1983). *The Political Economy of Demographic Change.* London: Heinemann.

Ferri, E. (1993). *Life at 33: The Fifth Follow-up of the National Child Development Study.* London: National Children's Bureau.

Freedman, J., et al. (1988). *Property and Marriage: An Integrated Approach.* London: Institute for Fiscal Studies.

Fry, J., D. Brooks, and I. McColl (1984). *NHS Data Book.* Lancaster: MTP Press.

Glass, D. (1967). *Population Policies and Movements in Europe.* Oxford: Oxford University Press.

Goodman, A., and S. Webb (1994). *For Richer, For Poorer.* London: Institute for Fiscal

Studies.

Graham, H. (1984). *Women, Health and the Family.* Brighton: Wheatsheaf.

—— (1986). *Caring for the Family.* London: Health Education Council.

Greve, J. (1991). *Homelessness in Britain.* York: Joseph Rowntree Foundation.

Ham, C. (1985). *Health Policy in Britain: The Politics and Organisation of the National Health Service.* 2nd ed. London: Macmillan.

Harris, J. (1993). *Private Lives, Public Spirit.* Oxford: Oxford University Press.

Harrop, A., and P. Moss (1993). 'Trends in Mothers' and Fathers' Employment in the 1980s'. Paper presented to the conference 'Two Decades of Social Change', Oxford, July 1993.

Haskey, J. (1982). 'The Proportion of Marriages Ending in Divorce'. *Population Trends* 27: 4–8.

—— (1989a). 'Current Prospects for the Proportion of Marriages Ending in Divorce'. *Population Trends* 55: 34–7.

—— (1989b). 'One-Parent Families and their Children in Great Britain: Numbers and Characteristics'. *Population Trends* 55: 27–33.

—— (1993). 'Trends in the Numbers of One-Parent Families in Great Britain'. *Population Trends* 71: 26–33.

——, and K. Kiernan (1989). 'Cohabitation in Britain: Characteristics and Estimated Numbers of Cohabiting Partners'. *Population Trends* 58: 23–32.

Heath, A., M. Colton, and J. Aldgate (1989). 'The Education of Children In and Out of Care'. *British Journal of Social Work* 19: 447–60.

——, M. Colton, and J. Aldgate (1994). 'Failure to Escape: A Longitudinal Study of Foster Children's Educational Attainment'. *British Journal of Social Work* 24: 241–60.

——, and D. McMahon (1992). 'Changes in Values'. In Jowell, R., et al., eds. *British Social Attitudes: The 9th Report.* Aldershot: Gower.

Hills, J. (1993). *The Future of Welfare.* York: Joseph Rowntree Foundation.

Holmans, A., S. Nandy, and A. Brown (1987). 'Household Formation and Dissolution and Housing Tenure: A Longitudinal Perspective'. *Social Trends* 17: 20–8.

Johnson, P., and G. Stark (1989). *Taxation and Social Security 1979–1989: The Impact on Household Incomes.* London: Institute for Fiscal Studies.

——, G. Stark, and S. Webb (1989). *Alternative Tax and Benefit Policies for Families with Children.* London: Institute for Fiscal Studies.

Joseph Rowntree Foundation (1985). *Inquiry into British Housing.* York: Joseph Rowntree Foundation.

—— (1991). *Inquiry into British Housing.* 2nd Report. York: Joseph Rowntree Foundation.

Joshi, H. (1985). *Motherhood and Employment: Change and Continuity in Postwar Britain.* OPCS Occasional Paper 35. London: OPCS.

——, ed. (1989). *The Changing Population of Britain.* Oxford: Basil Blackwell.

——, and H. Davies (1993). 'Mothers' Human Capital and Childcare in Britain'. *National Institute Economic Review* Nov. 1993.

Kay, J., and M. King (1990). *The British Tax System.* 5th ed. Oxford: Oxford University Press.

Kiernan, K. (1989). 'The Family: Formation and Fission.' In Joshi, 1989.

—— (1992). 'Men and Women at Work and at Home'. In Jowell, R., et al., eds. *British Social Attitudes: The 9th Report.* Aldershot: Gower.

——, and V. Estaugh (1993). *Cohabitation: Extra-Marital Childbearing and Social Policy.* London: Family Policy Studies Centre.

——, and M. Wicks. (1990). *Family Change and Future Policy.* London: Family Policy Studies Centre.

Klein, R. (1989). *The Politics of the NHS.* 2nd ed. Harlow: Longman.

Laing, R. (1977). *Bird of Paradise and Politics of Experience.* Penguin.

Lampard, R. (1990). 'An Examination of the Relationship between Marital Dissolution and Unemployment.' ESRC Social Change and Economic Life Initiative Working Paper 17.

Lasch, C. (1977). *Haven in a Heartless World.* New York: Basic Books.

Laslett, P., ed. (1972). *Household and Family in Past Time: Comparative Studies in the Size and Structure of the Domestic Group over the Last Three Centuries.* Cambridge: Cambridge University Press.

Leaper, R. (1980). 'Introduction to the Beveridge Report'. *Social Policy and Administration* 1980: 3–13.

Leathard, A. (1980). *The Fight for Family Planning.* London: Macmillan.

Leete, R. (1989). *Changing Patterns of Family Formation and Dissolution in England and Wales 1964–1976.* London: HMSO.

Lewis, J. (1991). 'Models of Equality for Women: The Case of State Support for Children in Twentieth-Century Britain'. In Bock and Thane, 1991.

Maclean, M., and J. Eekelaar (1993). 'Child Support: The British Solution'. *International Journal of Law and the Family* 205.

MacKaim, and J. Kurczewki, eds. (1994). *Families, Politics and the Law.* Oxford: Oxford University Press.

Maclennan, D. (1994). *A Competitive UK Economy: The Challenges for Housing Policy.* York: Joseph Rowntree Foundation.

Malpass, P., and A. Murie (1990). *Housing Policy and Practice.* 3rd ed. London: Macmillan.

Marsh, C. (1991). *Hours of Work of Women and Men in Britain.* London: HMSO.

Martin, J., and C. Roberts (1984). *Women and Employment: A Lifetime Perspective.* London: HMSO.

McRae, S. (1991). *Maternity Rights in Britain: The Experience of Women and Employers.* London: Policy Studies Institute.

Melhuish, E., and P. Moss (1991). *Day Care for Young Children: International Perspectives.* London: Routledge.

Meltzer, H. (1994). *Day Care Services for Children.* London: HMSO.

Millham, S., et al. (1986). *Lost in Care.* Aldershot: Gower.

Moss, P. (1994). 'Statistics on Early Childhood Services: Placing Britain in an International Context.' In Ball, 1994.

Murphy, M., and O. Sullivan (1985). 'Housing Tenure and Family Formation in Contemporary Britain'. *European Sociological Review* 1: 230–43.

——, and O. Sullivan (1986). 'Unemployment, Housing and Household Structure among Young Adults'. *Journal of Social Policy* 15: 205–22.

Murray, C. (1990). *The Emerging British Underclass.* London: The Institute of Economic Affairs.

Niner, P. (1989). *Housing Needs in the 1990s.* London: National Housing Forum.

Noble, M., et al. (1989). *The Other Oxford: Low Income Households in Oxford.* Oxford: Department of Social and Administrative Studies.

Office of Health Economics (1992). *Compendium of Health Statistics.* 8th ed. London: Office of Health Economics.

Oppenheim, C. (1993). *Poverty: The Facts.* London: Child Poverty Action Group.

Osborn, A., N. Butler, and A. Morris (1984). *The Social Life of Britain's Five Year Olds.* London: Routledge and Kegan Paul.

Owen, C., and P. Moss (1989). 'Patterns of Preschool Provision in English Local Authorities'. *Journal of Educational Policy* 4: 309–28.

Packman, J. (1993). 'From Prevention to Partnership: Child Welfare Services across Three Decades'. In Pugh, G., ed. *Thirty Years of Change for Children.* London: National Children's Bureau.

Payne, J. (1987). 'Does Unemployment Run in Families? Some Findings from the General Household Survey.' *Sociology* 21: 199–214.

—— (1989). 'Unemployment and Family Formation Among Young Men'. *Sociology* 23: 171–91.

Penn, H., and K. Riley (1992). *Managing Services for the Under Fives.* Harlow: Longman.

Phillips, R. (1989). *Putting Asunder: A History of Divorce in Western Society.* Cambridge: Cambridge University Press.

Pizzey, E. (1974). *Scream Quietly or the Neighbours Will Hear.* Harmondsworth: Penguin Books.

Power, C., O. Manor, and J. Fox (1993). *Health and Class: The Early Years.* London: Chapman and Hall.

Preschool Playgroups Association (1993). *Counting the Cost of Childcare.* London: PPA.

—— (1994). *The Way Forward.* London: PPA.

Pugh, G., et al. (1987). *Partnership in Action: Working with Parents in a Pre-School Centre.* London: National Children's Bureau.

Randall, G. (1989). *Homeless and Hungry.* London: Centrepoint.

Ringen, S., and B. Halpin (1995). *The Standard of Living of Children.* Oxford: Department of Applied Social Studies and Social Research.

Rowntree, S., and G. Lavers (1951). *Poverty and the Welfare State.* London: Longmans.

Schofield, R., D. Revier, and A. Bideau, eds. (1993). *The Decline of Mortality in Europe.* Oxford: Clarendon Press.

Schweinhart, L., H. Barnes, and D. Weikart (1993). *Significant Benefits: The High/Scope Perry Preschool Study through Age 27.* Ypsilanti, Michigan: High/Scope Press.

Scott, J. (1990). 'Women and the Family'. In Jowell, R., et al., eds. *British Social Attitudes: The 7th Report.* Aldershot: Gower.

——, M. Braun, and D. Alwin (1993). 'The Family Way'. In Jowell, R., et al., eds. *International Social Attitudes: The 10th BSA Report.* Aldershot: Gower.

Shaw, C. (1990). 'Fertility Assumptions for 1989-Based Population Projections for England and Wales'. *Population Trends* 61: 17–23.

Silburn, R. (1991). 'Beveridge and the War-Time Consensus'. *Social Policy and Administration*: 80–6.

Simons, J. (1974). 'Great Britain'. In *Population Policy in Developed Countries.* New York: McGraw-Hill.

—— (1986a). 'Culture, Economy and Reproduction in Contemporary Europe'. In Coleman, D., and R. Schofield, eds. *The State of Population Theory: Forward from Malthus.* Oxford: Basil Blackwell, 256–78.

—— (1986b). 'How Conservative are British Attitudes to Reproduction?' *Quarterly Journal of Social Affairs* 2: 41–54.

Smith, G. (1975). *Educational Priority.* Vol. 4: The West Riding Project. London: HMSO.

Smith, T. (1992). 'Family Centres, Children in Need and the Children Act 1989.' In Gibbons, J., ed. *The Children Act 1989 and Family Support: Principles into Practice.* London: HMSO.

—— (1995). *Family Centres and Bringing up Young Children.* London: HMSO.

Social Services Inspectorate (1994). *National Inspection of Services to Disabled Children and their Families.* London: HMSO.

Stacey, M. (1988). *The Sociology of Health and Healing.* London: Unwin Hyman.

Sylva, K. (1994). 'The Impact of Early Learning on Children's Later Development.' In Ball, 1994.

Taylor, L., ed. (1970). *The Optimum Population for Britain*. London: Academic Press.

Teitelbaum, M. (1984). *The British Fertility Decline*. Princeton, New Jersey: Princeton University Press.

Thane, P. (1991). 'Visions of Gender in the Making of the British Welfare State: The Case of Women in the British Labour Party and Social Policy, 1906–1945'. In Bock and Thane, 1991.

Townsend, P., N. Davidson, and M. Whitehead (1988). *Inequalities in Health*. London: Penguin Books.

Utting, D. (1995). *Family and Parenthood: Supporting Families, Preventing Breakdown*. York: Joseph Rowntree Foundation.

——, J. Bright, and H. Henricson (1993). *Crime and the Family: Improving Childrearing and Preventing Delinquency*. London: Family Policy Studies Centre.

van der Eyken, W. (1984). 'Day Nurseries in Action: A National Study of Local Authority Day Nurseries in England, 1975–1983'. Final Report December 1984. University of Bristol: Department of Child Health (Unpublished report).

Wedge, P., and H. Prosser (1973). *Born to Fail?* London: Arrow Books.

——, and J. Essen (1982). *Children in Adversity*. London: Pan Books.

Wiggins, R., and J. Bynner (1993). 'Social Attitudes'. In Ferri, 1993.

Witherspoon, S. (1988). 'Interim Report: A Woman's Work'. In Jowell, R., et al., eds. *British Social Attitudes: The 5th Report*. Aldershot: Gower.

——, and G. Prior (1991). 'Working Mothers: Free to Choose?' In Jowell, R., L. Brook, and B. Taylor, eds. *British Social Attitudes: The 8th Report*. Aldershot: Dartmouth/SCPR.

Young, M., and P. Willmott (1973). *The Symmetrical Family*. London: Routledge and Kegan Paul.

CANADA

Abella, R. (1984). *Report of the Royal Commission on Equality and Employment*. Ottawa: Minister of Supply and Services Canada.

Adams, I., et al. (1971). *The Real Poverty Report*. Edmonton: MG Hurtig Ltd.

Adams, O., and D. Nagnur (1990). 'Marrying and Divorcing: A Status Report for Canada'. In McKie and Thompson, 142–5.

Adsett, M. (1995). 'An Exploration into the Relationship Between Changes in Family Formation and the Relative Cost of Housing in Canada, 1951–1991'. Paper presented at the annual meetings of the Canadian Sociology and Anthropology Association, Montreal, Quebec, 7 June 1995.

Akbari, A. (1995). 'The Impact of Immigrants on Canada's Treasury, circa 1990'. In D. DeVortez, ed. *Diminishing Returns*. Toronto: C. D. Howe Institute, 113–27.

Allen, D. (1993). 'Welfare and the Family: The Canadian Experience'. *Journal of Labor Economics* 11(1): S201–S223.

Allen, R. (1971). *The Social Passion: Religion and Social Reform in Canada 1914–1928*. Toronto: University of Toronto Press.

Anderson, G. (1992). *Housing Policy in Canada*. Ottawa: Canada Mortgage and Housing Corporation.

Anderson, K., et al., eds. (1988). *Family Matters: Sociology and Contemporary Canadian Families*. Scarborough: Nelson Canada.

Archer, K. (1991). 'The New Democrats, Organized Labour and the Prospects of Electoral

Reform'. In Bakvis, 313–43.

Armitage, A. (1988). *Social Welfare in Canada*. Toronto: McClelland and Stewart.

—— (1993a). 'Family and Child Welfare in First Nation Communities'. In Wharf, 1993a, 131–71.

—— (1993b). 'The Policy and Legislative Context'. In Wharf, 1993a, 37–63.

Armstrong, P., and H. Armstrong (1988). 'The Conflicting Demands of "Work" and "Home"'. In Anderson, K., et al., 113–40.

Arnup, K. (1994). *Education for Motherhood: Advice for Mothers in Twentieth-Century Canada*. Toronto: University of Toronto Press.

Asner, E., and D. Livingstone (1990). 'Household Class, Divisions of Labour and Political Attitudes in Steeltown'. Paper presented at Canadian Socialist Association Meetings, Victoria, British Columbia.

Avakumovic, I. (1978). *Socialism in Canada*. Toronto: McClelland and Stewart.

Baines, C., P. Evans, and S. Neysmith (1991). *Women's Caring: Feminist Perspectives on Social Welfare*. Toronto: McClelland and Stewart.

Baker, M. (1985). *Equality for Women: Past and Present Efforts to Improve Women's Status*. Ottawa: Library of Parliament, Research Branch.

—— (1990). 'The Perpetuation of Misleading Family Models in Social Policy: Implications for Women'. *Canadian Review of Social Work* Summer: 169–82.

—— (1993). *Families in Canadian Society*. 2nd ed. Toronto: McGraw–Hill Ryerson.

——, ed. (1994a). *Canada's Changing Families: Challenges to Public Policy*. Ottawa: The Vanier Institute of the Family.

—— (1994b). 'Family and Population Policy in Québec: Implications for Women'. *Canadian Journal of Women and the Law* 7(1): 116–32.

—— (1995). *Canadian Family Policies: Cross-National Comparisons*. Toronto: University of Toronto Press.

——, ed. (1996). *Families: Changing Trends in Canada*. 3rd ed. Toronto: McGraw–Hill Ryerson.

——, and D. Lero (1996). 'Division of Labour: Paid Work and Family Structure'. In Baker, M., ed. *Families: Changing Trends in Canada*. 3rd ed. Toronto: McGraw–Hill Ryerson.

——, and M. Robeson (1986). 'Trade Union Reactions to Women Workers and Their Concerns'. In Lundy, K., and B. Warme, eds. *Work in the Canadian Context*. 2nd ed. Toronto: Butterworths, 296–309.

Bakvis, H., ed. (1991). *Canadian Political Parties: Leaders, Candidates and Organization*. Royal Commission on Electoral Reform and Party Financing, vol. 13. Ottawa: Minister of Supply and Services Canada.

Bala, N. (1991). 'An Introduction to Child Protection Problems'. In Bala, Hornick, and Vogl, 1–16.

——, and M. Bailey (1990–91). 'Canada: Controversy Continues Over Spousal Abortion and Support'. *Journal of Family Law* 29(2): 303–15.

——, and K. Clarke (1981). *The Child and the Law*. Toronto: McGraw–Hill Ryerson Limited.

——, J. Hornick, and R. Vogl, eds. (1991). *Canadian Child Welfare Law*. Toronto: Thompson Educational Publishing, Inc.

Balakrishnan, T., E. Lapierre-Adamczyk, and K. Krotki (1993). *Family and Childbearing in Canada: A Demographic Analysis*. Toronto: University of Toronto Press.

Ball, A. (1988). 'Organizing Working Women: The Women's Labour Leagues'. *Canadian Dimension* 21(8): 18–21.

Barnhorst, D., and L. Johnson, eds. (1991). *The State of the Child in Ontario*. Toronto: Oxford University Press.

——, and B. Walter (1991). 'Child Protection Legislation in Canada'. In Bala, Hornick, and Vogl, 17–32.

Barrett, G., and M. Cragg (1995). 'Dynamics of Canadian Welfare Participation'. Discussion Paper No. 95–05. Vancouver: University of British Columbia.

——, et al. (1994). 'The Interaction of Unemployment Insurance and Social Assistance'. Human Resources Development. Evaluation Brief #18.

Battle, K., and L. Muszynski (1995). *One Way to Fight Child Poverty*. Ottawa: Caledon Institute of Social Policy.

——, and S. Torjman (1993). *Opening the Books on Social Spending*. Ottawa: Caledon Institute of Social Policy.

Baumann, A., and H. Connor (1993). 'Women's Health Status in Canada'. In World Health Organization. *Women's Health and Development: A Global Challenge*. Boston: Jones & Bartlett Publishers, 123–7.

Beach, C., and G. Slotsve (1993). 'Polarization of Earnings in the Canadian Labour Market'. Paper presented at the John Deutsch Institute conference on 'Stabilization, Growth and Distribution: Linkages in the Knowledge Era'. Queen's University, Kingston, Ontario, 14–16 October 1993.

Beaudry, M., and L. Aucoin-Larade (1989). 'Who Breastfeeds in New Brunswick, When and Why?' *Canadian Journal of Public Health* 80(3): 166–72.

Beaujot, R. (1986). 'Dwindling Families'. *Policy Options* 7(Sept.): 3–7.

—— (1990). 'The Family and Demographic Change in Canada: Economic and Cultural Interpretations and Solutions'. *Journal of Comparative Family Studies* 21(1): 25–38.

—— (1991). *Population Change in Canada. The Challenge of Policy Adaptation*. Toronto: McClelland and Stewart.

Bégin, M. (1992). 'The Royal Commission on the Status of Women in Canada: Twenty Years Later'. In Backhouse, C., and D. Flaherty, eds. *Challenging Times: The Women's Movement in Canada and the United States*. Montreal and Kingston: McGill–Queen's University Press, 21–38.

Belliveau, J., J. Oderkirk, and C. Silver (1994). 'Common-Law Unions: The Quebec Difference'. *Canadian Social Trends* 33: 8–12.

Bernadi, M. (1992). 'The Impact of Public International Law on Canadian Constitutional and Criminal Law and Child Health'. In Knoppers, 43–150.

Bertoia, C., and J. Drakich (1993). 'The Fathers' Rights Movement: Contradictions in Rhetoric and Practice'. *Journal of Family Issues* 14(4): 592–615.

Betcherman, G., and R. Morissette (1993). 'Recent Youth Labour Market Experiences'. Paper presented at the Canadian Employment Research Forum Workshop on Youth Labour Adjustment, Vancouver, 25 June 1993.

Beveridge, W. (1942). *Social Insurance and Allied Services: Report by Sir William Beveridge*. London: Macmillan.

Blake, D. (1991). 'Party Competition and Electoral Volatility: Canada in Comparative Perspective'. In Bakvis, H., ed. *Representation, Integration and Political Parties in Canada*. Royal Commission on Electoral Reform and Party Financing in Canada, vol. 14. Ottawa: Minister of Supply and Services Canada, 253–73.

Blakeney, M. (1992). 'Canadians in Subsidized Housing'. *Canadian Social Trends* Winter: 20–4.

Blank, R., and M. Hanratty (1993). 'Responding to Need: A Comparison of Social Safety Nets in Canada and the United States'. In Card, D., and R. Freeman, eds. *Small Differences That Matter: Labour Markets and Income Maintenance in Canada and the United States*. Chicago: University of Chicago Press, 191–231.

Blomqvist, A., and D. Brown (1994). *Limits to Care*. Toronto: C. D. Howe Institute.

Blood, R., and D. Wolfe (1960). *Husbands and Wives*. Glencoe, Illinois: Free Press.

Boadway, R., and H. Kitchen (1984). *Canadian Tax Policy*. Canadian Tax Paper No. 76. Toronto: Canadian Tax Foundation.

Boyd, M. (1984). *Canadian Attitudes Toward Women: Thirty Years of Change*. Ottawa: Labour Canada, Women's Bureau.

Bozinoff, L., and P. MacIntosh (1991a). 'Majority of Canadians Believe Two-Child Family Ideal'. *The Gallup Report* 22 April 1991.

——, and P. MacIntosh (1991b). 'Public Perceives Gender Inequality in Canadian Society'. *The Gallup Report* 9 December 1991.

——, and P. MacIntosh (1991c). 'Public Queried on Battery of Lifestyle Issues'. *The Gallup Report* 2 August 1991.

——, and P. MacIntosh (1992). 'Faithfulness, Sex Most Important for Successful Marriage'. *The Gallup Report* 13 February 1992.

Brennan, J., ed. (1985). *Building the Co-operative Commonwealth*. Regina: Canadian Plains Research Centre.

Burch, T., and A. Madan (1986). *Union Formation and Dissolution: Results from the 1984 Family History Survey*. Statistics Canada, Catalogue 99–963E. Ottawa: Supply and Services Canada.

Burke, M. (1990). 'Cooperative Housing: A Third Tenure Form'. *Canadian Social Trends* Spring: 11–14.

——, et al. (1991). 'Caring for Children'. *Canadian Social Trends* 22(Autumn): 12–15.

Burtch, B. (1994). *Trials of Labour: The Re-emergence of Midwifery*. Montreal and Kingston: McGill–Queen's University Press.

Callahan, M. (1993). 'Feminist Approaches: Women Recreate Child Welfare'. In Wharf, 1993a, 172–209.

Campaign 2000 (1994). *Investing in the Next Generation: Policy Perspectives on Children and Nationhood*. Toronto: Campaign 2000.

Campeau, F. (1992). 'Children's Right to Health Care under Quebec Civil Law'. In Knoppers, 209–57.

Canada Communication Group (1994). *The New Face of Government: A Guide to the New Federal Government Structure*. 2nd ed. Ottawa: Minister of Supply and Services.

Canada, Department of Finance (1992). *Federal–Provincial Study on the Cost of Government and Expenditure Management*. Ottawa: Minister of Finance.

Canada, Department of National Health and Welfare (1992). *The Child Tax Benefit: A White Paper on Canada's New Integrated Child Tax Benefit*. Ottawa: Minister of Supply and Services Canada.

Canada, Federal/Provincial/Territorial Family Law Reform Committee (1995). *Report and Recommendations on Child Support: Summary*. Ottawa: Minister of Public Works and Government Services Canada.

Canada, Government of (1994). *National Longitudinal Survey of Children: Overview of Survey Instruments*. Cat. 94–02. Ottawa: Human Resources Development Canada and Statistics Canada.

Canada, Health and Welfare (1986). *Historical Statistics on Family Allowances*. Ottawa: Minister of National Health and Welfare.

—— (1988). *Promoting Healthy Weights: A Discussion Paper*. Ottawa: Minister of Supply and Services.

—— (1989). *Nutrition Recommendations: A Call for Action*. Ottawa: Minister of Supply and Services.

—— (1990). *Action Towards Healthy Eating*. Ottawa: Minister of Supply and Services.
—— (various years). *Inventory of Income Security Programs in Canada*. Ottawa: Minister of National Health and Welfare.
Canada, House of Commons (1991). *Canada's Children: Investing in Our Future*. Report of the Sub-Committee on Poverty of the Standing Committee on Health and Welfare, Social Affairs, Seniors and the Status of Women (Chair: Barbara Greene, MP). Ottawa: House of Commons.
Canada, Human Resources and Labour (1993). *Family-Related Leave and Benefits*. Ottawa: Human Resources and Labour Canada.
Canada, Human Resources Development (1994a). *Improving Social Security in Canada*. Ottawa: Department of Human Resources Development.
—— (1994b). *Income Security for Children: A Supplementary Paper*. Ottawa: Human Resources Development.
—— (1994c). *Overview: Income Security Programs*. Ottawa: Minister of Supply and Services.
—— (1994d). *Reforming the Canada Assistance Plan: A Supplementary Paper*. Ottawa: Human Resources Development.
—— (1995). *Canada. Security, Opportunities and Fairness: Canadians Renewing Their Social Programs*. Report of the Standing Committee on Human Resources Development. Ottawa: Human Resources Development.
Canada, Minister of National Health and Welfare (1974). *Social Security in Canada*. Ottawa: Information Canada.
Canada Mortgage and Housing Corporation (CMHC) (1987). *A Consultation Paper on Housing Renovation*. Ottawa: CMHC.
—— (1993). *Housing Statistics*. Ottawa: CMHC.
Canada, Senate. Special Senate Committee on Poverty (1971). *Poverty in Canada*. Ottawa: Information Canada.
Canada, Status of Women (1986). *Report of the Task Force on Child Care*. Ottawa: Minister of Supply and Services.
—— (1989). *Dimensions of Equality: An Update of the Federal Government Work Plan for Women*. Ottawa: Status of Women Canada.
—— (1992). 'Measuring the Dimensions of Equality'. *Perspectives* 5(3): 3–7.
—— (1994). *Perspectives* 7(2).
Canada, Task Force on Child Care (1986). *Report of the Task Force on Child Care*. Ottawa: Supply and Services Canada.
Canadian Council on Social Development (CCSD) (1992). 'CCSD Calls for Social Rights to be Included in the Constitution'. *Perception* 16(1): 13–18.
—— (1993). 'Annual Report 1992–1993'. *Perception* 17(2): 1–7.
Canadian Institute of Child Health (CICH) (1989). *The Health of Canada's Children: A CICH Profile*. Ottawa: CICH.
—— (1994). *The Health of Canada's Children: A CICH Profile*. 2nd ed. Ottawa: CICH.
Cassidy, H. (1988). 'The Canadian Welfare Council in the Post-War Era'. *Perception* 12(3): 22–4.
CCSD. *See* Canadian Council on Social Development
Che-Alford, J. (1992). 'Canadians on the Move'. *Canadian Social Trends* 25(Summer): 32–4.
Child Welfare League of Canada (1994). *In Brief*. August.
CICH. *See* Canadian Institute of Child Health
CMHC. *See* Canada Mortgage and Housing Corporation
Coates, M. (1992). *Is There a Future for the Canadian Labour Movement?* Kingston, Ontario:

Industrial Relations Centre, Queen's University.

Cohen, G. (1992). 'Hard at Work'. *Perspectives on Labour and Income* 4(1): 8–14.

Cohen, M. (1993a). 'The Canadian Women's Movement'. In Pierson et al., 1–97.

—— (1993b). 'Social Policy and Social Services'. In Pierson et al., 264–320.

Colley, S. (1983). 'Free Universal Day Care: The OFL Takes a Stand'. In Briskin, L., and L. Yanz, eds. *Union Sisters: Women in the Labour Movement*. Toronto: Women's Educational Press, 307–21.

Corbett, G. (1981). *Barnardo Children in Canada*. Peterborough: Woodland Publishing.

Crean, S. (1988). *In the Name of the Fathers*. Toronto: Amanita Enterprises.

Crittenden, D. (1988). 'R.E.A.L. Women Don't Eat Crow'. *Saturday Night* May: 27–35.

Dennis, M., and S. Fish (1972). *Programs in Search of a Policy: Low Income Housing in Canada*. Toronto: A. M. Hakkert.

Doherty, G., et al. (in press). *Child Care: An Essential Component in Social and Economic Policies*. A background paper prepared for the Canadian Advisory Council on the Status of Women. Toronto: Centre for Urban and Community Studies, University of Toronto, Child Care Resource and Research Unit.

Dooley, M. (1989). 'The Demography of Child Poverty in Canada: 1973–1986'. Program for Quantitative Studies in Economics and Population. Research Report No. 251.

—— (1995). 'Lone-Mother Families and Social Assistance Policy in Canada'. In Richards, J., and W. Watson, eds. *Family Matters: New Policies for Divorce, Lone Mothers, and Child Poverty*. Toronto: C. D. Howe Institute: 35–104.

Drache, D., and D. Cameron, eds. (1985). *The Other Macdonald Report*. Toronto: James Lorimer and Company.

Dranoff, L. (1977). *Women in Canadian Life: Law*. Toronto: Fitzhenry and Whiteside.

Drover, G., P. Kerans, and D. Williams (1985). *Administering the Welfare State: Bipartism and Worker Management of Social Programs*. Ottawa: The Canadian Association of Social Workers.

Dumas, J. (1994). *Report on the Demographic Situation in Canada 1993*. Catalogue 91–209E, March. Ottawa: Statistics Canada.

——, and A. Bélanger (1994). *Report on the Demographic Situation in Canada 1994*. Catalogue 91–209E, November. Ottawa: Statistics Canada.

——, and Y. Lavoie (1990). *Report on the Demographic Situation in Canada 1990*. Statistics Canada. Catalogue #91–209, November. Ottawa: Supply and Services Canada.

—— (with Y. Lavoie) (1992). *Report on the Demographic Situation in Canada 1992*. Catalogue 91–209E, September. Ottawa: Statistics Canada.

——, and Y. Péron (1992). *Marriage and Conjugal Life in Canada*. Statistics Canada (Cat. #91–534E). Ottawa: Minister of Industry, Science and Technology.

Duxbury, L., and C. Higgins (1994). 'Families in the Economy'. In Baker, 1994a, 29–40.

Dyck, R. (1991). 'Links Between Federal and Provincial Parties and Party Systems'. In *Representation, IntHP LaserJet Series IIHPLASEII.PRS @d Livability*. Montreal: McGill University School of Architecture. (Unpublished masters thesis.)

Economic Council of Canada (1990). 'Good Jobs, Bad Jobs: Employment in the Service Economy'. Ottawa: Minister of Supply and Services Canada.

Eichler, M. (1988). *Families in Canada Today*. Toronto: Gage Educational Publishing Company.

Ergas, Y. (1990). 'Child-Care Policies in Comparative Perspective: An Introductory Discussion'. In *Lone-Parent Families. The Economic Challenge*. Paris: OECD Social Policy Studies No. 8, 173–200.

Ernst, A. (1992). 'From Liberal Continentalism to Neoconservatism: North American Free

Trade and the Policies of the C. D. Howe Institute'. *Studies in Political Economics* 39(Autumn): 109–40.

Esping-Andersen, G. (1990). *The Three Worlds of Welfare Capitalism*. Princeton: Princeton University Press.

Evans, R. (1984). *Strained Mercy: The Economics of Canadian Health Care*. Toronto: Butterworths.

Falls, G. (1993). *Government's Role in Housing*. Kingston: School of Policy Studies, Queen's University.

Ferguson, E. (1991). 'The Child-Care Crisis: Realities of Women's Caring'. In Baines, Evans, and Neysmith, 73–105.

Finn, E., ed. (1993). *Thirty-Six Ways the Tories have Hurt Canadians*. Ottawa: Canadian Centre for Policy Alternatives.

Freiler, C., and B. Kitchen (1990). 'Family Portrait'. *Perception* 14(2): 46–9.

Friendly, M. (1994). *Child Care Policy in Canada*. Don Mills, Ontario: Addison–Wesley Publishers Limited.

Fritzell, J. (1992). 'Income Inequality Trends in the 1980s: A Five Country Comparison'. Luxemburg Income Study, Working Paper #73.

Fulton, J. (1994). 'Families, Health and Health Care'. In Baker, 1994a, 89–102.

Fung, A. (1992). 'Low Income Rental Housing in Canada: Policies, Programs and Livability'. Montreal: McGill University School of Architecture. (Unpublished masters thesis.)

Galarneau, D. (1992). 'Alimony and Child Support'. *Perspectives on Labour and Income* 4(20): 8–21.

Gallup Canada (1994). 'Public Divided on Same Sex Spousal Benefits'. *The Gallup Poll* 25 April 1994.

Garfinkel, I., and P. Wong (1990). 'Child Support and Public Policy'. *Lone-Parent Families. The Economic Challenge*. Paris: OECD.

Genereux, A. (1991). 'The Protection Hearing'. In Bala, Hornick, and Vogl, 55–76.

Ghalam, N. (1993). *Women in the Workplace*. 2nd. ed. Statistics Canada, Cat. #71–534E. Ottawa: Minister of Industry, Science and Technology.

—— (1994). 'Women in the Workplace'. In *Canadian Social Trends*, vol. 2. Toronto: Thompson Educational Publishing, Inc., 141–5.

Glendon, M. (1987). *Abortion and Divorce in Western Law*. Cambridge, Massachusetts: Harvard University Press.

Goelman, H. (1992). 'Day Care in Canada'. In Lamb et al., 223–63.

Goldberg, M. (1994). 'The Adequacy of Social Assistance'. *Perception* 18(1): 22.

Gordon, M. (1988). *Social Security Policies in Industrialized Countries: A Comparative Analysis*. Cambridge: Cambridge University Press.

Gray, C. (1988). 'Why Can't Women Get Their Act Together?' *Chatelaine* November: 82–3, 232–40.

Greene-Finestone, L., et al. (1989). 'Infant Feeding Practices and Socio-Demographic Factors in Ottawa-Carleton'. *Canadian Journal of Public Health* 80(3): 173–76.

Gregg, A., and M. Posner (1990). *The Big Picture: What Canadians Think About Almost Everything*. Toronto: MacFarlane, Walter & Ross.

Guest, D. (1980). *The Emergence of Social Security in Canada*. Vancouver: University of British Columbia Press (reprinted 1985).

Gunter, L. (1992). 'Government Saving the Family from Government'. *Alberta Report* 19(11): 6–7.

Haskins, R. (1988). 'What Day Care Crisis?' *Regulation* 12(2): 13–21.

Hess, M. (1992). *The Canadian Fact Book on Income Security Programs*. Ottawa: The

Canadian Council on Social Development.

Hilton, K. (1993). 'Close Down the Food Banks'. *Canadian Dimension* August: 22–3.

Hossie, L. (1985). 'The Midwives Battle for Self-Rule'. *The Globe and Mail* (Toronto) 12 November 1985.

Hughes, J. (1993). '31% Favour Legalized Abortion under Any Circumstance'. *The Gallup Report* 2 August 1993.

Hurlburt, W. (1986). *Law Reform Commissions in the United Kingdom, Australia and Canada*. Edmonton: Juriliber Limited.

Johnson, A. (1985). 'Restructuring Family Allowances: "Good Policy at No Cost"?' In Ismael, J., ed. *Canadian Social Welfare Policy: Federal and Provincial Dimensions*. Kingston and Montreal: McGill–Queen's University Press, 105–19.

Johnson, H. (1990). 'Wife Abuse'. In McKie and Thompson, 173–6.

Kalbach, W., and W. McVey (1979). *The Demographic Basis of Canadian Society*. 2nd ed. Toronto: McGraw–Hill Ryerson.

Kamerman, S., and A. Kahn (1989a). 'Child Care and Privatization Under Reagan'. In Kamerman, S., and A. Kahn, eds. *Privatization and the Welfare State*. Princeton, New Jersey: Princeton University Press, 235–59.

Kelly, L. (1971). *Family Allowances and the Tax System*. Kingston: Industrial Relations Centre, Queen's University.

Kerans, P. (1990). 'Government Inquiries and the Issue of Unemployment: The Struggle for People's Imagination'. In Riches, G., and G. Ternowetsky, eds. *Unemployment and Welfare: Social Policy and the Work of Social Work*. Toronto: Garamond Press, 47–63.

Kerr, G. (1993). 'What's Going on with Food Banks?' *Perception* 17(2): 17–18.

Kesselman, J. (1979). 'Credits, Exemptions, and Demogrants in Canadian Tax-Transfer Policy'. In *Canadian Tax Journal* 27(6): 653–88.

—— (1993). 'The Child Tax Benefit: Simple, Fair, Responsive?' *Canadian Public Policy* 19(2): 109–32.

Kluck-Davis, C. (1991). 'Children's Habitat'. In Barnhorst and Johnson, 185–204.

Knoppers, B. (1992). *Canadian Child Health Law*. Toronto: Thompson Educational Publishing, Inc.

Krane, J. (1994). 'The Transformation of Women into Mother Protectors: An Examination of Child Protection Practices in Cases of Child Sexual Abuse'. Toronto: University of Toronto. (Unpublished doctoral thesis.)

Labour Canada, Women's Bureau (1984). *Maternity and Child Care Leave in Canada*. Ottawa: Labour Canada.

—— (1985). *Canadian Women and Job Related Laws, 1984*. Ottawa: Labour Canada.

—— (1990). *Women in the Labour Force 1990–91*. Ottawa: Labour Canada.

Lachapelle, R., and J. Henripin (1982). *The Demolinguistic Situation in Canada: Past Trends and Future Prospects*. Montreal: The Institute for Research on Public Policy.

Lamb, M., et al., eds. (1992). *Child Care in Context: Cross-Cultural Perspectives*. New Jersey: Lawrence Erlbaum Associates.

——, and K. Sternberg (1992). 'Sociocultural Perspectives on Nonparental Child Care'. In Lamb et al., 1–23.

La Novara, P. (1993). *A Portrait of Families in Canada*. Catalogue #89–523E. Ottawa: Statistics Canada.

Law Reform Commission of Nova Scotia (1993). *The Legal Status of the Child Born Outside of Marriage in Nova Scotia*. Halifax: Law Reform Commission of Nova Scotia.

Laycock, D. (1994). 'Reforming Canadian Democracy? Institutions and Ideology in the Reform Party Project'. *Canadian Journal of Political Science* 27(2): 213–47.

LEAF: *See* Women's Legal Education and Action Fund

Le Bourdais, C., and N. Marcil-Gratton (with D. Bélanger) (1994). 'Quebec's Pro-Active Approach to Family Policy: Thinking and Acting Family'. In Baker, 1994a, 103–15.

Lero, D., et al. (1992). *Canadian National Child Care Study: Parental Work Patterns and Child Care Needs.* Catalogue #89–529. Ottawa: Minister of Supply and Services.

——, and K. Johnson (1994). *110 Canadian Statistics on Work and Family.* Ottawa: The Canadian Advisory Council on the Status of Women.

Light, B., and R. Pierson (1990). *No Easy Road: Women in Canada 1920s to 1960s.* Toronto: New Hogtown Press.

Lindsay, C. (1992). *Lone-Parent Families in Canada.* Catalogue #89–522E, December. Ottawa: Minister of Industry, Science and Technology.

Lo, O., and P. Gauthier (1995). 'Housing Affordability Problems Among Renters'. *Canadian Social Trends* 36(Spring): 14–17.

Lynas, K. (1993). 'The Feminization of Parliament'. *Perception* 17(2): 9–11, 34.

MacIntyre, E. (1993). 'The Historical Context of Child Welfare in Canada'. In Wharf, 1993a, 13–36.

Mackie, R. (1995). 'Quebec's Birth Rate Drops for Fourth Year'. *The Globe and Mail* 8 July 1995: A4.

MacLeod, L. (1980). *Wife Battering in Canada: The Vicious Circle.* Ottawa: Canadian Advisory Council on the Status of Women.

—— (1989). *Wife Battering and the Web of Hope: Progress, Dilemmas and the Visions of Prevention.* Prepared for the Family Violence Prevention Division. Ottawa: Health and Welfare Canada.

Manitoba Law Reform Commission (1988). *The Manitoba Law Reform Commission: A Framework for the Future.* Winnipeg: Manitoba Law Reform Commission.

Marsh, L. (1943). *Report on Social Security for Canada.* Ottawa: E. Cloutier. (Reprinted in 1975 by the University of Toronto Press.)

Marshall, K. (1993). 'Employed Parents and the Division of Housework'. *Perspectives on Labour and Income.* Ottawa: Statistics Canada 5(3): 23–30.

Martin, S. (1989). *Women's Reproductive Health.* Ottawa: Canadian Advisory Council on the Status of Women.

Maynard, R. (1988). 'Were They Better Off Than We Are'. *Report on Business Magazine (The Globe and Mail)* May: 39–47.

McCall, M., and G. Robertson (1992). 'Legal Rights of Children to Health Care in the Common Law Jurisdictions of Canada'. In Knoppers, 151–208.

McDaniel, S. (1990). *Towards Family Policies in Canada With Women in Mind.* Ottawa: Canadian Research Institute for the Advancement of Women.

—— (1993). 'Where the Contradictions Meet: Women and Family Security in Canada in the 1990s'. In Ross, 1993, 163–80.

McElroy, M., and M. Horney (1981). 'Nash-Bargained Household Decisions: Toward a Generalization of the Theory of Demand'. *International Economic Review* 22(2): 333–49.

McGillivray, A. (1990). 'Abused Children in the Courts: Adjusting the Scales after Bill C-15'. *Manitoba Law Journal* 19: 549–79.

McGilly, F. (1990). *Canada's Public Social Services.* Toronto: McClelland and Stewart.

McKie, C. (1993). 'Demographic Change and Quality-of-Life Concerns in Postwar Canada'. In Ross, 1993, 107–34.

——, and K. Thompson (1990). *Canadian Social Trends.* Toronto: Thompson Educational Publishing, Inc.

McLaughlin, M. (1991). 'The Facts on Food and Shelter, 1990'. *Perception* 15(2): 21–3.

Mitchell, A. (1995a). 'Abortion Numbers Continue to Climb'. *The Globe and Mail* 13 July 1995: A1, A8.

—— (1995b). 'Vouchers Raise Doubts about Universal Care'. *The Globe and Mail* 29 November 1995: A8.

Moloney, J. (1989). 'On Maternity Leave'. In *Perspectives on Labour and Income*. Ottawa: Statistics Canada 1(1): 27–46.

Morissette, R., J. Myles, and G. Picot (1994). 'Earnings Inequality and the Distribution of Working Time in Canada'. *Canadian Business Economics* 2(3): 3–16.

Morton, M. (1988). 'Dividing the Wealth, Sharing the Poverty: The (Re)formation of "Family" in Law'. *The Canadian Review of Sociology and Anthropology* 25(2): 254–75.

—— (1990). 'Controversies Within Family Law'. In Baker, M., ed. *Families. Changing Trends in Canada.* 2nd ed. Toronto: McGraw–Hill Ryerson, 211–40.

Moscovitch, A., and G. Drover (1987). 'Social Expenditures and the Welfare State: The Canadian Experience in Historical Perspective'. In Moscovitch, A., and J. Albert, eds. *The Benevolent State.* Toronto: Garamond, 13–43.

Muir, B. (for Indian and Northern Health Services) (1988). *Health Status of Canadian Indians and Inuit.* Ottawa: Health and Welfare Canada.

Muszynski, L. (1988). *Is It Fair? What Tax Reform Will Do to You.* Ottawa: Canadian Centre for Policy Alternatives and The United Church of Canada.

Nakamura, A., and E. Diewert (1994). 'Reforming Our Public Income Support Programs'. Paper prepared for the School of Policy Studies' Conference on Labour Market Polarization and Social Policy. Queen's University, Kingston, Ontario, 27–28 January 1994.

National Action Committee on the Status of Women (1991). *Feminist Action* 5(3) February.

National Anti-Poverty Association (1989). *NAPO.* Ottawa: NAPO.

National Council of Welfare (1983). *Family Allowances For All?* Ottawa: Supply and Services.

—— (1987a). *Welfare in Canada: The Tangled Safety Net.* Ottawa: Minister of Supply and Services.

—— (1987b). *Testing Tax Reform: A Brief to the Standing Committee on Finance and Economic Affairs.* Ottawa: Minister of Supply and Services.

—— (1990). *Women and Poverty Revisited.* Ottawa: Minister of Supply and Services.

—— (1991). *Fighting Child Poverty.* Ottawa: Minister of Supply and Services.

—— (1992a). *The 1992 Budget and Child Benefits.* Ottawa: Minister of Supply and Services.

—— (1992b). *Welfare Reform.* Ottawa: Minister of Supply and Services Canada.

—— (1993a). *Incentives and Disincentives to Work.* Ottawa: Minister of Supply and Services Canada.

—— (1993b). *Welfare Incomes 1992.* Ottawa: Minister of Supply and Services.

—— (1994a). *A Blueprint for Social Security Reform.* Ottawa: Minister of Supply and Services.

—— (1994b). *Poverty Profile 1992.* Ottawa: Minister of Supply and Services.

—— (1995). *Social Security Background Papers, #1, #2, #3, #4.* Ottawa: Minister of Supply and Services.

National Forum on Family Security (1993). 'Keynote Paper'. In Ross, 1993, 1–18.

Nault, F., and E. Jenkins (1993). *Projections of Canada's Population With Aboriginal Ancestry, 1991–2016.* Catalogue 91–2016. Ottawa: Statistics Canada, Employment Equity Data Program.

Naylor, C., ed. (1992). *Canadian Health Care and the State.* Montreal and Kingston: McGill–Queen's University Press.

Nesmith, M. (1994). 'The Family'. *Maclean's* 107(25): 30–8.

Nett, E. (1981). 'Canadian Families in Social-Historical Perspective'. *Canadian Journal of Sociology* 6(3): 239–60.

Oderkirk, J. (1992). 'Food Banks'. *Canadian Social Trends* 24(Spring): 6–14.

Osberg, L. (1993). *Social Policy and the Demand Side*. Working Paper No. 93–13. Halifax: Dalhousie University.

—— (1995, forthcoming). 'The Equity/Efficiency Trade-Off in Retrospect'. *Canadian Business Economics*.

——, and S. Phipps (1992). 'A Social Charter for Canada'. In MacCallum, J., ed. *A Social Charter for Canada? Perspectives on the Constitutional Entrenchment of Social Rights*. Toronto: C. D. Howe Institute, 1–34.

——, and S. Phipps (1995). *The Role of Unemployment Insurance in the Income Security Framework: A Component Study of the Unemployment Regular Benefits Program*. Halifax: Dalhousie University.

——, S. Erksoy, and S. Phipps (1994a). *The Distribution of Income, Wealth and Economic Security: The Impact of Unemployment Insurance Reforms in Canada*. Working Paper No. 94–08. Halifax: Dalhousie University.

——, S. Erksoy, and S. Phipps (1994b). *How to Value the Poorer Prospects of the Young?* Working Paper No. 94–09. Halifax: Dalhousie University.

——, S. Erksoy, and S. Phipps (1994c). *Labour Market Impacts of the Canadian and U.S. Unemployment Insurance Systems*. Working Paper No. 94–12. Halifax: Dalhousie University.

——, S. Erksoy, and S. Phipps (1995, forthcoming). 'Unemployment, Unemployment Insurance and the Distribution of Income in Canada in the 1980s'. In Gustafsson, B., and E. Palmer, eds. *Distribution of Economic Well-being in the 1980s: An International Perspective*. Cambridge: Cambridge University Press.

Overall, C. (1993). *Human Reproduction: Principles, Practices, Policies*. Toronto: Oxford University Press.

Pelletier, R., F. Bundock, and M. Sarra-Bournet (1991). 'The Structures of Canadian Political Parties: How They Operate'. In Bakvis, 265–309.

Perry, J. (1989). *A Fiscal History of Canada: The Postwar Years*. Canadian Tax Paper No. 85. Toronto: Canadian Tax Foundation.

Peters, J. (1988). 'Changing Perspectives on Divorce'. In Anderson, K., et al., 141–62.

Phipps, S. (1993). 'Does Unemployment Insurance Increase Unemployment?' *Canadian Business Economics* 1(3): 37–50.

—— (1994). 'What is the Income "Cost" of a Child? Exact Equivalence Scales for Canadian Two Parent Families'. Halifax: Dalhousie University, Department of Economics.

—— (1995). 'Canadian Child Benefits: Behavioural Consequences and Income Adequacy'. *Canadian Public Policy* 21(1): 20–30.

——, and P. Burton (1992). 'What's Mine is Yours? The Influence of Male and Female Incomes on Patterns of Household Expenditure'. Discussion Paper No. 92–12. Halifax: Dalhousie University.

——, and P. Burton (1993). 'Collective Models of Household Behaviour: Implications for Economic Policy'. Paper presented at the Status of Women Economic Equality Workshop. Ottawa, Ontario, 29–30 November 1993.

——, and P. Burton (1995). 'Sharing within Families: Implications for the Measurement of Poverty among Individuals in Canada'. *Canadian Journal of Economics* 28(1): 177–204.

Picard, A. (1992). 'Quebec Budget'. *The Globe and Mail* 15 May 1992: A4.

Pierson, R. (1977). 'Women's Emancipation and the Recruitment of Women into the Labour

Force in World War II'. In Trofimenkoff, S., and A. Prentice, eds. *The Neglected Majority: Essays in Canadian Women's History.* Toronto: McClelland and Stewart, 125–45.

—— (1993). 'The Politics of the Body'. In Pierson et al., 98–185.

——, et al., eds. (1993). *Canadian Women's Issues, vol. 1: Strong Voices.* Toronto: James Lorimer & Company.

Pitsula, J. (1985). 'The CCF Government of Saskatchewan and Social Aid, 1944–1964'. In Brennan, 205–25.

Posterski, D., and R. Bibby (1988). *Canada's Youth: A Comprehensive Survey of 15–24 Year Olds.* Ottawa: Canadian Youth Foundation.

Powell, L. (1992). *Towards Child Care Policy Development in Canada.* Background paper prepared for the School of Policy Studies Program on Social Policy. Kingston: Queen's University.

Quebec, Government of (1989). *Reference Manual on the Youth Protection Act.* Quebec: Minister of Health and Social Services.

Ram, B. (1990). 'Intermarriage Among Ethnic Groups'. In Halli, S., F. Trovato, and L. Driedger, eds. *Ethnic Demography. Canadian Immigrant, Racial and Cultural Variations.* Ottawa: Carleton University Press, 213–27.

Rashid, A. (1990). 'Government Transfer Payments and Family Income'. *Perspectives on Labour Income* 2(3): 50–60.

REAL Women of Canada (1985). Brief to Members of Parliament. 19 November 1985.

—— (1986). Brief to Members of Parliament. 18 November 1986.

Revenue Canada, Taxation (1982). *1982 Taxation Statistics.* Ottawa: Minister of Supply and Services Canada.

—— (1987). *1987 Taxation Statistics.* Ottawa: Minister of Supply and Services Canada.

—— (1992). *1992 Taxation Statistics.* Ottawa: Minister of Supply and Services Canada.

Rice, J., and M. Prince (1993). 'Life of Brian: A Social Policy Legacy'. *Perception* 17(2): 6–8.

Richardson, C. (1988). *Court-Based Divorce Mediation in Four Canadian Cities: An Overview of Research Results.* Ottawa: Minister of Supply and Services.

Riches, G. (1986). *Food Banks and the Welfare Crisis.* Ottawa: Canadian Council on Social Development.

Ringen, S. (1987). *The Possibility of Politics: A Study in the Political Economy of the Welfare State.* Oxford: Clarendon Press.

Roberts, B. (1988). *Smooth Sailing or Storm Warning? Canadian and Quebec Women's Groups and the Meech Lake Accord.* Ottawa: Canadian Research Institute for the Advancement of Women.

Roeher Institute (1993). *Right off the Bat: A Study of Inclusive Child Care in Canada.* North York, Ontario: Roeher Institute.

Ross, D., ed. (1993). *Family Security in Insecure Times.* Ottawa: National Forum on Family Security.

——, and E. Shillington (1989). *A Profile of the Canadian Volunteer.* Ottawa: National Voluntary Organization.

——, E. Shillington, and C. Lochhead (1994). 'Poverty and Income Distribution in Canada and Abroad'. In *The Canadian Fact Book on Poverty: 1994.* Ottawa: The Canadian Council on Social Development, 109–15.

Routhier, A., and S. Labowka (1994). *Unemployment Insurance Provision of Special Benefits: Evaluation Synthesis and Issues.* Ottawa: Human Resources Development Canada.

Roy, M. (1994). 'What Does the BQ Stand For?' *Canadian Dimension* 28(1): 26–7.

Royal Commission on New Reproductive Technologies (1993). *Proceed with Care.* Ottawa: Minister of Government Services Canada.

Royal Commission on the Status of Women (1970). *Report of the Royal Commission on the Status of Women in Canada*. Ottawa: Information Canada.

Sarrasin, R. (1994). 'L'Evolution de la Politique Familiale Québecoise'. *Intervention* 99(Oct.): 7–16.

Scarth, S. (1993). 'Child Welfare at the Crossroads: Can the System Protect Canada's Most Vulnerable Children?' *Perception* 17(3): 5–8.

Seccombe, W. (1989). '"Helping Her Out": The Participation of Husbands in Domestic Labour When Wives Go Out to Work'. Toronto: Ontario Institute for Studies in Education. (Unpublished paper.)

'Serving the Needs of Children and Families'. (1991). *Health Promotion* 30(3): 14–15.

Sev'er, A. (1992). *Women and Divorce in Canada*. Toronto: Canadian Scholars' Press.

Sharif, N., and S. Phipps (1994). 'The Challenge of Child Poverty'. *Canadian Business Journal* 2(3): 17–30.

Siggner, A. (1986). 'The Socio-Demographic Conditions of Registered Indians'. In Ponting, J., ed. *Arduous Journey*. Toronto: McClelland and Stewart.

Sigurdson, R. (1994). 'Preston Manning and the Politics of Post-Modernism in Canada'. *Canadian Journal of Political Science* 27(2): 249–76.

Sillars, L. (1994). 'The Fraser Institute turns 20'. *Alberta Report* 21(27): 38–9.

Silver, C., and R. Van Diepen (1995). 'Housing Tenure Trends: 1951–1991'. *Canadian Social Trends* 36(Spring): 8–13.

Sinclair, J., D. Philips, and N. Bala (1991). 'Aboriginal Child Welfare in Canada'. In Bala, Hornick, and Vogl, 171–94.

Smith, V. (1994). 'Compared to Europe, Canada has No Reason to Feel Smug'. *The Globe and Mail* 20 January 1994: A6.

Statistics Canada (annual). *Births and Deaths*. Cat. #84–204. Ottawa: Minister of Industry, Science and Technology.

—— (1966). *Seasonally Adjusted Labour Force Statistics, January 1953–December 1966*. Cat. #71–201. Ottawa: Dominion Bureau of Statistics.

—— (1975). *Historical Labour Force Statistics. 1974*. Cat. #71–201. Ottawa: Minister of Industry, Trade and Commerce.

—— (1982). *Family Allowances and Related Programs 1982*. Social Security National Programs, vol. 4. Ottawa: Supply and Services.

—— (1983). *Historical Statistics of Canada*. 2nd ed. Ottawa: Supply and Services Canada.

—— (1985). *Unemployment Insurance Statistics*. Cat. #73–001. Ottawa: Minister of Supply and Services Canada.

—— (1988). *Industry Trends 1951–1986*. Cat. #93–152. Ottawa: Minister of Supply and Services Canada.

—— (1990a). *1990 General Social Survey*. Ottawa (microdata).

—— (1990b). *Current Demographic Analysis: New Trends in the Family*. Cat. #91–535E. Ottawa: Minister of Industry, Science and Technology.

—— (1991a). *Families: Number, Type and Size. The Nation*. Cat. #93–312. Ottawa: Statistics Canada.

—— (1991b). *Households and Families*. Vol. 2, Part 1. Cat. #93–510. Ottawa: Statistics Canada.

—— (1991c). *Where Does Time Go?* Cat. #11–612E #4. Ottawa: Minister of Industry, Science and Technology.

—— (1991d). *Historical Labour Force Statistics, 1991*. Cat. #71–201. Ottawa: Minister of Industry, Science and Technology.

—— (1992a). *Canadian National Child Care Survey: Introductory Report*. Ottawa: Minister of Industry, Science and Technology.

—— (1992b). *Parental Work Patterns and Child Care Needs*. Cat. #89–529E. Ottawa: Minister of Industry, Science and Technology.

—— (1992c). *Health Reports. Supplement No. 14. Births, 1990*. Cat. #82–003S14, vol. 14, no. 1. Ottawa: Minister of Supply and Services Canada.

—— (1993a). *Births 1992*. Cat. #84–210. Ottawa: Minister of Industry, Science and Technology.

—— (1993b). *Canada Yearbook 1994*. Ottawa: Minister of Industry, Science and Technology.

—— (1993c). *Families: Social and Economic Characteristics*. Cat. #93–320. Ottawa: Minister of Industry, Science and Technology.

—— (1993d). *Health Reports* 5 (4). Cat. #82–003S. Ottawa: Minister of Industry, Science and Technology.

—— (1993e). *Household Facilities and Equipment*. Cat. #64–202. Ottawa: Minister of Industry, Science and Technology.

—— (1993f). *Housing Costs and Other Characteristics of Canadian Households*. Cat. #93–330. Ottawa: Minister of Industry, Science and Technology.

—— (1993g). Initial Data Release from the 1992 *General Social Survey on Time Use*. Ottawa: Minister of Industry, Science and Technology.

—— (1993h). *An Overview of Child Care Arrangements in Canada*. Cat. #89–527E. Ottawa: Minister of Industry, Science and Technology.

—— (1993i). *Selected Birth and Fertility Statistics, Canada 1921–1990*. Cat. #82–553. Ottawa: Minister of Industry, Science and Technology.

—— (1993j). *Selected Infant Mortality and Related Statistics, Canada, 1921–1990*. Cat. #82–549. Ottawa: Minister of Industry, Science and Technology.

—— (1993k). *Therapeutic Abortions 1991*. Cat. #82–219. Ottawa: Minister of Industry, Science and Technology.

—— (1994a). *1991 Aboriginal People's Survey: 1) Disability, 2) Housing*. Cat. #89–535. Ottawa: Minister of Industry, Science and Technology.

—— (1994b). *The Labour Force*. Cat. #71–001. Ottawa: Minister of Industry, Science and Technology.

—— (1995a). *Profile of Canada's Aboriginal Population*. Cat. #94–325. Ottawa: Statistics Canada.

—— (1995b). *Women in Canada: A Statistical Report*. 3rd ed. Cat. #89–503E. Ottawa: Minister of Industry.

—— (1995c). *Unemployment Insurance Statistics. Annual Supplement*. Cat. #73–202S. Ottawa: Minister of Supply and Services Canada.

Steele, S. (1994). 'A National Mirror'. *Maclean's* 107(1): 12–13.

Stout, C. (1991). 'Common-Law: A Growing Alternative'. *Canadian Social Trends* 23(Winter): 18–20.

Strauss, S. (1992). 'Baby Boomlet Continues, Statistics Canada Reports'. *The Globe and Mail* 31 March 1992: A1, A5.

Strong-Boag, V. (1976). *The Parliament of Women: The National Council of Women 1893–1929*. Ottawa: National Museums of Canada.

—— (1982). 'Intruders in the Nursery: Childcare Professionals Reshape the Years One to Five, 1920–1940'. In Parr, J., ed. *Childhood and Family in Canadian History*. Toronto: McClelland and Stewart, 160–78.

Sutherland, N. (1976). *Children in English-Canadian Society: Framing the Twentieth*

Century Consensus. Toronto: University of Toronto Press.

Swift, K. (1995). *Manufacturing 'Bad Mothers': A Critical Perspective on Child Neglect.* Toronto: University of Toronto Press.

Syrtash, J. (1992). *Religion and Culture in Family Law.* Toronto: Butterworths.

Tarasuk, V., and H. Maclean (1990). 'The Institutionalization of Food Banks in Canada: A Public Health Concern'. *Canadian Journal of Public Health* 81(4): 331–2.

Taylor, M. (1987). *Health Insurance and Canadian Public Policy.* 2nd ed. Toronto: Institute of Public Administration of Canada.

Torjman, S. (1994a). 'Crests and Crashes: The Changing Tides of Family Income Security'. In Baker, 1994a, 69–87.

—— (1994b). 'Is CAP in Need of Assistance?' In Banting, K., and K. Battle, eds. *A New Social Vision for Canada? Perspectives on the Federal Discussion Paper on Social Security Reform.* Kingston: Queen's University School of Policy Studies, 99–113.

Townson, M. (1983). *A National System of Fully-Paid Parental Leave for Canada: Policy Choices, Costs and Funding Mechanisms.* Ottawa: Labour Canada.

—— (1985). 'Paid Parental Leave Policies: An International Comparison, with Options for Canada'. In *Child Care: The Employer's Role,* series 4. Background paper for *Report of the Task Force on Child Care.* Ottawa: Status of Women, 1–57.

Trocmé, N. (1991). 'Child Welfare Services'. In Barnhorst and Johnson, 63–91.

United Nations (1991). *World's Women 1970–1990: Trends and Statistics.* New York: United Nations.

United States Department of Health and Human Services (1990). *Social Security Programs Throughout the World.* Research Report #61. Washington: Department of Health and Human Services.

Ursel, J. (1992). *Private Lives, Public Policy. 100 Years of State Intervention in the Family.* Toronto: Women's Press.

Vanier Institute of the Family (VIF) (1993). *Inventory of Family and Supportive Policies and Programs in Federal, Provincial and Territorial Jurisdictions.* Ottawa: VIF.

—— (1994). *Profiling Canada's Families.* Ottawa: VIF.

Vayda, E., and R. Debec (1992). 'The Canadian Health Care System: A Developmental Overview'. In Naylor, D., ed. *Canadian Health Care and the State.* Montreal and Kingston: McGill–Queen's University Press, 125–40.

Vickers, J., P. Rankin, and C. Appelle (1993). *Politics as if Women Mattered: A Political Analysis of the National Action Committee on the Status of Women.* Toronto: University of Toronto Press.

VIF. *See* Vanier Institute of the Family

Vogl, R. (1991). 'Initial Involvement'. In Bala, Hornick, and Vogl, 33–54.

Wadhera, S., and W. Millar (1991). 'Patterns and Change in Canadian Fertility 1971–1988: First Births After Age 30'. *Health Reports* 3(2): 149–61.

——, and J. Strachan (1991). 'Births and Birth Rates, Canada, 1989'. *Health Reports* 3(2): 79–82.

Walder, D. (1985). 'Following the Gleam: The Political Philosophy of J. S. Woodsworth'. In Brennan, 43–56.

Wharf, B., ed. (1993a). *Rethinking Child Welfare in Canada.* Toronto: McClelland and Stewart.

—— (1993b). 'The Constituency/Community Context'. In Wharf, 1993a, 98–127.

White, J. (1993). *Sisters and Solidarity: Women and Unions in Canada.* Toronto: Thompson Educational Publishing, Inc.

Winnipeg Urban Aboriginal Community (1993). *The First Peoples Urban Circle: Choices*

for Self Determination. Ottawa: The Native Council of Canada.
Wong, G. (1994). 'Job Separation and the Passage to Unemployment and Welfare Benefits'. Prepared for the CERF Workshop on Income Assistance. Vancouver, British Columbia, 26–27 March 1994.
Women's Legal Education and Action Fund (LEAF) (1992). *LEAF Lines* 5(2) Fall.
Wood, C. (1988). 'Lifestyles: Strong Family Ties'. *Maclean's* 101(1): 48–9.
Wooley, F. (1994). 'Ending Universality: The Case of Child Benefits'. Paper presented at the CERF Workshop on Labour Markets and Income Support. University of British Columbia, 26 March 1994.

NEW ZEALAND

Angus, J., and W. Gray (1995). 'A Department of Social Welfare Policy Perspective on Rights and Responsibilities'. In *Rights and Responsibilities*, 79–84.
Atkin, B. (1992). 'Financial Support: The Bureaucratization of Personal Responsibility'. In Henaghan and Atkin.
Barclay, P., and J. Hills (1995). *Joseph Rowntree Foundation Inquiry into Income and Wealth*. 2 vols. York, England: Joseph Rowntree Foundation.
Beaglehole, A. (1993). *Benefiting Women: Income Support for Women, 1893–1993*. Wellington: Social Policy Agency, Department of Social Welfare.
Bollard, A., and R. Buckle, eds. (1987). *Economic Liberalisation in New Zealand*. Wellington: Allen and Unwin.
Boston, J. (1984). *Incomes Policy in New Zealand*. Wellington: Victoria University Press.
——, and Dalziel, P., eds. (1992). *The Decent Society? Essays in Response to National's Economic and Social Policies*. Auckland: Oxford University Press.
——, and Holland, M., eds. (1987). *The Fourth Labour Government: Radical Politics in New Zealand*. Auckland: Oxford University Press.
Bowie, R., and I. Shirley (1994). 'Political and Economic Perspectives on Recent Health Policy'. In Spicer, Trlin, and Walton, 298–322.
Bradshaw, J., et al. (1993). *Support for Children: A Comparison of Arrangements in Fifteen Countries*. UK Department of Social Security Research Report No. 21. London: HMSO.
Brashares, E. (1993). 'Assessing Income Adequacy in New Zealand'. *New Zealand Economic Papers* 27(2): 185.
Brosnan, P., and D. Rea (1992). 'Rogernomics and the Labour Market'. *New Zealand Sociology* 7(2): 188–221.
Bryn Mawr (1978). Report on New Zealand Accident Compensation Act, cited in the *Evening Post* 25 August 1978.
Budget '85 Task Force (1985). 'Benefits, Taxes, and the 1985 Budget'. Discussion paper. Wellington: Government Printer.
Butterworths (1993). *Family Law Journal*. Wellington: Butterworths/Bayleys Uniprint.
Cameron, J. (1990). *Why Have Children?* Christchurch: University of Canterbury Press.
Carmichael, G. (1982). 'Aspects of Ex-Nuptiality in New Zealand'. Canberra: Australian National University. (Unpublished doctoral thesis.)
—— (1984). 'Living Together in New Zealand: Data on Co-Residence at Marriage and on de Facto Unions'. *New Zealand Population Review* 10(3): 41–53.
Cartwright, S. (1985). 'Law and Population'. In ESCAP, 1985, 187–94.
Castles, F. (1985). *The Working Class and Welfare: Reflections on the Political Development of the Welfare State in Australia and New Zealand 1890–1980*. Wellington: Allen and Unwin.

444   *Bibliography*

—— (1988). *Australian Public Policy and Economic Vulnerability*. Sydney: Allen and Unwin.

——, R. Gerritsen, and J. Vowles, eds. (1996). *The Great Experiment: Labour Parties and Public Policy Transformation in Australia and New Zealand*. Auckland: Auckland University Press.

——, and I. Shirley (1996). 'Labour and Social Policy: Gravediggers or Refurbishers of the Welfare State'. In Castles, Gerritsen, and Vowles, 88–106.

Caygill, D. (1990). *Building Economic Growth: Economic Strategy*. Wellington: Minister of Finance.

Chatterjee, S. (1992). *Aspects of New Zealand's Economic Restructuring 1984–92: An Assessment*. Working Paper Series. Perth: Curtin University of Technology.

——, and C. Michelini (1983). *Balance of Payments Constraints and Feasible Growth Rates: The New Zealand Experience*. Massey Economic Papers, B8310. Palmerston North: Massey University Department of Economics.

Collins, S. (1987). *Rogernomics*. Wellington: Pitman.

Committee for the International Year of the Family (1994). *New Zealand Family Facts*. Newsletter March/April. Wellington: IYF Committee.

Condran, G., and F. Furstenburg (1994). 'Evolution du Bien-etre des Enfants et la Transformation de la Famille americaine'. *Population* 49(6): 1613–38.

Crean, P. (1982). *Survey of Low Income Families*. Christchurch: Low Incomes Working Party.

Crosby, A. (1986). *Ecological Imperialism: The Biological Expansion of Europe, 900–1900*. Cambridge: Cambridge University Press.

Dalziel, P. (1993). *Taxing the Poor, Key Economic Assumptions Behind the April 1991 Benefit Cuts: What are the Alternatives?* Wellington: New Zealand Council of Christian Social Services.

Davey, J. (1993). *From Birth to Death III*. Wellington: Victoria University Institute of Policy Studies.

Davidson, A. (1989). *Two Models of Welfare: The Origins and Development of the Welfare State in Sweden and New Zealand, 1888–1988*. Uppsala: Acta Universitatis Upsaliensis.

Davies, L., et al. (1993). 'Sole Parenting: A Different Demographic Perspective'. In *Ethnicity and Gender: Population Trends and Policies in the 1990s*. Conference proceedings. Wellington: Population Association of New Zealand and Te Puni Kokiri, 99–113.

——, and Jackson, N. (1993). *Women's Labour Force Participation in New Zealand: The Past 100 Years*. Wellington: Social Policy Agency.

Department of Social Welfare (1985–95). *Annual Reports*. Wellington: Department of Social Welfare.

—— (1987). *Income Maintenance and Taxation*. Working Paper No. 3. Wellington: Department of Social Welfare.

—— (1988). *State Financial Support for Children*. Paper prepared for the Royal Commission on Social Policy. Wellington: Department of Social Welfare.

—— (1995). *From Welfare to Well-being*. Wellington: Department of Social Welfare.

Department of Statistics (1961–1995). *Official Yearbook*. Wellington: Government Printer.

—— (1990). *The Fiscal Impact on Income Distribution 1987/88*. Wellington: Department of Statistics.

—— (1991). *New Zealand Social Trends: Incomes*. Wellington: Department of Statistics.

—— (1994). *New Zealand Now: Children*. Wellington: Statistics New Zealand.

Easting, S. (1994). *Women, Childcare and the State*. Palmerston North: Massey University.

——, and R. Fleming (1994). *Families, Money and Policy. Summary of the Intra Family Income Study and Discussions of Policy Issues*. Wellington: Intra Family Income Project.

Easton, B. (1976). 'Poverty in New Zealand: Estimates and Reflections'. *Political Science* 28(2). Reprinted in Easton, 1983, 264–79.

—— (1981). *Pragmatism and Progress: Social Security in the Seventies.* Christchurch: University of Canterbury Press.

—— (1983). *Income Distribution in New Zealand.* Research Paper No. 28. Wellington: New Zealand Institute of Economic Research.

—— (1986) *Wages and the Poor.* Wellington: Allen and Unwin.

——, ed. (1989). *The Making of Rogernomics.* Auckland: Auckland University Press.

—— (1990). 'Structural Change and Economic Growth in Postwar New Zealand'. Paper to the conference of the New Zealand Association of Economists, Wellington, February.

—— (1993). 'Poverty and Families: Priority or Piety?' Paper prepared for workshop 'Issues for Families', Wellington, October.

—— (1994a). 'Approaching Family Economic Issues: Holistically or Pathologically?' In *Rights and Responsibilities*, 94–99.

—— (1994b). 'Properly Assessing Income Adequacy in New Zealand'. (Unpublished manuscript.)

——, and Bowie, R. (1993). 'Some Aggregate Health Statistics: Through Time and Between Countries'. Paper presented at the National Conference of the Public Health Association of New Zealand, Wellington, 1993.

——, and R. Gerritsen (1996). 'Economic Reform: Parallels and Divergences'. In Castles, Gerritsen, and Vowles, 22–47.

Economic and Social Commission for Asia and the Pacific (ESCAP), Population Division, eds. (1985). *The Population Of New Zealand.* New York: United Nations.

—— (1986). *The Family, Fertility and Contraception in Asia and the Pacific: A Review of Seven Cross-Comparative, Micro-Demographic Country Studies*, vol. 1. Bangkok: United Nations.

ESCAP: *See* Economic and Social Commission for Asia and the Pacific

Family Centre and Business and Economic Research Ltd. (BERL) (1991). *The National Government Budgets of the First Year in Office: A Social Assessment.* Wellington: Sunday Forum.

Fleming, R., and S. Easting (1994). *The Intrafamily Income Study.* Wellington: Ministry of Women's Affairs and Massey University Social Policy Research Centre.

Galtry, J., and P. Callister (1995). 'Birth and the Early Months: The Issue of Parental Leave and Paid Work'. In Callister, P., et al., eds. *Striking a Balance: Families, Work and Early Childhood Education.* Wellington: New Zealand Council for Educational Research.

Gibbs, A. (1994). 'The Impact of the Changing Economy on Families'. Paper presented at the International Year of the Family Conference, Auckland, 30 November–2 December 1994.

Gibson, C. (1971). 'Demographic History of New Zealand'. Berkeley: University of California. (Unpublished doctoral thesis.)

Gough, I. (1995). 'Diverse Systems, Common Destination? A Comparative Study of Social Assistance in OECD Countries'. Paper presented at the International Sociological Association Conference on Comparative Research on Welfare State Reforms, University of Pavia, Italy, 14–17 September 1995.

Haines, L. (1989). *Work Today: Employment Trends to 1989.* Wellington: New Zealand Planning Council.

Hanson, E. (1980). *The Politics of Social Security: The 1938 Act and Some Later Developments.* Auckland: Auckland University Press.

Harbridge, R., ed. (1993). *Employment Contracts: New Zealand Experiences.* Wellington:

Victoria University Press.

Henaghan, M., and B. Atkin, eds. (1992). *Family Law Policy in New Zealand*. Auckland: Oxford University Press.

——, and P. Tapp (1992). 'Legally Defining the Family'. In Henaghan and Atkin.

Hoem, J. (1990). 'Social Policy and Recent Fertility Change in Sweden'. *Population And Development Review* 16(4): 735–48.

Hyman, P. (1994). *Women and Economics: A New Zealand Feminist Perspective*. Wellington: Bridget Williams.

International Labour Office (1949). *Systems of Social Security: New Zealand*. Geneva: ILO.

Jackman, S. (1993). *Child Poverty in Aotearoa/New Zealand*. Report from the New Zealand Council of Christian Social Services. Wellington: NZCCSS.

Jackson, N. (1994a). 'Youth Unemployment and the "Invisible Hand"': A Case for a Social Measure of Unemployment'. In Morrison, P., ed. *Labour, Employment and Work in New Zealand 1994*. Wellington: Victoria University.

—— (1994b). 'Youth Unemployment and the Core Family: Population, Policy and Political Economy'. Hamilton: University of Waikato. (Unpublished masters thesis.)

——, and I. Pool (1994). *Fertility and Family Formation in the 'Second Demographic Transition': New Zealand Patterns and Trends*. Christchurch: New Zealand Institute for Social Research and Development.

——, and I. Pool (1995). 'Familial Capacity: The Demographic Components of Caring Capacity'. In *Rights and Responsibilities*, 1–14.

——, and I. Pool (in press). 'Will the Real New Zealand Family Please Stand Up? Substantive and Methodological Factors Affecting Research and Policy on Families and Households'. *Social Policy Journal of New Zealand*. Wellington: Social Policy Agency, Department of Social Welfare.

James, B. (1985). 'Mill Wives: A Study of Gender Relations, Family and Work in a Single-Industry Town'. Hamilton: University of Waikato Department of Sociology. (Unpublished doctoral thesis.)

—— (1986) 'A Great Place to Raise a Family? New Zealand Family Policy and the Welfare State'. In Wilkes, C., ed. *Working Paper on the State*. Palmerston North: Massey University Department of Sociology, 128–209.

Jesson, B. (1987). *Behind the Mirror Glass: The Growth of Wealth and Power in New Zealand in the Eighties*. Auckland: Penguin.

—— (1989). *Fragments of Labour: The Story Behind the Labour Government*. Auckland: Penguin.

Jessop, B. (1987). 'The Political Economy of Thatcherism'. Seminar presented at Massey University, September 1987.

Johnstone, K., and I. Pool (1995). *New Zealand Families: Size, Income and Labour Force Participation*. Population Studies Centre Discussion Paper No. 7. Hamilton: University of Waikato.

Karoly, L. (1993). 'The Trend in Inequality Among Families, Individuals, and Workers in the United States: A 25-Year Perspective'. In Danziger, S., and P. Gottschalk, eds. *Uneven Tides: Rising Inequality in America*. New York: Russell Sage Foundation.

Katzenstein, P. (1985). *Small States in World Markets: Industrial Policy in Europe*. Ithaca and London: Cornell University Press.

Khawaja, M. (1985). 'Fertility Trends and Differentials'. In ESCAP, 1985.

Koopman-Boyden, P., and C. Scott (1984). *The Family and Government Policy*. Sydney: Allen and Unwin.

Labour Caucus (1994). *'On the Breadline': Impact of the Government's Housing Policy on Housing New Zealand Tenants 16*. Wellington: New Zealand Labour Party.

Le Rossignol, J., and W. Stewart (1910). *State Socialism in New Zealand*. London: George G. Harrap.

Lesthaeghe, R. (1991). *The Second Demographic Transition in Western Countries: An Interpretation*. Working Paper No. 2. Brussels: Inter-University Program in Demography.

Martin, B. (1995). *The New Zealand Family and Economic Restructuring in the 1980s*. Population Studies Centre Discussion Paper No. 4. Hamilton: University of Waikato.

—— (forthcoming). *Some Life Cycle Characteristics Associated with the Incomes of New Zealand Families*. Population Studies Centre Discussion Paper. Hamilton: University of Waikato.

Maxwell, G., and J. Robertson (1990). 'Child Support After Separation'. *Family Law Bulletin* 94: 106.

McCaw, P. (1982). *Report of the Task Force on Tax Reform*. Wellington: Government Printer.

McKay, R. (1981). *Children in Foster-care*. Wellington: Department of Social Welfare.

McKendry, C., and D. Muthummala (1993). *Health Expenditure Trends in New Zealand 1980–1991*. Wellington: Department of Health.

McPherson, M. (1992). 'Cohort Vulnerability to Lack of Family Support in Old Age: A Theoretical and Analytical Exploration'. Hamilton: University of Waikato. (Unpublished masters thesis.)

—— (1995). *Divorce in New Zealand: Recent Trends, Future Directions, Policy Implications and Research Needs*. Family Studies Monograph. Palmerston North: Social Policy Research Centre.

Ministry of Women's Affairs (1992). *Status of New Zealand Women 1992*. Wellington: Ministry of Women's Affairs.

—— (1993). *Briefing to the Incoming Government*. Wellington: Ministry of Women's Affairs.

Mitchell, D., and A. Harding (1993). *Changes in Poverty Among Families During the 1980s: Poverty Gap versus Poverty Head-Count Approaches*. National Centre for Social and Economic Modelling Discussion Paper No. 2. Canberra: University of Canberra Faculty of Management.

Morris, A. (1991). *Health Expenditure: How the Money was Spent and Who Benefited*. Wellington: Department of Health.

Mowbray, M. (1993a) *Incomes Monitoring Report 1981–1991*. Wellington: Social Policy Agency, Department of Social Welfare.

—— (1993b). *Social Environment Scan*. Wellington: Social Policy Agency, Department of Social Welfare.

——, and Dayal, N. (1994). The Fall and Rise (??) of Household Incomes. *Social Policy Journal of New Zealand* 2: 114–22.

Murphy, M. (1993). 'The Contraceptive Pill and Female Employment as Factors in Fertility Change in Britain, 1963–80: A Challenge to the Conventional View'. *Population Studies* 47(2): 221–44.

—— (in press). 'Household and Family Structures among Ethnic Minorities in Britain'. In Coleman, D., and J. Salt, eds. *Ethnic Minorities in Britain: Census Volume 1*. London: Office of Population Censuses and Surveys, HMSO.

New Zealand Council of Christian Social Services (NZCCSS) and the Salvation Army (1994). *Housing the Hungry: A Survey of Salvation Army Foodbank Recipients to Assess the Impact of the Government's Housing Reforms*. Wellington: NZCCSS and the Salvation Army.

New Zealand Council of Social Services (NZCSS) (1978). *Sharing Social Responsibility.* Wellington: NZCSS.

New Zealand Planning Council (NZPC) (1990). *Who Gets What? The Distribution of Income and Wealth in New Zealand.* Wellington: NZPC.

Oliver, W. (1977). 'The Origins and Growth of the Welfare State'. In Trlin, A., ed. *Social Welfare and New Zealand Society.* Wellington: Methuen.

—— (1978). 'An Uneasy Retrospect'. In Wards, I., ed. *Thirteen Facets.* Wellington: Government Printer, 41–65.

—— (1988). 'Social Policy in New Zealand: An Historical Overview'. In *Report of the Royal Commission on Social Policy*, vol. 1. Wellington: Royal Commission, 3–45.

O'Neill, C. (1985). 'Nuptiality and Marital Status'. In ESCAP, 1985, 193–208.

Oppenheimer, V. (1994). 'Women's Rising Employment and the Future of the Family in Industrial Societies'. *Population and Development Review* 20(2): 293–342.

Parker, W. (1995). 'De facto Property Rights: Time for Change?' In *Family Law Journal.* Wellington: Butterworths, 179–180.

People's Select Committee (1992). *Neither Freedom nor Choice: Report of the People's Select Committee.* Palmerston North: People's Select Committee.

Peron, Y., and E. Lapierre-Adamcyk (1986). 'Le cycle de la vie familiale comme cadre d'analyse de la statistique des familles'. *Les Familles d'Aujourd'hui.* Paris: AIDELF.

Pool, I. (1977). *The Maori Population of New Zealand, 1769–1971.* Auckland: Auckland University Press.

—— (1985) 'Mortality Trends and Differentials'. In ESCAP, 1985, 209–42.

—— (1987). *New Zealand Universities Until 2007: Demographic Structures and Changes.* Report prepared on behalf of The Universities Review Committee. Wellington: New Zealand Vice Chancellors Committee.

—— (1991). *Te Iwi Maori.* Auckland: Auckland University Press.

—— (1992). 'The New Zealand Family: Structural Changes in the Context of Shifts in Societal Values'. *New Zealand Population Review* 18(1 and 2): 69–86.

—— (1993). 'New Zealand's Two Health Transitions: A Comparative Analysis'. Proceedings of the Conference of the International Union for the Scientific Study of Population, vol. 1. Montreal and Liege: IUSSP, 419–27.

—— (1994) 'Cross-Comparative Perspectives on New Zealand Health'. In Spicer, Trlin, and Walton, 16–49.

—— (in press). 'Changes in the Structures of Families: Good News or Bad News?' Paper presented at the National Seminar on Supporting Children and Families through Family Changes, University of Otago, Dunedin.

——, and J. Sceats (1981). *Fertility and Family Formation in New Zealand.* Wellington: Ministry of Works, Town and Country Planning Branch.

——, et al. (1993). *Demographic Change and Family Policy: A Methodological Comment.* Population Studies Centre Discussion Paper No. 1. Hamilton: University of Waikato.

Prebble, M., et al. (1991). *Report of the Change Team on Targeting Social Assistance.* Wellington: Department of Prime Minister and Cabinet.

Puao-Te-Ata-Tu (1986). *The Report of the Ministerial Advisory Committee on a Maori Perspective for the Department of Social Welfare.* Wellington: Government Printer.

Rainwater, L. (1994). 'Family Equivalence as a Social Construction'. In Ekert-Jaffe, O., ed. *Standards of Living and Families: Observation and Analysis.* Paris: INED.

Rankin, K. (1991). *The Universal Welfare State: Incorporating Proposals for a Universal Basic Income.* Department of Economics Policy Discussion Paper Series No. 12. Auckland: University of Auckland.

Richardson, R. (1990). 'Statement by the Minister of Finance'. In Bolger, J., R. Richardson, and W. Birch. *Economic and Social Initiative, December 1990*. Wellington: Government Printer.
—— (1995). *Making a Difference*. Christchurch: Shoal Bay Press.
Rights and Responsibilities (1995). Papers from the International Year of the Family Symposium. Wellington: IYF Committee.
Rochford, M. (1993). *A Profile of Sole Parents from the 1991 Census*. Research Report Series No. 15. Wellington: Social Policy Agency, Department of Social Welfare.
——, et al. (1992). *A Profile of Sole Parents from the 1986 Census*. Research Report Series No. 13. Wellington: Department of Social Welfare.
Rosenberg, W. (1977). 'Full Employment: The Fulcrum of Social Welfare'. In Trlin, A., ed. *Social Welfare and New Zealand Society*. Wellington: Methuen, 45–60.
Royal Commission on Social Policy (1988). *April Report*, vols. 1–5. Wellington: Government Printer.
Royal Commission on Social Security (RCSS) (1972). *Social Security in New Zealand*. Wellington: Government Printer.
Salmond, G. (1985). 'Health and Morbidity'. In ESCAP, 1985, 269–302.
Santow, G. (1989). 'A Sequence of Events in Fertility and Family Formation?' In proceedings of the International Population Conference, vol. 3. Liege: International Union for the Scientific Study of Population, 217–29.
Saunders, P., G. Hobbes, and H. Stott (1989). *Income Inequality in Australia and New Zealand: International Comparisons and Recent Trends*. Social Welfare Research Centre Discussion Papers. Sydney: The University of New South Wales.
Saville-Smith, K., et al. (1994). *Bringing Home the Bacon: The Changing Relationship Between Family, State and Market in New Zealand in the 1980s*. Family and Societal Change, Research Report No. 3. Wellington: New Zealand Institute for Social Research and Development Ltd.
Sceats, J. (1981). 'Family Formation in Canada and New Zealand: An Analysis of the Timing and Spacing of Pregnancies'. *New Zealand Population Review* 7(3): 28–34.
—— (1988a). 'Abortion in a Low Fertility Country: New Zealand, a Case Study'. London: University of London. (Unpublished doctoral thesis.)
—— (1988b). 'Implications of Changes in New Zealand Family Formation and Household Structure'. In Crothers, C., and R. Bedford, eds. *The Business Of Population*. Wellington: New Zealand Demographic Society.
——, and A. Parr (1995). 'Induced Abortion: National Trends and a Regional Perspective'. In proceedings of the First National Conference of Termination of Pregnancy Providers, Wellington.
——, and I. Pool (1985a). 'Fertility Regulation'. In ESCAP, 1985, 178–92.
——, and I. Pool (1985b). 'Perinatal and Infant Mortality'. In ESCAP, 1985, 243–68.
Second New Zealand Sweating Commission (1990). *Across the Counter: The Lives of the Working Poor in New Zealand 1990*. Wellington: RSNZSC.
Select Committee on Women's Rights (1975). *The Role of Women in New Zealand Society*. Wellington: Government Printer.
Sewell, H. (1870). *Hansard*. New Zealand Parliamentary Debates, vol. 9. Wellington: Government Printer, 361.
Shipley, J., et al. (1991). *Social Assistance: Welfare that Works*. Wellington: Government Printer.
Shirley, I. (1982). 'Social Policy and Social Planning'. In Spoonley, P., D. Pearson, and I. Shirley, eds. *New Zealand: Sociological Perspectives*. Palmerston North: Dunmore

Press, 239–62.

—— (1990). 'New Zealand: The Advance of the New Right'. In Taylor, I., ed. *The Social Effects of Free Market Policies: An International Text*. London and New York: Harvester/Wheatsheaf.

—— (1991). 'Social Policy: Beyond the Welfare State'. In Saunders, P., and W. Encel, eds. *Social Policy in Australia: Options for the 1990s*. Proceedings of the National Social Policy Conference. New South Wales: Social Policy Research Centre, 61–84.

—— (1992). 'Social Services in a Market Economy'. In *Social Work Review* (July). Palmerston North: New Zealand Association of Social Workers, 6–9.

—— (1993). 'Experiments in the New Zealand Laboratory'. Paper presented at the Conference on Comparative Research on the Welfare State in Transition, Oxford University, September 1993.

—— (1994). 'Social Policy'. In Spoonley, P., D. Pearson, and I. Shirley, eds. *New Zealand Society*. Palmerston North: Dunmore Press, 130–145.

——, et al. (1990). *Unemployment in New Zealand*. Palmerston North: Dunmore Press.

Sinclair, K. (1980). *A History of New Zealand*. 2nd ed. London: A. Lane.

Spicer, J., A. Trlin, and J. Walton, eds. (1994). *Social Dimensions of Health and Disease: New Zealand Perspectives*. Palmerston North: Dunmore Press.

St. John, S. (1982). *The Impact of the 1982 Budget and Associated Issues on the Position of Families*. Working Papers Series No. 5. Auckland: University of Auckland Department of Economics.

—— (1983). *Financial Assistance for Families and the 1983 Budget*. Working Papers Series No. 8. Auckland: University of Auckland Department of Economics.

—— (1985). *The Impact of the 1985 Budget Changes on Families*. Working Paper Series No. 20. Auckland: University of Auckland Department of Economics.

—— (1989). *Family Assistance 1980/81 to 1988/89: Recent Directions in Family Policy*. Working Papers Series No. 52. Auckland: University of Auckland Department of Economics.

—— (1991). *The Core Family Unit: The Implications for Women*. Journal of Women's Studies. Auckland: Women's Studies Association.

—— (1994). *Delivering Financial Assistance to Families: An Analysis of New Zealand's Policies and the Case for Reform*. Policy Discussion Paper No. 18. Auckland: University of Auckland Department of Economics..

——, and Heynes, A. (1993). *The Welfare Mess*. Auckland: University of Auckland Department of Economics.

Stephens, R. (1992). 'Budgeting with the Benefits Cuts'. In Boston and Dalziel, 100–25.

—— (1994a). 'The Impact of Housing Expenditure on the Incidence and Severity of Poverty in New Zealand'. (Unpublished manuscript.)

—— (1994b). *The Incidence and Severity of Poverty in New Zealand, 1990–1991*. Wellington: Victoria University Department of Public Policy.

——, and J. Bradshaw (1996). 'The Generosity of New Zealand's Assistance to Families with Dependent Children'. *Social Policy Journal of New Zealand* 4(July): 53–75.

Sutch, W. (1966). *The Quest for Security in New Zealand 1840 to 1966*. Wellington: Oxford University Press.

Tennant, M. (1989). *Paupers and Providers: Charitable Aid in New Zealand*. Wellington: Allen and Unwin, and Historical Branches, Department of Internal Affairs.

—— (1994). *Children's Health, the Nation's Wealth: A History of Children's Health Camps*. Wellington: Bridget Williams Books and Historical Branch, Department of Internal Affairs.

Thomson, A. (1859). *The Story of New Zealand*. 2 vols. London: John Murray.

Treasury, The (1984). 'Economic Management'. Post-Election Briefing to the Incoming Government. Wellington: New Zealand Treasury.

—— (1987). 'Government Management'. Post-Election Briefing to the Incoming Government. Wellington: New Zealand Treasury.

van de Kaa, D. (1987). 'Europe's Second Demographic Transition'. *Population Bulletin* 42(1).

Van Moeseke, P. (1980). 'Aluminium Smelting in New Zealand: An Economics Appraisal (with Addendum)'. No. 8008. Dunedin: University of Otago.

Walsh, P. (1993). 'The State and Industrial Relations in New Zealand'. In Roper, B., and C. Rudd, eds. *State and Economy in New Zealand*. Auckland: Oxford University Press, 59–76.

Waring, M. (1988). *Counting for Nothing: What Men Value and What Women are Worth*. Wellington: Allen and Unwin/Port Nicholson Press.

West Auckland Women's Centre (1994). *Feeling Stretched: Women and Families in Transition*. West Auckland: West Auckland Women's Centre.

Whitwell, J. (1989). 'Monetary Policy: An Anti-Inflationary or an Anti-Employment Strategy?' Background paper prepared for the Social Policy Research Centre. Palmerston North: Massey University.

Wilkes, C., and I. Shirley (1984). *In the Public Interest: Health, Work and Housing in New Zealand*. Auckland: Benton Ross.

Woods, N. (1963). *Industrial Conciliation and Arbitration in New Zealand*. Wellington: Government Printer.

UNITED STATES

Ahlburg, D., and C. De Vita (1992). 'New Realities of the American Family'. *Population Bulletin* 47(2).

Aldous, J., and W. Dumon, eds. (1980). *The Politics and Programs of Family Policy*. Indiana: University of Notre Dame Press.

Bauer, G. (1991). Testimony. In Select Committee on Children, Youth and Families, 1991: 49–51.

Bianchi, S. (1990). 'America's Children: Mixed Prospects'. *Population Bulletin* 45(1).

——, and D. Spain (1986). *American Women in Transition*. New York: Russell Sage Foundation.

Bradshaw, J., et al. (1993). *Support for Children: A Comparison of Arrangements in Fifteen Countries*. Department of Social Security, Research Report No. 21. London: HMSO.

Bumpass, L., and K. Raley (1995). 'Redefining Single-Parent Families: Cohabitation and Changing Family Reality'. *Demography* 32(1): 97–109.

Butz, W., and M. Ward (1978). *Counter Cyclical US Fertility*. Santa Monica, California: Rand Corporation.

Cahan, E. (1989). *Past Caring: A History of US Preschool Care and Education for the Poor, 1820–1965*. New York: Columbia University, National Center for Children in Poverty.

Carlson, A. (1980). 'Families, Sex and the Liberal Agenda'. *The Public Interest* 58(Winter): 62–79.

Chafe, W. (1972). *The American Woman: Her Changing Social, Economic, and Political Roles, 1920–1970*. New York: Oxford University Press.

Cherlin, A. (1992). *Marriage, Divorce, and Remarriage*. 2nd ed. Cambridge, Massachusetts: Harvard University Press.

452   *Bibliography*

Clark, R., and R. Berkowitz (1995). *Federal Expenditures on Children.* Washington, DC: The Urban Institute.

Committee on Labor and Public Welfare, US Senate (1974). *American Families: Trends and Pressures, 1973.* Washington, DC: US Government Printing Office.

Committee on Ways and Means, US House of Representatives (1993, 1994). *The Green Book: Overview of Entitlement Programs.* Washington, DC: US Government Printing Office.

Congressional Budget Office (1988). *Trends in Family Income: 1970–1986.* Washington, DC: US Government Printing Office.

Congressional Research Service (1990). *Federal Programs for Children and Their Families.* Washington, DC: US Government Printing Office.

Danziger, S., and S. Danziger (1993). 'Child Poverty and Public Policy: Toward a Comprehensive Antipoverty Agenda'. *Daedalus* 122(1): 57–84.

Degler, C. (1980). *At Odds.* New York: Oxford University Press.

Easterlin, R. (1980). *Birth and Fortune.* New York: Basic Books.

Family Economics Research Group (1993). *Expenditure on a Child by Families, 1993: Technical Report.* Hyattsville, Maryland: Agricultural Research Service, US Department of Agriculture.

Freed, D., and H. Foster (1983). 'Family Law in the Fifty States: An Overview'. *Family Law Quarterly* 16(4): 289–383.

Friedman, S. (1992). *The Law of Parent-Child Relationships: A Handbook.* American Bar Association.

Garfinkel, I., and M. Melli (1990). 'The Use of Normative Standards in Family Law Decisions: Developing Mathematical Standards for Child Support'. *Family Law Quarterly* 24(2): 157–78.

Gershuny, J., and J. Robinson (1989). 'Historical Change in the Household Division of Labor'. *Demography* 25(4): 537–52.

Gettis, V., and M. Vinovskis (1992). 'History of Child Care in the United States Before 1950'. In M. Lamb, et al. *Child Care in Context.* Hillsdale, New Jersey: Lawrence Erlbaum, 185–206.

Glendon, M. (1977). *State, Law and Family: Family Law in Transition in the United States and Western Europe.* Oxford: North–Holland Publishing Co.

—— (1989). *The Transformation of Family Law: State, Law and Family in the United States and Western Europe.* Chicago: University of Chicago Press.

Grubb, N., and M. Lazerson (1982). *Broken Promises: How Americans Fail Their Children.* New York: Basic Books.

Haveman, R., and B. Wolfe (1994). *Succeeding Generations: On the Effects of Investment in Children.* New York: Russell Sage Foundation.

Hayes, C., ed. (1982). *Making Policies for Children.* Washington, DC: National Academy Press.

Hayghe, H. (1990). 'Family Members in the Workforce'. *Monthly Labor Review* 113(3): 14–19.

——, and S. Bianchi (1994). 'Married Mothers' Work Patterns'. *Monthly Labor Review* 117(6): 24–30.

Hernandez, D. (1992). 'When Households Continue, Discontinue, and Form'. Current Population Reports, Series P–23–179. Washington, DC: US Government Printing Office.

—— (1993a). *America's Children: Resources from Family, Government, and the Economy.* New York: Russell Sage Foundation.

Bibliography 453

—— (1993b). 'When Families Break Up'. *Population Profile of the United States, 1993*. Current Population Reports, Series P–23–185. Washington, DC: US Government Printing Office, 18–9.

Himmelfarb, G. (1995). *The De-Moralization of Society: From Victorian Virtues to Modern Values*. New York: Knopf.

Hofferth, S., and C. Hayes, eds. (1987). *Risking The Future*, vol. 2. Washington, DC: National Academy Press.

——, et al. (1991). *National Child Care Survey*. Washington, DC: The Urban Institute.

Hogan, D., and D. Lichter (1995). 'Children and Youth: Living Arrangements and Welfare'. In Farley, R., ed. *State of the Union: America in the 1990s*. Vol. 2: Social Trends. New York: Russell Sage Foundation.

Kahn, A., and S. Kamerman (1988). *Child Care: Facing the Hard Choices*. Westport, Connecticut: Greenwood Press, Auburn House.

——, and S. Kamerman (1992). *Integrating Services Integration: An Overview of Initiatives, Issues, and Possibilities*. New York: Columbia University, National Center for Children in Poverty.

Kamerman, S. (1976). *Developing a Family Impact Statement*. New York: Foundation for Child Development.

——, and A. Kahn (1976). *Social Services in the United States*. Philadelphia: Temple University Press.

——, and A. Kahn (1978). 'The United States'. In Kamerman, S., and A. Kahn, eds. *Family Policy: Government and Families in Fourteen Countries*. New York: Columbia University Press, 428–75.

——, and A. Kahn (1987). *The Responsive Workplace: Employers and a Changing Labor Force*. New York: Columbia University Press.

——, and A. Kahn (1988). *Mothers Alone: Strategies for a Time of Change*. Westport, Connecticut: Greenwood Press, Auburn House.

——, A. Kahn, and P. Kingston (1983). *Maternity Policies and Working Women*. New York: Columbia University Press.

Kenniston, K. (1977). *All Our Children: The American Family Under Pressure*. Report of the Carnegie Council on Children. New York: Harcourt Brace Jovanovich.

Klein, V., and A. Myrdal (1956). *Women's Two Roles*. London: Routledge.

Klerman, L. (1991). *Alive and Well? A Research and Policy Review of Health Programs for Poor Young Children*. New York: Columbia University, National Center for Children in Poverty.

Krause, H. (1986). *Family Law in a Nutshell*. St. Paul: West Publishing Co.

—— (1989). *Illegitimacy: Law and Social Policy*. New York: Bobbs–Merril Co.

Leonard, P., and R. Greenstein (1991). 'The New Budget Reconciliation Law: Progressive Deficit Reduction and Critical Social Investments'. Washington, DC: Center on Budget and Policy Priorities.

Levy, F., and R. Michel (1991). *The Economic Future of American Families: Income and Wealth Trends*. Washington, DC: The Urban Institute.

Lino, M. (1996). 'Income and Spending of Poor Households with Children'. *Family Economics and Nutrition Review* 9(1): 2–13.

——, and J. Guthrie (1994). 'The Food Situation of Families Maintained by Single Mothers: Expenditure, Shopping Behavior, and Diet Quality'. *Family Economics and Nutrition Review* 7(1): 9–21.

Lou Harris and Associates (1981). *Families At Work: The General Mills American Family Report, 1980–81*. Minneapolis: General Mills.

Lugaila, T. (1992). *Households, Families, and Children: A 30-Year Perspective*. US Bureau of the Census, Current Population Reports, Series P23–181. Washington, DC: US Government Printing Office.

Magee, E., and M. Pratt (1985). *1935–1985: 50 Years of US Federal Support to Promote the Health of Mothers, Children and Handicapped Children in America*. Vienna, Virginia: Information Sciences Research Institute.

McLanahan, S., and L. Casper (1995). 'Growing Diversity and Inequality in the American Family'. In Farley, R., ed. *State of the Union: America in the 1990s*. Vol. 2: Social Trends. New York: Russell Sage Foundation.

——, and G. Sandefur (1994). *Growing Up With a Single Parent: What Hurts, What Helps*. Cambridge, Massachusetts: Harvard University Press.

Miller, W. (1977). *Welfare and Values in America: A Review of Attitudes Toward Welfare and Welfare Policies in the Light of American History and Culture*. Durham, North Carolina: Duke University Institute of Policy Sciences and Public Affairs.

Moore, K. (1994). *Trends in Teenage Fertility*. Washington, DC: Child Trends.

Nasar, S. (1994). 'More Men in Prime of Life Spend Less Time Working'. *The New York Times* 1 December 1994.

National Advisory Commission on Civil Disorders (1981). *Report of the Kerner Commission*. Washington, DC: US Government Printing Office.

National Commission on Children (1991). *Beyond Rhetoric: A New American Agenda for Children and Families*. Washington, DC: US Government Printing Office.

National Conference on Social Welfare (1977). 'American Families in Transition: Approaches to Family Policy'. Washington, DC: NCSW.

National Research Council (1976). *Toward a National Policy for Children and Families*. Washington, DC: National Academy of Sciences.

Nelson, B. (1984). *Making an Issue of Child Abuse*. Chicago: University of Chicago Press.

Norton, A., and L. Miller (1992). *Marriage, Divorce, and Remarriage in the 1990s*. US Bureau of the Census, Current Population Reports, Series P23–180. Washington, DC: US Government Printing Office.

O'Connell, M. (1993). 'Where's Papa? Father's Role in Child Care'. *Population Bulletin* 20. Washington, DC: Population Reference Bureau.

OECD (1992). *The Tax/Benefit Position of Production Workers*. Paris: OECD.

—— (1994). *OECD in Figures, 1994*. Paris: OECD.

Omnibus Budget Reconciliation Act of 1990 (OBRA) (1990). P. L. 101–508. US Congress.

Peden, J., and F. Glahe, eds. (1986). *The American Family and the State*. San Francisco: Pacific Institute for Public Policy.

Pleck, J. (1985). *Working Wives/Working Husbands*. Beverly Hills, California: Sage.

Rainwater, L., and T. Smeeding (1995). 'Doing Poorly: The Real Income of American Children in a Comparative Perspective'. Working Paper No. 127, Luxemburg Income Study. Luxemburg: I. Walferdange.

Rice, R. (1977). *American Family Policy: Content and Context*. New York: Family Service Association of America.

Rothman, S. (1978). *Woman's Proper Place*. New York: Basic Books.

Ruggles, P. (1990). *Drawing the Line*. Washington, DC: The Urban Institute.

Select Committee on Children, Youth and Families, US House of Representatives (1986). *The Diversity and Strength of American Families*. Hearings. Washington, DC: US Government Printing Office.

—— (1991). *Reclaiming the Tax Code for American Families*. Hearings. Washington, DC: US Government Printing Office.

—— (1992a). *America's Families: Conditions, Trends, Hopes and Fears*. Hearings. Washington, DC: US Government Printing Office.

—— (1992b). *Federal Programs Affecting Children and Their Families, 1992*. Washington, DC: US Government Printing Office.

Shalit, R. (1993). 'Family Managers'. *The New Republic* 16 August 1993: 13.

Sherman, A. (1994). *Wasting America's Future*. Boston: Beacon Press.

Skocpol, T. (1992). *Protecting Soldiers and Mothers: The Political Origins of Social Policy in the United States*. Cambridge, Massachusetts: Harvard University Press.

Smolensky, E., S. Danziger, and P. Gottschalk (1988). 'The Declining Significance of Age in the United States: Trends in the Well-Being of Children and the Elderly Since 1939'. In Palmer, J., T. Smeeding, and B. Torrey, eds. *The Vulnerable*. Washington, DC: The Urban Institute, 29–54.

Social Security Administration (1993). 'Social Security Programs in the United States, 1993'. *Social Security Bulletin* 56(4): 3–82.

—— (1993, 1994). *Annual Statistical Supplement to the Social Security Bulletin*. Washington, DC: US Government Printing Office.

Steiner, G. (1976). *The Children's Cause*. Washington, DC: The Brookings Institution.

—— (1981). *The Futility of Family Policy*. Washington, DC: The Brookings Institution.

Steuerle, E. (1991). Testimony. In Select Committee on Children, Youth and Families, US House of Representatives, 1991.

Subcommittee on Children and Youth, US Senate (1973). *American Families: Trends and Pressures, 1973*. Hearings. Washington, DC: US Government Printing Office.

Subcommittee on Family and Human Services, US Senate (1983). *Broken Families*. Hearings. March and October, Parts 1 and 2. Washington, DC: US Government Printing Office.

Subcommittee on Human Resources (1993). Committee on Ways and Means, US House of Representatives. *Sources of the Increases in Poverty, Work Effort, and Income Distribution Data*. Washington, DC: US Government Printing Office.

Sweet, J., and L. Bumpass (1987). *American Families and Households*. New York: Russell Sage Foundation.

Thoennes, N., P. Tjaden, and J. Pearson (1991). 'The Impact of Child Support Guidelines on Award Adequacy, Award Variability, and Case Processing Efficiency'. *Family Law Quarterly* 25(3): 325–45.

Timmer, S., J. Eccles, and K. O'Brien (1985). 'How Children Use Time'. In Juster, T., and F. Stafford, eds. *Time, Goods, and Well-Being*. Ann Arbor, Michigan: University of Michigan.

Trout, J., and D. Mattson (1984). 'A 10-Year Review of the Supplemental Security Income Program'. *Social Security Bulletin* 47(1): 3–24.

US Bureau of the Census (1975). *Historical Statistics of the United States: Colonial Times to 1970*. Washington, DC: US Government Printing Office.

—— (1978). *Perspectives on American Fertility*. Current Population Reports, Series P23, No. 70. Washington, DC: US Government Printing Office.

—— (1990). *Studies in Household and Family Formation*. Current Population Reports, Series P23, No. 169. Washington DC: US Government Printing Office.

—— (1991a). *Fertility of American Women: June, 1990*. Current Population Reports, Series P20, No. 454. Washington, DC: US Government Printing Office.

—— (1991b). *Who's Minding the Kids?* Current Population Reports, Series P70–36. Washington, DC: US Government Printing Office.

—— (1992). *Poverty in the United States: 1991*. Current Population Reports, Series P–60,

No. 181. Washington, DC: US Government Printing Office.

—— (1993a). *Household and Family Characteristics: March, 1992.* Current Population Reports, Series P20–467, Table H. Washington, DC: US Government Printing Office.

—— (1993b). *Marital Status and Living Arrangements: March, 1993.* Current Population Reports, Series P20–468. Washington, DC: US Government Printing Office.

—— (1993c). *Measuring the Effect of Benefits and Taxes on Income and Poverty, 1992.* Current Population Reports, Series P–60–186RD. Washington, DC: US Government Printing Office.

—— (1993d). *Poverty in the United States: 1992.* Current Population Reports, Series P–60–185. Washington, DC: US Government Printing Office.

—— (1993e). *Money Income of Households, Families, and Persons in the United States: 1992.* Current Population Reports, Series P60–184. Washington, DC: US Government Printing Office.

—— (1993f). *School Enrollment: Social and Economic Characteristics of Students, October 1993.* Current Population Reports, Series P20–479. Washington, DC: US Government Printing Office.

—— (1994). *The Diverse Living Arrangements of Children: Summer 1991.* Current Population Reports, Series P70–38. Washington, DC: US Government Printing Office.

—— (1995). *Fertility of American Women: June 1994.* Current Population Reports, Series P20, No. 482. Washington, DC: US Government Printing Office.

US Department of Labor, Bureau of Labor Statistics (1992). 'Labor Month in Review'. *Monthly Labor Review* 115(6): 2.

Vinovskis, M. (1983). 'Early Childhood Education: Then and Now'. *Daedalus* 122(1): 151–76.

VCIS Research Notes (1993). American Public Welfare Association, Voluntary Cooperative Information System. Washington, DC: VCIS.

Weitzman, L. (1985). *The Divorce Revolution: The Unexpected Social and Economic Consequences for Women and Children in America.* New York: The Free Press.

Wells, R. (1973). 'Demographic Change and the Life Cycle of American Families'. In Rabb, T., and R. Rotberg, eds. *The Family in History.* New York: Harper Torchbooks, 85–94.

Weyrauch, W., and S. Katz (1983). *American Family Law in Transition.* Washington, DC: BNA.

Zill, N., and C. Rogers (1988). 'Recent Trends in the Well-Being of Children in the United States and Their Implications For Public Policy'. In Cherlin, A., ed. *The Changing American Family and Public Policy.* Washington, DC: The Urban Institute, 31–115.

Index

abortion 7, 17, 24, 33–34, 38, 41, 45, 82, 113, 119, 124, 181–82, 186, 188–89, 195, 197, 214, 217–19, 221, 223, 232, 280, 289, 311, 329, 332, 397, 398–99, 404, 406, 408, 411
adoption and foster care 7, 18, 52, 133, 172, 209, 218, 232, 241, 278, 280, 283, 308, 348, 389–92
Aid to Families with Dependent Children (AFDC) 20, 22, 357–59, 364–76, 378–80, 383, 387, 390, 393, 396, 399, 402–3, 407, 409–11
history of 351, 363, 365–366
alimony. *See* divorce: financial settlement
Australia 4, 16, 209–10, 213, 217, 220, 231, 266, 274, 289, 293, 298

baby boom 12, 34, 37, 106, 112, 201, 211, 220–25, 227, 239, 251, 312, 317, 320, 332
benefits 56. *See also* employment and parenting policies: benefits; family and child allowances; National Insurance; unemployment: insurance and benefits
in-kind 20, 253, 285, 308, 351, 392
means-tested 10, 19–20, 25, 60, 62, 67–68, 98–100, 254, 261, 266, 287, 365–66, 387, 410
universal 10, 19–20, 27, 32–33, 64, 68, 97, 100, 139, 145, 147, 159, 253, 255, 257, 266, 303
Beveridge Report 31, 66, 93, 145, 189
birth incentives 112, 152, 153
birth rate. *See* fertility
blacks 12–13, 15, 312, 314–16, 318–20, 322, 324, 338, 340, 350, 353–54, 364–66, 369, 391, 407, 408
Bloc Québécois 188, 194, 195
block grants 107, 155, 159, 163–64, 178, 193, 195, 363–64, 372, 383, 391, 399, 403

breastfeeding 161, 167
Bush, George 311, 344, 372

C. D. Howe Institute 184
Caesarean section 166
Caledon Institute of Social Policy 185
Campaign 2000 183–84
Canada Assistance Plan (CAP) 155–56, 158, 163, 177, 186, 193
Canada Evidence Act 174
Canada Health Act 118, 169, 186, 193
Canada Health and Social Transfer (CHST) 155–56, 158, 164, 193, 195
Canadian Advisory Council on the Status of Women 181
Canadian Charter of Rights and Freedoms 119–20, 122, 173
Canadian Council for Family Rights 182
Canadian Council on Social Development (CCSD) 179, 183
Carter, Jimmy 403–4
Catholic Church, Catholics 10, 106, 110–12, 146, 172–73, 195, 209, 364, 395, 398
child abuse and protection 23, 88–89, 160, 172–75, 180, 192–93, 197–99, 264, 282, 284, 309, 319, 389–91, 395, 399, 410
crimes against the foetus 120
child allowances. *See* family and child allowances
child care 3, 6–7, 10, 16, 18, 21, 27, 31, 44, 47, 53–54, 58, 70–79, 97, 105, 124, 128–29, 131, 136, 161–65, 181–85, 187, 192, 195, 199–201, 290, 335–36, 348, 395–99, 402, 408–9
employer provision of 60, 70–71, 75, 77, 100, 348, 397
history and development of 72–74, 161–62, 271, 341, 378–80
public funding and provision 7, 21, 22, 31, 70–71, 78, 91, 98, 100, 112, 153, 160, 162–63, 183, 186, 189–91, 194,

462   *Index*